*Major Problems in American
Foreign Relations*

MAJOR PROBLEMS IN AMERICAN HISTORY SERIES

GENERAL EDITOR
THOMAS G. PATERSON

Major Problems in American Foreign Relations

DOCUMENTS AND ESSAYS

CONCISE EDITION

EDITED BY

DENNIS MERRILL
UNIVERSITY OF MISSOURI–KANSAS CITY

THOMAS G. PATERSON
UNIVERSITY OF CONNECTICUT

HOUGHTON MIFFLIN COMPANY
Boston   New York

For
Theresa Hannon
Aaron M. Paterson

Publisher: Charles Hartford
Senior Consulting Editor: Jean L. Woy
Senior Development Editor: Jeffrey Greene
Project Editor: Reba Libby
Editorial Assistant: Deborah Berkman
Manufacturing Coordinator: Renée Ostrowski
Senior Marketing Manager: Sandra McGuire

Cover image: Signing of the Camp David Accords by Franklin McMahon, 1979. © Franklin McMahon/Corbis.

Printed in the U.S.A.

Library of Congress Catalog Card Number: 2005927709

ISBN: 0-618-37639-9

3456789-MV-09 08

Contents

C H A P T E R   5
The Monroe Doctrine
Page 116

C H A P T E R   6
Manifest Destiny, Texas, and the War with Mexico
Page 136

CHAPTER 7
The Spanish-American-Cuban-Filipino War
Page 163

CHAPTER 8
Woodrow Wilson, World War I, and the League Fight
Page 198

C H A P T E R   9
U.S. Entry into World War II
Page 235

C H A P T E R   1 0
The Origins of the Cold War
Page 275

C H A P T E R   1 1
Cold War Culture and the "Third World"
324

C H A P T E R   1 2
Cuba and the Missile Crisis
Page 365

C H A P T E R   1 3
The Vietnam War
Page 412

CHAPTER 14
The Cold War Ends and the Post–Cold War Era Begins
Page 453

CHAPTER 15
September 11, 2001, and Anti-Americanism in the Muslim World
Page 492

Maps

Maps

Preface

The terrorist attacks that struck United States soil on September 11, 2001, forcefully illustrated that we live in a global age. No barrier is unbreachable, it seems, for we are inextricably linked to the rest of the world. Newspaper headlines and television reports from around the globe bombard Americans every day, reminding us, sometimes to our discomfort, that the United States participates in an international community. In a world made interconnected and interdependent by instant communications, rapid transportation, information revolution, economic partnerships, travel and tourism, and a shared natural environment, we have discovered that everything—from gas at the pump to the clothes we buy to the air we breathe—carries the "global" tag. We know that a sizable portion of our tax dollars pays for foreign economic, military, and humanitarian aid; for overseas military and intelligence installations; and for interventions, wars, and covert operations intended to change the behavior of other people and governments. News of massacres, famines, and violent uprisings constantly arouses Americans' moral sensibilities. Terrorist cells operate through global networks and obtain international reach. Families worry about the hundreds of thousands of U.S. military personnel stationed abroad, many of them in harm's way. Holidays commemorate international events. The American people have long participated in international affairs—and so has their government; this book seeks to explain why, how, and where.

This new, concise edition of *Major Problems in American Foreign Relations* explores, in a single volume, America's many intersections with the world from the American Revolution to the present. The selections in this book, most of which have been drawn from the sixth edition of our two-volume edition, reveal that searching debate—among Americans and foreign peoples, and among scholars, that has surrounded most issues. Indeed, Americans have spiritedly debated one another about their place in the world, their wars, their territorial expansion, their overseas commitments, their trade policies, and the status of their principles and power; and with comparable vigor they have debated the people of other nations. In preparing for a revision of our two-volume *Major Problems in American Foreign Relations*, we heard from a number of instructors who wanted to expose their students to the reasoning and passion that informed these debates, but could not use the two-volume work because their courses cover the sweep of U.S. foreign relations history in one semester. This concise version is designed for a one-term course. To produce this shorter volume, we have combined parts of chapters, reduced the number and the length of selections, and in some cases cut back on the breadth of coverage. At the same time, we have taken care to choose topics that accent critical historical events and periods, illustrate enduring trends and major changes in American foreign relations, and draw into focus major themes and controversies in the scholarly literature.

We use the phrase *American Foreign Relations* in the title because the subject matter encompasses the myriad of ways in which peoples, cultures, economies, national governments, nongovernmental organizations, regional associations, and international institutions interact. The term *foreign policy* seems inadequate to account for this wide array of activities and actors because it focuses largely on governmental decisionmaking and on policy itself. *Diplomacy* falls short because it refers primarily to negotiations or communications among states and organizations. *International history* seems so broad a term that it loses meaning, while at the same time it underplays an appropriate emphasis on *American* foreign relations. The phrase *foreign relations* comes closest to the new emphases because it explains the totality of interactions—economic, cultural, political, military, environmental, and more— among peoples, organizations, states, and systems, and their impact upon American society. It shows how Americans from various walks of life have participated in the world community. It examines why and how American leaders devised policies to protect, manage, and extend U.S. interests abroad.

As always, we have integrated into our chapters some of the very best recent scholarship and available documents that raise original, thought-provoking questions and points of debate. This single volume edition includes foundational statements of American foreign policy principle, including George Washington's admonition against permanent alliances (1793), the Monroe Doctrine (1823), Woodrow Wilson's Fourteen Points (1918), and the Truman Doctrine (1947)—as well as recently released documents, including those drawn from former Communist archives on the recently concluded Cold War. It probes the meaning of Manifest Destiny in the early nineteenth century, and includes an up-to-date analysis of America's place in the international system at the beginning of the twenty-first century. The final chapter focuses on the terrorist attacks of September 11, 2001, the George W. Bush administration's war against terrorism, and the roots of anti-Americanism in the Muslim world. Selected essays and documents continue to reflect the growing scholarship on international cultural relations, and the impact of attitudes about class, gender, race, and national identity on world affairs—including a chapter on Cold War culture and the Third World. As always, we have included foreign voices and statements by people of color, so as to illuminate the wide array of participants in foreign relations and to suggest ways in which America influences other peoples and nations. We have also accented the importance of groups who share transnational commonalities—such as women's rights activists, relief and development workers, and international peace organizations—to illustrate how cultural, economic, and political internationalism have transformed foreign relations and spurred globalization.

Like other volumes in this series, *Major Problems in American Foreign Relations* approaches its subject in two ways: first, through primary sources; and second, through the interpretations of scholars. We invite readers to contend with a diversity of viewpoints and approaches on critical issues. Documents introduce each chapter's problem, identify key questions, reveal the flavor of the times, and convey the intensity of the debate. Through encounters with documents, students can immerse themselves in the historical moment, shape their own perspectives, and test the explanations of others. The essays demonstrate that different scholars read documents differently, come to quite different conclusions, or choose to focus on different aspects of an issue. Students' interaction with the documents and essays builds an appreciation for the complexity of historical problems, a fascination about historical inquiry, and a recognition that events and personalities once buried in the past carry contemporary meaning for students as both scholars and citizens. Introductions and headnotes in each chapter start this empowering and rewarding process. And suggestions for further reading at the end of each chapter provide resources for students who would like to do additional research.

Instructors and students who want to continue their study of foreign relations history are invited to join the Society for Historians of American Foreign Relations (SHAFR). This organization publishes a superb journal, *Diplomatic History,* as well as an informative newsletter, offers book, article, and lecture prizes and dissertation research grants, and holds an annual conference where scholars present their views and research results. Dues are reasonable. The organization has published a bibliographical work entitled *American Foreign Relations Since 1600: A Guide to the Literature* (2003), edited by Robert L. Beisner and Kurt W. Hanson, which is available for purchase. This indispensable guide includes citations of journal articles, books, memoirs, document collections, and other sources, organized by topic and period. For information on SHAFR, contact the SHAFR Business Office, Ohio State University, Department of History, 106 Dulles Hall, 230 West 17th Avenue, Columbus, OH 43210; email shafr@osu.edu or visit the official website at www.shafr.com. For on-line discussion of topics in the history of U.S. foreign relations, consult the electronic journal *H-DIPLO* web page at http://h-net2.msu.edu/~diplo.

We are very pleased to acknowledge the many generous people who have helped us with both documents and essays, advised us about content, and pointed out errors. Detailed and constructive written reviews for the two-volume edition helped guide our preparation of this concise edition. They were provided by Stanley J. Adamiak, University of Central Oklahoma; David L. Anderson, University of Indianapolis; Diane Shaver Clemens, University of California, Berkeley; John W. Coogan, Michigan State University; Gordon E. Harvey, University of Louisiana at Monroe; Robert B. Kane, Troy State University, Montgomery; Sharon Murphy, Nazareth College of Rochester; Kenneth E. Shewmaker, Dartmouth College; and Amy L. S. Staples, Middle Tennessee State University. The talented Houghton Mifflin staff deserves special thanks. Imaginative, thorough, and understanding, Houghton Mifflin's editors shaped this book for the better. We thank Senior Consulting Editor for History and Political Science Jean L. Woy; Senior Development Editor Frances Gay; Project Editor Reba Libby; Editorial Assistant Deborah Berkman; and Permissions Editor Mary Dalton-Hoffman.

We welcome comments, suggestions, and criticisms from students and instructors so that we can continue to improve this book.

D. M.
T. G. P.

CHAPTER 1

Approaching the Study of
American Foreign Relations

Why did the United States expand into a world power from the colonial era to the early twenty-first century? What were the enduring foreign policy principles and practices handed down by the nation's founders? What foreign relations guideposts did U.S. leaders and citizens establish as they interacted with their hemispheric neighbors? How did Americans conduct themselves on the world stage as they pursued the path to power? The explanations abound. Some scholars assert that the expansionist course was calculated and coherent, fueled by a thirst for territory, foreign markets and investment opportunities, and ultimately Great Power status. Others see America's growing engagement with the rest of the world as having been accidental or unplanned—a defensive response to external threats, designed to safeguard core values and U.S. national security, but a posture that nonetheless necessitated continental expansion, the acquisition of overseas bases, and the cultivation of military allies. Some argue that the urge to spread American power, and the American way of life, arose from ideological canon: a belief in America's "manifest destiny" to promote democracy, Christian civilization, and the international rule of law worldwide. Still others focus on American culture. Less self-conscious and less rigid than ideology, culture can be defined as an evolving constellation of values, beliefs, myths, language, symbols, and assumptions about what it means to be American, and what it means to be foreign. These perceptions grow out of cultural constructions of class, race, gender, religion, and national identity—negotiated by different groups within society and refashioned in light of international experiences. Finally, contemporary scholars also grapple with the phenomenon of globalization; that is, the increasing political, economic, cultural, technological, and environmental interconnectedness of the world. How has globalization reshaped American foreign relations? What role have nongovernmental groups (NGOs), and transnational advocates for human rights, international peace, environmental protection, and other global reforms played in U.S. foreign policy? To what extent has the globalizing process blurred boundaries and identities, and undermined the nation-state structure?

Related to the many questions about U.S. expansionism and the larger world are others that highlight how policy is made and how the process of decisionmaking itself shapes both the policy and the outcome. How have U.S. leaders gone about deciding to use the nation's power abroad, and has that exercise of power produced

1

the results intended? In this category, scholars explore the role of domestic politics: the structure of the federal union and the Constitution, the two party system, electoral contests, presidential-congressional relations, bureaucracies, interest groups and elites, the media and public opinion, and individuals whose personalities mold perceptions and influence decisions.

Most problems in American foreign relations have multicausal rather than singular explanations, and most historians agree that interests and ideals need not be mutually exclusive. But they still disagree on the weight that should be attached to each. Different approaches yield different conclusions about the nature of America's international behavior. Some scholars perceive the United States as a champion of global democracy, an exceptional or unique nation in its devotion to liberty and humanitarianism. Others maintain that the United States has been exceptional in its resolve to remain isolated from the rest of the world, an isolationism made possible by its geographical location in the Western Hemisphere, the political and military weakness of its neighbors, and its natural oceanic barriers—at least until the twentieth century. Some scholars question America's uniqueness, and portray the United States as an emerging Great Power whose leaders have always practiced "realpolitik" and held their own with Europe's most accomplished diplomats. More critical scholarship depicts the United States as an aggressive empire builder—which in the twentieth century led the world capitalist system and imposed its economic, cultural, and military hegemony around the globe. Finally, diplomatic style and technique also come under scrutiny. Some see the United States as internationalist in its willingness to broker alliances and multilateral undertakings. The case has been made by others that American leaders have jealously guarded their independence and more often than not opt to act unilaterally.

This chapter provides a sampling of different approaches to the study of American foreign relations and raises basic questions that run throughout this entire book. What have been the enduring fundamental characteristics and wellsprings of the American people and nation in a changing world? What can a historical perspective teach us about America and the world?

ESSAYS

In the opening essay, Thomas J. McCormick of the University of Wisconsin, Madison, introduces the "world systems theory" of international relations and emphasizes the U.S. rise to economic hegemony or dominance in a capitalistic world system comprising core, periphery, and semi-periphery countries. According to McCormick, individual nations experience mobility between the zones, including America's transformation from a semi-peripheral country in 1790 to a core country by 1890. By the mid–twentieth century the United States possessed the preponderant economic and military power and exercised political-ideological leadership, yet confronted the dilemma of all hegemons: the tendency to overinvest in overseas enterprise and military production, to neglect internal and civilian needs, and to fall into decline. In the second essay, Akira Iriye of Harvard University analyzes a subject that is in many ways connected to global economics: international cultural relations. He observes that Americans have long imagined themselves to be a uniquely multiethnic and freedom-loving people, and they have felt compelled to export their democratic culture. While racism and empire-building inhibited understanding of non-European cultures, the globalizing trends of the late nineteenth century increased U.S. contact with Latin America and Asia and stirred curiosity in foreign societies. The Americanization of world culture during the twentieth century often sparked localist opposition, but Iriye concludes that economic modernization universalized certain values, eroded the significance of geopolitics, and elevated the cultural dimension in international affairs.

Laura McEnaney of Vassar College, in the third essay, explores one aspect of American culture: gender. While gender analysis is often associated with women's history, she stresses that cultural constructions of femininity and masculinity are embedded in all relationships of power. Foreign relations historians use gender analysis to understand symbolic linkages between domestic insecurities relating to women's rights and external threats. Gendered language also reflects the world views of foreign policy officials—who often equate political and military weakness with femininity, and imperial leadership with manliness. In the fourth essay, Michael H. Hunt of the University of North Carolina-Chapel Hill analyzes American racism. He traces the belief in Anglo-Saxon racial superiority to Elizabethan England and the oppression of Africans and Native Americans in the British colonies. As the United States expanded across the continent and beyond, and brought additional non-Western people under its rule, white Americans ranked other societies according to a color-coded racial hierarchy. During the Cold War, when U.S. officials encountered decolonization in the "Third World," they relied on the paternalistic social science of "development" to justify U.S. economic, political, and military supervision.

Melvyn P. Leffler of the University of Virginia contends, in the fifth essay, that a blend of power politics, democratic values, and security concerns has defined American foreign policy since the early days of the republic. Placing official Washington's response to the terrorist attacks of September 11, 2001, and the U.S. war on Iraq that followed in 2003, in historical context, he disagrees with those who characterize President George W. Bush's doctrine of preemption, and willingness to act unilaterally, as having no precedent. Leffler emphasizes, however, that Bush's reliance on military force shortchanges the Wilsonian realization that in times of international crisis multilateral strategies and institutions may also advance U.S. interests and ideals. In the final selection, J. Garry Clifford of the University of Connecticut examines the foreign policy decisionmaking process. He stresses how bureaucratic politics—the give-and-take bargaining within the United States government—shapes the implementation, and therefore the outcome, of foreign policy. Because of all the tugging and hauling in policymaking, U.S. foreign relations do not always conform to its leader's intentions.

The World-System, Hegemony, and Decline

THOMAS J. McCORMICK

Since modern history began in the late fifteenth century, the earth's inhabitants have lived in three distinct types of environments: the capitalist world-system (or world economy), the external world (empires), or the minisystems of subsistence communities. For the past five hundred years, the dynamic growth and expansion of the world-system has been at the expense of the other two. The Ottoman Empire of the Turks disappeared, the Russian Empire of the Romanovs and the empire of the Manchus in China collapsed in revolutionary disarray, all victims of their archaic political systems and the inability of their quasi-feudal economies to compete with or

Adapted from Thomas J. McCormick, *America's Half-Century: United States Foreign Policy in the Cold War and After,* 1–7. © 1995 by Johns Hopkins University Press. Reprinted with permission of The Johns Hopkins University Press.

alternatively to insulate themselves from the more dynamic and efficient economies of the capitalist world-system. Likewise, the minisystems of Eastern Europe, Ireland, the Americas, Africa, and Asia were, over time and despite great resistance, wrenched away from their subsistence, village agriculture and integrated into a cash nexus and the world market. By the late twentieth century, the remnants of the external world of empires, the Soviet Union and the Peoples' Republic of China, had emerged from the containment and self-isolation of the Cold War and begun to experiment with market economies in place of command (planned) economies. Also by that time, the remaining isolated pockets of subsistence systems had virtually disappeared from the face of the earth. The revolutionary expansion of European capitalism and Mediterranean civilization, begun a half-millennium earlier, seemed about to reach its final, all-encompassing frontier. The world-system and the world itself seemed almost one—one world rather than three. . . .

During the [1980s], a number of academic observers have concluded that capitalism's tendency toward international fluidity eventually produced a configuration that could properly be described as a system, a combination of parts forming a complex, unitary whole. Fernand Braudel and Immanuel Wallerstein, in their epic studies of early European capitalism, concluded that such a system was in place by 1650. Others feel that it was not until the nineteenth century that an integrated global division of labor allowed capitalism to merit characterization as a system.

Studies advancing a world-system analysis (including this study) argue that there are three constants about that world-system, even though the particular forms it takes are always changing. First, there are always implicit geographical boundaries within that system, and they are essentially defined by the spatial limits of the world market economy at any given time. In our contemporary period, the term *free world* is essentially a synonym for the capitalist world-system. Cold War rhetoric may impart a more ideological twist to the phrase, but Nelson Rockefeller's chief aide got at its root in late 1941 when he declared that America was "committed to the fight for freedom of economic life and for freedom of the seas, in a word, the fight for a free world." Second, there is always a center or pole to the system, a dominant city that acts as the coordinating point and clearing house of international capital. Its location has shifted historically from the Mediterranean to Northern Europe to North America (and perhaps yet to Northeast Asia), but there is always a central metropolis, be it London in 1845 or New York in 1945.

Finally, the system consists of three successive zones, each performing a specialized function in a complex, international division of labor. *Core* countries (the First World) own most of the high-tech, high-profit enterprises. The *periphery* (the Third World) specializes in primary production of agricultural commodities and raw materials—they are the "hewers of wood and carriers of water." Between them, the *semiperiphery* (the Second World) performs intermediate functions of transport, local capital mobilization, and less complex, less profitable forms of manufacturing. Historically, there has been some limited mobility of individual nations between zones, including America's own transformation from a semiperipheral country in 1790 to a core country by 1890. Likewise, changing technology continually redefines what constitutes high-, intermediate-, or low-value enterprises. Textiles, steel, and shipbuilding might have been high-value activities in an earlier era but have become low- or intermediate-value in the contemporary age of electrical equipment. What remains constant are the zones themselves and the specialized (and unequally re-warded) division of labor among them. Hence, . . . [today] there is a world-system in which North America, Japan, and Europe constitute the core and specialize in electronics, capital goods, diversified agriculture, and finance; the less developed countries (LDCs) of Africa, Southeast Asia, and the Caribbean basin, as the periphery, specialize in nonpetroleum raw materials and single-crop agriculture; and the newly industrializing countries (NICs), Mexico, Brazil, South Africa, Israel, Iran, India, China, and those of Eastern Europe and the Pacific rim, as the semiperiphery, special-ize in shipping, petroleum, credit transactions, and consumer goods manufacturing.

The emergence of a capitalist world economy coincided with the emergence of the modern nation-state as the prevailing political unit of governance, and the nation-state has both fostered and inhibited the capitalist world economy. On one hand, nation-states have often provided crucial stimulation of economic growth and de-velopment: their banking, taxation, credit, and internal improvement policies have frequently aided domestic entrepreneurs in accumulating capital and minimizing risks. On the other hand, those same nation-states have often interfered with and impeded the fluidity and mobility of capital, goods, and labor across national boundaries. This nationalist bias is caused in part by nation-states being, by defini-tion, wedded to specific territories and committed to the defense and sustenance of their citizens. In part, too, it reflects the uneven pace of capitalist development among countries, and the unequal division of labor and rewards that results from it. The frequent consequence has been an attempt by "have-not" countries to overtake "have" countries through nationalistic economic measures, often referred to as mer-cantilistic policies in earlier periods and, in our own time, as import-substitution policies (i.e., substitution of indigenous products for those previously imported). Whatever the cause of this nationalist bias, the resulting farm subsidies, military spending, protective tariffs, navigation laws, capital controls, and restricted currency convertibility have constituted serious obstacles to a free world of economic inter-nationalism and interdependence in which capitalism, as a purely economic sys-tem, can realize its maximum efficiency and profitability. So, too, have the policies of territorial expansion that often accompany economic nationalism interfered, by seeking to monopolize whole regions of the earth for the benefit of a single national economy. Examples are the British mercantile empire of the eighteenth century and the Japanese Greater East Asian Co-Prosperity Sphere of the twentieth. In sum, nation-states have tended to pursue policies of economic autarky—capitalism in one country or one self-contained trading bloc—and such approaches limit the options of capital in pursuit of maximum rewards.

Hegemony historically has operated to soften the contradiction between the internationalist imperatives of capitalism and the nationalist biases of political nation-states. In the context of the world-system, hegemony means that one nation possesses such unrivaled supremacy, such predominant influence in economic power, military might, and political-ideological leadership, that no other power, or combination of powers, can prevail against it. Economic supremacy is the indis-pensable base of hegemony, for all other forms of power are possible with it and no others possible, for very long, without it. Any hegemonic power must, simulta-neously, contain the dominant financial center, possess a clear comparative advantage in a wide range of high-tech, high-profit industries, and function commercially as both the world's major exporter and its major importer. Beyond mere economic power, it must possess clear military superiority and ideological hegemony as well. By fear or respect, it must be able to exert its political will over the rest of the system and command deference to its principles and policies.

Hegemony and the balance of power have been on opposing sides of the contradiction between economic internationalism and national autarky or self-sufficiency. The balance of power attempts to use the alignment of forces and, if necessary, war, to prevent any one power from achieving such preponderance that it could impose economic internationalism on autarkic-minded nations. A single hegemonic power, however, has a built-in incentive to force other nations to abandon their national capitalism and economic controls and to accept a world of free trade, free capital flows, and free currency convertibility. As the world's dominant economic power, a hegemonic power has the most to gain from such a free world and the most to lose from nationalistic efforts to limit the free movement of capital, goods, and currencies. So the preponderant world power is unequivocally self-interested in using its economic power, as workshop and banker of the free world, to create institutions and ground rules that foster the internationalization of capital. It finds it inherently advantageous to use its political power as ideologue of the world-system to preach the universal virtues of freedom of the seas, free trade, open door policies, comparative advantage, and a specialized division of labor. It finds it necessary to use its military power as global policeman to protect the international system against external antagonists, internal rebellions, and internecine differences: to be judge, jury, and executioner, insuring that the ground rules of internationalism are not impeded by either friend or foe.

Only twice in the history of the capitalist world economy has hegemony triumphed over balance of power as the prevailing structure of the international system. Great Britain functioned as hegemonic center between roughly 1815 and 1870, and the United States did so between roughly 1945 and 1970. (Others argue that the Dutch republic did so as well, in the late seventeenth century, but the argument seems rather forced.) In each instance, world war was crucial to the formation of hegemony. It radically redistributed power and wealth in ironic fashion, denying hegemony to a European continental power while bestowing postwar supremacy on its balance of power adversary.

In the first instance, France attempted through its Napoleonic Wars (constituting the first truly world war) to impose its dominance on the Eurasian heartland, the very center of European capitalism. Great Britain attempted to thwart that ambition through its traditional balance of power politics, and it ultimately prevailed. But the wars and attendant revolutions were so long, so destructive, so destabilizing that they temporarily obliterated the old balance of power system and left Great Britain the tacit sovereign of the post-Napoleonic world. In the second instance (as we shall see in detail later), Germany, under both the Kaiser and Hitler, attempted to impose its dominance on the same Eurasian heartland, while Anglo-American balance of power diplomacy sought to prevent it. But the ironic consequence of World Wars I and II was, by denying hegemony to the Germans, to make it possible for the Americans to become the acknowledged leaders of the free world. In each case, hegemony made it nearly impossible for other core powers to use war as an instrument of diplomacy against each other—a Pax Britannica for the mid-nineteenth century and a Pax Americana for the mid-twentieth. In each case, hegemony blunted the forces of economic nationalism and facilitated greater global interdependence, enabling a freer and easier *exchange* of goods in the nineteenth century and the multinational *production* of goods in the twentieth.

Hegemony is always impermanent, as Great Britain discovered and the United States is discovering. Indeed, hegemony undermines the very economic supremacy upon which it necessarily must rest. Two related tendencies lead the preponderant power to neglect investment in its civilian research and production and to transform itself into a *rentier* nation and *warfare* state. There is a tendency to overinvest and lend overseas and to live off dividends and interests (renting out one's money, hence *rentier*). It happens because it is easy to do, since the hegemonic power is in a position to secure favorable treatment for its capital throughout the free world. It happens also because it is necessary, since higher wage bills make it more profitable to invest overseas than at home. The higher wage bills themselves are part of the burden of power: the necessity to demonstrate to managers and workers that there are ample economic rewards for supporting an internationalist foreign policy with their votes, tax dollars, and conscription.

The tendency to overinvest abroad is compounded by the tendency to overinvest in military production. Essential to the hegemonic power's capacity to act as global policeman, military research and production receive favored treatment from the government in the form of state-subsidized high profits. The government becomes a more predictable and more profitable customer than private individuals and corporate consumers. The end result is to divert capital from civilian to military production, to the neglect of modernization needs of the domestic industrial plant. This disinvestment, as some term it, erodes over time the economic underpinnings of hegemony and makes it more difficult to compete with other core powers who have avoided the pitfalls of similar disinvestment. Moreover, like a snowball rolling downhill, the problems compound as the hegemon grows aware of its decline. Confronted with declining profitability in the civilian sector, it is likely to stress military spending even more as the easiest way to assure its capitalists of adequate returns—often spending far in excess of any plausible military purposes. Relatedly, it is likely to exploit its continuing function as world policeman to extort special privileges from its competitors: favored treatment for its currency, its trade, and its investments in exchange for continued police protection. In short, it is likely to become even more of a rentier or warfare economy and speed up the very decline it is trying to retard.

The Importance of Culture

AKIRA IRIYE

From the beginning, Americans were interested in cultural themes in their foreign affairs. For one thing, at the time of the American Revolution the political and intellectual leaders were fond of stressing the multiethnic nature of the new republic. In most instances, to be sure, multiethnicity consisted of diverse European nationalities rather than distinctive racial groups. Compared with western European countries,

Akira Iriye, "The Importance of Culture" from "Cultural Relations and Policies," in Alexander De Conde, et al., *Encyclopedia of American Foreign Policy* (New York: Charles Scribner's, 2001), 410, 412–416, 418–419, 421–423. From *Encyclopedia of American Foreign Relations,* by Alexander De Conde, Macmillan Reference USA., © 2001 Macmillan Reference USA. Reprinted by permission of The Gale Group.

the United States seemed unique in that no nationality constituted a majority of the nation, even though those of English stock represented nearly half the population. There were Welsh, Irish, Germans, French, Scandinavians, and others whose admixture with, and adoption of the language of, the English-speaking Americans impressed European visitors for decades after the Revolution. This was as much a cultural as a political undertaking; to establish a republic made up of people from many countries who imagined themselves to belong to the same community required some shared memory, a sense of Americanness, to distinguish the new nation from all others. How such a republic could survive in a world consisting of sovereign states, on one hand, and of large empires, on the other, was the key question.

One way for the American people to assure themselves that this could be done was through developing a fairly precise image of themselves. The idea of the "city on a hill," and the idealized self-perception that the Americans had struggled for the "rights of man," not simply the rights of Englishmen, implied the coming into existence of a new kind of nation and assumed that others, too, would look to the United States as a land of freedom and opportunity. Conversely, Americans would carry out their mission to spread the blessings of civilization and liberty to the less fortunate in distant countries. If, as so many writers asserted, America was the most progressive land in the world, it was because it was a country without archaic encumbrances, where men and women from many countries would come and work together to build a new, ideal community. Anybody, theoretically, could join the undertaking. By the same token, what happened here would be of universal applicability. If various races and groups could join together in the United States to realize an earthly paradise, there was no reason why they could not do so elsewhere in the world. It was in this sense that America was called humankind's best hope. . . .

Europeans, of course, comprised the bulk of the population of the United States, and cultural ties across the Atlantic were quite important. At the same time, however, it was when Americans dealt, either directly or indirectly, with people outside Western civilization that their cultural self-awareness became most clearly articulated. For instance, they viewed Arabs, Hindus, or Chinese in the framework of their own self-definition. These people, in other words, would be judged in terms of their distance from the American ideals and of their capacity to approximate them—if not immediately, then in the future. It is not surprising that observers of non-European societies frequently argued about whether these societies would ever transform themselves and become more like America. The basic assumption was, of course, that at the moment they lacked most of the ingredients that made the United States so progressive. . . .

The situation did not change drastically after the Civil War, but there was a greater awareness of different civilizations than there had been earlier. Fundamentally this reflected the technological development of the last decades of the nineteenth century, when steam and electricity, as observers were fond of pointing out, narrowed distances between various parts of the world. One could travel far more easily and speedily than before, and news in one corner of the globe could be transmitted almost overnight to most other regions. Great migrations of people started from Asia to the American continent, and from Europe to Africa and South America. One saw more foreigners in one's lifetime than earlier. . . .

These were extremely interesting phenomena. . . . It may be said that toward the end of the nineteenth century, world history entered an age of globalization that had cultural, as well as political and economic, implications. Economically, the phenomenon has been referred to as modernization, a neutral term suggesting that any society with certain endowments may opt for change. Modernized nations would establish global networks of capital, goods, and technology, which in turn would help further modernize their economies and ways of life. . . .

Politically, the process of globalization was synonymous with what was then called, and has since been called, imperialism. The world was divided into those who established control over distant territories and those who became objects of such control. A handful of imperialist nations appropriated among themselves the vast lands of Africa, the Middle East, Asia, and the Pacific Ocean as colonies, semi-colonies, or spheres of influence. This was a military-political process, since control necessitated that a power structure be imposed upon alien peoples. Without such a regime, it was feared that local instability would create a chaotic condition and threaten the interests of a particular imperialist nation or invite the extension of power by its rivals. . . .

Americans had always been curious about other peoples and had cherished imports from distant lands. But in the age of globalization there arose serious interest not only in curios and exotica of strange peoples but also in the fine arts, religions, philosophies, and ways of life of other countries, especially in the East. . . .

This sort of serious interest in what would later be called cultural anthropology was quite visible at the end of the century. The World's Columbian Exposition of 1893, held at Chicago to commemorate the four hundredth anniversary of Christopher Columbus's voyage, provides a good case in point. Close to 30 million people visited the fair, which was spread over 686 acres of land in south Chicago. Most countries of the world participated, including Japan, which spent millions of dollars to construct buildings specifically for the fair and to present an exhibition of all aspects of traditional and contemporary life. Although this was not the first time that Americans had had an opportunity to examine Japanese artifacts closely—Japan had participated in the 1876 Centennial Exposition at Philadelphia—their observations led to awareness that Japanese culture was much more than a phenomenon to be appreciated in isolation from the rest of that people's life. If the Japanese craftsmen at the Columbian Exposition seemed polite, industrious, and capable of producing refined objects, this had to be related to the totality of Japanese history and values. Japanese civilization could not be understood only within the framework of Western moral standards. Indeed, it might be comparable on equal terms with American civilization. . . .

The Japanese were not the only heathens at Chicago. The Columbian Exposition coincided with the World Parliament of Religions, to which many non-Christian leaders were invited. From India came several prominent figures, including Swami Vivekananda, a Hindu leader noted for his belief that all religions contain truth. His arrival aroused much excitement among Americans. He not only attended the parliament but also traveled extensively in the United States. Americans were fascinated by his stress on religious toleration: "I preach nothing against the Great One of Galilee. I only ask the Christians to take in the Great Ones of India along with the Lord Jesus." . . .

By the time of World War I, the United States had established its position as the leading Western power, not only in industrial production, trade, and foreign loans and investments but also in armaments and political influence. While this was not the same thing as cultural hegemony, there is little doubt that the United States came to stand and speak for Western civilization at a time when the European countries were engaged in fratricidal conflicts and disputes. One reason why President Woodrow Wilson wanted to postpone American entry into the war was his fear for the survival of Western civilization. He came to see his country as a guardian of that precious tradition, a sentiment shared by an increasing number of British. . . .

Because the European countries lost population, productive capacity, morale, and prestige as a result of the war, the United States was able to replace European power and influence in international affairs. American technology, epitomized by the automobile, dominated the postwar world, as did popular American culture such as jazz, radio, and motion pictures. In Europe one talked of the "decline of the West" after Oswald Spengler's book of that title was published in 1918, but somehow the West that was declining did not seem to include the United States. . . . To understand modern society one looked at the United States. Whether one liked it or not, it seemed that Americanization was an inevitable phenomenon of the postwar world. . . .

While the interwar era, then, was a period of rapid Americanization, it is also true that the 1920s and the 1930s saw self-conscious opposition to, and even rejection of, the West by some non-Western countries. They began to assert their identity, no longer content to remain objects of Western expansion and receptacles of Western influence. This second trend, toward particularism, was already visible at the beginning of the century, when people everywhere noted signs that seemed to indicate the non-West's rise against the West. The Russo-Japanese War, which the Japanese took pains to characterize not as a racial conflict but as one between civilization and barbarism, nevertheless was cheered by non-Westerners from Egypt to China as a victory of a colored nation over a white nation. In the Near East and North Africa, Islam was becoming self-conscious and militant; Islamic spokesmen talked of an Arab renaissance and the coming jihad against the Christian West. Mosques began to be built in American cities. . . .

Intercultural relations after World War II were far more extensive and diverse than earlier. The United States became the virtual inheritor of European civilization, emerging as the strongest and richest country in the world, capable of supporting the arts and financing scholarly and artistic undertakings. European refugees enriched America's cultural life. For the first time it could be said that American art was in the vanguard of modern art, not a pale reflection of European works. The same was true of literature and music. . . . Moreover, American troops stationed in most parts of Europe transmitted American popular culture and lifestyles to the Old World. It became important for European intellectuals to study in the United States if they wished to keep abreast of developments in scholarship.

The impact on the non-Western world was no less great. American influence was transmitted through soldiers, officials, and businessmen who were scattered throughout Africa, the Middle East, and Asia. Consciously or unconsciously, they contributed to a deeper cultural involvement of America in other lands. America came to stand for what was fashionable and up-to-date. At the same time, Americans abroad collectively and individually increased their nation's awareness of other cultures and contributed to a greater appreciation of non-Western traditions. Many who were trained during the war as language specialists and intelligence officers retained their interest in foreign countries, and some of them became leaders in the postwar development of "area studies." American colleges began seriously teaching courses in non-Western civilizations and founded institutes to further research in these areas. There was also a flood of non-Europeans to the United States as war brides, students, and visitors. Through them Americans came into contact with non-Western ways of life. . . .

It would appear that the old opposition between globalization, on one hand, and local identities, on the other, gave way to the virtually universal forces of global interdependence and interpenetration after World War II. These forces were economic, social, and cultural. Modernization provided one easily recognizable framework to comprehend this phenomenon. In the wake of a war that had divided the globe, there resurfaced the idea that all the countries in the world were tending toward a more modern phase. Economic development, political democracy, and social justice appeared to be essential ingredients of modernity; and intellectuals discussed how such an outlook could be encouraged in a traditional society. Appreciation of non-Western civilizations often took the form of discovering elements in them that were potentially "modern." In this process, there grew some tolerance for cultural pluralism: not just greater appreciation for Japanese architecture, Chinese food, or Indian philosophy but economic, political, social changes in those countries. The hope was that through such changes, coupled with the new outlook in post-war America, foreigners and Americans would come to a better understanding of one another. They would develop a common vocabulary of mutual respect as they cooperated to bring about a more modern world. The pace of globalization was being accelerated in a changing world. U.S. cultural relations contributed to globalization and at the same time to an appreciation of diversity. This was a far more significant story than the vicissitudes of the Cold War, for ultimately it was the globalizing world that put an end to the Cold War, not the other way round.

It might be objected that the Cold War did have a globalizing aspect. Not only did it provoke fears of a nuclear conflagration that would annihilate the whole world, but the vocabulary of the geopolitical confrontation often had global connotations. The Soviet Union and its allies spoke of a worldwide people's struggle against the evils of capitalism and imperialism, while the United States and its partners accused the opponents of infringing upon such universal values as freedom and democracy. Moreover, both sides frequently used cultural means to wage Cold War: propaganda, student exchanges, conferences of intellectuals, and the like. . . . A cultural Cold War did exist, as did official cultural policies. But if such policies resulted in a growing interdependence among different parts of the world, it was more by accident than by design. What brought about the dissipation and, ultimately, the end of the Cold War were not these policies but the growing global consciousness, a product of cultural interpenetration, not of the geopolitical confrontation whose fundamental orientation was to divide the globe, not to unite it. . . .

The 1970s were . . . a remarkable decade in that it was the time when cultural diversity became a matter of serious concern in international affairs and, at the same time, when the number of nongovernmental organizations mushroomed, to supplement and in some instances even to supplant the work traditionally carried out by states. The two phenomena were interrelated in that both reflected the growth of civil society and by the same token, the decline of state authority. This was a circumstance that could be observed in the United States as well as in Soviet-bloc nations among the rich as well as developing countries. The rise of Islamic fundamentalism and its challenge to the power of both the United States (as in Iran) and the Soviet Union (as in Afghanistan) is but one extreme example of the emergence of religious and cultural diversity as a factor in international relations. And the fact that neither superpower was able to dislodge the religious fundamentalists by force indicated the growing importance of culture as a determinant of foreign affairs. . . .

How the challenge would be met, and whether . . . [an] international civil society would some day come to establish a more viable world order than sovereign states, were questions that fascinated statesmen and citizens alike as the twentieth century drew to a close. . . . The globalization of cultural activities, ranging from information technology to the spread of fast food, was continuing with its own momentum, promoted by multinational enterprise, international organizations, and many other nongovernmental entities. Sometimes globalization provoked opposition on the part of forces exemplifying cultural diversity, but this was a dualism that had always existed, as we have seen. What was remarkable as the century gave way to the new millennium was that the dualism was coming more and more to determine the shape of international political and economic, as well as cultural, affairs. Cultural relations were no longer marginal pursuits, if they ever were. For the United States as well as for others, culture was coming to claim center stage as they conducted their foreign affairs.

Gender Analysis and Foreign Relations

LAURA McENANEY

In the most basic sense, applying a gender analysis to the study of American foreign policy is an attempt to see things differently, or to see new things entirely. Like other tools of analysis, gender offers another angle, another peek into the complicated world of policymaking. Diplomatic historians who use gender analysis are no different than their colleagues in the field; they, too, seek answers to longstanding questions about the emergence of colonialism, the development of tariff and trade policies, the rise of anti-imperialist movements, the origins of the Cold War, and the like. The use of a gender analysis does not preclude the use of any of the customary methodologies of the historian; gender merely adds to the historian's toolbox. . . .

[T]he emergence of gender studies has made it possible for historians not only to find women but to see both women and men as gendered actors. Indeed, the research on women and femininity as historical subjects has inspired new investigation into

Laura McEnaney, "Gender Analysis and Foreign Relations," in Alexander De Conde et al., *Encyclopedia of American Foreign Policy* (New York: Charles Scribner's, 2001), 123–133. From *Encyclopedia of American Foreign Relations,* by Alexander De Conde, Macmillan Reference USA., © 2001 Macmillan Reference USA. Reprinted by permission of The Gale Group.

the histories of men and masculinity. This has opened a rich vein of scholarship that does not take men's participation in foreign affairs for granted; rather, it interrogates how masculine values and worldviews have shaped diplomacy, enabling students of foreign policy to see anew how normative ideas about manhood inform policy-makers' decision making in both domestic and international contexts.

But a gender analysis shows us more than masculinity in action; it offers a critical tool for understanding power in all of its guises. Seeing gender enables historians to scrutinize the organization of power in any arena, from the most public to the most intimate. Gender ideologies can represent relationships of power as innate, fixed, or biologically rooted, but gender history can make transparent the human agency behind those "natural" relationships. Gender analysis can also reveal how ideologies of masculinity and femininity are embedded in language and social structure; the language of warfare, for example, depends on gendered ideas of strength and weakness, protector and protected, which, in turn, shape how an institution like the military utilizes men and women to carry out American foreign policy. . . .

Cold War history offers an illustrative, although by no means exclusive, case of how gender analysis can affect the study of American foreign policy. It was in this field where scholars first began to commingle the study of politics, culture, and gender to expand traditional narratives of diplomatic history. . . .

Historians of the family and sexuality, for example, have explored how anti-communism and national security policies became manifest in everyday life. The ambient fear of nuclear annihilation, paired with concerns about the resilience of the nuclear family, spurred campaigns to "contain" the social forces that might prove disruptive to gender and family traditionalism. In fact, scholars have argued, postwar America's red scare was as much an attempt to root out nontraditional gender roles and sexual practices as it was an effort to secure America's foreign policy dominance. The preoccupation with national security abroad was bolstered by a security effort at home that enshrined "family values." According to popular cold warriors, with Joseph McCarthy being merely one of a chorus of voices, only heterosexual nuclear families with breadwinner fathers, stay-at-home mothers, and children could anchor a patriotic domestic security endeavor. Anything outside of that configuration was suspect, probably subversive, a potential menace to national security. . . .

[T]he first historians to do this work tended to look for a gender–foreign policy connection primarily in popular culture, leaving unanalyzed the gender content of the more traditional documents (letters, memos, telegrams, agency reports, treaties) found in presidential and security agency archives. In fact, there was arguably a kind of gendering of the sources themselves, whereby scholars who wanted to find gender in diplomacy tended to look at popular discourses (gendered feminine) rather than at the records of diplomacy (gendered masculine). This left the impression, as Amy Kaplan (1993) has argued, that gender "enters diplomatic history only through the aegis of culture." More recent scholarship on gender and Cold War foreign policy has built on these earlier approaches, and historians continue to fine-tune and adapt the methodologies of literary and cultural studies to traditional historical analysis of diplomacy. . . .

An examination of particular moments in Cold War history from the Truman, Eisenhower, and Kennedy administrations may help readers see how this work is done. Diplomatic historians have long debated questions about the emergence of chilly relations between the United States and the Soviet Union in the aftermath of World War II. Volumes have been written about how the two superpowers sought military, economic, and territorial advantages as they tried to construct a postwar world hospitable to their own interests. Many scholars have focused on the development of the doctrine of containment, foreshadowed by the 1947 Truman Doctrine (which pledged the United States to fight communism in Greece and Turkey), and then articulated more thoroughly by George Kennan, the State Department analyst who penned the now famous "long telegram" in early 1946, followed by the "Sources of Soviet Conduct" article in July 1947. Historians have scrutinized Kennan's policy recommendations and rhetorical flourishes for decades, but until the late 1990s, no historians had done a close textual analysis that incorporated gender analysis. In fact, the question of how gender has shaped the political assumptions, worldviews, and policies of cold warriors has yet to be asked in a systematic way for the whole of the Cold War. Nevertheless, new studies have yielded some compelling findings on particular episodes in Cold War history.

Using the insights of gender studies, historian Frank Costigliola found that George Kennan's writings were rife with gendered metaphors that represented the Cold War as an emotional, sexually charged struggle between a man and woman. Kennan's favorite analogies to describe the changing postwar relationship between the United States and the Soviet Union depended heavily on gender, family, and sexual ideologies and imagery. For example, Kennan likened the relationship between Soviet citizens and their government to a wife who becomes gradually disillusioned with her husband and seeks a divorce from him. Russian people, in general, were gendered feminine, Kennan's way of conveying his firm view that the Soviet citizenry was beholden to their cruel and despotic government, gendered as a hypermasculine authority figure. In his telegram, Kennan went so far as to portray the Soviet government as a rapist who tried to exert "unceasing pressure" with "penetration" into Western society. . . .

We can reach further back in time, to the nineteenth century, to apprehend gender meanings in American foreign policy. Kristin L. Hoganson's 1998 study about the operation of gender in the Spanish-American War, for example, nudges historians to confront difficult questions about the causal role of gender in American foreign policy decisions. Like the scholarship on gender and the Cold War, her study is premised on the notion "that the conduct of foreign policy does not occur in a vacuum, that political decision makers are shaped by their surrounding cultures," and that "inherited ideas about gender" are a part of that culture and thus shape profoundly the views of foreign policymakers. In the case of the Spanish-American War, Hoganson states that gender ideals "played an exceptionally powerful and traceable role" in the decision to go to war. Advocates of intervention in Cuba and the Philippines believed that international aggression would fortify American nationalism and manhood at the same time. They drew on nineteenth-century ideas about "manly" character and citizenship, arguing that a war for territorial and economic expansion would energize and rehabilitate American manhood, which, they claimed, had grown soft without the challenges of frontier expansion, agricultural production, and warrior experience. Layered upon these concerns was another: women's growing political activism and their insistence on the right to vote. An imperial war, according to interventionists, would certify gender traditionalism (man as protector, women as the protected) and restore the manly (and womanly) virtues and character that were the basis of American democracy. . . .

Whatever the century or whatever the case study, then, late-twentieth-century scholarship made big and insistent claims that gender ideologies were a fundamental part of foreign policy formulation. In all of the examples cited, it appears that gender shaped the identities of foreign policymakers themselves before they arrived in Washington, and that it continued to shape their assumptions, anxieties, aspirations, and actions once they were fully ensconced in diplomatic circles. . . .

[S]ince gender topics first appeared in the pages of diplomatic history journals, historians have debated the merits of gender analysis at conferences, in on-line forums, in journals, and in their own monographs. One of the reasons for this debate is that some of the gender-themed studies of American foreign relations gained momentum in fields outside of diplomatic history and, indeed, outside of the history discipline itself, in the more literary-focused arena of cultural studies. Skeptics of the gender approach have wondered aloud what diplomatic historians can learn from stories about sexual metaphors. . . . They have accused gender historians of paying too much attention to issues of representation at the cost of asking hard questions about causation. Some have argued that gender scholars have borrowed too heavily from other disciplines and have introduced questionable theories, methodologies, and insights into the field. . . .

While critics have argued that the new work on gender has better explained the connections between gender, culture, and diplomacy, rather than causation, those whose scholarship has been integral to this historiographical turn maintain that clear causation is hard to identify for any scholar, working on any problem, in any era. In fact, most gender scholars would agree that gender analysis does not explain reductively a single cause for a particular action, and that sometimes, gender meanings are not the most salient or significant aspects of a historical puzzle. Rather, they would argue, gender analysis abets the historian's effort to get closer to a reasonable and reliable set of explanations about a particular historical problem. Historians who seriously engage gender do not shy away from questions about causation, but they tend to approach overarching causal explanations with caution. The precise effect of George Kennan's "long telegram" on policymaking, for example, is impossible to discern, but it seems clear that his writings simplified what should have been a complex debate about Soviet intentions, and that his highly gendered, emotional musings naturalized—and thus rationalized—a set of diplomatic maneuvers that positioned the Soviets as unreliable allies and credible threats. In the case of the Spanish-American War, the societal panic about masculinity in decline reveals how gender "pushed" and "provoked" warfare as an antidote to the changes in nineteenth-century family and gender relations. . . .

Together, women's history and gender studies have enabled historians to conceive of foreign policy more broadly, inviting more actors, methods, and theories into the endeavor. A gender analysis offers one way to recast and expand the debates about the history of diplomacy. Its newness, relative to other approaches, has generated both excitement and skepticism, and as new work is published, historians will have new opportunities to debate its impact and merits.

The Racial Hierarchy

MICHAEL H. HUNT

Benjamin Franklin, that paragon of Enlightenment optimism, versatility, and virtue, was also a racist. He divided humanity according to skin color, assigning to each color characteristic traits. Indians he publicly condemned as "barbarous tribes of savages that delight in war and take pride in murder." His private correspondence depicted them as ignorant, congenitally lazy, vain, and insolent. An occasional blow was essential to keeping them in line; even a hint of weakness was an invitation to trouble. A slave owner whose printing establishment profited from slave sales, Franklin regarded blacks as lazy, thieving, and improvident. He defended the severity of slave codes as appropriate to a people "of a plotting Disposition, dark, sullen, malicious, revengeful, and cruel in the highest Degree." Even the "swarthy" German settlers in Franklin's Pennsylvania, derogated by him as "Palatine Boors," seemed undesirable aliens. They were worrisomely clannish, and some among them were even papists. . . .

Franklin's consciousness of color, fully shared by his contemporaries, figured prominently in the thinking of subsequent generations. Their conception of race, somewhat more elaborate and structured than Franklin's, was essentially hierarchical. They drew distinctions among the various peoples of the world on the basis of physical features, above all skin color and to a lesser extent head type . . . , and guided by those distinctions they ranked the various types of peoples in the world. Those with the lightest skin were positioned on the highest rung of the hierarchy, and those with the darkest skin were relegated to the lowest. In between fell the "yellow" Mongolians and Malays, the "red" American Indian, and the racially mixed Latino. Each color implied a level of physical, mental, and moral development, with white Americans setting themselves up as the unquestioned standard of measurement. . . .

This conception of race, defined by the poles of black and white, carried over into American foreign policy. By its grip on the thinking of the men who debated and determined that policy, by its influence over the press, and by its hold on the electorate, race powerfully shaped the way the nation dealt with other peoples. This included not just the Indian even before Franklin's day but also the peoples of Latin America, East Asia, and Europe. . . .

Americans inherited a rich legacy of racial thought from their immediate European ancestors. Westerners coming into contact with peoples of the "Third World" in the fifteenth century had already betrayed signs of racism. Well before Englishmen took that first step on the North American continent, they had absorbed Elizabethan myths about blacks and easily extrapolated them to other nonwhite peoples. These inherited views were greatly sharpened as Anglos began to contend with other expatriate Europeans, native Americans, and even Asians for a place on the new continent. For ambitious yet initially isolated British colonists, a picture of the world's peoples in which lightness of skin was tied to innate worth proved understandably attractive. Had there existed no ready-made Elizabethan notions about race, these colonists would surely have had to invent them. They used the racial hierarchy to underwrite their claim to lands they wanted and, once possession was secure, to justify the imposition of Anglo cultural values and institutions as well as the expulsion or political and economic subordination of lesser peoples. . . .

In the structure of American race thinking, Anglo-Saxonism—the belief that Americans and the British were one people united by uncommon qualities and common interests—occupied a central position. By the first half of the nineteenth century Americans had begun to claim with pride their place in a trans-Atlantic community of English-speaking people. Dimming memories of fratricidal conflict set off by the American revolution created the conditions favorable to the rise of Anglo-Saxonism in an increasingly firm national consciousness. School texts began to celebrate the trans-Atlantic tie. A poetic paean to "America and Britons" often reproduced in the 1830s and 1840s proclaimed, "The voice of blood shall reach, / More audibly than speech, / WE ARE ONE." . . .

The arrival of large numbers of disturbingly foreign immigrants sharpened the sensitivity to racial differences even within the circle of European whites. The nativism of the antebellum period had revealed early on the determination of ethnic Anglos to preserve their cultural hegemony against alien newcomers, then chiefly Irish and Germans. The concerns felt during that era proved mild, however, compared to the anxiety provoked by an ever greater influx of still more foreign peoples, from southern and eastern Europe, at the end of the century. From the racial comparisons then drawn by a defensive but culturally dominant Anglo elite, there emerged a clear and fixed pecking order even for whites. . . .

The popular vogue enjoyed by Darwinism further accentuated the tendency for Americans to think of themselves as a race in comparative and competitive terms and to locate themselves in an Anglo-Saxon community of interests. Given an optimistic twist, Darwinian notions served to reinforce preexisting ideas of Anglo-Saxon superiority. By the standards of industrial progress, military prowess, and international influence and control, Anglo-Saxons had an incontestable claim to the top of the racial heap. From that eminence they would point the way toward an era of unprecedented world peace and prosperity. Lesser races, awed and grateful, could follow the lead of the Anglo-Saxon—or drop to the bottom of the heap to meet their fate, ultimate extinction. . . .

[Theodore] Roosevelt's "strenuous" conception of national greatness dovetailed neatly with his preoccupation with race. Roosevelt read voraciously and wrote extensively on the subject; in expressing himself he could as easily employ formal pseudoscientific language as the cruder epithets of popular discourse. He regarded the world as a competitive arena for races no less than nations. The clash between civilized races and barbarian ones was inevitable; progress came only through the civilized man "subduing his barbarian neighbor." Not surprisingly Roosevelt considered Anglo-Saxons (he later came to prefer the term "English-speaking" people) the most advanced race. In 1881, in his first foray as an author, he described them as "bold and hardy, cool and intelligent." The American branch had been further strengthened by the frontier experience where lesser races had served as its "natural prey." With the frontier gone, Americans would have to confirm their mettle by joining their English cousins in the race for overseas territory and in the "warfare of the cradle" against the more prolific lower orders, chiefly eastern Europeans, Latin Americans, and blacks. . . .

[V]ery unlike Roosevelt, [Woodrow] Wilson was a belated convert to the notion that an assertive foreign policy was the key to national greatness. Not until the Spanish-American War did he give even perfunctory attention to foreign affairs. He appears at first to have shared the doubts of many Southerners about the desirability of annexing the Philippines. By November 1898, however, he seems to have reluctantly concluded that it was better for Spain to be displaced by the United States than by a power such as Germany or Russia. The United States stood for "the light of day, while theirs was the light of darkness." . . .

But Wilson did not share Roosevelt's fixation with great-power rivalry and racial struggle. True to his own heritage, Wilson focused instead on moral service that would gently help the weak and suffering and refine the American spirit. Good works abroad would test "our political character, our political capacity, our political principles, even our political organizations." Wilson directed his instinct for service toward an Asia in ferment. The United States had a duty, he contended, "to play a part, and a leading part at that, in the opening and transformation of the East." For example, the Philippines, which had drawn his attention to the Pacific in the first place, challenged Americans to learn colonial administration, introduce order, guide the "natives" through "a long apprenticeship" in self-government, and thereby demonstrate that "we have only their welfare at heart." . . .

[A]ttitudes toward race . . . persisted little changed into the interwar era. They flourished at home in the nativism of the 1920s, itself an encore to the hyperpatriotism and attacks on hyphenates that had marred the war years. With the foreign-born and their children accounting for an alarmingly high proportion of the population (over a fifth), defenders of the old stock and ancestral virtues stirred into action. Congress passed by overwhelming margins laws to keep out undesirable immigrants—Japanese, Filipinos, and southern and eastern Europeans. In the South, Midwest, Southwest, and Far West as many as five million Americans joined the Ku Klux Klan, drawn by its doctrine of white supremacy and its attacks on Catholics, Jews, and other outsiders. The racial hatreds of the time turned most ferociously against blacks, for whom lynchings were but the most brutal of a variety of reminders of their assigned place in the hierarchy of color. . . .

These racial attitudes bore striking fruit in the feelings of condescension and contempt that policymakers occasionally revealed. Franklin D. Roosevelt, advocate of the Good Neighbor policy toward Latin America, unwittingly revealed his feelings of superiority when he offered a backhanded compliment to what he described as "these South American things." He observed, "The think they are just as good as we are," and then broad-mindedly conceded that "many of them are." In Cuba in 1933 he demonstrated the strength of his paternalism when he acted on what he conceived to be "our duty" to prevent "starvation or chaos among the Cuban people." . . .

Japan's occupation of Manchuria in 1931 and the invasion of China proper six years later bothered the defenders of Anglo-Saxonism in the East. [Secretary of War Henry] Stimson and later Roosevelt and his secretary of state Cordell Hull worried that the militarists were in the ascendance. But American leaders also believed that the civilians still had a chance to regain control and reverse a policy of aggression if encouraged by an admonitory and if necessary hard-line U.S. stance.

Stimson, confident that his service in the Philippines had given him an insight into "the Oriental mind," was determined to defend the East Asian international order and a U.S. China policy characterized by a "real nobility." Both were threatened by the "virtually mad dogs" that had taken control in Japan. Staging public displays of disapproval, he also fussed and blustered at Japanese envoys in private. Hull, for his part, had by the late 1930s decided that the Japanese were barbarians at the gate intent on joining Hitler in driving the world back into the Dark Ages. Roosevelt bluntly told Japanese diplomats that their policy violated "the fundamental principles of peace and order." With his associates he was even blunter. The Japanese were indeed "the Prussians of the East"; they were "openly and unashamedly one of the predatory nations fundamentally at odds with American ideals; and they were "drunk with their dream of dominion." For Roosevelt it was clear on which side Japan stood in the sharpening global struggle "between human slavery and human freedom— between pagan brutality and the Christian ideal." . . .

World War II led to an unprecedented, decade-long mobilization and deployment of national power. No sooner had American leaders been assured of victory over the Axis than they set to work on stabilizing and reforming the postwar political and economic order, as well as on countering what they soon concluded was a serious Soviet threat to that order. By the end of 1950 the pattern of the Cold War was set as arms costs mushroomed, aid programs and alliances multiplied, American troops fought their first limited war in Korea, and Washington made the initial commitments that would lead to the second, in Indochina. . . .

After five years of gestation a policy geared to greatness and counterrevolution had taken shape. In Europe it quickly proved a success. The Marshall Plan, the largest of the postwar assistance programs, rescued the Continent's war-ravaged economies, while American-backed Christian Democrats drove the large French and Italian Communist parties from power. The North Atlantic Treaty Organization functioned no less effectively as a shield against the Red Army. West Germany, with its valuable manpower and industry, was not subjected to "pastoralization" (as punitive wartime plans had intended) but integrated into the alliance. . . .

Elsewhere along the containment line stretching from the Middle East to Northeast Asia, American leaders encountered greater difficulties. Indeed, not only here but throughout the "Third World" (in other words, lands unfamiliar to Americans, even those making up the foreign-policy elite) they would find military and political problems ambiguous, complex, intractable, and in the final analysis ill suited to a straightforward policy of containment modeled on the European experience. Rural economies more sorely pinched by poverty than those in Europe, leaders still struggling to end colonial control and give form to their national aspirations, and peoples largely immune to the appeal of American political values left the lands of Asia, Latin America, and Africa in ferment. American cold warriors constantly worried about the disorder these continents were prone to. Unsettled conditions not only made for infirm allies and fickle dependents but, more troubling still, invited Communist subversion or invasion.

Realizing that the solution of these problems was the precondition for the defense of the Third World, Washington came to embrace a policy of development. Development was the younger sibling of containment. While containment focused on the immediate problems of holding the Soviets and their leftist allies at bay, development was intended to provide long-term immunity against the contagion of communism. Like containment, development policy drew inspiration from the long-established ideology. But while containment underlined the obligations of a great nation to defend liberty, development theory drew its inspiration from the old American vision of appropriate or legitimate processes of social change and an abiding sense of superiority over the dark-skinned peoples of the Third World. Social scientists and policymakers often described the goals of development in abstract, neutral catchwords. They spoke of the modernization of traditional societies, nation building, or the stimulation of self-sustaining economic growth in once stagnant economies. In practice, though, these impressive new formulations amounted to little more than a restatement of the old ethnocentric platitudes about uplift and re-generation formerly directed at the Philippines, China, and Mexico. . . .

Condescending and paternalistic, development theory also carried forward the long-established American views on race. Changing domestic practices and inter-national conditions had, however, made untenable a hierarchy cast in explicitly racial terms. From the 1940s Jim Crow laws had fallen under mounting attack, culminating in the civil-rights movement of the late 1950s and early 1960s. Over that same period a hot war against Nazi supermen and a cold war in the name of freedom and the lib-eration of oppressed peoples had made racial segregation at home and pejorative references to race in public a serious embarrassment. Moreover, scientists had by then turned their backs on grand racial theories, thereby further undermining the legitimacy of thinking in terms of race. Policymakers, whose impulse to see the world in terms of a hierarchy was ever more at odds with the need for political discretion, found their way out of their bind by recasting the old racial hierarchy into cultural terms supplied by development theorists. No longer did leaders dare broadcast their views on barbarous or backward people, race traits, or skin color. It was instead now the attributes of modernity and tradition that fixed a people's or nation's place on the hierarchy.

Not surprisingly, though, the resulting rankings were strikingly similar to the ones assigned two centuries earlier by race-conscious ancestors. Americans could remain secure in the superiority of their own kind. Anglo-Americans were still on top, followed by the various European peoples. Then came the "Third World." The term, which gained currency in the 1950s and 1960s, defined the battleground between the democratic First World and the Second World of the socialist bloc that had emerged after World War II. The Cold War concern with the Third World as a zone of conflict rested on a sturdy bedrock of American thinking on race. Though the socialist monolith fell apart and the struggle for the political soul of the Third World sputtered on inconclusively, the idea of the Third World as a single entity survived, sustained by the American conviction of its backwardness and the re-pressed American consciousness of the color of its peoples. Black Africa occupied the lowest rung, just as black ghettos represented the lower reaches of American society. Higher up stood Asians and Latins, still exotic and still difficult to classify with exactitude because of the unstable mixture of attractive and repulsive character-istics assigned to them. An American society where skin color still powerfully defined an individual's place and prospects was unable to transcend the policy implications of long-nurtured assumptions about racial differences. The change in vocabulary had not altered the hierarchy; it had simply made more plausible the denial of any links to an unfashionably racist world view.

Security, Values, and Power

MELVYN P. LEFFLER

[I]n mid-September 2002, the Bush administration released a formal statement of its national security strategy. It ignited a storm of controversy. "The United States," reported the *Guardian,* "will not hesitate to strike pre-emptively against its enemies . . . and will never again allow its military supremacy to be threatened by a rival superpower." In an editorial three days later, the newspaper excoriated the Bush strategy. It "is arrogant, patronizing, complacent, amazingly presumptuous—but above all aggressive." Although other influential media outlets like *The Economist* and the *Financial Times* gave more nuanced responses, most European newspapers suggested that something new, profound and ominous was being introduced. "We must face facts," said *Le Monde Diplomatique.* "A new imperial doctrine is taking shape under George Bush."

In the United States as well as in the UK and Europe, a stream of critical articles poured forth, arguing that the new strategy was the product of a group of neo-conservative hawks, including Vice-President Dick Cheney and Deputy Secretary of Defense Paul Wolfowitz, who since the early 1990s had been advocating strategies of unilateralism, pre-emption and military hegemony. Their plan, wrote David Armstrong in *Harper's Magazine,* "is for the United States to rule the world. The overt theme is unilateralism, but it is ultimately a story of domination." . . .

The Bush administration prides itself on marrying power and values. "There is an old argument," emphasized Condoleezza Rice, between realists and idealists. "To oversimplify, realists downplay the importance of values. . . . Idealist emphasize the primacy of values. . . . As a professor," she went on to say, "I recognize that this debate has won tenure for . . . many generations of scholars. As a policymaker, I can tell you that these categories obscure reality."

She is quite right. The history of American foreign relations is not about the struggle between power and ideals, as it is so often portrayed, but about their intermingling. America's ideals have always encapsulated its interests. America's ideology has always been tailored to correspond with its quest for territory and markets. In short, power, ideology and interests have always had a dynamic and unsettled relationship with one another. But these relationships are more nuanced and complex than most people think. Power sometimes has been constrained by legislative-executive battles and the spectre of a garrison state; expansion has been circumscribed by the exigencies of domestic politics, racial attitudes and republican ideology; unilateralism has been tempered by the realization that alliances and multilateral strategies could be adopted if they advanced American interests.

So today, in many respects, Bush's national security strategies are more firmly rooted in the past than most people think. They are also more complex and more conflicted than either supporters or critics believe. The quest for military superiority, for example, is hardly new or noteworthy. Throughout its early history, the United States relied on the British navy to ward off European foes while deploying superior power

Melvyn P. Leffler, "Security, Values and Power," from "9/11 and the Past and Future of American Foreign Policy," *International Affairs* 79(5) (2003): 1045–1046, 1050–1051, 1053–1055, 1057, 1059–1062. Reprinted by permission of Blackwell Publishing.

on land against the Spanish, Mexicans and Native Americans. When they had to, American policy-makers mobilized additional force to deal with vexatious foes, as, for example, when Thomas Jefferson and James Madison built a small navy to cope with the attacks of the terrorists of their day, the so-called Barbary pirates. Frightened by the rise of German naval power in the early twentieth century and always chafing at British naval supremacy, the United States built a modern navy of its own and then demanded naval parity in the aftermath of the First World War. After the Second World War, chastened by the lessons learned from America's failure to build to treaty limits and by the attack on Pearl Harbor, Truman's intention was to preserve US military superiority. Although he was ready to discuss international control of atomic weapons, he sought to retain America's nuclear monopoly for as long as possible.

Although many contemporaries and historians defined US Cold War policies in terms of containment and deterrence, America's real strategy was to pursue a preponderance of power. US Cold War policies were always designed not so much to contain Soviet power and influence as to roll them back, and to transform the Kremlin's approach to international politics. . . .

If the quest for military superiority is not so different from what it was during the Cold War, neither is the strategy of pre-emption. . . .

Pre-emption has a long tradition in American history. In 1904 President Theodore Roosevelt announced a new corollary to the Monroe Doctrine, unilaterally asserting the right of the United States to intervene militarily in the western hemisphere to preserve order. "Pre-emptive imperialism" was designed to thwart prospective European interventions and protect the national security of the United States. The United States intervened repeatedly in Cuba, the Dominican Republic, Nicaragua and Haiti. In Nicaragua, US troops remained from 1912 to 1933 (with one brief interruption); in Haiti they stayed from 1915 to 1934; in the Dominican Republic from 1916 to 1924.

Pre-emption, then, is not new; but it has a place of special importance in the thinking of Bush's defense advisers. It is "fundamental," Wolfowitz told a joint congressional committee. "This is not a game we will ever win on defense. We'll only win it on offense."

Although this attitude is often portrayed as unique to a group of neoconservative hawks who have infiltrated the Bush administration, the truth of the matter is that the proclivity towards an offensive strategy, towards pre-emption and counterproliferation, had been evolving for a decade and had mustered bipartisan support long before Rumsfeld and Wolfowitz became household names. In a partially declassified presidential directive of 1995, Bill Clinton put his imprimatur on a new United States counterterrorism policy. The policy of the United States, the directive said, is "to deter and preempt, apprehend and prosecute . . . individuals who perpetrate or plan to perpetrate terrorist attacks." The United States, the directive went on to say, would seek to identify ". . . states that sponsor or support such terrorists, isolate them and extract a heavy price." . . .

Almost everyone in the United States who carefully examined national security issues in the 1990s grasped the growing threat of terrorism, the links with failing and rogue states, and the spectre of an attack on the United States with weapons of mass destruction. Many and diverse people called for preventive action. Many struggled, however reluctantly, with pre-emptive scenarios. Many grasped the reality that there were terrorist groups that were not likely to be deterred as states had been deterred. Many accepted the awful reality that technological developments, communications breakthroughs and porous borders made attacks with biological and chemical weapons more likely, indeed very likely. Experts might argue over the mix of policies, but few doubted that innovations in weapons technology and military tactics were needed, as were a vast array of preventive actions and pre-emptive options. The new threat—the nexus of terrorism, failing states, rogue governments, suicide bombers and weapons of mass destruction—made this mode of thinking unavoidable.

Like many of the experts who wrote these reports, Powell and Rice have stressed that pre-emption "must be treated with great caution." It is one tool, said Colin Powell, in a toolbox filled with tools. The number of cases in which it might be justified, insisted Condoleezza Rice, "will always be small. . . . It does not give a green light—to the United States or any other nation—to act first without exhausting other means. . . . The threat must be very grave. And the risks of waiting must far outweigh the risks of action."

Nor do US officials believe that root causes can be ignored. "We [have] got to act preventively," Wolfowitz told his congressional inquisitors. "And that isn't only by military means, or even only by intelligence means."

Wolfowitz, Rice, Powell and their colleagues embrace the idea of a democratic peace. They seek, by deploying American power to crush terrorists and by mobilizing American economic strength to foster growth, to expand the opportunities for democratic self-government everywhere. Their speeches are infused with a missionary zeal, with a conviction that freedom is good for individuals, for societies and for the international system. Their convictions are supported by research since the 1980s demonstrating that democratic nations do tend to be more peaceful when they deal with one another. Freedom, peace, order and self-interest are all intertwined. . . .

If the administration's strategy has deep and diverse historical roots, and if it reflects an awareness of the complex sources of terrorism, why, then, does it merit criticism? . . .

When faced with existential challenges in the twentieth century, the United States championed not a balance of power, but a community of power. As Woodrow Wilson solemnly pondered American intervention in the First World War, he said, "peace cannot . . . rest upon an armed balance of power." After the war, he insisted that the balance of power "should end now and forever." Lasting peace, he maintained, required "not a balance of power, but a community of power; not organized rivalries, but an organized common peace."

Wilson's alternative vision was of a community of power based on self-determination of peoples and the interdependence of nations. The central idea of this treaty, he maintained, is "that nations do not consist of their governments but consist of their people." People had the right to determine their own government and to live without fear. They had the right to travel on the seas freely and to trade on equal terms. They had the right to expect their governments to preserve order, govern justly and thwart revolutionary impulses. Governments, in turn, had a responsibility to limit their armaments and work together to preserve the peace. Peace would be made secure by the organized moral force of mankind, mobilized through the vehicle of the League of Nations. . . .

Woodrow Wilson called for a community of power precisely because he fore-saw that unilateral efforts to enhance security triggered arms races and multiplied perceptions of threat. He was not blind to the dangers lurking in a world of nation-states, but he believed they were best dealt with through multilateral institutions embodying notions of collective security. Wilson's community of power meant limiting armaments, expanding economic interdependence and, most of all, building norms, laws and institutions to modulate the competitive instincts of nations and to avert the security dilemmas that inevitably flow from unilateral actions, whether intended for good or evil.

Nowadays, scholars refer to these efforts in terms of the utility of "soft power." The Bush administration, as we have seen, is not unaware of the utility of soft power. Indeed, it seeks to capitalize on the resonance of American values, dissemi-nate its marketplace principles and utilize its economic prowess to mould a more peaceful world order. But balance of power thinking trumps the administration's understanding of soft power and inclines it to favour military priorities. Senator Richard Lugar, chairman of the Foreign Relations Committee, got to the heart of the matter in February 2003 when he politely admonished Secretary Powell for the paltry funds allocated to the non-military aspects of foreign policy. "Even after a healthy increase in the last fiscal year," Senator Lugar pointed out, "the U.S. foreign assistance, in constant dollars, has declined about 44 percent since Ronald Reagan's presidency in 1985 and about 18 per cent since the collapse of the Soviet Union in 1991." The United States, Lugar added, ranked last among the 21 major providers of aid to the developing world. . . .

At times of existential crisis in the past, at times when dangers seemed to loom very large and very close, Bush's predecessors sought to tackle root causes and establish lasting institutions. Wilson focused on the League; Franklin Roosevelt helped craft the IMF, the World Bank and the United Nations; Truman, Eisenhower and Kennedy sought to fashion the political and economic instruments that nur-tured the recovery of Germany and Japan and facilitated their peaceful integration into the international system. . . .

The point of these comparisons is not to glorify the past. Neither Wilson, nor Roosevelt, nor Truman ever renounced the use of power, or relinquished the free-dom to act unilaterally, or countenanced serious infringements of US sovereignty. But their apocalyptic fears and messianic zeal prompted a very different matrix of policies. . . .

[The Bush administration] should not be criticized for highlighting the threats that confront humankind. Their fear of weapons of mass destruction in the hands of terrorists or arbitrary governments is well founded; their belief that advances in technology abet the cause of terrorists is not erroneous; their understanding that porous borders provide opportunities for sabotage is not irrational: their conviction that weak states and rogue governments may provide safe havens for terrorists is grounded in reality. Like Wilson and Franklin Roosevelt, like Truman and the cold warriors who succeeded him, Bush rightly sees peril lurking in the international environment. . . .

As we have seen, Bush's policies are rooted in the traditional American matrix of values, interests and power. These variables have a dynamic and unstable rela-tionship to one another and can be configured in different ways, with strikingly dif-ferent implications. In the background of Bush's strategy lurks a recognition that pre-emption should not be a first option; that root causes cannot be ameliorated by the application of force; that a democratic peace can make for a more peaceful world; that multilateral institutions can multiply the strength of freedom-loving nations. The potential, therefore, exists for a different strategy; but its emergence will depend on the policies of America's friends abroad as well as on domestic politics and legislative-executive relations at home.

Bureaucratic Politics and Policy Outcomes

J. GARRY CLIFFORD

In the mid-1960s, when members of the Harvard Faculty Study Group on Bureaucracy, Politics, and Policy began to write their scholarly tomes, their sometime colleague in the mathematics department, the irreverent folk singer Tom Lehrer, inadvertently gave song to what came to be called the "bureaucratic politics" approach to the study of U.S. foreign policy. In his ballad about a certain German emigre rocket scientist, Lehrer wrote: "Once the rockets are up / Who cares where they come down? / That's not my department! / Said Wernher von Braun." Lehrer's ditty, by suggesting that government is a complex, compartmentalized machine and that those running the machine do not always intend what will result, anticipated the language of bureaucratic politics. The dark humor also hinted that the perspective might sometimes excuse as much as it explains about the foreign policy of the United States.

The formal academic version of bureaucratic politics came a few years later with the publication in 1971 of Graham T. Allison's *Essence of Decision*. Building on works by Warner R. Schilling, Roger Hilsman, Richard E. Neustadt, and other political scientists who emphasized informal bargaining within the foreign policy process, and adding insights from organization theorists such as James G. March and Herbert A. Simon, Allison examined the 1962 Cuban Missile Crisis to counter the traditional assumption that foreign policy is produced by the purposeful acts of unified national governments. Allison argued that instead of behaving like a "rational actor," the Kennedy administration's actions during the crisis were best explained as "outcomes" of standard operating procedures followed by separate organizations (the navy's blockade, the Central Intelligence Agency's U-2 overflights, and the air force's scenarios for a surgical air strike) and as a result of compromise and competition among hawks and doves seeking to advance individual and organizational versions of the national interest. Allison soon collaborated with Morton H. Halperin to formalize the bureaucratic politics paradigm. Other scholars followed with bureaucratic analyses of topics including American decision making in the Vietnam War, the nonrecognition of China, the Marshall Plan, U.S.-Turkish relations, the Antiballistic Missile (ABM) decision, nuclear weapons accidents, and U.S. international economic policy, as well as refinements and critiques of the Allison-Halperin model. The John F. Kennedy School of Government at Harvard made bureaucratic politics the centerpiece of its new public policy program, and Allison became its dean. In 1999, his framework long since hailed as "one of the most widely disseminated concepts in all of social sciences," Allison and Philip Zelikow prepared an extensive, revised edition of *Essence of Decision* to refute political science theorists who "explain state behavior by system-level or external factors alone."

The Allisonian message holds that U.S. foreign policy has become increasingly political and cumbersome with the growth of bureaucracy. Diversity and conflict permeate the policy process. There is no single "maker" of foreign policy. Policy flows instead from an amalgam of organizations and political actors who differ substantially on any particular issue and who compete to advance their own personal and organizational interests as they try to influence decisions. Even in the aftermath of such national disasters as Pearl Harbor or the terrorist attacks of September 2001, turf wars proliferate because agencies reflexively resist reorganization and scapegoat others to avoid blame. The president, while powerful, is not omnipotent; he is one chief among many. For example, President Ronald Reagan may have envisaged his Strategic Defense Initiative (or "Star Wars") as a workable program to shield entire populations from the threat of nuclear war, but hardliners in the Pentagon saw it primarily as an antiballistic missile defense that would gain a technological advantage over the Soviet Union and stifle public agitation for more substantial arms control proposals.

Even after a direct presidential decision the "game" does not end because decisions are often ignored or reversed. Just as Jimmy Carter thought he had killed the B-1 bomber, only to see it revived during the Reagan years, so too did Franklin D. Roosevelt veto a "Pacific First" strategy in 1942, whereupon the Joint Chiefs of Staff, in historian Mark Stoler's words, "formally submitted to his [FDR's] orders but did so in such a way as to enable them to pursue a modified version of their alternative strategy" for the rest of World War II. Because organizations rely on routines and plans derived from experience with familiar problems, those standard routines usually form the basis for options furnished the president. Ask an organization to do what it has not done previously, and it will usually do what the U.S. military did in Vietnam: It will follow existing doctrines and procedures, modifying them only slightly in deference to different conditions.

Final decisions are also "political resultants," the product of compromise and bargaining among the various participants. As Allison puts it, policies are "resultants in the sense that what happens is not chosen . . . but rather results from compromise, conflict, and confusion of officials with diverse interests and unequal influence; political in the sense [of] . . . bargaining along regularized channels among individual members of government." Similarly, once a decision is made, considerable slippage can occur in implementing it. What follows becomes hostage to standard operating procedures and the parochial interests of the actors and agencies doing the implementing. Even when a president personally monitors performance, as John F. Kennedy tried to do during the missile crisis, organizational routines and hierarchies are so rigid and complex that the president cannot micromanage all that happens. Not only did Kennedy not know that antisubmarine warfare units were routinely forcing Soviet submarines to the surface, thus precipitating the very confrontations he wanted to avoid, but the president was also unaware that NATO's nuclear-armed fighter-bombers had been put on a nuclear Quick Reaction Alert (QRA), thus escaping the tight personal controls he had placed on Jupiter missiles in Turkey and Italy.

The bureaucratic politics perspective also suggests that intramural struggles over policy can consume so much time and attention that dealing with external realities can become secondary. Virtually every study of nuclear arms negotiations from the Baruch Plan to START confirms the truism that arriving at a consensus among the various players and agencies within the U.S. government was more complicated, if not more difficult, than negotiating with the Soviets. Ironically, officials who are finely attuned to the conflict and compartmentalization within the American government often see unitary, purposeful behavior on the part of other governments. Recall the rush to judgment about the Soviet shooting down of a Korean airliner in autumn 1983 as compared to the embarrassed and defiant explanations emanating from Washington when a U.S. navy spy plane collided with a Chinese jet and crash-landed on Hainan Island in 2001. When NATO forces carried out long-planned war games (Operation Able Archer) in the aftermath of the KAL 007 shoot-down, Washington experts scoffed at intelligence reports that Soviet leaders genuinely feared a nuclear first strike, calling it a disinformation ploy. Only President Reagan, as one scholar has noted, worried that "[Andrei] Gromyko and [Yuri] Andropov are just two players sitting on top of a large military machine" and that panic and miscalculation might lead to Armageddon, so he told his startled senior advisers. Reagan's very next speech called for "nuclear weapons" to be "banished from the face of the earth."

Several important criticisms have been leveled at the bureaucratic politics approach. Some critics contend that ideological core values shared by those whom Richard J. Barnet has called "national security managers" weigh more in determining policy than do any differences attributable to bureaucratic position. The axiom "where you stand depends on where you sit" has had less influence, they argue, than the generational mindset of such individuals as McGeorge Bundy, Paul Nitze, John J. McCloy, and Clark Clifford, whose participation in the foreign policy establishment spanned decades and cut across bureaucratic and partisan boundaries. Because, as Robert S. McNamara later observed of the missile crisis, "you can't manage" crises amidst all the "misinformation, miscalculation, misjudgment, and human fallibility," other critics suggest that the framework lets decisionmakers off the hook by failing to pinpoint responsibility. Indeed, the president can dominate the bureaucracy by selecting key players and setting the rules of the game. Even though President Reagan once joked that "sometimes our right hand doesn't know what our far right-hand is doing," his defenders erred in absolving Reagan by blaming the Iran-contra affair on insiders "with their own agenda" who allegedly deceived the detached president by feeding him false information. Yet, as Theodore Draper has clearly demonstrated, at all top-level meetings on Iran-contra, President Reagan spoke more than any of his advisers, forcefully steered discussions, and made basic decisions, whether or not he subsequently approved every operational detail. The historian must be careful in each case to judge how much of the buck that stops with the president has already been spent by the bureaucracy. . . .

Yet such defeats in the bureaucratic politics approach may not hamper historians, who do not need models that predict perfectly. Unlike political scientists, they do not seek to build better theories or to propose more effective management techniques. Because the bureaucratic politics approach emphasizes state-level analysis, it cannot answer such system-level questions as why the United States has opposed revolutions or why East-West issues have predominated over North-South issues. It is better at explaining the timing and mechanics of particular episodes, illuminating proximate as opposed to deeper causes, and showing why outcomes were not what was intended. The bureaucratic details of debacles such as Pearl Harbor and the Bay of Pigs invasion are thus better understood than the long-term dynamics of war and peace. . . .

When can the framework be most helpful? Because organizations function most predictably in a familiar environment, major transformations in the international system (wars and their aftermaths, economic crises, the Sino-Soviet split) require the analyst to study how these changes produce, however belatedly, institutional adjustments in U.S. policies. Equally propitious, even for the pre-Cold War era, are military occupations wherein the often clashing missions of diplomats and military proconsuls ("striped pants" versus "gold braid," in Eric Roorda's formulation) complicate the management of empire from Managua to Manila. So too are political transitions that bring in new players pledged to reverse the priorities of their predecessors, and particularly those administrations in which the president, deliberately or not, encourages competition and initiative from strong-willed subordinates. Fiascos such as the U.S. failure to anticipate the attack on Pearl Harbor and the Iran-contra affair not only force agencies to reassess procedures and programs but, even better, often spawn official investigations that provide scholars with abundant evidence for bureaucratic analysis. Budget battles, weapons procurement, coordination of intelligence, war termination, alliance politics—in short, any foreign policy that engages the separate attentions of multiple agencies and agents—should alert the historian to the bureaucratic politics perspective.

Consider, for example, the complex dynamics of American entry into World War II. Looking at the period through the lens of bureaucratic politics reveals that FDR had more than Congress in mind when making his famous remark: "It's a terrible thing to look over your shoulder when you are trying to lead—and to find no one there." The institutional aversion to giving commissioned naval vessels to a foreign power delayed the destroyers-for-bases deal for several weeks in the summer of 1940, and only by getting eight British bases in direct exchange for the destroyers could Roosevelt persuade the chief of naval operations, Admiral Harold Stark, to certify, as required by statute, that these destroyers were no longer essential to national defense. According to navy scuttlebutt, the president threatened to fire Stark if he did not support what virtually every naval officer opposed and the admiral agonized before acquiescing. The army's initial opposition to peacetime conscription, FDR's dramatic appointment of Henry L. Stimson and Frank Knox to head the War and Navy departments in June 1940, his firing of Admiral James O. Richardson for his opposition to basing the Pacific fleet at Pearl Harbor, the refusal of the army and navy to mount expeditions to the Azores and Dakar in the spring of 1941, the unvarying strategic advice not to risk war until the armed forces were better prepared—all suggest an environment in which the president had to push hard to get the bureaucracy to accept his policy of supporting the Allies by steps short of war. Even the navy's eagerness to begin Atlantic convoys in spring 1941 and the subsequent Army Air Corps strategy of reinforcing the Philippines with B-17s were aimed in part at deploying ships and planes that FDR might otherwise have given to the British and the Russians. . . .

In sum, this essay should be read as a modest plea for greater attention to bureaucratic politics. The perspective can enrich and complement other approaches. By focusing on internal political processes we become aware of the tradeoffs within government that reflect the cooperative core values posited by the corporatists or neo-realists. In its emphasis on individual values and tugging and hauling by key players, bureaucratic politics makes personality and cognitive processes crucial to understanding who wins and why. Bureaucratic hawks, as Frank Costigliola has noted, often use emotion-laden, gendered language to prevail over their dovish colleagues. Although bureaucratic struggles may be over tactics more than strategy, over pace rather than direction, those distinctions may matter greatly when the outcome is a divided Berlin and Korea, a second atomic bomb, impromptu hostage rescue missions that fail, or a military "exit strategy" that precludes occupation of the enemy's capital. Too easily dismissed as a primer for managing crisis that should be avoided, the bureaucratic politics perspective also warns that when "governments collide," the machines cannot do what they are not programmed to do. Rather than press "delete" and conceptualize policy only as rational action, it is incumbent on historians to know how the machines work, their repertories, the institutional rules of the game, the rosters, and how the box score is kept. The peculiarities of the U.S. checks-and-balances system of governance make such analysis imperative. The British ambassador Edward Lord Halifax once likened the foreign policy processes in Washington to "a disorderly line of beaters out shooting; they do put the rabbits out of the bracken, but they don't come out where you would expect." Historians of American foreign relations need to identify the beaters and follow them into the bureaucratic forest because the quarry is much bigger than rabbit.

F U R T H E R   R E A D I N G

Shigeru Akita and Takeshi Matsuda, eds., *Look Backward at the Twentieth Century* (2000) (on world-systems theory)

Graham Allison and Philip Zelikow, *Essence of Decision: Explaining the Cuban Missile Crisis* (1999)

Giovanni, Arrighi, *The Long Twentieth Century* (1994) (on world capitalism)

William H. Becker and Samuel F. Wells, eds., *Economics and World Power* (1984)

Gail Bederman, *Manliness and Civilization* (1995)

Thomas Bender, *Rethinking American History in a Global Age* (2002)

David Campbell, *Writing Security* (1992) (on postmodern theory)

John M. Carrol and George C. Herring, eds., *Modern American Diplomacy* (1995)

J. Garry Clifford and Samuel R. Spencer Jr., *The First Peacetime Draft* (1986)

Carol Cohn, "War, Wimps, and Women: Talking Gender and Thinking War," in Miriam Cooke and Angela Woolacott, eds., *Gendering War Talk* (1993), 227–246

Frank Costigliola, "Unceasing Pressure for Penetration: Gender, Pathology, and Emotion in George Kennan's Formation of the Cold War," *Journal of American History* 83 (1997): 1309–1338

Robert Dallek, *The American Style of Foreign Policy* (1983)

Alexander DeConde, *Presidential Machismo* (2000)

Stefan Dudink et al., eds., *Masculinities in Politics and War* (2004)

Cynthia Enloe, *Bananas, Beaches, and Bases* (1989) (on gender)

Heidi Fehrenbach and Uta G. Poiger, eds., *Transactions, Transgressions, Transformations: American Culture in Western Europe and Japan* (2000)

Eric Foner, *Who Owns History?* (2002)

"Foreign Relations in the Early Republic: Essays from a SHEAR Symposium," *Journal of the Early Republic* 14 (1994): 453–495

Frank Füred, *The Silent War* (1998) (on race)

John Lewis Gaddis, *The Landscape of History* (2002)

Lloyd C. Gardner, ed., *Redefining the Past* (1986)

Jessica C. E. Gienow-Hecht et al., eds., *Culture and International Relations* (2003)

Craig Gorden, *Force and Statecraft* (1995)

Andre Gunder Frank and Barry Gills, *The World System* (1996)

Morton Halperin, *Bureaucratic Politics and Foreign Policy* (1974)

Michael J. Hogan and Thomas G. Paterson, eds., *Explaining the History of American Foreign Relations* (2004)

Kristin Hoganson, *Fighting for American Manhood* (1999)

Ole Holsti, *Public Opinion and American Foreign Policy* (1996)

G. John Ikenberry, ed., *American Foreign Policy: Theoretical Essays* (1999)

Amy Kaplan, *The Anarchy of Empire in the Making of U.S. Culture* (2002)

———— and Donald E. Pease, eds., *Cultures of United States Imperialism* (1993)

Charles Kindleberger, *The World Economy and National Finance in Historical Perspective* (1995)

Christina Klein, *Cold War Orientalism* (2003) (on U.S. and Asia)

Gabriel Kolko, *Century of War* (1994)

Walter LaFeber, "Liberty and Power: U.S. Diplomatic History, 1750–1945," in Susan Porter Benson et al., eds., *The New American History* (1997)

James N. Leiker, *Racial Borders* (2002)

Seymour Martin Lipset, *American Exceptionalism* (1996)

Charles S. Maier, Consigning the Twentieth Century to History: Alternative Narratives for the Modern Era," *American Historical Review* 105 (June 2000): 807–831

Gorden Martel, ed., *American Foreign Relations Reconsidered* (1994)

James McDougall, *Promised Land, Crusader State* (1995)

Laura McEnaney, *Civil Defense Begins At Home* (2000)

James K. Merriwether, *Proudly We Be Africans* (2002)

Charles E. Neu, "The Rise of the National Security Bureaucracy," in Louis Galambos, ed., *The New American State* (1987)

Richard E. Neustadt, *Presidential Power* (1990)

Frank A. Ninkovich, *Modernity and Power* (1994)

————, *The Wilsonian Century* (1999)

Ruth Roadh Pierson and Nupur Chaudhuri, *Nation, Empire, Colony* (1998) (on gender and race)

Mary A. Renda, *Taking Haiti* (2001) (on gender, race, and cultural paternalism)

Emily S. Rosenberg, *Financial Missionaries to the World* (2000) (on gender and dollar diplomacy)

Andrew J. Rotter, "Gender Relations, Foreign Relations: The United States and South Asia, 1947–1964," *Journal of American History* 81 (September 1994): 518–542

"Roundtable: Cultural Transfer or Cultural Imperialism," *Diplomatic History* 24 (Summer 2000): 465–528

David Ryan, *U.S. Foreign Policy in World History* (2000)

Arthur Schlesinger, Jr., *War and the American Presidency* (2004)

Joan W. Scott, *Gender and the Politics of History* (1999)

Robert Shaffer, "Race, Class, Gender and Diplomatic History," *Radical History Review* 70 (1998): 156–168

Tony Smith, *Foreign Attachments* (2000) (on ethnic groups and foreign relations)

Ann Laura Stoler, *Carnal Knowledge and Imperial Power* (2002)

"Symposium: African Americans and U.S. Foreign Relations," *Diplomatic History* 20 (1996): 531–650

"Symposium: Gender and U.S. Foreign Relations," *Diplomatic History* 18 (1994): 47–124

Immanuel Wallerstein, *The Capitalist World Economy* (1979)

Donald W. White, *The American Century* (1996)

William Appleman Williams, *The Tragedy of American Diplomacy* (1972)

Thomas W. Zeiller, "Just Do It? Globalization for Diplomatic Historians," *Diplomatic History* 25 (Fall 2001): 529–551

CHAPTER
2

The Origins of American Foreign Policy in the Revolutionary Era

Americans were once proud members of the British Empire. For more than 150 years that membership brought good profit at low cost and protection against the French in North America. But in the 1760s, after victory in the French and Indian War, Britain began to impose new taxes and regulations that shattered the relationship. In 1776 the American colonials chose independence through revolution. They selected the dangerous course not only because they perceived British treachery but also owing to their own New World sense of themselves as different from—indeed, superior to—the Old World of monarchy, relentless international rivalry, and corrupt institutions.

Geographic isolation from Europe helped to spawn such notions of exceptionalism, as did the doctrine of mission and God-favored destiny that the Puritans had etched on American memory. Colonials from New England to Georgia had, moreover, become accustomed to making their own decisions, governing themselves at the local level, and expanding their landholdings and commerce without much interference from the British crown and Parliament. Yet when Americans declared independence and then worked to gain and preserve it in a doubting and hostile world, they felt compelled to appeal to Europe for help and in 1778 signed an alliance with France. Once they achieved independence through the Treaty of Paris in 1783, they continued to navigate the shoals of Old World diplomacy in pursuit of commercial opportunities, an expanded frontier, and national security. They became uneasy that transatlantic linkages compromised what some scholars have labeled American "isolationism." At the same time, however, American leaders saw in their new treaties and nationhood the opportunity to reform traditional world politics and advance U.S. interests.

Engagement with the outside world also encouraged efforts to form a more perfect union at home. The need for a more coherent and respected foreign policy became a persuasive argument for a stronger central government and the adoption of the Constitution in 1789. The founders nonetheless confronted a host of international *challenges that spurred political and sectional divisions. Most vexing was the question of America's place in the larger Atlantic world. Britain failed to vacate fortified posts on American soil as called for in the Treaty of Paris, and refused to grant trade concessions to the former colony. The 1778 alliance with France became an encumbrance in 1792–1793 when the French Revolution entered a stormy stage that initiated war between republican France and monarchical Europe. During the administration of George Washington, Secretary of Treasury Alexander Hamilton led the Federalist party that denounced revolutionary France and the excesses of republicanism and urged better relations with Great Britain as a bastion of order and as America's chief trading partner. On the other hand, James Madison and Thomas Jefferson led a faction called the Republican party. While they disapproved of the violence that swept France, they applauded the French Revolution as a triumph for freedom from tyranny. They argued also that the United States, because its foreign trade was so dependent on the British, was compromising its sovereignty by favoring Great Britain. The debate reached a fever pitch with the signing of Jay's Treaty in 1794. The treaty defused Anglo-American tensions by forcing Britain to vacate finally its North American fortresses. But Republicans decried Jay's failure to wring major trade concessions from the British and predicted the treaty would poison relations with France. President Washington tried to cool political passions and summarize American diplomatic principles in his Farewell Address in 1796. But debate persisted, and not until 1800 did France and the United States temper their relations after two years of quasi war on the high seas by signing an agreement terminating the 1778 alliance.*

Historians have debated the relative importance of isolationism, expansionism, imperialism, and idealism as characteristics of early American foreign relations. And they have wondered to what extent American leaders understood and exercised power in eighteenth century world affairs. But they have agreed that Americans ardently claimed that their upstart republic had a unique international position that would transform the world community. Why Americans came to think so is explained by the documents and essays in this chapter.

DOCUMENTS

Document 1, from John Adams's autobiography depicting his views of 1775, recounts the case that this prominent Massachusetts attorney and politician made for ties with France, cautions against entanglement in Europe's wars, and urges neutrality for the future. The two treaties with France that followed (Documents 2 and 3) provided not only for alliance but for principles that would govern foreign commerce. The Treaty of Paris (Document 4), providing for American independence, was signed in Paris on September 3, 1783, and ratifications were exchanged on May 8, 1784. Document 5 presents those parts of the U.S. Constitution of 1789 that cover the making and execution of foreign policy.

Following the military victory against Great Britain and the establishment of federal union, the fledgling republic still struggled to forge a foreign policy. At stake during the 1790s, many thought, was the very survival of the new nation. After France and Britain went to war in February 1793, President Washington received the unanimous support of his cabinet to proclaim U.S. neutrality. But Document 6, Jay's Treaty, negotiated with Britain by Supreme Court Chief Justice John Jay and signed on November 19, 1794, became the focal point for vigorous public debate. Although the treaty passed the Senate on June 22 by the necessary two-thirds vote of 20-10, it continued to stir heated protest. The supporters of Thomas Jefferson and James Madison in Congress denounced Jay's Treaty as a pro-British, Federalist document, and recommended instead that commercial restrictions be imposed on Britain. Document 7, a fiery resolution of September 1795, passed by a Democratic-Republican society in South Carolina, gives testimony to the political firestorm. More than forty such organizations in the United States proclaimed themselves the protectors of political liberties against a privileged elite. They denounced secretly negotiated treaties and British trade restrictions and demanded alliance with France against Britain.

Believing that the political factionalism engulfing the United States threatened the well-being of the nation, George Washington addressed this danger in his farewell address on September 17, 1796. This statement (Document 8), written mostly by Treasury Secretary Alexander Hamilton, spoke not only to the turmoil of domestic politics but also to the appropriate posture for the United States in international relations. Many scholars have interpreted Washington's warning against "permanent alliances" as a declaration of isolationism that guided U.S. foreign policy until the Cold War era following the Second World War.

1. John Adams of Massachusetts Explains French Interest in American Independence and Cautions Against Alliance, 1775

Some gentlemen doubted of the sentiments of France; thought she would frown upon us as rebels, and be afraid to countenance the example. I replied to those gentlemen, that I apprehended they had not attended to the relative situation of France and England; that it was the unquestionable interest of France that the British Continental Colonies should be independent; that Britain, by the conquest of Canada and her naval triumphs during the last war, and by her vast possessions in America and the East Indies, was exalted to a height of power and preëminence that France must envy and could not endure. But there was much more than pride and jealousy in the case. Her rank, her consideration in Europe, and even her safety and independence, were at stake. The navy of Great Britain was now mistress of the seas, all over the globe. The navy of France almost annihilated. Its inferiority was so great and obvious, that all the dominions of France, in the West Indies and in the East Indies, lay at the mercy of Great Britain, and must remain so as long as North America belonged to Great Britain, and afforded them so many harbors abounding with naval stores and resources of all kinds, and so many men and seamen ready to assist them and man their ships; that interest could not lie; that the interest of France was so obvious, and her motives so cogent, that nothing but a judicial infatuation of her councils could restrain her from embracing us; that our negotiations with France ought, however, to be conducted with great caution, and with all the foresight we could possibly obtain; that we ought not to enter into any alliance with her, which should entangle us in any future wars in Europe; that we ought to lay it down, as a first principle and a maxim never to be forgotten, to maintain an entire neutrality in all future European wars; that it never could be our interest to unite with France in

This document can be found in Charles Francis Adams, ed., *The Works of John Adams, Second President: With a Life of the Author* (Boston: Charles C. Little and James Brown, 1850), II, 504–506.

the destruction of England, or in any measures to break her spirit, or reduce her to a situation in which she could not support her independence. On the other hand, it could never be our duty to unite with Britain in too great a humiliation of France; that our real, if not our nominal, independence, would consist in our neutrality. If we united with either nation, in any future war, we must become too subordinate and dependent on that nation, and should be involved in all European wars, as we had been hitherto; that foreign powers would find means to corrupt our people, to influence our councils, and, in fine, we should be little better than puppets, danced on the wires of the cabinets of Europe. We should be the sport of European intrigues and politics; that, therefore, in preparing treaties to be proposed to foreign powers, and in the instructions to be given to our ministers, we ought to confine ourselves strictly to a treaty of commerce; that such a treaty would be an ample compensation to France for all the aid we should want from her. The opening of American trade to her, would be a vast resource for her commerce and naval power, and a great assistance to her in protecting her East and West India possessions, as well as her fisheries; but that the bare dismemberment of the British empire would be to her an incalculable security and benefit, worth more than all the exertions we should require of her, even if it should draw her into another eight or ten years' war.

2. Treaty of Amity and Commerce with France, 1778

Article 2.   The most Christian King, and the United States engage mutually not to grant any particular Favour to other Nations in respect of Commerce and Navigation, which shall not immediately become common to the other Party, who shall enjoy the same Favour, freely, if the Concession was freely made, or on allowing the same Compensation, if the Con[c]ession was Conditional. . . .

Article 19.   It shall be lawful for the Ships of War of either Party & Privateers freely to carry whithersoever they please the Ships and Goods taken from their Enemies, without being obliged to pay any Duty to the Officers of the Admiralty or any other Judges; nor shall such Prizes be arrested or seized, when they come to and enter the Ports of either Party. . . .

Article 25.   . . . And it is hereby stipulated that free Ships shall also give a freedom to Goods, and that every thing shall be deemed to be free and exempt, which shall be found on board the Ships belonging to the Subjects of either of the Confederates, although the whole lading or any Part thereof should appertain to the Enemies of either, contraband Goods being always excepted. It is also agreed in like manner that the same Liberty be extended to Persons, who are on board a free Ship, with this Effect, that although they be Enemies to both or either Party, they are not to be taken out of that free Ship, unless they are Soldiers and in actual Service of the Enemies.

This document can be found in Hunter Miller, ed., *Treaties and Other International Acts of the United States of America* (Washington, D.C.: U.S. Government Printing Office, 1931), II, 3–29.

Article 26.   This Liberty of Navigation and Commerce shall extend to all kinds of Merchandizes, excepting those only which are distinguished by the name of contraband; And under this Name of Contraband or prohibited Goods shall be comprehended, Arms, great Guns, Bombs with the fuzes, and other things belonging to them, Cannon Ball, Gun powder, Match, Pikes, Swords, Lances, Spears, halberds, Mortars, Petards, Granades Salt Petre, Muskets, Musket Ball, Bucklers, Helmets, breast Plates, Coats of Mail and the like kinds of Arms proper for arming Soldiers, Musket rests, belts, Horses with their Furniture, and all other Warlike Instruments whatever. These Merchandizes which follow shall not be reckoned among Contraband or prohibited Goods, that is to say, all sorts of Cloths, and all other Manufacturers woven of any wool, Flax, Silk, Cotton or any other Materials whatever; all kinds of wearing Apparel together with the Species, whereof they are used to be made; gold & Silver as well coined as uncoin'd, Tin, Iron, Latten, Copper, Brass Coals, as also Wheat and Barley and any other kind of Corn and pulse; Tobacco and likewise all manner of Spices; salted and smoked Flesh, salted Fish, Cheese and Butter, Beer, Oils, Wines, Sugars and all sorts of Salts; & in general all Provisions, which serve for the nourishment of Mankind and the sustenence of Life; furthermore all kinds of Cotton, hemp, Flax, Tar, Pitch, Ropes, Cables, Sails, Sail Cloths, Anchors and any Parts of Anchors; also Ships Masts, Planks, Boards and Beams of what Trees soever; and all other Things proper either for building or repairing Ships, and all other Goods whatever, which have not been worked into the form of any Instrument or thing prepared for War by Land or by Sea, shall not be reputed Contraband, much less such as have been already wrought and made up for any other Use; all which shall be wholly reckoned among free Goods: as likewise all other Merchandizes and things, which are not comprehended and particularly mentioned in the foregoing enumeration of contraband Goods: so that they may be transported and carried in the freest manner by the Subjects of both Confederates even to Places belonging to an Enemy such Towns or Places being only excepted as are at that time beseiged, blocked up or invested.

3. Treaty of Alliance with France, 1778

Article 1.   If War should break out betwan [F]rance and Great Britain, during the continuance of the present War betwan the United States and England, his Majesty and the said united States, shall make it a common cause, and aid each other mutually with their good Offices, their Counsels, and their forces, according to the exigence of Conjunctures as becomes good & faithful Allies.

Article 2.   The essential and direct End of the present defensive alliance is to maintain effectually the liberty, Sovereignty, and independance absolute and unlimited of the said united States, as well in Matters of Gouvernement as of commerce. . . .

This document can be found in Hunter Miller, ed., *Treaties and Other International Acts of the United States of America* (Washington, D.C.: U.S. Government Printing Office, 1931), II, 35–41.

Article 5.   If the united States should think fit to attempt the Reduction of the British Power remaining in the Northern Parts of America, or the Islands of Bermudas, those Contries or Islands in case of Success, shall be confederated with or dependant upon the said united States.

Article 6.   The Most Christian King renounces for ever the possession of the Islands of Bermudas as well as of any part of the continent of North america which before the treaty of Paris in 1763, or in virtue of that Treaty, were acknowledged to belong to the Crown of Great Britain, or to the united States heretofore called British Colonies, or which are at this Time or have lately been under the Power of The King and Crown of Great Britain.

Article 7.   If his Most Christian Majesty shall think proper to attack any of the Islands situated in the Gulph of Mexico, or near that Gulph, which are at present under the power of Great Britain, all the said Isles, in case of success, shall appertain to the Crown of france.

Article 8.   Neither of the two Parties shall conclude either Truce or Peace with Great Britain, without the formal consent of the other first obtain'd; and they mutually engage not to lay down their arms, until the Independence of the united states shall have been formally or tacitly assured by the Treaty or Treaties that shall terminate the War. . . .

Article 11.   The two Parties guarantee mutually from the present time and forever, against all other powers, to wit, the united states to his most Christian Majesty the present Possessions of the Crown of [F]rance in America as well as those which it may acquire by the future Treaty of peace: and his most Christian Majesty guarantees on his part to the united states, their liberty, Sovereignty, and Independence absolute, and unlimited, as well in Matters of Government as commerce and also their Possessions, and the additions or conquests that their Confederation may obtain during the war, from any of the Dominions now or heretofore possessed by Great Britain in North America, conformable to the 5th & 6th articles above written, the whole as their Possessions shall be fixed and assured to the said States at the moment of the cessation of their present War with England.

4. Treaty of Peace Provides for American Independence, 1783

Article 1st.   His Britannic Majesty acknowledges the said United States, viz. New-Hampshire, Massachusetts Bay, Rhode-Island & Providence Plantations, Connecticut, New York, New Jersey, Pennsylvania, Delaware, Maryland, Virginia, North Carolina, South Carolina & Georgia, to be free sovereign & Independent States; that he treats with them as such, and for himself his Heirs & Successors,

---

This document can be found in Hunter Miller, ed., *Treaties and Other International Acts of the United States of America* (Washington, D.C.: U.S. Government Printing Office, 1931), II, 151–156.

relinquishes all Claims to the Government Propriety & Territorial Rights of the same & every Part thereof. . . .

Article 3d.   It is agreed that the People of the United States shall continue to enjoy unmolested the Right to take Fish of every kind on the Grand Bank and on all the other Banks of New-foundland, also in the Gulph of St. Lawrence, and at all other Places in the Sea where the Inhabitants of both Countries used at any time heretofore to fish. And also that the Inhabitants of the United States shall have Liberty to take Fish of every Kind on such Part of the Coast of New-foundland as British Fishermen shall use, (but not to dry or cure the same on that Island) And also on the Coasts Bays & Creeks of all other of his Britannic Majesty's Dominions in America, and that the American Fishermen shall have Liberty to dry and cure Fish in any of the unsettled Bays Harbours and Creeks of Nova Scotia, Magdalen Islands, and Labrador, so long as the same shall remain unsettled but so soon as the same or either of them shall be settled, it shall not be lawful for the said Fishermen to dry or cure Fish at such Settlement, without a previous Agreement for that purpose with the Inhabitants, Proprietors or Possessors of the Ground.

Article 4th.   It is agreed that Creditors on either Side shall meet with no lawful Impediment to the Recovery of the full Value in Sterling Money of all bona fide Debts heretofore contracted.

Article 5th.   It is agreed that the Congress shall earnestly recommend it to the Legislatures of the respective States to provide for the Restitution of all Estates, Rights and Properties which have been confiscated belonging to real British Subjects. . . . And that Persons of any other Description shall have free Liberty to go to any Part or Parts of any of the thirteen United States and therein to remain twelve Months unmolested in their Endeavours to obtain the Restitution of such of their Estates Rights & Properties as may have been confiscated. . . .

And it is agreed that all Persons who have any Interest in confiscated Lands, either by Debts, Marriage Settlements, or otherwise, shall meet with no lawful Impediment in the Prosecution of their just Rights.

Article 6th.   That there shall be no future Confiscations made nor any Prosecutions commenc'd against any Person or Persons for or by Reason of the Part, which he or they may have taken in the present War, and that no Person shall on that Account suffer any future Loss or Damage, either in his Person Liberty or Property; and that those who may be in Confinement on such Charges at the Time of the Ratification of the Treaty in America shall be immediately set at Liberty, and the Prosecutions so commenced be discontinued.

Article 7th.   There shall be a firm and perpetual Peace between his Britannic Majesty and the said States and between the Subjects of the one, and the Citizens of the other, wherefore all Hostilities both by Sea and Land shall from henceforth cease: All Prisoners on both Sides shall be set at Liberty, and his Britannic Majesty shall with all convenient speed, and without causing any Destruction, or carrying away any Negroes or other Property of the American Inhabitants, withdraw all his

Armies, Garrisons & Fleets from the said United States, and from every Port, Place and Harbour within the same; leaving in all Fortifications the American Artillery that may be therein: And shall also Order & cause all Archives, Records, Deeds & Papers belonging to any of the said States, or their Citizens, which in the Course of the War may have fallen into the Hands of his Officers, to be forthwith restored and deliver'd to the proper States and Persons to whom they belong.

Article 8th. The Navigation of the River Mississippi, from its source to the Ocean shall for ever remain free and open to the Subjects of Great Britain and the Citizens of the United States.

5. Foreign Policy Powers in the Constitution, 1789

Article I. *Section 8.* The Congress shall have power

To lay and collect taxes, duties, imposts, and excises, to pay the debts and provide for the common defense and general welfare of the United States; but all duties, imposts and excises shall be uniform throughout the United States;

To borrow money on the credit of the United States;

To regulate commerce with foreign nations, and among the several States, and with the Indian tribes;

To establish an uniform rule of naturalization, and uniform laws on the subject of bankruptcies throughout the United States;

To coin money, regulate the value thereof, and of foreign coin, and fix the standard of weights and measures; . . .

To define and punish piracies and felonies committed on the high seas and offenses against the law of nations;

To declare war, grant letters of marque and reprisal, and make rules concerning captures on land and water;

To raise and support armies, but no appropriation of money to that use shall be for a longer term than two years;

To provide and maintain a navy;

To make rules for the government and regulation of the land and naval forces;

To provide for calling forth the militia to execute the laws of the Union, suppress insurrections, and repel invasions;

To provide for organizing, arming, and disciplining the militia, and for governing such part of them as may be employed in the service of the United States, reserving to the States respectively the appointment of the officers, and the authority of training the militia according to the discipline prescribed by Congress;

To exercise exclusive legislation in all cases whatsoever, over such district (not exceeding ten miles square) as may, by cession of particular States, and the acceptance of Congress, become the seat of government of the United States, and to exercise like authority over all places purchased by the consent of the legislature of the State, in which the same shall be, for erection of forts, magazines, arsenals, dock-yards, and other needful buildings;—and

This document can be found in *United States Code,* 1994 ed. (Washington, D.C.: U.S. Government Printing Office, 1995), I, lv–lx.

To make all laws which shall be necessary and proper for carrying into execution the foregoing powers, and all other powers vested by this Constitution in the government of the United States, or in any department or officer thereof. . . .

Section 10.   No State shall enter into any treaty, alliance, or confederation; grant letters of marque and reprisal; coin money; emit bills of credit; make anything but gold and silver coin a tender in payment of debts; pass any bill of attainder, ex post facto law, or law impairing the obligation of contracts, or grant any title of nobility.

No State shall, without the consent of Congress, lay any imposts or duties on imports or exports, except what may be absolutely necessary for executing its inspection laws: and the net produce of all duties and imposts, laid by any State on imports or exports, shall be for the use of the treasury of the United States; and all such laws shall be subject to the revision and control of the Congress.

No State shall, without the consent of Congress, lay any duty of tonnage, keep troops or ships of war in time of peace, enter into any agreement or compact with another State, or with a foreign power, or engage in war, unless actually invaded, or in such imminent danger as will not admit of delay. . . .

Article II.   *Section 2.* The President shall be commander in chief of the army and navy of the United States, and of the militia of the several States, when called into the actual service of the United States; he may require the opinion, in writing, of the principal officer in each of the executive departments, upon any subject relating to the duties of their respective offices, and he shall have power to grant reprieves and pardons for offenses against the United States, except in cases of impeachment.

He shall have power, by and with the advice and consent of the Senate, to make treaties, provided two-thirds of the Senators present concur; and he shall nominate, and by and with the advice and consent of the Senate, shall appoint ambassadors, other public ministers and consuls. . . .

Article III.   *Section 1.* The judicial power of the United States shall be vested in one Supreme Court, and in such inferior courts as the Congress may from time to time ordain and establish. . . .

Section 2.   The judicial power shall extend to all cases, in law and equity, arising under this Constitution, the laws of the United States, and treaties made, or which shall be made, under their authority;—to all cases affecting ambassadors, other public ministers and consuls;—to all cases of admiralty and maritime jurisdiction;—to controversies to which the United States shall be a party;—to controversies between two or more States;—*between a State and citizens of another State;*—between citizens of different States;—between citizens of the same State claiming lands under grants of different States, and between a State, or the citizens thereof, and foreign states, citizens or subjects.

In all cases affecting ambassadors, other public ministers and consuls, and those in which a State shall be party, the Supreme Court shall have original jurisdiction. . . .

Article IV.   *Section 3.* The Congress shall have power to dispose of and make all needful rules and regulations respecting the territory or other property belonging to the United States; and nothing in this Constitution shall be so construed as to prejudice any claims of the United States, or of any particular State. . . .

Article VI.   This Constitution, and the laws of the United States which shall be made in pursuance thereof; and all treaties made, or which shall be made, under the authority of the United States, shall be the supreme law of the land; and the judges in every State shall be bound thereby, anything in the Constitution or laws of any State to the contrary notwithstanding.

6. Jay's Treaty, 1794

Article II.   His Majesty will withdraw all His Troops and Garrisons from all Posts and Places within the Boundary Lines assigned by the Treaty of Peace to the United States. This Evacuation shall take place on or before the first Day of June One thousand seven hundred and ninety six. . . .

Article III.   It is agreed that it shall at all Times be free to His Majesty's Subjects, and to the Citizens of the United States, and also to the Indians dwelling on either side of the said Boundary Line freely to pass and repass by Land, or Inland Naviga-tion, into the respective Territories and Countries of the Two Parties on the Conti-nent of America (the Country within the Limits of the Hudson's Bay Company only excepted) and to navigate all the Lakes, Rivers, and waters thereof, and freely to carry on trade and commerce with each other. But it is understood, that this Article does not extend to the admission of Vessels of the United States into the Sea Ports, Harbours, Bays, or Creeks of His Majesty's said Territories; nor into such parts of the Rivers in His Majesty's said Territories as are between the mouth thereof, and the highest Port of Entry from the Sea, except in small vessels trading bona fide between Montreal and Quebec, under such regulations as shall be established to prevent the possibility of any Frauds in this respect. Nor to the admission of British vessels from the Sea into the Rivers of the United States, beyond the highest Ports of Entry for Foreign Vessels from the Sea. The River Mississippi, shall however, according to the Treaty of Peace be entirely open to both Parties. . . .

Article VI.   Whereas it is alleged by divers British Merchants and others His Majesty's Subjects, that Debts to a considerable amount which were bónâ fide con-tracted before the Peace, still remain owing to them by Citizens or Inhabitants of the United States. . . . It is agreed that in all such Cases where full Compensation for such losses and damages cannot, for whatever reason, be actually obtained had and received by the said Creditors in the ordinary course of Justice, The United States will make full and complete Compensation for the same to the said Creditors. . . .

Article XII.   His Majesty Consents that it shall and may be lawful, during the time hereinafter Limited, for the Citizens of the United States, to carry to any of His Majesty's Islands and Ports in the West Indies from the United States in their own Vessels, not being above the burthen of Seventy Tons, any Goods or Merchan-dizes, being of the Growth, Manufacture, or Produce of the said States, which it is,

This document can be found in Hunter Miller, ed., *Treaties and Other International Acts of the United States of America* (Washington, D.C.: U.S. Government Printing Office, 1931), II, 245–264.

or may be lawful to carry to the said Islands or Ports from the said States in British Vessels, and that the said American Vessels shall be subject there to no other or higher Tonnage Duties or Charges, than shall be payable by British vessels, in the Ports of the United States; and that the Cargoes of the said American Vessels shall, be subject there to no other or higher Duties or Charges than shall be payable on the like Articles, if imported there from the said States in British vessels.

And His Majesty also consents that it shall be lawful for the said American Citizens to purchase, load and carry away, in their said vessels to the United States from the said Islands and Ports, all such articles being of the Growth, Manufacture or Produce of the said Islands, as may now by Law be carried from thence to the said States in British Vessels, and subject only to the same Duties and Charges on Exportation to which British Vessels and their Cargoes are or shall be subject in similar circumstances.

Provided always that the said American vessels do carry and land their Cargoes in the United States only, it being expressly agreed and declared that during the Continuance of this article, the United States will prohibit and restrain the carrying any Meolasses, Sugar, Coffee, Cocoa or Cotton in American vessels, either from His Majesty's Islands or from the United States, to any part of the World, except the United States, reasonable Sea Stores excepted. Provided, also, that it shall and may be lawful during the same period for British vessels to import from the said Islands into the United States, and to export from the United States to the said Islands, all Articles whatever being of the Growth, Produce or Manufacture of the said Islands, or of the United States respectively, which now may, by the Laws of the said States, be so imported and exported. And that the Cargoes of the said British vessels, shall be subject to no other or higher Duties or Charges, than shall be payable on the same articles if so imported or exported in American Vessels. . . .

Article XIII.   His Majesty consents that vessels belonging to the citizens of the United States shall be admitted and hospitably received in all the seaports and harbors of the British territories in the East Indies. And that the citizens of the said United States may freely carry on a trade between the said territories and the said United States, in all articles of which the importation or exportation respectively, to or from the said territories shall not be entirely prohibited. . . . But it is expressly agreed that the vessels of the United States shall not carry any of the articles exported by them from the said British territories to any port or place, except to some port or place in America. . . . It is also understood that the permission granted by this article is not to extend to allow the vessels of the United States to carry on any part of the coasting trade of the said British territories. . . .

Article XIV.   There shall be between all the dominions of His Majesty in Europe and the territories of the United States a reciprocal and perfect liberty of commerce and navigation. . . .

Article XV.   It is agreed, that no other or higher Duties shall be paid by the Ships or Merchandize of the one Party in the Ports of the other, than such as are paid by the like vessels or Merchandize of all other Nations. Nor shall any other or higher Duty be imposed in one Country on the importation of any articles, the growth, produce, or manufacture of the other, than are or shall be payable on the importation of the like articles being of the growth, produce or manufacture of any other Foreign Country. Nor shall any prohibition be imposed, on the exportation or importation of any articles to or from the Territories of the Two Parties respectively which shall not equally extend to all other Nations. . . .

Article XVIII. In order to regulate what is in future to be esteemed Contraband of war, it is agreed that under the said Denomination shall be comprized all Arms, and Implements serving for the purposes of war . . . as also Timber for Shipbuilding, Tar or Rosin, Copper in Sheets, Sails, Hemp, and Cordage, and generally whatever may serve directly to the equipment of Vessels, unwrought Iron and Fir planks only excepted, and all the above articles are hereby declared to be just objects of Confiscation, whenever they are attempted to be carried to an Enemy. . . .

Article XXIV. It shall not be lawful for any Foreign Privateers (not being Subjects or Citizens of either of the said Parties) who have Commissions from any other Prince or State in enmity with either Nation, to arm their Ships in the Ports of either of the said Parties, nor to sell what they have taken, nor in any other manner to exchange the same, nor shall they be allowed to purchase more provisions than shall be necessary for their going to the nearest Port of that Prince or State from whom they obtained their Commissions.

7. A Democratic-Republican Society
Blasts Jay's Treaty, 1795

The Franklin, or Republican Society of Pendleton county, having by the watchful vigilance of their standing committee, on a most pressing question, been called together to give their opinion on a public measure—a right they will not tamely relinquish, nor resign but with their lives!—having taken into consideration the ruinous treaty *proposed* and signed by John Jay, the American ambassador, with his Britannic majesty—a treaty, as detestable in its origin, as contemptible in its event!—a treaty which can never be enforced but by the bayonet!—having fully weighed it in all its articles—and taking into view, that when the complaints of a brave and powerful people are observed to increase in proportion to the wrongs they have suffered!— when, instead of sinking into submission, they are roused to resistance! the time must come at which every inferior consideration will yield to their security—to the general safety of the empire! . . .

    Resolved, That on the appointment of John Jay as an *extraordinary* ambassador to Britain, we were *led to believe* that our rights would have been vindicated with firmness, a reparation of our wrongs obtained!—On the contrary, *even after the signing of a treaty of amity,* our flag is the *common sport* of Britain, and our sailor fellow-citizens and property at their mercy.

This document can be found in the *City Gazette* (Charleston), October 28, 1795. It can also be found in Philip S. Foner, ed., *The Democratic Republican Societies, 1790–1800* (Westport, Conn.: Greenwood Press, 1976), 400–409.

Resolved, That we were induced by *profession* to believe our administration sympathized in the cause of an ally [France], wrestling for liberty—a great and re-generated people, who cherish in their utmost purity those sacred principles which have laid the foundation of OUR *freedom in the blood of our dearest citizens!*—but that ally has been treated with *insincerity, even at the moment our inveterate enemy, and the foe of human happiness, has been invited to our bosom! and when British tyranny and baseness can leave not a doubt on a single unprejudiced mind that we are about to give that nation* A FOOTING IN LAW AMONG US WHICH WILL BE CONVERTED TO OUR RUIN! . . .

Resolved, That so far as is depending on his own integrity and good wishes to the United States, we are still willing to behold in Washington THE SAME GOOD AND GREAT MAN! But, is it not possible, at least respecting Jay's treaty, that he may have been wrongly advised? . . .

Resolved, That we view with surprize the industry used not to disclose the articles of Mr. Jay's treaty—AFFECTING *and* PRACTISING *all the secrecy of* MONARCHY, *so opposite to open and republican principles.*—Will it, dare it be contended, that the people have no right to ask, nay, to *demand* information on the posture of their affairs?—Secrecy robs them of this right, and makes *twenty* greater than the *whole.* Is this republicanism?—is this liberty?—Monarchs and conclaves make a *trade of secrecy—it suits their designs*—but neither monarchs nor conclaves are, as yet, in unison with the sentiments, nor the wishes of the American people. There is no authorized secrecy in *our* government, and to infer such a right from the practices of other nations, is a prostitution of republican principles. The constitution of the United States gives to the president and Senate the power of making treaties, but it communicates no ability to hatch those things in darkness. A treaty! which is to be the supreme-law-of-the-land! and yet the people not to be informed of the terms of this law until binding upon them! until the opportunity for amendment is past!—Secrecy and mystery marked the conception, birth, and parentage of this lump of abortion and deformity. . . .

Resolved, That by the article regarding the West-India trade, nothing can be more evident than that Britain mediated to wrest from America the carrying trade, an immense share of which she has lately possessed, as appears by the astonishing increase of our seamen and shipping; but we trust 'twill never be forgotten that the protection of a free carrying trade was one of the primary objects for which the federal government was established.—Let not, then, our national government have the discredit of doing any thing by which the limits of our navigation may be fettered—Let us not concur with the British ministry in eminently promoting the British commerce at the expense of our own!—Not satisfied with the innumerable depradations on our shipping, the British government wants their real destruction by this insidious article, confining our vessels to seventy tons, mere boats, whilst they reserve to themselves the right of navigating in any size vessels they please, in the same pursuit of trade. By this deceptive article, we *alone* granted—have been prevented from exporting in our own bottoms any articles of West-India produce, and even of *cotton,* an article of our own growth, and becoming a very important one in this and the sister state of Georgia (even in our own district)—while the vessels of *Britain,* and *every other* nation, would be at liberty to export from American ports every article of West-India, and some of our own produce, to all parts of the world. . . .

Resolved, finally, That the vice-moderator, the corresponding secretary, and secretary of the society, do sign the foregoing resolutions—and that they be generally printed, as expressive of our abhorrence and detestation of a treaty—which gives to the English government more power over us a[s] states, than it ever claimed over us as colonies—and which, if Britain had been left to her generosity, *she would have been ashamed to propose!*—a treaty, involving in its pusilanimity, stupidity, ingratitude, and TREACHERY!—to blast the rising grandeur of our common country—of our infant empire!

8. President George Washington Cautions Against Factionalism and Permanent Alliances in His Farewell Address, 1796

I have already intimated to you the danger of parties in the State, with particular reference to the founding of them on geographical discriminations. Let me now take a more comprehensive view, and warn you in the most solemn manner against the baneful effects of the spirit of party generally.

This spirit, unfortunately, is inseparable from our nature, having its root in the strongest passions of the human mind. It exists under different shapes in all governments, more or less stifled, controlled, or repressed; but in those of the popular form it is seen in its greatest rankness and is truly their worst enemy.

The alternate domination of one faction over another, sharpened by the spirit of revenge natural to party dissension, which in different ages and countries has perpetrated the most horrid enormities, is itself a frightful despotism. But this leads at length to a more formal and permanent despotism. The disorders and miseries which result gradually incline the minds of men to seek security and repose in the absolute power of an individual, and sooner or later the chief of some prevailing faction, more able or more fortunate than his competitors, turns this disposition to the purposes of his own elevation on the ruins of public liberty.

Without looking forward to an extremity of this kind (which nevertheless ought not to be entirely out of sight), the common and continual mischiefs of the spirit of party are sufficient to make it the interest and duty of a wise people to discourage and restrain it.

It serves always to distract the public councils and enfeeble the public administration. It agitates the community with ill-founded jealousies and false alarms; kindles the animosity of one part against another; foments occasionally riot and insurrection. It opens the door to foreign influence and corruption, which find a facilitated access to the government itself through the channels of party passion. Thus the policy and the will of one country are subjected to the policy and will of another. . . .

Observe good faith and justice toward all nations. Cultivate peace and harmony with all. Religion and morality enjoin this conduct. And can it be that good policy does not equally enjoin it? It will be worthy of a free, enlightened, and at no

This document can be found in James D. Richardson, ed., *A Compilation of the Messages and Papers of the Presidents* (New York: Bureau of National Literature, 1897), I, 210–211, 213–215.

distant period a great nation to give to mankind the magnanimous and too novel example of a people always guided by an exalted justice and benevolence. . . .

In the execution of such a plan nothing is more essential than that permanent, inveterate antipathies against particular nations and passionate attachments for others should be excluded, and that in place of them just and amicable feelings toward all should be cultivated. The nation which indulges toward another an habitual hatred or an habitual fondness is in some degree a slave. It is a slave to its animosity or to its affection, either of which is sufficient to lead it astray from its duty and its interest. Antipathy in one nation against another disposes each more readily to offer insult and injury, to lay hold of slight causes of umbrage, and to be haughty and intractable when accidental or trifling occasions of dispute occur.

Hence frequent collisions, obstinate, envenomed, and bloody contests. The nation prompted by ill will and resentment sometimes impels to war the government contrary to the best calculations of policy. The government sometimes participates in the national propensity, and adopts through passion what reason would reject. At other times it makes the animosity of the nation subservient to projects of hostility, instigated by pride, ambition, and other sinister and pernicious motives. The peace often, sometimes perhaps the liberty, of nations has been the victim.

So, likewise, a passionate attachment of one nation for another produces a variety of evils. Sympathy for the favorite nation, facilitating the illusion of an imaginary common interest in cases where no real common interest exists, and infusing into one the enmities of the other, betrays the former into a participation in the quarrels and wars of the latter without adequate inducement or justification. It leads also to concessions to the favorite nation of privileges denied to others, which is apt doubly to injure the nation making the concessions by unnecessarily parting with what ought to have been retained, and by exciting jealousy, ill will, and a disposition to retaliate in the parties from whom equal privileges are withheld; and it gives to ambitious, corrupted, or deluded citizens (who devote themselves to the favorite nation) facility to betray or sacrifice the interests of their own country without odium, sometimes even with popularity, gilding with the appearances of a virtuous sense of obligation, a commendable deference for public opinion, or a laudable zeal for public good the base or foolish compliances of ambition, corruption, or infatuation.

As avenues to foreign influence in innumerable ways, such attachments are particularly alarming to the truly enlightened and independent patriot. How many opportunities do they afford to tamper with domestic factions, to practice the arts of seduction, to mislead public opinion, to influence or awe the public councils! Such an attachment of a small or weak toward a great and powerful nation dooms the former to be the satellite of the latter. Against the insidious wiles of foreign influence (I conjure you to believe me, fellow-citizens) the jealousy of a free people ought to be *constantly* awake, since history and experience prove that foreign influence is one of the most baneful foes of republican government. But that jealousy, to be useful, must be impartial, else it becomes the instrument of the very influence to be avoided, instead of a defense against it. Excessive partiality for one foreign nation and excessive dislike of another cause those whom they actuate to see danger only on one side, and serve to veil and even second the arts of influence on the other. Real patriots who may resist the intrigues of the favorite are liable to become suspected and odious, while its tools and dupes usurp the applause and confidence of the people to surrender their interests.

The great rule of conduct for us in regard to foreign nations is, in extending our commercial relations to have with them as little *political* connection as possible. So far as we have already formed engagements let them be fulfilled with perfect good faith. Here let us stop.

Europe has a set of primary interests which to us have none or a very remote relation. Hence she must be engaged in frequent controversies, the causes of which are essentially foreign to our concerns. Hence, therefore, it must be unwise in us to implicate ourselves by artificial ties in the ordinary vicissitudes of her politics or the ordinary combinations and collisions of her friendships or enmities.

Our detached and distant situation invites and enables us to pursue a different course. If we remain one people, under an efficient government, the period is not far off when we may defy material injury from external annoyance; when we may take such an attitude as will cause the neutrality we may at any time resolve upon to be scrupulously respected; when belligerent nations, under the impossibility of making acquisitions upon us, will not lightly hazard the giving us provocation; when we may choose peace or war, as our interest, guided by justice, shall counsel.

Why forego the advantages of so peculiar a situation? Why quit our own to stand upon foreign ground? Why, by interweaving our destiny with that of any part of Europe, entangle our peace and prosperity in the toils of European ambition, rivalship, interest, humor, or caprice?

It is our true policy to steer clear of permanent alliances with any portion of the foreign world, so far, I mean, as we are now at liberty to do it; for let me not be understood as capable of patronizing infidelity to existing engagements. I hold the maxim no less applicable to public than to private affairs that honesty is always the best policy. I repeat, therefore, let those engagements be observed in their genuine sense. But in my opinion it is unnecessary and would be unwise to extend them.

Taking care always to keep ourselves by suitable establishments on a respectable defensive posture, we may safely trust to temporary alliances for extraordinary emergencies.

Harmony, liberal intercourse with all nations are recommended by policy, humanity, and interest. But even our commercial policy should hold an equal and impartial hand, neither seeking nor granting exclusive favors or preferences; consulting the natural course of things; diffusing and diversifying by gentle means the streams of commerce, but forcing nothing; establishing with powers so disposed, in order to give trade a stable course, to define the rights of our merchants, and to enable the Government to support them, conventional rules of intercourse, the best that present circumstances and mutual opinion will permit, but temporary and liable to be from time to time abandoned or varied as experience and circumstances shall dictate; constantly keeping in view that it is folly in one nation to look for disinterested favors from another; that it must pay with a portion of its independence for whatever it may accept under that character; that by such acceptance it may place itself in the condition of having given equivalents for nominal favors, and yet of being reproached with ingratitude for not giving more. There can be no greater error than to expect or calculate upon real favors from nation to nation. It is an illusion which experience must cure, which a just pride ought to discard.

E S S A Y S

Historians disagree in their identification of the bedrock principles of American foreign policy and the attitudes of the founders toward the outside world. In the first essay, Lawrence S. Kaplan, long a professor of history at Kent State University, examines America's treaty of alliance with France, signed in 1778. He concludes that the young nation's diplomats disdained international commitments and begrudgingly accepted a political and military alliance with Paris only when it became essential to winning independence from Great Britain. According to Kaplan, the nation's founders were isolationist rather than internationalist in outlook, and they believed that revolutionary ideals and the national interest would be best served by steering clear of the European powers. The foreign policy debates of the 1790s between Federalists and Republicans centered on the means by which to steer clear of Europe's wars rather than the fundamental question of neutrality versus intervention. The isolationist strain, Kaplan suggests, remained a prominent feature of American foreign policy well into the twentieth century.

In the second essay, the historians Peter S. Onuf and Leonard J. Sadosky of the University of Virginia counter that isolationism was never an option for the new nation. They instead explore the interconnectedness between foreign relations and the evolving structure of the U.S. government. Faced with an array of international challenges—from overseas trade treaties, to diplomatic relations with native tribes, to transactions with North Africa's Barbary pirates—the leaders of the American Revolution not only embraced internationalism but were also spurred to replace in 1789 the decentralized federal government of the Articles of Confederation with the Constitution. According to Onuf and Sadosky, the founders concluded that only a more powerful centralized government could overcome America's weakness in the larger Atlantic world and prevent the various "state republics" from conducting separate and potentially conflicting foreign policies. Throughout the 1790s, Republican opposition to Federalist diplomacy arose only partly from differences over international diplomacy. The foreign policies of George Washington and his Federalist successor John Adams also turned into questions about the structure of the federal union, executive power, and states rights.

The Treaty of Alliance with France and American Isolationism

LAWRENCE S. KAPLAN

Isolationism has always held an elusive quality for American diplomatic historians. The term itself is no older than the 1920s, and fittingly is identified with a revulsion against the entanglements of world war. This rejection of Europe was undergirded by an earlier religious image of a New World arising out of the failure of the Old, sitting apart on its transatlantic bill. These Calvinist expectations of a New Jerusalem in turn received reinforcement from the secular thought of the Enlightenment, which contrasted the simple, egalitarian, free society of eighteenth-century America with the complex, class-ridden, war-plagued societies of Europe. As a consequence of this bifurcated vision of the world Washington's Farewell Address of 1796 became an

"The Treaty of Alliance with France and American Isolationism" from Lawrence S. Kaplan, ed., *The American Revolution and "A Candid World,"* (Kent State Univ. Press, 1977) 134–143, 145–157. Reprinted with permission of Kent State University Press.

enduring symbol of America's isolation. His message was directed against the French alliance of 1778, the first and only entangling political commitment to Europe the United States made until the framing of the North Atlantic Treaty in 1949.

For all but a few ideologues tied either to the mother country or to the wilderness, isolationism meant a freedom to enjoy access to all ports interested in receiving American products. It meant further a freedom from subservience to any foreign power, of the kind which had forced them into the service of a maternal economy or of dynastic wars in the past. Finally, it extended to a self-image of virtue and in-nocence that would be protected by advancing principles of peaceful relationships among nations.

The alliance with France violated these conceptions of America's position in the world. Conceivably, the potential contradiction between the profession of isolationism and the making of alliance lies in confusion over the meaning of "alliance." It may be resolved, according to [the historian] Felix Gilbert, by accepting an eighteenth-century understanding of alliances which embrace both commercial agreements and military obligations. There were no genuine distinctions between a treaty of commerce and a treaty of alliance. So when the Founding Fathers spoke of a foreign alliance as a desideratum, they could reconcile their wish for a commercial connection with refusal of political bonds. There is evidence enough in the language used by policymakers during the life of the twenty-three year alliance to buttress this thesis. Both the French and Americans intertwined the provisions of the treaty of amity and commerce with the claims of the treaty of alliance in the 1770s. And the model treaty of 1776 lumped political and commercial considerations together.

But there is also abundant evidence that the men who framed foreign policy during the Revolution recognized clearly the distinctions between the two kinds of treaties. They wanted France to be obligated in the Model Treaty without cost to themselves. They failed to entice the French under these terms, and they knew they failed. If they accepted political and military entanglement it was because they felt they had no choice. The most they could do would be to limit the potential damage subservience to France's national interest would have. . . .

That a successful defiance of England would require the help of Europe was understood even before separation was made official. The Continental Congress established a five-man Committee of Secret Correspondence on 19 November 1775, "for the sole purpose of corresponding with our friends in Great Britain, Ireland, and other parts of the world." Since the voices of America's friends in and out of Parliament had either been stilled or had turned away from the colonies, the "other parts of the world" became an immediate object of attention. The most notable part was France, England's familiar enemy, which had been periodically testing colonial discontent for ten years to see how it might be turned to its own advantage.

The French Court's interest was not ephemeral. Vergennes, the foreign minis-ter, welcomed the dispatch of Silas Deane, a former delegate to the Congress from Connecticut and merchant connected with Robert Morris's firm in Philadelphia. It was not coincidental that Morris was a member of the committee which presented the Model Treaty of 1776. Deane was joined by Arthur Lee, the committee's agent in London and colonial agent from Massachusetts. He was the brother of Richard Henry Lee, another member of the Committee of Secret Correspondence. The scene was set then both for the supply of munitions, weapons, and equipment to the colonies by indirect means from the French and Spanish Crowns which permitted a vital and massive infusion of energy to the colonial war effort and an opportunity for fiscal confusion and personal profit for the American agents involved in the transactions. In all these dealings the substance was commerce, not politics; trade, not military obligations.

The function France was performing should have fitted perfectly the message of Thomas Paine in his *Common Sense,* when he expressed a few months later that "the true interest of America is to steer clear of Europe's contentions, which she never can do while, by her dependence on Britain, she is made the makeweight in the scale of British politics." More than this, he asserted that "Our plan is commerce, and that, well attended to, will secure us the peace and friendship of Europe." It also reflected the thinking of John Adams who had been the prime mover in the summer of 1776 in drawing up a model treaty. His Plan of 1776 operated on the assumption that Europe would sue for America's trade and would promote America's independence to secure this advantage as well as to weaken British colonial power. France was the vital cog in the plan that would serve the war effort but without the price of entangling reciprocal obligations. Adams's language could not be plainer: "I am not for soliciting any political connection, or military assistance, or indeed, naval from France. I wish for nothing but commerce, a mere marine treaty with them."

As a consequence of a confidence bordering on truculence the American treaty plan of 1776 elaborated on liberal ideas of international law and freedom of the seas, ideas appealing to the philosophers of France and to the naval competitors of the great seapower of the day. More controversial in tone was the self-denial Article 9 would impose on the French, forcing the king to promise that "he shall never invade, nor, under any pretense, attempt to possess himself of any of the territories of the mainland which had been French or Spanish in the past. Almost grudgingly it seemed, the French would be permitted to keep whatever West Indian possessions they acquired by virtue of joining the Americans.

Such euphoria as this plan reflected dissipated rapidly in 1776. The war went badly for American arms and American morale. While the surreptitious aid given by the French and Spanish was substantial, it did not produce the desired effects on the war effort. As a result, the demands on France moved from commercial support to military assistance to a promise of reciprocal political and military obligation, in return for open adherence to the war. It was the Americans, and not the French, who became the suitor for an alliance. An increasingly nervous awareness that the world was not so well ordered as the Paine scenario had implied informed the advice given the ministers in France by the Committee of Secret Correspondence and its successor, the Committee of Foreign Affairs. Deane and Lee, joined by Franklin late in 1776, were permitted to relax the requirements for French aid. They were to assure the French of no future allegiance to Britain, of no trade advantages to any other power greater than to the French benefactor, and an additional agreement to make no termination of war, should the French enter it, without full notice to the French partner. . . .

The French foreign office listened and bided its time. Port officials returned British prizes Americans brought too openly into French cities. There was no acknowledgement of the declaration of American independence, even as supplies and soldiers found their way to America from France. It required the victory at Saratoga in the fall of 1777, and more important, signs of British accommodation to America's early war aims before France was willing to make an alliance formally and accept the price of war for its pains. And when the treaty was finally concluded, the brave words of Adams and Paine were forgotten. Not only did the United States reassure the French about the termination of the war and about commercial benefits, but a specific entanglement was made in Article 11, which was not to be found in the Model Treaty, in the form of mutual guarantees "from the present time and forever, to wit, the united states to his most Christian Majesty the present Possessions of the Crown of France in America as well as those which it may acquire by the future Treaty of peace. . . ." Thus the commissioners made an agreement which bound the United States for an indefinite future to the defense of a foreign power's territory in America, a sure guarantee of involvement in the European balance of power in any subsequent quarrel between Britain and France.

The American response was one of relief and gratitude. The Congress considered the treaty officially on 4 May 1778, and ratified it two days later with little commentary beyond directing the commissioners "to present the grateful acknowledgements of this Congress to his most Christian majesty for his truly magnanimous conduct respecting these States in the said generous and disinterested treaties." The only question raised by the commissioners concerned the mutual prohibitions of duties on exports between the United States and the French West Indies. These articles were removed. . . .

Generous as the French were, their interest in the success of the United States was always subordinated to their greater interests in their financial status, maintenance of the monarchical principle, and cultivation of their more important alliance with Spain. If America could achieve its objectives in war without clashing with France's other concerns, the French ally would gladly be of service, as long as the paternal guidance of His Most Christian Majesty would govern American behavior. But when it became apparent first to the new peace commission abroad—John Adams, John Jay, and Benjamin Franklin—and then to the Congress that France was prepared to accept less than the borders the United States wanted or the fisheries New England demanded, the relationship soon became uneasy. . . .

American restiveness was . . . openly expressed. A generalized anti-Gallican and anti-Catholic sentiment had its center in New England, but its vibrations were felt throughout the states. Friends of France like Jefferson were sorely disappointed over the quality of French military assistance. Distrust over the purposes of French aid was widespread from the beginnings of the alliance, as secret negotiations among the European powers between 1778 and 1782 evoked suspicions first of French disinterest in America's transappalachian ambitions, and then of the ally's collaboration with the British and Spanish in an attempt to confine the United States to the Atlantic littoral. These suspicions were justified, and most of the French *arrières pensées* [ulterior motives] about America were exposed before the war ended. Even more open were the pressures exerted by French officials in America to bend Congress's policies to France's wishes. [Chevalier de la] Luzerne, in the best manner of a patron chiding a client for his errors, made Congress revise its instruction to the American commission abroad from a general statement that the commission be guided by "the advice and opinion of the French peace negotiators" to a more specific mandate that it "undertake nothing in the negotiations for peace or truce without their knowledge and concurrence." Since the Court disliked John Adams, his appointment was broadened to include first two and then four commissioners.

But ironically as the war drew to a close, the Congress became more compliant rather than more resistant to French designs. The explanation for docility was not in the venality of [American] politicians on the [French] payroll, even though that roll was long, illustrious and well padded. It lies more in the increasing awareness of the fragility of the Confederation and in the psychological and financial drain of the long war with Britain. To men such as Robert R. Livingston, the first secretary for foreign affairs of the Confederation, and Robert Morris, its superintendent of finances from 1781 to 1783, there was no substitute for French support in this period.

Morris, in his critical capacity as finance minister, reveals this dependence clearly. Buoyed by the Franco-American victory at Yorktown, he expressed his surprise to Franklin in December 1781, that the United States made so many purchases in Holland. "If everything else were equal the generous conduct of France towards us has been such that I cannot but think every possible preference ought to be given to the manufacturers of that nation." Whether this sentiment reflected the state of his personal investments more than the national is less material than the importance he gave to the continuing French financial support. . . .

As for Livingston, he was alarmed at the freewheeling behavior of the commissioners who wandered over Europe denouncing the ally, dickering with the enemy, and ignoring the will of the Congress. Jay, prodded by Adams, had exposed a secret French memorandum which presumably would have ended the war, with the British and Spanish sharing territory between the mountains and the Mississippi; while Franklin concluded a separate agreement with the British which left the French no alternative but to accept. Jay's letter chafing at Congressional fetters discomfited Livingston. Jay insisted on the Americans accepting British terms if they were appropriate: "we are under no obligation to persist in the war to gratify this court. But can it be wise to instruct your commissioners to speak only as the French minister shall give them utterance."

Livingston was not alone in his nervousness. He represented the sense of the Congress preoccupied with financial cares and with the impediments to governance. While [Alexander] Hamilton could admit that it was "not improbably that it had been the policy of France to procrastinate the definite acknowledgemt. of our Independence . . . in order to keep us more knit to herself & untill her own interests could be negotiated," he preferred to compare French benevolence with British malevolence. Jay and his colleagues had erred in not showing preliminary articles to the ally before signing and in working out a separate and secret article on Florida boundaries with the British. There was a churlishness implicit in the commissioner's behavior. On balance, as [James] Madison suggested, the total role of France deserves gratitude, not reproach. . . .

The treaty [however] lost much of its significance to both parties after the war ended. France had too many other problems plaguing its society in the 1780s to place any priority on its American investment. With few immediate benefits on the horizon, subsidies to American journalists were no longer necessary, even if they could have been afforded. France's complaisance over America's inability to repay its debts reflects the comfort the government was able to take in a weak and divided nation that had only France to turn to for support, no matter how attenuated the relationship should become. . . .

France's failure, after the Revolution, to liberalize American commerce with the West Indies or its earlier unwillingness, as guarantor of the Peace of Paris, to help Americans push the British out of Northwest posts or to defend American shipping in the Mediterranean against Barbary pirates might have evoked stronger reactions from Americans. If they did not, a subliminal recognition of a counterpart guarantee to French possessions may have checked their anger. There was an underlying uneasiness over the French relationship experienced by American leaders of every persuasion. They agreed that the weakness of the Confederation required drastic remedies to cope with a hostile world. Madison and Jefferson, as well as Jay and Morris, believed that France as well as Spain and Britain was part of that world. For James Monroe the quarrel between him and Jay over the abortive treaty with Spain in 1786, which would have closed the Mississippi River to American shipping, excluded France; for both men France's role was that of Spain's patron. Similarly, Jefferson could join with Jay in deploring Franklin's consular agreement with France of 1782 for its apparent grant of excessive privileges to French consuls in America; they smacked of extraterritoriality. . . .

The record of the first few years of the Federal Union in which Jefferson and Hamilton shared power in the Cabinet discloses no significant shift in sentiment over the French alliance. While Hamilton and his followers moved quickly toward an appreciation of a strong British commercial connection and thereby to a depreciation of the French treaties, Jefferson did not find the treaties of alliance or of amity and commerce equally important to him. It is not that he advocated the termination of the connections. The threat of British reconquest and commercial enslavement appeared stronger to him than before, and France's role as a weapon to break loose from Britain's economic control appealed to him and to Madison in the House of Representatives. Moreover, the early phases of the French Revolution inspired pride in American contribution to France's political enlightenment. But the sluggish response of presumably liberal France to the secretary of state's overtures revived all his suspicions and annoyances. Revolutionary France should have none of the old regime's excuses for failing to accommodate the economic needs of the United States. When the National Assembly imposed special duties on all foreign ships carrying commerce to France, Jefferson found this "such an act of hostility against our navigation, as was not to have been expected from the friendship of that nation."

Many of these feelings receded when France and England went to war in 1793. France, now a republic, was challenged by British monarchism. And when Hamilton emerged openly as the powerful American champion of British interests, the role of France assumed a new character to the Jeffersonians. The alliance was pushed into the forefront of a Cabinet debate, by virtue of Hamilton's goading Washington into a proclamation of neutrality in the European war. The secretary of the treasury welcomed the Anglo-French crisis as an opportunity to break with France and realign American policy formally toward Britain. He could not have found a more sensitive issue with which to challenge his political opponents—Jefferson, Madison, Monroe and the Republican leaders of the North, George Clinton of New York, and Alexander Dallas of Pennsylvania. For neutrality was their object, as well as his, but it was an objective they did not wish to publicize in any way embarrassing to or injurious to the French war effort. Initially, they were willing to settle for a proclamation, provided that the word "neutrality" was excluded from the text.

What they wished to avoid was the potential conflict between the obligations of the treaty of alliance, which could bring them into war in defense of the French West Indies, and American vulnerability to British economic and naval power, which would make war a disaster for the United States. Consequently, they spent their energies in the spring of 1793, where possible, on the more acceptable subject raised by Hamilton: namely, the illegitimacy of the French republic as an excuse for breaking the alliance and refusing to accept its envoy. As Jefferson indignantly wrote to Gouverneur Morris in Paris, "We surely cannot deny to any nation that right whereon our own government is founded, that every one may govern itself according to whatever form it pleases." . . .

[T]he above sentiments were echoed and reinforced by the numerous democratic societies which sprang up throughout the country in 1793. Whether they were the heirs of the Sons of Liberty or spawns of the French Jacobin societies, they served to promote friendship with France and fidelity to the alliance. Their primary note, and that of Jeffersonian leadership as well, was that France was fighting America's battle abroad. And America's service to the alliance would not be belligerency, but economic aid for which neutrality was a prerequisite. But it would be "a fair neutrality," in Jefferson's words, in which American vessels carried goods to France from the West Indies, unimpeded according to liberal understandings of neutral rights, with produce for France and profit for America. Jefferson admitted that it would still be "a disagreeable pill to our friend."

The Jeffersonians deluded themselves in believing they could have both neutrality and the alliance. It is customary to blame the indiscretions of [French Ambassador Edmond] Genêt, the youthful French minister in 1793, for spoiling the delicate relationship between the two countries [by stoking anti-British sentiment in America and equipping privateers in U.S. ports]. But could the claims of the alliance, under the circumstances, have permitted the kind of neutrality Jefferson preferred? The British navy obviously had no intention of permitting what they called contraband goods to move from French colonial ports in American ships, even if it would stimulate resentment in the United States. The French would have permitted Americans to remain technically out of the war only because they saw other services the alliance could extract from the United States in the form of the transfer to supplies in American ships, the arming of privateers in American ports, and the staging of invasions in American territory. When these services were refused in the name of neutrality, the French then invoked the relationship of 1778. They were prepared to relieve the United States of the burden of defending West Indian islands only if the Americans would invoke and fulfill the articles of the treaty of commerce concerning freedom of the seas. For this occasion, France linked the two treaties.

Hamilton realized the sham of the alliance sooner than Jefferson. The Republicans erred first in thinking the proclamation would have been harmless if Hamilton had not perverted it. And they were mistaken later in emphasizing the unconstitutional action of the executive in taking the action, as if this was the source of the difficulties with the French. The secretary of state's stand on Genêt's attempts to arm vessels in American ports exposed a position on the treaties that violated its spirit, if not its letter. Did Article 24 of the Treaty of Amity and Commerce imply that this privilege would be open to the French, since it was specifically denied to the enemies of both countries? Jefferson's negative answer appeared to be a mean-spirited literal interpretation of the treaty, worthy of the Hamiltonians. The French construction was not unreasonable. But if compliance meant war with Britain, the Jeffersonians preferred embarrassment with France.

This does not mean that Madison, who led the Republicans from the Congress after Jefferson retired from the Cabinet in 1793, would have taken the next step of a treaty with the British, which outraged France's sensibilities even further. Whether Jay's Treaty was the work of Hamilton's prudence or guile, it was a logical extension of the American neutrality in the war and of America's dependence upon British trade channels. While the terms stipulated that nothing in the document would affect obligations already binding on the signatory powers, the contents made a mockery of the Franco-American treaties. Article 24, forbidding foreign privateers from arming their ships in American ports, did not grant to the British what had been denied to the French in 1793; but it explicitly denied this privilege to the "ally." At the same time, the treaty gave Britain exactly the same concession that France had enjoyed since 1778 in bringing prizes captured from France into this country, directly in conflict with the French treaty. Combined with the failure to challenge Britain's interpretation of neutral rights and Britain's inclusion of provisions as contraband, it was hardly surprising that France read betrayal of the alliance into Jay's Treaty.

France was right. Its anti-American measures, in the face of the American position, were not inordinate. Abandoned by the United States in the one area the Americans could help the French, the mistreatment of American vessels that followed Jay's Treaty in French waters, and the undeclared war against the new undeclared ally of Britain, could be considered fitting retribution. Certainly, some of the Jeffersonian reaction followed this line. Unhappy though they were with France's descending to Britain's level in depredations against American commerce, they felt France to be the injured party provoked by the Federalists anxious to serve monarchism above republicanism. Washington's farewell address was simply a Hamiltonian ploy to divert the nation from the real entangling connection, that of England. They cheered French victories on the Continent and toasted impending French invasions of England in 1795 and in 1797.

Yet visceral support for the French cause against Britain and the surrogate Britons among the High Federalists did not signify any surrender to France or to the French Revolution under the Directory. Jeffersonian distress over the damage to France in the Jay Treaty was based on the threat of war, initiated by either the Directory or the Federalists. The alliance was the touchstone of the relationship. In 1795 and 1796, when news of that treaty spread through Europe and discredited Monroe, the American minister to Paris, they feared the French government's denunciation of the alliance would be a prelude to full scale war. Similarly in 1798, after France had humiliated the American commissioners sent by President [John] Adams to Paris in the XYZ affair [by demanding bribes for the privilege of negotiating with the French foreign office], they opposed the administration's unilateral abrogation of the alliance as a *casus belli*. Alliance in these circumstances was a symbol of the status quo, not of American loyalty or even of gratitude.

While no specific information was available about France's imperial intentions in America, the treatment of European satellite nations did not go unnoticed even among partisans of France. The Directory's ambitions in Louisiana may not have been fully clear, but Madison had no hesitation about speculating on an angry France conspiring with the Spanish to disturb navigation on the Mississippi River. Jefferson gloomily predicted that there will be "new neighbors in Louisiana (probably the present French armies when disbanded)," which he equated with "a combination of enemies of that side where we are most vulnerable." And Monroe added an apocalyptic note by suggesting that if war should come, the Federalists would link America to England "as a feeble contemptible satellite." And if France wins, "we are then to experience that fate which she will then prescribe. . . ."

Such was the scenario projected by the Jeffersonians in the summer of 1798. From the floor of the Congress, they worked against voiding the treaties. Albert Gallatin, a Jeffersonian leader from Pennsylvania in the House, admitted France's violations of the Treaty of Commerce, but claimed that the alliance was not affected by French measures. If the Federalists had asked for the voiding of the Treaty of Commerce, he could understand the argument, although he made it clear that Jay's Treaty with England would deserve denunciation along with the French Treaty. Additionally, he protested the "novel" nature of the proceedings, since there was no precedent for legislatures to repeal treaties. This theme was developed at great length in the Philadelphia *General Advertiser,* where it was coupled with the state's rights thesis of government found in the Kentucky and Virginia Resolutions rejecting the Federalist Alien and Sedition laws of 1798 [which restricted alien resident rights and the right to dissent]. An editorial asked rhetorically: "is not every officer of a State Government sworn to uphold the Constitution of the United States? If the Federal Government passes laws contravening the Constitution, is it not a breach of oath in a state officer to carry such laws into effect? . . . If Congress can annul a contract with a foreign country because of its violation, will not the same justice operate to modifying or annulling a contract between states which is no longer regarded?"

The debate over the alliance was all the more spirited because the French treaties were mixed with suppression of states' rights, as well as with Hamiltonian ambitions for alliance with Britain. But how much specific meaning did it have beyond its function as a weapon of internecine political combat? Were the Jeffersonians willing to risk war with Britain for the sake of either of the treaties of 1778? The answers were negative. A preliminary examination of the press in 1798, in search of occasions which would celebrate the alliance—such as the twentieth anniversary of its signing or of Independence Day—yields no affirmative position on the treaties. In fact, the anniversary went almost unnoticed on 6 February; the cheers of the democratic societies had vanished along with the societies themselves. . . .

When it became apparent to Jeffersonians that the break between the Adams and the Hamiltonian Federalists was genuine and permanent and that the new mission to France intended seriously to reduce conflict to repair the breach with the ally, none of the opposition leaders took this to mean a reinstatement of the alliance. Jefferson put it clearly to Gerry, just returned from France in January 1799: "I am for free commerce with all nations; political connection with none; & little or no diplomatic establishment. And I am not for linking ourselves by new treaties with the quarrels of Europe." It is difficult to distinguish this sentiment from Washington's farewell address in 1796 or from President Jefferson's inaugural address in 1801.

Critics, over the years, have attributed such words of Jefferson, Madison, or Monroe to either a shrewd pitch for votes in the presidential campaign of 1800 or to the temporary shock over Napoleon Bonaparte's coup d'etat of 9 November 1799. That Bonapartism affected the Jeffersonian judgment of France is not in question. Madison deplored France's defection from civil authority and felt it "left America as the only Theatre on which true liberty can have a fair trial." Jefferson ruminated about men-on-horseback and made the connection between Bonaparte and Hamilton. If he could accept the former, and not the latter, it was only because France was fit for nothing better. The Consulate reflected the French lack of "the habit of self-government." . . .

When the Adams peace commissioners signed a new treaty with France in 1800 that terminated the alliance, there was not a single protest from Jefferson, his colleagues, or from the press which supported the new President. If Jefferson called it a "bungling" treaty, it was because it failed to win compensation for damages done to American shipping and because it might be regarded with hostility by the British. President Jefferson was not much moved by such American friends in France as Joel Barlow or Paine who praised a new maritime convention the French were supporting in favor of the liberal maritime rulings, which both countries had subscribed to in 1778. Neutral rights had lost their luster, if only because they had failed to affect British seapower. Jefferson pointedly agreed with George Logan, a devoted Pennsylvania peace seeker, that the United States ought to join no confederacies, even when they pursued laudable goals of freeing the seas for neutral trade: "It ought to be the very first object of our pursuits to have nothing to do with the European interests and politics." This is American isolationism.

American Internationalism and Federal Union

PETER S. ONUF AND LEONARD J. SADOSKY

Though Americans withdrew from the British Empire, transforming themselves from subjects of King George III into self-governing citizens, they remained connected to the wider world. The most basic building block of the state republic, the independent household, could not survive or prosper without access to markets for its surpluses at home and abroad. Overseas markets did not open spontaneously: to secure commercial privileges abroad, the American states had to engage in diplomatic relations with the sovereigns of Europe. But American politicians were necessarily concerned with much more than foreign affairs. Negotiations with Indian nations were critically important for the security of frontier regions, [as were] access to commercial opportunities, and the acquisition of new lands. . . .

Even before the United States had formally declared independence, American statesmen recognized the importance of trade for securing their place in the wider Atlantic states system. Between June and September 1776, John Adams led the Continental Congress in drafting a plan of a treaty with France. The "model treaty" would not constitute a conventional political or military alliance, but instead codified the reciprocal commercial rights and privileges to be enjoyed by French and

"American Internationalism and Federal Union" from Peter S. Onuf and Leonard J. Sadosky, *Jeffersonian America* (Malden, MA: Blackwell Publishers, 2000) 183–187, 194–201. Reprinted by permission of Blackwell Publishing.

American merchants, strictly defined contraband, and set up procedures for the capture and condemnation of prizes during wartime. Americans believed that the benefits of free trade with their states were so obvious as to compel France and other continental powers to recognize the United States and engage in commerce with them, even at the risk of war with Britain. These diplomatic hopes proved unrealistic, as ratification of the Franco-American military alliance along with a treaty of commerce in 1778 testifies. Yet the model treaty continued to serve as the basis for the Confederation's diplomacy throughout the 1780s. Commerce pushed Americans into the Atlantic states system, and it remained the source from which future conflicts flowed.

Commercial conflicts also represented the most compelling argument for a more centralized federal union. Sitting in Congress in 1784, Jefferson grappled with the dilemmas posed by commerce. If commercial competition divided the states, it could also unite them. "All the world is becoming commercial," he wrote George Washington. The sources of this were apparent. "Our citizens have had too full a taste of the comforts furnished by the arts & manufactures to be debarred the use of them." Thus, as he told John Jay, "Our people are decided in the opinion that it is necessary for us to take a share in the occupation of the ocean." The implications of this were obvious: because "we cannot separate ourselves" from the world of Atlantic commerce, full engagement with the diplomatic machinery of Europe would be necessary. With American ships and merchants traversing all corners of the Atlantic, "their property will be violated on the sea" and "in foreign ports," and Americans would face the prospect of insults and imprisonment for "pretended debts, contracts, crimes, contraband" and the like. Diplomacy was the only remedy for such eventualities. Consuls and commercial agents could protect American merchants and mariners operating aboard, [and] commercial compacts negotiated by American ministers would give them a framework within which to work. But ultimately Americans must be prepared to vindicate their rights by military force, particularly naval power. "Our commerce on the ocean and in other countries must be paid for by frequent war." If the majority of Americans were determined to follow through on their choice to become a commercial people, Jefferson recognized that American statesmen would be required to engage in the political, legal, and diplomatic systems of Europe.

As Jefferson and the other members of the Confederation's fledgling diplomatic corps sought to expand the sphere open to American commerce, it became obvious that a . . . "federal republic," or confederation that left the sovereignty of its member states intact, was radically insufficient. Only a strong union, a government "partly national, and partly federal," could sustain diplomatic initiatives abroad and contain interstate political and commercial competition at home. During his years as American minister to France, Jefferson constantly found himself combating negative images of American government, economy, and society under the Confederation. In early 1786, he confessed to Archibald Stuart that the "American reputation in Europe is not such as to be flattering to its citizens." It was both the "nonpaiment of our debts" and "the want of our energy in our government" that Jefferson identified as the key factors which "discourage a connection with us."

After Spain closed the Mississippi River to American navigation in 1784, the Confederation's secretary for foreign affairs, John Jay, entered into negotiations with Spanish minister Don Diego de Gardoqui. Because of the Confederation's weakness within the Atlantic states system, Jay found himself with few options, and acquiesced in the humiliating closure of the river in order to secure commercial concessions. European observers perceived a weak American government that lacked the financial, military, and political wherewithal to be a major player in the commercial life of the Atlantic states system. Although the United States was able to secure commercial treaties with small and medium-sized European powers such as the Netherlands (1782), Sweden (1783), and Prussia (1785), American diplomats such as Jefferson, Adams, and Jay found wresting beneficial commercial accords from the major European powers—Britain, France, and Spain—to be a most difficult endeavor. Hamilton pithily encapsulated the situation in *The Federalist,* noting that the "imbecility of our government even forbids" the European powers "to treat with us," and as a result "our ambassadors abroad are the mere pageants of mimic sovereignty."

The Confederation's weakness handicapped the diplomatic efforts to extend American commerce in other sectors of the Atlantic states system. In the Mediterranean, the nonexistence of an American navy imperilled American commercial prospects. For decades, the Barbary Regencies of North Africa engaged in the systematic capture, plunder, and ransom of any shipping in the Mediterranean that did not pay them an annual tribute. The question of how to respond to the depredations of the "Barbary pirates" became a perennial one for American policy-makers into the early decades of the nineteenth century. As the Confederation's highest-ranking diplomats in the Old World, Jefferson and Adams were called upon to implement Congress's policy of making treaties and paying tribute. Both personally disagreed with the policy. Adams favored an American naval build-up that could effectively police the Mediterranean and protect the American merchant marine; Jefferson preferred an immediate, outright war on all of the Barbary states. Yet both realized that the Confederation government had neither the funds nor the authority to support such aggressive policies. Congress's more conciliatory approach did not produce satisfactory results. Agent Thomas Barclay concluded a treaty of commerce with Morocco, the weakest of the four states, in 1786, but negotiations with Algiers, Tunis, and Tripoli would continue into the 1790s, and did not result in commercial treaties until the new federal government could bring its more substantial resources into play.

Diplomatic relations with American Indian communities followed a similarly tortuous course. Initially, American statesmen argued that the United States gained title to Indian lands through victory in the revolution: all Indians who lived within the boundaries of the United States as recognized by the Treaty of Paris (1783) were a "conquered" people. But it was much easier to formulate than to implement such a claim. Many American Indian communities remained connected to trading partners and potential allies in the European states system: they were powerful enough to resist American pretensions; through alliances with imperial powers they posed a credible challenge to the confederation governments. Negotiators on both the Indian and American sides of the treaty councils perceived that only a United States with a strong central government could offer commercial incentives to rival those offered by the agents of the European empires, or pose a realistic military threat to compel serious negotiation in the first place. Only a strong central government could restrain American settlers from perpetrating acts of violence on the frontier.

The new nation was at risk in every direction. Isolation was not a viable alternative for a commercial, enterprising people. Settlers demanded access to new (Indian) lands; planters, farmers, and merchants sought access to foreign markets on favorable terms. American diplomats were called upon to open avenues for all America's diverse produce and open ports to American shipping. On both sides of the Atlantic, American negotiators found this task to be almost impossible. A frustrated Jefferson captured the general mood in 1786, when he complained about British unwillingness to negotiate a commercial treaty: "Our overtures of commercial arrangement have been treated with a derision which shew their [the British government's] firm persuasion that we shall never unite to suppress their commerce or even to impede it." So, for Jefferson and his contemporaries, a stronger union between the American states became a strategy to combat their weaknesses, both perceived and real, within the Atlantic states system.

In the months preceding the Philadelphia Convention, James Madison [also] concluded that only a strong federal union could preserve republicanism in the separate states and preempt interstate conflict. Without a strong nationalizing force, the American states system would look increasingly like the European states system. In February 1787, Madison observed to Edmund Randolph that "the existing Confederacy is tottering to its foundation," and that some contemplated the adoption of "Monarchy" while other "individuals predict a partition of the States into two or more Confederacies." Madison himself believed the latter was more likely, and without "radical amendment" of the existing Confederation, it was a certainty. A partition of the union seemed a likely outcome if the Philadelphia Convention failed to create a workable restructuring of the confederacy, or if the Constitution that it produced was not ratified.

The federal Constitution of 1787 apparently resolved any ambiguity about the sovereignty of the states under the Confederation by establishing the exclusive authority of the general government over foreign policy, including relations with Indians. At the same time, however, Federalist advocates of ratification sought to assure skeptical voters that their more energetic union would secure the states in their remaining, undelegated rights. Republicanism would flourish in the separate states even while—and because—they ceased to exist as independent polities in the larger world. . . .

Throughout the 1790s, debates about how the federal government should conduct diplomacy in the Atlantic states system [again] often turned into questions about the structure of the federal union. This was the case in 1793, as Revolutionary France went to war with nearly all of Europe in the aftermath of the execution of Louis XVI. When the French National Convention dispatched a minister, Edmond Genêt, to the United States, the Washington administration was forced to decide whether to receive him and thus recognize the French Republic. Washington's cabinet was divided on the matter, with secretary of state Jefferson arguing for recognition and secretary of the treasury [Alexander] Hamilton arguing against. Revolutionary change in France raised controversial questions in the law of nations, most notably whether the Franco-American treaties of 1778 remained in effect after Louis's death. Did the French nation continue to exercise its sovereignty through the new republican regime? A related issue also polarized the cabinet. Jefferson and Hamilton agreed that the United States should steer clear of the European wars, whatever the language of the French treaty, but they divided over how this neutrality should be constitutionally determined and promulgated. Hamilton believed that a decision on neutrality hinged on the interpretation of a treaty, and therefore fell solely to the executive. Jefferson thought Congress should play the decisive role, "as the Executive cannot decide the question of war on the affirmative side, neither ought it to do so on the negative side." Washington decided on a compromise of sorts, recognizing Genêt and the treaties but unilaterally issuing the Proclamation of Neutrality on 22 April 1793.

Debate over the Proclamation simmered throughout the summer of 1793. It was largely a debate about means, not ends. Both Federalists and Republicans saw an Atlantic states system erupting into war and concluded that it was in the interest of the United States to remain neutral. But Republicans worried that the administration's responses to the transformation of the European system would transform the carefully balanced structures of the American states system. Conflicting partisan perspectives were fully elaborated in a polemical exchange between Hamilton (writing as "Pacificus") and Madison ("Helvedius"). Hamilton insisted that the ability to declare neutrality was part of the President's executive powers. "The legislative department is not the *organ* of intercourse between the United States and foreign nations," he asserted, "it is charged neither with *making* nor *interpreting* treaties." Because the neutrality proclamation simply stated and clarified, but did not in itself effect any change in the nation's situation, it fell well within the power of the President to execute the laws. Madison disagreed fundamentally. . . . . Pacificus's thinly-veiled agenda was to use plausible arguments about the interpretation of treaties to justify a dangerous concentration of power in the executive branch. . . . The clear language of the Constitution left no doubt about where the disputed power lay. Because of far-reaching implications of the treaty power, any ambiguity on this point was intolerable. "A treaty is not an execution of laws," Madison insisted, but "is, on the contrary, to have itself the force of a *law*," for indeed, the Constitution made any treaty "the supreme law of the land." As a result, treaties "have sometimes the effect of changing not only the external laws of the society, but operate also on the internal code." Here was the ultimate source of Republican fears about the course of Federalist diplomacy. An enterprising president and his minions could corrupt the Senate, depriving the legislature of its legitimate role in conducting foreign policy. Once the executive gained the upper hand, he could then make law, altering the delicate constitutional balance the Convention had struggled to establish and endangering the residual sovereignty of the state-republics. The machinery which would keep the spheres of the republican political cosmos separate and distinct was in danger.

These were the concerns that shaped the Republican response to the Jay Treaty two years later. The commercial treaty that John Jay negotiated with Britain in 1794 and 1795 became a subject of national controversy when it was ratified by the Senate and made public. To secure commercial reciprocity (equal trade restrictions on both sides) with Great Britain itself, Jay had allowed trade with the British West Indies to remain closed; he had also abandoned the principle of "free ships, free goods," acceding to the British "Rule of 1756," which stipulated that a trade not open to a neutral in peacetime could not be opened in time of war. The Jay Treaty also failed to stop either the British practice of seizing contraband from neutral ships or the impressment of sailors from American ships. Republican critics concluded that the administration had betrayed the principles of the model treaty of

1776 by accepting limitations on American sovereignty and limiting the commercial choices available to American producers.

Historians have exaggerated Jefferson's Anglophobia and love for Revolutionary France in explaining his opposition to the Jay Treaty. Jefferson was most disturbed by the prospect that the treaty would alter power relationships within both the Atlantic and American states systems. The treaty's abandonment of neutral rights, a key principle in Jefferson's understanding of the law of nations, was particularly upsetting. From the Republican perspective, American independence and sovereignty in the Atlantic system were inextricably linked. Favoring the commerce of one nation over another could reduce American producers to dependency; the sovereignty of dependent states and their ability to assert their rights under the law of nations was radically, perhaps fatally, compromised. . . .

At the same time, the Jay Treaty promised to alter the shape of the relations between sovereignties within the American states system. Writing to Madison in late 1795, Jefferson cast the problem in the starkest terms: the Federalists' campaign for the treaty was "the boldest act they have ever ventured to undermine the construction" and thus destroy the union. "For it is certainly an attempt of a party which finds they have lost their majority in one branch of the legislature to make a law by the aid of the other branch, and of the executive, under color of a treaty, which shall bind up the hands of the adverse branch from ever restraining the commerce of the patronation." This was the same specter Madison had raised in the "Helvidius" essays. The quest of particular interests for commercial advantage in the Atlantic trading system jeopardized the structure of the American union. If the administration party could use diplomacy to subvert the federal legislative process, how could the state-republics be safe from unconstitutional encroachments?

American Republicans were not alone in their alarm at the apparent tendency of administration policy. The French Directory saw the ratification of Jay's "English Treaty" as a sign of a *rapprochement* between Britain and its former colonies, thus revealing the hollowness of American claims to neutrality. French privateers, as well as what remained of the French Navy, began to interdict American merchantmen, mostly in the West Indies, ostensibly to search for contraband. Conciliatory initiatives by American minister James Monroe failed to end France's attacks on American shipping. In 1797, as domestic political frustration over the situation grew, President John Adams dispatched Charles Cotesworth Pinckney, John Marshall, and Elbridge Gerry to France for further negotiations. The peace mission ended in failure with the famous XYZ Affair, when French agents refused to begin talks until a bribe was paid. News of the XYZ Affair enraged public opinion in the United States and led Federalists to clamor for war. As Franco-American relations deteriorated during the ensuing "Quasi-War" of 1798–1800, an undeclared naval war largely fought in the Caribbean, the Adams administration put the nation on a war footing: building a new navy, making preparations to raise an army, and moving to stifle internal dissent. These last measures convinced Republicans that the fears they had been harboring for the past few years were all too justified.

Republicans were convinced that their opponents meant to exploit the war crisis to transform the federal Constitution. During the summer of 1798, the Federalists pushed the controversial Alien and Sedition Acts through Congress by narrow votes: the new legislation tightened naturalization requirements, made it easier for the federal government to deport resident aliens, and defined sedition so broadly as to make any criticism of the administration a crime.

The threat posed by the Alien and Sedition Acts was similar in kind to the earlier crises. In order to achieve ends within the realm of extra-state diplomacy, the Federalists were engaging in actions that fundamentally altered the rules of the American system. What made the crisis of 1798 different was that the assault on republicanism was so much larger in scope. Both the executive and legislative power had fallen into the hands of forces inimical to the republican experiment. With the Sedition Act, there was simply no protected space within which the perfect republic could be preserved. As in 1787, the metes and bounds of the American state system had to be clarified if they were going to be preserved at all.

As the machinery of government was directed against Republican newspaper editors and political operatives, Jefferson and Madison moved into action, drafting protest resolutions that were subsequently adopted by the Kentucky and Virginia legislatures respectively. Returning to what they claimed were the first principles of the federal charter, Jefferson and Madison argued that the Constitution was a *compact* among sovereign states. The states were not dissolved by joining the union, but retained the right to self-preservation as specified by the first law of nature. The "several states" were "not united on the principle of unlimited submission to their government," Jefferson wrote in his original draft of the Kentucky Resolutions, but were rather joined "by a compact under the style and title of Constitution for the U.S. and amendments thereto." The states had only delegated to the general government "certain definite powers, reserving each state to itself, the residuary mass of right to their own self-government." Though Madison's language was less strident, his Virginia Resolutions made the same point: "the powers of the federal government" resulted "from the compact to which the states are parties." Compact theory gave the states the sovereign power they needed to preserve their character as perfect republics.

Many historians have focused on the politically expedient, opportunistic character of Republican compact theory. But the doctrine of the Virginia and Kentucky Resolutions had a respectable enough pedigree, traceable to Antifederalist criticisms of the Constitution—and Federalist efforts to allay their opponents' anxieties. Compact theory grew logically out of a decade of increasingly polarized debate about the nature of the American union and the status of its component state-republics. Had Republicans wished merely to challenge the constitutionality of the Alien and Sedition Acts, they did not have to rethink the whole structure of the union. Republican John Dawson thus concluded (as would subsequent generations of legal scholars) that the Sedition Act was unconstitutional because it violated the First Amendment. By 1798, however, Republicans were no longer satisfied with a narrowly circumscribed debate about the constitutionality of specific administration measures. They were instead convinced that fundamental questions about both the nature of the federal union and the conduct of foreign relations hung in the balance. Federalists had been willing, even eager, to allow events within the realm of European and Atlantic diplomacy to alter the constitutionally prescribed distribution of sovereign powers within the American system. If the states did not retain a necessary measure of sovereignty, there would be no room within which citizens could fashion their perfect republics, and the whole republican experiment would fail. . . .

The experiences of the 1790s shaped Jefferson's policies as his party took power in the federal executive and legislature following the 1800 election. The intense party battles over the Proclamation of Neutrality, the Jay Treaty, and the Quasi-War confirmed Republican fears of the dangers of becoming entangled in European politics. Federalists efforts to promote particular American interests in the Atlantic states system had nearly undermined the sovereignty of states within the American union, as well as the balance between federal and state power that underlay the Madisonian "extended republic." If the independence of the state-republics was compromised, Jeffersonians feared, the republican experiment would fail. Jefferson's response to the Federalist ascendancy was an aggressive assertion of state sovereignty. While the Republican administrations slowly backed away from the extreme implications of the "Principle of '98," they remained sensitive to the distinctive, divergent interests of each state-republic.

The 1790s had thus revealed how dangerous the politics of the Atlantic system could be for the American states and their union. But withdrawal from the larger world was never an option. Republicans knew that the American republics could not survive and prosper without overseas trade. Jefferson and his followers sought to resolve this conundrum by ensuring that national commercial policy would secure and harmonize diverse interests across the continent. The pursuit of commerce would be made a national concern. The costs and benefits of Atlantic commerce would be borne by all Americans. Peace would be made with the Indians on the northwest and southwest borderlands; the navigation of the Mississippi, as well as the other rivers that ran through the Floridas, would be secured; and, most importantly, the rights of neutral American navigators on the Atlantic "frontier" would be ensured by enforcing a progressive interpretation of neutral rights. Success on all these fronts would vindicate the Jeffersonian conception of an extended, de-centered union of free state-republics.

FURTHER READING

Harry Ammon, *The Great Mission* (1973)

Joyce Appleby, *Capitalism and a New Social Order: The Republican Vision of the 1790s* (1984)

———, *Inheriting the Revolution* (2000)

Bernard Bailyn, *To Begin the World Anew* (2003)

Lance Banning, *Conceived in Liberty* (2004)

Doron S. Ben-Atar, *The Origins of Jeffersonian Commercial Policy and Diplomacy* (1993)

H. W. Brands, *The First American: The Life and Times of Benjamin Franklin* (2002)

Richard Brookhiser, *Gentleman Revolutionary: Gouverneur Morris, the Rake Who Wrote the Constitution* (2003)

Thomas E. Chavez, *Spain and the Independence of the United States* (2002)

Ron Chernow, *Alexander Hamilton* (2004)

Francis D. Cogliano, *Revolutionary America* (1999)

Jerald A. Combs, *The Jay Treaty* (1970)

John E. Crowley, *The Privileges of Independence* (1993)

Noble E. Cunningham Jr., *Thomas Jefferson v. Alexander Hamilton* (2000)

Alexander DeConde, *Entangling Alliance: Politics and Diplomacy Under George Washington* (1958)

Jonathan R. Dull, *A Diplomatic History of the American Revolution* (1985)

Marc Egnal, *A Mighty Empire: The Origins of the American Revolution* (1988)

Stanley Elkins and Eric McKitrick, *The Age of Federalism* (1993)

———, *His Excellency: George Washington* (2004)

Joseph Ellis, *The Founding Brothers* (2000)

"Essays Commemorating the Treaty of Paris in 1783," *International History Review* (1983)

James A. Field, "1789–1820: All Economists, All Diplomats," in William H. Becker and
    Samuel F. Wells Jr., eds., *Economics and World Power* (1984), 1–54

David M. Fitzsimmons, "Tom Paine's New World Order," *Diplomatic History* 19 (1995):
    569–582

"Foreign Relations in the Early Republic: Essays from a SHEAR Symposium," *Journal of
    the Early Republic* 14 (1994): 453–495

Felix Gilbert, *To the Farewell Address: Ideas of Early American Foreign Policy* (1961)

Mary A. Giunta, *Documents of the Emerging Nation* (1998)

David C. Hendrickson, *Peace Pact* (2003)

Don Higginbotham, *George Washington* (2002)

Reginald Horsman, *The Diplomacy of the New Republic* (1985)

James Huston, *John Adams and the Diplomacy of the American Revolution* (1980)

Walter Issacson, *Benjamin Franklin* (2003)

Lawrence S. Kaplan, *Alexander Hamilton: Ambivalent Anglophile* (2002)

Roger G. Kennedy, *Burr, Hamilton, and Jefferson* (1999)

Peggy Liss, *Atlantic Empires: The Network of Trade and Revolution, 1713–1826* (1983)

Frederick W. Marks III, *Independence on Trial: Foreign Affairs and the Making of the
    Constitution* (1973)

———, *The Presidency of George Washington* (1979)

David McCollough, *John Adams* (2001)

Drew R. McCoy, "Republicanism and American Foreign Policy: James Madison and the
    Political Economy of Commercial Discrimination, 1789 to 1794," *William and Mary
    Quarterly* 31 (1974): 633–646

Forrest McDonald, *Alexander Hamilton* (1979)

Robert Middlekauf, *Benjamin Franklin* (1996)

Edmund S. Morgan, *Benjamin Franklin* (2002)

Conor Cruise O'Brien, *The Long Affair: Thomas Jefferson and the French Revolution*
    (1996)

Peter S. Onuf and Nicholas Onuf, *Federal Union, Modern World* (1993)

Bradford Perkins, *The Creation of a Republican Empire, 1776–1865* (1993)

Merrill D. Peterson, *Thomas Jefferson and the New Nation* (1970)

Norman K. Risjord, *Jefferson's America* (2002)

Robert Rutland, *James Madison* (1987)

H. M. Scott, *British Foreign Policy in the Age of the American Revolution* (1990)

James Roger Sharp, *American Politics in the Early Republic* (1993)

Matthew Spalding and Patrick J. Garrity, *A Sacred Union of Citizens* (1996)

William Stinchcombe, *The XYZ Affair* (1981)

Reginald C. Stuart, *United States Expansionism and British North America, 1775–1871*
    (1988)

"Symposium: Early U.S. Foreign Relations," *Diplomacy History* 22 (1998): 63–120

Robert W. Tucker and David C. Hendrickson, *The Fall of the First American Empire* (1982)

William Earl Weeks, "New Directions in the Study of Early American Foreign Relations,"
    Diplomatic History 17 (1993): 73–96

John Edward Wilz, "American Isolationism: Its Colonial Origins," *Amerikastudien/American
    Studies* 21 (1976): 261–280

Gordon S. Wood, *The Americanization of Benjamin Franklin* (2004)

CHAPTER
3

The Louisiana Purchase

Behind the negotiations in Paris that produced the April 30, 1803, treaty whereby France sold the vast Louisiana Territory to the United States lay years of American interest in and anxiety over Louisiana and its port of New Orleans at the mouth of the Mississippi River. The waterway was the vital route down which western farmers shipped their goods to market. In 1800 Spain had secretly transferred Louisiana to France. When Americans heard about the deal, they worried that the French would strangle U.S. commerce by denying Americans the use of the port. The administration of Thomas Jefferson therefore pressed France to sell New Orleans to the United States. The French astounded American diplomats by offering to sell all of Louisiana. The "noble bargain," as French minister of foreign affairs Talleyrand called it, was consummated in a few days.

Through the purchase, the United States doubled in size, receiving 828,000 square miles of frontier land lacking precise boundaries. Napoleon Bonaparte's asking price for this substantial piece of his empire had been only $15 million, or just 3 cents an acre. Even before the completion of the purchase, Jefferson astutely recruited his twenty-nine-year-old private secretary, Captain Meriwether Lewis, to lead an expedition across the expansive and largely uncharted domain to the Pacific Ocean. Headed by Lewis and Lieutenant William Clark, and later joined by a young Shoshone woman named Sacajawea, who served as interpreter, the fifty-strong "Corps of Discovery" undertook a two-year journey (1804–1806) that yielded volumes of new knowledge relevant to both scientific inquiry and western commercial development.

Historians differ over the extent to which external and internal factors facilitated the purchase of Louisiana. Some have emphasized that the United States was simply lucky that it benefited from Napoleon's troubles with Great Britain and Santo Domingo and the prospect of European war. Others have stressed America's long imperial interest in the territory and constant beseeching of France. In other words, the purchase came to pass in part because Napoleon realized that Americans, moving west, threatened someday to overrun the territory. Whether Americans profited from Europe's turmoil or their own devices, they had added immensely to what Jefferson envisioned as an "empire of liberty"—an American land of successful, virtuous, republican farmers.

🌐 D O C U M E N T S

In Document 1, a letter of April 18, 1802, to American minister to France Robert R. Livingston, President Thomas Jefferson expresses alarm over the fate of Louisiana and the American export trade after he has learned of Spain's cession of the territory to France. Document 2, from the 1830 recollections of the French official François Barbé Marbois, presents First Consul Napoleon Bonaparte's explanations to his advisers in April 1803 as to why Louisiana should be sold to the United States. In an April 13, 1803, letter to Secretary of State James Madison, Document 3, Livingston recounts the steps leading to the Louisiana Purchase. Jefferson's rival, Alexander Hamilton, published a stinging critique of the president's policies on July 5, 1803. This selection, reprinted as Document 4, first appeared in the *New York Evening Post.* In it, Hamilton maintains that the American acquisition of Louisiana owed more to good fortune than to skillful diplomacy. Hamilton thus set into motion a debate that even today continues among scholars. Document 5 is a letter of instruction that President Jefferson wrote to Captain Meriwether Lewis on June 20, 1803, just prior to the launching of the two-year Lewis and Clark expedition that explored the geography, botany, native peoples, and commercial potential of the newly purchased territory.

1. President Thomas Jefferson Assesses the French Threat in New Orleans, 1802

The cession of Louisiana, and the Floridas by Spain to France, works most sorely on the United States. On this subject the Secretary of State has written to you fully, yet I cannot forbear recurring to it personally, so deep is the impression it makes on my mind. It completely reverses all the political relations of the United States, and will form a new epoch in our political course. Of all nations of any consideration, France is the one which, hitherto, has offered the fewest points on which we could have any conflict of right, and the most points of a communion of interests. From these causes, we have ever looked to her as our *natural friend,* as one with which we never could have an occasion of difference. Her growth, therefore, we viewed as our own, her misfortunes ours. There is on the globe one single spot, the possessor of which is our natural and habitual enemy. It is New Orleans, through which the produce of three-eighths of our territory must pass to market, and from its fertility it will ere long yield more than half of our whole produce, and contain more than half of our inhabitants. France, placing herself in that door, assumes to us the attitude of defiance. Spain might have retained it quietly for years. Her pacific dispositions, her feeble state, would induce her to increase our facilities there, so that her possession of the place would be hardly felt by us, and it would not, perhaps, be very long before some circumstance might arise, which might make the cession of it to us the price of something of more worth to her. Not so can it ever be in the hands of France: the impetuosity of her temper, the energy and restlessness of her character, placed in a point of eternal friction with us, and our character, which,

---

This document can be found in Jefferson to Livingston, 18 April 1802, Thomas Jefferson Papers, Series 1, Reel # 26, Manuscripts Division, Library of Congress.

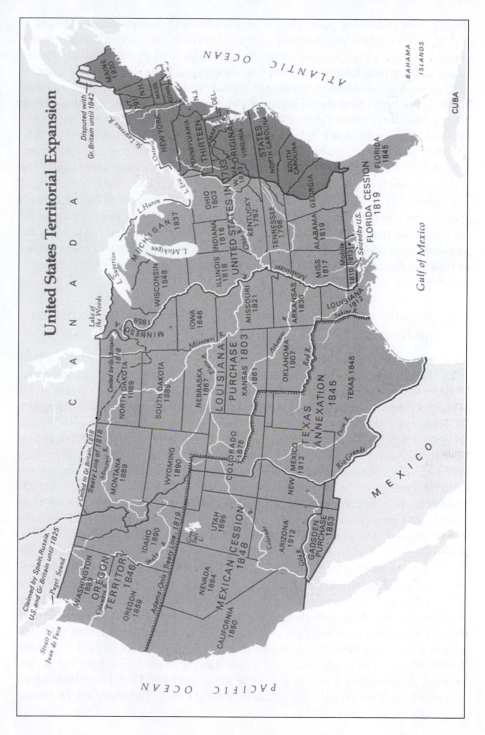

United States Territorial Expansion

though quiet and loving peace and the pursuit of wealth, is high-minded, despising wealth in competition with insult or injury, enterprising and energetic as any nation on earth; these circumstances render it impossible that France and the United States can continue long friends, when they meet in so irritable a position. They, as well as we, must be blind if they do not see this; and we must be very improvident if we do not begin to make arrangements on that hypothesis. The day that France takes possession of New Orleans, fixes the sentence which is to restrain her forever within her low-water mark. It seals the union of two nations, who, in conjunction, can maintain exclusive possession of the ocean. From that moment, we must marry ourselves to the British fleet and nation. We must turn all our attention to a maritime force, for which our resources place us on very high ground; and having formed and connected together a power which may render reinforcement of her settlements here impossible to France, make the first cannon which shall be fired in Europe the signal for the tearing up any settlement she may have made, and for holding the two continents of America in sequestration for the common purposes of the United British and American nations. This is not a state of things we seek or desire.

2. Napoleon Bonaparte, First Consul of France, Explains the Need to Sell Louisiana to the United States, 1803

I know the full value of Louisiana, and I have been desirous of repairing the fault of the French negotiator who abandoned it in 1763. A few lines of a treaty have restored it to me, and I have scarcely recovered it when I must expect to lose it. But if it escapes from me, it shall one day cost dearer to those who oblige me to strip myself of it than to those to whom I wish to deliver it. The English have successively taken from France, Canada, Cape Breton, Newfoundland, Nova Scotia, and the richest portions of Asia. They are engaged in exciting troubles in St. Domingo. They shall not have the Mississippi which they covet. Louisiana is nothing in comparison with their conquests in all parts of the globe, and yet the jealousy they feel at the restoration of this colony to the sovereignty of France, acquaints me with their wish to take possession of it, and it is thus that they will begin the war. They have twenty ships of war in the Gulf of Mexico, they sail over those seas as sovereigns, whilst our affairs in St. Domingo have been growing worse every day since the death of [General Charles Victor Emmanuel] Leclerc [in Santo Domingo]. The conquest of Louisiana would be easy, if they only took the trouble to make a descent there. I have not a moment to lose in putting it out of their reach. I know not whether they are not already there. It is their usual course, and if I had been in their place, I would not have waited. I wish, if there is still time, to take from them any idea that they may have of ever possessing that colony. I think of ceding it to the United States. I can scarcely say that I cede it to them, for it is not yet in our possession. If, however, I leave the least time to our enemies, I shall only transmit an empty title to those republicans whose friendship I seek. They only ask of me one

This document can be found in Barbé Marbois, *The History of Louisiana* (Philadelphia: Carey and Lea, 1830), 263–264, 274–275, 276, 312.

town in Louisiana, but I already consider the colony as entirely lost, and it appears to me that in the hands of this growing power, it will be more useful to the policy and even to the commerce of France, than if I should attempt to keep it. . . .

Irresolution and deliberation are no longer in season. I renounce Louisiana. It is not only New Orleans that I will cede, it is the whole colony without any reservation. I know the price of what I abandon, and I have sufficiently proved the importance that I attach to this province, since my first diplomatic act with Spain had for its object the recovery of it. I renounce it with the greatest regret. To attempt obstinately to retain it would be folly. I direct you to negotiate this affair with the envoys of the United States. Do not even await the arrival of Mr. [James] Monroe: have an interview this very day with Mr. [Robert] Livingston; but I require a great deal of money for this war, and I would not like to commence it with new contributions. For a hundred years France and Spain have been incurring expenses for improvements in Louisiana, for which its trade has never indemnified them. Large sums, which will never be returned to the treasury, have been lent to companies and to agriculturists. The price of all these things is justly due to us. If I should regulate my terms, according to the value of these vast regions to the United States, the indemnity would have no limits. I will be moderate, in consideration of the necessity in which I am of making a sale. But keep this to yourself. I want fifty millions [about $9,375,000] and for less than that sum I will not treat. . . .

Perhaps it will also be objected to me, that the Americans may be found too powerful for Europe in two or three centuries: but my foresight does not embrace such remote fears. Besides, we may hereafter expect rivalries among the members of the Union. The confederations, that are called perpetual, only last till one of the contracting parties finds it to its interest to break them, and it is to prevent the danger, to which the colossal power of England exposes us, that I would provide a remedy. . . .

This accession of territory . . . strengthens for ever the power of the United States; and I have just given to England a maritime rival, that will sooner or later humble her pride.

3. Robert R. Livingston, American Minister to France, Recounts the Paris Negotiations, 1803

By my letter of yesterday, you learned that the Minister [of the Treasury] had asked me whether I would agree to purchase Louisiana &c. On the 12th, I called upon him to press this matter further. He then thought proper to declare that his proposition was only personal, but still requested me to make an offer; and, upon declining to do so, as I expected Mr. Monroe the next day, he shrugged up his shoulders, and changed the conversation. Not willing, however, to lose sight of it, I told him I had been long endeavoring to bring him to some point; but, unfortunately, without effect: that I wished merely to have the negotiation opened by any proposition on his part; and, with that view, had written him a note which contained that request,

---

This document can be found in *State Papers and Correspondence Bearing Upon the Purchase of the Territory of Louisiana,* U.S. House of Representatives, 57th Congress, 2nd Session, Doc. No. 431 (Washington, D.C.: Government Printing Office, 1903), 159–163.

grounded upon my apprehension of the consequence of sending General [Jean Baptiste Jules] Bernadotte without enabling him to say a treaty was begun. He told me he would answer my note, but that he must do it evasively, because Louisiana was not theirs. I smiled at this assertion, and told him I had seen the treaty recognizing it; that I knew the Consul had appointed officers to govern the country, and that he had himself told me that General Victor was to take possession; that, in a note written by the express order of the First Consul, he had told me that General Bernadotte was to treat relative to it in the United States, &c. He still persisted that they had it in contemplation to obtain it, but had it not. I told him that I was very well pleased to understand this from him, because, if so, we should not commit ourselves with them in taking it from Spain, to whom, by his account, it still belonged; and that, as we had just cause of complaint against her, if Mr. Monroe concurred in opinion with me, we should negotiate no further on the subject, but advise our Government to take possession. He seemed alarmed at the boldness of the measure, and told me he would answer my note, but that it would be evasively. I told him I should receive with pleasure any communication from him, but that we were not disposed to trifle; that the times were critical, and though I did not know what instructions Mr. Monroe might bring, I was perfectly satisfied that they would require a precise and prompt notice; that I was very fearful, from the little progress I had made, that my Government would consider me as a very indolent negotiator. He laughed, and told me that he would give me a certificate that I was the most importunate he had met with. . . .

I told him that the United States were anxious to preserve peace with France; that, for that reason, they wished to remove them to the west side of the Mississippi; that we would be perfectly satisfied with New Orleans and the Floridas, and had no disposition to extend across the river; that, of course, we would not give any great sum for the purchase; that he was right in his idea of the extreme exorbitancy of the demand, which would not fall short of one hundred and twenty-five millions; that, however, we would be ready to purchase, provided the sum was reduced to reasonable limits. He then pressed me to name the sum. I told him that this was not worth while, because, as he only treated the inquiry as a matter of curiosity, any declaration of mine would have no effect. If a negotiation was to be opened, we should (Mr. Monroe and myself) make the offer after mature reflection. This compelled him to declare, that, though he was not authorized expressly to make the inquiry from me, yet, that, if I could mention any sum that came near the mark, that could be accepted, he would communicate it to the First Consul. I told him that we had no sort of authority to go to a sum that bore any proportion to what he mentioned; but that, as he himself considered the demand as too high, he would oblige me by telling me what he thought would be reasonable. He replied that, if we would name sixty millions, and take upon us the American claims, to the amount of twenty more, he would try how far this would be accepted. I told him that it was vain to ask anything that was so greatly beyond our means; that true policy would dictate to the First Consul not to press such a demand; that he must know that it would render the present Government unpopular, and have a tendency, at the next election, to throw the power into the hands of men who were most hostile to a connection with France; and that this would probably happen in the midst of a war. I asked him whether the few millions acquired at this expense would not be too dearly bought?

He frankly confessed that he was of my sentiments; but that he feared the Consul would not relax. I asked him to press this argument upon him, together with the danger of seeing the country pass into the hands of Britain. I told him that he had seen the ardor of the Americans to take it by force, and the difficulty with which they were restrained by the prudence of the President; that he must easily see how much the hands of the war party would be strengthened, when they learned that France was upon the eve of a rupture with England. He admitted the weight of all this: "But," says he, "you know the temper of a youthful conqueror; everything he does is rapid as lightning; we have only to speak to him as an opportunity presents itself, perhaps in a crowd, when he bears no contradiction. When I am alone with him, I can speak more freely, and he attends; but this opportunity seldom happens, and is always accidental. Try, then, if you can not come up to my mark. Consider the extent of the country, the exclusive navigation of the river, and the importance of having no neighbors to dispute you, no war to dread." I told him that I considered all these as important considerations, but there was a point beyond which we could not go, and that fell far short of the sum he mentioned. . . .

I speak now without reflection, and without having seen Mr. Monroe, as it was midnight when I left the Treasury Office, and is now near 3 o'clock. It is so very important that you should be apprized that a negotiation is actually opened, even before Mr. Monroe has been presented, in order to calm the tumult which the news of war will renew, that I have lost no time in communicating it. We shall do all we can to cheapen the purchase; but my present sentiment is that we shall buy. Mr. Monroe will be presented to the Minister to-morrow, when we shall press for as early an audience as possible from the First Consul. I think it will be necessary to put in some proposition to-morrow: the Consul goes in a few days to Brussels, and every moment is precious.

4. Federalist Alexander Hamilton Debunks Jefferson's Diplomacy, 1803

At length the business of New-Orleans has terminated favorably to this country. Instead of being obliged to rely any longer on the force of treaties, for a place of deposit, the jurisdiction of the territory is now transferred to our hands and in future the navigation of the Mississippi will be ours unmolested. This, it will be allowed, is an important acquisition; not, indeed, as territory, but as being essential to the peace and prosperity of our Western country, and as opening a free and valuable market to our commercial states. This purchase has been made during the period of Mr. Jefferson's presidency, and will, doubtless, give éclat to his administration. Every man, however, possessed of the least candor and reflection will readily acknowledge that the acquisition has been solely owing to a fortuitous concurrence of unforeseen and unexpected circumstances, and not to any wise or vigorous measures on the part of the American government.

This document can be found in the *New York Evening Post,* July 5, 1803. It can also be found in Harold C. Syrett, ed., *The Papers of Alexander Hamilton* (New York: Columbia University Press, 1979), XXVI, 129–136.

As soon as we experienced from Spain a direct infraction of an important article of our treaty [of 1795], in withholding the deposit of New Orleans, it afforded us justifiable cause of war, and authorized immediate hostilities. Sound policy unquestionably demanded of us to begin with a prompt, bold, and vigorous resistance against the injustice; to seize the object at once. And having this *vantage* ground, should we have thought it advisable to terminate hostilities by a purchase, we might then have done it on almost our own terms. This course, however, was not adopted. . . .

On the part of France, the short interval of peace had been wasted in repeated and fruitless efforts to subjugate St. Domingo; and those means which were originally destined to the colonization of Louisiana had been gradually exhausted by the unexpected difficulties of this ill-starred enterprise.

To the deadly climate of St. Domingo, and to the courage and obstinate resistance made by its black inhabitants, are we indebted for the obstacles which delayed the colonization of Louisiana till the auspicious moment when a [prospective] rupture between England and France gave a new turn to the projects of the latter, and destroyed at once all her schemes as to this favorite object of her ambition.

It was made known to Bonaparte that among the first objects of England would be the seizure of New-Orleans, and that preparations were even then in a state of forwardness for that purpose. The First Consul could not doubt that, if an English fleet was sent thither, the place must fall without resistance. It was obvious, therefore, that it would be in every shape preferable that it should be placed in the possession of a neutral power. And when, besides, some millions of money, of which he was extremely in want, were offered him to part with what he could no longer hold, it affords a moral certainty that it was to an accidental state of circumstances, and not to wise plans, that this cession, at this time, has been owing. We shall venture to add that neither of the ministers through whose instrumentality it was effected will ever deny this, or even pretend that, previous to the time when a rupture was believed to be inevitable, there was the smallest chance of inducing the First Consul, with his ambitious and aggrandizing views, to commute the territory for any sum of money in their power to offer. The real truth is, Bonaparte found himself absolutely compelled, by situation, to relinquish his darling plan of colonizing the banks of the Mississippi. And thus have the government of the United States, by the unforeseen operation of events, gained what the feebleness and pusillanimity of its miserable system of measures could never have acquired.

5. Jefferson Instructs Captain Meriwether Lewis on Exploration, 1803

The object of your mission is to explore the Missouri river, & such principal stream of it, as, by it's course & communication with the waters of the Pacific Ocean, may offer the most direct & practicable water communication across this continent, for the purposes of commerce.

This document can be found in Jefferson to Lewis, 20 June 1803, Thomas Jefferson Papers, Series I, Reel # 28, Manuscipts Division, Library of Congress.

Beginning at the mouth of the Missouri, you will take observations of latitude & longitude, at all remarkable points on the river, & especially at the mouths of rivers, at rapids, at islands & other places & objects distinguished by such natural marks & characters of a durable kind, as that they may with certainty be recognized hereafter. The courses of the river between these points of observation may be supplied by the compass, the log-line & by time, corrected by the observations themselves. The variations of the compass too, in different places, should be noticed.

The interesting points of portage between the heads of the Missouri & the water offering the best communication with the Pacific Ocean should also be fixed by observation, & the course of that water to the ocean, in the same manner as that of the Missouri. . . .

The commerce which may be carried on with the people inhabiting the line you will pursue, renders a knolege of these people important. You will therefore endeavor to make yourself acquainted, as far as a diligent pursuit of your journey shall admit,

with the names of the nations & their numbers;
the extent & limits of their possessions;
their relations with other tribes or nations;
their language, traditions, monuments;
their ordinary occupations in agriculture, fishing, hunting, war, arts, & the
  implements for these;
their food, clothing, & domestic accommodations;
the diseases prevalent among them, & the remedies they use;
moral & physical circumstances which distinguish them from the tribes
  we know;
peculiarities in their laws, customs & dispositions;
and articles of commerce they may need or furnish, & to what extent.

And considering the interest which every nation has in extending & strengthening the authority of reason & justice among the people around them, it will be useful to acquire what knolege you can of the state of morality, religion & information among them, as it may better enable those who endeavor to civilize & instruct them, to adapt their measures to the existing notions & practises of those on whom they are to operate.

Other object worthy of notice will be
the soil & face of the country, it's growth & vegetable productions;
  especially those not of the U.S.
the animals of the country generally, & especially those not known in the U.S.
the remains and accounts of any which may [be] deemed rare or extinct;
the mineral productions of every kind; but more particularly metals, limestone, pit coal & salpetre; salines & mineral waters, noting the temperature of the last, & such circumstances as may indicate their character.
Volcanic appearances.
climate as characterized by the thermometer, by the proportion of rainy, cloudy & clear days, by lightening, hail, snow, ice, by the access & recess of frost, by the winds prevailing at different seasons, the dates at which particular plants put forth or lose their flowers, or leaf, times of appearance of particular birds, reptiles or insects. . . .

In all your intercourse with the natives treat them in the most friendly & conciliatory manner which their own conduct will admit; allay all jealousies as to the object of your journey, satisfy them of it's innocence, make them acquainted with the position, extent, character, peaceable & commercial dispositions of the U.S. of our wish to be neighborly, friendly & useful to them, & of our dispositions to a commercial intercourse with them; confer with them on the points most convenient as mutual emporiums, & the articles of most desireable interchange for them & us. If a few of their influential chiefs, within practicable distance, wish to visit us, arrange such a visit with them, and furnish them with authority to call on our officers, on their entering the U.S. to have them conveyed to this place at public expense. If any of them should wish to have some of their young people brought up with us, & taught such arts as may be useful to them, we will receive, instruct & take care of them. Such a mission, whether of influential chiefs, or of young people, would give some security to your own party. Carry with you some matter of the kinepox, inform those of them with whom you may be of it' efficacy as a preservative from the small-pox; and instruct & incourage them in the use of it. This may be especially done wherever you winter. . . .

Should you reach the Pacific ocean [One full line scratched out, indecipherable. . . .] inform yourself of the circumstances which may decide whether the furs of those parts may not be collected as advantageously at the head of the Missouri (convenient as is supposed to the waters of the Colorado & Oregon or Columbia) as at Nootka sound or any other point of that coast; & that trade be consequently conducted through the Missouri & U.S. more beneficially than by the circumnavigation now practised.

On your arrival on that coast endeavor to learn if there be any port within your reach frequented by the sea-vessels of any nation, and to send two of your trusty people back by sea, in such way as shall appear practicable, with a copy of your notes. And should you be of opinion that the return of your party by the way they went will be eminently dangerous, then ship the whole, & return by sea by way of Cape Horn or the Cape of good Hope, as you shall be able.

ESSAYS

The historiographical debate over the Louisiana Purchase revolves around President Thomas Jefferson's decisionmaking and the deliberateness of American policy. Did the Jefferson administration follow a coherent strategy that persuaded Napoleon Bonaparte to sell Louisiana? Or was the United States simply the beneficiary of France's bad luck? Robert W. Tucker of the Johns Hopkins University and David C. Hendrickson of Colorado College argue in the opening essay that Jefferson sought territorial expansion but opposed the use of military force either unilaterally or bilaterally. Jefferson thus pursued a risky policy of conquest without war. Tucker and Hendrickson conclude that external factors—Napoleon's ill-fated attempt to quell the black slave rebellion in Santo Domingo (the French called it Saint Domingue) and the imminence of war in Europe between France and Britain—prodded Napoleon to sell Louisiana to the United States. Joyce Appleby of the University of California at Los Angeles takes a different approach in the second essay. She agrees that external factors in Europe and the Caribbean played into America's hands, but she also attributes the acquisition of

Louisiana to Jefferson's assertive diplomatic campaign to buy New Orleans, expand American trade, and gain western territory through conquest. Neither his abhorrence of war nor his belief in limited government could deter the third president from his dream of a continental empire inhabited by white settlers. Jefferson's resolute leadership and cultural ethnocentrism reflected the collective will of the people who had elected him.

Jefferson's Risky Diplomacy of Watching and Waiting

ROBERT W. TUCKER AND DAVID C. HENDRICKSON

On September 28, 1801, the Secretary of State forwarded a letter of instructions to the newly appointed Minister to France [Robert Livingston], then awaiting passage to Bordeaux. The minister's attention was directed to the information that a "transaction" had likely been concluded between France and Spain involving "the mouth of the Mississippi, with certain portions of adjacent territory." The impending change of neighbors, Madison wrote Livingston, "is of too momentous concern not to have engaged the most serious attention of the Executive." Livingston was instructed to take up the subject with the French government and to express the anxiety of the United States over the prospects and consequences of the rumored transfer of territory. The "tendency of a French neighborhood," the government in Paris was to be delicately reminded, must "inspire jealousies and apprehensions which may turn the thoughts of our citizens towards a closer connexion with her rival, and possibly produce a crisis in which a very favorable part of her dominions would be exposed to the joint operations of a naval and territorial power." Should, however, Livingston find the cession a fait accompli, or virtually so, he was to make every effort to preserve those rights of trade and navigation then obtaining between the United States and Spain. Additionally, he was to see whether France could not be induced to cede the Floridas—or at least West Florida—to this country, assuming these territories to be included in the cession. Such cession by France would at once prove that nation's good will and serve to reconcile the United States to an arrangement so much "disrelished" by them. But should the Floridas neither have been ceded to France nor their cession contemplated by France, efforts were to be made to dispose Paris in favor of "experiments on the part of the United States, for obtaining from Spain the cession in view."

Thus France was to be warned that a return to the Mississippi valley could result in an alliance between this country and England, an alliance that might well result at some future date in France being driven altogether from North America. But the threat was to remain less than explicit, lest it unnecessarily arouse the French and thereby jeopardize American rights in the use of the river. Alternatively, France might be induced to give part of the territories ceded to it in order to gain the good will of this country. The cession of West Florida to the United States would reconcile the latter to the French presence elsewhere, while relieving France of spoliation claims by American citizens. On the other hand, if Spain still possessed the Floridas, France might nevertheless be disposed to assist us in obtaining these lands in return for our favorable disposition toward its presence here. How France might undertake this role was not elaborated.

These instructions, drawn up at the outset of the Louisiana crisis, form a succinct summary of the principal features of Jeffersonian diplomacy, not only in the Louisiana crisis but also in the subsequent efforts to obtain the Floridas. Essentially the same considerations, but with greater urgency, were pressed by Jefferson in his famous letter to Livingston in April 1802. Although once our "natural friend," Jefferson wrote, in possessing New Orleans France must become "our natural and habitual enemy." By doing so, he warned, France must seal its own fate, for in taking New Orleans it would not only force America into alliance with Great Britain but require the United States "to turn all our attention to a maritime force, for which our resources place us on very high grounds." When war broke out again in Europe, the United States would seize the opportunity to tear up any settlement France had made, and would then hold "the two continents of America in sequestration for the common purposes of the united British and American nations." In such a contest of arms, France would immediately lose New Orleans. "For however greater her force is than ours compared in the abstract, it is nothing in comparison of ours when to be exerted on our own soil." . . .

While the French never succeeded in taking possession of New Orleans, save in a formal sense and even then only for the briefest of periods, until the time Napoleon decided to sell the colony American diplomacy had to prepare against that day. How serious were the American efforts and what effect did they have on the French? The first question can be answered with greater assurance than the second. To characterize the American efforts to propitiate Great Britain as serious is to take no little liberty with that term. It may be argued, of course, that the propitiation of British power was virtually impossible during the period England was at peace with France, that there was no incentive the Jefferson administration could hold out that would tempt London to jeopardize the peace by allying England with the United States in opposing French plans of empire in North America. Even so, the question concerning the nature of the American efforts to enlist British support would remain. At best, those efforts must be characterized as halfhearted and without real significance. Given the outlook of Republicans, this was understandable. If an alliance was almost by definition an illicit relationship, an alliance with Great Britain represented for Jefferson and his political associates something approaching a state of mortal sin. Perhaps this explains why Jefferson and Madison appear to have thought of an alliance with England not as a product of the union of political wills but as something that resulted from a kind of political immaculate conception. Whereas the benefits of alliance were desired, the act that produced those benefits was not. For that act meant, if it meant anything, that benefits had to be apparent on both sides.

There is no evidence that Jefferson ever seriously considered the prospect of an alliance from this perspective. His strategy was not directed to the end of actually concluding an alliance with Great Britain. Instead, it was one of appearing to be moving in this direction, with the expectation—or hope—that the object of this strategic feint would be persuaded that the appearance foreshadowed the reality. Thus the story of Jefferson's alliance diplomacy during the Louisiana crisis is a story of attempts to pressure the French into yielding by threatening that the United States would ally itself with England against France. On occasion, the French were told that Great

Britain was eager to conclude an alliance with this country. None of these threats reflected a discernible reality in the sense that the American government was, in fact, prepared to enter into an alliance or that the English were disposed to offer one. Instead, it was the threat that formed the sole reality of this diplomacy.

There is one apparent exception to this pattern and even it is not quite clear. In April 1803, when the crisis had moved close to its denouement, the President, with the support of a majority of his cabinet, decided that if the French proved intractable in the negotiations then in progress in Paris, [Special Envoy James] Monroe and Livingston should be instructed to enter into discussions with the British government "to fix principles of alliance." The instructions Madison wrote to the two envoys were based, in the main, on the supposition that "Great Britain and France are at peace, and that neither of them intend at present to interrupt it." In this situation, the instructions read, if the French government should either "meditate hostilities" or force the United States to initiate a war by closing the Mississippi, Monroe and Livingston were to communicate with the British government and "invite its concurrence in the war." It was to be made clear to Great Britain that although war depended on the choice of the United States alone, our choice of war in turn depended on Britain undertaking to participate in it. At the same time, Madison emphasized, the certainty of our choice of war "should not be known to Great Britain who might take advantage of the posture of things to press on the United States disagreeable conditions of her entering the war." . . . Monroe and Livingston were to conduct these negotiations with England if France, by denying free navigation of the Mississippi, made war inevitable. If, however, navigation was not disputed but the deposit alone was denied, the envoys were to make no explicit engagement, leaving to Congress the decision between war or further procrastination.

The instructions were addressed to a contingency that had already been excluded by France: closure of the Mississippi to navigation by the United States. The French had earlier undertaken to abide by Spain's obligations to this country once they succeeded to Louisiana. These obligations included the right of navigation and of deposit. In this context, what is significant about the instructions was not so much that they provided for situations that were very unlikely to arise but what they had to say about the nature of the administration's alliance diplomacy. For the alliance Monroe and Livingston were to conclude was an alliance Great Britain could not be expected to make. The instructions simply brushed aside the experience of the preceding year and a half. Although assuming that England was neither at war nor intending to enter upon war, the envoys were nevertheless to conclude an alliance the real value of which to Britain was apparent only if the nation were at war. But if that were to occur—if, the instructions read, war has "actually commenced, or its approach be certain"—the American ministers were to avail themselves of this change of circumstances "for avoiding the necessity of recurring to Great Britain, or, if the necessity cannot be avoided, for fashioning her disposition to arrangements which may be the least inconvenient to the United States." In brief, they were either to make no alliance or to make one that would carry virtually no obligations for the United States.

Even if it is concluded that the alliance diplomacy of the Jefferson administration had no solid basis and that it rested on little more than a kind of incantation, it does not follow that the party to whom it was primarily addressed was unaffected.

Whether this diplomacy was "real" or not, the result, after all, was what mattered. Did it impress the French sufficiently to lead them, when taken together with other considerations, to draw back or substantially alter a course they were otherwise intent on taking? . . .

If Jefferson's alliance diplomacy was to affect French behavior, it was desirable—even imperative—that it do so during that critical period when France was moving militarily to occupy Louisiana and to build up the defenses of the colony. In the French plan this was the period when France would be at peace with England. The French calculation was that England would not break the peace over Louisiana. The calculation was sound. The English in entering into peace negotiations with France had deliberately put aside the issue of Louisiana in deference to Paris. That issue could not attract Great Britain into responding to the alliance diplomacy of the United States, and the French appreciated this very well.

It was only if the peace broke down for other reasons that this diplomacy could evoke a British response. Indeed, in the event that peace broke down, the English did not need Jefferson's encouragement to prompt them to strike at France's colonial efforts both at sea and on land. Then this diplomacy would be directed to restraining England's efforts rather than to eliciting them and for fear that otherwise these efforts might pave the way for subsequent claims. It is quite true that when peace visibly began to break down, Napoleon was at pains to see that the United States did not ally itself with Great Britain. The abandonment of Louisiana readily accomplished that. Still, Napoleon did not abandon Louisiana because he was affected by Jefferson's alliance diplomacy, but for quite different reasons. Having once decided to abandon the colony, however, he did so in a manner he considered would best serve his interests. Not the least of those interests was the creation of a power in the New World that might in time provide a serious challenge to the maritime power of England.

The question of Jefferson's alliance diplomacy is closely related to that of the President's use of the threat of war. The prevailing view among historians is that Jefferson was quite willing to use military power in pursuit of his diplomatic aim and that he effectively threatened France with war should it claim New Orleans. Whether or not this view is well taken depends in no small measure on determining what constitutes a meaningful threat of force. The persuasion that Jefferson was quite willing to use military power is, in part at least, dependent on the fact—or what is so claimed—that he seriously threatened war. Did he?

A serious threat of war has the quality of imminence, if not of immediacy, and is dependent on the occurrence of a specified event. The significance of the temporal element is apparent. The longer the period of time that is entertained, the greater the possibility that changing circumstances may alter the will of the party making the threat. The element of specificity in defining the conditions or circumstances productive of war is also important. The more vague or ambitious the conditions, the more difficult it is for a threat of war to serve as a deterrent (and that, presumably, is its principal purpose). Jefferson's threat of war satisfied neither of these conditions. Indefinite in time and vague in circumstance, his threats to use force were all of a contingent and hypothetical nature, dependent on future developments that were likely to put the French at sufficient disadvantage as to make the prospect of this country resorting to force against them a credible one. But these were not the kinds of threats likely to command Napoleon's respectful attention. He might be deterred by a meaningful threat of force in the here and now. He could not be deterred by a hypothetical threat addressed to circumstances in which he already knew that his empire would be put at risk.

There is one apparent exception to this pattern of Jeffersonian threats and it is to be found in the famous letter of April 18, 1802. Although clearly containing a threat of war, the threat was contingent on an alliance with Great Britain. The letter contrasts markedly with the official instructions Madison wrote at the time to Livingston. In the latter, Livingston was directed to state that "a mere neighborhood could not be friendly to the harmony which both countries have so much an interest in cherishing; but if a possession of the mouth of the Mississippi is to be added to the other causes of discord, the worst events are to be apprehended." These threats of war, contingent and hypothetical though they were, undoubtedly reached the French, for as early as the beginning of 1802, Jefferson had told the French Chargé that a French occupation of New Orleans would lead to a rupture between the United States and France, an alliance between the United States and Great Britain, and, eventually, a war between this country and the occupant of New Orleans.

While Jefferson was voicing this to [French Chargé d'affaires Louis André] Pichon, however, his minister in Paris was assuring the French government that "as long as France conforms to the existing treaties between us and Spain, the government of the United States does not consider herself as having any interest in opposing the exchange." Madison's letter to Livingston of May 1, 1802, represented an abrupt change from the assurances the American minister had been giving the French, and Jefferson's private letter to Livingston amounted to an even more radical shift in policy.

The shift was more apparent than real, however, for it was not otherwise attended by a hardened diplomatic position. On the contrary, having delivered themselves privately and officially of hard-line positions, Jefferson and Madison seemed content to let matters rest. The impression was thereby given of a government that was not to be taken at its word, when that word was bellicose. This impression would have been confirmed had adversaries only been able to read the letter Jefferson wrote in October 1802 to Livingston. Having told Livingston in April that the closest possible relationship must be formed between this country and England, in October the President had again seen "all the disadvantageous consequences of taking a side" between France and Great Britain. While acknowledging that we may yet be forced into taking sides by a "more disagreeable alternative," in that event, Jefferson insisted, "we must countervail the disadvantages by measures which give us splendor and power, but not as much happiness as our present system." And after insisting in the spring of 1802 that war must be the inevitable result of a French occupation of New Orleans, Jefferson insisted in the fall of that year that "no matter at present existing between them and us is important enough to risk a break of peace,—peace being indeed the most important of all things for us, except the preserving an erect and independent attitude." . . .

It was not the appearance of French forces in New Orleans that formed the *casus belli* for the administration, but the denial of free navigation of the Mississippi. This position is apparent in the general instructions March 2, 1803, given Monroe and Livingston. The American commissioners were to try to buy New Orleans and the

Floridas. They might offer close to ten million dollars for this as well as guaranteeing France commercial privileges. The commissioners, if pressed, might also offer as an inducement a guarantee of the west bank of the Mississippi. But if France refused to sell any of its territory under any conditions, the two envoys were to secure the right of deposit, and hopefully to improve on the old right. Should even the right of deposit be denied, Monroe and Livingston were to be guided by instructions specially adapted to the case.

The conclusion of Henry Adams that the instructions "offered to admit the French without condition" is difficult to resist. The same must be said of the instructions Madison subsequently wrote Monroe and Livingston on April 18. Unaware that Napoleon had decided to sell Louisiana to the United States, Madison drafted the April instructions primarily to provide for the eventuality that France "should be found to meditate hostilities or to have formed projects which will constrain the United States to resort to hostilities." But war was to be judged inevitable only in the event that France "should avow or evidence a determination to deny to the United States the free navigation of the Mississippi." If France should not dispute the right of navigation and instead only deny deposit, the envoys were advised that "it will be prudent to adapt your consultations to the possibility that Congress may distinguish between the two cases, and make a question how far the latter right may call for an instant resort to arms, or how far procrastination of that remedy may be suggested and justified by the prospect of a more favorable conjuncture." . . .

At the same time, the administration took certain measures, including limited preparation, for the possibility of armed conflict. These measures were taken against the background of a military policy that had reduced the army from an authorized strength of 5,500 to 3,300 regulars. In his second annual message, on December 15, 1802, Jefferson had declared that no change in the nation's military establishment was "deemed necessary" and had contented himself with recommending to the Congress a "review" of the militia with the purpose of giving it "those improvements of which you find it susceptible." Two weeks before, the Secretary of War had ordered the reenlistment of every valuable soldier whose period of service was expiring, a step, however, that added nothing to the existing force.

Beginning early in 1803, several measures were taken along the Mississippi frontier to increase the defensive capability of fortified positions there. Of these posts, the largest and most important was Fort Adams, situated on the Mississippi River just above the border with Spain. It was Fort Adams that constituted the principal defensive bulwark against an offensive thrust from New Orleans, just as it was this post that would have provided the base for an assault on New Orleans. In March 1803, Fort Adams had a force of seven companies. In the same month two additional companies were ordered there. Since the companies were in all likelihood under strength, the size of the force at this critical post probably numbered no more than six hundred men. Elsewhere, the distribution of forces both along the southern frontier, where they would face the French, as well as on the northern frontier, where they faced the British, inevitably meant that the army was stretched very thin.

How significant were the various measures taken to improve the readiness of the forces in the western posts and what do they indicate about Jefferson's intentions? Judged by the view that Jefferson himself seemed to have taken of his administration's efforts, they do not appear to have been more than of modest significance.

Certainly, they scarcely seem to have been of such character as to have "left nothing to chance" in a showdown with Napoleon's forces. . . .

During the early winter of 1802–3, the expectation persisted that a French force would eventually be sent to New Orleans. There were no plans to contest its arrival by military means. Nor did the American government intimate, let alone declare, that the attempt by France to occupy New Orleans would be regarded by this country as a *casus belli*. It is true that by late winter, American authorities entertained strong doubt that the French would in fact attempt the military occupation of Louisiana. But this doubt was not the result of the preparatory military measures taken by the administration. It arose instead from the repeated failure of the French to mount an expedition because of the continuing demands of the Santo Domingo campaign as well as from the growing realization that war would soon be renewed between France and England. . . .

As late as the spring and early summer of 1802, the prospects for Napoleon's scheme of empire seemed quite bright to its architects. In fact, the stage was already being set for the disaster that would overtake the French by the late summer of that year. Napoleon had badly underestimated the requirements of the campaign on Santo Domingo, as the American Consul on the island had noted before his expulsion. The expedition sent out under [General Charles Victor Emmanuel] Leclerc was not nearly of the size that was needed to ensure against defeat. But to men who held the blacks in contempt, as did Napoleon and Leclerc, the prospect of defeat at their hands was not to be credited. Besides, Leclerc had waged a determined and ruthless campaign, one that by April had left French forces in control of all the principal towns and ports of the island. Although the French had paid a very heavy price in casualties for their successes, this did not appear to detract from what they saw as a victory. . . .

The optimism . . . did not last long. In July [1802], the storm suddenly broke over Leclerc's head. The French commander had been prudent enough not to attempt the immediate implementation of Napoleon's order restoring slavery. But rumors that slavery had been restored on Guadeloupe soon reached Santo Domingo, where they aroused the blacks to a fury that persisted until independence, and freedom, had been achieved. By July, Leclerc's forces were weakened by an outbreak of yellow fever that grew in violence as the summer progressed. By late summer, a badly depleted force was clearly on the defensive. Before Paris could respond to Leclerc's frantic calls for reinforcements, he too had succumbed to yellow fever in November 1802. Only with a new force of ten thousand troops did his successor, [Comte de] Rochambeau, manage to launch a new offensive that kept the French in the field as an effective fighting force.

Even if Jefferson was endowed with an unusual degree of prescience, it is unreasonable to assume that he clearly foresaw the various difficulties that would beset French plans. Certainly the disastrous decision to restore slavery on the island could not have been counted on. Nor was there reason to expect that yellow fever would strike with the intensity that it did. Jefferson might have hoped that the black rebels of Santo Domingo would continue indefinitely to consume French forces until Napoleon abandoned his colonial ambitions in the New World, but he could not prudently *count* on this outcome. Nor did he. As it turned out, the demands imposed by Santo Domingo, formidable though they were, could not preclude Napoleon from sending a force to occupy Louisiana. He might well have done so in the fall of

1802 and very nearly did so in the winter of 1803, only to be blocked from acting by unusual weather. For Jefferson, the expected difficulties on Santo Domingo provided time; but true deliverance from peril, he thought, lay elsewhere.

The central hope of Jefferson's Louisiana diplomacy was that Britain and France would again go to war. Had the French succeeded in occupying New Orleans, a renewed European war, which would have immediately isolated what forces France had deployed in the Western Hemisphere, might have allowed the United States to seize New Orleans at little cost. Or the United States might have acted in concert with Britain. Whether Jefferson would have employed force even under such favorable circumstances remains uncertain; he clearly hoped that the prospect of such an event would induce Napoleon to sell New Orleans to the United States, or at least to return Louisiana to Spain.

As events turned out, Jefferson's best hopes were realized. Napoleon did not succeed in sending an occupation force to New Orleans. By the time the weather permitted the departure of the military expedition, the English had blockaded it. Although still formally at peace with France, it was already apparent to the government in London that the die had been cast for a renewal of the hegemonic struggle. With the imminent renewal of the war, Napoleon had little to lose by getting what he could for Louisiana. Once at war, Louisiana could easily be taken from him by England and he doubtless thought that this loss was more than likely. By selling Louisiana to the United States, he would be able to finance a part of the coming war. Abandoning Louisiana, it is true, meant abandoning his grand plan of empire in the West. But that plan could not survive renewal of the war with England, and Napoleon appreciated this only too well. . . .

[Negotiation] was, indeed, Jefferson's true policy: to conquer without war or, if this proved impossible, to conquer without a costly war. If war was the nemesis that threatened to destroy everything the Republicans had achieved and still hoped to achieve, Jefferson's unwillingness to face squarely the prospect of war with France and to make serious preparations for it was surely understandable. At the same time, his policy involved considerable risk. It did so in the first instance because it was prepared to accept for the time being a French military presence in New Orleans. Once this force was there, its removal might well have proven to be a difficult task. There was no way of knowing how large this presence might ultimately become. Nor was the size the principal consideration. Instead, it was the commitment itself. Once New Orleans was occupied by French forces, it was reasonable to expect that the nature of the crisis would be transformed. With the military occupation, the French commitment in Louisiana would have deepened.

Second, Jefferson's policy involved risk because it gambled with the sentiments of the western people. The argument that time would work increasingly against the French by virtue of numbers alone necessarily assumed that these numbers could always be counted on to support the American government's cause. This assumption was at odds, though, with the view that the very presence of a foreign power in the Mississippi valley would raise the specter of secession. Earlier, Jefferson himself had given expression to this dread prospect; he had done so in circumstances that were far less ominous than those faced in Louisiana. Moreover, even if in the long run time did work against the French, there might still be an enormous price to pay before the demographic fact worked its inevitable way. And once it had done so, it might still have left a legacy of disunion in its wake.

The purchase of Louisiana has often been regarded as one of the greatest triumphs of American diplomacy. Half of a continent was gained without war. The gauge of Jefferson's success has been measured almost as much in the means as in the end. Foremost among the means, presumably, was a brilliant diplomacy the central feature of which was to play for time. For time, Jefferson quickly sensed, was the great enemy of Napoleon's design. In time, the terrible cost of the ill-conceived campaign on Santo Domingo would become apparent to all and would operate to constrain even a Napoleon. In time, the struggle between England and France, implacable adversaries as they were, was bound to be renewed. And in time, the American position in the Mississippi valley could only become stronger. The essence of Jefferson's strategy was to wait for these developments, to play for time until they could work their expected result. In this, historians have generally concluded, Jefferson was right. He used conditioning circumstances to his great advantage, just as he used to his advantage the threat of forming an alliance or of going to war. And this capitalizing on circumstances, it is argued, testified above all to his insight and skill rather than to his good fortune.

The favorable assessment of Jefferson's statecraft has often been further underlined by comparing it with the course of action recommended at the time by Alexander Hamilton. Two options, Hamilton declared, were open to the United States: "First, to negociate and endeavor to purchase, and if this fails to go to war. Secondly, to seize at once on the Floridas and New-Orleans, and then negociate," a course of action that required an immediate increase in the army and militia as well as the full cooperation and support of Great Britain. For this counsel, the leading Federalist opponent of Jefferson has since been criticized. Hamilton's advice, this criticism runs, would have involved us in a war with both France and Spain, a war for which we were utterly unprepared. In this war, we could not count on the support of Great Britain, then at peace with France. Hamilton was too intelligent not to realize that the course he advocated could result only in disaster. This being the case, critics have concluded, it represented little more than a political maneuver made to embarrass the administration of the day.

Clearly, Hamilton's advice was intended to put the administration in an unfavorable light. Was this advice so manifestly misguided, however, that it does not warrant serious consideration? A positive response can scarcely be supported by pointing out that Hamilton's position rested on the assumption that France would never sell. Whatever his hopes might have been, Jefferson was often as skeptical of the chances for purchase as was Hamilton. But Jefferson stopped well short of accepting the proposition that in the event efforts to purchase failed, the alternative was war. The President did not accept Hamilton's first course. The war that for Jefferson would result from the failure of purchase negotiations was not a war in the here and now, as it undoubtedly was for Hamilton. Instead, it was a war projected into the future and one that was dependent on the fulfillment of certain conditions. The immediate prospect and reality for Jefferson was not war but palliating and enduring until these conditions were met. But this course, to repeat, carried its own risks. It meant allowing a French occupation of New Orleans. And it meant relying on the cooperation and help of the British.

In the circumstances of the winter of 1803, prudence dictated Hamilton's course rather than Jefferson's. The immediate war proposed by Hamilton surely involved considerable risks. The seizure of New Orleans and the Floridas would likely have resulted in naval hostilities with France and Spain, hostilities for which the country was unprepared. Nor could the United States count on the help of England; short of war between France and England, such assistance was always uncertain. At the same time, the risks entailed by Hamilton's course did not include a French military force in New Orleans, a risk that Jefferson's course could not avoid taking. Moreover, Hamilton might well have calculated, in February 1803, that Great Britain and France were bound to go to war in the reasonably near future. If this calculation is not seen as unjustified in assessing Jefferson's diplomacy, there is no apparent basis for deeming it unjustified in considering Hamilton's proposal.

At the same time, these differences between Jefferson and Hamilton reflected a deeper and more significant difference separating the two men. Hamilton's proposal stemmed from an outlook which assumed that time might work against us, that we could not entrust our fortunes to the contingencies of circumstance, and that we had to resolve immediately to take our fate into our own hands as far as this was at all possible. By contrast, Jefferson's diplomacy reflected an outlook which assumed that time was on our side, that something would turn up to favor our fortunes, and that far more harm than good would result from an impatience to bring matters to a head. The difference, of course, was one of temperament. Yet it was also one that reflected sharply different attitudes toward force and the justification for its use.

Jefferson's Resolute Leadership and Drive Toward Empire

JOYCE APPLEBY

Jefferson premised his foreign policy goals on principle, but in clearing a path for American expansion he willingly took a detour through the duplicities of diplomacy. He was temperamentally peace-loving, but his yearning to see white families spread across the continent trumped his aversion to violence, or at least permitted him to threaten it. Jefferson coined the phrase about avoiding "foreign entanglements," usually attributed to Washington, yet his presidential ambitions drew him ever more deeply into international parleys. And, as in a good play, a voice emerged to taunt him for these inconsistencies.

Jefferson had been tormented during Adams's administration when it looked as if the Federalists' bellicosity would plunge the nation into war with France. His opponents mocked his moderating tendencies as unmanly. Never mind: his longing to cut taxes bolstered his craving for peace. Without a military buildup there would be no need for more revenue. All would have been well had Jefferson also not wanted to settle Americans across the North American continent. To achieve this bold objective would require foreign allies, not to mention compromises made to secure them. To create an "empire of liberty" and spread American institutions beyond the Mississippi, Jefferson was willing to prevaricate, deceive, and deal. . . .

Although Jefferson expressed his policies in the sonorous universals of natural law, we can see now that they were ethnocentric in design and spirit. Stirred by the loftiness of his ideals, he seemed oblivious to the fact that planting American institutions across the plains would obliterate the Indian cultures that had flourished there for generations. He seemed equally indifferent to the fact that his empowering of ordinary white men left ordinary black men with more masters and less freedom. The universal truths he spoke for bore the traces of a particular philosophical position. In such contradictions, most of his contemporaries were equally blind, but no other figure articulated Americans' sentiments in such elegant phrasing, so it has been Jefferson called to the bar of history for the white supremacist basis of American foreign policy.

When he first became involved in diplomacy, as minister to France and the nation's first secretary of state, Jefferson was the very embodiment of an innocent abroad. But, as is the way with innocence, it often sees things invisible to old eyes. His education was wrested from both experience and introspection, hope and despair. When he succeeded Benjamin Franklin in France in 1784, he was thrust into the thorny thickets of international commerce. With John Adams, minister to Great Britain, he assiduously promoted American trading interests, which he had previously understood through the narrow vision of a Southern planter. Charged with getting the best terms possible from America's creditors, the two diplomats also mastered the details of international finance. . . .

One more influence from Jefferson's five-year stint in France shaped his presidential foreign policy. This was the "model treaty" carried to France by the American peace commissioners at the end of the War for Independence. The treaty had laid out a grand plan for global free trade, with acknowledgment of the rights of neutral countries in times of war. Haughtily rejected by the Europeans—Britain refused to consider making any kind of commercial treaty with its erstwhile colonies—the treaty set forth a distinctive set of American principles that Jefferson ardently embraced. By those principles, America's farming families might freely dispatch their crops around the world without fear of embroilment in the constant warfare among European monarchies. Agrarian self-sufficiency never appealed to Jefferson; he plumped instead for a rural prosperity built on the export of America's bumper crops.

It's in the nature of optimists to underestimate the difficulty of achieving their heart's desire. And Jefferson was the Revolution's optimist. Optimism was both the engine and the spanner in his foreign policy. It goaded him to push where no one had pushed before—as in his zealous advocacy of freedom of the seas—and it immobilized him when those grim realities that pessimists focus upon blocked his path. Jefferson feared war and avoided it whenever possible, but he became bellicose when others thwarted his plans. Europe had not signed on to the Americans' idealistic view of international relations. Federalists grasped this truth, but for Jefferson to do so would have been to dam the springs of his own resourcefulness. With his rose-tinted view of the world, he imagined that stupidity, greed, and revenge would yield eventually to reason and virtue. *Eventually,* of course, is a variable term, and eight years proved an insufficient time for virtue and reason to deliver on his goals. But Jefferson made free trade and continental expansion the twin pillars of Republican foreign policy. Treaties were appraised and trades promoted under their aegis.

The audacity of a minor country perched on the Atlantic shelf of the North American continent plotting to expel the French, Spanish, and British who had been in North America since the sixteenth century still induces awe. When Jefferson became president, fewer than six million people lived in the United States. They were scattered up and down the Atlantic Coast. The frontier line ran through the western parts of the thirteen original states. Kentucky, Tennessee, and Vermont had been added to the union; Ohio, the first state formed from the Northwest Territory, was about to enter (in 1803). Only New York, Philadelphia, Baltimore, and Boston had populations larger than 25,000. Yet few leaders in the United States doubted that they could and should plant American farms, schools, and courthouses across the West. In this, Jefferson headed a popular cause. Only with difficulty did he give up the idea of annexing Canada to the United States, and he persisted in considering Cuba for the same treatment. With equal forcefulness, Americans disputed the right of the indigenous people to retain their ancestral homes. Believing profoundly in the superiority of their civilization, Americans acted as though this capacity conferred legitimacy upon their insatiable desire for land. . . .

Most of what Americans wanted to do in the early nineteenth century they could do without the help of the federal government. The one great exception was the acquisition of land in the West. Eastern leaders as well as those eager to move onto the frontier wanted to see the country's boundaries move westward. Timothy Dwight caught the spirit of America's continental expansion in his much-loved poem "Greenfield Hill":

> All hail, thou western world! By heaven design'd
> Th' example bright, to renovate mankind.
> Soon shall thy sons across the mainland roam
> And claim on far Pacific shores, their home . . .

Dwight wrote this in 1794, while Spain and Great Britain retained possession of the lands abutting the Pacific—and most of the territory between the two oceans as well.

So long as enfeebled Spain nominally controlled the area, Americans were at ease: Spain's dependence upon their trade and migration into the region made it likely that New Orleans and Florida would eventually become part of the United States. Louisiana's Spanish governor, the Baron de Carondelet, indicated as much when he warned his superiors that Americans—"a new and vigorous people"—were "advancing and multiplying in the silence of peace." All this changed in 1801 when Napoleon Bonaparte, the new ruler of France, secured from Spain a retrocession of Louisiana. Even worse for American expectations, the First Consul had grand plans to reestablish a French empire in the New World. Word of these ambitions startled Americans from their daydream of western territories dropping into their laps like so many ripe plums.

American independence and the quickening pace of the Atlantic trade enhanced the importance of New Orleans. Coveted by Britain as well as France, Spain, and the United States, this gateway to the Mississippi Valley became a prime target of European rivalries. People in the United States viewed New Orleans as more a necessity than a luxury. Federalists felt distress no less extreme than that of Republicans at the thought of having Napoleon on their doorstep. The parties differed only in approach, the Federalists favoring immediate conquest. As one wrote, both Spain and France must "be driven into the Gulf of Mexico, or we shall never sleep in peace." Jefferson was no less determined to thwart the rising power of France, but he preferred an assertive diplomatic campaign to buy the city, using threats, bullying, and explanations of cold realities, mixed with occasional pleas, to close the deal. No one asked what the Constitution had to say about expansion through conquest.

The president dispatched his protégé James Monroe to help Robert R. Livingston, America's ambassador to France, in the negotiations. As minister plenipotentiary and envoy extraordinary, Monroe was instructed to purchase New Orleans and the Floridas (U.S. officials were under the mistaken impression that Spain had returned East and West Florida to France as well).

Developments elsewhere in the Caribbean played into Jefferson's strategy of buying New Orleans. Santo Domingo, where French troops were struggling to defeat Haitian rebels, turned into a deathtrap. Renewed hostilities between France and Great Britain were imminent. Taking all this in and acting with typical impulsiveness, Napoleon decided to rid himself of the whole Louisiana Territory in one grand sale. In December 1803, the French governor officially delivered Louisiana to the United States, thirty-one short months after Jefferson had received the first credible reports of Louisiana's return to France in May 1801.

Once the purchase was clinched, some Federalists turned churlish. Hamilton denied that Jefferson's success was due to "any wise or vigorous measures on the part of the American government," laying success instead at the feet of "a fortuitous concurrence of unforeseen and unexpected circumstances" and "an over-ruling Providence." Others denied Jefferson political advantage by belittling the purchase; one commentator described Louisiana as a "wilderness unpeopled with any beings except wolves and wandering Indians," which would be "turned into additional states that confirm Virginia's dominance in the union." Another critic exclaimed in mock astonishment: "We are to give money of which we have too little for land of which we already have too much." It *was* a lot of land—883,000 square miles—and the $15 million purchase price was large enough to necessitate some fancy foreign borrowing. As big as Great Britain, France, Germany, Italy, Spain, and Portugal added together, the Louisiana territory almost doubled America's national domain. An immediate and portentous use was found for the "unpeopled" land when official notice that Indians would be moved west of the Mississippi appeared in the Louisiana Territory Act.

Jefferson, the strict constructionist, has been lambasted for violating his own principles in purchasing Louisiana. Yet if he had, no one seemed to care, for he alone gave serious thought to the constitutional implications of adding such a vast area to the country. During the negotiations, he drafted several versions of an amendment to the Constitution to cover the purchase, but he dropped them when Napoleon insisted on a response within six months. His cabinet members did not share his constitutional scruples—not even Madison, the putative father of the document. The pressure to seize the moment carried the day. The Constitution granted the president the power to negotiate treaties, and American officials regularly acquired land from Indians through treaties. What stretched the president's constitutionally sanctioned treaty-making powers was the incorporation of a foreign population into the union.

As it turned out, Jefferson proceeded cautiously in the matter of bringing the people of Louisiana into his "Empire of Liberty," denying them any of the privileges of self-government for a decade. Declaring the Creoles not yet ready for American freedoms, he carried Congress with him. Louisiana did not become a state until 1812. . . .

News of Lewis and Clark's safe return in October 1806 capped the triumph of the Louisiana Purchase. In many ways this was the high point of Jefferson's presidency. Lewis and Clark had found the headwaters of the Missouri, reached the Pacific, made contact with many new Indian tribes, scouted out the commercial possibilities of the farthest reaches of the continent, produced dozens of maps, collected flora, fauna, and minerals, preserved a vast amount of scientific information in written records, and returned with all but one of the members of their remarkable expedition unharmed. The two intrepid leaders made tangible with stories, reports, and artifacts the significance of the continent Americans were about to possess. The nation would stretch "from sea to shining sea." At the same time, memorials imploring Jefferson to run for a third term began flooding the White House mailbox. State legislatures, in what was a demonstration of the Republican party's strength, passed resolutions hailing the president as the champion of the rights of man. . . .

The leaders of the United States had dreamed of a continental destiny for three decades. The country had an army of settlers on the ground to oppose the designs on paper of European powers. With the labor of their burgeoning families, they could break sod and create complete communities within five years. As the last Spanish governor of Louisiana had said, the Americans were "advancing and multiplying in the silence of peace." Jefferson's determination to secure the continent for the white families of the United States represented but the audacious implementation of what had long been a general expectation. That he held it with the same intensity as the man on the frontier helps explain his pervasive popularity. No bewigged gentleman sat in the White House, detached from the dreams of his people. The successive expeditions sent out in relentless pursuit of information about the continent, and the steady buying up of Indian land in the Ohio River Valley, announced a collective will that was galvanized by a resolute leader and that would neither fade nor fail.

F U R T H E R   R E A D I N G

Stephen Ambrose, *Undaunted Courage* (1996) (on Meriwether Lewis)

Lance Banning, *The Jeffersonian Persuasion* (1978)

Albert H. Bowman, "Pichon, the United States, and Louisiana," *Diplomatic History* 1 (1977): 257–270

Noble E. Cunningham Jr., *In Pursuit of Reason: The Life of Thomas Jefferson* (1987)

George Dangerfield, *Chancellor Robert R. Livingston of New York, 1746–1813* (1960)

Alexander DeConde, *This Affair of Louisiana* (1976)

Joseph J. Ellis, *American Sphinx* (1997) (on Jefferson)

Robert B. Holtman, ed., *Napoleon and America* (1988)

Robert M. Johnstone Jr., *Jefferson and the Presidency* (1978)

Lawrence S. Kaplan, *"Entangling Alliances with None": American Foreign Policy in the Age of Jefferson* (1987)

———, *Thomas Jefferson: Westward the Course of Empire* (1998)

Jon Kukla, *A Wilderness So Immense* (2003)

James W. Lewis, *The American Union and the Problem of Neighborhood* (1998)

Drew R. McCoy, *The Elusive Republic* (1980)
Forrest McDonald, *The Presidency of Thomas Jefferson* (1976)
Dumas Malone, *Jefferson the President* (1970)
Peter S. Onuf, *Jefferson's Empire* (2000)
——— and Leonard J. Sadosky, *Jeffersonian America* (2001)
Bradford Perkins, *The Creation of a Republican Empire, 1776–1865* (1993)
Merrill D. Peterson, *Thomas Jefferson and the New Nation* (1970)
Norman K. Risjord, *Thomas Jefferson* (1994)
Malcolm J. Rohrbough, *The Trans-Appalachian Frontier* (1978)
Thomas P. Slaughter, *Exploring Lewis and Clark* (2003)
James R. Sofka, "The Jeffersonian Idea of National Security," *Diplomatic History* 21
     (1997): 519–544
Paul A. Varg, *Foreign Policies of the Founding Fathers* (1970)
Marvin R. Zahniser, *Uncertain Friendship* (1975)

CHAPTER
4

The War of 1812

In 1803 Europe exploded in war. As Britain and France battled furiously, the United States again became ensnarled in Europe's troubles. Through the Napoleonic Decree of November 1806, France declared the Continental System, designed to close Europe to British products and to force neutrals to cease trading with Britain. In response, Britain issued a series of Orders in Council, first on November 11, 1807, intended to blockade France and curb neutral commerce with Napoleon's nation. Trampling on neutral rights in these ways, both European powers seriously hampered U.S. foreign trade. Similarly insulting to the United States was the British practice of impressment: boarding American ships to seize sailors who had allegedly deserted from the Royal Navy. Americans also charged that British agents were stirring up Indian resistance to American settlers in the Northwest Territory. In fact, the Shawnee chieftain Tecumseh, who passionately struggled to preserve Indian lands, had sounded out the British regarding an alliance in order to contain U.S. expansionism.

Presidents Thomas Jefferson and James Madison retaliated against the European powers by launching their own commercial warfare, initiating restrictive measures to persuade the belligerents to respect U.S. neutrality and commerce. But nothing quieted the tempest; instead, the crosscurrents of decrees, orders, acts, and agreements emanating from both sides of the Atlantic only exacerbated the international rivalries. In the end, unable to sustain peace, the United States chose war— a war, some have suggested, that ranks as the second war for independence.

Why did the United States go to war in 1812? Historians debate several factors, including the defense of American national honor in the face of impressment and violations of neutral rights, injury to U.S. commerce and consequent fears of economic depression, removal of the Indians from the advancing white frontier, hunger for land and for conquest (especially of Canada), politics (Republicans' eagerness to strengthen their power), and the deeply felt need of Americans to revitalize and unify themselves during a time of wrenching domestic transformation and foreign threat. Other questions have likewise provoked differing scholarly perspectives: Did the United States, for example, wait too long to claim its rights and defend itself against humiliating assaults on its sovereignty? Was the War of 1812 a necessary war? Could it have been avoided? Were national leaders—Jefferson, Madison, and others—up to the task? Did they foolishly cling to a policy of commercial coercion that failed? Did policymakers have alternatives? Finally, what were the consequences of the War of 1812?

DOCUMENTS

In late June 1807 the British warship *Leopard* fired on, boarded, and seized sailors from the U.S. warship *Chesapeake*. In Document 1, a July 6 letter from Secretary of State James Madison to fellow Virginian and diplomat James Monroe, the future president expresses American outrage toward Britain. Responding to the Napoleonic Decree of 1806 and the British Orders in Council the following year, both of which disrupted neutral trade, the United States issued the Embargo Act of December 1807 (Document 2), by which it hoped to protect American vessels from capture, avoid disputes over neutral rights that might lead to war, and persuade belligerents to back down by denying them the benefits of American commerce. In a speech on January 19, 1809, Document 3, Federalist member of Congress from Massachusetts Josiah Quincy tries to calm calls for war by pointing out the United States's vulnerability to attack and questioning the assumption that Americans could seize Canada. Document 4, the Non-Intercourse Act of March 1, 1809, replaced the Embargo Act and freed American ships to trade with all other nations except Britain and France and promised renewed trade with either belligerent once neutral rights received appropriate respect.

As the Atlantic crisis escalated, Indian relations along the frontier also worsened. In a speech to Indiana's territorial governor, William Henry Harrison, on August 20, 1810, reprinted here as Document 5, the Shawnee chieftain Tecumseh denounces the U.S. government's practice of negotiating fraudulent land cessions and warns that he will seek British assistance in resisting further encroachment on Indian lands. The Shawnee leader, who with his brother "The Prophet" called for the revival of traditional Indian culture and Indian federation against white expansion, aligned with the British in the ensuing war and was killed in October 1813 at the Battle of the Thames. "War hawk" Henry Clay, a Republican member of Congress from Kentucky, delivered a thumping anti-British speech on December 31, 1811, Document 6. On June 1 of the following year, President Madison asked Congress to deliberate on the question of war. His message, Document 7, lists America's grievances. Document 8 is former President Thomas Jefferson's prediction, made in a private letter of August 4, 1812, that the United States would easily conquer Canada.

1. Secretary of State James Madison Protests British Impressment of Americans from the *Chesapeake*, 1807

The documents herewith inclosed . . . explain the hostile attack with the insulting pretext for it, lately committed near the Capes of Virga. [Virginia] by the British ship of war the Leopard on the American frigate the Chesapeake. [One] is a copy of the Proclamation issued by the President interdicting [*sic*], in consequence of that outrage, the use of our waters and every other accommodation, to all British armed ships.

This enormity is not a subject for discussion. The immunity of a National ship of war from every species and purpose of search on the high seas, has never been contested by any nation. G. B. would be second to none in resenting such a violation of her rights, & such an insult to her flag. . . .

But the present case is marked by circumstances which give it a peculiar die. The seamen taken from the Chesapeake had been ascertained to be native Citizens of the

This document can be found in the U.S. Department of State Records, National Archives, Washington, D.C. It can also be found in Gaillard Hunt, ed., *The Writings of James Madison* (New York: G. P. Putnam's Sons, 1908), VII, 454–455, 456, 458.

U. States; and this fact was made known to the bearer of the demand, and doubtless, communicated by him to his commander previous to the commencement of the attack. It is a fact also, affirmed by two of the men with every appearance of truth that they had been impressed from American vessels into the British frigate from which they escaped, and by the third, that having been impressed from a British Merchant ship, he had accepted the recruiting bounty under that duress, and with a view to alleviate his situation, till he could escape to his own Country. Add that the attack was made during a period of negociation, & in the midst of friendly assurances from the B. Governmt.

The printed papers herewith sent will enable you to judge of the spirit which has been roused by the occasion. It pervades the whole community, is abolishing the distinctions of party, and regarding only the indignity offered to the sovereignty & flag of the nation, and the blood of Citizens so wantonly and wickedly shed, demands in the loudest tone, an honorable reparation.

With this demand you are charged by the President. The tenor of his proclamation will be your guide in reminding the British Govt. of the uniform proofs given by the U. S. of their disposition to maintain faithfully every friendly relation . . . till at length no alternative is left but a voluntary satisfaction on the part of G. B. or a resort to means depending on the United States alone. . . .

The exclusion of all armed ships whatever from our waters is in fact so much required by the vexations and dangers to our peace experienced from their visits, that the President makes it a special part of the charge to you, to avoid laying the U. S. under any species of restraint from adopting that remedy. Being extended to all Belligerent nations, none of them could of right complain; and with the less reason, as the policy of *all* nations has limited the admission of foreign ships of war into their ports, to such numbers as being inferior to the naval force of the Country, could be readily made to respect its authority & laws. . . .

The President has an evident right to expect from the British Govt. not only an ample reparation to the U. S. in this case, but that it will be decided without difficulty or delay. Should this expectation fail, and above all, should reparation be refused, it will be incumbent on you to take the proper measures for hastening home according to the degree of urgency, all American vessels remaining in British ports; using for the purpose the mode least likely to awaken the attention of the British Government. Where there may be no ground to distrust the prudence or the fidelity of Consuls, they will probably be found the fittest vehikles for your intimations. It will be particularly requisite to communicate to our public ships in the Mediterranean the state of appearances if it be such as ought to influence their movements.

All negociation with the British Govt on other subjects will of course be suspended untill satisfaction on this be so pledged & arranged as to render negociation honorable.

2. The Embargo Act Forbids U.S. Exports, 1807

Be it enacted by the Senate and House of Representatives of the United States of America in Congress assembled, That an embargo be, and hereby is laid on all ships and vessels in the ports and places within the limits or jurisdiction of the

---

This document can be found in *Public Statutes at Large of the United States* (Boston: Little, Brown, and Company, 1861), II, 451–453.

United States, cleared or not cleared, bound to any foreign port or place; and that no clearance be furnished to any ship or vessel bound to such foreign port or place, except vessels under the immediate direction of the President of the United States: and that the President be authorized to give such instructions to the officers of the revenue, and of the navy and revenue cutters of the United States, as shall appear best adapted for carrying the same into full effect: *Provided,* that nothing herein contained shall be construed to prevent the departure of any foreign ship or vessel, either in ballast, or with the goods, wares and merchandise on board of such foreign ship or vessel, when notified of this act.

Sec. 2.   And be it further enacted, That during the continuance of this act, no registered, or sea letter vessel, having on board goods, wares and merchandise, shall be allowed to depart from one port of the United States to any other within the same, unless the master, owner, consignee or factor of such vessel shall first give bond, with one or more sureties to the collector of the district from which she is bound to depart, in a sum of double the value of the vessel and cargo, that the said goods, wares, or merchandise shall be relanded in some port of the United States, dangers of the seas excepted, which bond, and also a certificate from the collector where the same may be relanded, shall by the collector respectively be transmitted to the Secretary of the Treasury. All armed vessels possessing public commissions from any foreign power, are not to be considered as liable to the embargo laid by this act.

3. Massachusetts Federalist Josiah Quincy Denounces Calls for War, 1809

Again, sir, you talk of going to war against Great Britain, with, I believe, only one frigate, and five sloops of war, in commission! And yet you have not the resolution to meet the expense of the paltry, little navy, which is rotting in the Potomac. Already we have heard it rung on this floor, that if we fit out that little navy our Treasury will be emptied. If you had ever a serious intention of going to war, would you have frittered down the resources of this nation, in the manner we witness? You go to war, with all the revenue to be derived from commerce annihilated; and possessing no other resource than loans or direct or other internal taxes? You! a party that rose into power by declaiming against direct taxes and loans? . . . The general resources of our country are as well known in Europe as they are here. But we are about to raise an army of fifty thousand volunteers. For what purpose? I have heard gentlemen say "we can invade Canada." But, sir, does not all the world, as well as you, know that Great Britain holds, as it were, a pledge for Canada? And one sufficient to induce you to refrain from such a project, when you begin seriously to weigh all the consequences of such invasion? I mean that pledge which results from the defenceless state of your seaport towns. For what purpose would you attack Canada? For territory? No. You have enough of that. Do you want citizen refugees? No. You would be willing to dispense with them. Do you want plunder? This is the only hope an invasion of Canada can offer you. And is it not very doubtful whether she could not, in

This document can be found in *Annals of the Congress of the United States,* 12th Congress, 1st Session (Washington, D.C.: Gales and Seaton, 1853), 1114.

one month, destroy more property on your seaboard, than you can acquire by the most successful invasion of that Province? Sir, in this state of things, I cannot hear such perpetual outcries about war, without declaring my opinion concerning them.

4. The Non-Intercourse Act Replaces the Embargo Act, 1809

Sec. 3. That from and after the twentieth day of May next, the entrance of the harbors and waters of the United States and the territories thereof be, and the same is hereby interdicted to all ships or vessels sailing under the flag of Great Britain or France, or owned in whole or in part by any citizen or subject of either. . . . And if any ship or vessel sailing under the flag of Great Britain or France . . . [should] arrive either with or without cargo, within the limits of the United States or the territories thereof, such ship or vessel, together with the cargo, if any, which may be found on board, shall be forfeited, and may be seized and condemned in any court of the United States or the territories thereof. . . .

Sec. 11. That the President of the United States be, and he hereby is authorized, in case either France or Great Britain shall so revoke or modify her edicts, as that they shall cease to violate the neutral commerce of the United States, to declare the same by proclamation; after which the trade of the United States, suspended by this act, and by the [embargo] . . . may be renewed with the nation so doing.

5. Shawnee Chief Tecumseh Condemns U.S. Land Grabs and Plays the British Card, 1810

Since the peace [the Treaty of Fort Wayne, 1809] was made you have kill'd some of the Shawanese, Winebagoes Delawares and Miamies and you have taken our lands from us and I do not see how we can remain at peace with you if you continue to do so. You have given goods to the Kickapoos for the sale of their lands to you which has been the cause of many deaths amongst them. You have promised us assistance but I do not see that you have given us any.

You try to force the red people to do some injury. It is you that is pushing them on to do mischief. You endeavor to make destructions, you wish to prevent the Indians to do as we wish them to unite and let them consider their land as the common property of the whole you take tribes aside and advise them not to come into this measure and until our design is accomplished we do not wish to accept of your invitation to go and visit the President.

The reason I tell you this is—You want by your distinctions of Indian tribes in allotting to each a particular track of land to make them to war with each other. You never see an Indian come and endeavor to make the white people do so. You are

Document 4 can be found in *Public Statutes at Large of the United States* (Boston: Little, Brown, and Company, 1861), II, 528–533.

Document 5 can be found in Logan Esarey, ed., *Messages and Letters of William Henry Harrison* (Indianapolis: Indiana Historical Commission, 1922), VII, 463–469. It can also be found in David R. Wrone and Russell S. Nelson, *Who's the Savage: A Documentary History of the Native North American* (Greenwich: Fawcett Publishers, 1973), 218–221.

continually driving the red people when at last you will drive them into the great lake where they can't either stand or work. . . .

This land that was sold and the goods that was given for it was only done by a few. . . . If you continue to purchase of them [land from the chiefs] it will produce war among the different tribes and at last I do not know what will be the consequence to the white people. . . .

We shall have a great council at which all the tribes shall be present when we will show to those who sold that they had no right to sell the claim they set up and we will know what will be done with those chiefs that did sell the land to you. I am not alone in this determination it is the determination of all the warriors and red people that listen to me.

I now wish you to listen to me. If you do not it will appear as if you wished me to kill all the chiefs that sold you this land. I tell you so because I am authorized by all the tribes to do so. I am at the head of them all. I am a Warrior and all the Warriors will meet together in two or three moons from this. Then I will call for those chiefs that sold you the land and shall know what to do with them. If you do not restore the land you will have a hand in killing them. . . .

I wish you would take pity on all the red people and do what I have requested. If you will not give up the land and do cross the boundary of your present settlement it will be very hard and produce great troubles among us. How can we have confidence in the white people when Jesus Christ came upon the earth you kill'd and nail'd him on a cross, you thought he was dead but you were mistaken. . . .

Everything I have said to you is the truth the great spirit has inspired me and I speak nothing but the truth to you. In two moons we shall assemble at the Huron Village (addressing himself to the Weas and Pottawatomies) where the great belts of all the tribes are kept and there settle our differences.

I hope you will confess that you ought not to have listened to those bad birds who bring you bad news. I have declared myself freely to you and if you want any explanation from our Town send a man who can speak to us.

If you think proper to give us any presents and we can be convinced that they are given through friendship alone we will accept them. As we intend to hold our council at the Huron village that is near the British we may probably make them a visit. Should they offer us any presents of goods we will not take them but should they offer us powder and the tomahawk we will take the powder and refuse the Tomahawk.

6. Kentucky Republican Henry Clay Articulates U.S. Grievances Against Britain, 1811

What are we to gain by war, has been emphatically asked? In reply, he would ask, what are we not to lose by peace?—commerce, character, a nation's best treasure, honor! If pecuniary considerations alone are to govern, there is sufficient motive for the war. Our revenue is reduced, by the operation of the belligerent edicts, to

---

This document can be found in *Annals of the Congress of the United States,* 12th Congress, 1st Session (Washington, D.C.: Gales and Seaton, 1853), 599–602.

about six million of dollars, according to the Secretary of the Treasury's report. The year preceding the embargo, it was sixteen. . . .

He had no disposition to swell, or dwell upon the catalogue of injuries from England. He could not, however, overlook the impressment of our seamen; an aggression upon which he never reflected without feelings of indignation, which would not allow him appropriate language to describe its enormity. Not content with seizing upon all our property, which falls within her rapacious grasp, the personal rights of our countrymen—rights which forever ought to be sacred, are trampled upon and violated. The Orders in Council were pretended to have been reluctantly adopted as a measure of retaliation. The French decrees, their alleged basis, are revoked. England resorts to the expedient of denying the fact of the revocation, and Sir William Scott, in the celebrated case of the Fox and others, suspends judgment that proof may be adduced of it. And, at the moment when the British Ministry through that judge, is thus affecting to controvert that fact, and to place the release of our property upon its establishment, instructions are prepared for Mr. [Augustus John] Foster [British minister] to meet at Washington the very revocation which they were contesting. And how does he meet it? By fulfilling the engagement solemnly made to rescind the orders? No, sir, but by demanding that we shall secure the introduction into the Continent of British manufactures. England is said to be fighting for the world, and shall we, it is asked, attempt to weaken her exertions? If, indeed, the aim of the French Emperor be universal dominion (and he was willing to allow it to the argument), what a noble cause is presented to British valor. But, how is her philanthropic purpose to be achieved? By scrupulous observance of the rights of others; by respecting that code of public law, which she professes to vindicate, and by abstaining from self-aggrandizement. Then would she command the sympathies of the world. What are we required to do by those who would engage our feelings and wishes in her behalf? To bear the actual cuffs of her arrogance, that we may escape a chimerical French subjugation! We are invited, conjured to drink the potion of British poison actually presented to our lips, that we may avoid the imperial dose prepared by perturbed imaginations. We are called upon to submit to debasement, dishonor, and disgrace—to bow the neck to royal insolence, as a course of preparation for manly resistance to Gallic invasion! What nation, what individual was ever taught, in the schools of ignominious submission, the patriotic lessons of freedom and independence? Let those who contend for this humiliating doctrine, read its refutation in the history of the very man against whose insatiable thirst of dominion we are warned. . . .

He contended that the real cause of British aggression, was not to distress an enemy but to destroy a rival. A comparative view of our commerce with England and the continent, would satisfy any one of the truth of this remark. . . . It is apparent that this trade, the balance of which was in favor, not of France, but of the United States, was not of very vital consequence to the enemy of England. Would she, therefore, for the sole purpose of depriving her adversary of this commerce, relinquish her valuable trade with this country, exhibiting the essential balance in her favor—nay, more; hazard the peace of the country? No, sir, you must look for an explanation of her conduct in the jealousies of a rival. She sickens at your prosperity, and beholds in your growth—your sails spread on every ocean, and your numerous seamen—the foundations of a Power which, at no very distant day, is to make her tremble for naval superiority.

7. President James Madison Urges Congress to Declare War on Great Britain, 1812

Without going back beyond the renewal in 1803 of the war in which Great Britain is engaged, and omitting unrepaired wrongs of inferior magnitude, the conduct of her Government presents a series of acts hostile to the United States as an independent and neutral nation.

British cruisers have been in the continued practice of violating the American flag on the great highway of nations, and of seizing and carrying off persons sailing under it, not in the exercise of a belligerent right founded on the law of nations against an enemy, but of a municipal prerogative over British subjects. British jurisdiction is thus extended to neutral vessels in a situation where no laws can operate but the law of nations and the laws of the country to which the vessels belong. . . .

The practice, hence, is so far from affecting British subjects alone that, under the pretext of searching for these, thousands of American citizens, under the safeguard of public law and of their national flag, have been torn from their country and from everything dear to them; have been dragged on board ships of war of a foreign nation and exposed, under the severities of their discipline, to be exiled to the most distant and deadly climes, to risk their lives in the battles of their oppressors, and to be the melancholy instruments of taking away those of their own brethren. . . .

British cruisers have been in the practice also of violating the rights and the peace of our coasts. They hover over and harass our entering and departing commerce. To the most insulting pretensions they have added the most lawless proceedings in our very harbors, and have wantonly spilt American blood within the sanctuary of our territorial jurisdiction. The principles and rules enforced by that nation, when a neutral nation, against armed vessels of belligerents hovering near her coasts and disturbing her commerce are well known. When called on, nevertheless, by the United States to punish the greater offenses committed by her own vessels, her Government has bestowed on their commanders additional marks of honor and confidence.

Under pretended blockades, without the presence of an adequate force and sometimes without the practicability of applying one, our commerce has been plundered in every sea. . . .

Not content with these occasional expedients for laying waste our neutral trade, the cabinet of Britain resorted at length to the sweeping system of blockades, under the name of orders in council, which has been molded and managed as might best suit its political views, its commercial jealousies, or the avidity of British cruisers.

To our remonstrances against the complicated and transcendent injustice of this innovation the first reply was that the orders were reluctantly adopted by Great Britain as a necessary retaliation on decrees of her enemy proclaiming a general blockade of the British Isles at a time when the naval force of that enemy dared not issue from his own ports. . . .

This document can be found in the U.S. Department of State Records, National Archives, Washington, D.C. It can also be found in Gaillard Hunt, ed., *The Writings of James Madison* (New York: G. P. Putnam's Sons, 1908), VII, 454–455, 456, 458.

Abandoning still more all respect for the neutral rights of the United States and for its own consistency, the British Government now demands as prerequisites to a repeal of its orders as they relate to the United States that a formality should be observed in the repeal of the French decrees nowise necessary to their termination nor exemplified by British usage, and that the French repeal, besides including that portion of the decrees which operates within a territorial jurisdiction, as well as that which operates on the high seas, against the commerce of the United States should not be a single and special repeal in relation to the United States, but should be extended to whatever other neutral nations unconnected with them may be affected by those decrees. . . .

Anxious to make every experiment short of the last resort of injured nations, the United States have withheld from Great Britain, under successive modifications, the benefits of a free intercourse with their market, the loss of which could not but outweigh the profits accruing from her restrictions of our commerce with other nations. And to entitle these experiments to the more favorable consideration they were so framed as to enable her to place her adversary under the exclusive operation of them. To these appeals her Government has been equally inflexible, as if willing to make sacrifices of every sort rather than yield to the claims of justice or renounce the errors of a false pride. Nay, so far were the attempts carried to overcome the attachment of the British cabinet to its unjust edicts that it received every encouragement within the competency of the executive branch of our Government to expect that a repeal of them would be followed by a war between the United States and France, unless the French edicts should also be repealed. Even this communication, although silencing forever the plea of a disposition in the United States to acquiesce in those edicts originally the sole plea for them, received no attention. . . .

In reviewing the conduct of Great Britain toward the United States our attention is necessarily drawn to the warfare just renewed by the savages on one of our extensive frontiers—a warfare which is known to spare neither age nor sex and to be distinguished by features peculiarly shocking to humanity. It is difficult to account for the activity and combinations which have for some time been developing themselves among tribes in constant intercourse with British traders and garrisons without connecting their hostility with that influence and without recollecting the authenticated examples of such interpositions heretofore furnished by the officers and agents of that Government.

Such is the spectacle of injuries and indignities which have been heaped on our country, and such the crisis which its unexampled forbearance and conciliatory efforts have not been able to avert. . . .

Whether the United States shall continue passive under these progressive usurpations and these accumulating wrongs, or, opposing force to force in defense of their national rights, shall commit a just cause into the hands of the Almighty Disposer of Events, avoiding all connections which might entangle it in the contest or views of other powers, and preserving a constant readiness to concur in an honorable reestablishment of peace and friendship, is a solemn question which the Constitution wisely confides to the legislative department of the Government. In recommending it to their early deliberations I am happy in the assurance that the decision will be worthy the enlightened and patriotic councils of a virtuous, a free, and a powerful nation.

Having presented this view of the relations of the United States with Great Britain and of the solemn alternative growing out of them, I proceed to remark that the communications last made to Congress on the subject of our relations with France will have shewn that since the revocation of her decrees, as they violated the neutral rights of the United States, her Government has authorized illegal captures by its privateers and public ships, and that other outrages have been practiced on our vessels and our citizens. It will have been seen also that no indemnity had been provided or satisfactorily pledged for the extensive spoliations committed under the violent and retrospective orders of the French Government against the property of our citizens seized within the jurisdiction of France. I abstain at this time from recommending to the consideration of Congress definitive measures with respect to that nation, in the expectation that the result of unclosed discussions between our minister plenipotentiary at Paris and the French Government will speedily enable Congress to decide with greater advantage on the course due to the rights, the interests, and the honor of our country.

8. Former President Thomas Jefferson Predicts the Easy Conquest of Canada, 1812

I see, as you do, the difficulties and defects we have to encounter in war, and should expect disasters if we had an enemy on land capable of inflicting them. But the weakness of our enemy there will make our first errors innocent, and the seeds of genius which nature sows with even hand through every age and country, and which need only soil and season to germinate, will develop themselves among our military men. Some of them will become prominent, and seconded by the native energy of our citizens, will soon, I hope, to our force add the benefits of skill. The acquisition of Canada this year, as far as the neighborhood of Quebec, will be a mere matter of marching, and will give us experience for the attack of Halifax the next, and the final expulsion of England from the American continent. Halifax once taken, every cock-boat of hers must return to England for repairs. Their fleet will annihilate our public force on the water, but our privateers will eat out the vitals of their commerce. Perhaps they will burn New York or Boston. If they do, we must burn the city of London, not by expensive fleets or congreve rockets, but by employing an hundred or two Jack-the-painters, whom nakedness, famine, desperation and hardened vice, will abundantly furnish from among themselves. We have a rumor now afloat that the orders of council are repealed. The thing is impossible after [Foreign Secretary] Castlereagh's late declaration in Parliament, and the re-construction of a [Spencer] Percival ministry.

I consider this last circumstance fortunate for us. The repeal of the orders of council would only add recruits to our minority, and enable them the more to embarrass our march to thorough redress of our past wrongs, and permanent security for the future. This we shall attain if no internal obstacles are raised up. The exclusion

---

This document can be found in H. A. Washington, *The Writings of Thomas Jefferson* (Washington, D.C.: Taylor and Maury, 1854), VI, 75–76.

of their commerce from the United States, and the closing of the Baltic against it, which the present campaign in Europe will effect, will accomplish the catastrophe already so far advanced on them.

E S S A Y S

In the opening essay, Garry Wills of Northwestern University roundly criticizes the Republican policy of economic coercion that was initiated on Secretary of State James Madison's advice during the Jefferson presidency and stubbornly pursued through the outbreak of war in 1812. Wills argues that Madison was naive to believe that commercial pressure would coerce Great Britain to halt the impressment of U.S. sailors and that the fourth president became easy prey for both British and French diplomats, who "suckered" him into believing they would honor America's neutral rights. Madison also failed to restrain attacks by U.S. militia on western Indian tribes—who, in turn, ultimately aligned with the British. As tensions with the British and Indians grew, Madison manipulated a reluctant Congress to support war and undertook an ill-fated gambit of seizing Canada and denying its products to the empire— one last futile effort at commercial warfare to force a settling of America's grievances. The second essay, by Steven Watts of the University of Virginia, takes a different approach to the war by exploring Americans' hopes and fears in the early nineteenth century. Identifying social and cultural anxieties generated by the nation's shift to a market economy, Watts finds that many Americans welcomed war as a way to test and affirm their core values, unite the nation through patriotic fervor, and revitalize a "noble" American character that they felt had become challenged by commercial greed.

Economic Coercion and the Conquest of Canada: Madison's Failed Diplomacy

GARRY WILLS

The superpowers of the day, France and England, were . . . locked in the death grip of the Napoleonic wars. The foreign ministers the United States had to deal with—men like Talleyrand in France, Canning and Castlereagh in England, Godoy in Spain— were playing for high stakes in Europe, and the devious Napoleon was manipulating them all. The United States was a marginal player, sometimes no more than a distraction, in this showdown—though [James] Madison thought it was the key to the whole situation. Only the government that allied itself with America, he believed, could hope to prevail. As early as 1793 he had dreamed of solving the world's problems by using American commerce as a weapon of peaceful coercion: "In this attitude of things, what a noble stroke would be an embargo? It would probably do as much good as harm at home, and would force peace on the rest of the world, and perhaps liberty along with it." It was a dream he would labor to make real as secretary of state. . . .

So [President Thomas] Jefferson proposed a Madisonian embargo. Congress passed the bill [the Embargo Act of December 1807]. Some legislators thought it was a way of buying time to come up with other measures, meanwhile keeping our ships at home to avoid danger. Some thought it was itself a preparation for war ([Treasury Secretary Albert] Gallatin hoped it was). Many did not believe Jefferson meant to maintain it indefinitely (it would go on for fifteen months). Defiance of it began immediately and escalated, as did Jefferson's determination to support it with force. The exports of America were barely a fifth in 1808 of what they had been in 1807. The depression this caused led to outright defiance of the law, which Jefferson grimly mobilized troops to enforce. He called on the regular army, on inspectors, on informers to wage war on smugglers. . . .

Madison was still saying that Congress must "make the Embargo proof against the frauds which have evaded it, which can be done with an effect little apprehended abroad"—that is, Congress could become even more draconian in punishment, without alerting other nations to the degree of resistance being mounted. But in fact the French and British already knew how unpopular the embargo was at home— they learned this not only from their representatives in America, but from smugglers who succeeded in evading the patrols and took their products abroad. Foreign governments professed satisfaction that the policy was hurting America more than it did them. John Armstrong, United States minister to France, wrote of the embargo, "Here it is not felt, and in England . . . it is forgotten."

Finally, Congress could take no more. Against the urgings of Madison, it voted to end the embargo. As a kind of gratuitous insult to Jefferson, the date of its expiration was set for the day he would be leaving office. [Congress replaced the Embargo Act with the Non-Intercourse Act in March 1809.] . . .

It seemed for a time that Madison would be blessed, early in his first term, with the kind of fortunate break that Jefferson enjoyed with the Louisiana Purchase. Shortly after his inauguration in March 1809, the British representative in Washington, David Erskine, reported that his government was ready to lift the Orders in Council that denied America neutral trading rights with other countries and their colonies. On April 19, the president used an authority given him by Congress to lift the nonintercourse act with whichever country, England or France, first removed its own trade barriers against the United States. Though the proclamation was not to take effect until June 10 (to allow time for promulgating its new trade terms over the ocean and back), six hundred ships left American shores during that interval, confident of free entry by June.

Even Madison's Federalist enemies, along with dissidents in his own party, now vied with each other to praise him. The wisdom of the embargo was retrospectively vindicated. England had been forced to truckle and Madison rubbed in his victory, telling Erskine that the captain of the British ship that had fired with insufficient warning on the USS *Chesapeake* should be handled "with what is due from His Britannic Majesty to his own honor"—a suggestion that the king had been dishonorable to that point. . . .

While the nation was rejoicing at this vindication of neutral trading rights, Madison, following Jefferson's example, left Washington for a summer break at his own plantation. While he was there, news began to trickle in from British newspapers that England was *not* lifting its Orders in Council. Erskine had exceeded his instructions, omitting three conditions for England's repeal of the Orders, including a continued right of the British to intercept and board American ships. Erskine was instantly recalled in disgrace, and it was announced that Francis James Jackson, a man notorious for war crimes, was being sent to replace him. The national euphoria over the end of conflict with England gave way to anger, disbelief, a desire to punish England, and a sense that Madison had been gulled.

How had the misunderstanding arisen? As [the historian Robert] Rutland puts it, "Madison heard what he wanted to hear." Not for the last time, Madison leaped at what he thought *should* be true before he could verify that it was true. He had predicted all along that England could not stand up to commercial pressure from America. [British foreign secretary George] Canning's instructions to Erskine tried to excuse British interception of American ships bound for France by saying that this was merely executing Americans' own laws, since Congress had forbidden ships to trade with France in response to Napoleon's Berlin decree against neutrals. Canning's supposed "concession" was a denial of American sovereignty over its own ships, and Madison had taken it as a matter for future discussion, not a hard condition for suspending the Orders in Council. Erskine let the misinterpretation stand, in his eagerness to strike an agreement.

It was mere wishful thinking for Madison, like Jefferson before him, to think that the British would give up the right to intercept American ships and to press back into service runaway British sailors. The 1806 treaty that James Monroe had negotiated in London was rejected by President Jefferson because it did not require an end to impressments at sea. But Monroe had good reasons for giving up on that condition. The British navy could not survive if it let its seamen escape to American ships, where they were better paid and flogged less often. The Napoleonic struggle had made control of the sea both difficult and necessary for England. Their press gangs at home had already forced British citizens by the thousands into service. . . .

In the search of American ships for British deserters, some ex-seamen who had become American citizens were taken. In fact, Americans with accents reflecting immigration were taken, too. The United States government was naturally angered by this; but it refused to take steps that would have prevented it. American ships could have refused to hire British subjects. The government could have issued certificates allowing employment only to American seamen. British deserters could have been quarantined in ports. But American merchants did not want any of these steps taken. They depended too heavily on British seamen. When Gallatin surveyed the overseas commercial trade in 1807, he found that roughly nine thousand British seamen were engaged in it—over a third of the overseas crews working under the American flag. Excluding these workers "would materially injure our navigation." Madison, as secretary of state, passed on these findings to President Jefferson, with a covering comment: "I fear that the number of British seamen may prove to be rather beyond our first estimate." Jefferson responded by calling off any efforts to check the employment of non-Americans: "Mr. Gallatin's estimate of the number of foreign seamen in our employ renders it prudent I think to suspend all propositions respecting our non-employment of them . . . our best course is to let the negotiation take a friendly nap."

The merchants whose vessels were being stopped preferred that invasion of their rights to the drying up of their work pool. But so long as the United States made no concessions on this employment of deserters, it was idle to suppose that England would give up seagoing impressments . . . yet Madison for years maintained the naive belief that the English, under pressure, would rather give up impressment (that is, give up their fleet) than give up American trade. . . .

With the failure of the great British breakthrough, Madison was back where he began—or, rather, he was worse off than before. The embargo had failed. The non-intercourse provision that followed had not only failed, but was about to expire. What could be substituted for it, if anything? What would Congress let the president try next? Gallatin, without much hope for his own new proposal, had Nathaniel Macon, as chairman of the proper committee, submit a plan to the House of Representatives on December 19, 1809. It would exclude British and French ships, but not British or French goods carried by other vessels. It was an attempt to keep some revenue from duties while maintaining the opposition to violators of our neutrality. The House and Senate took some things from Macon's bill, added some things to it, and then re-jected it on March 16, 1810, just after the end of Madison's first year in office. It was time to start all over again.

Macon submitted another bill as chairman, which became known as Macon's Bill Number 2, though he was neither the author nor a supporter of it. This turned the old nonintercourse logic upside down. The former said that trade was banned with the great powers' ships until one or other power recognized America's neutral rights, upon which trade would be resumed with it. Macon Number 2 said that trade would be *resumed* with both until one recognized neutrality, upon which it would be *withdrawn* from the other. This was a weird form of reverse blackmail, saying in effect, "We will be nice to you both until one is nice in return, upon which we will turn nasty toward the other."

Though the bill was called "miserable feeble puff" at the time, it gave rise to more wishful thinking on Madison's part. His hopes for accord with England had been based on his belief that England could not do without American commerce. His hope for accord with France was that Napoleon wanted America as an ally against England, a role that Madison was willing to play if that could be done with-out actually going to war with England. His expectations were unrealistic on both grounds—that Napoleon needed our alliance, and that he would purchase it with-out obliging us to join with him in war. The mere willingness to entertain offers from Napoleon was an affront to the British, who had an ideology resembling America's in the Cold War. England felt that it was defending the free world against the international tyranny of Bonapartism, their equivalent of Bolshevism. Anyone who was not with them in that struggle was against them; and small nations could be pushed around on the way to getting at the real enemy. Madison's mistake was to take each British shove as proving that America was the main enemy, not merely a little obstacle in the way. . . .

Napoleon responded to Macon Number 2 on August 2, 1810. He promised to repeal his former bans on neutral trade (the Berlin and Milan decrees) on Novem-ber 1, so long as America had imposed nonintercourse with England by then. He made this assurance in a letter issued by his foreign secretary, the Duc de Cadore. When this was delivered to our minister in France, John Armstrong, there had been no discussion of what other measures besides the Berlin and Milan decrees might be observed by Napoleon. He had in fact issued the Decree of Rambouillet in March, which absorbed Holland and authorized the confiscation of American and other ships in all the harbors of his empire. He had no intention of reversing this policy.

The mention of Berlin and Milan was a ruse to trap America into conflict with England. And it worked. Thanks to the provincialism and naivete that had been relatively harmless in his prior roles, Madison had been suckered again. . . . By the time Madison discovered that Napoleon was not observing the terms of Macon Number 2, the bill had done its work. A momentum toward war with England had been accelerated, and would become irreversible, even after England (unlike France) *did* meet the terms of Macon Number 2. . . .

The prospects for war were strengthened by news from the West, of a clash with Indians manufactured by the governor of the Indiana Territory, William Henry Harrison, who was disturbed by the organizing genius of a Shawnee religious leader, the Prophet, and his warrior brother, Tecumseh. Harrison had negotiated eight Indian treaties for Jefferson, and the Shawnee brothers were uniting people to prevent any further bargaining away of their lands. (They were thought to have murdered some chiefs who signed the treaties.) Like most western governors, Harrison had trouble calling up, organizing, and paying the Indiana militia. He wanted regular troops, and Madison's weak secretary of war, William Eustis, gave him some, ordering that they be used only for defensive purposes. But it was easy for Harrison to take any clash with Indians as an attack calling for a "defensive" counteroffensive. That is what he did while Tecumseh was away in the South organizing the Creek tribes. Harrison took the opportunity to march his troops to Prophetstown on the Tippecanoe River. He camped near the town on November 7, 1811, and left his camp without early-morning lookouts, though that is the time when Indians often attacked. They did so in this case, inflicting and taking heavy casualties. The Indians withdrew when they ran out of ammunition, and Harrison marched into Prophetstown, which had been abandoned overnight. The Prophet had escaped.

Harrison, under criticism from his own men, rushed a self-serving announcement of victory to Washington, and Madison reported it as such on December 18, saying it had brought peace to the frontier. Actually, it brought greater worries— the Prophet and Tecumseh were still active—and more demand for troops from other uneasy governors. When reports began to reach Washington contradicting Harrison's account, Secretary Eustis told Madison it would be bad for military morale to investigate them—though Madison showed his distrust of Harrison in later dealings with him. The legend of Tippecanoe lived on unchallenged, and became a basis for Harrison's successful presidential campaign in 1840.

On November 5, shortly before news of Tippecanoe reached Washington, Madison sent to Congress the message he and Monroe had conceived at [the president's Virginia plantation] Montpelier, one that Gallatin tried to soften. It said that British actions "have the character as well as the effect of war" and, in conveying "my deep sense of the crisis in which you are assembled," expressed confidence that "Congress will feel the duty of putting the United States into an armor and attitude demanded by the crisis and corresponding with the national spirit and expectations." As a follow-up he had the secretary of war ask that ten thousand regular troops be raised. It has often been thought that Madison had war thrust upon him by a Congress controlled by "war hawks" from the West. But Congress was hesitant and doubtful, unwilling to vote for the taxes that would make war preparation a reality. It made some war moves that were actually meant to evade the issue. . . .

Some have thought that Madison shilly-shallied his way into war, dragged by others, stalled by doubts. Rutland claims he was little more than a leaf riding the surface of a torrent. . . . But Madison created some of the pressures that worked on the public and himself. His readiness, for instance, to seize on the unconfirmed evidence of French cooperation came from his determination to have a showdown with England, to work out his commercial strategy to its logical conclusion. . . .

In fact, the maneuvering toward war gave Madison an opportunity to use his old collaborative methods, working with a more public partner. Here his partner was Monroe—and, at one remove, Henry Clay [of Kentucky], who was working Congress up to a declaration of war. A good example of Madison's indirect approach was the way he timed the release of dispatches from England, selected for their intransigence, to create indignation in Congress. . . .

Another means Madison used to ratchet up the war spirit was a new embargo, planned by Madison, Monroe, and Clay, and presented to Congress on March 11 [and passed later that month]. . . .

That such background maneuverings were necessary to heat Congress toward a declaration of war became clear when Madison finally asked for that declaration, on June 1 (just before everyone's summer departure from the fetid city). Though the House, under Clay's leadership, quickly passed the declaration (seventy-eight to forty-five), it was a close-run matter in the Senate, which took two weeks of secret session to pass the measure by a vote of eighteen to thirteen. The vote in both houses was purely partisan, no Federalist voting for the war, several Clintonian Republicans [followers of New Yorkers George and DeWitt Clinton] voting against it. Madison gave five reasons for going to war with England: 1) impressment, 2) blockades preventing safe departure from the American coast, 3) blockades preventing safe arrival at other shores, 4) confiscation of neutral trade at sea, and 5) the incitement of Indian hostility in the Northwest. The four maritime violations were not new, and were overlapping as he listed them. The Indian hostility was caused more from American expansion than British instigation (the Indians fled to the British from campaigns like that at Tippecanoe), but this grievance had to be listed, in order to bring Henry Clay's western constituents into the effort. Madison, far from being pushed into war by a bellicose Congress, had to drag his own hesitant party into it, past the determined obstruction of the Federalists. What had made Madison, the former pacifist, become a "war hawk"? One thing—Canada.

[The historian] J. C. A. Stagg has shown how important Canada was in Madison's own war thinking. All through the 1790s, Madison had downplayed the commercial importance of Canada. To advance and defend his plan for the embargo, he had to say that the bulk of England's trade from North America could come only from the United States. Canada's exports were insufficient to make up for an American embargo. When the embargo was canceled, however, Madison performed one of those drastic reversals that mark his career. All of a sudden, Canada became vital to British survival. The United States could now subdue England by taking over Canada and denying *its* products to the empire. This switch was partly based on some real changes in the world situation. Napoleon had cut off much of England's supplies from Europe, so it did depend more on Canada for certain goods, especially for the vast amounts of timber the British fleet required. Madison could not know—though he might have allowed for the possibility—that this situation would be rapidly altered, as it was in 1812, right after Madison went to war, when Napoleon met repulse in both Russia and Spain, and England's old markets were opening up to them again.

But ideology had more to do with Madison's analysis than did the course of events. He found in the new assessment of Canada a way to maintain his idée fixe of three decades, that England could be tamed by commercial pressure. Now the pressure would come after a conquest of Canada—but that initial easy victory would actually *prevent* full-scale war. Britain, feeling helpless without Canadian timber, would finally grant America its rights as a neutral nation. He had changed his estimate of Canada to avoid changing his basic concept. As Stagg puts it, "Madison's decision to wage war for Canada was not basically inconsistent with the diplomacy of peaceful commercial restriction he had advocated prior to 1812."

The initial war aim, therefore, was to conquer Canada in 1812, before England could reinforce its troops or deploy the fleet to assist them. That schedule had two even closer deadlines built into it—enough progress should have been made by November to assure Madison's re-election, and enough of Canada should be in American hands by December to allow setting up defensible winter quarters there. As a minimum, Montreal should be taken, so the winter pause could be devoted to assembling resources for taking Quebec. As it turned out, no part of Canada was taken in 1812. Rather, Canada conquered the Michigan Territory. The United States had rushed into a war without military staff organization, supply depots, or a credit system worked out for dealing with military contractors. William Eustis, the secretary of war, spent much of his time looking at catalogues for supplying shoes and uniforms. . . .

Why did America go to war? And why with England rather than with France? French seizures of American shipping were not as common as English harassment, but they were, in principle, the same violations of sovereignty. But Americans had never been the subjects of France. There was special humiliation in any submission exacted by a former master. The new war promised to conclude the unfinished business of the Revolution. Impressment, exclusion from markets, smugglers' ties with Canada, Indian ties with British agents in the West—all these made some chafe as if they were still under the thumb of King George. But none of this would have justified the war unless an easy target seemed to offer itself. England's military force was deeply engaged in the war with Napoleon, which left its western remnant of empire exposed. Canada, it was thought, could be seized before England had the time or spare men and ships to rush aid to it. Once taken, it could be used as a bargaining chip for settling all American grievances, to be restored under terms if at all.

Crusade to Revitalize the American Character

STEVEN WATTS

[My book] *The Republic Reborn* . . . attempts to contribute to a more comprehensive and nuanced understanding of war and its role in the development of modern Western society. Perhaps influenced by a boyhood in Springfield, Illinois, where the currents of the Civil War still run strong, or by coming of age in a period of

Steven Watts, *The Republic Reborn: War and the Making of Liberal America, 1790–1820.* (Baltimore: The Johns Hopkins University Press), 1987.

intense agitation over the Vietnam conflict, I always have suspected that war involves far more than foreign affairs, strategic maneuver, or power politics. Several trenchant studies encountered over the years—Richard Slotkin's *Regeneration Through Violence* [1973], George Frederickson's *The Inner Civil War* [1965], and Richard Hofstadter's "Cuba, the Philippines, and Manifest Destiny" [1951], among others—reinforced this suspicion by suggesting that the attraction that war holds for Americans has sprung less from calculating assessments of policy and power and more from some fundamental national dynamic of social psychology, cultural aspiration, and sense of collective experience. Indeed, as the sources began to speak from the American early republic, it became apparent that what was projected onto the looming conflict of 1812—fantasies and nightmares, visceral emotions and lofty ideals—often influenced people's views and actions more than a detached analysis of policy and instrumentality. For many citizens, the British confrontation appeared as an immense blank slate on which they wrote their hopes and fears. It also appeared evident that the stuff of this projection emerged from wrenching historical change in the early-nineteenth-century republic. . . .

The commercial growth, geographic expansion, and challenges to traditional authority that had begun to appear in the mid-1700s gained unstoppable force after the War for Independence. From 1790 to 1820 several revolutionary developments reshaped social and economic life. In agriculture, as new historical research has made us aware, significant commercialization began to occur. A large commodity-producing region took shape in a great arc from Virginia through the mid-Atlantic states to New York in response to European demand for foodstuffs. Beginning in the early 1800s, rapidly growing cotton production in the South also entangled that region increasingly in the web of international trade. In terms of commerce, equally drastic changes occurred. As a result of European preoccupation with the Napoleonic Wars, in the fifteen years after 1793 the American portion of the carrying and reexport trade became the largest in the Atlantic world. The three decades after 1790 also encompassed rapid expansion of both "household" and "extensive" manufactures, especially in the mills of New England and the Delaware Valley. This virtual explosion of economic activity took place against the backdrop of a massive geographical expansion beginning in the early 1790s. Heading westward over the Appalachians to the frontiers of the Old Northwest and Southwest, restless Americans by 1820 had brought into statehood nearly all the territory east of the Mississippi River.

Yet more was involved than mere growth. The *nature* of social and economic experience also changed fundamentally in America's early national decades. With rapid commercial expansion, the pervasive "household economy" began to lose its grip under pressure from "intraregional markets" spreading into the countryside from growing urban areas. The export of grain, meat, timber, and cotton further encouraged the market motive of production for profit. According to [the historian] Thomas Cochran, commercialization in the 1790s also ignited a "business revolution" of systemization: incorporation, sophisticated bookkeeping procedures, and the creation of wholesale commission houses, banks, insurance companies. But even more important, this expansive economic growth between 1790 and 1820 brought significant alterations in the social relations of production. While dynamic commercial development placed a disproportionate "concentration of wealth" in the hands of merchant businessmen, a general aura of opportunity spurred an ethos of entrepreneurialism and self-made success. This held true for those eastern farmers making market connections to urban centers, western farmers seeking independence and social advancement on the frontier, and urban master craftsmen engaging in capitalist-oriented production. As social and labor historians have discovered, the early republic marked the first emergence of a "new dichotomy between Labor and Capital" in areas where urban growth and manufacturing development began to flourish. So Americans not only overturned the moral economy and household system of colonial tradition, but also began to replace the social notion of paternalism with a new sense of competitive individualism.

In other words, the development of America after the Revolution involved the consolidation of a market economy *and* a market society. Both are necessary for the existence of liberal capitalism. While mere trade had existed for some time in the colonies, extensive markets and a social system based on individual competition did not congeal until the early nineteenth century. . . .

Appeals for unity and self-sacrifice composed a constant refrain among Republican war advocates in the months surrounding the declaration of war. In late May 1812 a mass meeting in Baltimore of "democratic citizens" approved a series of resolutions castigating the British and demanding war. The group implored, "Let us act with one heart, and with one hand; let us shew to an admiring world, that however we may differ among ourselves about some of our internal concerns, yet in the great cause of our country, the American people are animated by one soul and one spirit." The *Western Intelligencer* of Worthington, Ohio, confidently echoed, "Nothing united the public mind so much as danger." Richard Rush, in a grand oration before members of the Madison administration and both houses of Congress on July 4, 1812, proclaimed, "May there be a willing, a joyful immolation of all selfish passions on the altar of a common country." *Niles' Weekly Register* approvingly described mounting war fever: "From all quarters of the country—from the mountain tops of the interior, we have a common expression of the public will." The *Richmond Enquirer* urged Americans to embrace war with a spirit of unanimity and "like wise men sacrifice minor objects to the great end we have in view." The editors put the matter even more succinctly in another editorial: "Forget self, and think of America."

Such invocations may be dismissed in part as jingoistic rhetoric common to any national crisis. Yet the singular social pressures in the early American republic bestowed on such appeals a deeper urgency. While a liberalizing society of self-made men had raised dreams of ambition among early-nineteenth-century Americans, it also had created disquieting fears of greed and dissipation. As the cases of [Philip] Freneau, [Henry] Clay, and [Charles] Ingersoll suggest, such tensions helped shape a complex social desire for war as a means of surmounting avarice, weakened character, and social faction. The experiences of these men reveal a pattern of compensation: war's appeal in 1812 involved twin seductions of sacrifice to the common good and social regeneration. As [the scholar] Michael Walzer observed, the often brutal race of life in a capitalist society engenders sporadic desires for "civism," or immersion of self in a larger common purpose. Consequently, calls for widespread citizen involvement can appeal to a submerged yearning for solidarity. Thus war emerged partly as a social movement in early-nineteenth-century America. In a liberalizing society riven with tension, war against Great Britain beckoned as a crusade for civism, and hence renewal.

Notions of war as an adhesive for America's social factions featured prominently in the political discussions preceding the conflict. . . . [M]any Jeffersonians hoped that the threat of foreign power would weld together feuding combinations in the liberalizing republic. "War . . . if called for must be gone into with a vigor that will give the nation but one arm," editorialized the *National Intelligencer* in May 1812, and success would depend on "the undivided exertions of the whole nation against a common enemy." Governor William Plumer, addressing the New Hampshire legislature on the impending war less than a month later, put the matter even more forcefully. "Union is the vital strength of a nation, particularly so of a republic, whose authority rests on *public opinion,*" he proclaimed. "Our union is our safety—*a house divided against itself cannot stand.*"

Polemicists and orators consistently envisioned war as an instrument for extinguishing party rancor. In December 1811 Governor Benjamin Smith urged the North Carolina legislature to endorse a national policy of armed resistance, declaring, "Let us strive . . . to discard all party bickerings, and promote a spirit of harmony and good will." Much farther to the north, Massachusetts Governor Elbridge Gerry made a similar appeal to citizens of his state in early 1812. Speaking in favor of war preparations, he argued that party spirit should vanish. Instead, liberty demanded that Americans "consecrate at her shrine a COALITION OF PARTIES." Prowar newspapers concurred, urging submersion of party bickering in the larger national war crusade. Republican organs like the *Kentucky Gazette* and *Niles' Weekly Register* admitted that "party contentions may be necessary to keep up the public stamina, and secure the government from corruption—but when the question shall be fairly put—for, or against our country—the honest man will not hesitate on his course."

Advocates often depicted the War of 1812 as a gratifying and transcendent commitment for the liberal individual. In contrast to the mean pursuit of self-interest, war appeared to its supporters as an exercise in traditional republican virtue, or self-sacrifice to the public good. One newspaper, on the eve of hostilities, praised "a war, to which not one distillation from the subtle, anti-republican essences of ambition or aggrandizement has contributed." The *National Intelligencer,* in a series of editorials from May to July 1812, unfolded this notion of war as noble sacrifice. On May 5 it urged Congress to go beyond private interests and formulate a more aggressive policy in behalf of the "*general welfare.*" . . .

The social crusade for war in 1812 revived traditional veneration for virtue. It promised to strengthen weakened commercial character. It advanced nobler strivings in addition to those for profit and social betterment. But the venting of dissatisfaction, uncertainty, and strain over liberalizing change into the emotionally charged atmosphere of war had consequences that were even more far-reaching in the long run. It allowed early-nineteenth-century Americans to indulge both the entrepreneurial energy of ambition and the sacrifices of civism. Relegated to the war arena and ensconced in the armor of national survival, dissenting impulses were removed from day-to-day American social life. By relaxing the tension between dreams and disquietude for the self-made individual, purging him of guilt, and regenerating him, the War of 1812 comprised a long step toward assuring the hegemony of liberal society in America. . . .

By the summer of 1812, discipline and self-restraint had become watchwords of Republican prowar rhetoric. Military service appeared as precisely the sort of activity by which restless, ambitious Americans could learn discipline and self-command. The newspaper writer "Anti-Royalist," for instance, in January 1812 penned in the *National Intelligencer* an essay arguing that military life and "the manual exercise" would straighten out wayward young men. Drawing upon scenes of his own youthful army training, he recalled, "The most awkward boys became straight and graceful; puny ones were soon restored to health; strength and vigor attended upon all; the most untractable boys became obedient, and boys, who before ill comprehended the obligations of juvenile life, became strenuous asserters of and practical observers of every honourable institute of society." [Indiana Territory governor] William Henry Harrison echoed these sentiments. He urged the rising generation to enter military service, absorb its discipline, and internalize its "minute observances, which collectively form a beautiful and connected system." . . .

This notion of a war for character and self-control became especially evident in Jeffersonian depictions of the foreign enemy. In the eyes of many war advocates, the British symbolized all the dark passions that Americans were struggling against in the quest for self-regulation. If such perceptions often involved the projections of fantasy rather than fact, they nevertheless appeared quite real to their holders. Older ideological fears in the Puritan and republican traditions formed some of the foundation for this moral critique. Like Presbyterian minister Samuel Knox of Baltimore, Americans were fond of contrasting, in time-worn fashion, the peace and prosperity of America with Old World nations that drenched their lands in "human gore" and dealt in "injuries, violence, and bloodshed." . . .

Some Americans, such as Charles Ingersoll, focused on the British alliance with Indian raiders on the western frontier to raise images of violence, carnage, and lust. In a very long letter to his constituents defending the war, which was widely reprinted in eastern Republican newspapers, the congressman drew upon his stockpile of adjectives in condemning British libidinous outrages: "The massacre of captives and the poisoning of wounded," "foul and hellish slaughter," "refinements of barbarity which no savage ever exceeded," "rapine, rapes, and indiscriminate outrages," "their game of ruin, spoil, and havoc." . . .

This Republican reading of the 1812 conflict as moral struggle received a significant twist from John Stevens. Proclaiming *The Duty of Union in Just War,* and obviously confident about his own talents, he announced he would "judge of God's mind and will, from a view of his moral character." "I think it is a clear case, that God approves of the war in which we are now engaged for the defense of our just rights," Stevens declared confidently after assuring himself of the Deity's moral uprightness. Although a bit more brazen in tone than most such comments, Stevens' conviction reflected a widespread belief among Jeffersonians that the struggle with Great Britain enjoyed divine sanction. Their cultural campaign for morality, character, and sensual restraint—when combined with older Puritan and republican beliefs in the sacred destiny of the American "errand into the wilderness"—gave a strong boost to what one scholar has called the "civil religion" of the United States. In 1812 war summoned the republic's Christian Soldiers. . . .

But while some Jeffersonians found inspiration for war in an already-existing American Israel, others were attracted to it as a formative, chastening, revitalizing experience for the republic's religious character. Employing God in the service of bourgeois moralism, they recounted the sins of a people turning against him: pride, profanity, intemperance, lying, gaming and vain amusements, Sabbath-breaking, lewdness, and avarice. A Virginia Republican, for instance, in August 1812 contended that war was a punishment for sins that had tainted the moral character of America. He spoke at length on three of the most grievous: a lack of religious fervor, the growing use of liquor, and "the thirst for wealth." Prowar minister Solomon Aiken soberly explained the impending conflict in similar terms:

> It is for our iniquities and the abuse of divine favors. God hath given us the greatest liberty, civil and religious, of any Nation on earth. But what astonishing returns of ingratitude have we made. We have abused our liberties to great licentiousness, like Jeshurun of old, we have waxen fat, and kicked; we have rebelled against our God.

For these religious warriors, war offered a way for the republic to *renew* its divine covenant, and public discourse resounded with appeals for Americans to humble themselves before God, to gain victory. The Rev. Conrad Speece implored of his congregation in preparing them for a war, "Let us then repair to his throne of grace, to confess before him, with humble and contrite hearts, our own sins, and the sins of our country." . . .

On the afternoon of July 4, 1812, Richard Rush, the second son of Benjamin Rush, strode to the podium in the hall of the House of Representatives. A zealous and eloquent Jeffersonian, the young comptroller of the treasury had been chosen by President James Madison to defend officially the two-week-old declaration of war against Great Britain. Looking out at this grave celebration of American independence, the orator's eyes met those of the President, his cabinet, numerous congressmen, and assorted public officials and dignitaries. Carrying a heavy rhetorical burden, the young Philadelphian opened by castigating the British for their violations of American neutral rights and their instigation of Indian unrest on the frontier. Turning homeward, he also admonished his countrymen that decades of peace since the Revolution had created in America "an inordinate love of money, the rage of party spirit, and a willingness to endure even slavery itself rather than bear pecuniary deprivations or brave manly hazards." Thus Rush presented war not only as a defense of American rights but also as a regenerating cure for commercial dissipation. Nations and striving individuals were alike, he insisted, in that their well-being came only through "severe probations . . . by a willingness to encounter danger and by actually and frequently braving it."

Yet as it unfolded, Richard Rush's address put forward two other striking images that raised a submerged layer of meaning in his calls for war. First, he described the American republic as a young man struggling to find vigor, direction, and moral purpose. He contended that in the aftermath of revolution a young nation still in "the feebleness of youth" had been forced to submit to European economic regulation and foreign affairs structures. But now with war, Rush hoped, the growing republic "shall stand upon a pedestal whose base is fixed among ourselves." Military action proclaimed that "in the hope and purity of youth, we are not debased by the passions of old age." In the ringing words of the orator, war would make "ourselves more independent—privately and politically."

This imagery of youthful independence and destiny foreshadowed a second motif in Rush's symbolism. He queried rhetorically and emotionally that if Americans did not go to war in 1812, "where would be the spirit, where the courage of their slain fathers? Snatched and gone from ignoble sons?" Weaving a psychological fabric that contrasted the "noble" Founders with "the base conduct of those sons for whom they so gallantly fell," Rush vowed passionately to uphold the inheritance of the older generation: "We will wipe away all past stains; we will maintain our rights by the sword, or, like you, we will die! Then shall we render our ashes worthy to mingle with yours!"

Rush's emotional contrast of heroic Founding Fathers and searching, dissipated, death-seeking sons might seem histrionic and peculiar. Yet for such an important occasion—and for such an imposing and discriminating audience—Rush must have sifted his metaphors carefully for those most likely to find an emotional affinity. That he chose wisely was reflected in the fact that on the eve of war with Great Britain this refrain of Fathers and Sons sounded over and over again in Republican discourse. . . .

Yet if American Sons seemed eager to prove what they were not, they also were driven in 1812 to establish what they were. In many ways, war with Great Britain took shape as an oedipal struggle. Both respectful and resentful of their "heroic" Revolutionary forebears—and themselves set loose as individuals in the highly pressurized atmosphere of a competitive society—many early-nineteenth-century Americans were desperate to secure personal authority. Like John Quincy Adams, they sought to escape the paternal domination of the past and ascend to prominence in their own right. War promised a heroic means to do so. Hezekiah Niles, for example, acknowledged in 1811 that America's youth should try to emulate their fathers, but he added pointedly, "Most of the actors in the great scenes of those times have departed; a new generation supplies their place." An anonymous essayist in the summer 1812 *National Intelligencer* further illuminated this instinct for replacing the Fathers. The national crisis demanded that all Americans rally to the war effort, he wrote. Yet the author insisted that older patriots should now step aside for the "young, active, and enterprising." The Fathers had "done enough hitherto in preserving our liberties and nurturing us to manhood; let their sons now resume their stations, and ease them of their toils." . . .

Celebrations of peace in February 1815 barely contained American exultation. With much of Washington, D.C., still in ashes from the British assault only six months before, and rumors of further invasions still circulating, the peace treaty offered cathartic relief to a highly agitated citizenry. In addition, the decisive triumph of western troops over British regulars at New Orleans added an unexpectedly glorious conclusion to what had been a rather ignominious war. As elation swept through the republic, Jeffersonian rhetoric soared. . . .

From the outset Jeffersonians had endorsed the war in part to regenerate republican institutions. Troubled by years of European attacks on foreign commerce, and also by the seeming weakness and vacillation of the American response, they saw in war a chance to revitalize the strength and prove the efficacy of the young republic. During the actual hostilities, this instinct remained strong, if most of the time unfulfilled. As Vice-President Elbridge Gerry informed the Senate in May 1813, for example, the English war was a test "to determine, whether the republican system adopted by the people, is imbecile and transient, or whether it has force and duration worthy of the enterprise."

The conflict's glorious termination, however, finally told frustrated Jeffersonian Republicans what they wanted to hear. The young nation had met the Atlantic world's strongest monarchy and somehow fought her to a stand-off. Private and public discussion affirmed the republic's hard-won new respect in the community of nations and self-respect at home. As Secretary of State James Monroe wrote to the Senate barely a week after the announcement of peace, the war had "made trial of the strength and efficiency of our government," with the result that "our Union has gained strength, our troops honor, and the nation character." Congressman Jonathan Roberts of Pennsylvania testified to this strengthening effect on the nation in a private letter. The conflict's successful termination, he wrote to his brother on February 17, 1815, demonstrated that military prowess was not restricted to monarchies. "It is the triumph of virtue over vice, of republican men and republican principles over the advocates and doctrines of Tyranny."

Speaker of the House Henry Clay perhaps best represented the revitalizing effect of the War of 1812 on American republicanism. This young Liberal Republican had agitated for a declaration of war with just such hopes, and he managed to sustain them even through the darkest hours of the contest. With the 1815 peace, Clay was jubilant. "A great object of the war has been attained in the firm establishment of the national character," he wrote in a public letter in Washington. Back in Lexington, Kentucky, later in the year, the Speaker assured a banquet audience: "The immediate effects of the war were highly satisfactory. Abroad our character which at the time of its declaration was in the lowest state of degradation, was raised to the highest point of elevation." But it was not until a speech before Congress in January 1816 that Henry Clay offered a final assessment of the republic's new-found vigor:

> Have we gained nothing by the war? Let any man look at the degraded condition of the country before the war. The scorn of the universe, the contempt of ourselves; and tell me we have gained nothing by the war? What is our present situation? Respectability and character abroad—security and confidence at home. . . . Our character and constitution are placed on a solid basis never to be shaken. . . .

With the conclusion of the War of 1812, a grateful and vindicated [John C.] Calhoun [member of Congress from South Carolina] could only affirm that the United States had passed into an expansive new age. In a general sense, he believed that national pride had come to the young republic as a result of the "glory acquired in the late war, and the prosperity which had followed it." America's war-forged wealth and strength had been the will of God, Calhoun further insisted. "We are charged by Providence not only with the happiness of this great and rising people, but in a considerable degree with that of the human race," he told the House in early 1816. "We have a government of a new order. . . . If it succeed, as fondly hoped by its founders, it will be the commencement of a new era in human affairs."

This bright new age would become a certainty, Calhoun asserted, if Americans adopted a new political sensibility for their dynamic postwar society. In the months after peace, he urged his colleagues to draw on "the experience of the last war" to reject "the old imbecile mode" of conducting public affairs. For his part, in 1816 and 1817 the South Carolinian proposed a sweeping set of reforms—most eventually were adopted in some form—that not only inculcated lessons of the war but thoroughly recast traditional Jeffersonian doctrine in the mold of Liberal Republicanism. First, he proposed a revision of the republic's military organization wherein the militia would be taught "discipline and subordination" and supplemented with a larger defense establishment. To this end Calhoun suggested the creation of several military academies that would muster the self-made ethic of aspiring young men in the "middle" and "lower" ranks of American society. "Rich men, being already at the top of the ladder, have no further motive to climb," he pointed out. "It is that class of the community who find it necessary to strive for elevation, that furnishes you with officers." In numerous speeches, Calhoun also demanded construction of "a good system of roads and canals" and tariff protection to encourage the continued growth of domestic manufactures. These measures would unite in a home market "every branch of national industry, Agricultural, Manufacturing, and Commercial." As this confident Jeffersonian concluded in his great "Speech on Internal Improvements" of February 4, 1817, with such proposals "the strength of the community will be augmented, and its political prosperity rendered more secure." . . .

The gratifying denouement of the War of 1812 brought the history of the American early republic to a close. Victory—or perhaps more realistically, survival—in 1815 overwhelmed both dissent against liberalizing change and the past itself. Guided by energetic and innovative figures within the Jeffersonian Republican majority, the United States had ridden the vehicle of war to leave the world of eighteenth-century republicanism and enter that of nineteenth-century liberalism, and a new set of issues in public and private life, and a fresh array of problems, greeted them. More than thirty years later, venerable old Republicans like Charles J. Ingersoll still acknowledged and marveled at the war's influence. In an 1845 history of the conflict, he argued that its accomplishments—he described them as a boosting of "commerce, manufactures, navigation, agriculture, national character, the respect of nations, . . . and confidence in republican institutions"—had made it the equal of the Revolution in shaping the nation. The achievement of "moral, physical, and mental independence" was the lasting memorial of the 1812 ordeal, Ingersoll concluded.

F U R T H E R   R E A D I N G

James Banner, *To the Hartford Convention* (1970)

Lance Banning, *The Sacred Fire of Liberty: James Madison and the Founding of the Federal Republic* (1995)

Roger Brown, *The Republic in Peril* (1964)

Gregory E. Dowd, *A Spirited Resistance* (1992) (on American Indians)

R. David Edmunds, *The Shawnee Prophet* (1983)

Clifford L. Egan, *Neither Peace nor War: Franco-American Relations, 1803–1812* (1983)

Richard J. Ellings, *Embargoes and World Power* (1985)

Kenneth J. Hagan, *This People's Navy* (1991)

Ronald L. Hatzenbuehler and Robert L. Ivie, *Congress Declares War* (1983)

Donald R. Hickey, *The War of 1812* (1989)

Reginald Horsman, *The Causes of the War of 1812* (1962)
Ralph Ketcham, *James Madison* (1971)
Dumas Malone, *Jefferson the President* (1970–1974)
John C. Niven, *Henry Clay* (1991)
Bradford Perkins, *The Creation of a Republican Empire* (1993)
Robert V. Remini, *The Battle of New Orleans* (1999)
———, *Henry Clay* (1991)
Robert A. Rutland, *James Madison* (1987)
———, *Madison's Alternatives* (1975)
———, *The Presidency of James Madison* (1990)
———, ed., *The James Madison Encyclopedia* (1992)
Marshall Smelser, *The Democratic Republic: 1800–1815* (1968)
Burton Spivak, *Jefferson's English Crisis* (1979)
J. C. A. Stagg, "Between Black Rock and a Hard Place: Peter B. Porter's Plan for an
    Invasion of Canada," *Journal of the Early American Republic* 19 (1999): 385–422
———, *Mr. Madison's War* (1983)
John Sugden, *Tucumseh: A Life* (1998)
Anthony F. C. Wallace, *Jefferson and the Indians* (2001)
J. Leitch Wright Jr., *Britain and the American Frontier, 1783–1815* (1975)

CHAPTER
5

The Monroe Doctrine

In the early 1820s, events at home and abroad posed new threats to the well-being of the young American nation. Although the Missouri Compromise of 1820 calmed an immediate political crisis over slavery, it left a bitter legacy that eventually would produce a civil war. Meanwhile, Spanish colonies in Latin America, under such leaders as the legendary Simón Bolívar, were rebelling against Spain. North Americans cheered their southern neighbors for breaking the chains of their imperial master. Yet, judging Latin Americans inferior because they were Catholics of mixed blood, and predicting that they could not create the democratic institutions necessary to sustain their newfound independence, the United States refrained from overtly supporting the new nations that emerged. Secretary of State John Quincy Adams, moreover, feared that if the United States extended formal diplomatic recognition to the new governments, Spain might renege on the Transcontinental Treaty (1819) that had added the Floridas to the U.S. empire. While Adams urged delay, Henry Clay of Kentucky, like Adams a contender for the presidency, demanded U.S. recognition. In 1822 the Monroe administration finally recognized the states of Argentina, Chile, Gran Colombia, Mexico, and Peru. Spain fumed and plotted, intent on restoring its empire. What would the United States do, contemporaries wondered, if Europe's Holy Alliance (Russia, Spain, Austria, and France) sent military forces to destroy the new Latin American governments?

On December 2, 1823, President James Monroe gave his annual message to Congress. He stated principles that drew on the past and became guides for American diplomacy in the future. He declared that the Western Hemisphere was no longer open to European colonization, that the Old and New Worlds were so different that the United States would abstain from European wars, and that the European powers should not intervene forcefully in the Americas. Monroe designed these three points—noncolonization, two spheres, and nonintervention—to warn the monarchies of Europe against crushing the new Latin American states and to deter Russia from encroaching on the Pacific coast.

Great Britain, which had profited commercially from the breakup of the Spanish mercantile system and therefore did not welcome a restoration of Spanish rule in South America, approached the United States with the idea of issuing a joint declaration of opposition to European intervention. North Americans, who also realized economic benefits from the dismantling of the Spanish Empire, shared British worries about the European threat. Monroe's "doctrine" constituted the independent U.S. answer to the European menace.

116

Historians rank the Monroe Doctrine as a cardinal and lasting statement of American foreign policy. The traditional interpretation holds that the Monroe Doctrine represented a defense of American ideals, security, and commerce—an affirmation of the national interest. More critical scholars have placed the Monroe Doctrine within the American expansionist tradition and have pointed out that the declaration may have meant "hands-off" for the Europeans, but it permitted "hands-on" for the United States. Others have argued that domestic American politics, especially the presidential ambitions of the principal policymakers, and the pressure of public opinion helped shape a key decision: to reject the British overture in favor of a unilateral American proclamation.

🌎 D O C U M E N T S

A major architect of the Monroe Doctrine, Secretary of State John Quincy Adams, welcomed Latin America's breakaway from Spain, but he hesitated to extend diplomatic recognition to the new governments. One of his fears was that recognition might ensnare the United States in Latin American–European crises and, by dangerously enlarging U.S. commitments abroad, might undermine the nation at home. In Document 1, a July 4, 1821, speech, Adams explains his hesitation and warnings.

Document 2 is British foreign secretary George Canning's appeal of August 20, 1823. In this letter to Richard Rush, American minister in London, Canning asks the United States to join Great Britain in a declaration against possible European intervention to restore the Latin American states to Spanish rule. President James Monroe consulted not only his cabinet but also former presidents Thomas Jefferson and James Madison about Canning's proposal. In a letter of October 24, included here as Document 3, Jefferson advised Monroe to cooperate with Britain. Document 4, from Adams's diary, is an account of the cabinet discussion of November 7. Adams argued successfully against an Anglo-American declaration. Document 5 is the president's annual message to Congress on December 2, 1823—the Monroe Doctrine.

The last two documents represent Latin American reactions to the Monroe Doctrine. In Document 6, a July 2, 1824, letter to Secretary Adams from José María Salazar, Colombia's minister in the United States, the Colombian government asks for clarification of the Monroe Doctrine: Exactly how did the United States intend to resist European intervention? (Adams evasively replied that the president would consult with Congress and talk with the Europeans.) Document 7, from the pen of Juan Bautista Alberdi, a prominent Argentine intellectual who wrote prolifically on political topics in the 1840s and 1850s, considers the Monroe Doctrine a self-interested U.S. effort to separate the Western Hemisphere from Europe and to deny Spanish America true independence.

1. Secretary of State John Quincy Adams Warns Against the Search for "Monsters to Destroy," 1821

And now, friends and countrymen, if the wise and learned philosophers of the elder world, the first observers of nutation and aberration, the discoverers of maddening ether and invisible planets, the inventors of Congreve rockets and Shrapnel shells,

---

This document can be found in John Quincy Adams, "An Address, Delivered at the Request of the Committee of Arrangement for Celebrating the Anniversary of Independence at Washington of the Fourth of July, 1821, Upon the Occasion of Reading the Declaration of Independence" (Cambridge, Mass.: University Press, 1821) (pamphlet).

should find their hearts disposed to enquire what has America done for the benefit of mankind? Let our answer be this: America, with the same voice which spoke herself into existence as a nation, proclaimed to mankind the inextinguishable rights of human nature, and the only lawful foundations of government. America, in the assembly of nations, since her admission among them, has invariably, though often fruitlessly, held forth to them the hand of honest friendship, of equal freedom, of generous reciprocity. She has uniformly spoken among them, though often to heedless and often to disdainful ears, the language of equal liberty, of equal justice, and of equal rights. She has, in the lapse of nearly half a century, without a single exception, respected the independence of other nations while asserting and maintaining her own. She has abstained from interference in the concerns of others, even when conflict has been for principles to which she clings, as to the last vital drop that visits the heart. She has seen that probably for centuries to come, all the contests of that Aceldama the European world, will be contests of inveterate power, and emerging right. Wherever the standard of freedom and Independence has been or shall be unfurled, there will her heart, her benedictions and her prayers be. But she goes not abroad, in search of monsters to destroy. She is the well-wisher to the freedom and independence of all. She is the champion and vindicator only of her own. She will commend the general cause by the countenance of her voice, and the benignant sympathy of her example. She well knows that by once enlisting under other banners than her own, were they even the banners of foreign independence, she would involve herself beyond the power of extrication, in all the wars of interest and intrigue, of individual avarice, envy, and ambition, which assume the colors and usurp the standard of freedom. The fundamental maxims of her policy would insensibly change from *liberty* to *force.* . . . She might become the dictatress of the world. She would be no longer the ruler of her own spirit. . . .

[America's] glory is not *dominion,* but *liberty.* Her march is the march of the mind. She has a spear and a shield: but the motto upon her shield is, *Freedom, Independence, Peace.* This has been her Declaration: this has been, as far as her necessary intercourse with the rest of mankind would permit, her practice.

2. British Foreign Secretary George Canning Proposes a Joint Declaration, 1823

Is not the moment come when our Governments might understand each other as to the Spanish American Colonies? And if we can arrive at such an understanding, would it not be expedient for ourselves, and beneficial for all the world, that the principles of it should be clearly settled and plainly avowed?

For ourselves we have no disguise.

1. We conceive the recovery of the Colonies by Spain to be hopeless.
2. We conceive the question of the recognition of them, as Independent States, to be one of time and circumstances.

This document can be found in William R. Manning, ed., *Diplomatic Correspondence of the United States Concerning the Independence of the Latin-American Nations* (New York: Carnegie Endowment for International Peace, 1925), III, 1478–1479.

3. We are, however, by no means disposed to throw any impediment in the way of an arrangement between them, and the mother country by amicable negotiation.
4. We aim not at the possession of any portion of them ourselves.
5. We could not see any portion of them transferred to any other Power, with indifference.

If these opinions and feelings are as I firmly believe them to be, common to your Government with ours, why should we hesitate mutually to confide them to each other; and to declare them in the face of the world?

If there be any European Power which cherishes other projects, which looks to a forcible enterprize for reducing the Colonies to subjugation, on the behalf or in the name of Spain; or which meditates the acquisition of any part of them to itself, by cession or by conquest; such a declaration on the part of your government and ours would be at once the most effectual and the least offensive mode of intimating our joint disapprobation of such projects.

It would at the same time put an end to all the jealousies of Spain with respect to her remaining Colonies—and to the agitation which prevails in those Colonies, an agitation which it would be but humane to allay; being determined (as we are) not to profit by encouraging it.

Do you conceive that under the power which you have recently received, you are authorized to enter into negotiation, and to sign any Convention upon this subject? Do you conceive, if that be not within your competence, you could exchange with me ministerial notes upon it?

Nothing could be more gratifying to me than to join with you in such a work, and, I am persuaded, there has seldom, in the history of the world, occurred an opportunity when so small an effort, of two friendly Governments, might produce so unequivocal a good and prevent such extensive calamities.

3. Thomas Jefferson Advises President James Monroe to Cooperate with Britain, 1823

The question presented by the letters you have sent me, is the most momentous which has ever been offered to my contemplation since that of Independence. That made us a nation, this sets our compass and points the course which we are to steer through the ocean of time opening on us. And never could we embark on it under circumstances more auspicious. Our first and fundamental maxim should be, never to entangle ourselves in the broils of Europe. Our second, never to suffer Europe to intermeddle with cis-Atlantic affairs. America, North and South, has a set of interests distinct from those of Europe, and peculiarly her own. She should therefore have a system of her own, separate and apart from that of Europe. While the last is laboring to become the domicile of despotism, our endeavor should surely be to make our hemisphere that of freedom. One nation, most of all, could disturb us in this pursuit; she now offers to lead, aid, and accompany us in it. By acceding to her proposition, we detach her from the bands, bring her mighty weight into the scale of free government, and emancipate

This document can be found in H. A. Washington, ed., *The Writings of Thomas Jefferson* (Washington, D.C.: Taylor and Maury, 1854), VII, 315–317.

a continent at one stroke, which might otherwise linger long in doubt and difficulty. Great Britain is the nation which can do us the most harm of any one, or all on earth; and with her on our side we need not fear the whole world. With her then, we should most sedulously cherish a cordial friendship; and nothing would tend more to knit our affections than to be fighting once more, side by side, in the same cause. . . .

But we have first to ask ourselves a question. Do we wish to acquire to our own confederacy any one or more of the Spanish provinces? I candidly confess, that I have ever looked on Cuba as the most interesting addition which could ever be made to our system of States. The control which, with Florida Point, this island would give us over the Gulf of Mexico, and the countries and isthmus bordering on it, as well as all those whose waters flow into it, would fill up the measures of our political well-being. Yet, as I am sensible that this can never be obtained, even with her own consent, but by war; and its independence, which is our second interest, (and especially its independence of England,) can be secured without it, I have no hesitation in abandoning my first wish to future chances, and accepting its independence, with peace and the friendship of England, rather than its association, at the expense of war and her enmity.

I could honestly, therefore, join in the declaration proposed, that we aim not at the acquisition of any of those possessions, that we will not stand in the way of any amicable arrangement between them and the Mother country; but that we will oppose, with all our means, the forcible interposition of any other power, as auxiliary, stipendiary, or under any other form or pretext, and most especially, their transfer to any power by conquest, cession, or acquisition in any other way. I should think it, therefore, advisable, that the Executive should encourage the British government to a continuance in the dispositions expressed in these letters, by an assurance of his concurrence with them as far as his authority goes; and that as it may lead to war, the declaration of which requires an act of Congress, the case shall be laid before them for consideration at their first meeting, and under the reasonable aspect in which it is seen by himself.

4. Adams Argues Against a Joint Anglo-American Declaration in the Cabinet Meeting of November 7, 1823

Cabinet meeting at the President's from half-past one till four. Mr. [John] Calhoun, Secretary of War, and Mr. [Samuel] Southard, Secretary of the Navy, present. The subject for consideration was, the confidential proposals of the British Secretary of State, George Canning, to R. Rush, and the correspondence between them relating to the projects of the Holy Alliance upon South America. There was much conversation, without coming to any definite point. The object of Canning appears to have been to obtain some public pledge from the Government of the United States, ostensibly against the forcible interference of the Holy Alliance between Spain and South America; but really or especially against the acquisition to the United States themselves of any part of the Spanish-American possessions.

This document can be found in Charles Francis Adams, ed., *Memoirs of John Quincy Adams Comprising Portions of His Diary from 1795 to 1848* (Philadelphia: J. B. Lippincott, 1875), VI, 177–179.

Mr. Calhoun inclined to giving a discretionary power to Mr. Rush to join in a declaration against the interference of the Holy Allies, if necessary, even if it should pledge us not to take Cuba or the province of Texas; because the power of Great Britain being greater than ours to *seize* upon them, we should get the advantage of obtaining from her the same declaration we should make ourselves.

I thought the cases not parallel. We have no intention of seizing either Texas or Cuba. But the inhabitants of either or both may exercise their primitive rights, and solicit a union with us. They will certainly do no such thing to Great Britain. By joining with her, therefore, in her proposed declaration, we give her a substantial and perhaps inconvenient pledge against ourselves, and really obtain nothing in return. Without entering now into the enquiry of the expediency of our annexing Texas or Cuba to our Union, we should at least keep ourselves free to act as emergencies may arise, and not tie ourselves down to any principle which might immediately afterwards be brought to bear against ourselves.

Mr. Southard inclined much to the same opinion.

The President was averse to any course which should have the appearance of taking a position subordinate to that of Great Britain. . . .

I remarked that the communications recently received from the Russian Minister, Baron Tuyl, afforded, as I thought, a very suitable and convenient opportunity for us to take our stand against the Holy Alliance, and at the same time to decline the overture of Great Britain. It would be more candid, as well as more dignified, to avow our principles explicitly to Russia and France, than to come in as a cock-boat in the wake of the British man-of-war.

This idea was acquiesced in on all sides, and my draft for an answer to Baron Tuyl's note announcing the Emperor's determination to refuse receiving any Minister from the South American Governments was read.

5. The Monroe Doctrine Declares the Western Hemisphere Closed to European Intervention, 1823

At the proposal of the Russian Imperial Government, made through the minister of the Emperor residing here, a full power and instructions have been transmitted to the minister of the United States at St. Petersburg to arrange by amicable negotiation the respective rights and interests of the two nations on the northwest coast of this continent. . . . In the discussions to which this interest has given rise and in the arrangements by which they may terminate the occasion has been judged proper for asserting, as a principle in which the rights and interests of the United States are involved that the American continents, by the free and independent condition which they have assumed and maintain, are henceforth not to be considered as subjects for future colonization by any European powers. . . .

It was stated at the commencement of the last session that a great effort was then making in Spain and Portugal to improve the condition of the people of those countries, and that it appeared to be conducted with extraordinary moderation. It

---

This document can be found in James D. Richardson, ed., *A Compilation of the Messages and Papers of the Presidents* (New York: Bureau of National Literature, 1897), II, 778, 786–788.

need scarcely be remarked that the result has been so far very different from what was then anticipated. Of events in that quarter of the globe, with which we have so much intercourse and from which we derive our origin, we have always been anxious and interested spectators. The citizens of the United States cherish sentiments the most friendly in favor of the liberty and happiness of their fellow-men on that side of the Atlantic. In the wars of the European powers in matters relating to themselves we have never taken any part, nor does it comport with our policy so to do. It is only when our rights are invaded or seriously menaced that we resent injuries or make preparation for our defense. With the movements in this hemisphere we are of necessity more immediately connected, and by causes which must be obvious to all enlightened and impartial observers. The political system of the allied powers is essentially different in this respect from that of America. This difference proceeds from that which exists in their respective Governments; and to the defense of our own, which has been achieved by the loss of so much blood and treasure, and matured by the wisdom of their most enlightened citizens, and under which we have enjoyed unexampled felicity, this whole nation is devoted. We owe it, therefore, to candor and to the amicable relations existing between the United States and those powers to declare that we should consider any attempt on their part to extend their system to any portion of this hemisphere as dangerous to our peace and safety. With the existing colonies or dependencies of any European power we have not interfered and shall not interfere. But with the Governments who have declared their independence and maintained it, and whose independence we have, on great consideration and on just principles, acknowledged, we could not view any interposition for the purpose of oppressing them, or controlling in any other manner their destiny, by any European power in any other light than as the manifestation of an unfriendly disposition toward the United States. In the war between those new Governments and Spain we declared our neutrality at the time of their recognition, and to this we have adhered, and shall continue to adhere, provided no change shall occur which, in the judgment of the competent authorities of this Government, shall make a corresponding change on the part of the United States indispensable to their security.

The late events in Spain and Portugal shew that Europe is still unsettled. Of this important fact no stronger proof can be adduced than that the allied powers should have thought it proper, on any principle satisfactory to themselves, to have interposed by force in the internal concerns of Spain. To what extent such interposition may be carried, on the same principle, is a question in which all independent powers whose governments differ from theirs are interested, even those most remote, and surely none more so than the United States. Our policy in regard to Europe, which was adopted at an early stage of the wars which have so long agitated that quarter of the globe, nevertheless remains the same, which is, not to interfere in the internal concerns of any of its powers; to consider the government *de facto* as the legitimate government for us; to cultivate friendly relations with it, and to preserve those relations by a frank, firm, and manly policy, meeting in all instances the just claims of every power, submitting to injuries from none. But in regard to those continents circumstances are eminently and conspicuously different. It is impossible that the allied powers should extend their political system to any portion of either continent without endangering our peace and happiness; nor can anyone believe that our southern brethren, if [left] to themselves, would adopt it of their own accord. It is equally impossible, therefore, that we should behold such interposition in any form with indifference.

6. Colombia Requests an Explanation of U.S. Intentions, 1824

My Government has seen with the greatest pleasure the Message of the President of the United States, a work very worthy of its author, and which expresses the public sentiments of the people over whom he presides: it cannot be doubted, in virtue of this document, that the Government of the United-States endeavours to oppose the policy and ultimate views of the Holy Alliance, and such appears to be the decision of Great Britain from the sense of the Nation, some acts of the Ministry, and the language of her Commissioners in Bogotá.

In such circumstances the Government of Colombia is desirous to know in what manner the Government of the United-States intends to resist on its part any interferences of the Holy Alliance for the purpose of subjugating the new Republics or interfering in their political forms: if it will enter into a Treaty of Alliance with the Republic of Colombia to save America in general from the calamities of a despotic system; and finally if the Government of Washington understands by foreign interference the employment of Spanish forces against America at the time when Spain is occupied by a French Army, and its Government under the influence of France and her Allies.

It appears that it is already in the situation intended by this declaration, since it [is] generally asserted that an expedition has sailed from Cadiz destined for the coasts of Peru composed of the Ship Asia and of some frigates and brigs; there is no doubt that Spain does not furnish this force by herself alone in her present state of despotism and anarchy, without an army, without a marine and without money. This Nation notwithstanding its spirit of domination would have ere now decided for peace had it not been assisted for war.

In the name of my Government therefore, and reposing on the sympathy of the United States, I request the said explanations which may serve for its government in its policy and its system of defence.

7. Juan Bautista Alberdi of Argentina Warns Against the Threat of "Monroism" to the Independence of Spanish America, n.d.

The revolution for independence has not eliminated the Europeanized civilization of the new world: it has only changed its form. What exists in America [North, Central, and South] continues to be an aspect of what exists in Europe. There is an intimate solidarity of interests and destinies among the peoples of both continents.

They are not two *worlds,* as the figurative expression goes; they are not two planets with beings of separate races, rather they are parts of one geographical and political world.

Document 6 can be found in William R. Manning, ed., *Diplomatic Correspondence of the United States Concerning the Independence of the Latin-American Nations* (New York: Carnegie Endowment for International Peace, 1925), II, 1281–1282.

Document 7 can be found in Juan Bautista Alberdi, *La Doctrina de Monröe y la America Española*, ed. by Raimundo Rodriquez (Buenos Aires: Nuevo Meridión, 1987), 103–104, 117–118, 123–124. Translated from the Spanish by Miriam Biurci. The essay was probably written in the 1840s–1850s.

The seas bring peoples together rather than separating them.

Without the sea, Chile would have no communication with Europe. The idea of a land voyage of three thousand leagues is unheard of. The community of business interests is proof of the solidarity of interests and destinies of both continents. The doctrine attributed to Monroe, is a contradiction, the daughter of egoism. Even though the United States owes everything to Europe, it wants to isolate America from Europe, from any influence that does not emanate from the United States, which will make the United States the only custom house for the civilization of transatlantic origin. Monroe wanted to make his country the *Porto-Bello of American liberty.* . . . [Porto Bello, on the isthmus of Panama, was one of the most important commercial centers in the Spanish empire—a symbol of Spanish control.]

Although the *Monroe* [D]octrine is antithetical to the doctrines of the *Holy* Alliance in Spanish America, with regard to the America of Spanish origin, it is as ominous as the doctrines of the Holy Alliance. Both have as their objective the conquest of Spanish America: one for the benefit of *Spain,* the other for the benefit of the *United* States.

Both doctrines are the expression of two ambitions, the object of which is Spanish America.

Between the colonial annexation of South America by a European nation and colonial annexation by the United States, what is the difference? Which is preferable for South America? As far as annexation is concerned, neither: independence is better. In other words, neither *monroism* nor *holy alliance.* But let us compare the results of these two annexations, the practical examples of which are Havana and Texas. Havana, though a colony, is Spanish. Texas, though free, has died for the Spanish race. *Havana* lives, even if it is enslaved; of *Texas,* the only thing left is the soil.

Thus, the colonial annexation by Europe is the conservation of the race and the species with loss of liberty. Annexation by the United States is the loss of the race and its being as it acquires liberty . . . as is well understood by the living, not by the dead. Between the two annexations, let the devil choose. . . .

Those who are not, in any respect, in agreement over the intervention of Europe, accommodate themselves to the idea of a *protectorate* by the *United States* over the entire American continent.

Apart from the absurdity of such a protectorate—due to its impracticality—it is not honorable to the independence of the South American republics, as any *protectorate* is not honorable, wherever it emanates from and whoever exercises it.

All *protectorates* are humiliating because they are the denial of the means to *independence,* from which is derived, in practice, the *right* to be.

🌐 *E S S A Y S*

In the first selection, James E. Lewis, Jr., of Kalamazoo College portrays the Monroe Doctrine as a defensive—but ineffective—initiative. As Latin America's independence movements against Spain gained steam, the Monroe administration feared both European intervention to reclaim lost empire and competition from the newly established states for commercial and territorial advantage in the Western Hemisphere. Monroe's unilateral proclamation, according to Lewis, was designed to fend off Europe, encourage

Latin Americans to adopt peaceful, liberal political and economic institutions, and enhance U.S. prestige. Lewis concludes that the gambit failed, and in the end Latin American independence and U.S. security were bolstered mainly by British military power and Anglo-French diplomacy. William E. Weeks of San Diego State University, in the second essay, interprets the Monroe Doctrine not as a failed defensive measure but rather as a successful step toward empire-building. Taken together with the Transcontinental Treaty of 1819, by which Spain ceded the Floridas and territories reaching to the Pacific coast, Monroe's proclamation kept Europe at bay, advanced the United States as the dominant hemispheric power, and provided a justification for future U.S. intervention in Latin America. Indeed, American presidents and diplomats would again and again cite the Monroe Doctrine as they sought to create a U.S. dominated order in the Western Hemisphere. In 1904, President Theodore Roosevelt even declared a "corollary" to the doctrine, claiming a U.S. "police power" in the Caribbean and justifying U.S. military and political intervention in the region.

Ineffective Defense, at Best

JAMES E. LEWIS JR.

Even as he devoted more time to maritime issues with Europe during his second term as secretary of state, [John Quincy] Adams also focused more attention on changing conditions in the Western Hemisphere. American policymakers had closely followed and carefully responded to revolutionary upheaval in Spanish America for more than a decade before March 1821. In general, especially after the War of 1812, their response had been determined more by conditions on their borders and in Europe than by developments in Spanish America. The final ratification of the Transcontinental Treaty [by which Spain sold Florida to the United States and agreed to a transcontinental border] in February 1821 made it possible for [President James] Monroe and Adams to reevaluate these developments and rethink their policies. What they discovered proved deeply unsettling to them. By the fall of 1821, the revolutionaries had defeated Spanish troops and toppled Spanish authority in all of the mainland colonies. The emergence of independent nations in Spanish America simultaneously reinvigorated and threatened the original logic of the Founders. For the first time, American policymakers had to address the situation that the Founders had feared—the existence of a multitude of independent nations in the Western Hemisphere. Monroe and Adams responded by encouraging the new Spanish American nations to adopt political, diplomatic, and commercial principles that they believed would promote peace and prosperity in the New World. When they faced a European challenge to their goal of an independent, republican New World in the fall of 1823, they tried to counter it with what would later be called the Monroe Doctrine. Their efforts did not meet even their short-term goals and left unresolved the long-term question of how to react to the radical changes in the Western Hemisphere.

Though it was subsequently a subject of frequent debate and controversy, American policy toward the Spanish American revolutions was established, at least

James E. Lewis Jr., "Ineffective Defense at Best," in *John Quincy Adams: Policymaker for the Union* (Wilmington, DE: Scholarly Resources, 2001), 85–95. Reprinted by permission of Roman & Littlefield Publishers.

in general terms, shortly after the War of 1812. Uncertain about the actual state of Spanish America, convinced of the inveterate hostility of the European powers (particularly the Holy Alliance of Russia, Spain, Austria, and France), and alarmed by the demonstrated weakness of the United States, the Madison administration had crafted a policy of neutrality in the conflict between Spain and its colonies. As defined by the administration, neutrality did allow trading with both parties, but did not include recognizing the independence of the colonies if that risked embroiling the United States in a war with Spain and possibly other European nations. Monroe and Adams continued this cautious approach, even though they often differed over whether they could eliminate the dangers by coordinating recognition with Great Britain, France, and Russia. Once they learned in November 1819 that the fate of the Transcontinental Treaty was entangled with the question of recognition, Monroe and Adams became even more reluctant to act. Over the next fourteen months, recognition remained a hostage to the uncertain fate of the treaty.

The final ratification of the treaty in February 1821 did not ensure a change of policy, however. In a meeting with [Speaker of the House Henry] Clay in March 1821, Adams "acknowledge[d that] nothing had hitherto occurred to weaken in [his] mind the view which [he] had taken of this subject from the first." He "had never doubted" that the end result of the struggle would be the "entire independence" of the Spanish Americans. But he did not expect them to "establish free or liberal institutions of government." He argued that the United States must remain neutral, which in his view, unlike Clay's, did not yet allow for recognition. "The principle of neutrality to *all* foreign wars was," he believed, "fundamental to the continuance of our liberties and of our Union." This fierce commitment to neutrality appeared publicly in the Fourth of July oration that Adams delivered, at the request of Congress, in the Capitol four months later. Adams predicted that the principles of the Declaration of Independence would move the people to rise against tyranny in the future in Europe, as at present in South America. In these anticolonial and antimonarchial struggles, the United States would be "the well-wisher to the freedom and independence of all." But, he insisted, it should "[go] not abroad in search of monsters to destroy"; "by once enlisting under other banners than her own," the United States would find itself drawn into countless wars. In time, its own "freedom and independence" would be imperiled as it embarked upon a career of "dominion and power." Such a powerful and public statement of noninterventionist principles left little room for Monroe and Adams to risk recognizing the Spanish American nations as long as their struggle against Spain continued.

Within a year of Adams's conversation with Clay and Fourth of July oration, however, the administration, encouraged by the secretary of state, decided to recognize Buenos Aires, Chile, Colombia, Mexico, and Peru—all of Spain's mainland colonies. Monroe and Adams abandoned their old opposition to recognition without abandoning their old concerns. They still found few signs of political stability or republican government among the Spanish Americans; in fact, there was new evidence that some of the rebel colonies might agree to import a minor European prince as a king if that would help to reconcile Spain to their independence. Monroe and Adams still worried, moreover, about the hostility of the European powers, who forcibly overthrew the republican government of Naples in early 1821. Writing to Adams that July, Monroe asserted that the United States had "much to apprehend from the hostile feeling of many of the sovereigns of Europe towards us"; "war with them," he calculated, "is not an improbable event." Finally, Monroe and Adams still accepted that the United States could not risk a war. The Missouri Crisis, the Panic of 1819, and the election campaign had badly divided the people and the government; even more important, the reduction in federal revenues resulting from the Panic had given [Secretary of the Treasury William H.] Crawford's supporters in Congress the votes that they needed to cut the army and navy. What had changed by early 1822 that made possible a new policy was not the conditions that had always weighed against recognition, but the character of the contest between Spain and its colonies. By November 1821, new reports from Central and South America, particularly Peru and Mexico, had convinced Adams that "the Spanish authorities [were] falling away in every part of that continent."

Monroe and Adams now faced a dramatically altered situation. From their perspective, the United States had suddenly gained five indisputably independent neighbors in the Western Hemisphere with necessarily conflicting interests. All of the fears that the Founders had expressed in the 1780s when they predicted disunion in North America were revived on a much larger scale in the early 1820s. Applying the logic of the Founders, Monroe and Adams believed that an independent New World might develop in one of two ways. The new Spanish American nations might fall under the control, formal or informal, of the European powers. The New World would become merely an extension of the European balance of power, involving its nations in Europe's wars and surrounding the United States with hostile monarchies. Or the Spanish American states might retain their independence and behave like any sovereign nation. As such, they would use commercial regulations and military forces to compete with each other and with the United States for land, trade, and influence. Monroe and Adams deemed neither of these prospects compatible with American interests. In either case, the United States would have to seek foreign alliances, adopt a more centralized—and, thus, less republican—government, and accept new limits on its trade and expansion. The goals of the Revolution—goals that had been secured and advanced for three decades by the American union—seemed to be in jeopardy.

The administration responded to these concerns in the first weeks of 1822 by deciding to extend formal diplomatic recognition to five Spanish American nations. None of the earlier obstacles to recognition had disappeared, but now Monroe and Adams had to weigh the long-term threat of an independent New World against the immediate risk of a war with Spain and possibly other European powers. As Monroe understood, under these conditions, there was "*danger* in standing *still* or moving *forward*." In early 1822, Monroe and Adams concluded that the long-term threat of "standing *still*" was more important. They hoped that, by recognizing the new states before any other nation, they could shape the Western Hemisphere's emerging political system into the form that best suited American interests. Opening formal relations with the new states would enable Monroe and Adams to promote throughout Spanish America the diplomatic, political, and commercial principles of the United States. The new nations would be encouraged to model themselves upon their northern neighbor—distancing themselves from European affairs, organizing themselves into weak republican governments, and committing themselves to liberal principles of neutral rights and open commerce. If the Spanish American states adopted this model, they would limit the means through which they could promote their interests, just as the United States had. As a result, they would be less dangerous neighbors. Monroe and Adams trusted that the general adoption of these principles would benefit the new states as well as the United States, even though it would only ameliorate, rather than eliminate, the inherent dangers of competition between sovereign neighbors.

When the administration finally sent its first ministers to the new states—Caesar A. Rodney to Buenos Aires and Richard C. Anderson to Colombia—a year later, Adams prepared their initial instructions with these goals in mind. He fully appreciated the importance of his work, informing Monroe that "the foundations of the future permanent intercourse political and commercial between the United States and the new Spanish American nations must be laid in the instructions for these diplomatic missions." These foundations would rest on what Adams saw as the shared interest of the United States and the Spanish American states "that they should all be governed by republican institutions, politically and commercially independent of Europe." Republican government, diplomatic isolation from Europe, and liberal commerce would be pressed upon Spanish America in order to secure independence, republicanism, and prosperity in the United States. Rodney and Anderson were directed to discourage the Spanish Americans from forming any connections with the European powers since such ties were "always connected with systems of subserviency to *European* interests." At the same time, they were to encourage their hosts to adopt written constitutions that protected individual rights and subordinated military to civilian rule. Finally, they were to urge the new states to sign commercial treaties that included at least most-favored-nation status, if not reciprocity, and that asserted a broad view of neutral rights. Adams had no doubt that it was for the welfare of "our sisters of the southern continent . . . , no less than for that of the world, that they should found themselves" from the beginning upon "the principles upon which *our* confederated republic is founded."

The same thinking that produced the decision to recognize in the winter of 1822 and that shaped the first set of instructions in the spring of 1823 determined the administration's response to a new crisis that fall. In October, the administration learned that France, Russia, and Austria—having invaded Spain to topple the constitutional government and restore the king the preceding spring—intended to assist Spain in regaining control of its colonies. This information came from [Ambassador Richard] Rush in London, along with a British proposal for a joint statement in which the two powers would declare their opposition to outside interference in Spanish America and disavow any intention of acquiring territory from Spain's empire. Adams received confirmation of Rush's news about the plans of the Holy Alliance from the Russian minister in Washington, Baron Hendrik de Tuyll van Serooskerken. The crisis raised two interconnected questions for the administration. How should it react to the Holy Alliance's threat to the Spanish American states? And how should it respond to Great Britain's proposal for a joint statement? In the month before Congress met in early December, the cabinet discussed these questions at great length. Monroe, Adams, and the other cabinet members did not entirely agree about the developing situation or the appropriate response. Adams tended to see less danger of an Allied invasion and more peril from the British proposal than the president or the secretary of war, for example. But all could agree that it was precisely because they had recognized the Spanish American nations and had committed the United States to an independent, republican New World that they needed to respond at all.

Working from the logic of the earlier decision to recognize the Spanish American states, the administration believed that the United States had to check the Allied threat and that it had to try, at least, to do so without accepting the British proposal. In reconceptualizing the New World at the time of recognition, Monroe and Adams had defined new interests for the United States. In doing so, they had also identified new ways in which it could be threatened by Europe. Intervention by the Holy Alliance in Spanish America would revive all of the dangers that recognition had been intended to remove. Even if the Allied effort to restore Spanish authority ultimately failed, and Adams always believed that it would, the attempt itself seemed certain to undermine American goals in the region. Within each state, loyalists and monarchists would gain strength, while military leaders would retain power that should have been surrendered to civilian governments. The Allies would eventually abandon their effort to restore Spanish control, but Adams feared that they would then seek dominion for themselves. "The ultimate result of their undertaking," he predicted to the cabinet, "would be to recolonize [the new states], partitioned out among themselves." With France established in Buenos Aires and Mexico and Russia entrenched in Peru, Chile, and California, the administration's worst fears would be realized.

From the beginning of the cabinet debates, Monroe and Adams looked for ways to check the Holy Alliance without accepting the British proposal. "The President," Adams noted in his diary, "was averse to any course which should have the appearance of taking a position subordinate to that of Great Britain." Adams certainly agreed. In an oft-quoted statement, he asserted that "it would be more candid, as well as more dignified, to avow our principles explicitly to Russia and France, than to come in as a cock-boat in the wake of the British man-of-war." But Monroe and Adams were not merely looking for a way to maintain appearances. On [the] one hand, because Great Britain had not yet recognized the new states, it was not committed to their independence as the United States was. Without such a common commitment, Adams worried that any joint statement would "[rest] only upon a casual coincidence of interests" that would leave the British free to change their policy whenever they wished. On the other hand, Monroe and Adams calculated that, by acting alone, the United States could thwart the plans of the Holy Alliance and enhance its own influence in Spanish America. Unilateral action, in Monroe's thinking, would have a "better effect with our southern neighbours, as well as with Russia & other allied powers." Believing that Russia, in particular, feared Anglo-American cooperation, the administration would hold out to the Holy Alliance the possibility of preventing it simply by abandoning the Spanish American invasion. By checking the Allied threat without British support, Monroe and Adams would also help to prevent the spread of British influence in the new states. The alternative of following Great Britain's lead or, worse yet, allowing it to act alone, Adams warned, "would throw them completely into her arms, and . . . make them her Colonies instead of those of Spain."

Almost immediately, Adams concluded that this crisis had to be met with a multifaceted, but coordinated, response. After the first cabinet discussion of this matter, he informed Monroe that the instructions to Rush addressing the British proposal and the reply to de Tuyll, as well as new instructions for the ministers in Russia and France, "must all be parts of a combined system of policy and adapted to each other." Monroe, Adams noted, "fully concurred." Eventually, the elements of this "combined system of policy" included as well instructions for the new minister to Chile, meetings with the Colombian minister in Washington, and the dispatching of a secret agent to Europe. The most public facet of this response, at the time, and the most significant, subsequently, however, was the president's annual message to Congress. In time, the three paragraphs from the message that dealt with this crisis would be known as the Monroe Doctrine. They asserted three crucial principles that derived from the administration's new appraisal of the United States's hemispheric interests. The first informed the European powers, especially Great Britain and Russia, that the Western Hemisphere was no longer open to new colonization. The second addressed the current crisis directly by warning the Allies that the United States would view "any attempt on their part to extend their system to any portion of this hemisphere as dangerous to our peace and safety." The third reaffirmed that the United States would not involve itself in Europe's "internal concerns." With this message, the administration publicly took a bold, unilateral stand against the Holy Alliance, "mak[ing] an American cause," as Adams wished, "and adher[ing] inflexibly to [it]."

At home, this bold stand received widespread praise. Public meetings, private letters, and newspaper editorials all tended to support the forcefulness of the administration's public position. Both houses of Congress quickly sought ways to "[echo] back the Sentiments of the President's message" through resolutions. On the evening that the message was sent to Congress, Adams sought out Clay's opinion. Though they had usually battled over Spanish American policy during the preceding six years, the speaker of the House informed the secretary of state that he strongly approved of the administration's publicly expressed willingness to resist the Holy Alliance's threatened invasion. Two months later, he moved a resolution in the House that would have placed Congress squarely behind this policy. It was not just at home, moreover, that Monroe's message sparked such favorable comments. Among European liberals and Spanish American revolutionaries, it was immediately celebrated for its republican sentiments and its diplomatic stance. "The manly message of the President of the U.S. and the spirited feeling of the people at large and their representatives," the Marquis de Lafayette apprised Adams from France, "have produced an admirable and timely impression" in Europe.

But Monroe's annual message can be understood only in the context of the other elements of the administration's "combined system of policy." Taking all of its elements together, this policy was more tentative and more flexible than the message alone would suggest. The instructions for the new minister to France, for example, directed him to explain the message to his hosts, but warned him to "avoid any measure by which the Government might be prematurely implicated." The instructions for Rush made perfectly clear the administration's, particularly the president's, desire to keep open its options. As Adams drafted these instructions, Monroe insisted that they preserve even the possibility of accepting the original British proposal for a joint statement. If the crisis deepened despite the position taken publicly in the message and privately through diplomacy, Monroe reasoned, a joint statement, however unappealing in the abstract, might offer the only means of preventing an Allied invasion of Spanish America. Even after they received dispatches from London and Paris in late December reporting that a series of Anglo-French meetings had defused the crisis, Monroe and Adams watched Europe closely, prepared to revise their stand as necessary. "The policy of Great Britain & of Continental Europe, with regard to South America," Adams argued as late as May 1824, "is not yet fully disclosed."

Monroe and Adams continued to await new developments and remained ready "to adapt our own measures in reference to them."

The limits to the administration's position, as publicly and boldly stated in the president's message, emerged clearly in the months after its publication. The most important of these limits had been present from the beginning. Even though the message had warned that the United States would view any interference by the Holy Alliance in the affairs of the Spanish American states "as the manifestation of an unfriendly disposition toward [itself]," the administration had never intended to support its words with force, at least not if it had to act alone. "It does not follow, from what has been said," Monroe insisted in early December 1823, "that we should be bound to engage in war," particularly if Great Britain remained neutral. Monroe and Adams always realized that, if the Holy Alliance persisted with its plans, they might have to retreat from their unilateral stand; they prepared their instructions to keep open their options for such a contingency. Because British diplomacy had checked the Allied threat before the message reached Europe (in fact, before it was ever written), the limits to the administration's public position were exposed not by the response of the European powers, but by the reaction of the Spanish American states. In a way that Monroe and Adams had never imagined, some of the Spanish American states embraced the message. In July 1824, the Colombian minister asked the administration to fulfill its stated principles by signing an alliance and supporting his country against French pressures. Monroe and Adams refused. Trying to cover their retreat, Adams explained that the message addressed only "a deliberate and concerted system of the allied Powers to exercise force." Even in that case, the administration would act only with the support of Congress and "a previous understanding" with Great Britain.

The Monroe Doctrine's greater immediate impact was upon an ongoing territorial dispute over the Pacific Northwest. Four powers had claims in this region when Adams entered office in 1817. Spain's (which became Mexico's) had been limited to south of the 42nd parallel by the Transcontinental Treaty; the United States and Great Britain had agreed to joint occupation of their claims for a period of ten years in the Convention of 1818. But Russian pretensions remained unlimited and undefined. In the fall of 1821, the czar tried to strengthen his position by issuing a ukase [royal decree] closing both coasts and the waters of the Pacific north of 51° north latitude to foreigners. Adams immediately protested, but the limits of the respective Russian, British, and American claims remained undetermined. In the spring and summer of 1823, Adams worked to repel advancing Russian claims that seemed likely to push British claims further south. He hoped for a tripartite convention, to last for ten years, that would permit navigation, fishing, and commerce in any unoccupied areas of the coast while limiting Russian settlement to north of 55°, American settlement to south of 51°, and British settlement to the area in between. Such negotiations would almost certainly have failed in the face of a British insistence upon the freedom to settle as far north as 57° and as far south as the Columbia River. The Monroe Doctrine—by rebuffing the British proposal of a united stand against the Holy Alliance and asserting American opposition to new colonization in the New World—led the British to excuse themselves from these talks. In April 1824, the United States and Russia easily concluded a convention in St. Petersburg that included much that Adams sought, though it shifted the limit of Russian settlement south to 50°40′.

The final collapse of Spain's continental empire during the early 1820s posed significant challenges for Monroe and Adams; in the short-term, at least, their responses failed to achieve their goals. The ultimate success of the Spanish American revolutions held tremendous promise—opening new markets for American trade and, in Adams's thinking, rendering it "impossible that the old exclusive and excluding Colonial system should much longer endure anywhere." But it also reinvigorated the fears about how neighboring sovereignties interact with each other—and how such interactions could endanger the goals of the American Revolution—that had led the Founders to construct "a more perfect union" in the 1780s. Monroe and Adams responded to this challenge by trying to promote throughout the New World the principles that they trusted would ease competition between its states. They looked to recognition itself to begin this process. Its early effects were not encouraging. Nine months after recognition was announced, Adams "observed that those countries were yet all in a convulsive and revolutionary state." Faced with a new external challenge to their efforts in Spanish America a year later, Monroe and Adams stayed true to their new assessment of American interests, devising a set of measures that could check an Allied invasion without expanding British influence or risking an unwelcome war. But, although the Monroe Doctrine acquired tremendous significance in American policymaking eventually, it had no impact upon the crisis it was written to address. With the crisis resolved by Anglo-French diplomacy, Monroe and Adams quickly retreated from the message's implications.

The Age of Manifest Destiny Begins

WILLIAM E. WEEKS

In the courts of Europe the United States' sudden acquisition of both the Floridas and an expanded western domain [through the Transcontinental Treaty of 1819, signed with Spain] caused concern. The Americans had taken another giant step toward becoming the preeminent New World empire. The British press characterized the treaty as further proof of the ambitious, aggressive, expansionist ways of their former colonies.

To [Secretary of State John Quincy] Adams, however, the treaty was partial fulfillment of a divine plan: Europe, he wrote in his diary, must be "familiarized with the idea of considering our proper dominion to be the continent of North America." Expansion across the continent was "as much the law of nature . . . as that the Mississippi should flow to the sea. Until Europe shall find it a settled geographical element that the United States and North America are identical, any effort on our part to reason the world out of the belief that we are ambitious will have no other effect than to convince them that we add to our ambition hypocrisy."

Although the adroit use of force and diplomacy had produced for [President James] Monroe and Adams a spectacular victory in the confrontation with Spain, the threat of European intervention in the Latin American revolutions remained. Tsar Alexander I of Russia had by no means resigned himself to the destruction of a fellow monarch's colonial empire, and he labored intensely for a consensus

From William E. Weeks, *Building the Continental Empire: American Expansion from the Revolution to the Civil War* (Chicago: Ivan R. Dee, 1996), 53–58. Copyright © 1996 by William E. Weeks, by permission of Ivan R. Dee, Publisher.

among his "Holy Allies" that intervention in the New World was in the interest of conservative regimes across Europe. . . .

Yet these European efforts to reinstall reactionary regimes concerned the British as much as they did the Americans. Having gained access to the rapidly developing markets of South America as a consequence of the revolutionary upheaval, London did not wish to assist the reestablishment of a colonial regime whose first move likely would be to end British trading privileges. George Canning, who assumed the office of foreign secretary upon the suicide of [Lord] Castlereagh in 1821, followed the ambiguous course charted by his predecessor—offering to assist Spain in a negotiated end to the struggles but flatly opposing armed intervention. Canning finally made British policy explicit in October 1823 during a conference with French minister Duke de Polignac, in which each side pledged not to intervene militarily in the South American rebellions.

Canning also looked to the United States to bolster Britain's position opposing European intervention. A joint Anglo-American declaration of principle, perhaps even a full-scale alliance, would guarantee the abstention of the other European powers in Western Hemisphere affairs. In this spirit Canning, in August 1823, approached American minister Richard Rush with a startling offer: would the American government join the British in publicly declaring their mutual desire that the Latin American states remain free, independent, and not subject to transfer to any other European power? Would the Monroe administration consider making a statement publicly asserting this common position and mutually pledging that "We aim not at the possession of any portion of them ourselves"?

Canning's proposal created a sensation among American elite opinion. Aligning with Britain seemed to offer a way to guarantee that no further European (that is to say, non-British) intervention in the Western Hemisphere would occur. Both Monroe and former president James Madison were inclined to accept Britain's offer of a de facto alliance. Jefferson was enthusiastic about the possibilities. He advised Monroe that "By acceding to her [Britain's] proposition, we . . . bring her mighty weight into the scale of free government, and emancipate a continent at one stroke. . . . Great Britain is the nation which can do us the most harm of any one . . . and with her on our side we need not fear the whole world." The Americans seemed ready formally to ally themselves with their former mother country. . . .

John Quincy Adams assessed matters from a more nuanced perspective. Ever suspicious of the British bearing gifts, Adams perceived that the real motive behind the offer was to induce the United States to renounce publicly further acquisitions of territory. What about Texas and Cuba, which might someday desire annexation to the Union? Adams argued to the other members of the cabinet that "we should at least keep ourselves free to act as emergencies may arise, and not tie ourselves down to any principle that might be brought to bear against ourselves. . . . It would be more candid, as well as more dignified," Adams contended, "to avow our principles explicitly to Russia and France, than to come in as a cockboat in the wake of the British man-of-war. . . . We should separate it from all European concerns, disclaim all intentions of interfering with these, and make the stand altogether for an American cause."

Adams recognized the essential fact of the matter: Canning, through his actions and statements, had made Britain's opposition to European intervention unshakable. Therefore, why should the United States take part in a joint declaration by which it would gain nothing, and at the cost of a pledge of not to expand? With British policy certain and clear, Monroe and Adams were in a position "to avow [their] position explicitly to Russia and France" without making further commitments. The stage was now set for a formal declaration of these principles.

This occurred on December 2, 1823, in the president's seventh annual message to the Congress. The State of the Union address, as the annual message later became known, was an ideal vehicle for policy pronouncements to the public, to the European diplomatic corps, and to posterity. Buried amid the president's remarks on a range of issues were three paragraphs of profound long-term significance for both American and world history. The principles articulated, far from being primarily the result of cabinet infighting, as one historian has recently suggested, were in fact long aspired to by American political leaders. Only now were conditions favorable to their being raised to the level of holy writ, almost on a par with the Declaration of Independence.

The first of Monroe's principles was that of "noncolonization": ". . . the American continents, by the free and independent condition which they have assumed and maintain, are henceforth not to be considered as subjects for future colonization by any European powers. . . ." This bold prohibition on further colonization was bolstered by an equally vigorous statement against foreign intervention: "We owe it, therefore, to candor and amicable relations existing between the United States and those powers to declare that we should consider any attempt on their part to extend their system to any portion of this hemisphere as dangerous to our peace and safety. . . . It is impossible that the allied powers should extend their political system to any portion of either continent without endangering our peace and happiness. . . ." In effect, Monroe had defined the American security zone to include the entire Western Hemisphere. A justification was in place for future U.S. interventions throughout Latin America.

Having said, in effect, "Europe Hands Off!" the Western Hemisphere, Monroe assured European governments that the United States had no intention of intervening directly in the ongoing Greek struggle for independence from Turkey, in spite of widespread American ideological sympathy for the Greeks. By asserting the "doctrine of the two spheres," the third principle of his policy, Monroe declared the United States supreme in the Western Hemisphere while mollifying European concerns by pledging nonintervention in continental affairs. . . .

The bold American statement had an inspirational effect on many South American patriot movements that interpreted Monroe's message as an offer of a pan-American alliance. Recognition of the South American independence movements had finally begun in 1822, and hopes arose that an era of hemispheric cooperation was dawning. Yet Adams and Monroe had no intention of multilateralizing their new policy. Don José Maria Salazar, the new Colombian minister to the United States, queried Adams on the implications of the president's remarks. Would the United States "enter into treaty of alliance with the Republic of Colombia to save America in general from the calamities of a despotic system"? Adams rejected the offer of alliance and assured Salazar the U.S. government would determine the timing and appropriateness of any collective response.

Most immediately affected by Monroe's new policy was Russia. Tsar Alexander had made his power felt in the Western Hemisphere in 1821 when he issued a ukase, or royal decree, claiming exclusive Russian control of the northwest American coast as far south as the 51st parallel, and prohibiting foreign vessels from approaching to within one hundred miles of the coast. Now, faced with the depletion of fur-bearing animals, the financial difficulties of the Russian-American Company (a fur-trading monopoly he had chartered in 1799), and mounting U.S. opposition to his ukase and to further Russian colonization, Alexander capitulated. In April 1824 Russia agreed to allow American vessels near-unrestricted access to the Northwest Coast and its adjoining waters.

For Adams and Monroe it was the capstone of eight years of brilliant diplomacy. In a precarious position in 1817, by 1824 the American nation and the American empire stood on firmer ground than ever before. From a position of relative insecurity the United States had emerged as the supreme power in the Western Hemisphere. The Louisiana Purchase had been perfected, the Floridas secured, a transcontinental claim had been staked, and the prospect of European intervention in the hemisphere greatly reduced. The age of Manifest Destiny had begun.

FURTHER READING

Harry Ammon, *James Monroe* (1970)
———, "Monroe Doctrine: Domestic Politics or National Decision?" *Diplomatic History* 5 (Winter 1981): 53–70
Samuel Flagg Bemis, *John Quincy Adams and the Foundations of American Foreign Policy* (1949)
Kinley J. Brauer, "1820–1860: Economics and the Diplomacy of American Expansionism," in William H. Becker and Samuel F. Wells Jr., eds., *Economics and World Power* (1984)
Edward P. Crapol, "John Quincy Adams and the Monroe Doctrine: Some New Evidence," *Pacific Historical Review* 48 (1974): 413–418
Noble E. Cunningham Jr., *The Presidency of James Monroe* (1996)
George Dangerfield, *The Awakening of American Nationalism, 1815–1828* (1965)
Michael F. Holt, *Political Parties and American Political Development from the Age of Jackson to the Age of Lincoln* (1992)
John J. Johnson, *A Hemisphere Apart* (1990)
Lawrence S. Kaplan, "The Monroe Doctrine and the Truman Doctrine: The Case of Greece," *Journal of the Early Republic* 13 (1993): 1–21
Howard Kushner, *Conflict on the Northwest Coast: American-Russian Rivalry in the Pacific Northwest, 1790–1867* (1975)
Walter LaFeber, ed., *John Quincy Adams and American Continental Empire* (1965)
Lester D. Langley, *The Americas in the Age of Revolution* (1996)
———, *Struggle for the American Mediterranean* (1976)
James E. Lewis Jr., *The American Union and the Problem of Neighborhood* (1998)
Paul C. Nagel, *John Quincy Adams* (1997)
Lynn Hudson Parsons, *John Quincy Adams* (1999)
Bradford Perkins, *Castlereagh and Adams* (1964)
Dexter Perkins, *A History of the Monroe Doctrine* (1955)
Robert V. Remini, *John Quincy Adams* (2002)
Greg Russell, *John Quincy Adams* (1995)
Norman E. Saul, *Distant Friends* (1991) (U.S.-Russia)
Charles Sellers, *The Market Revolution: Jacksonian America, 1815–1846* (1991)
William E. Weeks, *John Quincy Adams and American Global Empire* (1992)
William Appleman Williams, *The Contours of American History* (1961)

CHAPTER
6

Manifest Destiny, Texas, and the War with Mexico

🌐

The 1840s witnessed an expansionist surge that netted new territories for the United States. After the threat or use of force and much debate, the territories of Texas, Oregon, and California became part of the expanding American empire. From infancy the United States had been expansionist and had moved steadily westward, enlarging its territory, pushing out its boundaries, and removing Native Americans. In the 1840s, expansionism took a new name. A journalist proclaimed that it was the United States's "Manifest Destiny" to extend its reach to the Pacific Ocean. In that decade, Oregon joined the American empire, and President James K. Polk took the nation to war against Mexico.

The origins of the Mexican-American War (1846–1848) can be traced to Spain's decision in 1819 to allow North American colonists, led by Moses Austin and his son Stephen, to settle in the Mexican province of Texas. Lured by the availability of cheap, fertile land, the settlers—who included many slaveholding southern planters—swelled in number to more than 15,000 within a decade. Tensions flared between the colonists and the new, independent Mexico when the central government in Mexico City required Texans to accept membership in the Roman Catholic church and to abolish slavery. In a further attempt to clamp down on the American migrants, Mexican president Antonio López de Santa Anna in 1830 abolished the province's legislature and marched his army into Texas. Led by the legendary Sam Houston, the indignant Texans rebelled in 1836. Although the rebels suffered a costly defeat at the Alamo mission in San Antonio, they regrouped and quickly secured Texan independence. The United States's annexation of the Lone Star Republic and the admission of Texas to the Union in 1845 soon sparked a new conflict. War broke out between the United States and Mexico along the disputed Texas border in 1846; and two years later, a defeated Mexico, in the Treaty of Guadalupe Hidalgo, transferred one-half of its national domain to the United States.

What explains this burst of territorial acquisitiveness? President James K. Polk's ardent expansionism? A cumulative and traditional American expansionism? Idealism? Racism? Security concerns? Commercial interest? The answers vary, as the selections in this chapter indicate.

🌐 *D O C U M E N T S*

On December 12, 1835, the commander in chief of Texas's rebel army, Sam Houston, issued a proclamation to his fellow citizens. The fiery pronouncement, Document 1, summarizes Texas's complaints against Mexican authorities and beseeches all Texans to join the struggle for independence. In Document 2, a memoir written in 1837, Mexico's Antonio López de Santa Anna defends his efforts to crush the Texas revolution. The colorful leader, renowned for leading the bloody assault in 1836 against badly outgunned rebels at the Alamo, disputes the legitimacy of Texan nationhood and condemns clandestine U.S. support for the uprising.

John L. O'Sullivan is credited with having popularized the idea of Manifest Destiny, which ultimately rationalized the United States's annexation of Texas and other territories. As the editor of the *Democratic Review,* he flamboyantly sketched an unbounded American future of democratic mission and territorial expansion. Document 3 is taken from his "The Great Nation of Futurity," published in 1839. James K. Polk became president in 1845. An avowed expansionist, he hungrily eyed Mexican lands and territories in the Southwest and disputed boundaries in the Northwest. Document 4, Polk's inaugural address of March 4, 1845, makes the case for the United States's absorbing Texas and Oregon. Document 5 is Polk's war message of May 11, 1846, in which the president presents U.S. grievances and asks Congress to declare war against Mexico.

The outbreak of the war, American territorial ambitions, and the ultimate U.S. triumph ignited considerable debate. In Document 6, the Wilmot Proviso, drafted by Representative David Wilmot of Pennsylvania, the author seeks to keep slavery out of any territory won from Mexico. Although the House passed this amendment to an appropriations bill in 1846 and again in 1847, the Senate turned it down, thereby exposing deep divisions over whether limits ought to be placed on expansion.

In Document 7, a speech delivered in the U.S. Senate on March 23, 1848, the leader of the Whig party, Daniel Webster of Massachusetts, denounces the acquisition of new territories as an abuse of executive power and an unconscionable act of aggression against Mexico. Webster predicts that the admission of new states from the former Mexican territories will alter the balance of power in the Senate between southern slaveholding and northern free states, disrupting the Union. The final selection, Document 8, is an excerpt from the collective views of a group of Mexican leaders, first translated into English and published in 1850. They portray the United States as an aggressive, expansionist power, condemn the annexation of Texas, and accuse Washington of having provoked war in 1846 by sending General Zachary Taylor's forces across the disputed Texas-Mexico border. Disarray in the Mexican government and politics, they acknowledged, eased the U.S. drive to acquire Texas.

1. Commander Sam Houston's Battle Cry for Texan Independence from Mexico, 1835

Your situation is peculiarly calculated to call forth all your manly energies. Under the Republican constitution of Mexico, you were invited to Texas, then a wilderness. You have reclaimed and rendered it a cultivated country. You solemnly swore to

---

This document can be found in *Texan and Emigrants Guide,* Nacogdoches,Texas, January 2, 1836.

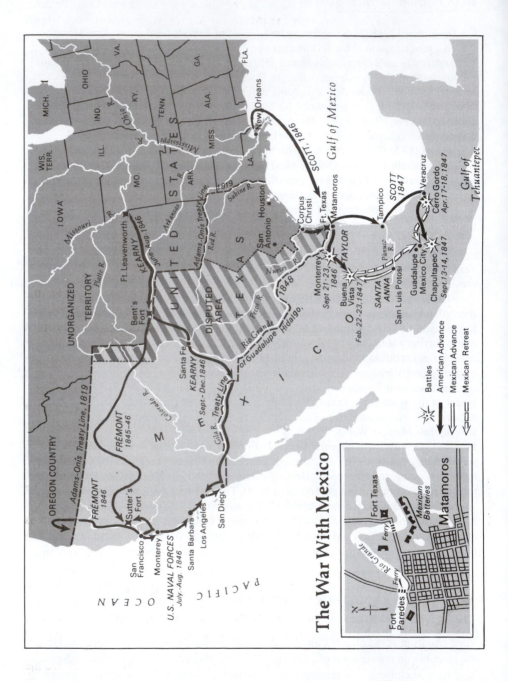

The War With Mexico

Thomas G. Paterson et al., *American Foreign Relations,* Sixth Edition. Copyright © 2005 by Houghton Mifflin Company. Used by permission of Houghton Mifflin Company.

support the Constitution and its laws. Your oaths are yet inviolate. In accordance with them, you have fought with the [Mexican] liberals against those who sought to overthrow the Constitution in 1832 when the present usurper was the champion of liberal principles in Mexico. Your obedience has manifested your integrity. You have witnessed with pain the convulsions of the interior and a succession of usurpations. You have experienced in silent grief the expulsion of your members from the State Congress. You have realized the horrors of anarchy and the dictation of military rule. The promises made to you have not been fulfilled. Your memorials for the redress of grievances have been disregarded and the agents you have sent to Mexico have been imprisoned for years without enjoying the rights of trial agreeable to law. Your constitutional executive has been deposed by the bayonets of a mercenary soldiery while your State Congress has been dissolved by violence, and its members either fled or were arrested by the military force of the country. The federation has been dissolved, the Constitution declared at an end, and centralism has been established. . . .

The usurper dispatched a military force to invade the colonies and exact the arms of the inhabitants. The citizens refused the demand, and the invading force was increased. The question then was shall we resist the oppression and live free, or violate our oaths and bear a despot's stripes? The citizens of Texas rallied to the defense of their constitutional rights. They have met four to one and by their chivalry and courage, they have vanquished the enemy with a gallantry and spirit which is characteristic of the justice of our cause. . . .

Since our army has been in the field, a consultation of the people, by their representatives, has met and established a provisional government. This course has grown out of the emergencies of the country; the army has claimed its peculiar care. We were without law and without a constitutional head. The Provisional Executive and the General Council of Texas are earnestly engaged in their respective duties preparing for every exigency of the country and I am satisfied from their zeal, ability and patriotism, that Texas will have everything to hope from their exertions in behalf of the principles which we have avowed. . . .

Citizens of Texas, your rights must be defended. The oppressors must be driven from our soil. Submission to the laws and union among ourselves will render us invincible; subordination and discipline in our army will guarantee to us victory and renown. Our invader has sworn to extinguish us or sweep us from the soil. He is vigilant in his work of oppression and has ordered to Texas ten thousand men to enforce the unhallowed purposes of his ambition. His letters to his subalterns in Texas have been intercepted and his plans for our destruction have been disclosed. Departing from the chivalric principles of warfare, he has ordered arms to be distributed to a portion of our population for the purpose of creating in the midst of us a servile war. The hopes of the usurper were inspired by a belief that the citizens of Texas were disunited and divided in opinion and that alone has been the cause of the present invasion of our rights. He shall realize the fallacy of his hopes in the union of her citizens and their ETERNAL RESISTANCE to his plans against constitutional liberty. We will enjoy our birthright or perish in its defense. . . .

Let the brave rally to our standard.

2. General Antonio López de Santa Anna Defends Mexican Sovereignty over Texas, 1837

Santa Anna, whether conqueror or conquered, whether free or in chains, yea, I swear it before the world, did not in Texas debase the Mexican name in which he glories and takes pride. . . .

[In] November, 1835, [I took] charge of a war from which I could have been excused, for the fundamental law of the country offered me a decorous excuse that my broken health made all the more honorable. Nevertheless, aware of the adverse circumstances I have expressed, I still desired to try to serve my country. In a few days I gathered six thousand men, clothed and equipped. At the cost of immense sacrifices, rising above obstacles that seemed insuperable, this force set out from San Luis towards the end of December, 1835. . . .

Let it be said now in order to avoid repetition: the war against Texas has been as just on the part of the Mexican government as the lack of the slightest attempt on the part of those who forced it upon Mexico has been to try to justify their action. Few of the colonists, properly speaking, have taken up arms in the struggle. The soldiers of [Colonel William Barret] Travis at the Alamo, those of [Captain James W.] Fannin at Perdido, the riflemen of Dr. [James] Grant, and [Sam] Houston himself and his troops at San Jacinto, with but few exceptions, were publicly known to have come from New Orleans and other points of the neighboring republic exclusively for the purpose of aiding the Texas rebellion without ever having been members of any of the colonization grants.

Some Mexicans, partisans of a former system of government, thought, perhaps in good faith, that the only effect of fanning the fire of war in Texas would be a political change in accord with their opinion. Their shortsighted ambition must be a terrible lesson to them as well as a source of eternal remorse. Too late, they now deplore having placed in jeopardy the integrity of our national territory.

Our country found itself invaded not by an established nation that came to vindicate its rights, whether true or imaginary; nor by Mexicans who, in a paroxysm of political passion, came to defend or combat the public administration of the country. The invaders were all men who, moved by the desire of conquest, with rights less apparent and plausible than those of [the Spanish conquistadors Hernán] Cortés and [Francisco de] Pizarro, wished to take possession of that vast territory extending from Béxar to the Sabine belonging to Mexico. What can we call them? How should they be treated? All the existing laws, whose strict observance the government had just recommended, marked them as pirates and outlaws. The nations of the world would never have forgiven Mexico had it accorded them rights, privileges, and considerations which the common law of peoples accords only to constituted nations.

This document can be found in Carlos E. Castañeda, ed., *The Mexican Side of the Texas Revolution, 1836* (Dallas: P. L. Turner Co., 1928), 5–8, 16–17.

3. Democratic Publicist John L. O'Sullivan Proclaims America's Manifest Destiny, 1839

The American people having derived their origin from many other nations, and the Declaration of National Independence being entirely based on the great principle of human equality, these facts demonstrate at once our disconnected position as regards any other nation; that we have, in reality, but little connection with the past history of any of them, and still less with all antiquity, its glories, or its crimes. On the contrary, our national birth was the beginning of a new history, the formation and progress of an untried political system, which separates us from the past and connects us with the future only; and so far as regards the entire development of the natural rights of man, in moral, political, and national life, we may confidently assume that our country is destined to be the great nation of futurity.

It is so destined, because the principle upon which a nation is organized fixes its destiny, and that of equality is perfect, is universal. It presides in all the operations of the physical world, and it is also the conscious law of the soul—the self-evident dictates of morality, which accurately defines the duty of man to man, and consequently man's rights as man. Besides, the truthful annals of any nation furnish abundant evidence, that its happiness, its greatness, its duration, were always proportionate to the democratic equality in its system of government. . . .

What friend of human liberty, civilization, and refinement, can cast his view over the past history of the monarchies and aristocracies of antiquity, and not deplore that they ever existed? What philanthropist can contemplate the oppressions, the cruelties, and injustice inflicted by them on the masses of mankind, and not turn with moral horror from the retrospect?

America is destined for better deeds. It is our unparalleled glory that we have no reminiscences of battle fields, but in defence of humanity, of the oppressed of all nations, of the rights of conscience, the rights of personal enfranchisement. Our annals describe no scenes of horrid carnage, where men were led on by hundreds of thousands to slay one another, dupes and victims to emperors, kings, nobles, demons in the human form called heroes. We have had patriots to defend our homes, our liberties, but no aspirants to crowns or thrones; nor have the American people ever suffered themselves to be led on by wicked ambition to depopulate the land, to spread desolation far and wide, that a human being might be placed on a seat of supremacy.

We have no interest in the scenes of antiquity, only as lessons of avoidance of nearly all their examples. The expansive future is our arena, and for our history. We are entering on its untrodden space, with the truths of God in our minds, beneficent objects in our hearts, and with a clear conscience unsullied by the past. We are the nation of human progress, and who will, what can, set limits to our onward march? Providence is with us, and no earthly power can. We point to the everlasting truth on the first page of our national declaration, and we proclaim to the millions of

This document can be found in "The Great Nation of Futurity," *The United States Magazine and Democratic Review* 6 (November 1839): 426–430. It can also be found in Norman A. Graebner, ed., *Manifest Destiny* (Indianapolis: Bobbs-Merrill Co., 1968), 15–21.

other lands, that "the gates of hell"—the powers of aristocracy and monarchy—"shall not prevail against it."

The far-reaching, the boundless future will be the era of American greatness. In its magnificent domain of space and time, the nation of many nations is destined to manifest to mankind the excellence of divine principles; to establish on earth the noblest temple ever dedicated to the worship of the Most High—the Sacred and the True. Its floor shall be a hemisphere—its roof the firmament of the star-studded heavens, and its congregation an Union of many Republics, comprising hundreds of happy millions, calling, owning no man master, but governed by God's natural and moral law of equality, the law of brotherhood—of "peace and good will amongst men." . . .

Yes, we are the nation of progress, of individual freedom, of universal enfranchisement. Equality of rights is the cynosure of our union of States, the grand exemplar of the correlative equality of individuals; and while truth sheds its effulgence, we cannot retrograde, without dissolving the one and subverting the other. We must onward to the fulfilment of our mission—to the entire development of the principle of our organization—freedom of conscience, freedom of person, freedom of trade and business pursuits, universality of freedom and equality. This is our high destiny, and in nature's eternal, inevitable decree of cause and effect we must accomplish it. All this will be our future history, to establish on earth the moral dignity and salvation of man—the immutable truth and beneficence of God. For this blessed mission to the nations of the world, which are shut out from the life-giving light of truth, has America been chosen; and her high example shall smite unto death the tyranny of kings, hierarchs, and oligarchs, and carry the glad tidings of peace and good will where myriads now endure an existence scarcely more enviable than that of beasts of the field. Who, then, can doubt that our country is destined to be *the great nation* of futurity?

4. President James K. Polk Lays Claim to Texas and Oregon, 1845

I regard the question of annexation as belonging exclusively to the United States and Texas. They are independent powers competent to contract, and foreign nations have no right to interfere with them or to take exceptions to their reunion. Foreign powers do not seem to appreciate the true character of our Government. Our Union is a confederation of independent States, whose policy is peace with each other and all the world. To enlarge its limits is to extend the dominions of peace over additional territories and increasing millions. The world has nothing to fear from military ambition in our Government. While the Chief Magistrate and the popular branch of Congress are elected for short terms by the suffrages of those millions who must in their own persons bear all the burdens and miseries of war, our Government can not be otherwise than pacific. Foreign powers should therefore look on the annexation of Texas to the United States not as the conquest of a nation seeking to

This document can be found in James D. Richardson, ed., *A Compilation of the Messages and Papers of the Presidents* (New York: Bureau of National Literature, 1897), V, 2230–2231.

extend her dominions by arms and violence, but as the peaceful acquisition of a territory once her own, by adding another member to our confederation, with the consent of that member, thereby diminishing the chances of war and opening to them new and ever-increasing markets for their products.

To Texas the reunion is important, because the strong protecting arm of our Government would be extended over her, and the vast resources of her fertile soil and genial climate would be speedily developed, while the safety of New Orleans and of our whole southwestern frontier against hostile aggression, as well as the interests of the whole Union, would be promoted by it.

In the earlier stages of our national existence the opinion prevailed with some that our system of confederated States could not operate successfully over an extended territory, and serious objections have at different times been made to the enlargement of our boundaries. These objections were earnestly urged when we acquired Louisiana. Experience has shown that they were not well founded. The title of numerous Indian tribes to vast tracts of country has been extinguished; new States have been admitted into the Union; new Territories have been created and our jurisdiction and laws extended over them. As our population has expanded, the Union has been cemented and strengthened. . . .

None can fail to see the danger to our safety and future peace if Texas remains an independent state or becomes an ally or dependency of some foreign nation more powerful than herself. Is there one among our citizens who would not prefer perpetual peace with Texas to occasional wars, which so often occur between bordering independent nations? Is there one who would not prefer free intercourse with her to high duties on all our products and manufactures which enter her ports or cross her frontiers? Is there one who would not prefer an unrestricted communication with her citizens to the frontier obstructions which must occur if she remains out of the Union? Whatever is good or evil in the local institutions of Texas will remain her own whether annexed to the United States or not. None of the present States will be responsible for them any more than they are for the local institutions of each other. They have confederated together for certain specified objects. Upon the same principle that they would refuse to form a perpetual union with Texas because of her local institutions our forefathers would have been prevented from forming our present Union. Perceiving no valid objection to the measure and many reasons for its adoption vitally affecting the peace, the safety, and the prosperity of both countries, I shall on the broad principle which formed the basis and produced the adoption of our Constitution, and not in any narrow spirit of sectional policy, endeavor by all constitutional, honorable, and appropriate means to consummate the expressed will of the people and Government of the United States by the reannexation of Texas to our Union at the earliest practicable period.

Nor will it become in a less degree my duty to assert and maintain by all constitutional means the right of the United States to that portion of our territory which lies beyond the Rocky Mountains. Our title to the country of the Oregon is "clear and unquestionable," and already are our people preparing to perfect that title by occupying it with their wives and children. But eighty years ago our population was confined on the west by the ridge of the Alleghanies. Within that period—within the lifetime, I might say, of some of my hearers—our people, increasing to many millions, have filled the eastern valley of the Mississippi, adventurously ascended the

Missouri to its headsprings, and are already engaged in establishing the blessings of self-government in valleys of which the rivers flow to the Pacific. The world beholds the peaceful triumphs of the industry of our emigrants. To us belongs the duty of protecting them adequately wherever they may be upon our soil. The jurisdiction of our laws and the benefits of our republican institutions should be extended over them in the distant regions which they have selected for their homes. The increasing facilities of intercourse will easily bring the States, of which the formation in that part of our territory can not be long delayed, within the sphere of our federative Union. In the meantime every obligation imposed by treaty or conventional stipulations should be sacredly respected.

5. Polk Asks Congress to Declare War on Mexico, 1846

The strong desire to establish peace with Mexico on liberal and honorable terms, and the readiness of this Government to regulate and adjust our boundary and other causes of difference with that power on such fair and equitable principles as would lead to permanent relations of the most friendly nature, induced me in September last to seek the reopening of diplomatic relations between the two countries. . . . An envoy of the United States repaired to Mexico with full powers to adjust every existing difference. But though present on the Mexican soil by agreement between the two Governments, invested with full powers, and bearing evidence of the most friendly dispositions, his mission has been unavailing. The Mexican Government not only refused to receive him or listen to his propositions, but after a long-continued series of menaces have at last invaded our territory and shed the blood of our fellow-citizens on our own soil.

It now becomes my duty to state more in detail the origin, progress, and failure of that mission. . . . On the 10th of November, 1845, Mr. John Slidell, of Louisiana, was commissioned by me as envoy extraordinary and minister plenipotentiary of the United States to Mexico, and was intrusted with full powers to adjust both the questions of the Texas boundary and of indemnification to our citizens. . . .

Mr. Slidell arrived at Vera Cruz on the 30th of November, and was courteously received by the authorities of that city. But the Government of General [José Joaquín de] Herrera was then tottering to its fall. The revolutionary party had seized upon the Texas question to effect or hasten its overthrow. Its determination to restore friendly relations with the United States, and to receive our minister to negotiate for the settlement of this question, was violently assailed, and was made the great theme of denunciation against it. The Government of General Herrera, there is good reason to believe, was sincerely desirous to receive our minister; but it yielded to the storm raised by its enemies, and on the 21st of December refused to accredit Mr. Slidell upon the most frivolous pretexts. These are so fully and ably exposed in the note of Mr. Slidell of the 24th of December last to the Mexican minister of foreign relations, herewith transmitted, that I deem it unnecessary to enter into further detail on this portion of the subject.

This document can be found in James D. Richardson, ed., *A Compilation of the Messages and Papers of the Presidents* (New York: Bureau of National Literature, 1897), VI, 2288–2292.

Five days after the date of Mr. Slidell's note General Herrera yielded the Government to General [Mariano] Paredes without a struggle, and on the 30th of December resigned the Presidency. This revolution was accomplished solely by the army, the people having taken little part in the contest; and thus the supreme power in Mexico passed into the hands of a military leader. . . .

In my message at the commencement of the present session I informed you that upon the earnest appeal both of the Congress and convention of Texas I had ordered an efficient military force to take a position "between the Nueces and the Del Norte." This had become necessary to meet a threatened invasion of Texas by the Mexican forces, for which extensive military preparations had been made. The invasion was threatened solely because Texas had determined, in accordance with a solemn resolution of the Congress of the United States, to annex herself to our Union, and under these circumstances it was plainly our duty to extend our protection over her citizens and soil.

This force was concentrated at Corpus Christi, and remained there until after I had received such information from Mexico as rendered it probable, if not certain, that the Mexican Government would refuse to receive our envoy.

Meantime Texas, by the final action of our Congress, had become an integral part of our Union. The Congress of Texas, by its act of December 19, 1836, had declared the Rio del Norte to be the boundary of that Republic. Its jurisdiction had been extended and exercised beyond the Nueces. The country between the river and the Del Norte had been represented in the Congress and in the convention of Texas, had thus taken part in the act of annexation itself, and is now included within one of our Congressional districts. Our own Congress had, moreover, with great unanimity, by the act approved December 31, 1845, recognized the country beyond the Nueces as a part of our territory by including it within our own revenue system, and a revenue officer to reside within that district has been appointed by and with the advice and consent of the Senate. It became, therefore, of urgent necessity to provide for the defense of that portion of our country. Accordingly, on the 13th of January last instructions were issued to the general in command of these troops to occupy the left bank of the Del Norte. This river, which is the southwestern boundary of the State of Texas, is an exposed frontier. From this quarter invasion was threatened; upon it and in its immediate vicinity, in the judgment of high military experience, are the proper stations for the protecting forces of the Government. . . .

The Army moved from Corpus Christi on the 11th of March, and on the 28th of that month arrived on the left bank of the Del Norte opposite to Matamoras, where it encamped on a commanding position, which has since been strengthened by the erection of fieldworks. A depot has also been established at Point Isabel, near the Brazos Santiago, 30 miles in the rear of the encampment. The selection of this position was necessarily confided to the judgment of the general in command.

The Mexican forces at Matamoras assumed a belligerent attitude, and on the 12th of April General Ampudia, then in command, notified General Taylor to break up his camp within twenty-four hours and to retire beyond the Nueces River, and in the event of his failure to comply with these demands announced that arms, and arms alone, must decide the question. But no open act of hostility was committed until the 24th of April. On that day General Arista, who had succeeded to the command of the Mexican forces, communicated to General Taylor that "he considered hostilities commenced and should prosecute them." A party of dragoons of 63 men and officers were on the same day dispatched from the American camp up the Rio del Norte, on its left bank, to ascertain whether the Mexican troops had crossed or were preparing to cross the river, "became engaged with a large body of these troops, and after a short affair, in which some 16 were killed and wounded, appear to have been surrounded and compelled to surrender." . . .

. . . Upon the pretext that Texas, a nation as independent as herself, thought proper to unite its destinies with our own she has affected to believe that we have severed her rightful territory, and in official proclamations and manifestoes has repeatedly threatened to make war upon us for the purpose of reconquering Texas. In the meantime we have tried every effort at reconciliation. The cup of forbearance had been exhausted even before the recent information from the frontier of the Del Norte. But now, after reiterated menaces, Mexico has passed the boundary of the United States, has invaded our territory and shed American blood upon the American soil. She has proclaimed that hostilities have commenced, and that the two nations are now at war.

As war exists, and, notwithstanding all our efforts to avoid it, exists by the act of Mexico herself, we are called upon by every consideration of duty and patriotism to vindicate with decision the honor, the rights, and the interests of our country.

6. The Wilmot Proviso Raises the Issue of Slavery in New Territories, 1846

Provided, That, as an express and fundamental condition to the acquisition of any territory from the Republic of Mexico by the United States, by virtue of any treaty which may be negotiated between them, and to the use by the Executive of the moneys herein appropriated, neither slavery nor involuntary servitude shall ever exist in any part of said territory, except for crime, whereof the party shall first be duly convicted.

7. Massachusetts Senator Daniel Webster Protests the War with Mexico and the Admission of New States to the Union, 1848

The members composing the other House . . . [have] passed a resolution affirming that "the war with Mexico was begun unconstitutionally and unnecessarily by the Executive Government of the United States." I concur in that sentiment. I hold that to be the most recent, authentic expression of the will and the opinions of the people of the United States. There is another proposition, not so authentically announced hitherto, but in my judgment equally true—equally capable of demonstration—and that is, that this war was begun, has been continued, and is now prosecuted, for the great and leading purpose of the acquisition of new territory. . . . Every intelligent man

---

Document 6 can be found in *Congressional Globe,* 29th Congress, 1st Session (August 8, 1846), 1217.

Document 7 can be found in *Congressional Globe,* 30th Congress, 1st Session (March 23, 1848), 530–535.

knows that there is a strong desire in the heart of the Mexican citizen to retain the territories belonging to that republic. We know that the Mexican people part with their territory—if part they must—with regret, with pangs of sorrow. That we know. . . .

This war was waged for the purpose of creating new States, near the southern portion of the United States, out of Mexican territory, and with such population as might be found resident therein. I have opposed that project. I am against the creation of new States. I am against the acquisition of territory to form new States. . . .

But we think we must take territory. For the sake of peace, we must take territory! This is the will of the President! If we do not take it, we may fare worse! Mr. Polk will take no less! That is fixed upon! He is immovable! He has put down his foot! He had put it down, sir, on "fifty-four forty," [America's northern-most claim along the Oregon-Canadian border] but it didn't stay! I speak of the President of the United States as I speak of all Presidents, without disrespect; but I know no reason why his opinions, his will, his purpose declared to be fixed, should control us, any more than our purpose formed upon equally conscientious motives, and I may add, formed under as high responsibilities, should control him. . . .

I have found, sir, in the course of thirty years' experience, that whatever measure the Executive Government embraces and pushes, is quite likely to succeed. There is a giving way somewhere. If the Executive Government acts with uniformity, steadiness, entire unity of purpose, sooner or later it is quite apt enough—according to my construction of history, too apt—to effect its purpose. . . .

I never could, and I never should, bring myself to be in favor of the admission of any States into the Union as slaveholding States, and I might have added, any State at all. Now, as I have said, in all this I acted under the resolutions of the State of Massachusetts—certainly concurrent with my own judgment, so often repeated, and reaffirmed by the unanimous consent of all men of all parties; that I could not well go through the series of pointing out, not only the impolicy, but the unconstitutionality of such annexation. A case presented is this: If a State proposes to come into the Union, and to come in as a slave State; then there is an augmentation of the inequality in the representation of the people, which already exists—an inequality already existing, with which I do not quarrel, and which I never will attempt to alter, but shall preserve as long as I have a vote to give, or any voice in this Government, because it is a part of the original compact. Let it stand. But then there is another consideration of vastly more general importance even than that—more general, because it affects all the States, free and slaveholding; and it is, that if States formed out of territories thus thinly populated come into the Union, they necessarily, inevitably break up the relation existing between the two branches of the Government, and destroy its balance. They break up the intended relation between the Senate and the House of Representatives. If you bring in new States, any State that comes in must have two Senators. She may come in with fifty or sixty thousand people or more. You may have, from a particular State, more Senators than you have Representatives. Can anything occur to disfigure and derange the form of government under which we live more signally than that? . . .

Sir, we take New Mexico and California. Who is weak enough to think that there is an end? Why, do we not hear it avowed every day, that it is proper for us also to take Sonora and Tamaulipas, and other provinces or States of northern Mexico? Who thinks that the hunger for dominion will stop here of itself? Somebody has said that this acquisition is so mean, and lean, and unsatisfactory, that we shall seek no further. In my judgment, sir, you may believe that, if you can believe that a rapacious animal that has made one unproductive foray won't try for a better! . . .

. . . I think I see a course adopted that is likely to turn the Constitution under which we live into a deformed monster—into a curse rather than a blessing—into a great frame of unequal government, not founded on popular representation, but founded in the grossest inequalities; and I think, if it go on—for there is danger that it will go on—that this government will be broken up.

8. Mexican Patriots Condemn U.S. Aggression, 1850

To explain then in a few words the true origin of the war, it is sufficient to say that the insatiable ambition of the United States, favored by our weakness, caused it. . . .

. . . Texas has over the greater part of Mexico the advantage of inclosing within its borders, beautiful and navigable rivers, the only blessing wanting in almost all the other parts of our richly endowed country. Texas, by its fertility and riches, by its climate and position, possesses all the elements requisite for prosperity in agriculture, industry, commerce, and navigation.

The profit which would accrue from the possession of this land stimulated the United States to procure it at any price. . . .

A short time before the independence of Mexico, in the year 1819, the Spanish government granted to Moses Austin the requisite authority to form a colony in Texas. This concession was owing principally to the zeal that animated the King of Spain for the dissemination and protection of the Catholic religion. Moses Austin had represented his sect as disheartened and dispersed, and begged that these lands might be given to him as an asylum, where the immigrants could and would enter for the exercise of their faith.

Stephen Austin, the son and heir of Moses, continued the work commenced by his father, and made a beginning of a vast enterprise by colonizing, in 1820, between the Brasos and Colorado rivers. The emancipation of our Republic opened a wide door to immigration. They received with open arms the strangers who touched our soil. But the political inexperience of our national governors converted into a fountain of evils a benevolent and purely Christian principle. Immigration, which ought to have equalized the laborious arms to agriculture, manufacture, and commerce, finally resulted in the separation of one of the most important states. It was this which involved us soon in actual, disastrous war. . . .

On the 12th April, 1844, the President of the United States made a treaty with Texas relative to the incorporation of that country into the Union. This treaty was not ratified by the Senate; the usurpation remained for the present suspended, which was soon, however, effected in a new way. . . .

At this time, more properly than before, it would have been exact justice to have immediately made war on a power that so rashly appropriated what by every title belonged to us. This necessity had increased to a point, that the administrations which had successively been intrusted with our affairs, upon consideration,

This document can be found in Ramón Alcarez et al., eds., *The Other Side: Or Notes for the History of the War Between Mexico and the United States,* trans. Albert C. Ramsey (New York: Wiley, 1850), 2, 9, 15–16, 23–24, 25, 26, 27–28, 29–30, 32.

had all agreed in the principle, that a decree of annexation should be viewed as a *casus belli*—a cause of war. . . .

At the close of the year 1844, a new revolution having overturned the government of General Santa Anna, intrusted in the interim to General [Antonio] Canaliso, elevated to power D. José Joaquin de Herrera, the President of the Council. . . .

The policy which this party [the Decembrists] pursued differed entirely from that observed by the former administrations. They acted upon the principle, in the firm belief that the Department of Texas had from the year 1830 been lost for ever; from which it was madness to suppose that our victorious eagles could be borne to the other side of the Sabine. They therefore decided on negotiation, and war on no account: for we were wanting in essentials the most indispensable. . . .

Notwithstanding . . . public clamor raised in opposition, [General Herrera's administration] persisted with firmness in the path proposed to be taken. To the end to open negotiations relating to this object, they formally asked and Congress passed a decree on the 17th May, 1845, conceding authority to it to hear the propositions which Texas had made, and to arrange or conclude a treaty which should be suitable and honorable to the Republic. The propositions presented were the four following: 1st. The independence of Texas was recognised. 2d. Texas agreed not to annex or subject herself to any other country. 3d. Limits and conditions were reserved for a final treaty. 4th. Texas was ready to submit the points in dispute about territories and other subjects to the decision of arbitrators. . . .

These preliminaries caused the belief that it would not be difficult to obtain a satisfactory arrangement. But the subsequent conduct of Texas finally resolved itself into annexation with the American Union. Whether it was owing to a breaking with this nation or because an arrangement was incompatible with the motions and revolutions it had against the government of the Decembristas, the negotiations were suspended, and soon this interesting question was left to the fate of arms. . . .

The year 1846 witnessed at its commencement new rules figuring in the political drama, having been elevated to power by another revolution. General [Mariano] Paredes pronounced in San Luis against Herrera. A few days were sufficient for this shameful revolution to become a triumph the most complete. Then Mr. Slidell renewed his suit, in considering that, although the old had been terminated by a refusal, still, as the business now went into new hands to be transacted, it was a favorable opportunity to see if he should meet in them a better disposition. The matter again underwent a revision in the council of the government, which repeated the reasons on which the former had been based, concluding with a renewal of the declaration that it could not admit Mr. Slidell further than Plenipotentiary *ad hoc* for the question of Texas. The government made this known to the Envoy, who now could do no more than ask for his passports, and withdraw from the Republic.

General Paredes, on the 21st of March of the same year, declared that peace not being compatible with the maintenance of the rights and independence of the nation, he should defend its territory. . . .

While the United States seemed to be animated by a sincere desire not to break the peace, their acts of hostility manifested very evidently what were their true intentions. Their ships infested our coasts; their troops continued advancing upon our territory, situated at places which under no aspect could be disputed. Thus violence and insult were united: thus at the very time they usurped part of our territory, they

offered to us the hand of treachery, to have soon the audacity to say that our obsti-
nacy and arrogance were the real causes of the war.

To explain the occupation of the Mexican territory by the troops of General
[Zachary] Taylor, the strange idea occurred to the United States that the limits of
Texas extended to the Rio Bravo del Norte. . . .

From the acts referred to, it has been demonstrated to the very senses, that the
real and effective cause of this war that afflicted us was the spirit of aggrandizement of the United States of the North, availing itself of its power to conquer us.
Impartial history will some day illustrate for ever the conduct observed by this Republic against all laws, divine and human, in an age that is called one of light, and
which is, notwithstanding, the same as the former—one of *force and violence.*

E S S A Y S

Historians have extensively probed the roots of expansionism in the 1840s. In the first
essay, Anders Stephanson of Columbia University examines the ideology of Manifest
Destiny that guided American expansionism. Studying the writings of the Jacksonian
newspaper editor John O'Sullivan, he concludes that a misguided and ethnocentric
idealism, undergirded by a belief in American exceptionalism and Anglo-Saxon racism,
contributed significantly to the quest for territory in the 1840s. In the second essay,
Thomas R. Hietala of Grinnell College in Iowa questions the role of ideology in American expansionism. Although Hietala acknowledges that the idea of Manifest Destiny
served as a legitimizing myth, he concludes that hard-headed interests—especially a
desire for western land, Pacific ports, and markets—motivated the Polk administration
to use force to acquire territory and empire.

The Ideology and Spirit of Manifest Destiny

ANDERS STEPHANSON

"In *America,*" a foreign observer wrote from afar in 1848, "we have witnessed the
conquest of Mexico and have rejoiced at it." The defeated nation hitherto had been
"exclusively wrapped up in its own affairs, perpetually rent with civil wars, and
completely hindered in its development." The best it could have hoped for in those
circumstances was economic subjection to Britain. From a Mexican viewpoint,
therefore, it was "an advance" now to be "forcibly drawn into the historical
process" and "placed under the tutelage of the United States." Thus the opinion of
Friedrich Engels.

Later in life, Engels would become more critical of such historical "advances."
In this he was at one with his American contemporary Walt Whitman. The great poet,
editor of the Democratic *Brooklyn Eagle* during the war, had found "miserable,
inefficient Mexico" totally incompatible "with the great mission of peopling the

New World with a noble race." I cite these two figures at the outset to indicate the political span of typical mid-nineteenth-century Western notions of progress. It is good to bear that range in mind when we now [turn] to John O'Sullivan and the ideology of Jacksonian expansionism, which he expressed better than anyone else. Not only did O'Sullivan coin the phrase "manifest destiny," but his political sallies formed a veritable summa of the arguments of this type. His journal, the *Democratic Review,* is in fact more interesting as a source here than the widely disseminated "penny press," which echoed the same sentiment but evinced less of the revealing ambivalence and ambiguity.

O'Sullivan, after consulting [Andrew] Jackson and [Martin] Van Buren, founded the *Review* in 1837 in order to give the Jacksonian movement intellectual and political presence in the domain of highbrow culture, which was then dominated by staid and conservative forces. Under his editorial guidance, the *Review* became the liveliest and most interesting journal of its kind. A whole constellation of future literary "greats" appeared in it. [Nathaniel] Hawthorne, a strong Democratic supporter, contributed from the start, but the new publication also opened its pages to Henry David Thoreau and Edgar Allan Poe, neither of whom was a Jacksonian. O'Sullivan mixed liberality of literary taste with a strongly polemical line, set by himself, in political affairs. It was the peculiar mixture of partisan politics and cultural openness that gave the journal its character. Though it never achieved great circulation, it was read by important people and became such a thorn in the side of conservatives that the *American Whig Review* was revamped in 1845 into a political counterpart.

Reduced to simple propositions, the views of O'Sullivan and his contemporaries now seem overblown and jejune. To maintain a sense for the rhetorical flavor (and of our historical distance from it), therefore, I shall make use of some extensive quotation.

O'Sullivan, as a good Jacksonian, spent the first years attacking the combined evils of consolidated government and banking aristocracy. Following Van Buren, he was also fully aware that he had "to stand aloof from the delicate and dangerous topic of Slavery and Abolition." In these early campaigns against what he typically called "delusive theories and fatal heresies," there was already a strongly destinarian conception of the United States:

> The last order of civilization, which is the democratic, received its first permanent existence in this country. . . . A land separated from the influences of ancient arrangement, peculiar in its position, productions, and extent, wide enough to hold a numerous people, admitting, with facility, intercommunication and trade, vigorous and fresh from the hand of God, was requisite for the full and broad manifestation of the free spirit of the new-born democracy. Such a land was prepared in the solitudes of the Western hemisphere.

As "the nation of human progress," with Providence in support and "a clear conscience unsullied by the past," the United States was obviously unstoppable in its "onward march." Others had better take heed:

> The far-reaching, the boundless future will be the era of American greatness. In its magnificent domain of space and time, the nation of many nations is destined to manifest to mankind the excellence of divine principles; to establish on earth the noblest temple ever dedicated to the worship of the Most High—the Sacred and the True.

> For this blessed mission to the nations of the world, which are shut out from the life-giving light of truth, has America been chosen; and her high example shall smite unto death the tyranny of kings, hierarchs, and oligarchs, and carry the glad tidings of peace and good will where myriads now endure an existence scarcely more enviable than that of beasts of the field.

Democracy was in fact nothing "but Christianity in its earthly aspect—Christianity made effective among the political relations of men" by elimination of "the obstacles reared by artificial life." History was a providential plan whose end was to be played out in the specially designed space of America, where Jacksonianism had made manifest and transparent the universal truth of democracy. The cause of humanity was identical with that of the United States; and that cause was "destined to cease only when every man in the world should be finally and triumphantly redeemed." In short, Christianity, democracy, and Jacksonian America were essentially one and the same thing, the highest stage of history, God's plan incarnate.

This would seem to leave the Democrats with nothing much to do except the administration of things and vigilant preservation of the sacred Origin. Yet O'Sullivan still saw need for battle against residual forces of corruption and enemies of truth. Culturally, there was also a tendency to ape European models, "bending the new to foreign idolatry, false tastes, false doctrines, false principles." However, as the very embodiment of historical truth, the people would see to the problem of false idols as well. His conclusion was indeed that the United States would not be led astray because it represented such a sharp break with the past. The "last order" in history was a completely new and completely *clean* civilization, free "from ancient arrangement" and so also free to choose destiny. "The scenes of antiquity" were of interest only as "lessons of avoidance." The future, and the future alone, was what mattered. (Herman Melville, after the Mexican War, put it more poetically: "The Past is a text-book of tyrants; the Future is the Bible of the Free.") The nation, then, was bound by nothing except its founding principles, the eternal and universal principles. It existed, as the "great nation of futurity," only in a perpetual present centered on projects and expectations.

Not much, however, was said about this "futurity," or about what the United States might actually do, other than being marvelous, to smite the tyrants of the world unto death. But gradually after [James K.] Polk's ascendency over Van Buren in 1844, the idea of acquiring boundless expanses of land became prominent. For this land would preserve in neo-Jeffersonian fashion the original moment of freedom as perpetual genesis, struggle, and appropriation. Expansion would afford the swelling masses of the future, the "men of simple habits and strong hands," the opportunity of carving out a properly independent American existence, away from the claws of "the great monopoly paper-coining machine." This utopian impulse was unthinkingly coupled in O'Sullivan, as in so many other Jacksonians, with one speculative scheme after another, in his case wholly without success.

Jacksonian virtue, he firmly believed, translated into a pacific posture vis-à-vis foreign powers. Since people and government were constitutionally identical and the people only wanted "freedom to trade," American foreign policy would always be marked by "*peace* and *good-faith*." In keeping with this concept, the *Review* followed an expansionist but pacific line, differing markedly from the many jingoistic elements within the party. War and blustering talk of national honor were inherently bad, peace and negotiation inherently good. The British, meanwhile, were singled out as particularly nasty exponents of the old anti-ethic of slaughter and conquest. In India and Afghanistan, they had engaged in "constant aggression, without any shadow of excuse or apology." Good thing, then, that the American system did not offer any "pretext of excuse for such wholesale oppression, robbery, and murder."

It is interesting to see this attitude come under pressure during the exciting but stressful sequence of Texas-Oregon-Mexico, which offered some evidence of both "pretexts" and "robbery," engineered by none other than a Jacksonian president. The least difficult question to face here was Oregon. As early as 1843 the *Review* took a maximalist stance, based on a critique of the "monopolistic" Hudson Bay Company. But when the issue heated up, the journal became a voice of moderation on the Democratic side, quietly suggesting extension along the forty-ninth parallel and carefully avoiding bellicose rhetoric. When one author indicated that war, while generally a bad thing, would finally liberate Americans from their cultural "thraldom" to Britain and cleanse "the political atmosphere," he was rebuked in an editorial note that declared war "an unmixed evil in its moral influences" that could never have any "benefits on the national spirit and character." War with the British, cads though they were, would ultimately be a great calamity.

In his short-lived popular paper the *Morning Star,* however, O'Sullivan maintained the original maximalism, while not calling for war. It was in this context that, on December 27, 1845, he proclaimed

> The right of *our manifest destiny* to overspread and to possess the whole continent which providence has given us for the development of the great experiment of liberty and federated self government. [Italics added]

Congress, at the time, was debating Oregon, and a member of the Whig opposition, in the course of denouncing the idea of "a universal Yankee nation," picked up the expression for ridicule, thus inadvertently helping to make it a staple of the political language of American history. But O'Sullivan and others had deployed the two words constantly. He had in fact used the expression six months earlier with regard to Texas annexation without any special notice.

The Oregon issue had barely been settled before the *Review,* in a sudden change of tone, published a lyrical ode to the coming fusion of England's manufacturing and American agriculture through the mechanism of free trade. The occasion was the repeal of the restrictive British corn laws and the commercial visions of American exports that this induced: "the Anglo-Saxon race" would be reunited (under American dominance) and prosperity ensue for all. The new economic theme articulated an underlying fact: powerful Britain, land of the Anglo-Saxons, was not Mexico. The two could not be conceived in the same frame.

A kind of geographical determinism originally governed O'Sullivan's views on Texas. Anyone, he said in April 1844, who "cast a glance over the map of North America" would see that Texas was "a huge fragment, artificially broken off" from its proper continental setting, a setting "symmetrically planned and adapted in its grand destiny" and duly "in the possession of the race sent there for the providential purpose." An impartial observer, therefore, would have to conclude that Texas "*must*, sooner or later, come together into one homogeneous unity" with the rest. Reading maps and spatial configurations in such a manner was common in the educated Western world of the nineteenth century. From a religious viewpoint, it was obvious that God had laid out the landscape with some intention in mind.

From a rationalist perspective it was obvious that nature was not an accidental heap of materials but a system whose inner logic could be uncovered by scientific analysis. The two perspectives generally could indeed be reconciled in "natural theology": the real was rational and thus subject to inherent, natural laws, which in turn had been divinely engineered. In the United States, geographical rationalism had a most reputable pedigree. Jefferson had considered New Orleans a "natural" (hence rightful) possession of the United States, and his comprehension of the Floridas followed the same pattern. Henceforth, cartographically minded politicians would find various "natural borders" to invoke, depending on the historical moment: The St. Lawrence River, the Mississippi, the Rocky Mountains, Hudson Bay, the Gulf of Mexico, the Pacific, the North American continent, even the Sandwich Islands (Hawaii). By the 1850s, it was in fact possible to think of the Caribbean islands as "naturally" American on account of their being the natural, effluvial result of the Mississippi.

Having read his map, O'Sullivan was less sure how to make the natural occur in real life. He was still wedded to the principle of morally impeccable expansion and insisted, therefore, that Mexico must agree before Texas annexation could take place. Such a "poor neighbour" ought not to be bullied. But by early 1845, after his political switch to Polk, he was favoring immediate annexation, now finding the neighborly complaints "the most insolent farce ever attempted even by the bombastic absurdity of Mexican conceit and imbecility." Worse still was the "traitorous Anti-Americanism" at home that was attempting to depict annexation by "misrepresentation and sophism" as "an act of national rapacity, spoliation, and bad faith," whereas in fact the behavior of "our great, pacific and friendly Union" had been extraordinarily restrained. It was with great satisfaction, therefore, that he took note in mid-1845 of the congressional assent to annexation:

> Texas has been absorbed into the Union in the inevitable fulfillment of the general law which is rolling our population westward. . . . It was disintegrated from Mexico in the natural course of events, by a process perfectly legitimate on its own part, blameless on ours; and in which all the censures due to wrong, perfidy and folly, rest on Mexico alone.

He went on to predict that California would be the next candidate for annexation: "Already the advance guard of the irresistible army of Anglo-Saxon emigration has begun to pour down upon it, armed with the plough and the rifle, and marking its trail with schools and colleges, courts and representative halls, mills and meeting-houses." The reality was less idyllic. In 1848, when California did become American territory, the condition of its Hispanic population deteriorated markedly; and when "the irresistible army of Anglo-Saxon emigration" came marching in to pursue land, gold, and profits, it was as usual a genocidal catastrophe for the Indian population.

Once Texas had been secured, O'Sullivan was remarkably quick in speculating on the virtues of gobbling up all of Mexico, laying out before the war the parameters of what would turn into a heated debate only in late 1847. He assumed that the southern neighbor would "become an integral portion of these United States at some future period" but thought it not a good idea for the moment because "the entire Mexican vote would be substantially below our national average both in purity and intelligence." Inclusion might also give rise to consolidated rule from the federal center, always something to be dreaded. Still, the march was on and so an obvious dilemma had arisen: "Democracies must make their conquests by moral agencies. If these are not sufficient, the conquest is robbery." His solution was pacific penetration by *commercial means,* which would "beget a community of interest between us" while suitably instilling in the Mexicans "confidence and respect for our institutions." Americans would gain an outlet for their right to pursue their interest and Mexicans would learn the ways of the future in good time. Through the "moral" education emanating from commerce, then, "the whole of this vast continent is destined one day to subscribe to the Constitution of the United States," whereas "a sword drawn to hasten the event" would detract from its value.

He wrote this to stem a flood of enthusiastic annexationism within his own party in the wake of the Texas victory. There was already a danger, as he saw it, that the United States would "be obliged, in self-defense, to assume an aggressive attitude towards Mexico," in which case it would be exceedingly difficult to avoid "an end short of absolute subjugation." And on that note the matter rested. The *Review* remained conspicuously low-key when war actually did break out. Nothing substantial was in fact said on the subject of Mexico between October 1845 and February 1847. A certain unease about Polk's war was probably one reason; another, more prosaic, was that O'Sullivan sold the journal in 1846, and though he continued to write editorials now and then, the polemics about foreign affairs declined in frequency. He himself commenced a private campaign to persuade the administration to buy Cuba. Polk was won over to the idea, but the ensuing proposal to the Spanish government was rebuffed in no uncertain terms. O'Sullivan then shifted his focus to conquering the islands by conspiring with Cuban interests in the United States, but the ensuing expeditions failed and almost got him convicted of breaking American neutrality laws.

Apprehensions about the legitimacy of the war against Mexico were gone, in any event, when the *Review* resumed serious coverage in 1847. Racial inflections now marked the tone, and the narrative was framed around how constant had been the historical advance of the American "race of hardy pioneers." Thus "barbarism" and "the savages" were said to have given way naturally to "the intelligent and peaceful settler," a process that differed fundamentally and favorably from European models of military invasion. While Americans had shown "democratic energy and enterprise" in "driving back the Indians, or annihilating them as a race," the Spanish conquerors of Mexico had showed no such spirit of mission. But if Christianization, civilization, and cultivation of the land had been sadly lagging, change was now in the works because of "the descent of the northern race." Yet because "the degraded Mexican-Spanish" were in no state to receive the "virtues of the Anglo-Saxon race," there could be no talk of any "political union." That same degradation, however, also made peaceful "accommodation" impossible: the opponent was simply incapable of acting reasonably. The only feasible result of the war, therefore, was "the annihilation" of Mexico "as a nation." Americans were obliged to seize control of the country and "settle its affairs." What O'Sullivan had feared in 1845 had seemingly come to pass.

Yet the Mexican vanishing act, however the *Review* imagined it, could not occur in the near future for there were millions of them; and while one might envisage a time when "every acre of the North American continent" would be peopled "by citizens of the United States," the task of settling the affairs of Mexico was, on balance, fraught with danger to the true spirit of America. A drawn-out effort would stimulate domestic militarism and so create vested interests dominated by the Whigs. Better, then, to take California and New Mexico against proper payment and let time take care of the rest. Nothing, at any rate, was more important than keeping the millions of "proverbially indolent" out of the American "political family."

Thus the prospect of dilution of American purity caused the *Review* to shrink before the actual task of extensive rearrangement of Mexico's affairs. Earlier, O'Sullivan had in fact singled out "homogeneity" as *the* factor that would make the American empire a lasting one. Its territory would be enormous, but similarity of "laws and institutions" would nevertheless make it "compact"; and the people themselves would also "be homogeneous." Other empires, past and present, had fallen precisely because of their "dissimilar and hostile materials." Hence, while "England must fade" and "the colossus of Russia must crumble," the empire of freedom would remain.

And so, one is bound to say, it has happened. The United States would have to go through a wrenching civil war to achieve unity, and the ensuing American empire would eventually be anything but homogeneous in population. But it has lasted in no small measure because of its insistence on constitutional homogeneity, its refusal of any room for territorialized differences of any significance within its continental compass. The precondition of that success, on the other hand, lay in the contradictory process, expressed with unconscious irony above, of peaceable settlers engaged in lofty acts of annihilation. Peace and annihilation were seemingly two sides of the same coin. Meanwhile, the other two empires are now in fact gone, a century or so later than O'Sullivan probably expected but partly for the very reasons he indicated: heterogeneity and "hostile materials." His early notion, it should be added, of elevating Mexico to American standards through the blessings of free trade, achieving the manifest destiny through economic flows, has a certain late-twentieth-century ring to it.

It may be suitable, in view of the general content of the *Review,* to end this exposition in a literary vein with a sonnet by William Gilmore Simms, a leading southern intellectual. His poem appeared in early 1846 under the title "Progress in America":

> The adventurous Spaniard crack'd th' Atlantic's shell—
>   Though not for him to penetrate the core.
> The good old Norman stock will do as well,
>   Nay, better; a selected stock of old
>   With blood well-temper'd, resolute and bold;
> Set for a mighty work, the way to pave
>   For the wrong'd nations, and, in one great fold,
> Unite them, from old tyrannies to save!
> We do but follow out our destiny,
>   As did the ancient Israelite—and strive,
> Unconscious that we work at His decree,
>   By Whom alone we triumph as we live!

These heroic commonplaces of American chosenness expressed a spirit that was least of all "unconscious," as the poet paradoxically argued. Seldom has there been a more articulated, explicit awareness of working His decrees in every way.

Empire by Design, Not Destiny

THOMAS R. HIETALA

The recurring emphasis on material factors in the Democrats' speculations about the need for expansion raises some important questions about the purported idealism of both "Jacksonian Democracy" and manifest destiny. To O'Sullivan and other Democrats, previous territorial acquisitions had been indispensable to the success of the American political and economic system. And though the Jacksonians were convinced of the superiority of popular government, they were much less certain about its viability. Their ambitions for a continental empire represented much more than simple romantic nationalism: they demanded land because they regarded it as the primary prerequisite for republican government and for an economy and society based upon individual acquisitiveness, geographical and social mobility, and a fluid class structure. These beliefs—best expressed by O'Sullivan but articulated by other Democrats as well—were crucial to most Jacksonian policies, especially those promoting territorial and commercial expansion. To consider manifest destiny in the context of such principles of political economy is a way of making more comprehensible the sustained drive for empire in the 1840s.

Misconceptions about manifest destiny still influence Americans' impressions about their nation's history. Although the civil rights struggle and the Vietnam War have led many Americans to question several of the prevailing orthodoxies of United States history, popular attitudes about the country's past—the self-concept of Americans and their definition of their nation's role in world affairs—have shown a remarkable resiliency, despite the challenges of revisionist scholars. Prevailing ideas about westward expansion are inextricably linked to the values associated with American exceptionalism and mission, fundamental components of the Jacksonian creed. The persistence of manifest destiny ideology under radically different political, economic, and military realities since the 1840s attests to the significant impact these legitimizing myths of empire have had on popular beliefs about United States history. Since continental expansion gave birth to and nurtured so many nationalistic myths, a reevaluation of the historical circumstances that spawned them is an essential exercise in the reassessment of the American past. . . .

Jacksonians exalted the pioneer as the epitome of the common man, and they celebrated American expansion as an integral part of their mission to obtain a better nation and a better world based on individual freedom, liberalized international trade, and peaceful coexistence. The Democrats equated American progress with global progress and repeatedly argued that European oligarchs were actually opposing the interests of their own people by trying to discourage the expansion of the United States. Geographically and ideologically separated from Europe, the United States, under Jacksonian direction, tried to improve its democratic institutions, utilize the land's rich resources, and demonstrate to the world the superiority of a system allowing free men to compete in a dynamic society. Consequently, the impact of the pioneering process transcended the concerns of the frontiersmen. In forming

---

"a more perfect union" on a continually expanding frontier, Americans thought that they were actually serving the cause of all mankind.

Such a melding of exceptionalism and empire permitted the Jacksonians the luxury of righteous denunciation of their critics at home and abroad. Their domestic foes could be paired with European monarchs as spokesmen for an old order of aristocracy, privilege, and proscription; American expansionism and the Jacksonian domestic program, on the other hand, represented the antithesis of traditional systems. Since territorial acquisitions and Democratic policies fostered opportunity and democracy, they liberated men from oppressive social and economic relationships. The Jacksonians' program promised so much for so little; no wonder messianic imagery appeared so frequently in their rhetoric.

Skeptical Whigs often challenged the Democrats' sincerity, however, sensing that the Jacksonians' motives for aggrandizement were more selfish than they usually admitted. The Democrats' rhetoric proved more resilient than the Whigs' trenchant criticisms of "manifest destiny," however, and so subsequent generations of Americans have underestimated the extent and the intensity of opposition to the policies behind expansionism in the 1840s, especially the Mexican War. . . .

The expansionism of the 1840s acquires a new significance, however, when it is considered within the context of the cultural, social, and political factors that motivated the Jacksonians to pursue a continental empire. In promoting the acquisition of new lands and new markets, the Democrats greatly exaggerated the extent of European hostility to the United States and refused to admit the duplicity and brutality behind their own efforts to expand their nation's territory and trade. By joining their concepts of exceptionalism and empire, the expansionists found a rationale for denying to all other nations and peoples, whether strong or weak, any right to any portion of the entire North American continent. If a rival was strong, it posed a threat to American security and had to be removed; if a rival was weak, it proved its inferiority and lent sanction to whatever actions were taken by pioneers or policy makers to make the territory a part of the United States.

The confusion surrounding expansion results in part from the ambivalence of the Jacksonians themselves, who demonstrated both compassion and contempt in their policies, depending on the racial and ethnic identities of the peoples to be affected by Democratic measures. Generous and humane toward impoverished Americans and poor immigrants from Europe, the Democrats showed far less concern for nonwhites whom they dispossessed or exploited in the process of westward expansion and national development. Removal, eclipse, or extermination—not acculturation and assimilation—awaited the Indians, blacks, and mixed-blood Mexicans on the continent. Despite occasional statements to the contrary, the expansionists regarded the incorporation of nonwhite peoples into the country as both unlikely and undesirable. Without hint of hypocrisy the Jacksonians sought lenient naturalization laws and opportunities for newcomers while strenuously defending policies to separate Indians and Mexicans from their lands and programs to relocate blacks to Africa and Central America. . . .

Jeffersonian ideology, especially its romantic agrarianism, its fear of industrialization, and its conviction that the United States had a natural right to free trade, contributed significantly to the ideology of manifest destiny. To the Jeffersonians and Jacksonians, American farms raised good republican citizens as well as corn, cotton, and wheat: cultivated fields produced virtuous, cultivated people. Whatever the realities of the late Jacksonian period, the expansionists insisted that agricultural societies fostered opportunity and political equality, the essential features of American uniqueness. Moreover, the neo-Jeffersonians contended that only industrial nations became international predators; agricultural countries were self-contained and did not need colonies or privileged markets. These misconceptions cloak some of the more unflattering aspects of antebellum economy and society: slavemasters, not sturdy yeomen, dominated the social and political life of the South; the country's most important export crops, cotton and tobacco, were produced by forced labor; Indians were cruelly dispossessed of their lands and often their culture to make room for American producers; "go-ahead" Americans frequently seemed more interested in land speculation schemes than in patient tilling of the soil; and the United States, like other empires, did prey upon other peoples and nations to augment its wealth, power, and security.

The fact that the United States acquired contiguous rather than noncontiguous territory makes American aggrandizement no less imperial than that of other empires of the mid-nineteenth century. The United States enjoyed several advantages that facilitated its enlargement and made it more antiseptic. Mexico's weakness, the inability of Indian tribes to unite and resist dispossession, the decline of France and Spain as colonizing powers in the New World, and geographical isolation from Europe all served the interests of the United States as it spread across the continent. In addition, the preference for an anticolonial empire embodied in the concept of a confederated Union also contributed to American success. But many Democrats wanted to venture beyond the continent, and had the party not become so divided during and after the Mexican War, the Polk administration probably would have taken steps to add Yucatán and Cuba to the United States, thereby extending the empire into the Caribbean.

The urge to expand beyond the continent was diminished by the fact that the continent itself was incredibly rich in resources. Those abundant resources provided the basis for unparalleled economic growth at home and power in relations with countries abroad. The expansionists regarded the nation's productivity as an irresistible weapon that could counterbalance the military strength of Europe. Here, again, an old Jeffersonian perception dating back to the 1790s came into play: the world desperately needed American commerce and would sacrifice a great deal to obtain it. Although the expansionists never had cause to drive the masses of Europe to starvation and revolution through an embargo on grain and cotton, their speculations on the subject showed them to be far more imperial than philanthropic in their attitudes toward their nation's wealth.

Distressed by many trends in American life, the Democrats formulated their domestic and foreign policies to safeguard themselves and their progeny for a potentially dismal future. They hoped to prevent domestic disturbances by acquiring additional territory and markets. Other measures were also devised to protect the country from various perils: the Democrats discouraged the growth of manufacturing and monopolistic banking, attempted to minimize the conflict over slavery, encouraged the sale and settlement of the national domain, and tried to discredit the efforts of dissidents to form third parties that might jeopardize the two-party system. . . .

Another myth of manifest destiny concerns the role of military power in American expansion. On May 11, 1846, President Polk informed Congress that "after reiterated menaces, Mexico has passed the boundary of the United States, has invaded our territory and shed American blood upon the American soil." War had begun, Polk observed, in spite of "all our efforts to avoid it." Much evidence, however, raises doubts about just how hard Polk tried to prevent war. Six weeks before Polk's war message, for example, Captain William S. Henry, a subordinate commander in [General Zachary] Taylor's army en route to the city of Matamoras, noted in his journal, "Our situation is truly extraordinary: right in the enemy's country (to all appearance), actually occupying their corn and cotton fields, the people of the soil leaving their homes, and we, with a small handful of men, marching with colors flying and drums beating, right under the very guns of one of their principal cities, displaying the star-spangled banner, as if in defiance, under their very nose." This army's purpose was not limited to the defense of Texas. It is true that the United States claimed the Rio Grande as the border; it is also true that the United States, in the person of James K. Polk, claimed that the nation had a "clear and unquestionable" title to Oregon up to 54° 40′. But the issue for the Polk administration was not the validity of various boundary claims, but rather the issue of whether military pressure could force Mexico to relinquish the disputed territory between the Nueces and Rio Grande, and the undisputed territories of New Mexico and California besides. The Democrats chose war to defend an unclear and questionable title in the Southwest but retreated from a supposedly clear and unquestionable title in the Northwest. The hypocrisy did not escape the Whigs. . . .

Polk . . . acted as imperially as any of his twentieth-century successors. Democratic process and an aggressive foreign policy were as incompatible in the mid-nineteenth century as in the twentieth, as congressional critics frequently noted. In late 1846, for example, Whig Garrett Davis pointed out that the founding fathers had "entrusted to the president the national shield," but they had intentionally given the national sword and "the entire war power" to Congress. "To make war is the most fearful power exerted by human government," Davis warned, a power too momentous to be placed in any one man's hands. That admonition was out of fashion for two decades after World War II, but Vietnam gave it new meaning. In the 1840s and in the 1960s, Congress was remiss in its responsibility to scrutinize how American military power was used, for what purposes, and under what pretenses. In both cases a scheming president misled Congress into sanctioning a wider war than anticipated. . . .

Orthodox historical "truths" possess considerable resiliency. By extolling the virtues and achievements of a self-conscious people, they appeal to nationalistic feeling, and through constant repetition they acquire an aura of unquestioned certainty over time. The idealism of westward expansion embodied in the concept of manifest destiny persists because it helps to reconcile American imperialism with an extremely favorable national image. The assumed benevolence and the supposedly accidental nature of American expansion are convenient evasions of the complexities of the past. In accepting the rhetoric of American mission and destiny, apologists for the expansionists of the 1840s have had to minimize or ignore much historical evidence. Perhaps more to the point, defenders of American exceptionalism and innocence have actually had to slight other crucial motives for expansion that the Democrats themselves often candidly admitted.

Though the phrase *manifest destiny* appears repeatedly in the literature of American foreign relations, it does not accurately describe the expansionism of the 1840s.

It is one of many euphemisms that have allowed several generations of Americans to maintain an unwarranted complacency in regard to their nation's past, a complacency that has contributed in a fundamental way to the persistent quandary the United States has faced in trying to define a realistic role for itself in a world that seldom acts according to American precepts. Geographical isolation and a powerful exceptionalist ideology have insulated the United States from the complexities of culture and historical experience affecting other peoples, leaving Americans susceptible to myths and misconceptions at home and abroad. Often unaware of their own history, Americans frequently misunderstand foreign cultures and experiences as well. Myths and misconceptions often fill the void created by ignorance of history.

The expansionists of the 1840s should not be permitted to expropriate many of the best American ideals for their own purposes. . . . [They exploited] American exceptionalist ideology to ennoble their ambitions for riches and dominion. But rhetoric could not hide the chauvinism, aggressiveness, and design that were essential components of continental expansion. The United States used many tactics to expand its domain, and like other empires it created legitimizing myths to sanction that expansion. Some Americans, however, challenged the validity of those myths and condemned the conduct they excused. But critics of national policy seldom reach generations other than their own, for history—especially American history—often records only the dominant voices of the past. That the United States has changed dramatically since attaining its continental empire is obvious. That the American people have reassessed their basic assumptions about themselves, their national experience, and their approach to other nations is not so obvious.

FURTHER READING

Jeremy Adelman and Stephen Aaron, "From Borderlands to Borders: Empires, Nation-States, and the People in Between in North American History," *American Historical Review* 104 (June 1999): 814–841

K. Jack Bauer, *Zachary Taylor* (1985)

Maurice G. Baxter, *One and Inseparable: Daniel Webster and the Union* (1984)

Paul H. Bergeron, *The Presidency of James K. Polk* (1987)

Albert Boime, *The Magisterial Gaze: Manifest Destiny in American Landscape Painting* (1991)

Gene Brack, *Mexico Views Manifest Destiny, 1821–1846* (1975)

Kinley Brauer, "The Great American Desert Revisited: Recent Literature and Prospects for the Study of American Foreign Relations, 1815–1861," *Diplomatic History* 3 (1989): 395–417

Charles H. Brown, *Agents of Manifest Destiny* (1980)

Richard Griswold del Castillo, *The Treaty of Guadalupe-Hidalgo* (1990)

Nathan J. Citino, "The Global Frontier: Comparative History and the Frontier-Borderlands Approach in American Foreign Relations" in *Explaining the History of American Foreign Relations,* ed. Michael J. Hogan and Thomas G. Paterson (2004), 194–211

Richard Drinnon, *Facing West* (1980)

John Eisenhower, *So Far from God: The U.S. War with Mexico* (1989)

William H. Goetzmann, *New Lands, New Men* (1987)

Norman A. Graebner, *Manifest Destiny* (1968)

Neal Harlow, *California Conquered* (1982)

Sam W. Haynes, *James K. Polk and the Expansionist Impulse* (2002)

Reginald Horsman, *Race and Manifest Destiny* (1981)

Albert L. Hurtado, *Intimate Frontiers* (1999) (on gender and culture)

Robert W. Johannsen, *To the Halls of Montezuma* (1985)

Howard Jones and Donald A. Rakestraw, *Prologue to Manifest Destiny* (1995)

Wilbur D. Jones, *The American Problem in British Diplomacy, 1841–1861* (1974)

Amy Kaplan, *The Anarchy of Empire in the Making of U.S. Culture* (2002)

Ernest M. Lander Jr., *Reluctant Imperialists: Calhoun, the South Carolinians, and the Mexican War* (1980)

Thomas M. Leonard, *James K. Polk* (2000)

Robert E. May, *Manifest Destiny's Underworld* (2002) (on filibusters)

Frederick Merk, *Manifest Destiny and Mission in American History* (1963)

Christopher Morris and Sam W. Haynes, eds., *Manifest Destiny and Empire* (1998)

Anna K. Nelson, *Secret Agents: President Polk and the Search for Peace with Mexico* (1988)

Gregory H. Nobles, *American Frontiers* (1997)

Glenn W. Price, *Origins of the War with Mexico: The Polk-Stockton Intrigue* (1967)

W. Dirk Raat, *Mexico and the United States* (1993)

Leonard L. Richards, *The Life and Times of Congressman John Quincy Adams* (1986)

Cecil Robinson, ed., *The View from Chapultepec* (1989)

Jaime E. Rodriguez, *Down from Colonialism: Mexico's Nineteenth Century Crisis* (1983)

——— and Kathryn Vincent, *Myths, Misdeeds, and Misunderstandings* (1997) (on Mexican-U.S. relations)

Ramón Eduardo Ruíz, *Triumphs and Tragedies* (1992)

John H. Schroeder, *Mr. Polk's War* (1973)

John Seigenthaler, *James K. Polk* (2001)

Paul A. Varg, *United States Foreign Relations, 1820–1860* (1979)

Josefina Vázquez and Lorenzo Meyer, *The United States and Mexico* (1985)

David J. Weber, *The Mexican Frontier, 1821–1846* (1982)

———, *"From Hell Itself": The Americanization of Mexico's Northern Frontier, 1821–1846* (1983)

Richard Bruce Winders, *Crisis in the Southwest* (2002) (on Texas)

CHAPTER
7

The Spanish-American-
Cuban-Filipino War

Sectional strife over slavery and the Civil War cooled the expansionist fervor of the
early nineteenth century. But once the national crisis had subsided, expansionists
again took up the call, spurred along by the new globalizing trends of the late
nineteenth century. The industrial revolution, transoceanic telegraph cables, and
steam-powered shipping connected nations and peoples as never before. Overseas
trade expanded, American consumers increasingly coveted imported goods, Christian
missionaries scoured Asia in search of converts, the U.S. navy sought overseas
coaling stations, and America exchanged a growing number of travelers and
tourists with distant lands. U.S. officials during the late 1890s enunciated the
"Open Door" policy—appealing to the great powers of Europe and Japan to
surrender special trading privileges in dynastic China and elsewhere in favor of
free trade. At the same time, post–Civil War leaders decreed it to be America's manly
duty and civilizing mission to acquire colonies for itself in the Caribbean and
Pacific regions. The U.S. government did not pursue an expansionist policy in all
cases. For example, Congress approved Secretary of State William H. Seward's
(1861–1869) acquisition of the immense Alaska territory, and the tiny Midway
Islands, but rejected President Ulysses S. Grant's attempt to annex the Dominican
Republic in the Caribbean. Congress embraced the cause of "Pan Americanism,"
but it maintained high tariffs that stifled inter-American trade. After the 1860s,
the United States nonetheless pushed its territorial, commercial, and cultural frontiers farther abroad and became a major participant in the international power
struggles of the early twentieth century.

    The United States reached a diplomatic crossroads in 1898 when it intervened
in colonial rebellions in Cuba and in the Philippines, both against Spain. Cubans
launched their revolt in 1895, and by the end of the following year, rebel forces
controlled two-thirds of the island's territory. Beleaguered Spanish officials tried to
halt the deterioration of their imperial position by implementing the reconcentrado
policy, which uprooted rural populations and forced them into government-run
concentration camps. The unsanitary conditions and high death rates in the camps,
and Spain's brutal repression of the Cuban rebels, shocked people around the
world, including many North Americans. U.S. businesses on the island, especially

entrenched in the sugar industry, worried about their investment of some $50 million. The administration of William McKinley encouraged Spain to negotiate an end to the violence, but both Spaniards and Cubans proved intransigent. The publication in early February 1898 of a private letter written by the Spanish minister in Washington, Enrique Dupuy de Lôme, harshly critical of President McKinley's leadership, added further fuel to the crisis. When the Maine exploded in Havana harbor on February 15, killing 266 crew members, many Americans instantly blamed Spanish authorities and the public clamor for war intensified. Impatient with revolutionary disorder so near the United States and thinking diplomacy unworkable, McKinley asked Congress in April 1898 for authority to take up arms against Spain.

The United States and Spain initially came to blows over Cuba, but the first major battle of the war occurred elsewhere in the Spanish empire. Admiral George Dewey's victory over the Spanish flotilla in Manila Bay on May 1, 1898, thrilled most Americans, but the nation soon faced the question of what to do with the Philippines. Although the United States at first joined with Emilio Aguinaldo's Filipino anticolonial forces, the McKinley administration opposed Philippine independence. Wishing to secure commercial and military advantages, McKinley decided the entire archipelago should be annexed as a U.S. colony. The Treaty of Paris signed by a defeated Spain on December 10, 1898, ceded all of the Philippines— along with Guam and Puerto Rico—to the United States. "Anti-Imperialists" opposed the acquisition of the Philippines, arguing that empire would violate the principle of self-determination, be expensive to hold, empower the president at Congress's expense, and incorporate within the republic "undesirable" non-Anglo-Saxon subjects. After a contentious debate, the U.S. Senate on February 6, 1900, approved the Treaty of Paris. From 1899 to 1902 U.S. troops crushed a Philippine insurrection that cost 5,000 Americans and over 200,000 Filipino lives. As the Philippine-American war raged, President McKinley vowed to prepare his "little brown brothers" for democratic self-rule and U.S. officials planned programs to promote education, and the building of roads, harbors, and hospitals.

Most scholars agree that the war with Spain marked a turning point in the history of U.S. foreign relations. Having secured overseas colonial possessions, the United States moved quickly to expand its empire and in 1903 gained a naval base and the right to intervene militarily in Cuban affairs by requiring Cuba's new government to attach the U.S.-authored Platt Amendment to the country's constitution. The acquisition of a transoceanic canal zone in Panama the same year, followed by a string of U.S. military occupations in the Caribbean and Central America further established U.S. hegemony in Latin America. Thus did the United States emerge as an important player in the vigorous, great power rivalry that reshaped international relations during the late nineteenth and early twentieth centuries. Why did the United States decide to fight Spain? Some historians argue that humanitarian concerns for Cuba, amplified by a sensationalist press, demanded it. Others maintain that war arose from a deliberate policy of expansionism driven by economic, military, and cultural motives, which denied Cuba its true independence. In assessing William McKinley's leadership, some scholars portray the president as a weak, ineffectual politician swept along by the winds of public opinion. Others see in him a calculating chief executive who believed in empire and skillfully maneuvered toward war.

This chapter addresses these issues and poses one last, fundamental set of questions. Was Washington's ultimate object in going to war a dependent Cuba, incapable of resisting U.S. hegemony? Or did the United States seek to provide Cuba with the *gift of independence from colonial rule? Finally, how did the Philippines figure into the imperial vision? Grappling with these questions helps to understand America's rise as a modern global power.*

⊕ D O C U M E N T S

José Martí, the political and intellectual leader of the Cuban independence movement, returned home in April 1895 from exile in the United States, hoping to direct the final stages of the rebellion. But Martí lost his life in a skirmish with Spanish troops on the morning of May 19, 1895. In his last letter, Document 1, he warns fellow rebel Manuel Mercado about U.S. imperialism and lashes out at those Cubans who advocated compromise with Spain or annexation to the "monster" of the north. In mid-December 1897 the Spanish minister to the United States, Enrique Dupuy de Lôme, sent a letter to a senior Spanish official that described President William McKinley as a weak, self-seeking politician. Intercepted by a rebel sympathizer and leaked to William Randolph Hearst's *New York Journal,* the de Lôme letter, reprinted here as Document 2, helped turn McKinley sour on Spain and galvanized support for Cuba. During the spring of 1898 a growing chorus of Congressional critics, including members of McKinley's Republican party, denounced Spain's harsh repression of the rebel movement, including Madrid's *reconcentrado* policy. Document 3, a political cartoon that appeared in April 1898, demonstrates that the press and the public often viewed the confrontation with Spain as a test of American manliness. The illustration depicts Cuba as a ravished woman, victimized by a brutalizing Spain—as Uncle Sam prepares to defend Cuba's feminine virtue. Document 4, another cartoon published the following month, calls into question President William McKinley's decisiveness and manhood by portraying the commander in chief as an old woman trying to sweep back popular pressures for war. During late March and early April the McKinley administration's posture toward Spain stiffened as Washington's attempts at arbitration proved futile. Madrid agreed to end reconcentration and seek an armistice, but resisted U.S. mediation. Cuba's rebels demanded independence and spurned talks altogether. In his war message of April 11, 1898, Document 5, President McKinley explains why he thought the United States had to take up arms.

War with Spain immediately raised the issue of Cuba's postwar status. Would the island be granted independence, or would it become a dependent of the United States? Following negotiations with the McKinley administration, Congress on April 20, 1898, passed the Teller Amendment. The fourth article of that joint resolution, which appears as Document 6, disavowed any U.S. attempt to annex Cuba. Military success in the Philippines, and Spain's cession of the archipelago to the United States in the Treaty of Paris, also raised the question of Filipino independence. After the defeat of Spanish colonial rule, fighting broke out in February 1899 between U.S. troops and Emilio Aguinaldo's nationalist forces. With the Treaty of Paris still pending before the U.S. Senate, debate erupted in the United States between imperialists and anti-imperialists over the war in the Philippines and overseas empire. The Platform of the Anti-Imperialist League (October 17, 1899), Document 7, spoke eloquently against empire. On November 21, 1899, President McKinley defended his decision to colonize the Philippines to a visiting delegation of Methodist church leaders. Reprinted as Document 8, McKinley portrays the United States as a reluctant imperialist and insists the decision to retain the Philippines derived from Christian conscience. As war raged in the Philippines, Congress passed the Platt Amendment, Document 9, which placed substantial restrictions on Cuba's independence. Written in Washington in 1901, attached to Cuba's constitution in 1902, and included in the U.S.-Cuba treaty signed May 22, 1903, it remained in force until it was abrogated in 1934.

1. Cuban Nationalist José Martí Cautions Against Annexation to the United States, 1895

Now I can write, now I can tell you how tenderly and gratefully and respectfully I love you and that home [Cuba] which I consider my pride and responsibility. I am in daily danger of giving my life for my country and duty, for I understand that duty and have the courage to carry it out—the duty of preventing the United States from spreading through the Antilles as Cuba gains its independence, and from overpowering with that additional strength our lands of America. All I have done so far, and all I will do, is for this purpose. I have had to work quietly and somewhat indirectly, because to achieve certain objectives, they must be kept under cover; to proclaim them for what they are would raise such difficulties that the objectives could not be realized.

The same general and lesser duties of these nations—nations such as yours and mine that are most vitally concerned with preventing the opening in Cuba (by annexation on the part of the imperialists from there and the Spaniards) of the road that is to be closed, and is being closed with our blood, annexing our American nations to the brutal and turbulent North which despises them—prevented their apparent adherence and obvious assistance to this sacrifice made for their immediate benefit.

I have lived in the monster [the United States] and I know its entrails; my sling is David's. At this very moment—well, some days ago—amid the cheers of victory with which the Cubans saluted our free departure from the mountains where the six men of our expedition walked for fourteen days, a correspondent from the [*New York*] *Herald,* who tore me out of the hammock in my hut, told me about the annexationist movement. He claimed it was less to be feared because of the unrealistic approach of its aspirants, undisciplined or uncreative men of a legalistic turn of mind, who in the comfortable disguise of their complacency or their submission to Spain, halfheartedly ask it for Cuba's autonomy. They are satisfied merely that there be a master—Yankee or Spanish—to support them or reward their services as go-betweens with positions of power enabling them to scorn the hardworking masses—the country's halfbreeds, skilled and pathetic, the intelligent and creative hordes of Negroes and white men. . . .

I am doing my duty here. The Cuban war, a reality of higher priority than the vague and scattered desires of the Cuban and Spanish annexationists, whose alliance with the Spanish government would only give them relative power, has come to America in time to prevent Cuba's annexation to the United States, even against all those freely used forces. The United States will never accept from a country at war, nor can it incur, the hateful and absurd commitment of discouraging, on its account and with its weapons, an American war of independence, for the war will not accept annexation. . . .

The formation of our utilitarian yet simple government can still take two more months, if it is to be stable and realistic. Our spirit is one, the will of the country, and I know it. But these things are always a matter of communication, influence, and accommodation. In my capacity as representative, I do not want to do anything that may appear to be a capricious extension of it. I arrived in a boat with General Máximo Gómez and four others. I was in charge of the lead oar during a storm, and we landed at an unknown quarry on one of our beaches. For fourteen days I carried my rifle and knapsack, marching through bramble patches and over hills. We gathered people along the way. In the benevolence of men's souls I feel the root of my affection for their suffering, and my just desire to eliminate it. The countryside is unquestionably ours to the extent that in a single month I could hear but one blast of gunfire.

2. Spanish Minister Enrique Dupuy de Lôme Criticizes President William McKinley, 1897

The situation here [in Washington, D.C.] remains the same. Everything depends on the political and military outcome in Cuba. The prologue of all this, in this second stage (phase) of the war, will end the day when the colonial cabinet shall be appointed and we shall be relieved in the eyes of this country of a part of the responsibility for what is happening in Cuba, while the Cubans, whom these people think so immaculate, will have to assume it.

Until then, nothing can be clearly seen, and I regard it as a waste of time and progress, by a wrong road, to be sending emissaries to the rebel camp, or to negotiate with the autonomists who have as yet no legal standing, or to try to ascertain the intentions and plans of this Government. The [Cuban] refugees will keep on returning one by one, and as they do so will make their way into the sheepfold, while the leaders in the field will gradually come back. Neither the one nor the other class had the courage to leave in a body and they will not be brave enough to return in a body.

The message has been a disillusion to the insurgents, who expected something different; but I regard it as bad (for us).

Besides the ingrained and inevitable bluntness with which is repeated all that the press and public opinion in Spain have said about [Spanish governor-general Valeriano] Weyler, it once more shows what [President William] McKinley is, weak and a bidder for the admiration of the crowd, besides being a would-be politician who tries to leave a door open behind himself while keeping on good terms with the jingoes of his party.

Nevertheless, whether the practical results of it [the presidential message to Congress] are to be injurious and adverse depends only upon ourselves.

I am entirely of your opinions; without a military end of the matter nothing will be accomplished in Cuba, and without a military and political settlement there will always be the danger of encouragement being given to the insurgents by a part of the public opinion if not by the Government.

I do not think sufficient attention has been paid to the part England is playing.

This document can be found in John Bassett Moore, *A Digest of International Law* (Washington, D.C.: Goverment Printing Office, 1906), VI, 176–177.

Nearly all the newspaper rabble that swarms in your hotels are Englishmen, and while writing for the *Journal* they are also correspondents of the most influential journals and reviews of London. It has been so ever since this thing began. As I look at it, England's only object is that the Americans should amuse themselves with us and leave her alone, and if there should be a war, that would the better stave off the conflict which she dreads but which will never come about.

It would be very advantageous to take up, even if only for effect, the question of commercial relations, and to have a man of some prominence sent hither in order that I may make use of him here to carry on a propaganda among the Senators and others in opposition to the [Cuban] junta and to try to win over the refugees.

3. "Peace—But Quit That": Uncle Sam Defends Cuba's Feminine Virtue, 1898

This document can be found in *New York World* in *Review of Reviews,* April 1898. The President and Fellows of Harvard College: from HOLLIS #001975444.

4. "Another Old Woman Tries to Sweep Back the Sea": Critics Lampoon President McKinley as Indecisive and Unmanly, 1898

5. McKinley Asks Congress to Authorize War on Spain, 1898

Obedient to that precept of the Constitution which commands the President to give from time to time to the Congress information of the state of the Union and to recommend to their consideration such measures as he shall judge necessary and expedient, it becomes my duty to now address your body with regard to the grave crisis that has arisen in the relations of the United States to Spain by reason of the warfare that for more than three years has raged in the neighboring island of Cuba.

I do so because of the intimate connection of the Cuban question with the state of our own Union and the grave relation the course which it is now incumbent upon the nation to adopt must needs bear to the traditional policy of our Government if it

Document 4 can be found in *New York Journal* in *Review of Reviews,* May 1898. The President and Fellows of Harvard College: from HOLLIS # 001975444.

Document 5 can be found in John Bassett Moore, *A Digest of International Law* (Washington, D.C.: Government Printing Office, 1906), VI, 211–223.

is to accord with the precepts laid down by the founders of the Republic and religiously observed by succeeding Administrations to the present day.

The present revolution is but the successor of other similar insurrections which have occurred in Cuba against the dominion of Spain, extending over a period of nearly half a century, each of which during its progress has subjected the United States to great effort and expense in enforcing its neutrality laws, caused enormous losses to American trade and commerce, caused irritation, annoyance, and disturbance among our citizens, and, by the exercise of cruel, barbarous, and uncivilized practices of warfare, shocked the sensibilities and offended the humane sympathies of our people. . . .

Our people have beheld a once prosperous community reduced to comparative want, its lucrative commerce virtually paralyzed, its exceptional productiveness diminished, its fields laid waste, its mills in ruins, and its people perishing by tens of thousands from hunger and destitution. We have found ourselves constrained, in the observance of that strict neutrality which our laws enjoin and which the law of nations commands, to police our own waters and watch our own seaports in prevention of any unlawful act in aid of the Cubans.

Our trade has suffered, the capital invested by our citizens in Cuba has been largely lost, and the temper and forbearance of our people have been so sorely tried as to beget a perilous unrest among our own citizens, which has inevitably found its expression from time to time in the National Legislature, so that issues wholly external to our own body politic engross attention and stand in the way of that close devotion to domestic advancement that becomes a self-contained commonwealth whose primal maxim has been the avoidance of all foreign entanglements. All this must needs awaken, and has, indeed, aroused, the utmost concern on the part of this Government, as well during my predecessor's term as in my own. . . .

The war in Cuba is of such a nature that, short of subjugation or extermination, a final military victory for either side seems impracticable. The alternative lies in the physical exhaustion of the one or the other party, or perhaps of both—a condition which in effect ended the ten years' war [Cuba's separatist uprising, 1868–1878] by the truce of Zanjon. The prospect of such a protraction and conclusion of the present strife is a contingency hardly to be contemplated with equanimity by the civilized world, and least of all by the United States, affected and injured as we are, deeply and intimately, by its very existence.

Realizing this, it appeared to be my duty, in a spirit of true friendliness, no less to Spain than to the Cubans, who have so much to lose by the prolongation of the struggle, to seek to bring about an immediate termination of the war. To this end I submitted on the 27th ultimo, as a result of much representation and correspondence, through the United States minister at Madrid, propositions to the Spanish Government looking to an armistice until October 1 for the negotiation of peace with the good offices of the President.

In addition I asked the immediate revocation of the order of reconcentration, so as to permit the people to return to their farms and the needy to be relieved with provisions and supplies from the United States, cooperating with the Spanish authorities, so as to afford full relief.

The reply of the Spanish cabinet was received on the night of the 31st ultimo. It offered, as the means to bring about peace in Cuba, to confide the preparation thereof to the insular parliament, inasmuch as the concurrence of that body would be necessary to reach a final result, it being, however, understood that the powers reserved by the constitution to the central Government are not lessened or diminished. As the Cuban parliament does not meet until the 4th of May next, the Spanish Government would not object for its part to accept at once a suspension of hostilities if asked for by the insurgents from the general in chief, to whom it would pertain in such case to determine the duration and conditions of the armistice. . . .

With this last overture in the direction of immediate peace, and its disappointing reception by Spain, the Executive is brought to the end of his effort. . . .

The grounds for . . . intervention may be briefly summarized as follows:

First. In the cause of humanity and to put an end to the barbarities, bloodshed, starvation, and horrible miseries now existing there, and which the parties to the conflict are either unable or unwilling to stop or mitigate. It is no answer to say this is all in another country, belonging to another nation, and is therefore none of our business. It is specially our duty, for it is right at our door.

Second. We owe it to our citizens in Cuba to afford them that protection and indemnity for life and property which no government there can or will afford, and to that end to terminate the conditions that deprive them of legal protection.

Third. The right to intervene may be justified by the very serious injury to the commerce, trade, and business of our people and by the wanton destruction of property and devastation of the island.

Fourth, and which is of the utmost importance. The present condition of affairs in Cuba is a constant menace to our peace and entails upon this Government an enormous expense. With such a conflict waged for years in an island so near us and with which our people have such trade and business relations; when the lives and liberty of our citizens are in constant danger and their property destroyed and themselves ruined; where our trading vessels are liable to seizure and are seized at our very door by war ships of a foreign nation; the expeditions of filibustering that we are powerless to prevent altogether, and the irritating questions and entanglements thus arising—all these and others that I need not mention, with the resulting strained relations, are a constant menace to our peace and compel us to keep on a semi war footing with a nation with which we are at peace. . . .

In view of these facts and of these considerations I ask the Congress to authorize and empower the President to take measures to secure a full and final termination of hostilities between the Government of Spain and the people of Cuba, and to secure in the island the establishment of a stable government, capable of maintaining order and observing its international obligations, insuring peace and tranquillity and the security of its citizens as well as our own, and to use the military and naval forces of the United States as may be necessary for these purposes.

And in the interest of humanity and to aid in preserving the lives of the starving people of the island I recommend that the distribution of food and supplies be continued and that an appropriation be made out of the public Treasury to supplement the charity of our citizens.

The issue is now with the Congress. It is a solemn responsibility. I have exhausted every effort to relieve the intolerable condition of affairs which is at our doors. Prepared to execute every obligation imposed upon me by the Constitution and the law, I await your action.

Yesterday, and since the preparation of the foregoing message, official information was received by me that the latest decree of the Queen Regent of Spain directs

General Blanco, in order to prepare and facilitate peace, to proclaim a suspension of hostilities, the duration and details of which have not yet been communicated to me.

This fact, with every other pertinent consideration, will, I am sure, have your just and careful attention in the solemn deliberations upon which you are about to enter. If this measure attains a successful result, then our aspirations as a Christian, peace-loving people will be realized. If it fails, it will be only another justification for our contemplated action.

6. The Teller Amendment Disavows the U.S. Annexation of Cuba, 1898

The United States hereby disclaims any disposition or intention to exercise sovereignty, jurisdiction, or control over said island [Cuba] except for the pacification thereof, and asserts its determination when that is accomplished to leave the government and control of the island to its people.

7. American Anti-Imperialist League Platform, 1899

We hold that the policy known as imperialism is hostile to liberty and tends toward militarism, an evil from which it has been our glory to be free. We regret that it has become necessary in the land of Washington and Lincoln to reaffirm that all men, of whatever race or color, are entitled to life, liberty and the pursuit of happiness. We maintain that governments derive their just powers from the consent of the governed. We insist that the subjugation of any people is "criminal aggression" and open disloyalty to the distinctive principles of our Government.

We earnestly condemn the policy of the present National Administration in the Philippines. It seeks to extinguish the spirit of 1776 in those islands. We deplore the sacrifice of our soldiers and sailors, whose bravery deserves admiration even in an unjust war. We denounce the slaughter of the Filipinos as a needless horror. We protest against the extension of American sovereignty by Spanish methods.

We demand the immediate cessation of the war against liberty, begun by Spain and continued by us. We urge that Congress be promptly convened to announce to the Filipinos our purpose to concede to them the independence for which they have so long fought and which of right is theirs.

The United States have always protested against the doctrine of international law which permits the subjugation of the weak by the strong. A self-governing state cannot accept sovereignty over an unwilling people. The United States cannot act upon the ancient heresy that might makes right.

Imperialists assume that with the destruction of self-government in the Philippines by American hands, all opposition here will cease. This is a grievous error. Much as we abhor the war of "criminal aggression" in the Philippines, greatly as we regret that the blood of the Filipinos is on American hands, we more deeply resent the betrayal of American institutions at home. The real firing line is not in

Document 6 can be found in John Bassett Moore, *A Digest of International Law* (Washington, D.C.: Government Printing Office, 1906), VI, 226.

Document 7 can be found in Frederic Bancroft, ed., *Speeches, Correspondence, and Political Papers of Carl Schurz* (New York: G. P. Putnam's Sons, 1913), VI, 77–79.

the suburbs of Manila. The foe is of our own household. The attempt of 1861 was to divide the country. That of 1899 is to destroy its fundamental principles and noblest ideals.

Whether the ruthless slaughter of the Filipinos shall end next month or next year is but an incident in a contest that must go on until the Declaration of Independence and the Constitution of the United States are rescued from the hands of their betrayers. Those who dispute about standards of value while the foundation of the Republic is undermined will be listened to as little as those who would wrangle about the small economies of the household while the house is on fire. The training of a great people for a century, the aspiration for liberty of a vast immigration are forces that will hurl aside those who in the delirium of conquest seek to destroy the character of our institutions.

We deny that the obligation of all citizens to support their Government in times of grave National peril applies to the present situation. If an Administration may with impunity ignore the issues upon which it was chosen, deliberately create a condition of war anywhere on the face of the globe, debauch the civil service for spoils to promote the adventure, organize a truth-suppressing censorship and demand of all citizens a suspension of judgment and their unanimous support while it chooses to continue the fighting, representative government itself is imperiled.

We propose to contribute to the defeat of any person or party that stands for the forcible subjugation of any people. We shall oppose for reelection all who in the White House or in Congress betray American liberty in pursuit of un-American ends. We still hope that both of our great political parties will support and defend the Declaration of Independence in the closing campaign of the century.

We hold, with Abraham Lincoln, that "no man is good enough to govern another man without the other's consent. When the white man governs himself, that is self-government, but when he governs himself and also governs another man, that is more than self-government—that is despotism. Our reliance is in the love of liberty which God has planted in us. Our defense is in the spirit which prizes liberty as the heritage of all men in all lands. Those who deny freedom to others deserve it not for themselves, and under a just God cannot long retain it."

We cordially invite the cooperation of all men and women who remain loyal to the Declaration of Independence and the Constitution of the United States.

8. McKinley Preaches His Imperial Gospel, 1899

Hold a moment longer! Not quite yet, gentlemen! Before you go I would like to say just a word about the Philippine business. I have been criticized a good deal about the Philippines, but don't deserve it. The truth is I didn't want the Philippines, and when they came to us, as a gift from the gods, I did not know what to do with them. When the Spanish War broke out [Admiral George] Dewey was at Hongkong, and I ordered him to go to Manila and to capture or destroy the Spanish fleet, and he had to; because, if defeated, he had no place to refit on that side of the globe, and if the Dons were victorious they would likely cross the Pacific and ravage our Oregon and

This document can be found in James Rusling, "Interview with President William McKinley," *Christian Advocate* (January 22, 1903), 17. It can also be found in Charles S. Olcott, *William McKinley* (Boston: Houghton Mifflin Company, 1916), II, 109–111.

California coasts. And so he had to destroy the Spanish fleet, and did it! But that was as far as I thought then.

When I next realized that the Philippines had dropped into our laps I confess I did not know what to do with them. I sought counsel from all sides—Democrats as well as Republicans—but got little help. I thought first we would take only Manila; then Luzon; then other islands perhaps also. I walked the floor of the White House night after night until midnight; and I am not ashamed to tell you, gentlemen, that I went down on my knees and prayed Almighty God for light and guidance more than one night. And one night late it came to me this way—I don't know how it was, but it came: (1) That we could not give them back to Spain—that would be cowardly and dishonorable; (2) that we could not turn them over to France and Germany—our commercial rivals in the Orient—that would be bad business and discreditable; (3) that we could not leave them to themselves—they were unfit for self-government—and they would soon have anarchy and misrule over there worse than Spain's was; and (4) that there was nothing left for us to do but to take them all, and to educate the Filipinos, and uplift and civilize and Christianize them, and by God's grace do the very best we could by them, as our fellow-men for whom Christ also died. And then I went to bed, and went to sleep, and slept soundly, and the next morning I sent for the chief engineer of the War Department (our map-maker), and I told him to put the Philippines on the map of the United States (pointing to a large map on the wall of his office), and there they are, and there they will stay while I am President!

9. The Platt Amendment Restricts Cuba's Independence, 1903

Article I.   The Government of Cuba shall never enter into any treaty or other compact with any foreign power or powers which will impair or tend to impair the independence of Cuba, nor in any manner authorize or permit any foreign power or powers to obtain colonization or for military or naval purposes, or otherwise, lodgment in or control over any portion of said island.

Article II.   The Government of Cuba shall not assume or contract any public debt to pay the interest upon which, and to make reasonable sinking-fund provision for the ultimate discharge of which, the ordinary revenues of the Island of Cuba, after defraying the current expenses of the Government, shall be inadequate.

Article III.   The Government of Cuba consents that the United States may exercise the right to intervene for the preservation of Cuban independence, the maintenance of a government adequate for the protection of life, property, and individual liberty, and for discharging the obligations with respect to Cuba imposed by the Treaty of Paris on the United States, now to be assumed and undertaken by the Government of Cuba. . . .

This document can be found in Charles I. Bevans, comp., *Treaties and Other International Agreements of the United States of America, 1776–1949* (Washington, D.C.: Government Printing Office for Department of State, 1971), VI, 1116.

Article V.   The Government of Cuba will execute, and, as far as necessary, extend the plans already devised, or other plans to be mutually agreed upon, for the sanitation of the cities of the island, to the end that a recurrence of epidemic and infectious diseases may be prevented, thereby assuring protection to the people and commerce of Cuba, as well as to the commerce of the Southern ports of the United States and the people residing therein. . . .

Article VII.   To enable the United States to maintain the independence of Cuba, and to protect the people thereof, as well as for its own defense, the Government of Cuba will sell or lease to the United States lands necessary for coaling or naval stations, at certain specified points, to be agreed upon with the President of the United States.

E S S A Y S

In the first essay, Walter LaFeber of Cornell University, disagrees with scholars who have portrayed U.S. entry into the war as an accident of history—a reaction to momentary, irrational impulses. He argues that the economic depression and domestic social crisis of the 1890s helped launch a search for foreign markets and overseas influence. While William McKinley did not initially want war with Spain, the president concluded that he could best obtain his economic and expansionist goals through armed force. An astute politician, McKinley maneuvered through a minefield of domestic and international pressures and ultimately led the nation to war on his terms. In the second essay, Kristin Hoganson of the University of Illinois-Champaign/Urbana analyzes an additional social crisis of the 1890s—the crisis in American manhood—to explain the decision for war. Threatened by the assertive, suffrage-seeking "New Woman" of the late nineteenth century, and having had no war to prove their manliness since the days of Lincoln, American jingoists, according to Hoganson, cast Cuba as a damsel in distress and Uncle Sam as her chivalrous male protector in order to make the case for U.S. intervention. Hoganson questions McKinley's decisiveness, and she concludes that the president only reluctantly succumbed to the drumbeat for war when he realized that gendered ideas about leadership made armed conflict politically necessary. But in the last selection, Louis A. Pérez Jr. of the University of North Carolina at Chapel Hill claims that U.S. leaders had long desired to annex Cuba and that intervention came at a time when a rebel victory seemed imminent. Convinced that the Spanish could no longer hold back the tide of Cuban nationalism, and that Cuba's racially mixed population was incapable of self-government, Washington intervened and ultimately imposed the Platt Amendment to quell instability, protect U.S. interests, and assert U.S. hegemony.

Preserving the American System

WALTER LAFEBER

The "splendid little war" of 1898, as Secretary of State John Hay termed it at the time, is rapidly losing its splendor. . . . Over the past decade few issues in the country's diplomatic history have aroused academics more than the causes of the Spanish-American War, and in the last several years the argument has become not merely

Walter LaFeber, "That 'Splendid Little War' in Historical Perspective," *Texas Quarterly,* 11 (1968), 89–98. Reprinted by permission of the author.

academic, but a starting point in the debate over how the United States evolved into a great power, and more particularly how Americans got involved in the maelstrom of Asian nationalism. The line from the conquest of the Philippines in 1898 to the attempted pacification of Vietnam in 1968 is not straight, but it is quite traceable, and if Frederick Jackson Turner was correct when he observed in the 1890s that "The aim of history, then, is to know the elements of the present by understanding what came into the present from the past," the causes of the war in 1898 demand analysis from our present viewpoint.

Historians have offered four general interpretations to explain these causes. First, the war has been traced to a general impulse for war on the part of American public opinion. This interpretation has been illustrated in a famous cartoon showing President William McKinley, in the bonnet and dress of a little old lady, trying to sweep back huge waves marked "Congress" and "public opinion," with a very small broom. The "yellow journalism" generated by the Hearst-Pulitzer rivalry supposedly both created and reflected this sentiment for war. A sophisticated and useful version of this interpretation has been advanced by [the historian] Richard Hofstadter. Granting the importance of the Hearst-Pulitzer struggle, he has asked why these newspaper titans were able to exploit public opinion. Hofstadter has concluded that psychological dilemmas arising out of the depression of the 1890s made Americans react somewhat irrationally because they were uncertain, frightened, and consequently open to exploitation by men who would show them how to cure their frustrations through overseas adventures. In other words, the giddy minds of the 1890s could be quieted by foreign quarrels.

A second interpretation argues that the United States went to war for humanitarian reasons, that is, to free the Cubans from the horrors of Spanish policies and to give the Cubans democratic institutions. That this initial impulse resulted within ten months in an American protectorate over Cuba and Puerto Rico, annexation of the Philippines, and American participation in quarrels on the mainland of Asia itself, is explained as accidental, or, more familiarly, as done in a moment of "aberration" on the part of American policymakers.

A third interpretation emphasizes the role of several Washington officials who advocated a "Large Policy" of conquering a vast colonial empire in the Caribbean and Western Pacific. By shrewd maneuvering, these few imperialists pushed the vacillating McKinley and a confused nation into war. Senator Henry Cabot Lodge, of Massachusetts, Captain Alfred Thayer Mahan, of the U.S. Navy, and Theodore Roosevelt, Assistant Secretary of the Navy in 1897–1898, are usually named as the leaders of the "Large Policy" contingent.

A fourth interpretation believes the economic drive carried the nation into war. This drive emanated from the rapid industrialization which characterized American society after the 1840s. The immediate link between this industrialization and the war of 1898 was the economic depression which afflicted the nation in the quarter-century after 1873. Particularly important were the 1893–1897 years when Americans endured the worst of the plunge. Government and business leaders, who were both intelligent and rational, believed an oversupply of goods created the depression. They finally accepted war as a means of opening overseas markets in order to alleviate domestic distress caused by the overproduction. For thirty years the economic interpretation dominated historians' views of the war, but in 1936

Professor Julius Pratt conclusively demonstrated that business journals did not want war in the early months of 1898. He argued instead the "Large Policy" explanation, and from that time to the present, Professor Pratt's interpretation has been pre-eminent in explaining the causes of the conflict.

As I shall argue in a moment, the absence of economic factors in causing the war has been considerably exaggerated. At this point, however, a common theme which unites the first three interpretations should be emphasized. Each of the three deals with a superficial aspect of American life; each is peculiar to 1898, and none is rooted in the structure, the bed-rock, of the nation's history. This theme is important, for it means that if the results of the war were distasteful and disadvantageous (and on this historians do largely agree because of the diverse problems which soon arose in the Philippines and Cuba), those misfortunes were endemic to episodes unique to 1898. The peculiarities of public sentiment or the Hearst-Pulitzer rivalry, for example, have not reoccurred; the wide-spread humanitarian desire to help Cubans has been confined to 1898; and the banding together of Lodge, Mahan, and Roosevelt to fight for "Large Policies" of the late 1890s was never repeated by the three men. Conspiracy theories, moreover, seldom explain history satisfactorily.

The fourth interpretation has different implications. It argues that if the economic was the primary drive toward war, criticism of that war must begin not with irrational factors or flights of humanitarianism or a few stereotyped figures, but with the basic structure of the American system.

United States foreign policy, after all, is concerned primarily with the nation's domestic system and only secondarily with the systems of other nations. American diplomatic history might be defined as the study of how United States relations with other nations are used to insure the survival and increasing prosperity of the American system. Foreign policymakers are no more motivated by altruism than is the rest of the human race, but are instead involved in making a system function at home. Secretary of State, as the Founding Fathers realized, is an apt title for the man in charge of American foreign policy.

Turning this definition around, it also means that domestic affairs are the main determinant of foreign policy. When viewed within this matrix, the diplomatic events of the 1890s are no longer aberrations or the results of conspiracies and drift; American policymakers indeed grabbed greatness with both hands. As for accident or chance, they certainly exist in history, but become more meaningful when one begins with [the British historian] J. B. Bury's definition of "chance": "The valuable collision of two or more independent chains of causes." The most fruitful approach to the war of 1898 might be from the inside out (from the domestic to the foreign), and by remembering that chance is "the valuable collision of two or more independent chains of causes."

Three of these "chains" can be identified: the economic crisis of the 1890s which caused extensive and dangerous maladjustments in American society; the opportunities which suddenly opened in Asia after 1895 and in the Caribbean and the Pacific in 1898, opportunities which officials began to view as poultices, if not cure-alls, for the illnesses at home; and a growing partnership between business and government which reached its nineteenth-century culmination in the person of William McKinley. In April 1898, these "chains" had a "valuable collision" and war resulted.

The formation of the first chain is the great success story of American history. Between 1850 and 1910 the average manufacturing plant in the country multiplied its capital thirty-nine times, its number of wage-earners nearly seven times, and the value of its output by more than nineteen times. By the mid-1890s American iron and steel producers joked about their successful underselling of the vaunted British steel industry not only in world markets, but also in the vicinity of Birmingham, England, itself. The United States traded more in international markets than any nation except Great Britain.

But the most accelerated period of this development, 1873–1898, was actually twenty-five years of boom hidden in twenty-five years of bust. That quarter-century endured the longest and worst depression in the nation's history. After brief and unsatisfactory recoveries in the mid-1880s and early 1890s, the economy reached bottom in 1893. Unparalleled social and economic disasters struck. One out of every six laborers was unemployed, with most of the remainder existing on substandard wages; not only weak firms but many companies with the best credit ratings were forced to close their doors; the unemployed slept in the streets; riots erupted in Brooklyn, California, and points in between, as in the calamitous Pullman Strike in Chicago; Coxey's Army of broken farmers and unemployed laborers made their famous march on Washington; and the Secretary of State, Walter Quentin Gresham, remarked privately in 1894 that he saw "symptoms of revolution" appearing. Federal troops were dispatched to Chicago and other urban areas, including a cordon which guarded the Federal Treasury building in New York City.

Faced with the prospect of revolution and confronted with an economy that had almost ground to a stop, American businessmen and political officials faced alternative policies: they could attempt to re-examine and reorient the economic system, making radical modifications in the means of distribution and particularly the distribution of wealth; or they could look for new physical frontiers, following the historic tendency to increase production and then ferreting out new markets so the surplus, which the nation supposedly was unable to consume, could be sold elsewhere and Americans then put back to work on the production lines.

To the business and political communities, these were not actually alternatives at all. Neither of those communities has been known historically for political and social radicalism. Each sought security, not new political experiments. Some business firms tried to find such security by squashing competitors. Extremely few, however, searched for such policies as a federal income tax. Although such a tax narrowly passed through Congress in 1894, the Supreme Court declared it unconstitutional within a year and the issue would not be resurrected for another seventeen years. As a result, business and political leaders accepted the solution which was traditional, least threatening to their own power, and (apparently) required the least risk: new markets. Secretary of the Treasury John G. Carlisle summarized this conclusion in his public report of 1894: "The prosperity of our people, therefore, depends largely upon their ability to sell their surplus products in foreign markets at remunerative prices."

This consensus included farmers and the labor movement among others, for these interests were no more ingenious in discovering new solutions than were businessmen. A few farmers and laborers murmured ominously about some kind [of] political and/or economic revolution, but Richard Hofstadter seems correct in suggesting that in a sense Populism was reactionary rather than radical. The agrarians in the Populist movement tended to look back to a Jeffersonian utopia. Historians argue this point, but beyond dispute is the drive by farmers, including Populists, for foreign markets. The agrarians acted out of a long and successful tradition, for they had sought overseas customers since the first tobacco surplus in Virginia three hundred and fifty years before. Farmers initially framed the expansionist arguments and over three centuries created the context for the growing consensus on the desirability of foreign markets, a consensus which businessmen and others would utilize in the 1890s.

The farmers' role in developing this theme in American history became highly ironic in the late nineteenth century, for businessmen not only adopted the argument that overseas markets were necessary, but added a proviso that agrarian interests would have to be suppressed in the process. Industrialists observed that export charts demonstrated the American economy to be depending more upon industrial than agrarian exports. To allow industrial goods to be fully competitive in the world market, however, labor costs would have to be minimal, and cheap bread meant sacrificing the farmers. Fully comprehending this argument, agrarians reacted bitterly. They nevertheless continued searching for their own overseas markets, agreeing with the industrialists that the traditional method of discovering new outlets provided the key to prosperity, individualism, and status.

The political conflict which shattered the 1890s revolved less around the question of whether conservatives could carry out a class solution than the question of which class would succeed in carrying out a conservative solution. This generalization remains valid even when the American labor movement is examined for its response to the alternatives posed. This movement, primarily comprised of the newly-formed American Federation of Labor, employed less than 3 per cent of the total number of employed workers in nonfarm occupations. In its own small sphere of influence, its membership largely consisted of skilled workers living in the East. The AFL was not important in the West or South, where the major discontent seethed. Although Samuel Gompers was known by some of the more faint-hearted as a "socialist," the AFL's founder never dramatized any radical solutions for the restructuring of the economy. He was concerned with obtaining more money, better hours, and improved working conditions for the Federation's members. Gompers refused, moreover, to use direct political action to obtain these benefits, content to negotiate within the corporate structure which the businessman had created. The AFL simply wanted more, and when overseas markets seemed to be a primary source of benefits, Gompers did not complain. As [the historian] Louis Hartz has noted, "wage consciousness," not "class consciousness," triumphed.

The first "chain of causes" was marked by a consensus on the need to find markets overseas. Fortunately for the advocates of this policy, another "chain," quite complementary to the first, began to form beyond American borders. By the mid-1890s, American merchants, missionaries, and ship captains had been profiting from Asian markets for more than a century. Between 1895 and 1900, however, the United States for the first time became a mover-and-pusher in Asian affairs.

In 1895 Japan defeated China in a brief struggle that now appears to be one of the most momentous episodes in the nineteenth century. The Japanese emerged as the major Asian power, the Chinese suddenly seemed to be incapable of defending their honor or existence, Chinese nationalism began its peculiar path to the 1960s, and European powers which had long lusted after Asian markets now seized a golden opportunity. Russia, Germany, France, and ultimately Great Britain initiated policies designed to carve China and Manchuria into spheres of influence. Within a period of months, the Asian mainland suddenly became the scene of international power politics at its worst and most explosive.

The American reaction to these events has been summarized recently by Professor Thomas McCormick: "The conclusion of the Sino-Japanese War left Pandora's box wide open, but many Americans mistook it for the Horn of Plenty." Since the first American ship sailed to sell goods in China in 1784, Americans had chased that most mysterious phantom, the China Market. Now, just at the moment when key interest groups agreed that overseas markets could be the salvation of the 1890s crisis, China was almost miraculously opening its doors to the glutted American factories and farms. United States trade with China jumped significantly after 1895, particularly in the critical area of manufactures; by 1899 manufactured products accounted for more than 90 percent of the nation's exports to the Chinese, a quadrupling of the amount sent in 1895. In their moment of need, Americans had apparently discovered a Horn of Plenty.

But, of course, it was Pandora's box. The ills which escaped from the box were threefold. Least important for the 1890s, a nascent Chinese nationalism appeared. During the next quarter-century, the United States attempted to minimize the effects of this nationalism either by cooperating with Japan or European powers to isolate and weaken the Chinese, or by siding with the most conservative groups within the nationalist movement. Americans also faced the competition of European and Japanese products, but they were nevertheless confident in the power of their newly-tooled industrial powerhouse. Given a "fair field and no favor," as the Secretary of State phrased the wish in 1900, Americans would undersell and defeat any competitors. But could fair fields and no favors be guaranteed? Within their recently-created spheres of influence European powers began to grant themselves trade preferences, thus effectively shutting out American competition. In 1897, the American business community and the newly-installed administration of William McKinley began to counter these threats.

The partnership between businessmen and politicians, in this case the McKinley administration, deserves emphasis, for if the businessman hoped to exploit Asian markets he required the aid of the politician. Americans could compete against British or Russian manufacturers in Asia, but they could not compete against, say, a Russian manufacturer who could turn to his government and through pressure exerted by that government on Chinese officials receive a prize railroad contract or banking concession. United States businessmen could only compete against such business-government coalitions if Washington officials helped. Only then would the field be fair and the favors equalized. To talk of utilizing American "rugged individualism" and a free enterprise philosophy in the race for the China market in the 1890s was silly. There consequently emerged in American policy-making a classic example of the business community and the government grasping hands and, marching shoulder to shoulder, leading the United States to its destiny of being a major power on a far-Eastern frontier. As one high Republican official remarked in the mid-1890s: "diplomacy is the management of international business."

William McKinley fully understood the need for such a partnership. He had grown to political maturity during the 1870s when, as one Congressman remarked, "The House of Representatives was like an auction room where more valuable considerations were disposed of under the speaker's hammer than in any other place on earth." Serving as governor of Ohio during the 1890s depression, McKinley learned firsthand about the dangers posed by the economic crisis (including riots in his state which he terminated with overwhelming displays of military force). The new Chief Executive believed there was nothing necessarily manifest about Manifest Destiny in American history, and his administration was the first in modern American history which so systematically and completely committed itself to helping businessmen, farmers, laborers, and missionaries in solving their problems in an industrializing, supposedly frontierless America. Mr. Dooley caught this aggressive side of the McKinley administration when he described the introduction of a presidential speech: "Th' proceedin's was opened with a prayer that Providence might r-remain undher th' protection iv th' administration."

Often characterized as a creature of his campaign manager Mark Hanna, or as having, in the famous but severely unjust words of Theodore Roosevelt, the backbone of a chocolate eclair, McKinley was, as Henry Adams and others fully understood, a master of men. McKinley was never pushed into a policy he did not want to accept. Elihu Root, probably the best mind and most acute observer who served in the McKinley cabinets, commented that on most important matters the President had his ideas fixed, but would convene the Cabinet, direct the members toward his own conclusions, and thereby allow the Cabinet to think it had formulated the policy. In responding to the problems and opportunities in China, however, McKinley's power to exploit that situation was limited by events in the Caribbean.

In 1895 revolution had broken out in Cuba. By 1897 Americans were becoming increasingly belligerent on this issue for several reasons: more than $50,000,000 of United States investments on the island were endangered; Spaniards were treating some Cubans inhumanely; the best traditions of the Monroe Doctrine had long dictated that a European in the Caribbean was a sty in the eye of any red-blooded American; and, finally, a number of Americans, not only Lodge, Roosevelt, and Mahan, understood the strategic and political relationship of Cuba to a proposed isthmian canal. Such a canal would provide a short-cut to the west coast of Latin America as well as to the promised markets of Asia. Within six months after assuming office, McKinley demanded that the island be pacified or the United States would take a "course of action which the time and the transcendent emergency may demand." Some Spanish reforms followed, but in January 1898, new revolts wracked Havana and a month later the "Maine" dramatically sank to the bottom of Havana harbor.

McKinley confronted the prospect of immediate war. Only two restraints appeared. First, a war might lead to the annexation of Cuba, and the multitude of problems (including racial) which had destroyed Spanish authority would be dumped on the United States. Neither the President nor his close advisers wanted to leap into the quicksands of noncontiguous, colonial empire. The business community comprised a second restraining influence. By mid-1897 increased exports, which removed part of the agricultural and industrial glut, began to extricate the country from its quarter-century of turmoil. Finally seeing light at the end of a long

and treacherous tunnel, businessmen did not want the requirements of a war economy to jeopardize the growing prosperity.

These two restraints explain why the United States did not go to war in 1897,
and the removal of these restraints indicates why war occurred in April 1898. The
first problem disappeared because McKinley and his advisers entertained no ideas
of warring for colonial empire in the Caribbean. After the war Cuba would be freed
from Spain and then ostensibly returned to the Cubans to govern. The United States
would retain a veto power over the more important policy decisions made on the
island. McKinley discovered a classic solution in which the United States enjoyed
the power over, but supposedly little of the responsibility for, the Cubans.

The second restraint disappeared in late March 1898, exactly at the time of
McKinley's decision to send the final ultimatum to Madrid. The timing is crucial.
Professor Pratt observed in 1936 that the business periodicals began to change their
antiwar views in mid-March 1898, but he did not elaborate upon this point. The
change is significant and confirms the advice McKinley received from a trusted
political adviser in New York City who cabled on March 25 that the larger corporations would welcome war. The business journals and their readers were beginning
to realize that the bloody struggle in Cuba and the resulting inability of the United
States to operate at full-speed in Asian affairs more greatly endangered economic
recovery than would a war.

McKinley's policies in late March manifested these changes. This does not
mean that the business community manipulated the President, or that he was repay-
ing those businessmen who had played vital roles in his election in 1896. Nor does it
mean that McKinley thought the business community was forcing his hand or circumscribing his policies in late March. The opinions and policies of the President
and the business community had been hammered out in the furnace of a terrible
depression and the ominous changes in Asia. McKinley and pivotal businessmen
emerged from these unforgettable experiences sharing a common conclusion: the nation's economy increasingly depended upon overseas markets, including the whole
of China; that to develop these markets not only a business-government partnership
but also tranquillity was required; and, finally, however paradoxical it might seem,
tranquillity could be insured only through war against Spain. Not for the first or last
time, Americans believed that to have peace they would have to wage war. Some, including McKinley, moved on to a final point. War, if properly conducted, could result
in a few select strategic bases in the Pacific (such as Hawaii, Guam, and Manila)
which would provide the United States with potent starting-blocks in the race for
Asian markets. McKinley sharply distinguished between controlling such bases and
trying to rule formally over an extensive territorial empire. In the development of the
"chains of causes" the dominant theme was the economic, although not economic in
the narrow sense. As discussed in the 1890s, business recovery carried most critical
political and social implications.

Some historians argue that McKinley entered the war in confusion and annexed
the Philippines in a moment of aberration. They delight in quoting the President's
announcement to a group of Methodist missionaries that he decided to annex the
Philippines one night when after praying he heard a mysterious voice. Most interesting, however, is not that the President heard a reassuring voice, but how the voice
phrased its advice. The voice evidently outlined the points to be considered; in any

case, McKinley numbered them in order, demonstrating, perhaps, that either he, the voice, or both had given some thought to putting the policy factors in neat and logical order. The second point is of particular importance: "that we could not turn them [the Philippines] over to France or Germany—our commercial rivals in the Orient—that would be bad business and discreditable. . . ." Apparently everyone who had been through the 1890s knew the dangers of "bad business." Even voices.

Interpretations which depend upon mass opinion, humanitarianism, and "Large Policy" advocates do not satisfactorily explain the causes of the war. Neither, however, does Mr. Dooley's famous one-sentence definition of American imperialism in 1898: "Hands acrost th' sea an' into somewan's pocket." The problem of American expansion is more complicated and historically rooted than that flippancy indicates. George Eliot once observed, "The happiest nations, like the happiest women, have no history." The United States, however, endured in the nineteenth century a history of growing industrialism, supposedly closing physical frontiers, rapid urbanization, unequal distribution of wealth, and an overdependence upon export trade. These historical currents clashed in the 1890s. The result was chaos and fear, then war and empire. In 1898 McKinley and the business community wanted peace, but they also sought benefits which only a war could provide. Viewed from the perspective of the 1960's, the Spanish-American conflict can no longer be viewed as only a "splendid little war." It was a war to preserve the American system.

Manhood, Chivalry, and McKinley's Reluctant Decision for War

KRISTIN HOGANSON

Why did *Cuba libre* strike such a powerful chord in the United States? The leading explanation offered by historians is that humanitarian sentiments and democratic principles of self-government underlay the broad backing commanded by the Cubans. This explanation clarifies why Americans sided with the Cuban revolutionaries over their Spanish opponents, but it does not account for the depth of Americans' commitment to the Cubans, for destitute and disfranchised residents of the United States failed to provoke a comparable outpouring of support. As one prolabor essayist noted, "The poor in the tenement houses of our cities are in worse extremes than the down-trampled population of Cuba, but what patriot suggests war to free them?"

The sympathy extended to the Cubans seems particularly incongruous when race is added to the picture. In the late nineteenth century, white Americans frequently invoked racial beliefs to justify denying self-government to people of color. Why, then, were so many white Americans distraught over the Cubans' political status? Sen. Orville H. Platt (R, Conn.) drew attention to this incongruity when he pointed out that men who did not seem outraged at the news of a recent lynching in

Adapted from Kristin Hoganson, *Fighting for American Manhood: How Gender Politics Provoked the Spanish-American and Philippine-American Wars* (New Haven: Yale University Press, 1998), 44–51, 54–57, 61–62, 64, 68, 99, 101–106. Copyright © 1998 by Yale University. Reprinted by permission of Yale University.

Texas (in which a man was covered with kerosene and burned to death on a public platform in the presence of seven thousand cheering witnesses) were not "shedding tears over the sad fate of Maceo [a mixed-race Cuban general]." Although there was some debate over the whiteness of the Cuban revolutionaries, it was quite clear that whatever they were, "Anglo-Saxons" they were not. Taken as a whole, the Cuban revolutionaries undoubtedly had more African blood than their Spanish rulers. Given the racial prejudices, poverty, and political injustice tolerated within the United States, it appears that something more than humanitarian sympathy and democratic principles lay behind the outpouring of support for the Cubans.

The key to the Cubans' appeal can be found in the numerous press accounts that treated them and their cause sympathetically: many of these portrayed the Cuban revolutionaries in chivalric terms. [The historians] Michael Hunt and Amy Kaplan have considered one aspect of this in their respective studies of U.S. foreign policy and romance novels. Both find that nineteenth-century Americans often viewed Cuba metaphorically, as a maiden longing to be rescued by a gallant knight. Strange though it may seem, this interpretation fit into a larger chivalric understanding of Cuban affairs, for favorable accounts also characterized the Cuban revolution as a heroic crusade that merited the fraternal assistance of American men. In their effort to cast the Cuban revolution in chivalrous terms, sympathizers did not stop at presenting it metaphorically—they also portrayed real Cuban men and women as if they were the protagonists of one of the adventure-filled romance novels that were so popular at the time. The tendency to depict Cuban revolutionaries as if they were the heroes and heroines of a chivalric drama helps explain why so many white Americans were well-disposed toward the mixed-race Cubans. To many Americans, chivalric standards represented the highest ideals of manhood and womanhood. Hence, the Cubans' positive gender images deflected attention from negative racial stereotypes.

If it seems odd that Americans strongly sympathized with the Cubans, it seems especially odd that they insisted on viewing a national liberation movement in chivalric terms. They did so because of domestic concerns: sympathizers looked to the Cubans as models of gallantry because they feared that chivalric standards were endangered within the United States. Many of those who fretted about a decline in chivalry regarded the assertive [politically active and suffrage seeking] New Woman as evidence of that decline, for at the heart of chivalry was the juxtaposition of feminine vulnerability and masculine power. An essay in *Popular Science Monthly* illustrates this conviction: "We know that the tenderness, affection, and sympathy which are the essential grace and charm of womanhood, as well as the courage, disinterestedness, and chivalric sentiment which form the nobility of manhood, have sprung from that very relation of strong to weak, protector and protected, which have for ages subsisted among all the civilized races." In the chivalric paradigm, women were the protected, men the protectors. Women were, in the words of the antisuffragist Helen Kendrick Johnson, "the inspiring force," men, "the organizing and physical power." Because the chivalric paradigm enshrined men's monopoly on political power, women who pushed for a greater public role seemed to pose a fundamental challenge to the standard. . . .

Because American women seemed ever less inclined to assume the role of an appreciative audience for male exploits, aspiring American knights and women who preferred pedestals to politics turned to Cuban women as models of femininity. In contrast to activist American women, Cuban women often appeared to be ideal romantic heroines. Americans found evidence for this view in narratives that described Cuban women as natural "home-bodies" and "chaste spouses and slaves to duty." Those who fretted about assertive New Women were captivated by reports that Cuban women, "the most feminine and simple women in the world," spent their time worshiping their husbands rather than meddling in men's affairs. As the *New York Tribune* reported, "The 'New Woman' is altogether unknown in Havana. There is not even a woman's club there. In fact, in this regard the city is actually mediaeval." Their image as acquiescent, traditional women made Cuban women seem to be perfect feminine foils for assertive American women. . . .

Although some sensational tales of the Cuban revolution described Cuban Amazons who fought alongside men, the chroniclers of the Amazons were careful to note that it was only the exigencies of war that turned Cuban women into fighters: ordinarily they were extremely feminine. The author Nathan Green effusively described Cuban women's fury in battle but then depicted the women as pitiful wrecks as soon as the fighting was over. "While the fighting lasts they show no emotion," he wrote, "but when the last shot is fired, I have seen women throw themselves on the ground and give way to a delirium of grief." . . .

If the first reason for the chivalric paradigm's powerful appeal was apprehension about the assertive New Woman, the second had to do with American men. Those who bemoaned the decline in chivalry often held American men partially accountable, their logic being that if men had upheld their side of the chivalric pact, then women would not be so eager to enter public life. According to this line of thought, the seeming decline in gallantry reflected a deterioration in manly character. Rep. John S. Williams (D, Miss.) drew attention to men's failings when he exclaimed, "In this latter end of the nineteenth century, men seem to think not only that 'the age of chivalry has gone,' but that this magnificent piece of humanity that God has created and which we call man . . . is nothing but a miserable money-making machine. . . . Poetry goes out from him; imagination ceases to exist with him. Chivalry is dead; manhood itself is sapped." . . .

To men frustrated by the standardized routines of an ever more industrialized society, Cuban men represented adventure and male display. To those disturbed by the prospect of degeneracy in a world of civilized comforts, Cuban men stood for a hardier manhood. And, perhaps most important, to those concerned about the civic virtue that American democracy was thought to rest upon, Cuban men seemed ideal citizens: fraternal-minded men willing to sacrifice themselves for a noble cause. Recognizing the appeal of such chivalric attributes as respect for women, martial prowess, and honorable objectives, sympathetic authors did their best to make the revolutionaries' story appear, as one article put it, "more like the wonders of a romance than like the authentic annals of our time." . . .

According to the conventions of chivalric novels, only a fiend would deny such heroic men that which they so valiantly struggled to attain. Cuban sympathizers did not disappoint these expectations in their descriptions of the Spaniards. Their critical assessments of the "proud Castilians" led numerous American readers to conclude that Spanish men, once known for the chivalry, had degenerated since the days of Don Quixote. The author Stephen Bonsal contributed to the Spaniards' degenerate image in his book *The Real Condition of Cuba To-Day* (1897). "It is not alone in prowess or in success that Spanish arms have fallen since the days they fought the Moors," wrote Bonsal. " . . . The decay has been even more strongly marked in the decadence of their chivalry." The most glaring evidence of Spanish men's decadent chivalry was the atrocities they committed against helpless civilians. American publications commonly presented the Spanish-Cuban War as a war waged against noncombatants, primarily women and children. As Davis said in reference to the Spanish policy of reconcentration, "In other wars men have fought with men, and women have suffered indirectly because the men were killed, but in this war it is the women, herded together in towns like cattle, who are going to die, while the men, camped in the fields and mountains, will live."

If the shocking stories of starved and butchered civilians that frequently appeared in pro-Cuban newspapers left any doubts about the Spaniards' chivalry, stories that depicted the Spanish soldiers as sexual predators worked to put these doubts to rest. One chronicle said that during General Valeriano Weyler's command (Weyler was in charge of the Spanish forces in Cuba from 1896 to 1897), "women dared not leave their homes. In many cases they were dragged out by the Spanish and by the drunken rabble of the town, who had license given to them at the same time that protection was withdrawn from the homes." Similarly, the author James Hyde Clark maintained that licentious Spanish soldiers violated and then killed "scores of young women," and Green contended that Weyler used his women prisoners in orgies, forced women to dance naked before his troops, and raped daughters in front of their parents. Accounts of bestial Spanish rapists paralleled the contemporary image, assiduously promoted by white supremacists, of dark-skinned rapists. But gender and racial stereotypes were at odds with each other in these stories from Cuba, for it was the white, Germanic Weyler and his Spanish associates who apparently brutalized women and the mixed-race Cuban men who respected them. . . .

Building on the many stories of victimized Cuban women, writers who endorsed the Cuban cause characterized the colonial relation between Spain and Cuba as one of lustful bondage. These accounts portrayed the entire island as a pure woman who was being assaulted by Spain. One such narrative described Cuba as "a country that Spain has never loved, but has always wished to hold in bondage for lust and brutality." A drama on the Cuban revolution (presented in Yiddish to enthusiastic audiences in the Bowery) based its plot on this allegory: it featured a dastardly Spanish villain who tried to force himself on an attractive Cuban maiden. The political cartoons that depicted Cuba as a ravished woman also promoted the idea of rape as a metaphor for the Spanish colonial endeavor. To add to the drama of the story, sympathizers played on Cuba's sobriquet, Queen of the Antilles, in their pleas on behalf of the revolution. "Queen of the Antilles!" Beautiful Cuba! For ages she has writhed under the oppression of the haughty Castilian," exclaimed one pro-Cuban account. Picturing the Spaniards as unchivalrous ravishers made their power seem immoral and illegitimate—a challenge to the principles of chivalry, which held that true women should be venerated and protected. It made the Spanish presence in Cuba appear to be an insult to the honor of Cuban women and the Cuban men charged with protecting them. . . .

Although the seemingly chivalrous Cuban cause captured Americans' imaginations because of domestic concerns, the chivalric paradigm had powerful foreign policy implications. By casting the Cuban revolution in metaphorical terms, it helped

Americans make the leap from sympathizing with individuals to opposing Spanish colonial power. By making Spanish power seem thoroughly corrupt, the paradigm suggested that humanitarian aid or limited political reforms were inadequate to settle the Cuban issue. It thus helped jingoes build their case for U.S. military intervention. This was no accident. The chivalric understanding of the Cuban revolution appealed to people who were not jingoes, but jingoes embraced chivalric imagery and metaphors with singular enthusiasm. They turned to the chivalric paradigm to deepen American's interest in Cuban affairs and to propose a course of action for the United States. . . .

To further implicate the United States in the unfolding Cuban drama, jingoes declared that the United States was more than a spectator—that it had a role in the romance. After the *New York Journal* reported that the Spaniards had strip-searched three Cuban women on an American vessel, jingoes called for recognition of Cuban belligerency, even for U.S. intervention, to end such unchivalrous deeds. Rep. David A. De Armond (D, Mo.) was one of the jingoes who pressed for a strong response. "Young ladies stripped and searched on board an American vessel by Spaniards, bearded, booted, and spurred!" he exclaimed in his plea for action. What made the strip-searches particularly offensive was not so much their effects on Cuban women—after all, the press reported more horrifying stories of rape and murder—but that they occurred on American ships. Jingoes presented them as insults to American men's ability to protect the honor of women. Senator Allen made this clear when, after describing the strip-search, he said he found it "absolutely humiliating" that the Spanish could commit such atrocities while American leaders "sit idly and supinely here." Richard Harding Davis, the writer who broke the story, agreed. Even after admitting that a female detective, not male soldiers, had stripped the young women, he continued to regard it as a grave affront to American honor. The true issue, he said, was that the demonstration of Spanish power on the American ship undercut the dignity of the United States. Davis was so ashamed by the incident that he cited it as grounds for intervention in the Spanish-Cuban War.

As they voiced their outrage over the nation's reluctance to protect victimized Cuban women, jingoes were mindful of the sympathy shown by a number of American women for the beleaguered Cubans and particularly for Cuban women. The same interest in women's well-being that led thousands of American women to join temperance and purity crusades in the 1880s and 1890s contributed to American women's empathy for their Cuban "sisters." Women who sympathized with the Cubans made their sentiments known in a variety of ways, starting with letters to political leaders. A *Christian Herald* leaflet that implored mothers to "think of the wretchedness of these poor, heart-broken mothers of Cuba" motivated one woman to write her senator to urge him to do something to end the suffering on the island. Women also indicated their views from the galleries of Congress. Perhaps most noticeable were the members of the Daughters of the American Revolution (DAR), who applauded congressmen who made assertive speeches on Cuba. Some of the women who sympathized with the Cubans were in political leaders' own households. A handful of prominent political wives in the nation's capital made their sympathies clear by establishing the National Relief Fund in Aid of Cuba. Other political wives expressed their positive feelings for the Cubans more discreetly in Washington social functions. . . .

[But] by appealing to American men to take a stance in favor of chivalric principles, jingoes couched the Cuban issue as one for men to resolve. The emphasis they
placed on brotherhood and male honor helped to keep women on the sidelines of the
Cuban debate. The chivalric paradigm implied that American women should plead
on behalf of their Cuban sisters but that they should not lead rescuing crusades, much
less fraternal expeditions. These, it implied, were men's responsibility. Indeed, according to the paradigm, the Cuban issue was nothing less than a test of American
manhood. If American men were truly chivalrous, they should enter the lists.

Significantly, when jingoes held up American men as knightly rescuers, they
often wrote Cuban men out of the romance. They implied that intervening American
men would take the place of Cuban men who were unable to protect Cuban women
because they were at the front, had been killed, or lacked the ability to do so. By
removing Cuban men from the picture, the rescue paradigm sketched a hierarchical
relation between the United States and Cuba. Viewing relations with Cuba as a
chivalric rescue implied that the maidenly Cubans would submit to American governance just as the heroines of chivalric novels voluntarily submitted to their heroic
rescuers. The rescue paradigm thus lent itself to imperial ambitions for Cuba as well
as to the jingoes' desire to foster chivalric relations between men and women. . . .

On the night of February 15, 1898, the U.S. battleship *Maine,* which had been
sent to Havana to protect American citizens after an outbreak of riots, exploded
and sank in Havana harbor. Two hundred and sixty-six men died in the disaster.
President [William] McKinley responded to the crisis by appointing a court of
naval inquiry. The court's report, submitted on March 25, attributed the explosion to
an external source. Although the commission admitted that it could not determine
who was responsible, suspicion came to rest on Spain. Not only did Spain have a
reputation for perfidy, but, to many Americans, it appeared that only the Spanish
government had the technological capabilities to commit such an act. Americans
were outraged at the thought of the Spaniards striking in the dark without giving
the sleeping crew a chance to fight. "Splendid sport, indeed! How chivalric!" exclaimed one senator, who, well-versed in the chivalric paradigm for understanding
the Spanish-Cuban war, interpreted the incident as yet another manifestation of
Spanish treachery.

Americans who blamed the disaster on Spain regarded it as a challenge to
American men, particularly because Spain refused to apologize or offer reparations
and instead suggested that the men of the *Maine* were at fault. Sen. Richard R.
Kenney (D, Del.) captured the leading sentiment of the day in his response to the
supposed Spanish insult: "American manhood and American chivalry give back the
answers that innocent blood shall be avenged, starvation and crime shall cease,
Cuba shall be free. For such reasons, for such causes, American[s] can and will
fight. For such causes and for such reasons we should have war." . . .

As he contemplated how to respond to the sinking of the *Maine,* McKinley faced
a number of issues: humanitarian concerns, the interests of American businessmen
in Cuba, the impact of a war on the entire American economy, and the potential for
coaling stations and strategic bases. Added to these were concerns for his reputation
and credibility as a leader and the implications of his image for his party. McKinley
suffered the constraint of being a first-term president in a political system that valued
a military style of manliness in its leaders. McKinley was deeply sensitive to public

opinion. As he assessed the tenor of the war debate, he undoubtedly realized that his perceived cowardice in foreign affairs was undermining his credibility as a leader, that it threatened to sink his administration along with the *Maine*.

The president had good reason to be apprehensive about charges of cowardice because, regardless of his youthful Civil War record [he had served as an Army officer], he was not universally esteemed as a great military hero or a forceful leader. The up-and-coming Theodore Roosevelt was not alone in thinking that despite his military record, McKinley was "not a strong man." The sedate McKinley did not embody the new standards of active, athletic, aggressive manhood. He had never enjoyed hunting, and when he tried fishing once as president, in his frock coat and silk hat, he capsized the boat and ruined his shoes and pants. The clean-shaven McKinley was the only president between Andrew Johnson and Woodrow Wilson not to have a beard or mustache, signs of masculinity. . . .

Besides appearing physically soft, McKinley appeared to lack the independence central to manliness. His opponents ridiculed him as a puppet of Marcus A. Hanna, who had risen to the Senate after running McKinley's campaign. A joke of the time questioned whether Hanna would still be president if McKinley died. Detractors accused McKinley of being a tool of his Wall Street advisers. "Take my word for it," said Representative [William] Sulzer, "the American people will never consent to be governed by any man who is not big enough to own himself." McKinley seemed not only overly dependent on Hanna and other wealthy backers, but also incapable of managing his own finances. Nineteenth-century men were expected to provide for their families, but McKinley had gone bankrupt in 1893. Although his Republican biographers maintained that McKinley had handled his business failure in a "manly way," their praise was defensive. . . .

A calculating politician, McKinley no doubt realized that he needed to demonstrate he still had backbone lest he lose his ability to lead a political system that equated military valor and leadership. Highly conscious of public opinion, he surely knew that many American men thought war was necessary to defend American honor and avenge the dead sailors from the *Maine*. In Congress, Republicans and Democrats alike were citing their constituents' eagerness to fight. Rep. Joseph Wheeler (D, Ala.) announced that the "chivalrous men who fought in that terrible conflict from 1861 to 1865, and their equally noble sons, inspired as they are by the fame earned by their sires, all stand ready to place their lives and treasure on the altar of duty." . . .

Assurances that men were eager to fight made efforts to avoid war seem incongruous with manly sentiment. If the masses of American men wanted to fight, why didn't McKinley? A *New York Journal* cartoon that depicted McKinley in a bonnet and apron futilely trying to sweep back a stormy sea conveyed the spreading (and, to McKinley, threatening) conviction that if the president countered the will of American men, he would become as politically potent as a feebleminded old woman.

In addition to worrying about losing the respect of the masses of American men, McKinley worried about losing leadership to Congress. After McKinley's message of March 28, the *Washington Post* reported that the president was afraid he would not be able to prevent Congress from acting on its own. On March 30 the *Post* noted, "If the President desires to lead the procession . . . he will be accorded every opportunity of doing so. If not, the ranks will be closed and the President will be under the necessity of falling in behind." Congressmen underscored the point that the president must act or lose his stature as a leader. In a letter of April 4, Sen. Joseph B. Foraker (R, Ohio) said that Congress had been waiting for the president to take the lead on the war issue, to no avail. The president, said Foraker, "disappointed all of us very seriously with his message about the *Maine* disaster and we made up our minds that we would not wait on his any longer." "The responsibility is now on Congress," said Sen. Marion Butler (Pop., N.C.) on April 12. "We must remove the humiliation that is upon us as a nation."

As Congress grew increasingly restive, even the president's erstwhile supporters began to question the manliness of his policies. Senator [John C.] Spooner commented that "we have borne the methods of Spain in Cuba with patience approaching pusillanimity. We can tolerate it no longer." Republicans begged the administration to make war for party survival. McKinley could appear to exhibit backbone by searching for a peaceful settlement for a while, but he could not hold back indefinitely. He knew that if Congress took the initiative in pressing for war, he might not regain his stature as a leader. A president who reluctantly followed the ranks into war would find it difficult to regain the confidence of men who interpreted politics in terms of military metaphors.

It is difficult to determine the degree to which McKinley's need to maintain his manly image affected his decision to push for war because he did not record his reasoning. He wrote few letters, left almost no personal papers, and said little in conversation. But friends believed that McKinley did not want war. They viewed him as a man who deeply desired peace. McKinley's associates were convinced that the president was pushed into war to satisfy Congress and public opinion. Senator [William E.] Chandler believed that the president advised delay because he was unwilling to give a war message to a Congress he knew would accept nothing else. Chandler attributed the president's increasingly bellicose attitude toward Spain to "the rising temper of the country and Congress especially." Although Chandler did not mention the aspersions on McKinley's manhood, these were an important component of the country's "rising temper." Placing the assaults on the president's manliness in the larger context of a political culture based on military manhood leads to the conclusion that the need to appear manly to an aggressive constituency helped make war seem politically necessary to the president.

On March 30 McKinley burst into tears as he told a friend that Congress was trying to drive the nation into war. He remembered the Civil War as a horrible conflict and had hoped that international arbitration would replace war as a means of settling international disputes. McKinley did not want war, but neither did he want to wreck his presidency. Aware of his growing reputation as a spineless leader and recognizing that Republican legislators would be unwilling to go along with a new peace initiative, McKinley drafted a message in early April that put the Cuban matter into the hands of the infamously bellicose Congress.

After McKinley delivered his message on April 11, jingoes continued to criticize him for his refusal to resoundingly cry for war. As one critic said, everybody except "the bankers and the ladies felt a sense of shame in reading the message of the President." Such calumny discouraged McKinley from seeking a last-minute solution to the crisis. On April 19 Congress submitted a resolution to the president authorizing him to intervene to end the war in Cuba. McKinley felt he had no choice but to sign, although he knew the resolution would surely lead to war. Spain immediately severed diplomatic relations with the United States. On April 22 the United States imposed a naval blockade of Cuba; on April 24 Spain declared war; and on April 25 McKinley asked Congress to declare war. Congress did so eagerly, predating the start of war to April 21.

McKinley's scanty personal records mean that arguments about his motives (gender-based or otherwise) ultimately must be based on conjecture. But even though McKinley did not record his rationale, the debate over his backbone shows that gendered ideas about leadership limited the range of politically viable options available to him. McKinley's backbone became a central issue in the debate over war because political activists, whether Republicans, Democrats, or Populists, believed that manly character mattered in politics. Men from across the country agreed that the character of the nation's leaders attested to the acceptability of their policies, and following the *Maine* disaster, increasing numbers of men demanded a militant leader. Aware of the links between manhood, military prowess, and political power (indeed, eager to take advantage of them in the campaign of 1896), McKinley reached the logical conclusion that war was politically imperative. His decision to join the jingoes was less a reflection of his courage or cowardice, strength or weakness, than an acknowledgement that the political system he operated in would not permit any other course of action.

Derailing Cuban Nationalism and Establishing U.S. Hegemony

LOUIS A. PÉREZ JR.

[By 1898] Spanish sovereignty in Cuba was coming to an end, or so it appeared. And appearances influenced outcomes. Of course, whether Cubans would have actually gone on to defeat Spain, then or thereafter, or even at all, cannot be demonstrated. What can be determined and documented, however, is that all parties involved had arrived at the conclusion that the days of Spanish rule in Cuba were numbered. This was the perception that, in the end, served as the basis on which the vital policy decisions were made and actions were taken.

Spanish authorities openly predicted defeat in Cuba. "Spain is exhausted," former president Francisco Pi y Margall concluded. "She must withdraw her troops and recognize Cuban independence before it is too late." The failure of autonomy, the Madrid daily *El Nuevo Régimen* editorialized, left only one alternative: "Negotiate on the basis of independence." *La Epoca* reached a similar conclusion. "In reality," observed the Madrid daily, "Cuba is lost to Spain."

Cubans, too, sensed that the end was near. A new optimism lifted separatist morale to an all-time high. Never had they been so openly certain of triumph as they were in early 1898. "This war cannot last more than a year," [General] Máximo Gómez exulted in January 1898. "This is the first time I have ever put a limit to it." [Rebel

Adapted from Louis A. Pérez Jr., *The War of 1898: The United States and Cuba in History and Historiography* (Chapel Hill: University of North Carolina Press, 1998), pp. 10–14, 18–21, 29–30, 32–35.

president] Bartolomé Masó agreed; in a "Manifesto" to the nation he confidently proclaimed: "The war for the independence of our country is nearing the end." . . .

U.S. officials were also among those who concluded that the Spanish cause was hopeless. "Spain herself has demonstrated that she is powerless either to conciliate Cuba or conquer it," former U.S. minister to Spain Hannis Taylor wrote in late 1897; "her sovereignty over [Cuba] is . . . now extinct." Secretary of State John Sherman agreed: "Spain will lose Cuba. That seems to me to be certain. She cannot continue the struggle." Assistant Secretary of State William Day warned grimly that the end was imminent. "The Spanish Government," he observed, "seems unable to conquer the insurgents." In a confidential memorandum to the White House, Day went further: "To-day the strength of the Cubans [is] nearly double . . . and [they] occupy and control virtually all the territory outside the heavily garrisoned coastal cities and a few interior towns. There are no active operations by the Spaniards. . . . The eastern provinces are admittedly 'Free Cuba.' In view of these statements alone, it is now evident that Spain's struggle in Cuba has become absolutely hopeless. . . . Spain is exhausted financially and physically, while the Cubans are stronger." . . .

In early 1898 the McKinley administration contemplated the impending denouement with a mixture of disquiet and dread. If Spanish sovereignty was untenable, Cuban pretension to sovereignty was unacceptable. The Cuban insurrection threatened more than the propriety of colonial administration; it also challenged the U.S. presumption of succession, for in contesting Spanish rule Cubans were advancing the claim of a new sovereignty. For much of the nineteenth century, the United States had pursued the acquisition of Cuba with resolve, if without results. The success of the Cuban rebellion threatened everything. In 1898 Cuba was lost to Spain, and if Washington did not act, it would also be lost to the United States. The implications of the "no transfer" principle [of the Monroe Doctrine] were now carried to their logical conclusion. If the United States could not permit Spain to transfer sovereignty to another power, neither could the United States allow Spain to relinquish sovereignty to Cubans.

Opposition to Cuban independence was a proposition with a past, possessed of a proper history, one that served to form and inform the principal policy formulations of the nineteenth century. Only the possibility of the transfer of Cuba to a potentially hostile foreign country seemed to trouble the United States more than the prospect of Cuban independence. Cuba was far too important to be turned over to the Cubans. Free Cuba raised the specter of political disorder, social upheaval, and racial conflict: Cuba as a source of regional instability and inevitably a source of international tension. Many had long detected in the racial heterogeneity of the island portents of disorder and dissolution. "Were the population of the island of one blood and color," John Quincy Adams affirmed in 1823, "there could be no doubt or hesitation with regard to the course which they would pursue, as dictated by their interests and their rights. The invasion of Spain by France would be the signal for *their* Declaration of Independence." However, Adams continued, in "their present state . . . they are not competent to a system of permanent self-dependence." Secretary of State Henry Clay gave explicit definition and enduring form to U.S. opposition to Cuban independence. "The population itself . . . ," Clay insisted, "is incompetent, at present, from its composition and amount, to maintain self government." This view was reiterated several decades later by Secretary of State

Hamilton Fish, who looked upon a population of Indians, Africans, and Spaniards as utterly incapable of sustaining self-government. . . .

Nor was the McKinley administration any more sympathetic to the prospects of Cuban independence. "I do not believe that the population is to-day fit for self-government," McKinley's minister to Spain, Stewart L. Woodford, commented in early March 1898. Woodford characterized the insurgency as "confined almost entirely to negroes," with "few whites in the rebel forces." Under the circumstances, he asserted, "Cuban independence is absolutely impossible as a permanent solution of the difficulty, since independence can only result in a continuous war of races, and this means that independent Cuba must be a second Santo Domingo." Several days later Woodford again invoked the specter of racial strife: "The insurgents, supported by the great majority of the blacks, and led by even a minority of enterprising and resolute whites, will probably be strong enough to prevent effective good government. . . . This would mean and involve continuous disorder and practical anarchy. . . . Peace can hardly be assured by the insurgents through and under an independent government." He concluded: "I have at last come to believe that the only certainty of peace is under our flag. . . . I am, thus, reluctantly, slowly, but entirely a convert to the early American ownership and occupation of the island." . . .

There was nothing further to be gained by delay. On the contrary, continued postponement could only benefit the Cubans. On April 11 McKinley forwarded his message to Congress. The portents of his purpose were clear: no mention of Cuban independence, nothing about recognition of the Cuban provisional government, not a hint of sympathy with Cuba Libre, nowhere even an allusion to the renunciation of territorial aggrandizement—only a request for congressional authorization "to take measures to secure a full and final termination of hostilities between the Government of Spain and the people of Cuba, and to secure in the island the establishment of a stable government, capable of maintaining order and observing its international obligations." The U.S. purpose in Cuba, McKinley noted, consisted of "forcible intervention . . . as a neutral to stop the war." The president explained: "The forcible intervention of the United States . . . involves . . . hostile constraint upon both the parties to the contest."

The war was thus directed against both Spaniards and Cubans, a means by which to neutralize the two competing claims of sovereignty and establish by force of arms a third one. . . .

News of McKinley's April 11 message to Congress, proposing intervention without recognition, immediately provoked hostile reactions from the Cuban leadership. "We will oppose any intervention which does not have for its expressed and declared object the independence of Cuba," [Cuban revolutionary party leader] Gonzalo de Quesada vowed. [Cuban legal counsel] Horatio Rubens released a statement bluntly warning the U.S. government that an intervention such as McKinley had proposed would be regarded as "nothing less than a declaration of war by the United States against the Cuban revolutionists." The arrival of a U.S. military expedition to Cuba under such circumstances, Rubens predicted, would oblige the insurgents to "treat that force as an enemy to be opposed, and, if possible, expelled." He added: "[T]he Cuban army will . . . remain in the interior, refusing to cooperate, declining to acknowledge any American authority, ignoring and rejecting the intervention to every possible extent. Should the United States troops succeed in expelling the Spanish; should the United States then declare a protectorate over the island—however provisional or tentative—and seek to extend its authority over the government of Cuba and the army of liberation, we would resist with force of arms as bitterly and tenaciously as we have fought the armies of Spain." The State Department, in fact, had dreaded this reaction. As early as March 24, [Assistant] Secretary [William] Day indicated that unless the United States recognized the Cubans, "or make some arrangement with them when we intervene, we will have to overcome both the Spaniards and Cubans."

The cause of Cuba Libre had wide support in Congress, and defenders of the Cuban cause mounted sustained efforts to secure recognition of Cuban independence. Seven days passed between the arrival of the president's message and the final war resolution on April 18, almost all of which were given to acrimonious debate and intense political maneuvering by the administration and its congressional supporters to defeat pro-independence resolutions. Compromise was reached when Congress agreed to forgo recognition of independence in exchange for McKinley's acceptance of a Joint Resolution in which Article Four, the Teller Amendment, served as a disclaimer of mischievous intentions. . . .

The Joint Resolution calmed Cuban misgivings. Persuaded that the intervention made common cause with separatist objectives, Cubans prepared to cooperate with their new allies. No matter that the United States refused to recognize the republic, as long as Washington endorsed the goals for which the republic stood. "It is true," [General] Calixto García conceded, "that they have not entered into an accord with our government; but they have recognized our right to be free and independent and that is enough for me." . . .

The question of Cuban independence, of course, had not been resolved. In the weeks and months that followed the cessation of hostilities, the McKinley administration moved determinedly to evade, circumvent, or otherwise nullify the purpose if not the purport of the Teller Amendment. Cubans were simply not ready to govern themselves, U.S. officials proclaimed after the war. "Self-government!" General William Shafter thundered in response to a reporter's question. "Why those people are no more fit for self-government than gunpowder is for hell." General Samuel Young insisted that "the insurgents are a lot of degenerates, absolutely devoid of honor or gratitude. They are no more capable of self-government than the savages of Africa." General William Ludlow agreed. "We are dealing here in Cuba," he reported to Washington, "with a relatively uninstructed population, whose sensibilities are easily aroused but who lack judgment, who are wholly unaccustomed to manage their own affairs, and who readily resort to violence when excited or thwarted. . . . The whole structure of society and business is still on too slender and tottering basis to warrant putting any additional strain upon it."

The implications were clearly drawn. The United States could hardly release Cuba into the family of nations so utterly ill-prepared for responsibilities in self-government. One cabinet member announced bluntly that President McKinley did not intend to expel Spain only to turn the island "over to the insurgents or any other particular class or faction." General Leonard Wood, the U.S. military governor of Cuba, articulated administration thinking succinctly. "When the Spanish-American war was declared," he insisted, "the United States took a step forward, and assumed a position as protector of the interests of Cuba. It became responsible for the welfare of the people, politically, mentally and morally."

The rationale to retain control over Cuba was established immediately after the war and found justification in the very congressional resolution that had promised independence. The Joint Resolution was reexamined and reinterpreted. Had not the Teller Amendment stipulated the necessity for "pacification"? Swift and striking, the new consensus formed around the proposition that "pacification" implied more than simply the cessation of hostilities. It also meant stability. "It is true," editorialized the *Philadelphia Inquirer,* "that the Congressional resolutions . . . set forth that we, as a nation, had no designs upon Cuba, and that our sole object was to free it. But these resolutions went further. They also declared it to be our intention to see to it that a stable government should be formed." The *New York Times* made a similar point, but with far more ominous implications: "The pledge we made by no means binds us to withdraw at once, nor does full and faithful compliance with its spirit and letter forbid us to become permanent possessors of Cuba if the Cubans prove to be altogether incapable of self-government. A higher obligation than the pledge of the resolution of Congress would then constrain us to continue our government of the island." The United States, insisted the *New York Tribune,* "is not repudiating, but is scrupulously and exactly fulfilling the obligation it assumed in the Act of Intervention. It did not then recognize the independence or sovereignty of the so-called Cuban Republic. It did not promise to establish that republic, or to put the insurgents in control of the island. It avowed the intention of pacifying the island." . . .

By 1901 the definition of pacification had undergone final transfiguration as an extension of U.S. interests. What circumstances would satisfy U.S. notions of "pacification," the *Philadelphia Inquirer* asked—and answered: "As soon as the Cubans show themselves able and ready to govern the Island in accordance with American principles of order, liberty, and justice, it is to be assumed that this Government will be ready to fulfill its pledge and relinquish control to them. It is not to be assumed that it will do so one day before that time." Leonard Wood was unequivocal. To end the occupation without having established prior control over Cuba, Wood predicted, would be tantamount to inviting European powers to occupy every harbor of the island. The United States demanded some definition of a "special relationship" as a precondition for the completion of "pacification," and hence compliance with "independence." And this "special relationship" necessarily required defining the terms by which the new government of Cuba would be obliged to act in a manner consistent with U.S. interests, even if this meant violating the spirit of the Teller Amendment. The United States, Secretary of War Elihu Root explained years later, insisted on "vitalizing the advice" to be offered to the Cuban government. "'Advice' meant, in this connection, more than the advice a man might give to his client; it meant 'enforceable advice,' like the advice which Great Britain might give to Egypt." Senator [Orville] Platt expressed his preference for "very much more stringent measures" but understood, too, that "when they concede to us the right of intervention and naval stations . . . that the United States gets an effective moral position, and which becomes something more than a moral position." Platt was categorical. "All that we have asked," he responded in defense of the amendment that would bear his name, "is that the mutual relations [between Cuba and the United States] shall be defined and acknowledged coincidentally with the setting up of Cuba's new government. In no other way could a stable government be assured in Cuba, and until such assurance there could be no complete 'pacification' of the island, and no surrender of its control."

The passage of the Platt Amendment in 1901 fulfilled the U.S. purpose. The new Cuban republic was to be shorn of all essential properties of sovereignty prior to its creation. The Cuban government was denied authority to enter into "any treaty or other compact with any foreign power or powers," denied, too, the authority to contract a public debt beyond its normal ability to repay, and obliged to cede national territory to accommodate a U.S. naval station. Lastly, Cubans were required to concede to the United States "the right to intervene" for the "maintenance of a government adequate for the protection of life, property and individual liberty." . . .

Acceptance of the Platt Amendment, Cubans were told, was the minimum condition for ending the military occupation. "We should . . . make our requests and desires known to Cuba," Representative [Townsend] Scudder insisted, "and thereafter, if necessary, these requests should be put in the form of an ultimatum. . . . The probability is that Cuba will yield; but if she does not do so readily, then our troops must remain until an absolute understanding is reached." Elihu Root was equally adamant. "Under the act of Congress they can never have any further government in Cuba, except the intervening Government of the United States until they have acted," Root pronounced. "No constitution can be put into effect in Cuba, and no government can be elected under it, no electoral law by the Convention can be put into effect, and no election held under it until they have acted upon this question." Root's point was unambiguous: "There is only one possible way for them to bring about the termination of the military government and make either the constitution or electoral law effective; that is to do the whole duty they were elected for."

Cubans eventually acquiesced. The choice before the assembly, delegate Manuel Sanguily understood, was limited independence or no independence at all. "Independence with restrictions is preferable to the [U.S.] military regime," he explained in casting his vote to accept the Platt Amendment. Enrique Villuendas agreed. "There is no use objecting to the inevitable," he conceded. "It is either annexation or a Republic with an amendment." The Platt Amendment was incorporated into the Cuban Constitution of 1901 as an appendix and subsequently ratified into fixed bilateral relations by way of the Permanent Treaty of 1903. . . .

The Platt Amendment thus brought the U.S. purpose in 1898 to a successful conclusion. National interests were guaranteed, not—to be sure—by way of the direct succession of sovereignty so long foreseen. On the other hand, neither did sovereignty pass to a third party. The United States went to war, as it always said it would, to prevent the transfer of sovereignty of Cuba, in this instance to the Cubans themselves.

F U R T H E R   R E A D I N G

Teodoro Agoncillo, *A Short History of the Philippines* (1975)

Robert L. Beisner, *Twelve Against Empire* (1968)

———, *From the Old to the New Diplomacy* (1986)

Ken De Bevoise, *Agents of Apocalypse: Epidemic and Disease in Colonial Philippines* (1995)

H. W. Brands, *Bound to Empire* (1992) (on the Philippines)

Eric Breitbart, *A World on Display: Photographs from the 1904 Saint Louis World's Fair* (1997)

Warren I. Cohen, *America's Response to China* (2000)

Renato Constantino, *The Philippines* (1975)

A. B. Feuer, *America at War: The Philippines* (2002)

James A. Field Jr., "American Imperialism," *American Historical Review* 83 (1978): 644–688

Mark T. Gilderhos, *The Second Century: U.S.–Latin American Relations Since 1889* (2000)

Frank Golay, *Face of Empire: United States–Philippine Relations, 1898–1946* (1998)

Lewis L. Gould, *The Spanish-American War and William McKinley* (1983)

Robert Hannigan, *The New World Power* (2002)

Michael H. Hunt, *The Making of a Special Relationship* (1993) (on China)

Gilbert M. Joseph, et al., eds., *Close Encounters of Empire* (1998)

Stanley Karnow, *In Our Image* (1989) (on the Philippines)

Paul A. Kramer, "Empires, Exceptions, and Anglo-Saxons: Race and Rule Between the British and United States Empires, 1880–1910," *Journal of American History* 88 (March 2002): 1315–1353

Walter LaFeber, *The American Search for Opportunity, 1865–1913* (1993)

———, *The New Empire* (1998)

Brian Linn, *The Philippine War* (2000)

Eric T. Love, *Race Over Empire* (2004)

Glenn A. May, *Battle for Batangas* (1991)

———, *Social Engineering in the Philippines* (1980)

Stuart Creighton Miller, *"Benevolent Assimilation"* (1982) (on the Philippines)

Joyce Milton, *The Yellow Kids* (1989) (on journalism)

Ian Mugridge, *The View from Xanadu* (1995) (on William Randolph Hearst)

Ivan Musicant, *Empire by Default* (1998)

John L. Offner, *An Unwanted War* (1992)

Thomas G. Paterson, "United States Intervention in Cuba: Interpretations of the Spanish-American-Cuban-Filipino War," *History Teacher* 29 (May 1996): 341–361

Louis A. Pérez, *Cuba Between Empires* (1988)

———, *Cuba and the United States* (1990)

———, *On Becoming Cuban* (1999)

David M. Pletcher, *The Diplomacy of Trade and Investment* (1998)

Vicente Rafael, *White Love* (2000) (on the Philippines)

Hyman Rickover, *How the Battleship "Maine" Was Destroyed* (1976)

Emily S. Rosenberg, *Spreading the American Dream* (1982)

———, *Financial Missionaries to the World* (1999)

James Carlos Rowe, *Literary Culture and U.S. Imperialism* (2000)

Robert W. Rydell et al., *Fair America: World's Fairs in the United States* (2000)

Michael Salmon, *The Embarrassment of Slavery* (2001) (on the Philippines)

Peggy Samuels and Harold Samuels, *Remembering the Maine* (1998)

Thomas Schoonover, *Uncle Sam's War of 1898 and the Origins of Globalization* (2004)

Peter W. Stanley, *Reappraising an Empire* (1984)

David Trask, *The War with Spain in 1898* (1981)

Richard E. Welch, *Response to Imperialism* (1979) (on the Philippines)

William L. Williams, "United States Indian Policy and the Debate over Philippine Annexation: Implications for the Origins of American Imperialism," *Journal of American History* 66 (1980): 810–831

Fareed Zakaria, *Wealth to Power: The Unusual Origins of America's World Role* (1998)

CHAPTER
8

Woodrow Wilson,
World War I,
and the League Fight

In August 1914 Europe descended into war. Then an imperial power and an active trader on the high seas, the United States became ensnared in the deadly conflict. Until April 1917, however, President Woodrow Wilson struggled to define policies that would protect U.S. interests and principles, end the carnage, and permit him to shape the terms of the peace settlement. The president protested violations of U.S. neutral rights—dramatized by the sinking of the Lusitania by a German submarine in May 1915, lectured the belligerents to respect international law, and offered to mediate a "peace without victory." When his peace advocacy faltered and Germany launched unrestricted submarine warfare, Wilson asked a divided but ultimately supportive Congress for a declaration of war.

Once the United States became a belligerent, Wilson strove not only to win the war but to shape the postwar peace. He called for a nonvindictive peace treaty and urged creation of an association of nations to deter war. The president's Fourteen Points outlined his plans for shelving balance-of-power politics in favor of disarmament, open diplomacy, Open Door trade, and self-determination. Having tipped the balance in favor of the Allies, the United States helped to force Germany to surrender on November 11, 1918. In January of the following year, Wilson journeyed to the Versailles Palace near Paris to negotiate a peace treaty and a covenant for the League of Nations. European leaders sneered that Wilson was a dreamer, but millions of people on the Continent cheered his arrival and his appeals for a democratic and peaceful future.

At home, however, many Americans began to question Wilson's handling of foreign policy, especially after they learned that he had compromised many of his principles in order to win approval for his League. Some critics listened to his lofty rhetoric and wondered if the president had deluded himself into thinking he was the world's savior. Republican leaders, who had defeated Democrats in the 1918 congressional elections, calculated that Wilson was politically vulnerable. Supreme nationalists feared that an international organization would undermine American *sovereignty and violate George Washington's venerable advice to avoid permanent alliances. Wilson denounced the naysayers as narrow, backward-looking people, and refused to abandon the collective security provision of Article 10 of the League covenant. Unwilling to bargain with senators who demanded "reservations" (amendments), opposed by "irreconcilables" who would accept no league whatsoever, and laid low by a debilitating stroke suffered in the summer of 1919, Wilson lost the fight. The Senate rejected the peace treaty and U.S. membership in the League of Nations.*

In spite of the rejected treaty, America's participation in the First World War elevated the nation to Great Power status and globalized U.S. foreign relations. The ideals that Woodrow Wilson espoused, moreover, became a cornerstone of modern American foreign policy. Scholars have disagreed strongly in assessing "Wilsonianism." Why did Wilson's diplomacy fail? Some have labeled Wilson a messianic idealist, whose arrogant moralism led him to adopt an inconsistent neutrality during the early stages of World War I. Critics argue that he under-estimated the great-power nationalism of the Allies—and the influence of Senate Republicans—at war's end. Others have praised Wilson for his breadth of vision and his willingness to make America assume a vital role in the postwar peace. Still others have analyzed the impact of the adversarial two-party system, the con-frontational interplay between the executive and legislative branches of the U.S. government, and the toll taken by Wilson's deteriorating health.

Wilson's diplomacy sparked a debate over fundamental issues in American for-eign policy. How engaged in the world should the nation be and how should foreign policy be conducted? Because his policies weighed so heavily on the future, historians continue to debate Wilson's legacy. Should he be credited with designing a multi-lateral international system that, once adopted after World War II, preserved the peace for over a half-century? Or was Wilson's principal legacy the flawed Versailles treaty that unwisely punished Germany, left the United States absent from the League of Nations, and set the stage for the Second World War? To grapple with Wilsonianism and its legacy, is to reach for an understanding of America's place in twentieth-century world affairs.

D O C U M E N T S

When a German U-boat sank the British liner *Lusitania* on May 7, 1915, killing 1,198, including 128 Americans, President Woodrow Wilson sent a strong note to Berlin. The May 13 warning, Document 1, demands that Germany disavow submarine warfare and respect the right of Americans to sail on the high seas. In January 1917, Germany declared unrestricted submarine warfare, and Wilson broke diplomatic relations with Berlin. On April 2, after the sinking of several American vessels, the president asked Congress for a declaration of war. His war message, Document 2, outlines U.S. griev-ances against Germany. One of the few dissenters in the Senate—the war measure passed, 82 to 6—was Robert M. La Follette of Wisconsin. In his speech of April 4, Document 3, the great reform politician reveals his fear of an American "war machine."

President Wilson issued his Fourteen Points in a speech on January 8, 1918, reprinted here as Document 4. Articles 10 through 16 of the Covenant of the League of Nations hammered out at the Paris Peace Conference in 1919 are included as Docu-ment 5. Wilson explained during his busy western U.S. speaking tour in September 1919 that these provisions would prevent wars. Excerpts from his speeches are featured in

Document 6. Led by Senator Henry Cabot Lodge of Massachusetts, critics worked to add "reservations" to the covenant through a Lodge resolution dated November 19, 1919, Document 7. But neither an amended peace treaty (which contained the covenant) nor an unamended treaty passed the Senate.

1. The First *Lusitania* Note Demands That Germany Halt Submarine Warfare, 1915

The Government of the United States has been apprised that the Imperial German Government considered themselves to be obliged by the extraordinary circumstances of the present war and the measures adopted by their adversaries in seeking to cut Germany off from all commerce, to adopt methods of retaliation which go much beyond the ordinary methods of warfare at sea, in the proclamation of a war zone from which they have warned neutral ships to keep away. This Government has already taken occasion to inform the Imperial German Government that it cannot admit the adoption of such measures or such a warning of danger to operate as in any degree an abbreviation of the rights of American shipmasters or of American citizens bound on lawful errands as passengers on merchant ships of belligerent nationality; and that it must hold the Imperial German Government to a strict accountability for any infringement of those rights, intentional or incidental. It does not understand the Imperial German Government to question those rights. It assumes, on the contrary, that the Imperial Government accept, as of course, the rule that the lives of noncombatants, whether they be of neutral citizenship or citizens of one of the nations at war, can not lawfully or rightfully be put in jeopardy by the capture or destruction of an unarmed merchantman, and recognize also, as all other nations do, the obligation to take the usual precaution of visit and search to ascertain whether a suspected merchantman is in fact of belligerent nationality or is in fact carrying contraband of war under a neutral flag.

The Government of the United States, therefore, desires to call the attention of the Imperial German Government with the utmost earnestness to the fact that the objection to their present method of attack against the trade of their enemies lies in the practical impossibility of employing submarines in the destruction of commerce without disregarding those rules of fairness, reason, justice, and humanity, which all modern opinion regards as imperative. It is practically impossible for the officers of a submarine to visit a merchantman at sea and examine her papers and cargo. It is practically impossible for them to make a prize of her; and, if they can not put a prize crew on board of her, they can not sink her without leaving her crew and all on board of her to the mercy of the sea in her small boats. These facts it is understood the Imperial German Government frankly admit. We are informed that, in the instances of which we have spoken, time enough for even that poor measure of safety was not given, and in at least two of the cases cited, not so much as a warning was received. Manifestly submarines can not be used against merchantmen,

This document can be found in U.S. Department of State, *Papers Relating to the Foreign Relations of the United States, 1915, Supplement* (Washington, D.C.: Government Printing Office, 1928), 393–396.

as the last few weeks have shown, without an inevitable violation of many sacred principles of justice and humanity.

American citizens act within their indisputable rights in taking their ships and in traveling wherever their legitimate business calls them upon the high seas, and exercise those rights in what should be the well-justified confidence that their lives will not be endangered by acts done in clear violation of universally acknowledged international obligations, and certainly in the confidence that their own Government will sustain them in the exercise of their rights.

2. President Woodrow Wilson Asks Congress to Declare War Against Germany, 1917

On the third of February last I officially laid before you the extraordinary announce-ment of the Imperial German Government that on and after the first day of February it was its purpose to put aside all restraints of law of humanity and use its submarines to sink every vessel that sought to approach either the ports of Great Britain and Ireland or the western coasts of Europe or any of the ports controlled by the enemies of Germany within the Mediterranean. That had seemed to be the object of the Ger-man submarine warfare earlier in the war, but since April of last year the Imperial Government had somewhat restrained the commanders of its undersea craft in con-formity with its promise then given to us that passenger boats should not be sunk and that due warning would be given to all other vessels which its submarines might seek to destroy, when no resistance was offered or escape attempted, and care taken that their crews were given at least a fair chance to save their lives in their open boats. The precautions taken were meagre and haphazard enough, as was proved in dis-tressing instance after instance in the progress of the cruel and unmanly business, but a certain degree of restraint was observed. The new policy has swept every restriction aside. Vessels of every kind, whatever their flag, their character, their cargo, their destination, their errand, have been ruthlessly sent to the bottom without warning and without thought of help or mercy for those on board, the vessels of friendly neutrals along with those of belligerents. Even hospital ships and ships carrying relief to the sorely bereaved and stricken people of Belgium, though the latter were provided with safe conduct through the proscribed areas by the German Government itself and were distinguished by unmistakable marks of identity, have been sunk with the same reckless lack of compassion or of principle.

I was for a little while unable to believe that such things would in fact be done by any government that had hitherto subscribed to the humane practices of civi-lized nations. International law had its origin in the attempt to set up some law which would be respected and observed upon the seas, where no nation had right of dominion where lay the free highways of the world. By painful stage after stage has that law been built up, with meagre enough results, indeed, after all was ac-complished that could be accomplished, but always with a clear view, at least of what the heart and conscience of mankind demanded. This minimum of right the German Government has swept aside under the plea of retaliation and necessity

---

This document can be found in *Congressional Record*, LV (April 2, 1917), Part 1, 102–104.

and because it had no weapons which it could use at sea except these which it is impossible to employ as it is employing them without throwing to the winds all scruples of humanity or of respect for the understandings that were supposed to underlie the intercourse of the world. I am not now thinking of the loss of property involved, immense and serious as that is, but only of the wanton and wholesale destruction of the lives of noncombatants, men, women, and children, engaged in pursuits which have always, even in the darkest periods of modern history, been deemed innocent and legitimate. Property can be paid for; the lives of peaceful and innocent people cannot be. The present German submarine warfare against commerce is a warfare against mankind.

It is a war against all nations. American ships have been sunk, American lives taken, in ways which it has stirred us very deeply to learn of, but the ships and people of other neutral and friendly nations have been sunk and overwhelmed in the waters in the same way. There has been no discrimination. The challenge is to all mankind. Each nation must decide for itself how it will meet it. The choice we make for ourselves must be made with a moderation of counsel and a temperateness of judgment befitting our character and our motives as a nation. We must put excited feeling away. Our motive will not be revenge or the victorious assertion of the physical might of the nation, but only the vindication of right, of human right, of which we are only a single champion. . . .

With a profound sense of the solemn and even tragical character of the step I am taking and of the grave responsibilities which it involves, but in unhesitating obedience to what I deem my constitutional duty, I advise that the Congress declare the recent course of the Imperial German Government to be in fact nothing less than war against the government and people of the United States; that it formally accept the status of belligerent which has thus been thrust upon it; and that it take immediate steps not only to put the country in a more thorough state of defense but also to exert all its power and employ all its resources to bring the Government of the German Empire to terms and end the war. . . .

Does not every American feel that assurance has been added to our hope for the future peace of the world by the wonderful and heartening things that have been happening within the last few weeks in Russia? Russia was known by those who knew it best to have been always in fact democratic at heart, in all the vital habits of her thought, in all the intimate relationships of her people that spoke their natural instinct, their habitual attitude towards life. The autocracy that crowned the summit of her political structure, long as it had stood and terrible as was the reality of its power, was not in fact Russian in origin, character, or purpose; and now it has been shaken off and the great, generous Russian people have been added in all their naive majesty and might to the forces that are fighting for freedom in the world, for justice, and for peace. Here is a fit partner for a League of Honour.

One of the things that has served to convince us that the Prussian autocracy was not and could never be our friends is that from the very outset of the present war it has filled our unsuspecting communities and even our offices of government with spies and set criminal intrigues everywhere afoot against our national unity of counsel, our peace within and without, our industries and our commerce. . . . That it means to stir up enemies against us at our very doors the intercepted note to the German Minister at Mexico City [the Zimmerman telegram] is eloquent evidence.

We are accepting this challenge of hostile purpose because we know that in such a government, following such methods, we can never have a friend; and that in the presence of its organized power, always lying in wait to accomplish we know not what purpose, there can be no assured security for the democratic governments of the world. We are now about to accept gauge of battle with its natural foe to liberty and shall, if necessary, spend the whole force of the nation to check and nullify its pretensions and its power. We are glad, now that we see the facts with no veil of false pretence about them, to fight thus for the ultimate peace of the world and for the liberation of its peoples, the German peoples included: for the rights of nations great and small and the privilege of men everywhere to choose their way of life and of obedience. The world must be made safe for democracy. . . .

It is a distressing and oppressive duty, Gentlemen of the Congress, which I have performed in thus addressing you. There are, it may be, many months of fiery trial and sacrifice ahead of us. It is a fearful thing to lead this great peaceful people into war, into the most terrible and disastrous of all wars, civilization itself seeming to be in the balance. But the right is more precious than peace, and we shall fight for the things which we have always carried nearest our hearts—for democracy, for the right of those who submit to authority to have a voice in their own governments, for the rights and liberties of small nations, for a universal dominion of right by such a concert of free peoples as shall bring peace and safety to all nations and make the world itself at last free. To such a task we can dedicate our lives and our fortunes, everything that we are and everything that we have, with the pride of those who know that the day has come when America is privileged to spend her blood and her might for the principles that gave her birth and happiness and the peace which she has treasured. God helping her, she can do no other.

3. Senator Robert M. La Follette
Voices His Dissent, 1917

The poor, sir, who are the ones called upon to rot in the trenches, have no organized power, have no press to voice their will upon this question of peace or war; but, oh, Mr. President, at some time they will be heard. I hope and I believe they will be heard in an orderly and a peaceful way. I think they may be heard from before long. I think, sir, if we take this step, when the people to-day who are staggering under the burden of supporting families at the present prices of the necessaries of the life find those prices multiplied, when they are raised a hundred percent, or 200 percent, as they will be quickly, aye, sir, when beyond that those who pay taxes come to have their taxes doubled and again doubled to pay the interest on the nontaxable bonds held by Morgan and his combinations, which have been issued to meet this war, there will come an awakening; they will have their day and they will be heard. It will be as certain and as inevitable as the return of the tides, and as resistless, too. . . .

Just a word of comment more upon one of the points in the President's address. He says that this is a war "for the things which we have always carried nearest to our hearts—for democracy, for the right of those who submit to authority to

---

This document can be found in *Congressional Record*, LV (April 4, 1917), Part 1, 226, 228.

have a voice in their own government." In many places throughout the address is this exalted sentiment given expression. . . .

But the President proposes alliance with Great Britain, which, however liberty-loving its people, is a hereditary monarchy, with a hereditary ruler, with a hereditary House of Lords, with a hereditary landed system, with a limited and restricted suffrage for one class and a multiplied suffrage power for another, and with grinding industrial conditions for all the wageworkers. The President has not suggested that we make our support of Great Britain conditional to her granting home rule to Ireland, or Egypt, or India. We rejoice in the establishment of a democracy in Russia, but it will hardly be contended that if Russia was still an autocratic Government, we would not be asked to enter this alliance with her just the same. Italy and the lesser powers of Europe, Japan in the Orient; in fact all of the countries with whom we are to enter into alliance, except France and newly revolutionized Russia, are still of the old order—and it will be generally conceded that no one of them has done as much for its people in the solution of municipal problems and in securing social and industrial reforms as Germany. . . .

Who has registered the knowledge or approval of the American people of the course this Congress is called upon in declaring war upon Germany? Submit the question to the people, you who support it. You who support it dare not do it, for you know that by a vote of more than ten to one the American people as a body would register their declaration against it.

In the sense that this war is being forced upon our people without their knowing why and without their approval, and that wars are usually forced upon all peoples in the same way, there is some truth in the statement; but I venture to say that the response which the German people have made to the demands of this war shows that it has a degree of popular support which the war upon which we are entering has not and never will have among our people. The espionage bills, the conscription bills, and other forcible military measures which we understand are being ground out of the war machine in this country is the complete proof that those responsible for this war fear that it has no popular support and that armies sufficient to satisfy the demand of the entente allies can not be recruited by voluntary enlistments.

4. Wilson Proclaims U.S. War Aims: The Fourteen Points, 1918

I. Open covenants of peace, openly arrived at, after which there shall be no private international understandings of any kind but diplomacy shall proceed always frankly and in the public view.

II. Absolute freedom of navigation upon the seas, outside territorial waters, alike in peace and in war, except as the seas may be closed in whole or in part by international action for the enforcement of international covenants.

III. The removal, so far as possible, of all economic barriers and the establishment of an equality of trade conditions among all the nations consenting to the peace and associating themselves for its maintenance.

This document can be found in *Congressional Record,* LVI (January 8, 1918), Part 1, 680–682.

IV. Adequate guarantees given and taken that national armaments will be reduced to the lowest point consistent with domestic safety.

V. A free, open-minded, and absolutely impartial adjustment of all colonial claims, based upon a strict observance of the principle that in determining all such questions of sovereignty the interests of the populations concerned must have equal weight with the equitable claims of the government whose title is to be determined.

VI. The evacuation of all Russian territory and such a settlement of all questions affecting Russia as will secure the best and freest cooperation of the other nations of the world in obtaining for her an unhampered and unembarrassed opportunity for the independent determination of her own political development and national policy and assure her of a sincere welcome into the society of free nations under institutions of her own choosing; and, more than a welcome, assistance also of every kind that she may need and may herself desire. The treatment accorded Russia by her sister nations in the months to come will be the acid test of their good will, of their comprehension of her needs as distinguished from their own interests, and of their intelligent and unselfish sympathy.

VII. Belgium, the whole world will agree, must be evacuated and restored, without any attempt to limit the sovereignty which she enjoys in common with all other free nations. No other single act will serve as this will serve to restore confidence among the nations in the laws which they have themselves set and determined for the government of their relations with one another. Without this healing act the whole structure and validity of international law is forever impaired.

VIII. All French territory should be freed and the invaded portions restored, and the wrong done to France by Prussia in 1871 in the matter of Alsace-Lorraine, which has unsettled the peace of the world for nearly fifty years, should be righted, in order that peace may once more be made secure in the interest of all.

IX. A readjustment of the frontiers of Italy should be effected along clearly recognizable lines of nationality.

X. The peoples of Austria-Hungary, whose place among the nations we wish to see safeguarded and assured, should be accorded the freest opportunity of autonomous development.

XI. Rumania, Serbia, and Montenegro should be evacuated; occupied territories restored; Serbia accorded free and secure access to the sea; and the relations of the several Balkan states to one another determined by friendly consul along historically established lines of allegiance and nationality; and international guarantees of the political and economic independence and territorial integrity of the several Balkan states should be entered into.

XII. The Turkish portions of the present Ottoman Empire should be assured a secure sovereignty, but the other nationalities which are now under Turkish rule should be assured an undoubted security of life and an absolutely unmolested opportunity of autonomous development, and the Dardanelles should be permanently opened as a free passage to the ships and commerce of all nations under international guarantees.

XIII. An independent Polish state should be erected which should include the territories inhabited by indisputably Polish populations, which should be assured a free and secure access to the sea, and whose political and economic independence and territorial integrity should be guaranteed by international covenant.

XIV. A general association of nations must be formed under specific covenants for the purpose of affording mutual guarantees of political independence and territorial integrity to great and small states alike.

5. Articles 10 Through 16 of the League of Nations Covenant, 1919

Article 10.   The Members of the League undertake to respect and preserve as against external aggression the territorial integrity and existing political independence of all Members of the League. In case of any such aggression or in case of any threat or danger of such aggression the Council shall advise upon the means by which this obligation shall be fulfilled.

Article 11.   Any war or threat of war, whether immediately affecting any of the Members of the League or not, is hereby declared a matter of concern to the whole League, and the League shall take any action that may be deemed wise and effectual to safeguard the peace of nations. . . .

It is also declared to be the friendly right of each Member of the League to bring to the attention of the Assembly or of the Council any circumstance whatever affecting international relations which threatens to disturb international peace or the good understanding between nations upon which peace depends.

Article 12.   The Members of the League agree that if there should arise between them any dispute likely to lead to a rupture, they will submit the matter either to arbitration or to inquiry by the Council, and they agree in no case to resort to war until three months after the award by the arbitrators or the report by the Council.

In any case under this Article the award of the arbitrators shall be made within a reasonable time, and the report of the Council shall be made within six months after the submission of the dispute.

Article 13.   The Members of the League agree that whenever any dispute shall arise between them which they recognise to be suitable for submission to arbitration and which cannot be satisfactorily settled by diplomacy, they will submit the whole subject-matter to arbitration. . . .

Article 14.   The Council shall formulate and submit to the Members of the League for adoption plans for the establishment of a Permanent Court of International Justice. The Court shall be competent to hear and determine any dispute of an international character which the parties thereto submit to it. The Court may also give an advisory opinion upon any dispute or question referred to it by the Council or by the Assembly.

This document can be found in U.S. Department of State, *Papers Relating to the Foreign Relations of the United States, 1919* (Washington, D.C.: Government Printing Office, 1942–1947), XIII, 83–89.

Article 15. If there should arise between Members of the League any dispute likely to lead to a rupture, which is not submitted to arbitration in accordance with Article 13, the Members of the League agree that they will submit the matter to the Council. . . .

Article 16. Should any Member of the League resort to war in disregard of its covenants under Articles 12, 13 or 15, it shall *ipso facto* be deemed to have committed an act of war against all other Members of the League, which hereby undertake immediately to subject it to the severance of all trade or financial relations, the prohibition of all intercourse between their nationals and the nationals of the covenant-breaking State, and the prevention of all financial, commercial or personal intercourse between the nationals of the covenant-breaking State and the nationals of any other State, whether a Member of the League or not.

It shall be the duty of the Council in such case to recommend to the several Governments concerned what effective military, naval or air force the Members of the League shall severally contribute to the armed forces to be used to protect the covenants of the League.

6. Wilson Defends the Peace Treaty and League, 1919

Indianapolis, Indiana, September 4

You have heard a great deal about article 10 of the covenant of the league of nations. Article 10 speaks the conscience of the world. Article 10 is the article which goes to the heart of this whole bad business, for that article says that the members of this league, that is intended to be all the great nations of the world, engage to respect and to preserve against all external aggression the territorial integrity and political independence of the nations concerned. That promise is necessary in order to prevent this sort of war from recurring, and we are absolutely discredited if we fought this war and then neglect the essential safeguard against it. You have heard it said, my fellow citizens, that we are robbed of some degree of our sovereign independent choice by articles of that sort. Every man who makes a choice to respect the rights of his neighbors deprives himself of absolute sovereignty, but he does it by promising never to do wrong, and I can not for one see anything that robs me of any inherent right that I ought to retain when I promise that I will do right, when I promise that I will respect the thing which, being disregarded and violated, brought on a war in which millions of men lost their lives, in which the civilization of mankind was in the balance, in which there was the most outrageous exhibition ever witnessed in the history of mankind of the rapacity and disregard for right of a great armed people. We engage in the first sentence of article 10 to respect and preserve from external aggression the territorial integrity and the existing political independence not only of the other member States, but of all States, and if any member of the league of nations disregards that promise, then what happens? The council of the league advises what should be done to enforce the respect for that covenant on the part of the nation

This document can be found in *Congressional Record,* LVIII (September 1919): Part 5, 5001–5002, 5005; Part 6, 5593, 6244–6245, 6249, 6254; Part 7, 6417, 6422.

attempting to violate it, and there is no compulsion upon us to take that advice except the compulsion of our good conscience and judgment. So that it is perfectly evident that if in the judgment of the people of the United States the council adjudged wrong and that this was not a case of the use of force, there would be no necessity on the part of the Congress of the United States to vote the use of force. But there could be no advice of the council on any such subject without a unanimous vote, and the unanimous vote includes our own, and if we accepted the advice we would be accepting our own advice, for I need not tell you that the representatives of the Government of the United States would not vote without instructions from their Government at home, and that what we united in advising we could be certain that the American people would desire to do. There is in that covenant not only not a sur-render of the independent judgment of the Government of the United States, but an expression of it, because that independent judgment would have to join with the judgment of the rest.

But when is that judgment going to be expressed, my fellow citizens? Only after it is evident that every other resource has failed, and I want to call your attention to the central machinery of the league of nations. If any member of that league or any nation not a member refuses to submit the question at issue either to arbitration or to discussion by the council, there ensues automatically, by the engagements of this covenant, an absolute economic boycott. There will be no trade with that nation by any member of the league. There will be no interchange of communication by post or telegraph. There will be no travel to or from that nation. Its borders will be closed. No citizen of any other State will be allowed to enter it and no one of its citizens will be allowed to leave it. It will be hermetically sealed by the united action of the most powerful nations in the world. And if this economic boycott bears with unequal weight, the members of the league agree to support one another and to relieve one another in any exceptional disadvantages that may arise out of it. . . .

I want to call your attention, if you will turn it up when you go home, to article 11, following article 10 of the covenant of the league of nations. That article, let me say, is the favorite article in the treaty, so far as I am concerned. It says that every matter which is likely to affect the peace of the world is everybody's business; that it shall be the friendly right of any nation to call attention in the league to anything that is likely to affect the peace of the world or the good understanding between na-tions, upon which the peace of the world depends, whether that matter immediately concerns the nation drawing attention to it or not.

St. Louis, Missouri, September 5

There can hereafter be no secret treaties. There were nations represented around that board—I mean the board at which the commission on the league of nations sat, where 14 nations were represented—there were nations represented around that board who had entered into many a secret treaty and understanding, and they made not the least objection to promising that hereafter no secret treaty should have any validity whatever. The provision of the covenant is that every treaty or international understanding shall be registered, I believe the word is, with the gen-eral secretary of the league, that the general secretary shall publish it in full just so soon as it is possible for him to publish it, and that no treaty shall be valid which is not thus registered. It is like our arrangements with regard to mortgages on real estate, that until they are registered nobody else need pay any attention to them. And so with the treaties; until they are registered in this office of the league nobody, not even the parties themselves, can insist upon their execution. You have cleared the deck thereby of the most dangerous thing and the most embarrassing thing that has hitherto existed in international politics.

Sioux Falls, South Dakota, September 8

I can not understand the psychology of men who are resisting it [the treaty]. I can not understand what they are afraid of, unless it is that they know physical force and do not understand moral force. Moral force is a great deal more powerful than physical. Govern the sentiments of mankind and you govern mankind. Govern their fears, govern their hopes, determine their fortunes, get them together in concerted masses, and the whole thing sways like a team. Once get them suspecting one another, once get them antagonizing one another, and society itself goes to pieces. We are trying to make a society instead of a set of barbarians out of the governments of the world. I sometimes think, when I wake in the night, of all the wakeful nights that anxious fathers and mothers and friends have spent during those weary years of this awful war, and I seem to hear the cry, the inarticulate cry of mothers all over the world, millions of them on the other side of the sea and thousands of them on this side of the sea, "In God's name, give us the sensible and hopeful and peaceful processes of right and of justice."

America can stay out, but I want to call you to witness that the peace of the world can not be established without America. America is necessary to the peace of the world. And reverse the proposition: The peace and good will of the world are necessary to America. Disappoint the world, center its suspicion upon you, make it feel that you are hot and jealous rivals of the other nations, and do you think you are going to do as much business with them as you would otherwise do? I do not like to put the thing on that plane, my fellow countrymen, but if you want to talk business, I can talk business. If you want to put it on the low plane of how much money you can make, you can make more money out of friendly traders than out of hostile traders. You can make more money out of men who trust you than out of men who fear you.

San Francisco, California, September 17

The Monroe doctrine means that if any outside power, any power outside this hemisphere, tries to impose its will upon any portion of the Western Hemisphere the United States is at liberty to act independently and alone in repelling the aggression; that it does not have to wait for the action of the league of nations; that it does not have to wait for anything but the action of its own administration and its own Congress. This is the first time in the history of international diplomacy that any great government has acknowledged the validity of the Monroe doctrine. Now for the first time all the great fighting powers of the world except Germany, which for the time being has ceased to be a great fighting power, acknowledge the validity of the Monroe doctrine and acknowledge it as part of the international practice of the world.

They [critics] are nervous about domestic questions. They say, "It is intolerable to think that the league of nations should interfere with domestic questions," and whenever they begin to specify they speak of the question of immigration, of the question of naturalization, of the question of the tariff. My fellow citizens, no competent or authoritative student of international law would dream of maintaining that these were anything but exclusively domestic questions, and the covenant of the league expressly provides that the league can take no action whatever about matters which are in the practice of international law regarded as domestic questions.

San Francisco, California, September 18

In order that we may not forget, I brought with me the figures as to what this war [First World War] meant to the world. This is a body of business men and you will understand these figures. They are too big for the imagination of men who do not handle big things. Here is the cost of the war in money, exclusive of what we loaned one another: Great Britain and her dominions, $38,000,000,000; France, $26,000,000,000; the United States, $22,000,000,000 (this is the direct cost of our operations); Russia, $18,000,000,000; Italy $13,000,000,000; and the total, including Belgium, Japan, and other countries, $123,000,000,000. This is what it cost the Central Powers: Germany, $39,000,000,000, the biggest single item; Austria-Hungary, $21,000,000,000; Turkey and Bulgaria, $3,000,000,000; a total of $63,000,000,000, and a grand total of direct war costs of $186,000,000,000—almost the capital of the world. The expenditures of the United States were at the rate of $1,000,000 an hour for two years, including nighttime with daytime. The battle deaths during the war were as follows: Russia lost in dead 1,700,000 men, poor Russia that got nothing but terror and despair out of it all; Germany, 1,600,000; France, 1,385,000; Great Britain, 900,000; Austria, 800,000; Italy, 364,000; the United States, 50,300 dead. The total for all the belligerents, 7,450,200 men—just about seven and a half million killed because we could not have arbitration and discussion, because the world had never had the courage to propose the conciliatory methods which some of us are now doubting whether we ought to accept or not.

San Diego, California, September 19

It is feared that our delegates will be outvoted, because I am constantly hearing it said that the British Empire has six votes and we have one. I am perfectly content to have only one when the one counts six, and that is exactly the arrangement under the league. Let us examine that matter a little more particularly. Besides the vote of Great Britain herself, the other five votes are the votes of Canada, of South Africa, of Australia, of New Zealand, and of India. We ourselves were champions and advocates of giving a vote to Panama, of giving a vote to Cuba—both of them under the direction and protectorate of the United States—and if a vote was given to Panama and to Cuba, could it reasonably be denied to the great Dominion of Canada? Could it be denied to that stout Republic in South Africa, that is now living under a nation which did, indeed, overcome it at one time, but which did not dare retain its government in its hands, but turned it over to the very men whom it had fought? Could we deny it to Australia, that independent little republic in the Pacific, which has led the world in so many liberal reforms? Could it be denied New Zealand? Could we deny it to the hundreds of millions who live in India? But, having given these six votes, what are the facts? For you have been misled with regard to them. The league can take no active steps without the unanimous vote of all the nations represented on the council, added to a vote of the majority in the assembly itself. These six votes are in the assembly, not in the council. The assembly is not a voting body, except upon a limited number of questions, and whenever those questions are questions of action, the affirmative vote of every nation represented on the council is indispensable, and the United States is represented on the council.

Salt Lake City, Utah, September 23

I am not going to stop, my fellow citizens, to discuss the Shantung provision [which shifted control of the area from Germany to Japan] in all its aspects, but what I want to call your attention to is that just so soon as this covenant is ratified every nation in the world will have the right to speak out for China. And I want to say very frankly, and I ought to add that the representatives of those great nations themselves admit, that Great Britain and France and the other powers which have insisted upon similar concessions in China will be put in a position where they will have to reconsider them. This is the only way to serve and redeem China, unless, indeed, you want to start a war for the purpose. At the beginning of the war and during the war Great Britain and France engaged by solemn treaty with Japan that if she would come into the war and continue in the war, she could have, provided she in the meantime took it by force of arms, what Germany had in China. Those are treaties already in force. They are not waiting for ratification. France and England can not withdraw from those obligations, and it will serve China not one iota if we should dissent from the Shantung arrangement; but by being parties to that arrangement we can insist upon the promise of Japan—the promise which the other Governments have not matched—that she will return to China immediately all sovereign rights within the Province of Shantung. We have got that for her now, and under the operations of article 11 and of article 10 it will be impossible for any nation to make any further inroads either upon the territorial integrity or upon the political independence of China.

Denver, Colorado, September 25

The adoption of the treaty means disarmament. Think of the economic burden and the restraint of liberty in the development of professional and mechanical life that resulted from the maintenance of great armies, not only in Germany but in France and in Italy and, to some extent, in Great Britain. If the United States should stand off from this thing we would have to have the biggest army in the world. There would be nobody else that cared for our fortunes. We would have to look out for ourselves, and when I hear gentlemen say, "Yes; that is what we want to do; we want to be independent and look out for ourselves" I say, "Well, then, consult your fellow citizens. There will have to be universal conscription. There will have to be taxes such as even yet we have not seen. There will have to be concentration of authority in the Government capable of using this terrible instrument. You can not conduct a war or command an army by a debating society. You can not determine in community centers what the command of the Commander in Chief is going to be; you will have to have a staff like the German staff, and you will have to center in the Commander in Chief of the Army and Navy the right to take instant action for the protection of the Nation." America will never consent to any such thing.

7. Senator Henry Cabot Lodge Proposes Reservations to the League Covenant, 1919

1. . . . In case of notice of withdrawal from the league of nations, as provided in said article [Article 1], the United States shall be the sole judge as to whether all its international obligations . . . have been fulfilled, and notice of withdrawal . . . may be given by a concurrent resolution of the Congress of the United States.

2. The United States assumes no obligation to preserve the territorial integrity or political independence of any other country . . . under the provisions of article 10, or to employ the military or naval forces of the United States under any article of the treaty for any purpose, unless in any particular case the Congress, which . . . has the sole power to declare war . . . shall . . . so provide.

3. No mandate shall be accepted by the United States under article 22 . . . except by action of the Congress of the United States.

4. The United States reserves to itself exclusively the right to decide what questions are within its domestic jurisdiction. . . .

5. The United States will not submit to arbitration or to inquiry by the assembly or by the council of the league of nations . . . any questions which in the judgment of the United States depend upon or relate to . . . the Monroe doctrine; said doctrine is to be interpreted by the United States alone and is . . . wholly outside the jurisdiction of said league of nations. . . .

6. The United States withholds its assent to articles 156, 157, and 158 [Shantung clauses]. . . .

7. The Congress of the United States will provide by law for the appointment of the representatives of the United States in the assembly and the council of the league of nations, and may in its discretion provide for the participation of the United States in any commission. . . . No person shall represent the United States under either said league of nations or the treaty of peace . . . except with the approval of the Senate of the United States. . . .

9. The United States shall not be obligated to contribute to any expenses of the league of nations . . . unless and until an appropriation of funds . . . shall have been made by the Congress of the United States.

10. If the United States shall at any time adopt any plan for the limitation of armaments proposed by the council of the league . . . it reserves the right to increase such armaments without the consent of the council whenever the United States is threatened with invasion or engaged in war. . . .

14. The United States assumes no obligation to be bound by any election, decision, report, or finding of the council or assembly in which any member of the league and its self-governing dominions, colonies, or parts of empire, in the aggregate have cast more than one vote.

This document can be found in *Congressional Record,* LVIII (November 19, 1919), Part 9, 877–878.

In the first essay, Thomas J. Knock of Southern Methodist University delivers a sympathetic but not uncritical assessment of Wilson. Knock argues that Wilson drew upon both progressive and conservative internationalists in pursuing neutrality toward Europe's war but rallied a left-of-center coalition to win reelection in 1916, advance his liberal domestic agenda, and mediate a "peace without victory." Once America entered the war, however, the president failed to win support for his controversial peace treaty, including the League of Nations, primarily because the backing of the progressives he needed for victory eroded in the face of wartime reaction both at home and abroad. In the second essay, the Dutch scholar Jan Wilhelm Schulte-Nordholt presents a more biting critique of Wilson and Wilsonianism. While admiring the president's commitment to peace, Schulte-Nordholt depicts a strong-willed dreamer who lost touch with reality. Driven by his culturally arrogant belief that the United States could provide an appropriate model for world peace, Wilson underestimated the complexities of international politics. At Paris, the Versailles negotiators manipulated the president, who conceded too much in order to save the League. The flawed peace, Schulte-Nordholt concludes, helped sow the seeds of the Second World War. Tony Smith of Tufts University takes on Wilson's critics in the last essay. Focusing on the Treaty of Versailles and the League, Smith praises Wilson's blueprint for a new world order based on the principles of liberal internationalism. Wilsonianism, he observes, wedded the urge for national self-determination to democracy and called for collective security and a liberal economic regime to contain German power and guarantee the peace. Answering foreign-policy "realists" who have accused Wilson of failing to comprehend power politics, Smith asks if there was a better way at the time for America to defend its interests and stabilize Europe. Smith downplays Wilson's impact on the international crises of the 1920s and 1930s and points to the Wilsonian resurgence after World War II as proof of Wilson's far-sightedness.

From Peace to War: Progressive Internationalists Confront the Forces of Reaction

THOMAS J. KNOCK

As the historian Frederick Jackson Turner once remarked, the age of reform in the United States was "also the age of socialistic inquiry." Indeed, by 1912, the Socialist Party of America and its quadrennial standard-bearer, Eugene Debs, had attained respectability and legitimacy. The party's membership exceeded 115,000, and some 1,200 socialists held public office in 340 municipalities and twenty-four states. As many as three million Americans read socialist newspapers on a regular basis. Julius Wayland's *Appeal to Reason,* with 760,000 weekly subscribers, ranked among the most widely read publications in the world.

The general cast of the four-way presidential campaign of 1912 also lent credence to Turner's observation. Notwithstanding the conservatism of the incumbent, William Howard Taft, the impact of progressivism on the two main parties, in tandem with the success of the Socialist party, caused a certain blurring of traditional

---

This is an original essay written for this volume based on *To End All Wars: Woodrow Wilson and the Quest for a New World Order* (New York: Oxford University Press, 1992).

political lines. To millions of citizens, a vote for either Woodrow Wilson, the progressive Democrat, Theodore Roosevelt, the insurgent "Bull Moose" who bolted the Republicans to form the Progressive party, or Debs, the Socialist, amounted to a protest against the status quo of industrial America. And that protest, from top to bottom, sanctioned an unfolding communion between liberals and socialists practically unique in American history.

In this new age of progressive reform and socialistic inquiry, it would be Woodrow Wilson's opportunity and challenge to reconcile and shape domestic and foreign concerns in ways that no previous chief executive had ever contemplated. . . .

Feminists, liberals, pacifists, socialists, and reformers of varying kinds filled the ranks of the progressive internationalists. Their leaders included many of the era's authentic heroes and heroines: Jane Addams of Hull House, the poet-journalist John Reed, Max Eastman of the *Masses,* the civil-rights crusader Oswald Garrison Villard, and Lillian Wald of New York's Henry Street Settlement, to name a few. For them the search for a peaceful world order provided a logical common ground. Peace was indispensable to change itself—to the survival of the labor movement, to their campaigns on behalf of women's rights and the abolition of child labor, and to social justice legislation in general. If the war in Europe were permitted to rage on indefinitely, progressive internationalists believed, then the United States could not help but get sucked into it; not only their great causes, but also the very moral fiber of the nation would be destroyed should its resources be diverted from reform to warfare. Thus, their first goal (and one in keeping with Wilson's policy of neutrality) was to bring about a negotiated settlement of the war.

The Woman's Peace party, founded in January 1915, in Washington, D.C., and led by Jane Addams, played a pivotal role in the progressive internationalist movement. Guided by the principle of "the sacredness of human life," the platform of the Woman's Peace party constituted the earliest manifesto on internationalism advanced by any American organization throughout the war. The party's "program for constructive peace" called for an immediate armistice, international agreements to limit armaments and nationalize their manufacture, a reduction of trade barriers, self-determination, machinery for arbitration, and a "Concert of Nations" to supersede the balance-of-power system. The platform also pressed for American mediation of the war. Its authors made sure that the president received all of their recommendations. . . .

Many progressive internationalists regarded the reactionary opponents of domestic reform and the advocates of militarism and imperialism as twins born of the same womb; they watched with alarm as the champions of "preparedness" mounted what they viewed as an insidious offensive to thwart social and economic progress at home, as well as disarmament and the repudiation of war as an instrument of foreign policy. In response to the preparedness movement, liberal reformers and leading socialists joined forces to establish the American Union Against Militarism (AUAM). Within months, the AUAM had branches in every major city in the country. When, in the wake of the *Lusitania* disaster, Wilson introduced legislation to increase substantially the size of the army and navy, it appeared that he had surrendered to the enemy. Then, too, a competing, conservative vision of internationalism was vying for national attention.

The program of the conservative internationalists was different in both subtle and conclusive ways. It was developed by the organizers of the League to Enforce

Peace (LEP), founded in June 1915, and led by former president William Howard Taft and other Republicans prominent in the field of international law. Within two years, they had established four thousand branches in forty-seven states. The LEP's platform, "Warrant from History," called for American participation in a world parliament, which would assemble periodically to make appropriate changes to international law and employ arbitration and conciliation procedures to settle certain kinds of disputes. While more or less endorsing the general principle of collective security, most conservative internationalists also believed that the United States should build up its military complex and reserve the right to undertake independent coercive action whenever the "national interest" was threatened. Unlike progressive internationalists, the LEP did not concern itself with self-determination or advocate disarmament or even a military standoff in Europe. These internationalists were openly pro-Allied; in fact, the slogan, "The LEP does *not* seek to end the present war," appeared on their letterhead in the autumn of 1916.

Throughout that year, Wilson met and corresponded with representatives of both wings of the new internationalist movement. In May 1916, for example, he delivered an important address before a gathering of the LEP, the occasion for his first public affirmation on behalf of American membership in some kind of postwar peacekeeping organization. Yet Wilson's sympathies lay decidedly with the progressive internationalists. Two weeks earlier, for the first time, he had articulated to persons other than his absolute confidants his ideas for a "family of nations," during a lengthy White House colloquy with leaders of the AUAM.

The AUAM stood neither for "peace at any price" nor against "sane and reasonable" military preparedness, Lillian Wald explained to the president; but they were anxious about those agents of militarism who were "frankly hostile to our institutions of democracy." Wilson contended that his preparedness program conformed to his interlocutors' criteria—that it would provide adequate security "without changing the spirit of the country" and that one of his motives for it was to achieve a league of nations. "[I]f the world undertakes, as we all hope it will undertake, a joint effort to keep the peace, it will expect us to play our proportional part," he said. "Surely that is not a militaristic ideal. That is a very practical, possible ideal." . . .

Wilson could not have made a truly plausible case for a new diplomacy and a league—nor would he have been continued in office—if, at the same time, he had not been willing and able to move plainly to the left of center in American politics. Indeed, the array of social justice legislation he pushed through Congress on the eve of his reelection campaign gave legitimacy to his aspirations in foreign affairs like nothing else could have. Wilson could boast of a number of accomplishments for his first two years in office: the Underwood Tariff, the Clayton Antitrust Act, the Federal Reserve System, and the Federal Trade Commission. Then, as his polestar moved comparatively leftward with the approach of the 1916 campaign, he put two "radicals" (Louis D. Brandeis and John Hessin Clarke) on the Supreme Court. Over the protests of conservatives in and out of Congress, he secured passage of the Adamson Act, which established the eight-hour day for railroad workers, and the Keating-Owen bill, which imposed restrictions on child labor. Finally, he had defused the conservatives' appeal to jingoism with his "moderate" preparedness program, which, in conjunction with the Revenue Act of 1916, yielded the first real tax on wealth in American history. . . .

But this was only the half of it. As the complement to his advanced progressivism, Wilson also made American membership in a league of nations one of the cardinal themes of his campaign, a theme that complemented the Democratic chant, "He Kept Us Out Of War!" His utterances on the league exerted a significant impact on the outcome. [The leftist journalist] Max Eastman predicted that Wilson would win reelection because "he has attacked the problem of eliminating war, and he has not succumbed to the epidemic of militarism." Indeed, his speeches on the league constituted "the most important step that any President of the United States has taken towards civilizing the world since Lincoln." Herbert Croly, the influential editor of the *New Republic,* threw his support to Wilson not only on the grounds of the president's domestic record but also because he had "committed himself and his party to a revolutionary doctrine": American participation in a postwar league of nations. . . .

In any event, the election returns suggested that Wilson and the progressive internationalists had not merely checked the reactionaries; they had presided over the creation of a left-of-center coalition that seemed to hold the balance of political power in the United States. Precisely what all of this portended for future domestic struggles could hardly be predicted. As for foreign policy, the deeper meaning of their victory was unmistakable. "[T]he President we reelected has raised a flag that no other president has thought or perhaps dared to raise," [the left-liberal journalist] Amos Pinchot submitted. "It is the flag of internationalism."

American neutrality was a fragile thing. Wilson had always shared the conviction of fellow peace seekers that the best way to keep the country out of the war was to try to bring about a negotiated settlement. Twice, to that end, in 1915 and 1916, he had sent his personal emissary, Colonel Edward M. House, to Europe for direct parlays with the heads of all the belligerent governments. These appeals had proved futile. Now, fortified by reconfirmation at the polls, he decided on a bold stroke. In a climactic attempt to end the war, he went before the Senate on January 22, 1917, and called for "peace without victory." In this address, Wilson drew together the strands of progressive internationalist thought and launched a penetrating critique of European imperialism, militarism, and balance-of-power politics—the root causes of the war, he said. In their stead, he held out the promise of a "community of nations"—a new world order sustained by procedures for the arbitration of disputes between nations, a dramatic reduction of armaments, self-determination, and collective security. The chief instrumentality of this sweeping program was to be a league of nations. Thus, Wilson began his ascent to a position of central importance in the history of international relations in the twentieth century.

Responses to the address varied. The governments of both warring coalitions, still praying for decisive victory in the field, either ignored it or received it with contempt. Many pro-Allied Republicans, such as Senator Henry Cabot Lodge of Massachusetts, heaped scorn upon the very notion of "peace without victory" and wondered exactly what membership in a league might entail. Nonetheless, Wilson's manifesto met with an unprecedented outpouring of praise from progressive groups at home and abroad. . . .

One week later, Germany announced the resumption of unrestricted submarine warfare against all flags. After three American ships were sunk without warning, public opinion shifted markedly. On March 20, the cabinet unanimously recommended full-fledged belligerency. Wilson, too, had concluded that after some thirty months of neutrality, war had "thus been thrust upon" the United States. "But," the secretary of interior recorded in his diary, "he goes unwillingly."

In his address to Congress on April 2, 1917, the president explained why neutrality no longer seemed tenable and outlined the measures necessary for getting the country on a war footing. He then turned to more transcendent matters. His goals were the same as when he had addressed the Senate in January; he said, "The world must be made safe for democracy. Its peace must be planted upon the tested foundations of political liberty. We have no selfish ends to serve. We desire no conquest, no dominion. We seek no indemnities for ourselves, no material compensation for the sacrifices we shall freely make." He implied that Americans would be fighting to establish some degree of "peace without victory," or, as he put it, "for a universal dominion of right by such a concert of free nations as shall bring peace and safety to all nations and the world itself at last free"—a program now attainable apparently only through the crucible of war. . . .

Then, just as the United States entered the war, Russia, staggering under the relentless blows of the German army, was seized by revolutionary upheaval. By the end of 1917, the Bolshevik leaders, V. I. Lenin and Leon Trotsky, pulled their ravaged nation out of the war. They thereupon issued proclamations on behalf of a democratic peace based on self-determination and summoned the peoples of Europe to demand that their governments—the Allies and the Central Powers alike—repudiate plans for conquest.

In the circumstances, Wilson really had no choice but to respond to the Bolshevik challenge. In his Fourteen Points Address, of January 8, 1918, the most celebrated speech of his presidency, he reiterated much of the anti-imperialist "peace without victory" formula and once again made the League of Nations the capstone. In answer to Lenin's entreaty to stop the war, he argued that German autocracy and militarism must be crushed so that humanity could set about the task of creating a new and better world. Wilson's endeavor to remove the suspicions hanging over the Allied cause and rally doubters to see the war through to the bitter end succeeded magnificently. The popular approbation that greeted the Fourteen Points in both Europe and America approached phenomenal proportions. (Even Lenin hailed the address as "a great step ahead towards the peace of the world.") But as before, the Allied governments declined to endorse or comment on Wilson's progressive war aims.

At home, Wilson's own immediate priorities inexorably shifted toward the exigencies of war mobilization. And, in part owing to stinging Republican criticism of "peace without victory" and, later, the Fourteen Points as the basis for the postwar settlement, he refused to discuss his plans for the League in any concrete detail throughout the period of American belligerency. He also neglected to lay essential political groundwork for it at home. By the autumn of 1918, important segments among both conservative and progressive internationalists had grown disenchanted with Wilson, albeit for entirely different reasons.

This development would prove to be as unfortunate as the partisan opposition led by the president's arch-nemeses, Theodore Roosevelt and Henry Cabot Lodge. For example, Wilson grievously offended Taft by frustrating the wartime efforts of the LEP and other conservative internationalists, who wanted to make formal plans for the League of Nations in cooperation with the British government. (There were, of course, serious ideological differences between his and Taft's conception of the League, but Wilson might have found a way to use the Republican-dominated LEP to defuse some of the incipient senatorial criticism.)

Perhaps just as consequential, Wilson failed to nurture the left-of-center coalition of 1916, a dynamic political force that, had it remained intact, might have made it possible for him to secure and validate American leadership in a peacekeeping organization intended to serve progressive purposes. But he began to lose his grip on his former base of support as a tidal wave of anti-German hysteria and superpatriotism swept over the country in 1917–1918. Like a giant wrecking machine, "One Hundred Percent Americanism," as it was known, had the potential to batter the progressive wing of the American internationalist movement to ruins. In every part of the United States, acts of political repression and violence (sanctioned by federal legislation) were committed against German-Americans as well as pacifists and radicals. Only at risk of life or limb did antiwar dissenters express their views in public. For example, for speaking out against American participation in the war, Eugene Debs was sentenced to ten years in prison. The postmaster general denied second-class mailing privileges to such publications as the *Milwaukee Leader,* the *Appeal to Reason,* and the *Masses,* virtually shutting them down. The majority of progressive internationalists steadfastly supported the war effort, but they could not abide these kinds of violations of basic First Amendment rights, for which, ultimately, they held Wilson responsible. And so, because he acquiesced in the suppression of civil liberties, Wilson himself contributed to a gradual unraveling of his coalition.

The circumstances in which the war ended compounded the larger problem. By September 1918, the combined might of the Allied and American armies had pushed the enemy back toward Belgium. On October 6, German Chancellor Max von Baden appealed to Wilson to take steps for the restoration of peace based on the Fourteen Points. The armistice was signed on November 11. Meanwhile, a midterm congressional election more important than most presidential elections in American history had taken place. Against the Wilsonian peace plan, the Republicans launched a fiercely partisan, ultraconservative campaign. This time around, endorsements on behalf of the administration by leading progressives outside the Democratic party hardly matched those of the 1916 contest. Even so, the centralization of the wartime economy and the core of Wilson's foreign policy placed him far enough to the left to make all Democrats vulnerable to Republican charges that they were "un-American." Most historians maintain that Wilson committed the worst blunder of his presidency in countering the attacks: He asked the public for a vote of confidence—an ostensibly partisan appeal to sustain the Democrats' control of Congress. When the Republicans won majorities of forty-five in the House and two in the Senate, they could claim that the president, who planned to attend the Paris Peace Conference personally, had been repudiated. The Republicans also thereby gained control over congressional committees, including the Senate Foreign Relations Committee, which would be chaired by Lodge.

Yet despite these political setbacks, the Fourteen Points had acquired the status of sacred text among the war-weary peoples of Europe, and "Wilson" was becoming something more than the name of a president. Italian soldiers placed his picture in their barracks. An old woman said she heard that in America "there was a great saint who is going to make peace for us." Romain Rolland, the French Nobel laureate, pronounced him the greatest "moral authority" in the world. The whole world seemed to come to a halt to honor Wilson when he arrived in Europe. Into the streets and piazzas of Paris, London, Rome, and Milan, millions of people turned out to hail "the Moses from Across the Atlantic." . . .

Whereas he could not have prevailed without the massive outpouring of public support, Wilson still had to pay a heavy price for the League. If he was adored by the "common people," the statesmen of Europe—David Lloyd George, Georges Clemenceau, and Vittorio Orlando—held grave reservations about a Wilsonian peace. They were also keen students of American politics. Fully aware of the arithmetic of the Senate, they used their acceptance of the covenant as a lever to gain concessions on other vital and contentious issues.

For instance, Wilson was compelled to swallow a less-than-satisfactory compromise on the disposition of captured enemy colonies, which the Allies (in particular, Australia and South Africa) coveted for themselves. Clemenceau, on threat of withdrawal of his certification of the League, demanded for France military occupation of the Rhineland; Orlando claimed for Italy the Yugoslav port city of Fiume; and the Japanese insisted on retaining exploitative economic privileges in China's Shantung province. On several occasions, Wilson was able to moderate the more extreme Allied demands and uphold at least the spirit of the Fourteen Points. But, then, on verge of physical collapse, he permitted the Allies to impose upon Germany a huge reparations burden and, on top of everything else, a "war-guilt" clause—saddling it with the moral responsibility for allegedly having started the war. Wilson tried to take comfort in the hope that, once the "war psychosis" had receded, the League would be in position to arbitrate and rectify the injustices contained in the peace treaty itself. After six long months of often acrimonious deliberations, however, the signing of that document in the Hall of Mirrors at Versailles, on June 28, 1919, was at best a fleeting triumph for the exhausted president.

By the time Wilson returned to the United States in the summer of 1919, thirty-two state legislatures and thirty-three governors had endorsed the covenant. According to a *Literary Digest* poll, the vast majority of nearly 1,400 newspaper editors, including a majority of Republican editors, advocated American membership in some kind of league. Had a national referendum been held at just that moment, the country almost certainly would have joined. The reasons for its failure to do so are still debated by historians. To begin, Wilson had already lost the active support of most left-wing progressives, not to mention that of the socialists. Many liberals, too, shook their heads in dismay upon reading the Versailles settlement. They believed that, regardless of his motives, he had forsaken the Fourteen Points; that he had conceded too much to the Allies in the territorial compromises; and that vindictiveness, not righteousness, had ruled at the Paris conclave. In short, they feared that the League of Nations would be bound to uphold an unjust peace.

The great debate also coincided with the opening phase of the Red Scare, an even more hysterical and pervasive manifestation of "One Hundred Percent Americanism" whose focus had shifted from the German menace to the threat of bolshevism. Deterioration of civil liberties continued to discourage many progressive internationalists from giving Wilson's crusade their full devotion. . . .

In the Senate on the one hand sheer partisanship motivated much of the opposition. Until the autumn of 1918, Wilson had been the most uniformly successful (if controversial) president since Lincoln. What would become of the Republican party, a friend asked Senator Lodge, if Wilson got his League and the Democrats could boast of "the greatest constructive reform in history"? On the other hand, many of the senatorial objections were grounded in ideological principles. Most Republicans acknowledged that the United States should cooperate with the Allies and play its part in upholding the peace settlement; but they also believed that Wilson had consigned too many vital national interests to the will of an international authority. (At one point, Wilson had frankly admitted, "Some of our sovereignty would be surrendered.") The Republicans found Article X of the covenant particularly troubling. It obliged contracting nations to "preserve as against external aggression the territorial integrity and political independence of all Members of the League." Thus, at least on paper, the United States might be required to take part in some far-flung military intervention in which it had no compelling interest; at the same time, the United States apparently would be prevented from using its military power unilaterally whenever it wanted to. Although during the peace conference he had responded to early criticisms and amended the covenant—to provide for withdrawal from the League and nominally to exempt the Monroe Doctrine and domestic matters (such as immigration) from its jurisdiction—Wilson had not done enough to assuage the anxieties of the majority of Republicans.

Then, too, a small but sturdy knot of senators known as the "irreconcilables" flat-out opposed the League in any form. Not all of the fifteen or so irreconcilables were partisans or reactionaries (though most, like Albert Fall, were); several of them, including Robert La Follette and George Norris, were bona-fide progressives who based their opposition on convictions similar to those of many liberals and socialists. Irreconcilable or no, only a few of Wilson's opponents were strict isolationists. No one had cut through to the crux of the debate with more discernment than Gilbert M. Hitchcock of Nebraska, the Democratic leader in the Senate, when he observed, "Internationalism has come, and we must choose what form the internationalism is to take." The *Appeal to Reason,* though disillusioned with the president and highly dubious of his labors, was harsher: Republicans feared Wilson's League because it placed restrictions on "America's armed forces . . . [and] the commercial and territorial greed of American capitalists." The Lodge crowd hardly advocated isolationism, but rather "the internationalism of unrestrained plunder and competition."

By summer's end, the Senate Foreign Relations Committee, dominated by Republicans and irreconcilables and with Lodge at the helm, had formulated forty-six amendments as the conditions for ratification; by autumn, these had evolved into formal reservations—curiously, fourteen in number. The most controversial one pertained to Article X of the covenant: "The United States assumes no obligation to preserve the territorial integrity or political independence of any country . . . unless in any particular case the Congress . . . by act or joint resolution [shall] so provide." . . .

Meanwhile, Wilson held a series of White House meetings with groups of Republicans known as "mild reservationists" and tried to persuade them to ratify the treaty as it was written. In fact, there was very little difference between their views and those of the senators called "strong reservationists." Hence, none of these conferences changed anyone's mind. Then, against the advice of his personal physician and the pleading of the First Lady, Wilson determined that he must take his case directly to the American people and let them know what was at stake. For three weeks in September 1919, he traveled ten thousand miles by train throughout the Middle and Far West, making some forty speeches to hundreds of thousands of people.

Wilson appealed to his audiences on both the intellectual and the emotional level. Despite the importance of Article X, he told them, military sanctions probably would not have to come into play very often—in part because of the deterrent manifest within the threat of collective force, in part because of the cooling-off provisions in the arbitration features of the League, and in part because disarmament, which he heavily emphasized, would help to eliminate most potential problems from the start. He also addressed the question of sovereignty, as it related to the Senate's concern over arbitration and the hindrance to unilateral action that League membership implied: "The only way in which you can have impartial determinations in this world is by consenting to something you do not want to do." And the obvious corollary was to agree to refrain from doing something that you *want* to do, for there might be times "when we lose in court [and] we will take our medicine."

But there could be no truly effective League without America's participation. Should Americans turn their backs, he said, they would have to live forever with a gun in their hands. And they could not go in grudgingly or on a conditional basis. The "Lodge Reservations" would utterly "change the entire meaning of the Treaty." If the League were thus crippled, he would feel obliged to stand "in mortification and shame" before the boys who went across the seas to fight and say to them, "'You are betrayed. You fought for something that you did not get.'" . . .

As the crowds grew larger and the cheers louder, Wilson looked more haggard and worn out at the end of each day. His facial muscles twitched. Headaches so excruciating that he could hardly see recurred. To keep from coughing all night, he slept propped up in a chair. At last, his doctor called a halt to the tour and rushed him back to Washington. Two days later, on October 2, he suffered a stroke that nearly killed him and permanently paralyzed the left side of his body. From that point onward, Wilson was but a fragile husk of his former self, a tragic recluse in the White House, shielded by his wife and doctor.

The Senate roll was called three times, in November 1919 and March 1920. But whether on a motion to ratify the treaty unconditionally or with the fourteen Lodge reservations attached to it, the vote always fell short of a two-thirds majority. In November 1920, Warren G. Harding, the Republican presidential candidate, won a landslide victory over the Democrat, James M. Cox. The Republicans were only too happy to interpret the returns as the "great and solemn referendum" that Wilson had earlier said he had wanted for his covenant. "So far as the United States is concerned," Lodge now declared, "that League is dead."

In surveying the ruins, many historians have cited the president's stroke as the primary factor behind the outcome. A healthy Wilson, they argue, surely would have grasped the situation and strived to find a middle ground on the question of reservations. Other historians have maintained that his refusal to compromise was consistent with his personality throughout his life, that he would never have yielded to the Republicans (especially to Lodge), regardless of the state of his health. Although there is merit in both of these interpretations—the stroke and Wilson's personality are of obvious relevance—neither provides a complete explanation. They do not take adequate account of the evolution of the League idea, the ideological gulf that had always separated progressive and conservative internationalism, or the domestic political conditions that had taken shape long before the treaty was in the Senate.

In a very real sense, Wilsonian, or progressive, internationalism had begun at home, as part of the reform impulse in the "age of socialistic inquiry." By the touchstone of Wilson's advanced reform legislation and his synthesis of the tenets of the New Diplomacy, progressive internationalists had been able to define the terms of the debate and claim title to the League until 1917–1918—that is, until "One Hundred Percent Americanism" released uncontrollable forces that overwhelmed them. Wilson contributed to this turn of events by losing sight of the relationship between politics and foreign policy—by refusing to acknowledge his administration's culpability in the wartime reaction and by declining to take any action to combat it. . . .

Whatever the central cause of his historic failure, Wilson's conservative and partisan adversaries earnestly believed that his was a dangerously radical vision, a new world order alien to their own understanding of how the world worked. His severest critics among progressive internationalists believed he had not done enough to rally the people to his side and resist the forces of reaction—either in America or at the Paris Peace Conference. Wilson's response to them was a cry of anguish. "What more could I have done?" he asked historian William E. Dodd shortly before leaving the presidency. "I had to negotiate with my back to the wall. Men thought I had all power. Would to God I had had such power." His voice choking with emotion, he added, "The 'great' people at home wrote and wired every day that they were against me."

On all counts, and no doubt for all concerned, it had been, as Dodd himself concluded, "one long wilderness of despair and betrayal, even by good men."

The Peace Advocate Out of Touch with Reality

JAN WILHELM SCHULTE-NORDHOLT

We are in many respects Woodrow Wilson's heirs. That is why it is of great importance to us to make out what kind of man he was, how he came to his exalted and advanced ideas, and why in the end he failed. That is my purpose. . . . I want to examine more closely the life of a man who sought a solution to problems that are still ours, and who was therefore the first great advocate of world peace. He was, as it were, a whole peace movement all by himself.

I almost wrote "apostle of peace," but this phrase is too strong. It makes it seem that I had at least to some extent a work of hagiography in mind. Far from it! History is about people, their dreams and their failures. It would be all too easy to paint Woodrow Wilson as the great prophet who was always wiser than his fellow men. The purpose of a biography ought not to be to turn a human being into a figure of puppetry; to change the metaphor, to press him into flat uniformity. Was Wilson a prophet, an idealist, a dissembler, a practical man, a revolutionary reformer? He was to some small extent all of these. Like most great men, indeed like most people, Wilson was a bundle of contradictions. That is what makes him so fascinating. He

Adapted from *Woodrow Wilson: A Life for Peace* (1991) by Jan W. Schulte-Nordholt, trans./ed. by Rowen, Herbert. Reprinted by permission of the University of California Press.

was many things: a scholar driven by deep feelings; a poet who found his vocation in politics; a Christian consumed by his need for recognition; a lonely man who thought he understood mankind; a practical man who became fossilized in all too lofty dreams; a reasonable man full of turbulent passions. It is this paradoxical personality that I have tried to respect, . . . the irritating, moving grandeur of a self-willed man who played an immense role in history and whose importance has become extraordinarily great in our own times, even though he failed so wretchedly. That is why his life story is a dramatic tale, almost a Greek tragedy, with a catharsis at the end that still drains and raises our emotions. . . .

The outbreak of the war [in 1914] affected the president deeply. It shocked his sensitive nature. We read for example in a letter to [his assistant Edward] House in August: "I feel the burden of the thing almost intolerably from day to day." Two months later he wrote in the same vein but at greater length to Walter Page, the ambassador in London:

> The whole thing is vivid in my mind, painfully vivid, and has been almost ever since the struggle began. I think my thought and imagination contain the picture and perceive its significance from every point of view. I have to force myself not to dwell upon it to avoid the sort of numbness that comes from deep apprehension and dwelling upon elements too vast to be yet comprehended or in any way controlled by counsel.

Here we see once again in Wilson the tension between feeling and detachment.

This only emphasizes the importance of the question of how neutral he really was or wanted to be. His first personal reactions were emotionally favorable to the Allies. He was, after all, imbued with English values and ideals. The French ambassador to Washington, Jules Jusserand, wondered what "the great doctrinaire" in the White House was thinking, but the president soon gave his answer, as it were, to the English ambassador, Sir Cecil Spring-Rice. Spring-Rice informed Sir Edward Grey, the English foreign secretary, that Wilson had admitted to him that everything he held dear was now at stake. The president, he added, spoke with deep emotion. The ambassador, who knew the man he was dealing with, quoted a few lines from Wordsworth's sonnets about English freedom written during the Napoleonic wars. He knew them by heart, Wilson said with tears in his eyes. (Spring-Rice, as it happened, was also playing up to Grey, who, like Wilson, was passionately fond of Wordsworth.)

In his personal feelings Wilson was not in the slightest neutral. House heard him inveigh against everything German—government and people and what he called abstract German philosophy, which lacked spirituality! But he was quite able to separate his personal opinions and his official duties. In the first place, he understood that neutrality was necessary, that the American people were totally set against intervention. But he was also moved by the great goal that he had glimpsed since the beginning of the war, a possibility that fitted his character like a glove. It makes its appearance in his call for neutrality, for he did not merely issue a scrupulously formal official declaration, as any other president would have done. He did more, accompanying this declaration with a personal call to the people to remain truly neutral in thought and words. America, he reminded them, was composed of many peoples and too great sympathy for one or the other side could bring division among them.

Unity was even more necessary for another reason as well. This was the grand ideal that he now made public officially for the first time and which henceforth would inspire him and more and more involve him in international complications. America, he announced, was chosen to mediate, as only America could, just because it was neutral. He spoke in an exalted, religious tone, as he liked to do on so many other occasions. It was as if the war at last made possible things that all his life he had dreamed of—his country as the model and the very leader of the whole world, and himself called and chosen as the leader of his country and the maker of the future. . . .

One thing led to another. The arms shipments [to the Allies] led to loans. [William Jennings] Bryan, the pacifist-minded secretary of state, doubted that this flow of funds, which went almost entirely to the Entente, was really neutral. In good biblical fashion, he saw money as the root of all evil. Was it not written in Scripture that where one's treasure was, one's heart was too? He was able to convince Wilson that steps had to be taken against these loans, and American bankers were therefore warned on August 15, 1914, that such credits were "inconsistent with the true spirit of neutrality." But such a splendid position could not be maintained in the long run. Arms deliveries continued to grow, and the American economy could not do without them. In the spring of 1915 Bryan's idealistic approach was abandoned and one loan after another was floated in the United States. When America entered the war in 1917, the loans to the Allies had risen to more than two billion dollars, while those to the Central Powers amounted to no more than $27,000,000. . . .

War brings all international agreements into question, for war is unpredictable and full of surprises, always different from what anyone could have imagined. This was never so painfully evident as in the question of submarine warfare, since submarines were a weapon without equal, but operated effectively only by surprise. A multitude of notes discussed and debated the question of their surprise attacks. What was the status of the fine agreements about merchant ships in wartime? The answer was clear: a warship might halt, search, seize, and even sink a merchantman, but only after prior warning and giving civilian travelers the opportunity to leave safely. But a submarine that adhered to such rules would of course become defenseless and useless.

When the war broke out, German ships were swept off the seas, Germany was blockaded, and the Germans desperately turned to the submarine as a means of breaking the Allied stranglehold. The initial successes of the U-boats in the autumn of 1914 brought a sudden resurgence of hope, and the German military command slowly realized what a powerful weapon it had in its hands. On February 4, 1915, the German government published an official declaration putting a blockade around the British islands: in a zone around Great Britain, all enemy ships, including merchant vessels, would be attacked without warning. Neutral ships were advised to avoid these regions, since the Allied ships could always be disguised with neutral flags. . . .

The submarine weapon made it much more difficult for the United States, like all nonbelligerents, to remain neutral. Neutrality became a dilemma as never before. Was it neutral to waive fundamental rights of free navigation? Wasn't this itself a serious breach of international law, a grave derogation of morality in a world where morality seemed more and more on the wane?

Wilson, a man of principle, protested, but in so doing he reduced his chances for mediation. A sharp note was sent to Berlin, declaring that the policy set forth in the German note was "so unprecedented in naval warfare that this Government is reluctant to believe that the Imperial Government of Germany in this case contemplates it as possible." The American government would hold the German government fully responsible for the consequences. This seemed like plain talk, but what would happen if American rights were really challenged could not be foreseen. It was nonetheless probable that once such a stand on principle was taken, a conflict would result. . . .

Wherever the inspiration for the phrase ["peace without victory"] came from, the address that the president made to the Senate on January 22 [1917] was genuine Wilson from beginning to end. It was a plea, splendid, grandiose, and vague, for America's involvement in a future world order. That order—an organization of the peoples with its own force—had to come, he said. The question was, what kind of force? This was and remained the point of difficulty. For Wilson, the moralist who knew that without human inspiration and dedication the finest promises are empty, had in mind a "force" that was greater than the force of any country or alliance, which was "the organized major force of mankind." The nations must come to an agreement and then the old system of the "balance of power" would give way to a "community of power." And that could happen only if there was true reconciliation, upon the basis of a "peace without victory," a peace among equals.

That did not bring pleasure to everyone's ears, he realized. But he had to say it, for his intention was "only to face realities and to face them without soft concealments." Dreamers want so much to be taken for realists! . . .

He spoke in the name of the United States of America, the unique and superior country, as he himself liked to call it, forward-looking and in the lead in the service of mankind. All liberal-thinking people everywhere, in Europe and in America, rejoiced at his words. But conservatives (must we call them the realists?) on both sides of the ocean shook their heads over such empty phrases. Among the first of these, as we know, were persons in Wilson's own backyard, his closest advisers. [Secretary of State Robert] Lansing had warned against the term "peace without victory." What did it really mean? And, most of all, how would these words be taken in the Allied countries? But, Lansing tells us, Wilson did not want to listen. "I did not argue the matter, especially as I knew his fondness for phrasemaking and was sure that it would be useless to attempt to dissuade him." . . .

As was to be expected, [Republican Senator Henry Cabot] Lodge surpassed all the others in his hostility to Wilson. In an angry speech to the Senate he wielded the full resources of his logic to tear apart the arguments of his enemy. What did it mean to say that America had no interest in the peace terms but only in the peace? How can men be required to wage war not to win, so that all their sacrifices were in vain, "a criminal and hideous futility"? . . . How could the "organized major force of mankind" be applied? Voluntarily, or automatically, or compulsorily? When the idea of a league was broached two years earlier, he had been greatly attracted to it, but the more he thought about it, the more problems he saw. It could not be made effective by "high-sounding phrases, which fall so agreeably upon the ear, when there is no thought behind it." Does it mean that the small nations can, by majority vote, involve the large nations in war? "Are we prepared to commit ourselves to a purely general proposition without knowing where we are going or what is to be demanded of us, except that we shall be compelled to furnish our quota of military and naval forces to the service of a league in which we shall have but one voice?" A league for peace meant readiness to wage war against any country that did not obey its decisions. What if it decided that Japan and China should have the right of migration anywhere, and Canada, Australia, and New Zealand declined to accept the decision? Or California, for that matter?

The points made by Lodge were fundamental, which is why I present them at such length. Already at this time, in January 1917, the lines of division were drawn which would define the great debate and the great tragedy of 1919. On one side stood the idealist, on the other the realist, and on both sides more than personal animosity was involved. Furthermore, a political alliance was beginning to take shape that slackened during the war years but operated with full force in 1919; it brought together the Republican isolationists from the West, who were also idealists, for the most part from the Progressive camp, and the Republican internationalist realists, [Senator William] Borah on the one side and Lodge on the other. It was an alliance that would bring disaster to Wilson, but in 1917 he could not foresee that. . . .

Wilson shrank from taking the final step [after the German decision in late January 1917 to launch unrestricted submarine warfare], not out of fear, not out of unsullied pacifism, but because his whole conception of mediating between the belligerents (and thereby saving white civilization) would be shattered. This was the principal reason for his hesitation. And so he talked during these weeks in almost pacifist terms about war and imperialism, spoke out in anger against the support for war from right-wing circles, which he described as "Junkerthum trying to creep in under the cover of the patriotic feeling of the moment." . . .

[The journalist] Walter Lippmann, who looked at him with cool rationality and was among those bitterly disappointed with him after 1919, draws for us nonetheless a portrait of Wilson in his book *Men of Destiny,* showing the orator of light learning about darkness. He gazed in March 1917, says Lippmann, "in the bottomless pit." He was "an anguished prophet," full of compassion and doubt, a man who experienced the tragedy of his time and therefore was able, with overwrought absoluteness, to see the league of nations as the only justification of his action.

With this as his justification he went into the war, not out of economic interest, not because of the violation of the neutral rights of the United States, although these played a part, but in order to bring about genuine peace. Only if America took part could it have a voice in the peace. Mediation through participation would be more effective than neutrality, he now believed. To a delegation of pacifists led by Jane Addams, he said on February 28 that "as head of a nation participating in the war, the President of the United States would have a seat at the Peace Table, but that if he remained the representative of a neutral country he could at best only 'call through a crack in the door.'" Personal ambition and general interest concurred in what we may call a mission. The man and his times seemed to fit each other like the two halves of a piece of fruit. . . .

Of all the impressive sermons that Wilson preached to his people and to the world, none became so famous as his "Fourteen Points" speech of January 8, 1918. It attained a breadth and depth, in space and in time, greater than that of all the others. Not that it is his finest address; there are others, such as the "peace without victory" speech of a year earlier and the declaration of war of April 1917, which are more splendid in rhetoric and wider in vision. But this time Wilson was more practical, adding as it were deed to words; he developed a practical program that was of importance for the whole world. . . .

All in all, the Fourteen Points seemed practical and responsible. How lightly they skipped over historical problems would only become evident in Paris. But there was also a fourteenth point, a panacea for all the shortcomings now and later, a League of Nations: "A special association of nations must be formed under specific covenants for the purpose of affording mutual guarantees of political independence and territorial integrity to great and small states alike." This short sentence carried a heavy burden, too heavy as it turned out. In these few words the future world peace was settled, totally and permanently. For Wilson everything revolved around it; he did not see the difficulties and he did not want to see them, and this would in the end bring his downfall. . . .

In general Wilson's principles more and more broke loose from reality and lived their own lives. Self-determination was one such principle. During the war it became one of the major foundations of Wilson's new world order. We shall never subject another people, he had said back in 1915, "because we believe, we passionately believe, in the right of every people to choose their own allegiance and be free of masters altogether."

Only very slowly, as the reality of Europe began to come closer, did he discover the dangerous consequences of the principle. In the discussion with Spring-Rice on January 3 . . . , he wondered whether it was in fact possible to apply it consistently. The example of the threatening dismemberment of Austria-Hungary was probably in his thoughts when he said: "Pushed to its extreme, the principle would mean the disruption of existing governments to an undefinable extent. Logic was a good and powerful thing but apart from the consideration of existing circumstances might well lead to very dangerous results." The Englishman must have heard this with satisfaction, for the British Empire was not about to grant self-determination to all its peoples.

Later, in Paris, many began to realize the difficulties and dangers in this splendid principle. Lansing hit the nail on the head in a confidential memorandum, in which he wondered what self-determination would mean for the Irish, Indians, Egyptians, and South African Boers. What would happen with the Muslims in Syria and Palestine, and how did that fit in with the idea of Zionism, to which Wilson was very sympathetic. "The phrase is simply loaded with dynamite. It will raise hopes which can never be realized." It was the dream of an idealist, he said, and it is clear whom Lansing really had in mind.

As Wilson himself came to see, he had to be very cautious in Paris when trying to put his great principles into practice. He acknowledged that when he had first spoken of self-determination he had not realized that there were so many peoples who would claim it as their right. . . .

Wilson did not underestimate the devastation in Europe, but he retained his nineteenth-century American optimism. His whole existence was tied up with it; he could not live without hope. He clung to the idea of a grand radical cure, to a mystical faith in the mankind of the future, who were purified by events and repented. He had to represent that mankind; he had to make a new peace.

That is why he had to go to Paris [after the German surrender in late 1918]. . . . He was overwhelmed by his mission. His Czech colleague Thomas Masaryk, who understood him well ("now, we were both professors") warned him about the European statesmen: "But he wouldn't listen, for he was too filled with his plan for a League of Nations to take obstacles into account." . . .

Wilson's triumphal tour of Europe took him from Paris to London and then to Rome. Everywhere he was greeted as a savior, as the "Redeemer of Humanity"

(*Redentore dell' Humanità*) and "God of Peace" (*Dio di Pace*), in the words of the Italian banners. He spent weeks indulging in this pomp and circumstance, immersed in a sea of flags and songs, carried along by beautiful words that promised so much for the future. Justice! Peace! When we hear Wilson speak in these first weeks, everything is radiant. Sometimes a harsh sound breaks through, as when he replies to [Raymond] Poincaré, the president of France, who wants no reconciliation with the foe, that there exist "eternal principles of right and justice" which bring with them "the certainty of just punishment." But for the most part his outlook is peaceful. He speaks of the peoples who form "the organized moral force of men throughout the world," of the tide of good will: "There is a great tide running in the hearts of men. The hearts of men have never beaten so singularly in unison before. Men have never been so conscious of this brotherhood." . . .

Alas, there was in fact no moral tide that carried all with it. There was rather a divided Europe in which the peoples were driven at least as much by muddled feelings of rage and revenge as by lofty thoughts of right and reason. Wilson himself had experienced the impact of such vindictiveness during the off-year elections in the United States, and it was at least as prevalent in Europe. [French premier Georges] Clemenceau told the Chamber of Deputies at the end of December that he disagreed with Wilson, although he had, he said, the greatest admiration for the American president's "noble candor" (which was changed in the parliamentary journal to "noble grandeur"); he thereupon won a vote of confidence by a majority of 380 to 134. [British prime minister] Lloyd George triumphed equally convincingly in elections for the House of Commons just before Christmas. His coalition of Liberals and Tories, in which the latter were dominant, ran on an electoral program of hate and revenge against Germany with slogans like "Hang the Kaiser" and "Make Germany Pay," received no less than 526 of the 707 seats. It was not Lloyd George himself but the navy minister Sir Eric Geddes who uttered the notorious words, "We shall squeeze the German lemons until the pips squeak."

Wilson's moral majority therefore existed only in his poetic imagination. He was totally out of touch with reality. The Europeans did not know what to make of his fine words. They asked themselves whether he actually meant what he said. "I am one of the few people who think him honest," said Lloyd George to his friends. But he too was exasperated when the president blew his own horn loudly and gave no sign that he understood the sacrifices England had made: "Not a word of generous appreciation issued from his lips." Wilson, the American, could not establish an accepted character and place in Europe. The Europeans thought he was American, with his smooth, streamlined face, showing no emotion behind his shining glasses. . . .

In a word, the European leaders did not like Woodrow Wilson. From the start there was tension between them. Clemenceau, an old hand in politics, was not the man to come under the influence of Wilson's lofty words. He knew the United States; he had lived there just after the Civil War, spoke English well, and had married an American woman. He had no high opinion of American idealism, as was evident in the witticisms he made at Wilson's expense. God had needed only ten commandments, but Wilson fourteen, he jibed. . . . And, in reaction to the "peace without victory" speech, he wrote: "Never before has any political assembly heard so fine a sermon on what human beings might be capable of accomplishing if only they weren't human." In brief, this was classic realism confronting classic idealism. . . .

Wilson believed in his League of Nations as a remedy for all troubles, a miraculous cure that would work precisely because it was so entwined with the peace treaty itself. The treaty might not be perfect, he said in April, but with the League of Nations as an integral part of the treaty, there was a mechanism to improve its operation.

But actually it worked the other way round, a fact that Wilson completely missed. The delegates of the Allied countries exploited his League of Nations proposal to extract concessions from him; the peace turned out very badly because he repeatedly made compromises in order to save his beloved plan, carrying it through the bustling debates to safe harbor. . . . "The fact is," wrote the deeply disappointed [diplomat Henry] White in May, "that the League of Nations, in which he had been more deeply interested than anything else from the beginning, believing it to be the best if not the only means of avoiding war in the future, has been played to the limit by France and Japan in extracting concessions from him; to a certain extent by the British too, and the Treaty as it stands is the result." . . .

The history of the Versailles peace has called forth a welter of difficult questions. Was it too harsh, a *Diktatfrieden* that automatically elicited a reaction of revanche? Or was it, on the contrary, too mild a settlement, enabling the old forces in Germany to continue? In any case, is there a direct causal link between 1919 and 1933? Does the guilt for the disastrous consequences lie with the men who, in Paris, laid down the rules for the future? These are all questions that in their nature cannot be given a conclusive or logically satisfactory answer. But they are also questions that cannot be evaded. If this peace were not accepted, Wilson said many times on his swing through the West in the fall, there would be another war in twenty years. . . .

How horribly right he proved to be! What he predicted came about just as he said. But was he himself guiltless? Hadn't he written the whole scenario for that future? The defeat [of Germany] was a humiliation, not intended as such by him in his noble naïveté, but nonetheless felt as such by the vanquished. Humiliation led to dreams of revenge; the seeds of a new war were put into the soil. Of course, they would only grow when the climate was favorable, when events, primarily the Great Depression that began in 1929, permitted. But beyond question the seeds were planted by the peace of Versailles.

Wilsonianism: A Workable
Blueprint for a Broken World

TONY SMITH

The essential genius of Wilson's proposals for a new world order after World War I was that it had a vision of the proper ordering of domestic as well as international politics that was well suited to the development of political and economic forces worldwide in the twentieth century. Here was a period in Germany, Russia, and Eastern Europe where social forces were struggling over the modernization of the state,

Adapted from Tony Smith, *America's Mission: The United States and the Worldwide Struggle for Democracy in the Twentieth Century* (Princeton: Princeton University Press, 1994), 87, 102–109. © 1994 The 20th Century Fund, Inc. Published by Princeton University Press. Reprinted by permission of Princeton University Press.

where rival conceptions of national unity were trying to make government responsive through party government to nationalistic appeals for popular sovereignty. In domestic terms, Wilson respected the power of nationalism and favored national self-determination. States were presumed to be legitimate when they were democratically constituted, and it was expected that in most instances ethnic boundaries would make for the frontiers of countries. In the context of the world of 1918, such a proposal was radical; it accepted the dismemberment of empires (those of Austria-Hungary, Russia, and Turkey immediately; those of the Western European powers by implication thereafter), and it worked for the replacement of autocracies with democracies in Germany and the new nation-states to the East.

For international relations, Wilson called for a liberal economic regime and a system of collective security designed to preserve the peace. Again, his initiative was radical for it challenged the competitive mercantilistic practices that dictated much of world commerce with a more open trading system, just as it proposed to replace competitive balance of power thinking politically with what he called "a convenant of cooperative peace."

In short, the foundation of Wilson's order was the democratic nation-state; its superstructure was an international order of economic, military, and moral interdependence. Nationalism wed to democracy; democracies wed in peace, prosperity, and mutual respect embodied in international law and institutions: such was Wilson's essential vision, a form of liberalism he felt to be both necessary and appropriate for his era and essential to guarantee American national security. . . .

Wilson failed in his efforts both to root democratic forces in countries where they were struggling to take power and to establish a stable new configuration of power among the states of the continent. German democracy was not robust; Franco-German rapprochement did not occur; outside Czechoslovakia, democratic forces were weak in Eastern Europe; the Russian Revolution remained militant; communist parties in Western Europe sapped democratic forces; fascism came into power in Italy in 1922, encouraging like-minded movements to duplicate its success; no way was found to counter economic nationalism and the destructive impact of the Depression that began in 1929; collective security proved unable to halt Italian aggression in Ethiopia or Japanese attacks on China; and the American people and Congress refused to identify the national security with an active hand in the protection of liberal democracy in Europe.

Was there a better guide than Wilsonianism as to how America should defend its legitimate concerns in the founding of a stable European order friendly to this country's interests? Between 1940 and the early 1950s, the most influential thinkers in this country on the proper conduct of American foreign policy . . . took special pains to use Wilson as a negative example, a textbook study of how foreign policy should not be formulated. For these analysts, Wilsonianism stands for the American penchant to conduct its foreign conduct by moralizing about it, by assuming that somehow democracy is a panacea for the world's problems. In their eyes, liberal democratic internationalism betrays a vein of naive and utopian idealism ill-fitted to effective participation in global politics. The affliction did not start with Wilson nor end with him, but his presidency marks its high-water point. Realism, the dominant school of international relations theory in the United States, was founded at this time by these men and built its concepts by consciously pitting itself against the basic tenets of Wilsonianism.

Thus, referring to the settlement of 1919, [the diplomat and scholar] George Kennan wrote:

> This was the sort of peace you got when you allowed war hysteria and impractical idealism to lie down together in your mind, like the lion and the lamb; when you indulged yourself in the colossal conceit of thinking that you could suddenly make international life over into what you believed to be your own image; when you dismissed the past with contempt, rejected the relevance of the past to the future, and refused to occupy yourself with the real problems that a study of the past would suggest. . . .

[The journalist] Walter Lippmann's charges were even harsher, for they allege that Wilson's mistakes set the stage for the rise of fascism and the inability of the democracies to rally effectively to the challenge. . . .

How, then, should American foreign policy have been formulated? These writers consider themselves realists. They insist that the national interest should be determined rather strictly by calculations of the relative amount of power among states, with a view of preventing threats to the existence or independence of the United States. Seen from this perspective, the only obvious antagonist of the United States in world affairs at that time was Germany, which Washington should forthrightly have mobilized to contain. They have no patience with the "idealism" of a "utopian," "moralistic" crusade to change the character of international relations by making states democratic, such as Wilson advanced, for this talk only put a smokescreen over the essential matter of dealing with German power. . . .

In a word, the realists maintained that Wilson did not adequately appreciate the character of "power politics" or the "balance of power" in his deliberations, by which they meant the need to contain German power so that it would not dominate the continent, a turn of events that would have been seriously threatening to American national security. In Lippmann's view, for example, Wilson failed to explain to the American people why the country went to war: "The reasons he did give were legalistic and moralistic and idealistic reasons, rather than the substantial and vital reasons that the security of the United States demanded that no aggressively expanding imperial power, like Germany, should be allowed to gain the mastery of the Atlantic Ocean."

These charges ask for an indictment that the evidence does not warrant. Thus, Wilson was not a pacifist, and his proposals for disarmament are best understood as confidence-building measures among states, not as a reluctance to back commitments with force, as Lippmann suggested. Again, the League of Nations was not to have either financial or military resources independent of the states that participated in it, and its Council had to act by unanimous agreement; the League was not to be a world government. More, the call for self-determination was not intended as a blank check for secessionist movements. Wilson respected economic, strategic, and historical considerations that had to be weighed against nationalist feelings; it was only toward the end of the war that he finally resigned himself to the dismemberment of the Austro-Hungarian empire rather than to seeing it reconstituted as a democratic federalist structure.

But most importantly, Wilson intended the League to be the vehicle to bind the United States permanently to a management role in world affairs. Whatever the shortcomings of the details in his plan, American membership in the League might well have provided the check on Germany that Wilson's critics allege his naivete and moralizing prevented him from establishing.

For Wilson, the vital issue at the Peace Conference was the League; for his critics, it was Germany. Yet the League's very existence implicitly addressed the essential issue for Europe from 1871 until 1945 (and perhaps once again today): the German question. Given Germany's population, economic strength, militaristic history, political structure, and geography, could it live peacefully with its neighbors? Were the only alternatives to destroy it or be conquered by it? American leadership of the League portended that Germany might be contained by American power. Once contained, domestic reforms might be consolidated so that Germany could live with its neighbors by progressively shedding its militaristic elements in favor of developing itself as a democracy capable of interacting peacefully with the other states of Europe. But even without German reforms, membership in the League would automatically tie America into the European balance of power and so safeguard American national security.

Wilsonianism, did, therefore, meaningfully address the critical issue of what to do about Germany. If the League's fundamental purpose was to check aggression against weaker states created by the dismemberment of the Russian, Ottoman, and Austro-Hungarian empires after 1918, if its collateral ambition was to foster democratic government and liberal international economic exchange, then what better safeguard could be put on German power? As a way of addressing the growing presence of the Soviet Union in world affairs, it offered a useful forum as well.

In addition to the League, Wilson had two other ways of influencing Germany. His preferred approach was to control German power by absorbing it into a liberal economic, political, and military arrangement that would effectively integrate Germany with its neighbors (especially France) and the United States. Here was the germ of the American idea after 1945 to push for European integration based on Franco-German rapprochement. Wilson also agreed to join the British in guaranteeing France against German attack in a treaty independent of the League. The Senate defeated this latter project along with barring American membership in the League. . . .

Fail though it did at the time, the virtues of Wilson's policy for the postwar world were threefold. First, it acknowledged the fundamental political importance of nationalism, seeking to direct rather than to repress its energy. Second, it sought to channel the demands for popular sovereignty contained in nationalism in the direction of democratic government, and away from authoritarian or totalitarian regimes (though the latter—a particular curse of the twentieth century—was not yet clearly visible when Wilson was in office). Third, it attempted to provide a structure of international institutions and agreements to handle military and economic affairs among democratically constituted, capitalist states. In all of these respects, American national security thinking followed Wilson's lead after 1945. Again today, in the aftermath of the cold war, we can see the prescience of his proposals as we deliberate the problems of nationalism in Eastern Europe, the course of Western European integration based on Franco-German understanding, and the need for organizational mechanisms to provide for the peaceful formulation of a gamut of issues from the economic to the military.

It is commonly observed that politics as an art requires pursuing the desirable in terms of the possible. The dilemma of leadership is to decide when it is weakness to fail to exploit the inevitable ambiguities, and therefore possibilities, of the historical moment, and when it is foolhardy to attempt to overcome immovable constraints set by a combination of forces past and present. Since options are always open to some extent, greatness requires creating opportunities and taking risks within the limits set by history.

While the constraints of history nullified Wilson's hopes, his efforts did not totally contradict the forces of his time. Democratic nationalist forces did exist in Germany and parts of Eastern Europe. If it was unlikely that the Bolshevik Revolution would ever have turned in a democratic direction, it was not until 1921 (with the Tenth Party Congress, which established iron discipline within the Communist party, and with the crushing of the Kronstadt mutiny, a sailors' uprising against Lenin's rule) that its totalitarian cast was definitely set. If it was unlikely that democracy would consolidate itself in Germany given the rancors of the right, the splitting of the left, and the rigors of the Depression, it certainly was not until after 1930 that this became manifestly evident. Again, although the Senate had repudiated the League in 1919–20, it could reconsider its position, as at times the American government seemed interested in doing. In short, Wilson's gamble on the forces of democracy and collective security (which in practice would have been the balance of power under another name) was not totally unrealistic. And what were his other options? Indeed his greatness as a visionary comes from how close to success his program came. Suppose America had joined the League in good faith, an organization basically of his devising? By that single act, the course of history might have been changed, for it would have committed the United States to the maintenance of a European equilibrium containing Germany.

The best evidence of the power of Wilsonianism, however, comes from its resurgence in American foreign policy in the aftermath of World War II. Bretton Woods, the initial plans for the United Nations, the hopes for Western European integration that lay behind the occupation of Germany and the Marshall Plan—all this was essentially Wilsonian in inspiration (even when operationalized by people like [British economist John Maynard] Keynes and Kennan who saw themselves as opponents of Wilson's position in Paris in 1919). In the late 1940s, Wilsonianism was thus to have a success that it was denied in the early 1920s. But it was in the late 1980s that Wilson's time truly arrived. Of all the extraordinary developments connected with the end of the cold war in 1989, surely one of the most noteworthy was the way Soviet leader Mikhail Gorbachev's "new thinking" for Europe—with its insistence on the importance of national self-determination, democratic government, and collective security—echoed Wilson's appeals of seventy years earlier. . . .

Unlike most statesmen, then, Wilson deserves to be measured not on the basis of achieving the ends of his policy in their time, but by the magnitude of his efforts and the influence they continued to have in later years. Seen from the perspective of the mid-1990s, three-quarters of a century since he left office, Wilson's concern that nationalism abroad be turned in the direction of democratic government for the sake of the American national interest seems soundly conceived. Writing in 1889 on "Leaders of Men," Wilson had declared:

> Great reformers do not, indeed, observe time and circumstance. Theirs is not a service of opportunity. They have no thought for occasion, no capacity for compromise. They are early vehicles of the Spirit of the Age. They are born of the very times that oppose them. . . . Theirs to hear the inarticulate voices that stir in the night-watches, apprising the lonely sentinel of what the day will bring forth.

FURTHER READING

Lloyd Ambrosius, *Woodrow Wilson and His Legacy in American Foreign Relations* (2002)

H. W. Brands, *Woodrow Wilson* (2003)

Kendrick A. Clements, *The Presidency of Woodrow Wilson* (1992)

G. R. Conyne, *Woodrow Wilson: British Perspectives* (1992)

John W. Coogan, "Wilsonian Diplomacy in War and Peace," in *American Foreign Relations Reconsidered, 1890–1993,* ed. Gordon Martel (1994)

John Milton Cooper Jr., *Breaking the Heart of the World* (2001)

David E. Davis and Eugene P. Trani, *The First Cold War* (2000)

Richard R. Doerries, *Imperial Challenge: Ambassador Count von Bernstorff and German-American Relations, 1908–1917* (1989)

David M. Esposito, *The Legacy of Woodrow Wilson* (1996)

Byron Farrell, *Over There* (1999)

Robert H. Ferrell, *Woodrow Wilson and World War I* (1985)

David S. Foglesong, *America's Secret War Against Bolshevism* (1995)

Lloyd C. Gardner, *Safe for Democracy* (1984)

Hans W. Gatske, *Germany and the United States* (1980)

Ross A. Kennedy, "Woodrow Wilson, World War I, and American National Security," *Diplomatic History* 25 (Winter 2001): 1–31

William R. Keylor, *The Legacy of the Great War* (1998)

Henry Kissinger, *Diplomacy* (1994)

Antony Lentin, *Lloyd George, Woodrow Wilson, and the Guilt of Germany* (1985)

Arthur S. Link, *Wilson,* 5 vols. (1947–1965)

———, *Woodrow Wilson: Revolution, War, and Peace* (1979)

David W. McFadden, *Alternative Paths: Soviets and Americans, 1917–1920* (1993)

Margaret MacMillan, *Paris, 1919* (2003)

Herbert F. Margulies, *The Mild Reservationists and the League of Nations Controversy in the Senate* (1989)

John H. Mauer, *The Outbreak of the First World War* (1995)

Bert E. Park, *Ailing, Aging, Addicted: Studies of Compromised Leadership* (1993)

Ann R. Pierce, *Woodrow Wilson and Harry Truman* (2003)

Diane Preston, *"Lusitania": An Epic Tragedy* (2001)

Norman E. Saul, *War and Revolution* (2001)

Klaus Schwabe, *Woodrow Wilson, Revolutionary Germany, and Peacemaking, 1918–1919* (1985)

David Steigerwald, "The Reclamation of Woodrow Wilson," *Diplomatic History* 23 (Winter 1999): 79–99

John A. Thompson, *Woodrow Wilson* (2001)

Marc Trachtenburg, *Reparations in World Politics* (1980)

Barbara Tuchman, *The Zimmermann Telegram* (1958)

Robert W. Tucker, "The Triumph of Wilsonianism?" *World Policy Journal* 10 (1993–1994): 83–99

Edwin A. Weinstein, *Woodrow Wilson: A Medical and Psychological Biography* (1981)

William C. Widenor, *Henry Cabot Lodge and the Search for an American Foreign Policy* (1980)

Robert H. Zeiger, *America's Great War* (2001)

CHAPTER
9

U.S. Entry into World War II

The embittering experience of the First World War and the Versailles peacemaking bred a distaste for Europe's problems, and world politics in general, in the United States. Yet by the 1920s modern communications and transportation had made the world more interconnected and interdependent than ever before, and growing numbers of Americans enjoyed the benefits of international trade and investment. U.S. officials worked with private citizens to use nonmilitary methods, including trade and currency arrangements and disarmament treaties, to construct a prosperous and peaceful world order. The Great Depression of the 1930s, however, crippled the world marketplace and unleashed German and Japanese militarism. Once again Americans confronted questions of war and peace, neutrality or alliance.

Americans initially sought to avoid entanglement in the cascading crises that engulfed Europe and Asia. Congress passed neutrality acts, which banned arms sales and loans to belligerent nations in the event of war, and President Franklin D. Roosevelt publicly endorsed the United States's neutral stance. Recalling the horrors of World War I and beset by economic depression at home, many Americans embraced "isolationism," or what historians have called "independent internationalism." In Europe, France and Great Britain also remembered the Great War and refrained from challenging German aggression. Most dramatically, they adopted a policy of "appeasement" whereby they responded to Hitler's bellicose threats toward Czechoslovakia by recognizing German sovereignty over the Sudetenland, a German-speaking region of the country, in September 1938.

In March 1939 Hitler occupied the rest of Czechoslovakia, and in September he ordered his armies into Poland. Britain and France then abandoned appeasement, honored their alliance with Poland, and World War II commenced in Europe. Roosevelt and the nation gradually moved toward an interventionist posture, repealing the arms embargo portion of the Neutrality Acts in late 1939, arranging with British Prime Minister Winston S. Churchill to trade destroyers for bases in 1940, and gaining congressional approval to send Lend-Lease supplies to Britain in March 1941. Reluctant to challenge directly the nation's isolationist mood, and perhaps not fully convinced of America's need to take up arms, Roosevelt also won an unprecedented third term in the White House promising that American boys would not be sent to die in a foreign war. When Hitler turned his guns on Stalinist Russia in June 1941, Roosevelt opened the lend-lease spigot to the Soviet Union. The United States also initiated naval patrols to assist British shipping across the Atlantic, and America edged closer to war as its vessels traversed submarine-infested waters.

The German Onslaught 1939–1942

Thomas G. Paterson et al., *American Foreign Relations*, 6/e. Copyright © 2005 by Houghton Mifflin Company. Reprinted by permission of Houghton Mifflin Company.

When war came for the United States, however, it occurred 6,000 miles away from Europe, in Asia. For most of the twentieth century the United States had opposed Japanese expansion into China. When the Japanese sought access to vital raw materials and markets to relieve their economic stress in the 1930s, taking Manchuria and renaming it Manchukuo, Americans viewed Japanese imperialism as a violation of the Open Door, an assault on U.S. interests in Asia, and a threat to world order. Later in the decade, as the Sino-Japanese war escalated, the United States gradually expanded its navy, granted loans to China, and did not invoke the neutrality acts— thereby permitting China to buy arms from the United States. Yet Washington protested Japanese aggression in a manner designed not to provoke war with the Empire of the Sun. Certain that America's strategic priorities lay across the Atlantic in Europe, the Roosevelt administration hoped to avoid a two-front war.

Following conclusion of the Tripartite Pact among Japan, Germany, and Italy in September 1940 and Japan's acquisition of bases in northern French Indochina, the administration embargoed shipments of scrap iron and steel to the island nation. The crisis in the Pacific reached a critical juncture when Japanese troops, in July 1941, occupied all of French Indochina. In response, the Roosevelt White House froze

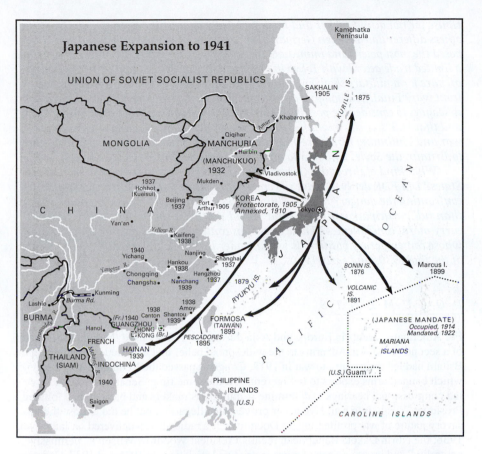

Thomas G. Paterson et al., *American Foreign Relations*, 6/e. Copyright © 2005 by Houghton Mifflin Company. Reprinted by permission of Houghton Mifflin Company.

Japanese assets in the United States, thereby denying Japan essential petroleum shipments. Tokyo and Washington exchanged proposals and counterproposals for the rest of the year, but to no avail. On December 7, in a surprise attack, Japanese pilots bombed the U.S. naval base at Pearl Harbor in the Hawaiian Islands, decimating the U.S. fleet and leaving more than 2,400 American military personnel dead. One day later the United States declared war on Japan, and on December 11 Germany declared war on the United States.

Historians have long debated U.S. intervention in World War II. While most agree that German, Italian, and Japanese militarism threatened world peace, they disagree over the significance of that threat to the United States. They also debate President Franklin D. Roosevelt's handling of the crisis. The most widely shared view is that Nazi racial ideology, Germany's resources, and Hitler's personal ambition produced a hate-driven aggression that aimed at world domination. Some scholars praise the Roosevelt administration for recognizing the threat, preparing an isolationist public for action, and aiding the anti-Axis nations by all possible means—including ultimately, U.S. military intervention. Other writers agree that the United Stated faced preeminent danger, but they criticize the Roosevelt White

House for not acting earlier and more forcefully against the aggressor states. Still others differentiate between German and Japanese aggression and argue that Hitler posed the most potent and immediate threat to U.S. interests. Thus, why not negotiate a limited trade accord with Tokyo in order to dodge or delay a conflict in the Pacific, prepare for a military showdown in Europe, and avoid a resource-stretching, two-front war? Finally, although a distinct minority, some scholars have challenged their colleagues to consider the possibility that Hitler's capabilities have been exaggerated, and that U.S. security might have been best protected by avoiding entry into the war and continuing FDR's pre-Pearl Harbor policy of sending large-scale assistance to Britain, the Soviet Union, and other anti-Axis nations.

What kind of threat did German and Japanese aggression pose to the United States? Did FDR deftly manage the crisis—or was he too forceful, or too timid, in confronting the danger? Did the United States realistically have any option other than full participation in the Second World War? Did the various policy options carry moral consequences? These questions continue to hold meaning for a nation whose contemporary position as world leader is historically traceable to the events of the late 1930s and early 1940s.

D O C U M E N T S

For Americans, events in Europe and Asia during the 1930s raised the ominous specter of a second world war. Adhering to the widespread belief that U.S. trade and shipping to Britain had led the country to war in 1917, Congress passed the Neutrality Act of 1935, which banned arms exports to belligerents. At the same time, Senator Gerald P. Nye led congressional hearings to determine if munitions makers and bankers had lobbied President Wilson into war. Nye never proved the allegation, but he did expose the unsavory nature of war profiteering. In Document 1, a radio speech delivered on January 6, 1936, the North Dakota Republican recalls President Woodrow Wilson's "permissive neutrality" and urges passage of more restrictive legislation. In 1936 and 1937, Congress bolstered the neutrality laws by banning loans to belligerents and prohibiting U.S. travel on belligerent ships.

World events, however, overtook U.S. policy. Tension between the United States and Japan escalated following a clash between Japanese and Chinese troops at the Marco Polo bridge, south of Beijing, in July 1937 and after Japan's full-fledged invasion of China. In an obvious reference to what Japanese leaders called the "China incident," President Franklin D. Roosevelt told a Chicago audience on October 5, 1937, that aggressors should be "quarantined" (Document 2). Although FDR offered no concrete policies, the administration in the following months began to send modest amounts of aid to China. The Japanese were not deterred. Document 3, an official Japanese statement of November 3, 1938, following a string of military victories in China, proclaimed the establishment of a "new order" in Asia. Hard-liners in the State Department urged the United States to punish Japan with economic measures, including the abrogation of the 1911 U.S.-Japan commercial treaty and sanctions on exports. The treaty lapsed in January 1940, but the Roosevelt administration for the moment refrained from implementing additional trade sanctions.

War broke out in Europe when Germany invaded Poland in September 1939 and Britain and France came to Poland's defense. Modifying his earlier endorsement of neutrality, Roosevelt now persuaded Congress to allow arms sales on the basis of "cash and carry." The German military rapidly advanced through Europe, and in September 1940 Germany, Italy, and Japan concluded their Tripartite Pact alliance.

Roosevelt devised new ways to assist the Allies without entering the war. Document 4 is FDR's December 1940 proposal for Lend-Lease, a program that allowed the United States to lease Britain massive amounts of military equipment, circumventing Britain's cash flow crisis and the Neutrality Act's ban on monetary loans. The president's program won congressional approval in March 1941. The United States edged closer to war after FDR authorized U.S. naval patrols part way across the Atlantic to protect Lend-Lease shipping. In response to an attempted torpedoing of the U.S. destroyer *Greer* by a German U-boat submarine in September 1941—the *Greer* had been signaling submarine locations to British bombers—FDR denounced Hitler's "rattlesnakes of the Atlantic" and called for a new policy of "shoot on sight" to protect U.S. vessels. His speech of September 11, 1941, is reprinted here as Document 5.

Of course, the incident that led to U.S. entry into the war occurred on the other side of the world. On July 25, 1941, following Japan's invasion of the southern portion of French Indochina, the Roosevelt administration froze Japanese assets. Document 6, the final negotiating points adopted by the imperial government on November 5, 1941, sets forth two options for a settlement with the United States: Plan A, which called for a Japanese withdrawal from China only after a successful Sino-Japanese truce had been reached; and Plan B, a more limited and pragmatic understanding that skirted the China issue but pledged that Japan would advance no farther south than Indochina in exchange for an unfreezing of Japanese assets and resumption of normal trade with the United States. Document 7, a restatement of Washington's proposals to Japan dated November 26, 1941, rejected compromise and sought to roll back Japanese expansionism and revive Washington's cherished Open Door principle. The Japanese dismissed the final U.S. bargaining position, and on December 7, 1941, Japanese planes descended on Pearl Harbor. Document 8 is Roosevelt's war message delivered to Congress on December 8, 1941. Three days later Germany declared war against the United States.

1. Senator Gerald P. Nye Cites the Lessons of History and Advocates Neutrality, 1936

Neutrality is to be had if we are willing to pay the price of abandonment of expectation of profits from the blood of other nations at war. But it defies any man to write a neutrality program that would long endure and succeed in keeping us neutral if the policy contemplated a business boom or even "business as usual" in America while other nations are at war and wanting supplies from our mines, fields and factories. . . .

We saw the last European war until 1917 as one in no degree our business. . . . We rejoiced at the moment that leadership of our Government was showing greatest determination to keep America out of that war, a leadership affording a policy that was presumed to be a guarantee of our neutrality. That neutrality policy is now known as a permissive or a discretionary policy, with its administration in no degree mandatory upon the President. That the policy failed, and that miserably, is record. . . .

The [Woodrow] Wilson permissive neutrality policy held that it was not an unneutral act for America to sell munitions to nations at war so long as it was our policy

From Nye radio address 6 January 1936, Gerald P. Nye Papers, Herbert Hoover Library, West Branch, Iowa.

to sell to both sides alike, and free trade in munitions was the result. Suddenly we became enraged, discovering that this permissive policy of neutrality was based upon international law defining our rights as a neutral upon the high seas, that Great Britain was not recognizing or abiding by that law. Britain, by her blockade, was interfering with our American commerce with Germany, writing new contraband definitions, searching and seizing the cargoes of American ships destined for Germany or even neutral ports which Great Britain suspicioned might be for ultimate German use. By reason of these practices we were losing even our normal trade with the Central Powers. We didn't like this interference with our trade and profits. President Wilson wrote notes of protest to Britain—notes which when now compared with those of protest later dispatched to Germany, sound like an apology. We were placated, however, with larger orders from the Allies which much more than offset our loss of trade with Germany. These Allied orders were tremendous and caused us to quite overlook the fact that our neutral policy was no longer one finding us furnishing munitions to both sides. It was our increasing commerce with the Allies upon which our prosperity now depended. Who doesn't remember how bitterly severe were our notes of protest to Germany when Germany, in retaliation of the British blockade, used the submarine to destroy commerce upon which the Allies were dependent. But, while this business with the Allies was maintaining a marvelous prosperity for us and while we were counting as a great thing so long as we kept out of it, we were nevertheless highly resolved to continue our neutrality "so called."

The Allies soon exhausted their own means of buying from us. They needed American credit. Our permissive neutrality policy of the hour forbade loans and credits, but it appears that such pressure was brought as caused the administrators of that policy to turn their back upon it. It was concluded, by that administration, that while loans should be prohibited to any nation at war, credits would be countenanced. Our own economic well-being was so dependent upon the continuing boom market of war that we would only cut our own throats by refusing the credit that would let the Allies continue buying from us! So, for a time, the Allies bought upon credit furnished by Americans. But the time comes when individual credit is exhausted and the Allies need large loans if they are to continue buying American supplies. If these loans couldn't be had Europe couldn't continue buying from us! Somewhere the strings were pulled that caused our neutrality administrators to permit loans to the Allies contrary to our neutrality policy—a discretionary policy. To have insisted against loans would have ended the profits and the prosperity of Americans flowing from Europe's war!

Ah, business continues good; prosperity remains on every hand! War isn't such a bad thing when we don't have to be in it! "But," we said, "look at those Germans; they are destroying American cargoes going to England and France and sinking English passenger vessels with Americans on board! Maybe something ought to be done about it! But, whatever we do, let's not get into that war!" That was our reasoning at the hour. How childish it all was—this expectation of success in staying out of a war politically while economically we stayed in it; how childish this permissive flip-flop neutrality policy of ours and our belief that we could go on and on supplying the sinews of war to one or even both sides and avoid ourselves being ultimately drawn into the engagement with our lives and our fortunes at stake.

Well, to make a long story short, our prosperity, which at the moment was our commerce with the Allies, demanded a more and more warlike attitude on our part. Our rights on the high seas, our commerce is declared in jeopardy! . . .

After we had started stretching our permissive American neutrality policy to accommodate our commercial interests the Allied powers were never in doubt as to what America would ultimately do. They saw what we didn't seem to realize, namely, that where our pocketbook was there would we and our hearts ultimately be. . . .

Insistence now upon establishment of a mandatory policy of neutrality is no reflection upon any one man. It is only fair to say that the present [Franklin D.] Roosevelt determination to keep us out of war is no higher than was that expressed by Wilson. Yet . . . while the Wilson administration was declaring itself neutral, parts of that administration were actually contemplating the hour when we would ultimately get into the war without a doubt as to which side we would enter on. . . .

Based upon such facts and such experience Senator [Bennet Champ] Clark [D–Mo.] and I today introduced in the Senate a bill proposing a strict policy of neutrality, the enforcement of which shall at once be not permissive or at the discretion of the President, but mandatory upon him. The bill presents requirements and advantages roughly stated as follows:

First, at the outbreak of war between other nations the President shall by proclamation forbid the exportation of arms, ammunition and implements of war for the use of those nations, and that the President shall, not "may" but shall, extend this embargo to other nations if and when they may become engaged in such war.

Second, the bill proposes an embargo on other items of commerce which may be considered essential war materials, such as oil, and provides that the President shall forbid exportation to nations at war of these materials beyond what was the average annual exportation of these materials to those nations during the five-year period preceding the outbreak of war.

Third, the bill requires that the President shall upon the outbreak of war between foreign states proclaim that the buyer of any and all articles to or through the field of operations of belligerent states shall be at the risk solely of the buyer and the bill provides that the buyers shall be without redress in any court of the United States. Thus, it will be seen, there is provided a strict "cash and carry" basis with buyers taking their own risk in accomplishing delivery of supplies they buy from us in time of war.

Fourth, the bill requires that the President shall require American passengers to refrain from traveling on the vessels of belligerent states, and provides that passengers who ignore this requirement at once forfeit their right to protection of the United States. Thus we can avoid a repetition of the Lusitania experience.

Fifth, the bill introduced today does with loans and credits to time of war precisely what it does with war materials—it embargoes and limits them. . . .

There are those who will insist that this measure is too severe. We, who sponsor it, feel that in the light of experience, nothing short of those provisions is deserving of the title of a neutrality policy and we beg the confidence of the people of the land in it not as an instrument that will completely prevent war, but as one that will make it extremely difficult for the United States to be drawn into another foreign war that becomes our war only because of selfish interests that profit from the blood spilled in the wars of other lands.

2. President Franklin D. Roosevelt Proposes to "Quarantine" Aggressors, 1937

Some fifteen years ago the hopes of mankind for a continuing era of international peace were raised to great heights when more than sixty nations solemnly pledged themselves not to resort to arms in furtherance of their national aims and policies. The high aspirations expressed in the Briand-Kellogg Peace Pact and the hopes for peace thus raised have of late given way to a haunting fear of calamity. The present reign of terror and international lawlessness began a few years ago.

It began through unjustified interference in the internal affairs of other nations or the invasion of alien territory in violation of treaties; and has now reached a stage where the very foundations of civilization are seriously threatened. The landmarks and traditions which have marked the progress of civilization toward a condition of law, order and justice are being wiped away.

Without a declaration of war and without warning or justification of any kind, civilians, including vast numbers of women and children, are being ruthlessly murdered with bombs from the air. In times of so-called peace, ships are being attacked and sunk by submarines without cause or notice. Nations are fomenting and taking sides in civil warfare in nations that have never done them any harm. Nations claiming freedom for themselves deny it to others.

Innocent peoples, innocent nations, are being cruelly sacrificed to a greed for power and supremacy which is devoid of all sense of justice and humane considerations. . . .

The peace-loving nations must make a concerted effort in opposition to those violations of treaties and those ignorings of humane instincts which today are creating a state of international anarchy and instability from which there is no escape through mere isolation or neutrality.

Those who cherish their freedom and recognize and respect the equal right of their neighbors to be free and live in peace must work together for the triumph of law and moral principles in order that peace, justice and confidence may prevail in the world. There must be a return to a belief in the pledged word, in the value of a signed treaty. There must be recognition of the fact that national morality is as vital as private morality. . . .

There is a solidarity and interdependence about the modern world, both technically and morally, which makes it impossible for any nation completely to isolate itself from economic and political upheavals in the rest of the world, especially when such upheavals appear to be spreading and not declining. There can be no stability or peace either within nations or between nations except under laws and moral standards adhered to by all. International anarchy destroys every foundation for peace. It jeopardizes either the immediate or the future security of every nation, large or small. It is, therefore, a matter of vital interest and concern to the people of the United States that the sanctity of international treaties and the maintenance of international morality be restored.

This document can be found in U.S. Department of State, *Papers Relating to the Foreign Relations of the United States, Japan: 1931–1941* (Washington, D.C.: Government Printing Office, 1943), I, 379–383.

The overwhelming majority of the peoples and nations of the world today want to live in peace. They seek the removal of barriers against trade. They want to exert themselves in industry, in agriculture and in business, that they may increase their wealth through the production of wealth-producing goods rather than striving to produce military planes and bombs and machine guns and cannon for the destruction of human lives and useful property.

In those nations of the world which seem to be piling armament on armament for purposes of aggression, and those other nations which fear acts of aggression against them and their security, a very high proportion of their national income is being spent directly for armaments. It runs from thirty to as high as fifty percent. We are fortunate. The proportion that we in the United States spend is far less— eleven or twelve percent.

How happy we are that the circumstances of the moment permit us to put our money into bridges and boulevards, dams and reforestation, the conservation of our soil and many other kinds of useful works rather than into huge standing armies and vast supplies of implements of war.

I am compelled and you are compelled, nevertheless, to look ahead. The peace, the freedom and the security of ninety percent of the population of the world is being jeopardized by the remaining ten percent who are threatening a breakdown of all international order and law. Surely the ninety percent who want to live in peace under law and in accordance with moral standards that have received almost universal acceptance through the centuries, can and must find some way to make their will prevail.

The situation is definitely of universal concern. The questions involved relate not merely to violations of specific provisions of particular treaties; they are questions of war and of peace, of international law and especially of principles of humanity. It is true that they involve definite violations of agreements, and especially of the Covenant of the League of Nations, the Briand-Kellogg Pact and the Nine Power Treaty. But they also involve problems of world economy, world security and world humanity.

It is true that the moral consciousness of the world must recognize the importance of removing injustices and well-founded grievances; but at the same time it must be aroused to the cardinal necessity of honoring sanctity of treaties, of respecting the rights and liberties of others and of putting an end to acts of international aggression.

It seems to be unfortunately true that the epidemic of world lawlessness is spreading.

When an epidemic of physical disease starts to spread, the community approves and joins in a quarantine of the patients in order to protect the health of the community against the spread of the disease.

It is my determination to pursue a policy of peace. It is my determination to adopt every practicable measure to avoid involvement in war. It ought to be inconceivable that in this modern era, and in the face of experience, any nation could be so foolish and ruthless as to run the risk of plunging the whole world into war by invading and violating, in contravention of solemn treaties, the territory of other nations that have done them no real harm and are too weak to protect themselves adequately. Yet the peace of the world and the welfare and security of every nation, including our own, is today being threatened by that very thing.

3. Japan Envisions a "New Order" in Asia, 1938

What Japan seeks is the establishment of a new order which will insure the permanent stability of East Asia. In this lies the ultimate purpose of our present military campaign.

This new order has for its foundation a tripartite relationship of mutual aid and co-ordination between Japan, Manchoukuo [the name Japan gave to Manchuria in February 1932], and China in political, economic, cultural and other fields. Its object is to secure international justice, to perfect the joint defence against Communism, and to create a new culture and realize a close economic cohesion throughout East Asia. This indeed is the way to contribute toward the stabilization of East Asia and the progress of the world.

What Japan desires of China is that that country will share in the task of bringing about this new order in East Asia. She confidently expects that the people of China will fully comprehend her true intentions and that they will respond to the call of Japan for their co-operation. Even the participation of the Kuomintang Government would not be rejected, if, repudiating the policy which has guided it in the past and remolding its personnel, so as to translate its re-birth into fact, it were to come forward to join in the establishment of the new order.

Japan is confident that other Powers will on their part correctly appreciate her aims and policy and adapt their attitude to the new conditions prevailing in East Asia. For the cordiality hitherto manifested by the nations which are in sympathy with us, Japan wishes to express her profound gratitude.

The establishment of a new order in East Asia is in complete conformity with the very spirit in which the Empire was founded; to achieve such a task is the exalted responsibility with which our present generation is entrusted. It is, therefore, imperative to carry out all necessary internal reforms, and with a full development of the aggregate national strength, material as well as moral, fulfill at all costs this duty incumbent upon our nation.

Such the Government declare to be the immutable policy and determination of Japan.

4. FDR Proposes Lend-Lease Aid to Great Britain, 1940

December 17, 1940, Press Conference

Now, what I am trying to do is to eliminate the dollar sign, and that is something brand new in the thoughts of practically everybody in this room, I think—get rid of the silly, foolish old dollar sign. All right!

Well, let me give you an illustration: Suppose my neighbor's home catches fire, and I have got a length of garden hose four or five hundred feet away; but, my Heaven, if he can take my garden hose and connect it up with his hydrant, I may

---

Document 3 can be found in U.S. Department of State, *Papers Relating to the Foreign Relations of the United States, Japan: 1931–1941* (Washington, D.C.: Government Printing Office, 1943), I, 477–478.

Document 4 can be found in Dec. 17 remarks from *Complete Presidential Press Conferences of Franklin D. Roosevelt* (New York: DaCapo Press, 1972), XV–XVI (1940), 353–355. Dec. 29 radio address in *Department of State Bulletin* 4 (1941): 3–8.

help him to put out his fire. Now what do I do? I don't say to him before that operation, "Neighbor, my garden hose cost me $15; you have got to pay me $15 for it." What is the transaction that goes on? I don't want $15—I want my garden hose back after the fire is over. All right. If it goes through the fire all right, intact, without any damage to it, he gives it back to me and thanks me very much for the use of it. But suppose it gets smashed up—holes in it—during the fire; we don't have to have too much formality about it, but I say to him, "I was glad to lend you that hose; I see I can't use it any more, it's all smashed up." He says, "How many feet of it were there?" I tell him, "there were 150 feet of it." He said, "All right, I will replace it." Now, if I get a nice garden hose back, I am in pretty good shape. In other words, if you lend certain munitions and get the munitions back at the end of the war, if they are intact—haven't been hurt—you are all right; if they have been damaged or deteriorated or lost completely, it seems to me you come out pretty well if you have them replaced by the fellow that you have lent them to. . . .

December 29, 1940, Radio Address

This is not a fireside chat on war. It is a talk on national security; because the nub of the whole purpose of your President is to keep you now, and your children later, and your grandchildren much later, out of a last-ditch war for the preservation of American independence and all of the things that American independence means to you and to me and to ours. . . .

Never before since Jamestown and Plymouth Rock has our American civilization been in such danger as now.

For, on September 27, 1940, by an agreement signed in Berlin, three powerful nations, two in Europe and one in Asia, joined themselves together in the threat that if the United States interfered with or blocked the expansion program of these three nations—a program aimed at world control—they would unite in ultimate action against the United States.

The Nazi masters of Germany have made it clear that they intend not only to dominate all life and thought in their own country, but also to enslave the whole of Europe, and then to use the resources of Europe to dominate the rest of the world. . . .

Some of our people like to believe that wars in Europe and in Asia are of no concern to us. But it is a matter of most vital concern to us that European and Asiatic war-makers should not gain control of the oceans which lead to this hemisphere. . . .

Does anyone seriously believe that we need to fear attack while a free Britain remains our most powerful naval neighbor in the Atlantic? Does anyone seriously believe, on the other hand, that we could rest easy if the Axis powers were our neighbor there?

If Great Britain goes down, the Axis powers will control the continents of Europe, Asia, Africa, Australasia, and the high seas—and they will be in a position to bring enormous military and naval resources against this hemisphere. It is no exaggeration to say that all of us in the Americas would be living at the point of a gun—a gun loaded with explosive bullets, economic as well as military. . . .

There are those who say that the Axis powers would never have any desire to attack the Western Hemisphere. This is the same dangerous form of wishful thinking which has destroyed the powers of resistance of so many conquered peoples.

The plain facts are that the Nazis have proclaimed, time and again, that all other races are their inferiors and therefore subject to their orders. And most important of all, the vast resources and wealth of this hemisphere constitute the most tempting loot in all the world. . . .

The experience of the past two years has proven beyond doubt that no nation can appease the Nazis. No man can tame a tiger into a kitten by stroking it. There can be no appeasement with ruthlessness. There can be no reasoning with an incendiary bomb. We know now that a nation can have peace with the Nazis only at the price of total surrender. . . .

The American appeasers ignore the warning to be found in the fate of Austria, Czechoslovakia, Poland, Norway, Belgium, the Netherlands, Denmark, and France. They tell you that the Axis powers are going to win anyway; that all this bloodshed in the world could be saved; and that the United States might just as well throw its influence into the scale of a dictated peace, and get the best out of it that we can.

They call it a "negotiated peace." Nonsense! Is it a negotiated peace if a gang of outlaws surrounds your community and on threat of extermination makes you pay tribute to save your own skins?

Such a dictated peace would be no peace at all. It would be only another armistice, leading to the most gigantic armament race and the most devastating trade wars in history. And in these contests the Americas would offer the only real resistance to the Axis powers. . . .

The proposed "new order" is the very opposite of a United States of Europe or a United States of Asia. It is not a government based upon the consent of the governed. It is not a union of ordinary, self-respecting men and women to protect themselves and their freedom and their dignity from oppression. It is an unholy alliance of power . . . to dominate and enslave the human race.

The British people are conducting an active war against this unholy alliance. Our own future security is greatly dependent on the outcome of that fight. Our ability to "keep out of war" is going to be affected by that outcome.

Thinking in terms of today and tomorrow, I make the direct statement to the American people that there is far less chance of the United States getting into war if we do all we can now to support the nations defending themselves against attack by the Axis than if we acquiesce in their defeat, submit tamely to an Axis victory, and wait our turn to be the object of attack in another war later on.

If we are to be completely honest with ourselves, we must admit there is risk in *any* course we may take. But I deeply believe that the great majority of our people agree that the course that I advocate involves the least risk now and the greatest hope for world peace in the future.

The people of Europe who are defending themselves do not ask us to do their fighting. They ask us for the implements of war, the planes, the tanks, the guns, the freighters, which will enable them to fight for their liberty and our security. Emphatically we must get these weapons to them in sufficient volume and quickly enough, so that we and our children will be saved the agony and suffering of war which others have had to endure.

Let not defeatists tell us that it is too late. It will never be earlier. Tomorrow will be later than today.

Certain facts are self-evident.

In a military sense Great Britain and the British Empire are today the spearhead of resistance to world conquest. They are putting up a fight which will live forever in the story of human gallantry.

There is no demand for sending an American Expeditionary Force outside our own borders. There is no intention by any member of your Government to send such a force. You can, therefore, nail any talk about sending armies to Europe as deliberate untruth.

Our national policy is not directed toward war. Its sole purpose is to keep war away from our country and our people.

Democracy's fight against world conquest is being greatly aided, and must be more greatly aided, by the rearmament of the United States and by sending every ounce and every ton of munitions and supplies that we can possibly spare to help the defenders who are in the front lines. It is no more unneutral for us to do that than it is for Sweden, Russia, and other nations near Germany to send steel and ore and oil and other war materials into Germany every day.

We are planning our own defense with the utmost urgency; and in its vast scale we must integrate the war needs of Britain and the other free nations resisting aggression. . . .

As planes and ships and guns and shells are produced, your Government, with its defense experts, can then determine how best to use them to defend this hemisphere. The decision as to how much shall be sent abroad and how much shall remain at home must be made on the basis of our over-all military necessities.

We must be the great arsenal of democracy. For us this is an emergency as serious as war itself. We must apply ourselves to our task with the same resolution, the same sense of urgency, the same spirit of patriotism and sacrifice, as we would show were we at war.

5. Roosevelt Orders the U.S. Navy to "Shoot on Sight," 1941

The Navy Department of the United States has reported to me that on the morning of September fourth the United States destroyer *Greer*, proceeding in full daylight toward Iceland, had reached a point southeast of Greenland. She was carrying American mail to Iceland. She was flying the American flag. Her identity as an American ship was unmistakable.

She was then and there attacked by a submarine. Germany admits that it was a German submarine. The submarine deliberately fired a torpedo at the *Greer*, followed later by another torpedo attack. In spite of what Hitler's propaganda bureau has invented, and in spite of what any American obstructionist organization may prefer to believe, I tell you the blunt fact that the German submarine fired first upon this American destroyer without warning, and with deliberate design to sink her.

Our destroyer, at the time, was in waters which the Government of the United States had declared to be waters of self-defense—surrounding outposts of American protection in the Atlantic.

This document can be found in *Public Papers and Addresses of Franklin D Roosevelt, 1941* (New York: Harper and Brothers, 1950), 384–392.

In the North of the Atlantic, outposts have been established by us in Iceland, in Greenland, in Labrador and in Newfoundland. Through these waters there pass many ships of many flags. They bear food and other supplies to civilians; and they bear matériel of war, for which the people of the United States are spending billions of dollars, and which, by Congressional action, they have declared to be essential for the defense of our own land.

The United States destroyer, when attacked, was proceeding on a legitimate mission. . . .

This was piracy—piracy legally and morally. It was not the first nor the last act of piracy which the Nazi Government has committed against the American flag in this war. For attack has followed attack.

A few months ago an American flag merchant ship, the *Robin Moor,* was sunk by a Nazi submarine in the middle of the South Atlantic, under circumstances violating long-established international law and violating every principle of humanity. The passengers and the crew were forced into open boats hundreds of miles from land, in direct violation of international agreements signed by nearly all Nations including the Government of Germany. No apology, no allegation of mistake, no offer of reparations has come from the Nazi Government. . . .

Five days ago a United States Navy ship on patrol picked up three survivors of an American-owned ship operating under the flag of our sister Republic of Panama—the *S.S. Sessa.* On August seventeenth, she had been first torpedoed without warning, and then shelled, near Greenland, while carrying civilian supplies to Iceland. It is feared that the other members of her crew have been drowned. In view of the established presence of German submarines in this vicinity, there can be no reasonable doubt as to the identity of the flag of the attacker.

Five days ago, another United States merchant ship, the *Steel Seafarer,* was sunk by a German aircraft in the Red Sea two hundred and twenty miles south of Suez. She was bound for an Egyptian port. . . .

In the face of all this, we Americans are keeping our feet on the ground. . . .

But it would be inexcusable folly to minimize such incidents in the face of evidence which makes it clear that the incident is not isolated, but is part of a general plan.

The important truth is that these acts of international lawlessness are a manifestation of a design which has been made clear to the American people for a long time. It is the Nazi design to abolish the freedom of the seas, and to acquire absolute control and domination of these seas for themselves.

For with control of the seas in their own hands, the way can obviously become clear for their next step—domination of the United States—domination of the Western Hemisphere by force of arms. Under Nazi control of the seas, no merchant ship of the United States or of any other American Republic would be free to carry on any peaceful commerce, except by the condescending grace of this foreign and tyrannical power. The Atlantic Ocean which has been, and which should always be, a free and friendly highway for us would then become a deadly menace to the commerce of the United States, to the coasts of the United States, and even to the inland cities of the United States. . . .

To be ultimately successful in world mastery, Hitler knows that he must get control of the seas. He must first destroy the bridge of ships which we are building across the Atlantic and over which we shall continue to roll the implements of war to help destroy him, to destroy all his works in the end. He must wipe out our patrol on sea and in the air if he is to do it. He must silence the British Navy.

I think it must be explained over and over again to people who like to think of the United States Navy as an invincible protection, that this can be true only if the British Navy survives. And that, my friends, is simple arithmetic.

For if the world outside of the Americas falls under Axis domination, the shipbuilding facilities which the Axis powers would then possess in all of Europe, in the British Isles, and in the Far East would be much greater than all the shipbuilding facilities and potentialities of all of the Americas—not only greater, but two or three times greater—enough to win. Even if the United States threw all its resources into such a situation, seeking to double and even redouble the size of our Navy, the Axis powers, in control of the rest of the world, would have the manpower and the physical resources to outbuild us several times over.

It is time for all Americans, Americans of all the Americas to stop being deluded by the romantic notion that the Americas can go on living happily and peacefully in a Nazi-dominated world. . . .

No tender whisperings of appeasers that Hitler is not interested in the Western Hemisphere, no soporific lullabies that a wide ocean protects us from him—can long have any effect on the hard-headed, far-sighted, and realistic American people.

Because of these episodes . . . we Americans are now face to face not with abstract theories but with cruel, relentless facts.

This attack on the *Greer* was no localized military operation in the North Atlantic. This was no mere episode in a struggle between two Nations. This was one determined step toward creating a permanent world system based on force, on terror, and on murder. . . .

There has now come a time when you and I must see the cold, inexorable necessity of saying to these inhuman, unrestrained seekers of world conquest and permanent world domination by the sword: "You seek to throw our children and our children's children into your form of terrorism and slavery. You have now attacked our own safety. You shall go no further."

Normal practices of diplomacy—note writing—are of no possible use in dealing with international outlaws who sink our ships and kill our citizens.

One peaceful Nation after another has met disaster because each refused to look the Nazi danger squarely in the eye until it actually had them by the throat.

The United States will not make that fatal mistake.

No act of violence, no act of intimidation will keep us from maintaining intact two bulwarks of American defense: First, our line of supply of matériel to the enemies of Hitler; and second, the freedom of our shipping on the high seas.

No matter what it takes, no matter what it costs, we will keep open the line of legitimate commerce in these defensive waters.

We have sought no shooting war with Hitler. We do not seek it now. But neither do we want peace so much, that we are willing to pay for it by permitting him to attack our naval and merchant ships while they are on legitimate business.

I assume that the German leaders are not deeply concerned, tonight or any other time, by what we Americans or the American Government say or publish about them. We cannot bring about the downfall of Nazism by the use of long-range invective.

But when you see a rattlesnake poised to strike, you do not wait until he has struck before you crush him.

These Nazi submarines and raiders are the rattlesnakes of the Atlantic. They are a menace to the free pathways of the high seas. They are a challenge to our sovereignty. They hammer at our most precious rights when they attack ships of the American flag—symbols of our independence, our freedom, our very life. . . .

In the waters which we deem necessary for defense, American naval vessels and American planes will no longer wait until Axis submarines lurking under the water, or Axis raiders on the surface of the sea, strike their deadly blow—first.

Upon our naval and air patrol—now operating in large number over a vast expanse of the Atlantic Ocean—falls the duty of maintaining the American policy of freedom of the seas—now. That means, very simply, very clearly, that our patrolling vessels and planes will protect all merchant ships—not only American ships but ships of any flag—engaged in commerce in our defensive waters. They will protect them from submarines; they will protect them from surface raiders. . . .

It is no act of war on our part when we decide to protect the seas that are vital to American defense. The aggression is not ours. Ours is solely defense. . . .

The orders which I have given as Commander in Chief of the United States Army and Navy are to carry out that policy—at once. . . .

I have no illusions about the gravity of this step. I have not taken it hurriedly or lightly. It is the result of months and months of constant thought and anxiety and prayer. In the protection of your Nation and mine it cannot be avoided.

The American people have faced other grave crises in their history—with American courage, and with American resolution. They will do no less today.

They know the actualities of the attacks upon us. They know the necessities of a bold defense against these attacks. They know that the times call for clear heads and fearless hearts.

And with that inner strength that comes to a free people conscious of their duty, and conscious of the righteousness of what they do, they will—with Divine help and guidance—stand their ground against this latest assault upon their democracy, their sovereignty, and their freedom.

6. Japan Proposes Two Diplomatic Options to the United States, November 1941

Plan A

The most important pending matters in negotiations between Japan and the United States are: 1) the stationing and withdrawal of troops in China and French Indochina; 2) nondiscriminatory trade in China; 3) interpretation and observance of the Tripartite Pact; and 4) the Four Principles [see Document 7]. These matters are to be moderated to the following extent:

1) The stationing and withdrawal of troops in China.

Setting aside for the moment our reasons for stationing troops, we shall moderate our stance to the following extent, considering that the United States has

Excerpts from *Japan's Decision for War: Records of the 1941 Policy Conferences.* Edited and translated by Nobutaka Ike. Copyright © 1967 by the Board of Trustees of the Leland Stanford Junior University, renewed 1995 by the author. Used with permission of Stanford University Press, www.sup.org.

(a) attached great importance to the stationing of troops for an indeterminate period of time, (b) objected to the inclusion of this item in the terms for a peace settlement, and (c) called for a clearer expression of intent regarding the withdrawal of troops:

> Japanese forces dispatched to China because of the China Incident shall occupy designated areas of north China and Mongolia and Hainan island for as long as is necessary after peace is concluded between Japan and China. The evacuation of other forces shall commence the minute peace is concluded, in accordance with separate arrangements made between Japan and China, and shall be completed within two years.
>
> Note: Should the United States ask what "for as long as is necessary" means, we shall reply to the effect that our goal is roughly 25 years.

2) The stationing and withdrawal of troops in French Indochina.

The United States entertains misgivings that Japan has territorial ambitions in French Indochina and is attempting to make it into a base for military advances into adjacent territories. In recognition of this, we shall moderate our stance to the following extent:

> The Japanese government respects the territorial sovereignty of French Indochina. Japanese troops currently dispatched to French Indochina will be immediately evacuated upon the settlement of the China Incident or upon the establishment of a just peace in the Far East.

3) Nondiscriminatory treatment in trade with China.

In the event that there is no prospect of securing complete agreement to our previous proposal of September 25, we shall deal with this issue on the basis of the following proposal:

> The Japanese government acknowledges that the principle of nondiscrimination will be applied in the entire Pacific region and China as well, insofar as that principle is applied throughout the world.

4) Interpretation and observance of the Tripartite Pact.

We shall respond on this matter by making it even clearer that we have no intention of unduly broadening our interpretation of the right of self defense; that as far as interpreting and observing the Tripartite Pact is concerned, the Japanese government will act on its own discretion, as we have frequently elaborated before; and that we think that the United States already understands this fully.

5) As for what the United States calls its four principles, we shall avoid with all our might their inclusion in anything formally agreed to between Japan and the United States (whether that be the Draft Understanding or other declarations).

Plan B

1) Both Japan and the United States shall promise not to make any advances by military force into Southeast Asia and the South Pacific region, other than French Indochina.

2) The governments of Japan and the United States shall cooperate together so as to guarantee the procurement of necessary resources from the Dutch East Indies.

3) The governments of Japan and the United States shall together restore trade relations to what they were prior to the freezing of assets, and the United States will promise to supply Japan with the petroleum it needs.

4) The United States government shall not engage in such actions as may hinder efforts toward peace by Japan and China

Notes

1) If it is necessary to do so, there is no objection to promising that if the present agreement is concluded, Japanese forces now stationed in southern Indochina are prepared, with the approval of the French government, to transfer to northern French Indochina, and that these Japanese forces will withdraw from French Indochina upon settlement of the China Incident or the establishment of a just peace in the Pacific region.

2) If it is also necessary to do so, additional insertions may be made to the provisions regarding nondiscriminatory treatment in trade and those regarding interpretation and observance of the Tripartite Pact in the existing proposals (last plans).

7. Washington Rejects Japan's Proposals and Reaffirms the Open Door, November 1941

Section I   Draft Mutual Declaration of Policy

The Government of the United States and the Government of Japan both being solicitous for the peace of the Pacific affirm that their national policies are directed toward lasting and extensive peace throughout the Pacific area, that they have no territorial designs in that area, that they have no intention of threatening other countries or of using military force aggressively against any neighboring nation, and that, accordingly, in their national policies they will actively support and give practical application to the following fundamental principles upon which their relations with each other and with all other governments are based:

1. The principle of inviolability of territorial integrity and sovereignty of each and all nations.
2. The principle of non-interference in the internal affairs of other countries.
3. The principle of equality, including equality of commercial opportunity and treatment.
4. The principle of reliance upon international cooperation and conciliation for the prevention and pacific settlement of controversies and for improvement of international conditions by peaceful methods and processes.

The Government of Japan and the Government of the United States have agreed that toward eliminating chronic political instability, preventing recurrent economic

---

This document can be found in U.S. Department of State, *Papers Relating to the Foreign Relations of the United States, Japan: 1931–1941* (Washington, D.C.: Government Printing Office, 1943), II, 768–769.

collapse, and providing a basis for peace, they will actively support and practically apply the following principles in their economic relations with each other and with other nations and peoples:

1. The principle of non-discrimination in international commercial relations.
2. The principle of international economic cooperation and abolition of extreme nationalism as expressed in excessive trade restrictions.
3. The principle of non-discriminatory access by all nations to raw material supplies.
4. The principle of full protection of the interests of consuming countries and populations as regards the operation of international commodity agreements.
5. The principle of establishment of such institutions and arrangements of international finance as may lend aid to the essential enterprises and the continuous development of all countries and may permit payments through processes of trade consonant with the welfare of all countries.

Section II   Steps to Be Taken by the Government of the United States and by the Government of Japan

The Government of the United States and the Government of Japan propose to take steps as follows:

1. The Government of the United States and the Government of Japan will endeavor to conclude a multilateral non-aggression pact among the British Empire, China, Japan, the Netherlands, the Soviet Union, Thailand and the United States.
2. Both Governments will endeavor to conclude among the American, British, Chinese, Japanese, the Netherland and Thai Governments an agreement whereunder each of the Governments would pledge itself to respect the territorial integrity of French Indochina and, in the event that there should develop a threat to the territorial integrity of Indochina, to enter into immediate consultation with a view to taking such measures as may be deemed necessary and advisable to meet the threat in question. Such agreement would provide also that each of the Governments party to the agreement would not seek or accept preferential treatment in its trade or economic relations with Indochina and would use its influence to obtain for each of the signatories equality of treatment in trade and commerce with French Indochina.
3. The Government of Japan will withdraw all military, naval, air and police forces from China and from Indochina.
4. The Government of the United States and the Government of Japan will not support—militarily, politically, economically—any government or regime in China other than the National Government of the Republic of China with capital temporarily at Chungking.
5. Both Governments will give up all extraterritorial rights in China, including rights and interests in and with regard to international settlements and concessions, and rights under the Boxer Protocol of 1901.

   Both Governments will endeavor to obtain the agreement of the British and other governments to give up extraterritorial rights in China, including rights in international settlements and in concessions and under the Boxer Protocol of 1901.

6. The Government of the United States and the Government of Japan will enter into negotiations for the conclusion between the United States and Japan of a trade agreement, based upon reciprocal most-favored-nation treatment and reduction of trade barriers by both countries, including an undertaking by the United States to bind raw silk on the free list.

7. The Government of the United States and the Government of Japan will, respectively, remove the freezing restrictions on Japanese funds in the United States and on American funds in Japan.

8. Both Governments will agree upon a plan for the stabilization of the dollar-yen rate, with the allocation of funds adequate for this purpose, half to be supplied by Japan and half by the United States.

9. Both Governments will agree that no agreement which either has concluded with any third power or powers shall be interpreted by it in such a way as to conflict with the fundamental purpose of this agreement, the establishment and preservation of peace throughout the Pacific area.

10. Both Governments will use their influence to cause other governments to adhere to and to give practical application to the basic political and economic principles set forth in this agreement.

8. Roosevelt Delivers His War Message to Congress, 1941

Yesterday, December 7, 1941—a date which will live in infamy—the United States of America was suddenly and deliberately attacked by naval and air forces of the Empire of Japan.

The United States was at peace with that Nation and, at the solicitation of Japan, was still in conversation with its Government and its Emperor looking toward the maintenance of peace in the Pacific. Indeed, one hour after Japanese air squadrons had commenced bombing in Oahu, the Japanese Ambassador to the United States and his colleague delivered to the Secretary of State a formal reply to a recent American message. While this reply stated that it seemed useless to continue the existing diplomatic negotiations, it contained no threat or hint of war or armed attack.

It will be recorded that the distance of Hawaii from Japan makes it obvious that the attack was deliberately planned many days or even weeks ago. During the intervening time the Japanese Government has deliberately sought to deceive the United States by false statements and expressions of hope for continued peace.

The attack yesterday on the Hawaiian Islands has caused severe damage to American naval and military forces. Very many American lives have been lost. In addition American ships have been reported torpedoed on the high seas between San Francisco and Honolulu.

Yesterday the Japanese Government also launched an attack against Malaya.

Last night Japanese forces attacked Hong Kong.

Last night Japanese forces attacked Guam.

Last night Japanese forces attacked the Philippine Islands.

This document can be found in U.S. Department of State, *Papers Relating to the Foreign Relations of the United States, Japan: 1931–1941* (Washington, D.C.: Government Printing Office, 1943), II, 793–794.

Last night the Japanese attacked Wake Island.

This morning the Japanese attacked Midway Island.

Japan has, therefore, undertaken a surprise offensive extending throughout the Pacific area. The facts of yesterday speak for themselves. The people of the United States have already formed their opinions and well understand the implications to the very life and safety of our Nation.

As Commander-in-Chief of the Army and Navy I have directed that all measures be taken for our defense.

Always will we remember the character of the onslaught against us.

No matter how long it may take us to overcome this premeditated invasion, the American people in their righteous might will win through to absolute victory.

I believe I interpret the will of the Congress and of the people when I assert that we will not only defend ourselves to the uttermost but will make very certain that this form of treachery shall never endanger us again.

Hostilities exist. There is no blinking at the fact that our people, our territory, and our interests are in grave danger.

With confidence in our armed forces—with the unbounded determination of our people—we will gain the inevitable triumph—so help us God.

I ask that the Congress declare that since the unprovoked and dastardly attack by Japan on Sunday, December seventh, a state of war has existed between the United States and the Japanese Empire.

ESSAYS

In the first essay, Gerhard Weinberg, of the University of North Carolina, lays out the case for U.S. military intervention in World War II. Weinberg, whose research unearthed a second book authored by Hitler after *Mein Kampf,* argues that the German dictator pursued a global agenda that included plans to conquer the United States. Wartime exigencies forced Hitler to delay, but never abandon, the development of naval and air capabilities for a trans-Atlantic attack. Germany's alliance with Japan in 1940 provided the Führer with a naval ally to help him advance his dream. According to Weinberg, President Roosevelt—unlike his isolationist critics—grasped the international dimensions of the threat, but still hoped to avoid war by aiding Britain, Russia, and China. Germany's relentless aggression, and Japan's determination to thrust southward across the Pacific, doomed any chance for peace. Weinberg concludes that U.S. entry into the war was both necessary and inevitable.

In the second essay, Bruce M. Russett of Yale University challenges conventional wisdom that the United States had little choice but to enter World War II. Russett argues that Hitler lacked the capability to achieve victory in Europe and posed no direct military threat to the United States. By late 1941 Britain's survival had already been assured by FDR's policy of providing assistance by all measures short of war, and Germany's imprudent invasion of the Soviet Union was doomed to end in a stalemate. As for Asia, Japan's conquest of China had reached a standstill by 1941, and until Washington slapped down a sweeping embargo on raw materials, including petroleum, Japan had been determined to avoid war with the United States. Thus, U.S. entry into the Second World War was unnecessary and avoidable. Russett explains in his updated preface that when he first published his work in 1972, the Vietnam War had moved him to ponder the legacies of World War II, including an exaggerated sense of power that has led postwar America to undertake military interventions globally.

The Global Threat and the Case for War

GERHARD WEINBERG

The initial reaction of both the leadership and the public in the United States to the outbreak of war in Europe was essentially similar and uniform. The overwhelming majority blamed Germany for starting the war; the overwhelming majority hoped that Britain and France would win; the overwhelming majority wanted to stay out of the war. The near unanimity on these three basic issues did not extend, however, to two other subsidiary but in practice critical matters: the real prospects of the Allies and the policy to be followed by the United States toward them.

There were those in the United States who thought it made no difference who won, but for many, the prospect of the victory of the Allies was not only the preferred but the most likely outcome of the conflict. As German victory in Poland was followed by a quiet winter, more of the public began to doubt the ability of Britain and France to defeat her; and their doubt, not surprisingly, increased with German victories in Scandinavia and the West in the spring of 1940. President Roosevelt's views on this subject appear to have been somewhat different—and in retrospect a great deal more far-sighted—than those of many others. He certainly always hoped for an Allied victory over Germany, but he was very skeptical of Western power. . . .

These perceptions of the President must be kept in mind in assessing and understanding the practical steps Roosevelt urged on Congress and the American people. He believed that Nazi Germany and its allies threatened the whole world, including the Western Hemisphere, and he very much hoped to keep the United States out of the war. Unlike, Stalin, who believed that the best way to avert war from the Soviet Union was to help the Germans fight the Western Powers, Roosevelt thought that the most likely prospect for continual avoidance of war was to assist Britain and France in defeating Germany. Because he believed, correctly as we now know, that the Western Powers were deficient in weapons of war, he considered the prohibition on the sale of weapons to them in the neutrality laws a bonus for the early rearmament of the aggressors and a major handicap for the Allies. He would, therefore, try again to have the neutrality laws changed.

Roosevelt hoped that this could be done on a non-partisan or bi-partisan basis, and in the initial stages tried to involve the 1936 Republican President and Vice-Presidential candidates, Alfred Landon, and Frank Knox, in the process. In the Congress, however, a bitter debate, largely though not entirely on partisan lines, ensued. The issue divided the country. What came to be a standard pattern over the next two years emerged. On the one side were those who believed that, both to stay out of war and to assist Britain and France, neutrality law revision was in the country's interest. A few took this side because they expected or wanted the United States to join the Allies. Against this position were those, generally called isolationists and

Adapted from Gerhard Weinberg, *A World at Arms: A Global History of World War II* (Cambridge: Cambridge University Press, 1994), 84–86, 178–180, 182, 239–241, 243–246, 249–252, 256–257, 261–263. Source notes in original text have been omitted. Copyright © 1994 by Cambridge University Press. Reprinted with the permission of Cambridge University Press.

later strongly identified with the America First Committee, who believed that the best way to stay out of the war was to do nothing to assist Britain and France or to help them to help themselves; and some took this side because they thought that it might be just as well if Germany won or at least that it made little difference to the United States if she did so.

In the weeks before the outbreak of war, the isolationists had won on the issue of allowing others to buy arms in the United States, when Roosevelt had proposed it as a way of warning Germany that American arsenals would be open to those certain to control the seas if Germany started a war. Now that the Germans had started it, the isolationists lost. After a lengthy and bitter struggle, during which Roosevelt, as he put it, was "walking on eggs," the Congress approved what had come to be called "cash and carry" early in November; the President signed the bill on November 4. . . .

Hitler's view of the United States was based on an assessment that this was a weak country, incapable because of its racial mixture and feeble democratic government of organizing and maintaining strong military forces. The antagonism of Americans, both in government and among the public, toward Germany was therefore no cause for worry. Certain that Allied victory in World War I was the result of Germany's having been stabbed in the back by the home front, he was never interested in the American military effort in that conflict or any possible renewal of it. He had long assumed that Germany would have to fight the United States after conquering Eurasia, and he had begun preparations toward that end both in airplane and naval construction. The outbreak of war in Europe in 1939, however, forced a temporary postponement in the program to construct a big navy of huge battleships and numerous other surface ships. . . .

For years Hitler [also] had been calling for an airplane capable of bombing the United States, and work on such a plane had been under way since 1937. The realization of this project, however, was still not imminent in 1940, and the Germans could only push forward with it in the hope that by the time the planes were ready, refueling in the Portuguese Azores would be possible and would increase the possible bomb load. The prerequisites for war with the United States were being worked on, but it was obvious that they would take time to complete. While the preparations went forward, a project which was thought to be much simpler and capable of completion long before the huge blue-water navy and swarms of four-engined bombers had been built was to be carried out by Germany's victorious army: the invasion of the Soviet Union and the defeat of that country so that huge portions of it could be annexed and settled by German farmers, and the area's metal and oil resources harnessed to the subsequent campaign against the United States.

The whole project of crushing France and England had, after all, been undertaken only as a necessary preliminary, in Hitler's eye, to the attack in the East which would enable Germany to take the living space, the *Lebensraum,* he believed she needed. And it is too often forgotten in retrospect that in his view the campaign in the West was always expected to be the harder one. If in World War I Germany had struggled unsuccessfully in the West though victorious in the East, the fortunate willingness of the Soviet Union to assist her in winning in the West this time could make it all the easier to win in the East against inferior Slavs ruled by incompetent Jews, as Hitler believed. . . .

In view of this background it should not be surprising that already in mid and late May of 1940, as soon as it became clear that the German offensive in the West was going forward as quickly and successfully as Hitler could possibly hope, he began to turn his thoughts to the attack on the Soviet Union. He was beginning to discuss this project with his military associates in late May, and in June had them starting on the first preparations of plans for such an operation. Initially conceived of as an offensive to be launched in the fall of 1940, the campaign was expected to last only a few weeks. If the mighty French army, which had stopped the Germans in the last war, could be crushed in six weeks and the British driven ignominiously from the continent, then victory in the East would take hardly any time at all. The concept of a "one-front" war always meant one *land* front to Hitler, so that the question of whether or not England remained in the war after the defeat of France was initially irrelevant to the timing of an attack in the East.

During the latter part of July, the preliminary discussion of the new offensive coincided with the recognition that Britain would not withdraw from the war. Far from discouraging Hitler, this had the opposite effect of making him all the more determined to attack the Soviet Union. In his eyes, the British were staying in the war in expectation of the Soviet Union and United States replacing France as Britain's continental ally, something he assumed the English invariably needed. This quick destruction of the Soviet Union would not only remove one of these two hopes but would indirectly eliminate the other as well. Once Japan was reassured by the German attack on the Soviet Union against any threat to her home islands from the Pacific territories of Russia, she could strike southwards into the areas she had long coveted, and such an action would necessarily draw American attention and resources into the Pacific. The destruction of Russia, accordingly, would serve as an indirect means of forcing Britain out of the war as well as opening up the agricultural land and raw materials of the Soviet Union for German settlement and exploitation.

In those same days, however, as the indirect fight against England was added to the original aims of the invasion of Russia, Hitler came to the conclusion that the attack in the East had best be launched in the early summer of 1941 rather than in the fall of 1940. Influenced it would seem by the arguments of his immediate military advisors that the transfer of German forces from the West to the East, their refitting for new operations, and the needed logistical preparations in an area of underdeveloped transportation facilities meant risking that the short campaign could not be completed victoriously before the onset of winter, Hitler had decided by the end of July that it made more sense to wait until the following year when the whole operation could be completed in one blow. . . .

The limited industrial resources of Germany at their relatively low level of mobilization were not, however, capable of coping simultaneously with the preparations for the new land campaign in the East and the construction of the great battleship navy. Once again—as in September 1939—these projects had to be postponed. Victory over the Soviet Union would release the necessary resources for a resumption of construction on the big ships; in the interim, Germany would concentrate at sea on the blockade of Great Britain by submarines and airplanes.

The postponement of fleet building, in turn, had immediate implications for Germany's direct and indirect relations with the United States. In the direct sense, it meant that the German submarines were instructed to be careful of incidents with the United

States, and Hitler ordered restraint on a navy ever eager to strike at American ship-ping. Simultaneously, in the indirect sense the position and role of Japan with its great navy became more important in German eyes. As already mentioned, Hitler antici-pated that an attack on the Soviet Union would help propel Japan forward in Asia, thus tying up the United States in the Pacific in the years that Germany was still building her own surface navy. Between the decision to attack Russia and the implementation of that decision, however, there were now the intervening months to consider.

It was in this context that lining up Japan with the Axis came to be seen as in-creasingly important, a process which met the interests of the new leadership which had come to power in Tokyo in the days of decision in Berlin. The Tripartite Pact of Germany, Italy and Japan was not signed until September 27, but the new impetus from Berlin, in spite of earlier German unhappiness with Japan, needs to be seen in the context of the decisions of late July. Furthermore, the slow dawning on Ger-many's leaders of the realization that England was not going to give in operated to reinforce the policy choice previously made. A Japanese attack on Britain's posses-sions in Southeast Asia, particularly on Singapore, could not help but assist Ger-many's own fight against the United Kingdom. . . .

The American President hoped to avoid open warfare with Germany altogether. He urged his people to aid Great Britain, and he devised and proposed, as we shall see, a whole variety of ways to do just that and to make sure that the aid actually reached its destination; but he hoped until literally the last minute that the United States could stay out of the war. There has been almost as much argument about Roosevelt's foreign policy in 1940–41 among historians as there was among con-temporaries. Several types of recently available sources confirm dramatically the reliability of a number of long-known statements made by Roosevelt at the time but not always taken as accurate indications of his views.

On August 22, 1940, when trying to get the support of the chairman of the Senate Naval Affairs Commission for the destroyers for bases deal, Roosevelt en-gaged the argument that such a step might lead to war with Germany because of re-taliatory acts by the latter. He argued that if the Germans wanted to go to war with the United States, they would always find an excuse to do so, but that the United States would not fight unless attacked. At the end of the year, when explaining his policy in detail to the American high commissioner in the Philippines, he stressed the global aspects of the aid to Britain policy but again asserted that the country could and should stay out of the war in both Europe and the Far East unless herself attacked. When recordings of press conferences made in the White House in the fall of 1940 became available recently, and it turned out that a machine had been inadvertently left turned on, extraordinarily similar remarks by Roosevelt in private conversation came to light. On October 4 and on October 8, he explained to political and administrative associates that the United States would not enter the war unless the Germans or Japanese actually attacked; even their considering themselves at war with the United States would not suffice. We know that in practice he would follow that approach in December 1941 towards Hungary, Romania, and Bulgaria, trying unsuccessfully for half a year to persuade those countries that they might find it wiser to withdraw their declarations of war on the United States.

The picture of Roosevelt trying and hoping to avoid war has been reinforced by what we now know about the breaking of German codes. Although the Americans told the British of their successes in breaking the major Japanese diplomatic code already in September 1940, and provided them with a machine for reading such messages themselves in January 1941, the British did not reciprocate with information on their breaking of German enigma machine codes until April 1941. Thereafter cooperation became more and more extensive. For the rest of 1941, the knowledge of German naval dispositions gained from the reading of naval messages was regularly and carefully utilized to *avoid* incidents, when it could very easily have been used to *provoke* them. The famous Presidential order to shoot at German submarines on sight, thus, was more to frighten them off than to provoke them. Aware of German orders to submarines to avoid incidents, the President could push forward with his program of aid to Britain knowing that at worst there might be isolated incidents in the Atlantic.

The general assumption of many that countries are either at war or at peace with each other was not shared by Roosevelt, who knew that the American navy had originated in the quasi-war with France at the turn of the eighteenth to the nineteenth century and that more recently Japan and the Soviet Union had engaged in bloody encounters at specific points in East Asia while continuing to have diplomatic relations and without entering into general hostilities with each other. Some of Roosevelt's advisors did think the United States should or would have to enter the war to assure the defeat of Hitler, but there is no evidence that the President himself abandoned his hope that the United States could stay out. He had been proved right in his belief that Britain could hold on in 1940—against the view of many; he would be proved right in his expectation that the Soviet Union could hold on in 1941—again against the view of many. In a way he would be proved right on the question of formal American entrance into the war. We now have his comments on October 8, 1940; "the time may be coming when the Germans and the Japs [sic] will do some fool thing that would put us in. That's the only real danger of our getting in . . ."

Lord Lothian, the British ambassador to the United States, was one of the few who understood the desire of Roosevelt to help England within the limits of the politically and legally feasible but to stay out of the war if at all possible. As Britain's ability to pay for supplies was nearing its end, he persuaded a reluctant Churchill to lay the financial facts openly before the President, and Lothian himself in public exposed the fact that England was running out of money. Out of this approach came Roosevelt's call for the Lend-Lease program, a massive system of Congressional appropriation for the purpose of providing assistance to Britain in wartime which was subsequently extended to other countries. Following great pressure by Roosevelt, [Secretary of State Cordell] Hull, and Secretary of the Treasury Henry Morgenthau—the administration's key figure on the issue—for Britain to come up with as much gold and dollars from the sale of investments as possible, and a very noisy debate in the public arena as well as in Congress, the bill, cleverly labeled H.R. 1776 to reassure House Majority Leader John McCormack's Irish constituents, became law on March 11, 1941. The first appropriation of seven billion dollars had been voted before the month was out.

Passage of this legislation in intense and widely reported debate signaled the American public's belief that the threat posed by Germany was great enough to merit drastic American support of Germany's enemies. Most still hoped to stay out of hostilities, but by contrast with the identical Soviet hopes of those months, the way to realize that hope was seen to be the massive shipment of supplies to Hitler's enemies rather than to Hitler. Simultaneously, this process assisted in the more efficient and effective building up of America's own rearmament program. . . .

The British [military] disasters in the Mediterranean in the spring of 1941 led to anguished debates in Washington as to what to do. The most important new step to aid Britain that the United States took was the result of Roosevelt's shift in favor of sending American troops to Iceland to replace the British garrison there, a step he had earlier refrained from taking in the face of a request from Iceland. The Americans, furthermore, drew for themselves the conclusion that part of the British military trouble had been caused by their divided command structure, with a resulting American emphasis on the power of theater commanders. In the immediate situation, they worried about what would happen if the Germans were now to seize the Spanish and Portuguese islands in the Atlantic the way they had taken Crete and thereby shift the battle in that theater decisively to their advantage. The Germans, however, moved east, not west, with the result that the new puzzle facing Washington was whether to extend aid to the Soviet Union and how to divide the scarce available supplies between the British and the Soviets while still building up America's own military power. . . .

The President quickly determined to send the Soviet Union whatever help could be provided; the fact that he placed his closest confidante, Harry Hopkins, in charge of this endeavor testifies to the importance he attached to it. Hopkins was sent to Moscow to get the whole project moving and took along Colonel Philip Faymonville, a strong believer in the ability of the Red Army to hold out, to handle aid at the Russian end. Knowing of popular opposition to aid to the Soviet Union, Roosevelt worked hard to try to have people see that this dictatorship was less threatening than the immediate menace of the German dictatorship, and he was especially concerned about calming the widespread concern over the lack of religious freedom in the Soviet Union. There were great worries and enormous difficulties, some growing out of the fact that there had been such vast differences between United States and Soviet policies in the preceding years. The Moscow conferences of early August 1941 produced an agreement on major shipments of military supplies in the face of the preference of United States and British military leaders who preferred to keep what weapons were coming off the assembly lines for their own forces. In the face of the German advances in the East, which if victorious would then free them for a renewed push in the Atlantic, Roosevelt pressed his associates to get the materials moving. In a way, he understood better than many contemporaries and most subsequent observers the anti-American component in Hitler's planning and hoped to preclude its success by making the German search for victory in the East as hard as possible. . . .

[Meanwhile,] [a]ll through 1940 and 1941 the Roosevelt administration tried to find ways to hold off Japan while the United States rearmed itself, aided Britain, and, after the German invasion of the Soviet Union, aided the latter. Concentrating primary attention on the Atlantic and the dangers there, the administration hoped to restrain Japan, possibly pry her loose from the Tripartite Pact, and figure out ways to keep her from expanding the war she had already started in China. The assistance provided to the Chinese Nationalists was one element in this policy. The end of the US–Japan trade agreement, which left the Japanese guessing as to the next American step, was another. Roosevelt did not want to take steps which might drive Japan to take radical action, but he was being pushed by a public opinion which objected to the United States selling Japan the materials it needed for the war against China; on this subject the same people who objected to aid for Britain for fear of war were among the most vociferous advocates of a forward policy in East Asia.

The hope of the administration that some accommodation could be reached with Japan which would restrain the latter by a combination of patient negotiations, continued American rearmament, and a passive stance in the Pacific, was dashed by the insistence of the Japanese government on a sweeping offensive in Southeast Asia; but for months there at least appeared to be a prospect of success. . . . On the Japanese side, the ambassador to the United States, Nomura Kichisaburo, really wanted peace with the United States. The Americans correctly believed this to be the case, and since several of the key figures in Washington, including the President and Secretary of State, knew and respected him, they did their best to accommodate him. Nomura, however, was not an experienced and skillful diplomat, frequently failed to inform his government accurately, and never recognized that . . . [Tokyo's] whole negotiating project was a fraud. . . . The hopeless confusion within the Japanese government, in which some elements did indeed still want peace with the United States, only confirmed Nomura's mistaken impressions.

On the American side, the hope that some way of avoiding war with Japan could still be found encouraged the President and Secretary of State to meet time and again with the Japanese ambassador, and later the special envoy sent to assist him. . . . It was their hope, furthermore, that the negotiations themselves might enable them to win enough time to rearm to such an extent that eventually the Japanese would give up any projects of new conquests altogether. In this regard, the two-ocean navy program looked to the distant future; for the time immediately ahead, the anticipated delivery of the new B-17 Flying Fortress 4-engine bomber was thought to be a possible deterrent. Quite exaggerated expectations were attached to the small numbers of these planes becoming available in 1941 and 1942, and it was seriously believed that their presence in the Philippines would make it possible to deter a Japanese attack southward—by the implied threat of fire-bombing the cities of Japan—or, if worse came to worse, to defend those islands effectively. Since all prior American planning had been based on the assumption that the islands in the Western Pacific could not be defended in the years before they were to attain independence anyway, this new concept showed how greatly illusions about small numbers of planes affected thinking in Washington in 1941. . . .

For months, the Germans had weighed the advantages of Japan's attacking the British in Southeast Asia, even if that also meant war with the United States. Each time they looked at the prospect, it looked better to them. Time and again the Japanese had shown their caution to be both excessive and at Germany's expense. There were innumerable German grievances over the failure of the Japanese to assist Germany in moving raw materials she needed from East and Southeast Asia. Unfavorable comparisons were made between what the United States was doing for Britain and what Japan was doing for its German ally. Over and over the Germans urged the Japanese to strike at Singapore: the way to destroy the British empire was to attack it while it was vulnerable, and that time was obviously now. To reassure the Japanese that such a move would not be dangerous for them, they provided Tokyo with one of their great intelligence scoops of the war: the capture in November, 1940, of a British

Cabinet report which showed that Britain could not and would not send major fleet units to East Asia in case of a Japanese attack.

From time to time, the Japanese would point out to the Germans that Japan would be ready to move in 1946, the year when the last United States forces were scheduled to leave the Philippines, to which the Germans responded by pointing out that by that time the war in Europe would be over and the American fleet doubled. Perhaps more important was the German assurance that if Japan could move against Singapore only if she struck the United States at the same time, then she could count on Germany to join her. . . .

[I]f the Japanese, who had hung back so long, took the plunge, then the naval deficit would automatically disappear. [Hitler] had thought of removing that discrepancy by a German sneak under-water attack on the United States navy in port. Told by his navy that this was impossible, there was the obvious alternative of Japan providing a navy for his side of the war; that the Japanese would do from above the water what he had hoped to do from underneath was not known to him beforehand, but that made no difference. The key point was that Japan's joining openly on the Axis side would provide a big navy right away, not after years of building, and hence remove the main objection to going to war with the United States now rather than later. It was therefore entirely in accord with his perception of the issues that he promised [Foreign Minister Yosuke] Matsuoka on April 4 that if Japan believed that the only way for her to do what the Germans thought they should do, namely attack the British, was also to go to war at the same time with the United States, they could move in the knowledge that Germany would immediately join them. This policy was fully understood in German headquarters and would be voiced repeatedly thereafter.

Because they held this point of view, the Germans were seriously alarmed by what they learned of a possible Japanese–United States accommodation growing out of the negotiations between the two countries. The dangerous converse of tension in the Pacific leading to war and the tying up of the United States fleet there was the possibility of a United States–Japanese agreement freeing the United States fleet for even greater employment in the Atlantic. Like the immediately involved negotiators in Washington and Tokyo, the Germans did not understand that this was all shadow-boxing . . . and the German government did what it could to discourage any agreement from the sidelines. (Had the Germans actually wanted to avoid a war with the United States, an opposite policy would, of course have been followed by Berlin.) . . .

The definitive Japanese decision to shift from concentrating on war with China to war against the Western Powers came in early June 1941. The hinge of decision was the shift from occupying *northern* French Indo-China, which was part of the war against China because that country could then be blockaded more effectively, to occupying *southern* Indo-China, which pointed in the opposite direction, that is, to war against the British and Dutch to the south and against the Americans in the Philippines and on the Pacific flank of the southern advance. . . .

Because of the insistence of the United States government on continuing negotiations and the desire of the Japanese ambassador in the United States (who was not informed about his government's intention) to do so also, the authorities in Tokyo had to reexamine the issues several times in October and November, always coming back to the same conclusion: now was the time to fight. In the process, [Prime

Minister Prince Fumimaro] Konoe became tired of the discussion of a policy he had himself launched and was replaced by War Minister Tojo Hideki, but there was no inclination within the government to reverse the course for war. The new Foreign Minister, Togo Shigenori, and Finance Minister Kaya Okinori had doubts but were overridden by the others. . . .

The Japanese had decided to provide a public explanation by making extensive demands on the United States which they expected to be refused and which could be increased if accepted. A lengthy memorandum was therefore sent to Washington following on earlier such demands. In between, they received and disregarded a restatement of the American position (which they afterwards for propaganda purposes called an ultimatum). All this was shadow-boxing. The Japanese government had decided on war; had kept this fact from their own diplomats in Washington so that these could appear to be negotiating in good faith; and instructed them to present a lengthy note in time for Japan to initiate hostilities. . . .

In reality, the Pearl Harbor attack proved a strategic and tactical disaster for Japan, though the Japanese did not recognize this. The ships were for the most part raised; by the end of December, two of the battleships [Admiral] Yamamoto [Isoroku] had imagined sunk were on their way to the West Coast for repairs. All but the *Arizona* returned to service, and several played a key role . . . in a great American naval victory in October 1944. Most of the crew members survived to man the rebuilding American navy. These tactical factors were outgrowths of the basic strategic miscalculation. As anyone familiar with American reactions to the explosion on the *Maine* or the sinking of the *Lusitania* could have predicted, an unprovoked attack in peacetime was guaranteed to unite the American people for war until Japan surrendered, thus destroying in the first minutes of war Japan's basic strategy. The hope that the American people would never expend the blood and treasure needed to reconquer from Japan all sorts of islands—most of which they had never heard of—so that these could be returned to others or made independent, became completely unrealistic with the attack on Pearl Harbor. The attainment of surprise guaranteed defeat, not victory, for Japan.

Others were eager to join Japan in war with the United States. The Germans and Italians had been asked by Japan to join in and enthusiastically agreed. Mussolini had already promised to join in on December 3 and now did so, an extraordinary situation given Italy's string of defeats. Hitler had repeatedly urged the Japanese to move against Britain and was positively ecstatic that they had acted at last. The idea of a Sunday morning air attack in peacetime was especially attractive to him. He had started his campaign against Yugoslavia that way a few months earlier; here was an ally after his own heart. Now there would be a navy of battleships and aircraft carriers to deal with the Americans. His own navy had been straining at the leash for years and could now sink ships in the North Atlantic to its heart's content. Since the Japanese had not told Hitler precisely when they planned to move, he had just returned to East Prussia from the southern end of the Eastern Front, where he had dealt with a crisis caused by a Soviet counter-offensive, when the news of Pearl Harbor reached him. It would take a few days to organize the proper ceremonies in Berlin on December 11, but that did not have to hold up the open hostilities he was eager to begin. In the night of December 8–9, at the earliest possible moment, orders were given to sink the ships of the United States and a string of countries in the Western Hemisphere.

Two days later Hitler told an enthusiastic Reichstag the good news of war with America. Those who really believed that Germany had lost World War I because of a stab-in-the-back, not defeat at the front, were certain that it was American military power which was the legend. For once the unanimity in the Reichstag mirrored near unanimity in the government of the Third Reich. The German government's only worry was that the Americans might get their formal declaration of war in before they could deliver one themselves; they would get their way.

President Roosevelt asked and obtained declarations of war against Germany and Italy from Congress in response to the German and Italian declarations, steps which those countries had followed up by a treaty with Japan promising never to sign a separate peace. When Romania, Hungary, and Bulgaria also declared war on the United States, the President tried to get these declarations withdrawn. Perhaps the peoples of those countries could live quite happily without having a war with the United States. But the effort to persuade them of this truth failed, and in June the Congress reciprocated. The whole world was indeed aflame.

Stalemate and the Case Against
U.S. Entry into the War

BRUCE M. RUSSETT

Whatever criticisms of twentieth-century American foreign policy are put forth, United States participation in World War II remains almost entirely immune. According to our national mythology, that was a "good war," one of the few for which the benefits clearly outweighed the costs. Except for a few books published shortly after the war and quickly forgotten, this orthodoxy has been essentially unchallenged. The isolationists stand discredited, and "isolationist" remains a useful pejorative with which to tar the opponents of American intervention in foreign land.

Such virtual unanimity on major policy matters is rare. World War I long ago came under the revisionists' scrutiny. The origins of the cold war have been challenged more recently, with many people asking whether the Soviet-American conflict was primarily the result of Russian aggressiveness or even whether it was the inevitable consequence of throwing together "two scorpions in a bottle." But all orthodoxy ought to be confronted occasionally, whether the result be to destroy, revise, or reincarnate old beliefs. Furthermore, this does seem an auspicious time to reexamine the standard credo about participation in World War II. Interventionism is again being questioned and Americans are groping toward a new set of principles to guide their foreign policy. Where should we intervene and where withdraw; where actively to support a "balance of power" and where husband our resources? A reexamination of the World War II experience is deliberately a look at a limiting case—an effort to decide whether, in the instance where the value of intervention is most widely accepted, the interventionist argument really is so persuasive. We

Adapted from Bruce M. Russett, *No Clear and Present Danger: A Skeptical View of American Entry into World War II* (New York: Harper and Row, 1972, 1997), 24–30, 41–48, 60–66, 88. Material has been retitled for this publication. Copyright © 1972 by Bruce M. Russett. Reprinted by permission of HarperCollins Publishers, Inc.

should consider the World War II experience not because intervention was obvious folly, but indeed because the case for American action there is strong. . . .

American participation in World War II brought the country few gains; the United States was no more secure at the end than it could have been had it stayed out. First, let us look at the "might have beens" in Europe. The standard justification of American entry into the war is that otherwise Germany would have reigned supreme on the continent, victor over Russia and Britain. With all the resources of Europe at the disposal of his totalitarian government, plus perhaps parts of the British fleet, Hitler would have posed an intolerable threat to the security of the United States. He could have consolidated his winnings, built his war machine, established bridge-heads in South America, and ultimately could and likely would have moved against North America to achieve world domination.

Several links in this argument might deserve scrutiny, but by far the critical one is the first, that Hitler would have won World War II. Such a view confuses the ability of Germany's enemies to *win* with their ability to achieve a *stalemate*. Also, it tends to look more at the military-political situation of June 1940 than at that of December 1941, and to confuse President Roosevelt's decision to aid Britain (and later Russia) by "all measure short of war" with an actual American declaration of war. Let me say clearly: I basically accept the proposition that German domination of all Europe, with Britain and Russia prostrate, would have been intolerable to the United States. By any of the classical conceptions of "power-balancing" and "national interest," the United States should indeed have intervened if necessary to prevent that outcome. . . .

I do not, therefore, argue that American nonbelligerent assistance to Britain was a mistake, quite the contrary. Yet that is just the point—by the end of 1941 Britain's survival was essentially assured. She might lose some colonies, her world position would be weakened, perhaps in the long run her independent existence would be threatened by the Germans in a second round of war. For the immediate future, nevertheless, Britain would live. Indeed, such a conclusion helps to make sense of Hitler's daring gamble in attacking Russia in the late spring of 1941. The British had made it through the worst patch, and only by a long and mutually-exhausting war could Germany hope to wear them down. At the least, German hopes for a quick end to the war had been irretrievably lost.

If British survival into 1941 raised the specter of deadlock or war of attrition to Hitler, the failure of his attack on Russia brought the specter to life. He had intended to invade the Soviet Union in mid-May 1941, but things had not gone well. His ally, Mussolini, had invaded Greece and met with repeated defeats. Hitler felt obliged to divert German troops from the Russian front to rescue the Italians and the German flank. His invasion of Russia, Operation Barbarossa, was thus delayed five weeks until June 22 when, without ultimatum or declaration of war, the troops moved east.

The attack itself was an admission that the war against Britain had gone badly. By some interpretations the German invasion of Russia was an attempt to secure the resources, especially oil, necessary to bring the British down in a long war of attrition; by others it was an effort to strike the Russians at a time of Hitler's choosing rather than wait for the Russians to come in on the British side later. Surely the prospect of being the weight in balance at the key moment would have been greatly tempting to Stalin. By either interpretation the attack accepted great risks, and was the last try with any hope of success to seize a clear victory.

With the onset of the Russian winter and Hitler's inability to take Moscow—Napoleon had at least managed that—the prospect of German failure was sharp. Looking back, we now can see that *this* was in fact the hinge of fate; the more visible turning a year later was more nearly the outward sign of a predetermined shift. . . .

The essential point is that the Russian success, like the British, occurred quite independently of American military action. . . .

Had America remained in the status of twilight belligerence Germany probably would not have been defeated, though as I have argued above, neither could it have won. Probably World War II would have ended in some sort of draw and negotiated settlement, or would have continued on for a decade or two with occasional truces for breathing spells—not unlike the Napoleonic Wars. Or perhaps most likely is some combination of the two, in which the negotiated peace was uneasy and soon broken. What I imagine, then, is a very long and bloody war, longer and even more bloody than the one that really was fought, with protracted savage fighting in east and central Europe. . . .

Some contemporaries of course took a more alarmist view, especially immediately after the fall of France. A *Fortune* magazine survey of Americans in July 1940 found that 63 percent expected that an Axis triumph would bring an immediate German attempt to seize territory in the Western Hemisphere; 43 percent expected an imminent attack on the United States. American army generals feared a Nazi invasion of South America, and to forestall it wanted a major base in Trinidad. The continued resistance of Britain calmed such alarm for a while, though it was to be revived in somewhat similar form in 1942 with the anticipation of German aerial attacks on American cities and towns. Seacoast areas were allotted major antiaircraft units. Blackout regulations were widely enforced. School children were taught how to crouch against basement walls clenching corks between their teeth in the event of bombardment. Fiorello LaGuardia, then head of the Office of Civilian Defense, wanted 50 million gas masks.

All of this of course seems more than a little absurd in light of known—then as well as now—German capabilities. Not a single German bomb ever did fall in North or South America. Any kind of troop landing required naval and logistic support utterly beyond Hitler's reach. After all, it was not until two and a half years of war, with vast shipping and naval superiority, and a base in Britain, that the Allies felt able to cross even the English Channel in an invasion the other way. The bogeyman of Nazi troops in America had no more substance than that, several years later, of Russian landings. . . .

Very possibly a stalemate would not have marked the end of Hitler's ambitions, but that is not really the point. For some time at least, Germany would not have been supreme as an immediate menace to the United States. One further step in still another war would first be required—the ultimate victory over Britain and/or Russia, and if that should in fact be threatened, the United States could still have intervened *then,* and done so while allies existed. By the end of 1941 the pressure for such intervention had really passed for *that* war. Even those who most heavily stress the dangers of Nazi subversion in North and South America grant that "There still would be ominous eddies, but by the summer of 1940 the Nazi cause was in retreat in the new world." . . .

Finally, we ought to confront the argument that sheer morality demanded American intervention against Hitler. I have deliberately left this issue aside, defining our concern to be only with the structure of the international system, the relative weight of power facing the United States and its potential allies. My argument has accepted the "realist" one that fears the concentration of great power in other hands regardless of the apparent goals, ideology, or morality of those wielding that power. Concern with the morality of others' domestic politics is an expensive luxury, and evaluations all too subject to rapid change. . . .

Yet some would maintain that Hitler was just too evil to tolerate, that the United States had a moral duty to exterminate him and free those under his rule. . . .

Still, in this context Hitler must be compared with Stalin, who was hardly a saint, and who as a result of the complete German collapse in 1945 emerged from the war with an immensely greater empire. We must remember the terror and paranoid purges of his rule, and such examples of Stalinist humanity as the starvation of millions of kulaks. The worst Nazi crimes emerged only in 1943 and later at Nuremberg. German "medical experiments" and extermination camps were unknown to the world in 1941. Though the Hitler regime had anything but a savory reputation then, the moral argument too is essentially one made in hindsight, not a primary motivation at the time war was declared. . . .

If one rejects the purely moral justification of American entry into the war against Hitler, no very effective moral brief can then be made for the war in the Pacific. True, the Japanese were often unkind conquerors, though this can easily be exaggerated by American memories of the Bataan death march and other horrors in the treatment of prisoners. Japanese occupation was often welcomed in the former European colonies of Southeast Asia, and Japan retains some reservoir of good will for its assistance, late in the war, of indigenous liberation movements. In any case it is Hitler, not Tojo, who is customarily presented as the personification of evil. Possibly Americans did have some vague obligation to defend Chinese independence, but more clearly than in Europe the basis for American participation has to be *realpolitik*. The case has to be founded on a conviction that Japan was too powerful, too dangerously expansionist without any apparent restraint, to have been left alone. An extreme but widely accepted version is given by an early chronicler of the war:

> Japan in the spring and summer of 1941 would accept no diplomatic arrangement which did not give it everything that it might win in the Far East by aggression, without the trouble and expense of military campaigns.

The evidence, however, shows quite a different picture both of intent and capability. Nor is it enough simply to assert that, because Japan attacked the United States at Pearl Harbor, America took no action to begin hostilities. This is formally true, but very deceptive. The Japanese attack would not have come but for the American, British, and Dutch embargo on shipment of strategic raw materials to Japan. Japan's strike against the American naval base merely climaxed a long series of mutually antagonistic acts. In initiating economic sanctions against Japan the United States undertook actions that were widely recognized in Washington as carrying grave risk of war. To understand this requires a retracing of the events of the preceding years. . . .

[The Japanese] apparently believed that their Empire's status as an independent world power depended on military equality with Russia and the United States in the Far East; that in turn depended on a hegemonical position, preferably economic but achieved by force if necessary, in the area of China. Though this seems strange now, an adequate view of Japanese policy in its contemporary context has to remember Tokyo's position as a latecomer to colonialism, in a world where France, Britain, and the United States all had their own spheres of influence.

Japanese forces made important initial gains by occupying most of the Chinese coast and most of China's industrial capacity, but with a trickle of American aid the nationalist armies hung on in the interior. By 1941 the Japanese armies were bogged down, and their progress greatly impeded by raw material shortages. . . .

Following the July 1941 freeze on Japanese assets in America, and the consequent cessation of shipment of oil, scrap iron, and other goods from the United States, Japan's economy was in most severe straits and her power to wage war directly threatened. Her military leaders estimated that her reserves of oil, painfully accumulated in the late 1930s when the risk of just such a squeeze became evident, would last at most two years. She was also short of rice, tin, bauxite, nickel, rubber and other raw materials normally imported from the Dutch East Indies and Malaya. Negotiations with the Dutch authorities to supply these goods, plus extraordinary amounts of oil from the wells of Sumatra, had failed, ostensibly on the grounds that the Dutch feared the material would be reexported to the Axis in Europe. The United States, and the British and Dutch, made it quite clear that the embargo would be relaxed only in exchange for Japanese withdrawal from air and naval bases in Indochina (seized in order to prosecute better the war against China) and an agreement which would have meant the end of the Japanese involvement in China and the *abandonment* of any right to station troops in that country, not just a halt to the fighting. The purpose of the Western economic blockade was to force a favorable solution to the "China incident."

Under these conditions, the High Command of the Japanese navy demanded a "settlement" of one sort or other that would restore Japan's access to essential raw materials, most particularly oil. Without restored imports of fuel the fleet could not very long remain an effective fighting force. While the navy might have been willing to abandon the China campaign, it was utterly opposed to indefinite continuation of the status quo. Either raw material supplies had to be restored by a peaceful settlement with the Western powers, or access to the resources in Thailand, Malaya, and the Indies would have to be secured by force while Japan still retained the capabilities to do so.

If the navy demanded either settlement or war, most members of the Japanese elite were opposed to any settlement which would in effect have meant withdrawal from China. No serious thought was given to the possibility of peace with Chiang's [Chinese leader Chiang Kai-shek's] government, for it would have meant the end of all hopes of empire in East Asia and even, it was thought, of influence on the continent of Asia. . . .

Having decided against withdrawal from China, failed to negotiate a settlement with America, and decided on the necessity of seizing supplies from Southeast Asia, [the Japanese] were faced with the need to blunt what they regarded as the inevitable American response. Thus they launched a surprise attack on Pearl Harbor to destroy any American capability for immediate naval offensive. For all the audacity of the strike at Hawaii, its aims were limited: to destroy existing United States offensive capabilities in the Pacific by tactical surprise. The Japanese High Command hoped only to give its forces time to occupy the islands of the Southwest Pacific, to extract those islands' raw materials, and to turn the whole area into a virtually impregnable line of defense which could long delay an American counteroffensive and mete out heavy casualties when the counterattack did come. . . .

[T]he Japanese attack on Pearl Harbor, and for that matter on Southeast Asia, [was] not evidence of any unlimited expansionist policy or capability by the Japanese government. It was the consequence only of a much less ambitious goal, centering on an unwillingness to surrender the position that the Japanese had fought for years to establish in China. When that refusal met an equal American determination that Japan should give up many of her gains in China, the result was war. Japanese expansion into Southeast Asia originated less in strength than in weakness; it was predominantly instrumental to the China campaign, not a reach for another slice of global salami. Of course there were Japanese political and military leaders with wider ambitions, but they were not predominant in policy-making.

Throughout the 1930s the United States government had done little to resist the Japanese advance on the Asian continent. There were verbal protests, but little more. Even in early 1941 Washington apparently would have settled for a *halt* in China, and saw little danger of a much wider move into Southeast Asia. But the application of economic sanctions against Tokyo was very successful; it was obviously hurting, and the moderate Premier Prince Konoye proposed a direct meeting with Roosevelt to try to reach an understanding. At about that point the American Government seems to have been so impressed with its success that it rebuffed Konoye's approach, demanding that he agree in advance on terms of a settlement. Konoye's cabinet fell, and American observers concluded—on the basis of untestable evidence that sounded a bit like sour grapes—that he could not have enforced a "reasonable" settlement in Japanese politics anyway. Washington then raised the ante, calling for a Japanese *withdrawal* from all occupied territory in China. Several officials in the State Department proposed settling for a halt, giving China a breathing spell that would have served it better for several more years of war while America made its main effort in the Atlantic. Hull considered and then rejected their plan for such a *modus vivendi,* which rather closely resembled the second of two Japanese proposals ("Plan B") that represented Tokyo's last efforts. Economic sanctions continued to provide a warm moral glow for those who disapproved of trading with an aggressor, but they then served to make inevitable an otherwise avoidable war which was peripheral to American vital interests and for which the country was ill-prepared. . . .

On purely strategic grounds some observers might argue that the danger was not from Germany, Italy, or Japan alone, but rather from their combination in an aggressive alliance encircling the Western Hemisphere. The rhetoric of the time could suggest such a threat, but in fact the Tripartite Pact of Germany and Italy with Japan had become quite fragile. As explained [previously] . . . it was designed to deter United States entry into either of the then still-separate conflicts. The Japanese foreign minister in early 1941, Yosuke Matsuoka, had negotiated the Pact and was by far its strongest supporter in the cabinet. He tried to persuade his colleagues to follow the German attack on Russia with a similar act by Japan, but failed and was deposed. Thereafter the Pact faded in importance to the Tokyo government. In considering their subsequent negotiations with the United States the Japanese leaders were fully willing to sacrifice the Pact in return for the necessary economic concessions. Had Hitler managed to get himself into war with America in the Atlantic he could not successfully have invoked the Pact unless the Japanese clearly had seen war to be in their own interests.

Moreover, this drift away from Germany was, it has been well argued, adequately known to American and British officials—Ambassadors [Joseph] Grew and [Britain's Sir Robert] Craigie, Cordell Hull, Roosevelt and Churchill—thanks in part to American ability to crack the codes used in all Japanese secret cables. [The historian Paul W. Schroeder has written:] "After Matsuoka's fall . . . no Axis leader was able even to keep up the pretense of expecting Japanese intervention in behalf of Germany and Italy." In the context of late 1941, therefore, the prospects of close cooperation among Germany, Italy and Japan were not very menacing. Given their very diverse long-run interests, and Hitler's racial notions, a "permanent" alliance surely does not seem very plausible. A special irony of the situation is that Roosevelt was particularly anxious to see Hitler beaten first, and that British and Dutch colonial possessions in Southeast Asia, which seemed essential to the European war, be unmolested. His belated insistence on Japanese evacuation from China then pushed the Axis back together and endangered his other goals. . . .

In retrospect, the fear that America would be left alone in the world against two great victorious empires in Europe and Asia seems terribly exaggerated. Clearcut victory was not in prospect for either, nor does the assumption that they could long have maintained a close alliance seem especially plausible. The critical American mistake may well have been in backing the Japanese into a corner, for without war in the Pacific the American conflict with Germany very possibly could have been held to limited naval engagements, but no clash of ground troops. In short, we might at most have fought a limited war.

These conclusions are highly speculative; the situation of the time cannot be reproduced for another run, searching for an alternate future. Perhaps I underestimate the risks that an American determination to avoid war would have entailed. On the other hand, the proposition that the war was unnecessary—in a real sense premature, fought before the need was sufficiently clearly established, though the need might well have become apparent later—is worth considering. Just possibly the isolationists were right in their essential perspective. . . .

I do not imagine that the United States should have carried on blithely in 1941 as though nothing were happening elsewhere in the world. Complete isolation would have been much worse than intervention. All Americans would agree that American strategic interests required substantial assistance to the belligerents against Germany. Both Britain and Russia had to be preserved as independent and powerful states. With a little less certainty I would also grant the need to keep a significant portion of China viable.

It seems, however, that those goals could have been achieved by the belligerents themselves, with great American economic and noncombatant military aid. As insurance, American rearmament had to go on. A sustained defense effort not less than what was later accepted during the cold war would have been required. That would imply 10 percent of the American GNP devoted to military purposes, as compared with about that amount actually expended in 1941 and a mere one and one-half percent in 1939. That much, incidentally, would with Lend-Lease have been quite enough to revive the economy from the depression and assuredly does not imply idle resources.

With this prescription I find myself at odds with the extreme critics of Roosevelt's policy, men who spoke at that time and again, briefly, after the war. Most of the President's military and economic acts seem appropriate and, in deed, necessary. I have no quarrel with the decisions for rearmament or to institute Selective Service, with revision of the Neutrality Act to permit "cash-and-carry" by belligerents (effectively by the Allies only), with the destroyers-for-bases exchange, with Lend-Lease, or with the decision to convoy American vessels as far as Iceland. Even the famous "shoot-on-sight" order, even as interpreted to allow American destroyers to seek out the sight of U-boats, seems necessary if the convoys were to be protected on the first stage of the critical lifeline to Britain. I do have some serious reservations about the way in which those decisions were publicly justified. . . . But the content of those decisions seems fully defensible. And irritating as they surely were, Hitler would probably have continued to tolerate them in preference to more active American involvement.

Only two major exceptions to the content of American policy in 1941 appear worth registering. One is the vote by Congress in mid-November 1941, at the President's behest, removing nearly all the remaining restrictions of the Neutrality Act. It permitted American ships to carry supplies all the way across the Atlantic, instead of merely as far as Iceland. This almost certainly would have been too much for Hitler to bear. . . .

The other and still more serious exception I take is with President Roosevelt's policy toward Japan as described [previously]. . . . It was neither necessary nor desirable for him to have insisted on a Japanese withdrawal from China. An agreement for a standstill would have been enough, and he did not make an honest diplomatic attempt to achieve it. He refused to meet Prince Konoye in the Pacific to work out a compromise, and after Konoye's fall he rejected, on Hull's advice, a draft proposal that could have served as a basis for compromise with the Japanese. We have no guarantee that agreement could have been reached, but here was at least some chance and the effort was not made. . . .

It would of course be unfair and inaccurate to trace all the developments cited in this chapter, and especially the adoption of interventionist policies, only back to 1940, just as it is wrong to think they emerged full-blown at the beginning of the cold war. One can find roots in our earlier Caribbean policy, in Woodrow Wilson's acts, in the war of 1898, and even earlier. But World War II, rather like monosodium glutamate, made pungent a host of unsavory flavors that had until then been relatively subdued. We cannot really extirpate contemporary "global policeman" conceptions from American thinking unless we understand how, in World War II, they developed and became ingrained.

Preface to the Twenty-fifth Anniversary Edition

[W]here did the book come from in my personal history? As I stated clearly in the original preface, it stemmed from my experience, as a scholar of American foreign policy, of the Vietnam War. Published at the height of the war, it originated from my disgust and represented my effort to understand why the war had happened and persisted. I believed then, and still do, that such standard interpretations as bureaucratic inertia on Pennsylvania Avenue, economic interest on Wall Street, or anti-communist ideology on Main Street, constitute at best partial explanations that missed a broader kind of ideological underpinning. I would characterize that ideological underpinning as a particular kind of "realist" view of international power politics that exaggerated both the necessity and the possibility of effectively exerting American military power all over the globe. A shorthand label for such a view now comes under the expression "imperial overstretch." And I believe that view was, for many Americans, born out of the experience of World War II. . . .

The fundamental problem with the World War II experience—rightly judged in some degree to be a success—was, in my view, that it led to an exaggerated sense of American power and wisdom; *hubris,* in effect. It seemed such a success that the limits and the particular circumstances of that success were ignored in subsequent policy. And that hubris led to the intervention in Vietnam, a military expedition for which the motivation and the need were far less clear than in World War II. Consequently, the national will for a total commitment in Vietnam was, properly, lacking, and thus the prospects for that intervention were poor. In other words, the construction put upon the World War II experience was an invitation to subsequent failure; to understand that failure, and to avoid repeating it, required some deconstruction of World War II's lessons. It required speculating about whether active American participation in the war could have been avoided, and if so, what the costs and benefits of such an alternative might have been. It was a task for historical evaluation as well as a practically oriented form of theoretical discussion.

FURTHER READING

Michael Barnhart, *Japan Prepares for Total War* (1987)
———, "The Origins of the Second World War in Asia and the Pacific: Synthesis Impossible?" *Diplomatic History* 20 (1996): 241–260
Charles A. Beard, *President Roosevelt and the Coming of the War, 1941* (1948)
Michael Beschloss, *Kennedy and Roosevelt* (1980)
Günter Bischof and Robert L. Dupont, eds., *The Pacific War Revisited* (1997)
Conrad Black, *Franklin Delano Roosevelt* (2003)
Dorothy Borg and Shumpei Okamoto, eds., *Pearl Harbor as History* (1973)
Thomas Buckley and Edwin B. Strong, *American Foreign and National Security Policies, 1914–1945* (1987)
Robert J. C. Butow, *The John Doe Associates* (1974)
Steven Casey, *Cautious Crusade* (2001) (on FDR and public opinion)
Thurston Clarke, *Pearl Harbor Ghosts* (2000)
J. Garry Clifford and Samuel R. Spencer Jr., *The First Peacetime Draft* (1986)
Warren I. Cohen, *Empire Without Tears* (1987)
———, *America's Response to China* (2000)
Wayne S. Cole, *Roosevelt and the Isolationists, 1932–1945* (1983)
Hilary Conroys and Harry Wray, eds., *Pearl Harbor Reexamined* (1990)
Robert Dallek, *Franklin D. Roosevelt and American Foreign Policy* (1979)
Kenneth R. Davis, *FDR* (1993)
Roger Dingman, *Power in the Pacific* (1976)
Robert A. Divine, *The Reluctant Belligerent* (1979)
Justus D. Doenecke, *Storm on the Horizon* (2000)
Justus D. Doenecke and Mark A. Stoler, *Debating Franklin D. Roosevelt's Foreign Policies* (2005)
John Dower, *Japan in War and Peace* (1993)

Barbara Rearden Farnham, *Roosevelt and the Munich Crisis* (2000)
Herbert Feis, *The Road to Pearl Harbor* (1950)
Frank Freidel, *Franklin D. Roosevelt: A Rendezvous with Destiny* (1990)
Lloyd Gardner, *Economic Aspects of New Deal Diplomacy* (1964)
Martin Gilbert, *Winston S. Churchill: Finest Hour, 1939–1941* (1983)
Patrick Hearden, *Roosevelt Confronts Hitler* (1987)
Waldo H. Heinrichs Jr., *Threshold of War* (1988)
Saburō Ienaga, *The Pacific War* (1978)
Akira Iriye, *The Globalizing of America* (1993)
———, *Pearl Harbor and the Coming of the Pacific War* (1999)
——— and Warren Cohen, eds., *American, Chinese, and Japanese Perspectives on Wartime
    Asia, 1931–1949* (1990)
Kenneth P. Jones, *U.S. Diplomats in Europe, 1919–1941* (1981)
Walter LaFeber, *The Clash* (1997) (on Japan)
Robert D. Lowe, ed., *Pearl Harbor Revisited* (1994)
Mark A. Lowenthal, *Leadership and Indecision* (1988) (on war planning)
Joseph A. Maiolo and Robert Boyce, eds., *The Origins of World War Two* (2003)
Frederick W. Marks III, *Wind over Sand* (1988) (on FDR)
Jonathan Marshall, *To Have and Have Not* (1995) (on raw materials and war)
Gorden Martel, ed., *The Origins of the Second World War Reconsidered* (1986)
James W. Morley, ed., *Japan's Road to the Pacific War: The Final Confrontation* (1994)
Norman Moss, *19 Weeks* (2003)
John Prados, *Combined Fleet Decoded* (2001)
Gordon W. Prange, *Pearl Harbor* (1986)
David Reynolds, *From Munich to Pearl Harbor* (2001)
Benjamin D. Rhodes, *United States Foreign Policy in the Interwar Period* (2001)
Emily S. Rosenberg, *A Date Which Will Live: Pearl Harbor in American Memory* (2003)
Arthur M. Schlesinger, Jr., "The Man of the Century," *American Heritage* May/June
    1994: 82–93 (on FDR)
David F. Schmitz, *Henry L. Stimson* (2000)
———, *The United States and Fascist Italy, 1922–1940* (1988)
Paul W. Schroeder, *The Axis Alliance* (1958)
Richard Steele, *Propaganda in an Open Society* (1985) (on FDR and the media)
Youli Sun, *China and the Origins of the Pacific War* (1993)
Charles C. Tansill, *Back Door to War* (1952)
John Toland, *Infamy: Pearl Harbor and Its Aftermath* (1982)
Cornelis A. Van Minnen and John F. Sears, eds., *FDR and His Contemporaries* (1992)
    (on foreign views)
D. C. Watt, *How War Came* (1989)
Lawrence Wittner, *Rebels Against War* (1984)
Roberta Wohlstetter, *Pearl Harbor: Warning and Decision* (1962)
Marvin R. Zahniser, *Then Came Disaster: France and the United States, 1918–1940*
    (2002)

CHAPTER
10

The Origins of the
Cold War

🌐

After American entry into the Second World War, Great Britain, the United States, and the Soviet Union formed the fifty-nation Grand Alliance, which in time forced the Axis to surrender. The Grand Alliance, however, collapsed soon after victory had been achieved. Strife had developed during the war itself, and the scramble for postwar position accentuated differences of power, interests, and ideology, especially between the United States and the Soviet Union. The emerging rivals disputed agreements struck at Yalta and Potsdam conferences near the end of the war, including those that sketched a framework for a United Nations organization, encouraged democratic institutions in postwar Europe, provided for German dismemberment and reparations, and ceded Poland and parts of East Europe to Moscow's control. Confrontation replaced compromise, and a new long war began—the Cold War.

While Soviet leaders came to see the United States as an expansionist power seeking world supremacy and threatening USSR security, U.S. leaders increasingly read the Soviet Union as a bullying, communist aggressor bent on grabbing territory, subjugating neighbors and disturbing the postwar peace through subversion. The Kremlin charged the United States with trying to encircle the Soviet Union; Washington claimed that it was only trying to contain the Soviet Union. Each side saw offense when the other saw defense. Fearing the future, the adversaries competed to build and enlarge spheres of influence, to attract allies, to enhance military capabilities, and to gain economic advantage.

Poland, Germany, Iran, Czechoslovakia, Greece, China, Korea, and many other nations became the diplomatic and military battlegrounds for the Cold War by mid-century. The Soviet Union and the United States never sent their troops into battle directly against one another. Instead, they cultivated and at times intimidated client states, constructed overseas bases and intelligence posts, intervened in civil wars, launched covert operations, sponsored exclusionist economic partnerships and foreign aid programs, and initiated propaganda campaigns in which they charged one another with conspiracy. They also pursued a dangerous and costly nuclear arms race— spurred by technological innovation and by national military and industrial establishments, as well as by Cold War politics at home. The destructiveness of the hydrogen bomb, first detonated in 1953, the poison of atmospheric testing, and the Orwellian nightmare of civil defense cast a vast shadow worldwide during the early Cold War.

The end of the Cold War in the late 1980s and early 1990s, and the question of who won or lost it, are treated in a later chapter of this book. Here we strive to understand why and how the Cold War began. In the past decade and a half, post–Cold War Russian, Eastern European, Chinese, and other archives have opened for the first time, providing illuminating but still limited new documentation. The new evidence, at times clarifying and at other times ambiguous (because Soviet leaders rarely stated their motives, even to one another, in unguarded terms) has by no means brought closure to debates about the Cold War. The documents of "the other side" nonetheless enable scholars to consider the interactive nature of Soviet-American relations, to understand better the impact of the superpower rivalry on client states, and to present new or revised perspectives on the origins of the Cold War.

Three areas of inquiry have intrigued scholars who explore the sources of the Cold War. First is the international context. The Second World War produced wrenching changes in the international system that increased the likelihood of postwar conflict. Power was redistributed, empires collapsed, and wartime destruction spawned social and economic dislocation. The United States and the Soviet Union each sought to influence the postwar world: defend against threats, exploit new opportunities, and enhance their stature. Which of the two was more responsible for the Cold War—or must they share responsibility?

Second, scholars study the national context of the Soviet Union and the United States. What drove them to become international activists? Some analysts stress power and security concerns: the Soviet preoccupation with the borderlands of Eastern Europe, and Washington's determination to plant air and naval bases around the globe to prevent a repetition of the attack on Pearl Harbor. Other writers highlight the centrality of economics: America's appetite for capitalist markets and investment opportunities, and Russia's desperate need for postwar reconstruction and reparations. Still others probe the role of ideology and the dramatic clash between democratic capitalism and authoritarian Marxism. In the United States, the influence of the Congress, political parties, and public opinion have warranted close examination. The dictatorial and secretive nature of Soviet communism also carried unique consequences for international relations. In addition to ideology, scholars deconstruct culture to divine how policymakers, the media, and the public in both countries may have fallen back on prevailing notions of race, ethnicity, class, gender, and national identity to decipher—as well as distort—the attitudes and behaviors of the other. Did the Cold War evolve because the two sides simply misunderstood one another, or because they understood each other very well, including their quite different national interests?

Third, historians assess the role of individuals, whose personalities, political ambitions, and styles of diplomacy influenced their nation's foreign relations. In the early Cold War, the personal imprints of President Harry S. Truman and Marshal Joseph Stalin stand out. Individual leaders usually define their nation's needs and goals, give voice to ideologies and cultural assumptions, and decide whether to negotiate or play politics with foreign policy. Some leaders are wise and patient, others shallow and impatient; some understand nuance and gray areas, others see extreme blacks and whites; some decisionmakers are driven blindly by ideology and entrenched interests, while others are more practical, knowledgeable, and flexible. In an accounting of the origins of the Cold War, how much weight should scholars give to Truman and Stalin as compared to systemic and national sources of conflict?

While the sources of the early Cold War were numerous and varied, we end with one overarching question: Was the Cold War inevitable, or were there viable alternatives to a half-century of mutual suspicion, militarization, and fear?

NORWAY

SWEDEN

FINLAND
To Russia

*Leased to Russia
until 1955*

L.
Ladoga

Gulf of Finland

• Leningrad

ESTONIA
to Russia

L. *Pskov*

NORTH
SEA

DENMARK

BALTIC SEA

To Russia
LATVIA

LITHUANIA
To Russia

SOVIET RUSSIA

To Russia
Niemen R.

U.S. ZONE

NETH.

BRITISH
ZONE

Berlin •

G E R M A N Y
W.   E.
RUSSIAN
ZONE

Danzig •
*To
Poland*

EAST
PRUSSIA
To Poland

Vistula R.

Oder R.

BEL.

Rhine R.

LUX.

FRENCH ZONE

UNITED
STATES
ZONE

C Z E C H O S L O V A K I A

P O L A N D

To Russia

Don R.

FRANCE

SWITZ.

FRENCH
U.S.

RUSSIAN
Vienna •

A U S T R I A
BRITISH

BRATISLAVA
BRIDGEHEAD
To Czech.

NORTHERN
BUKOVINA

SUBCARPATHIAN
RUTHENIA

BESSARABIA
To Russia

Dniester R.

Pruth R.

VENEZIA-GIULIA
To Yugoslavia

To France

Po R.

Trieste •

H U N G A R Y

R O M A N I A

Drava R.

I
T
A
L
Y

CORSICA

Rome •

ADRIATIC SEA

Y U G O S L A V I A

Danube R.

BLACK
SEA

DOBRUJA
*To
Bulgaria*

BULGARIA

SARDINIA

ALBANIA

G R E E C E   TURKEY

AEGEAN
SEA

SICILY

Changes in Europe
After World War II

MALTA (Br.)

Territorial Changes After World War II

DODECANESE IS.
(*To Greece
from Italy*)

CRETE

Notes: -The United States, British, and French Zones
of Germany merged in 1949 as the Federal
Republic of Germany.

-The Russian Zone of Germany became the
German Democratic Republic in 1949.

-The four zones of Austria merged in 1955 to
become the Federal Republic of Austria.

MEDITERRANEAN SEA

DOCUMENTS

On June 11, 1945, a group of scientists in Chicago who had been secretly developing an atomic bomb petitioned Secretary of War Henry L. Stimson to recognize the importance of future international (especially Soviet) agreement to prevent a nuclear-arms race. Headed by James Franck, the scientists' committee recommended against a surprise atomic attack on Japan and instead advocated a noncombatant use of the bomb on an island or in a desert, with international observers. But President Truman and his advisers rejected the Franck Committee's advice, presented as Document 1. On September 11, 1945, Stimson sent Truman a memorandum in which the secretary of war argued that "the problem" of the atomic bomb "dominated" Soviet-American relations. Stimson now urged that the United States approach the Soviet Union to discuss controls in order to reduce distrust, as Document 2 indicates.

Document 3, written by George F. Kennan, is his "long telegram" sent to Washington on February 22, 1946, from his post as attaché in the U.S. embassy in Moscow. Kennan pessimistically speculated on the motivations for Soviet behavior. His critique proved persuasive among Truman officials, and Kennan went on to serve as head of the State Department's Policy Planning Staff, where he helped to establish "containment" as U.S. Cold War doctrine. Document 4 is former British Prime Minister Winston S. Churchill's "iron curtain" speech of March 5, 1946, delivered in Fulton, Missouri, with an approving President Truman present. On September 27, 1946, Nikolai Novikov, Soviet ambassador to the United States, sent his own long telegram to his superiors in Moscow. Included as Document 5, Novikov's report described the United States as an expansionist power bent on world supremacy.

On March 12, 1947, the president addressed Congress to announce the "Truman Doctrine," or containment doctrine, in conjunction with a request for aid to Greece and Turkey. Much of the significant speech is reprinted here as Document 6. The Marshall Plan for European reconstruction soon followed. Suggested by Secretary of State George C. Marshall in June 1947, the aid program took form in the Economic Cooperation Act of 1948, which the president signed on April 3; the introduction to this legislation is included as Document 7. U.S. policy suffered two stunning setbacks in the early Cold War: the Soviet Union's successful test of an atomic bomb in September 1949, and the Communist triumph in the Chinese Civil War one month later. An excerpt from National Security Council Paper No. 68 (NSC-68), dated April 7, 1950, is reprinted as Document 8. Requested by the president, this alarmist report argued the need for a large military buildup.

1. The Franck Committee Predicts a Nuclear-Arms Race If the Atomic Bomb Is Dropped on Japan, 1945

The way in which the nuclear weapons, now secretly developed in this country, will first be revealed to the world appears of great, perhaps fateful importance.

One possible way—which may particularly appeal to those who consider the nuclear bombs primarily as a secret weapon developed to help win the present

---

This document can be found in "Political and Social Problems," June 11, 1945, Manhattan Engineering District Papers, National Archives, Washington, D.C. It can also be found in The Committee of Social and Political Implications, A Report to the Secretary of War, June 1945, *Bulletin of the Atomic Scientists* 1 (May 1, 1946): 2–4, 16.

war—is to use it without warning on an appropriately selected object in Japan. It is doubtful whether the first available bombs, of comparatively low efficiency and small in size, will be sufficient to break the will or ability of Japan to resist, especially given the fact that the major cities like Tokyo, Nagoya, Osaka and Kobe already will largely be reduced to ashes by the slower process of ordinary aerial bombing. Certain and perhaps important tactical results undoubtedly can be achieved, but we nevertheless think that the question of the use of the very first available atomic bombs in the Japanese war should be weighed very carefully, not only by military authority, but by the highest political leadership of this country. If we consider international agreement on total prevention of nuclear warfare as the paramount objective, and believe that it can be achieved, this kind of introduction of atomic weapons to the world may easily destroy all our chances of success. Russia, and even allied countries which bear less mistrust of our ways and intentions, as well as neutral countries, will be deeply shocked. It will be very difficult to persuade the world that a nation which was capable of secretly preparing and suddenly releasing a weapon, as indiscriminate as the rocket bomb and a thousand times more destructive, is to be trusted in its proclaimed desire of having such weapons abolished by international agreement. . . .

Thus, from the "optimistic" point of view—looking forward to an international agreement on prevention of nuclear warfare—the military advantages and the saving of American lives, achieved by the sudden use of atomic bombs against Japan, may be outweighed by the ensuing loss of confidence and wave of horror and repulsion, sweeping over the rest of the world, and perhaps dividing even the public opinion at home.

From this point of view a demonstration of the new weapon may best be made before the eyes of representatives of all United Nations, on the desert or a barren island. The best possible atmosphere for the achievement of an international agreement could be achieved if America would be able to say to the world, "You see what weapon we had but did not use. We are ready to renounce its use in the future and to join other nations in working out adequate supervision of the use of this nuclear weapon."

This may sound fantastic, but then in nuclear weapons we have something entirely new in the order of magnitude of destructive power, and if we want to capitalize fully on the advantage which its possession gives us, we must use new and imaginative methods. After such a demonstration the weapon could be used against Japan if a sanction of the United Nations (and of the public opinion at home) could be obtained, perhaps after a preliminary ultimatum to Japan to surrender or at least to evacuate a certain region as an alternative to the total destruction of this target.

It must be stressed that if one takes a pessimistic point of view and discounts the possibilities of an effective international control of nuclear weapons, then the advisability of an early use of nuclear bombs against Japan becomes even more doubtful—quite independently of any humanitarian considerations. If no international agreement is concluded immediately after the first demonstration, this will mean a flying start of an unlimited armaments race.

2. Secretary of War Henry L. Stimson Appeals for Atomic Talks with the Soviets, 1945

In many quarters it [atomic bomb] has been interpreted as a substantial offset to the growth of Russian influence on the continent. We can be certain that the Soviet Government has sensed this tendency and the temptation will be strong for the Soviet political and military leaders to acquire this weapon in the shortest possible time. Britain in effect already has the status of a partner with us in the development of this weapon. Accordingly, unless the Soviets are voluntarily invited into the partnership upon a basis of cooperation and trust, we are going to maintain the Anglo-Saxon bloc over against the Soviet in the possession of this weapon. Such a condition will almost certainly stimulate feverish activity on the part of the Soviet toward the development of this bomb in what will in effect be a secret armament race of a rather desperate character. There is evidence to indicate that such activity may have already commenced. . . .

To put the matter concisely, I consider the problem of our satisfactory relations with Russia as not merely connected with but as virtually dominated by the problem of the atomic bomb. Except for the problem of the control of that bomb, those relations, while vitally important, might not be immediately pressing. The establishment of relations of mutual confidence between her and us could afford to await the slow progress of time. But with the discovery of the bomb, they became immediately emergent. Those relations may be perhaps irretrievably embittered by the way in which we approach the solution of the bomb with Russia. For if we fail to approach them now and merely continue to negotiate with them, having this weapon rather ostentatiously on our hip, their suspicions and their distrust of our purposes and motives will increase. . . .

If the atomic bomb were merely another though more devastating military weapon to be assimilated into our pattern of international relations, it would be one thing. We could then follow the old custom of secrecy and nationalistic military superiority relying on international caution to prescribe the future use of the weapon as we did with gas. But I think the bomb instead constitutes merely a first step in a new control by man over the forces of nature too revolutionary and dangerous to fit into the old concepts. I think it really caps the climax of the race between man's growing technical power for destructiveness and his psychological power of self-control and group control—his moral power. If so, our method of approach to the Russians is a question of the most vital importance in the evolution of human progress. . . .

My idea of an approach to the Soviets would be a direct proposal after discussion with the British that we would be prepared in effect to enter an arrangement with the Russians, the general purpose of which would be to control and limit the use of the atomic bomb as an instrument of war and so far as possible to direct and encourage the development of atomic power for peaceful and humanitarian purposes.

This document can be found in Henry L. Stimson, Memorandum for the President, 11 September 1945, "Proposed Actions for Control of Atomic Bombs," Harry S. Truman Papers, PSF: General File, Folder: Atomic Bomb, Box 112, Harry S. Truman Presidential Library, Independence, Mo. It can also be found in Henry L. Stimson and McGeorge Bundy, *On Active Service in Peace and War* (New York: Harper and Brothers, 1948), 642–646.

Such an approach might more specifically lead to the proposal that we would stop work on the further improvement in, or manufacture of, the bomb as a military weapon, provided the Russians and the British would agree to do likewise. It might also provide that we would be willing to impound what bombs we now have in the United States provided the Russians and the British would agree with us that in no event will they or we use a bomb as an instrument of war unless all three Governments agree to that use. We might also consider including in the arrangement a covenant with the U.K. and the Soviets providing for the exchange of benefits of future developments whereby atomic energy may be applied on a mutually satisfactory basis for commercial or humanitarian purposes. . . .

I emphasize perhaps beyond all other considerations the importance of taking this action with Russia as a proposal of the United States—backed by Great Britain but peculiarly the proposal of the United States. Action of any international group of nations, including many small nations who have not demonstrated their potential power or responsibility in this war would not, in my opinion, be taken seriously by the Soviets. . . .

. . . The use of this bomb has been accepted by the world as the result of the initiative and productive capacity of the United States, and I think this factor is a most potent lever toward having our proposals accepted by the Soviets, whereas I am most skeptical of obtaining any tangible results by way of any international debate. I urge this method as the most realistic means of accomplishing this vitally important step in the history of the world.

3. Attaché George F. Kennan Critiques Soviet Foreign Policy in His "Long Telegram," 1946

At bottom of Kremlin's neurotic view of world affairs is traditional and instinctive Russian sense of insecurity. Originally, this was insecurity of a peaceful agricultural people trying to live on vast exposed plain in neighborhood of fierce nomadic peoples. To this was added, as Russia came into contact with economically advanced West, fear of more competent, more powerful, more highly organized societies in that area. But this latter type of insecurity was one which afflicted rather Russian rulers than Russian people; for Russian rulers have invariably sensed that their rule was relatively archaic in form, fragile and artificial in its psychological foundation, unable to stand comparison or contact with political systems of Western countries. For this reason they have always feared foreign penetration, feared direct contact between Western world and their own, feared what would happen if Russians learned truth about world without or if foreigners learned truth about world within. And they had learned to seek security only in patient but deadly struggle for total destruction of rival power, never in compacts and compromises with it.

It was no coincidence that Marxism, which had smouldered ineffectively for half a century in Western Europe, caught hold and blazed for first time in Russia.

This document can be found in U.S. Department of State, *Foreign Relations of the United States, 1946, Eastern Europe: The Soviet Union* (Washington, D.C.: Government Printing Office, 1969), VI, 699–701, 706–707.

Only in this land which had never known a friendly neighbor or indeed any tolerant equilibrium of separate powers, either internal or international, could a doctrine thrive which viewed economic conflicts of society as insoluble by peaceful means. After establishment of Bolshevist regime, Marxist dogma, rendered even more truculent and intolerant by Lenin's interpretation, became a perfect vehicle for sense of insecurity with which Bolsheviks, even more than previous Russian rulers, were afflicted. In this dogma, with its basic altruism of purpose, they found justification for their instinctive fear of outside world, for the dictatorship without which they did not know how to rule, for cruelties they did not dare not to inflict, for sacrifices they felt bound to demand. In the name of Marxism they sacrificed every single ethical value in their methods and tactics. Today they cannot dispense with it. It is fig leaf of their moral and intellectual respectability. Without it they would stand before history, at best, as only the last of that long succession of cruel and wasteful Russian rulers who have relentlessly forced country on to ever new heights of military power in order to guarantee external security of their internally weak regimes. This is why Soviet purposes must always be solemnly clothed in trappings of Marxism, and why no one should underrate importance of dogma in Soviet affairs. Thus Soviet leaders are driven [by?] necessities of their own past and present position to put forward a dogma which [apparent omission] outside world as evil, hostile and menacing, but as bearing within itself germs of creeping disease and destined to be wracked with growing internal convulsions until it is given final *coup de grace* by rising power of socialism and yields to new and better world. This thesis provides justification for the increase of military and police power of Russian state, for that isolation of Russian population from outside world, and for that fluid and constant pressure to extend limits of Russian police power which are together the natural and instinctive urges of Russian rulers. Basically this is only the steady advance of uneasy Russian nationalism, a centuries old movement in which conceptions of offense and defense are inextricably confused. But in new guise of international Marxism, with its honeyed promises to a desperate and war torn outside world, it is more dangerous and insidious than ever before.

It should not be thought from above that Soviet party line is necessarily disingenuous and insincere on part of all those who put it forward. Many of them are too ignorant of outside world and mentally too dependent to question [apparent omission] self-hypnotism, and who have no difficulty making themselves believe what they find it comforting and convenient to believe. Finally we have the unsolved mystery as to who, if anyone, in this great land actually receives accurate and unbiased information about outside world. In atmosphere of oriental secretiveness and conspiracy which pervades this Government, possibilities for distorting or poisoning sources and currents of information are infinite. The very disrespect of Russians for objective truth—indeed, their disbelief in its existence—leads them to view all stated facts as instruments for furtherance of one ulterior purpose or another. There is good reason to suspect that this Government is actually a conspiracy within a conspiracy; and I for one am reluctant to believe that Stalin himself receives anything like an objective picture of outside world. Here there is ample scope for the type of subtle intrigue at which Russians are past masters. Inability of foreign governments to place their case squarely before Russian policy makers—extent to which they are delivered up in their relations with Russia to good graces of obscure and unknown advisers who they never see and cannot influence—this to my mind is most disquieting feature of diplomacy in Moscow, and one which Western statesmen would do well to keep in mind if they would understand nature of difficulties encountered here. . . .

In summary, we have here a political force committed fanatically to the belief that with US there can be no permanent *modus vivendi,* that it is desirable and necessary that the internal harmony of our society be disrupted, our traditional way of life be destroyed, the international authority of our state be broken, if Soviet power is to be secure. This political force has complete power of disposition over energies of one of world's greatest peoples and resources of world's richest national territory, and is borne along by deep and powerful currents of Russian nationalism. In addition, it has an elaborate and far flung apparatus for exertion of its influence in other countries, an apparatus of amazing flexibility and versatility, managed by people whose experience and skill in underground methods are presumably without parallel in history. Finally, it is seemingly inaccessible to considerations of reality in its basic reactions. For it, the vast fund of objective fact about human society is not, as with us, the measure against which outlook is constantly being tested and reformed, but a grab bag from which individual items are selected arbitrarily and tendenciously to bolster an outlook already preconceived. This is admittedly not a pleasant picture. Problem of how to cope with this force [is] undoubtedly greatest task our diplomacy has ever faced and probably greatest it will ever have to face. It should be point of departure from which our political general staff work at present juncture should proceed. It should be approached with same thoroughness and care as solution of major strategic problem in war, and if necessary, with no smaller outlay in planning effort. I cannot attempt to suggest all answers here. But I would like to record my conviction that problem is within our power to solve—and that without recourse to any general military conflict. And in support of this conviction there are certain observations of a more encouraging nature I should like to make:

1. Soviet power, unlike that of Hitlerite Germany, is neither schematic nor adventuristic. It does not work by fixed plans. It does not take unnecessary risks. Impervious to logic of reason, and it is highly sensitive to logic of force. For this reason it can easily withdraw—and usually does—when strong resistance is encountered at any point. Thus, if the adversary has sufficient force and makes clear his readiness to use it, he rarely has to do so. If situations are properly handled there need be no prestige-engaging showdowns.

2. Gauged against Western World as a whole, Soviets are still by far the weaker force. Thus, their success will really depend on degree of cohesion, firmness and vigor which Western World can muster. And this is factor which it is within our power to influence.

3. Success of Soviet system, as form of internal power, is not yet finally proven. It has yet to be demonstrated that it can survive supreme test of successive transfer of power from one individual or group to another. Lenin's death was first such transfer, and its effects wracked Soviet state for 15 years. After Stalin's death or retirement will be second. But even this will not be final test. Soviet internal system will now be subjected, by virtue of recent territorial expansions, to series of additional strains which once proved severe tax on Tsardom. We here are convinced that never since termination of civil war have mass of Russian people

been emotionally farther removed from doctrines of Communist Party than they are today. In Russia, party has now become a great and—for the moment—highly successful apparatus of dictatorial administration, but it has ceased to be a source of emotional inspiration. Thus, internal soundness and permanence of movement need not yet be regarded as assured.

4. All Soviet propaganda beyond Soviet security sphere is basically negative and destructive. It should therefore be relatively easy to combat it by any intelligent and really constructive program.

4. Former British Prime Minister Winston Churchill Declares an "Iron Curtain" Has Descended on Europe, 1946

A shadow has fallen upon the scenes so lately lighted by the Allied victory. Nobody knows what Soviet Russia and its Communist international organization intends to do in the immediate future, or what are the limits, if any, to their expansive and proselytizing tendencies. I have a strong admiration and regard for the valiant Russian people and for my wartime comrade, Marshal Stalin. There is sympathy and good will in Britain—and I doubt not here also—toward the peoples of all the Russias and a resolve to persevere through many differences and rebuffs in establishing lasting friendships.

We understand the Russian need to be secure on her western frontiers from all renewal of German aggression. We welcome her to her rightful place among the leading nations of the world. Above all, we welcome constant, frequent, and growing contacts between Russian people and our own people on both sides of the Atlantic. It is my duty, however, to place before you certain facts about the present position in Europe.

From Stettin in the Baltic to Trieste in the Adriatic, an iron curtain has descended across the continent. Behind that line lie all the capitals of the ancient states of Central and Eastern Europe. Warsaw, Berlin, Prague, Vienna, Budapest, Belgrade, Bucharest, and Sofia, all these famous cities and the populations around them lie in the Soviet sphere and all are subject, in one form or another, not only to Soviet influence but to a very high and increasing measure of control from Moscow. Athens alone, with its immortal glories, is free to decide its future at an election under British, American, and French observation.

The Russian-dominated Polish government has been encouraged to make enormous and wrongful inroads upon Germany, and mass expulsions of millions of Germans on a scale grievous and undreamed of are now taking place. The Communist parties, which were very small in all these eastern states of Europe, have been raised to preeminence and power far beyond their numbers and are seeking everywhere to obtain totalitarian control. Police governments are prevailing in nearly every case, and so far, except in Czechoslovakia, there is no true democracy.

This document can be found in *Congressional Record*, XCII (1946, Appendix), A1145–A1147.

Turkey and Persia are both profoundly alarmed and disturbed at the claims which are made upon them and at the pressure being exerted by the Moscow government. An attempt is being made by the Russians in Berlin to build up a quasi-Communist party in their zone of occupied Germany by showing special favors to groups of left-wing German leaders. At the end of the fighting last June, the American and British Armies withdrew westward, in accordance with an earlier agreement, to a depth at some points of 150 miles on a front of nearly 400 miles, to allow the Russians to occupy this vast expanse of territory which the Western democracies had conquered.

If now the Soviet government tries, by separate action, to build up a pro-Communist Germany in their areas, this will cause new serious difficulties in the British and American zones, and will give the defeated Germans the power of putting themselves up to auction between the Soviets and the Western democracies. Whatever conclusions may be drawn from these facts—and facts they are—this is certainly not the liberated Europe we fought to build up. Nor is it one which contains the essentials of permanent peace.

In front of the iron curtain which lies across Europe are other causes for anxiety. In Italy the Communist party is seriously hampered by having to support the Communist-trained Marshall Tito's claims to former Italian territory at the head of the Adriatic. Nevertheless, the future of Italy hangs in the balance. Again, one cannot imagine a regenerated Europe without a strong France. . . .

However, in a great number of countries, far from the Russian frontiers and throughout the world, Communist fifth columns are established and work in complete unity and absolute obedience to the directions they receive from the Communist center. Except in the British Commonwealth, and in the United States, where communism is in its infancy, the Communist parties or fifth columns constitute a growing challenge and peril to Christian civilization. These are somber facts for anyone to have to recite on the morrow of a victory gained by so much splendid comradeship in arms and in the cause of freedom and democracy, and we should be most unwise not to face them squarely while time remains.

The outlook is also anxious in the Far East and especially in Manchuria. The agreement which was made at Yalta, to which I was a party, was extremely favorable to Soviet Russia, but it was made at a time when no one could say that the German war might not extend all through the summer and autumn of 1945 and when the Japanese war was expected to last for a further eighteen months from the end of the German war. In this country you are all so well informed about the Far East and such devoted friends of China that I do not need to expatiate on the situation there. . . .

Our difficulties and dangers will not be removed by closing our eyes to them; they will not be removed by mere waiting to see what happens; nor will they be relieved by a policy of appeasement. What is needed is a settlement, and the longer this is delayed, the more difficult it will be and the greater our dangers will become. From what I have seen of our Russian friends and allies during the war, I am convinced that there is nothing they admire so much as strength, and there is nothing for which they have less respect than for military weakness. For that reason the old doctrine of a balance of power is unsound. We cannot afford, if we can help it, to work on narrow margins, offering temptations to a trial of strength. If the Western democracies stand together in strict adherence to the principles of the United Nations Charter, their influence for furthering these principles will be immense and no one is likely to molest them. If, however, they become divided or falter in their duty, and if these all-important years are allowed to slip away, then indeed catastrophe may overwhelm us all.

5. Soviet Ambassador Nikolai Novikov Identifies a U.S. Drive for World Supremacy, 1946

The foreign policy of the United States, which reflects the imperialist tendencies of American monopolistic capital, is characterized in the postwar period by a striving for world supremacy. This is the real meaning of the many statements by President Truman and other representatives of American ruling circles: that the United States has the right to lead the world. All the forces of American diplomacy—the army, the air force, the navy, industry and science—are enlisted in the service of this foreign policy. . . .

Europe has come out of the war with a completely dislocated economy, and the economic devastation that occurred in the course of the war cannot be overcome in a short time. All of the countries of Europe and Asia are experiencing a colossal need for consumer goods, industrial and transportation equipment, etc. Such a situation provides American monopolistic capital with prospects for enormous shipments of goods and the importation of capital into these countries—a circumstance that would permit it to infiltrate their national economies. . . .

At the same time, there has been a decline in the influence on foreign policy of those who follow Roosevelt's course for cooperation among peace-loving countries. Such persons in the government, in Congress, and in the leadership of the Democratic party are being pushed farther and farther into the background. The contradictions in the field of foreign policy existing between the followers of [Henry] Wallace and [Claude] Pepper, on the one hand, and the adherents of the reactionary "bi-partisan" policy, on the other, were manifested with great clarity recently in the speech by Wallace that led to his resignation from the post of Secretary of Commerce. . . .

In the summer of 1946, for the first time in the history of the country, Congress passed a law on the establishment of a peacetime army, not on a volunteer basis but on the basis of universal military service. The size of the army, which is supposed to amount to about one million persons as of July 1, 1947, was also increased significantly. The size of the navy at the conclusion of the war decreased quite insignificantly in comparison with wartime. At the present time, the American navy occupies first place in the world, leaving England's navy far behind, to say nothing of those of other countries.

This document can be found in *Origins of the Cold War: The Novikov, Kennan, and Roberts "Long Telegram" of 1946,* Kenneth M. Jensen, editor, Washington: United States Institute of Peace, 1991. Translated by Kenneth M. Jensen and John Glad. Reprinted by permission.

Expenditures on the army and navy have risen colossally, amounting to 13 billion dollars according to the budget for 1946–47 (about 40 percent of the total budget of 36 billion dollars). This is more than ten times greater than corresponding expenditures in the budget for 1938, which did not amount to even one billion dollars.

Along with maintaining a large army, navy, and air force, the budget provides that these enormous amounts also will be spent on establishing a very extensive system of naval and air bases in the Atlantic and Pacific oceans. According to existing official plans, in the course of the next few years 228 bases, points of support, and radio stations are to be constructed in the Atlantic Ocean and 258 in the Pacific. . . .

One of the stages in the achievement of dominance over the world by the United States is its understanding with England concerning the partial division of the world on the basis of mutual concessions. The basic lines of the secret agreement between the United States and England regarding the division of the world consist, as shown by facts, in their agreement on the inclusion of Japan and China in the sphere of influence of the United States in the Far East, while the United States, for its part, has agreed not to hinder England either in resolving the Indian problem or in strengthening its influence in Siam and Indonesia.

In connection with this division, the United States at the present time is in control of China and Japan without any interference from England. . . .

In recent years American capital has penetrated very intensively into the economy of the Near Eastern countries, in particular into the oil industry. At present there are American oil concessions in all of the Near Eastern countries that have oil deposits (Iraq, Bahrain, Kuwait, Egypt, and Saudi Arabia). American capital, which made its first appearance in the oil industry of the Near East only in 1927, now controls about 42 percent of all proven reserves in the Near East, excluding Iran. Of the total proven reserves of 26.8 billion barrels, over 11 billion barrels are owned by U.S. concessions. . . .

The current relations between England and the United States, despite the temporary attainment of agreements on very important questions, are plagued with great internal contradictions and cannot be lasting.

The economic assistance from the United States conceals within itself a danger for England in many respects. First of all, in accepting the [U.S.] loan, England finds herself in a certain financial dependence on the United States from which it will not be easy to free herself. Second, it should be kept in mind that the conditions created by the loan for the penetration by American capital of the British Empire can entail serious political consequences. The countries included in the British Empire or dependent on it may—under economic pressure from powerful American capital—reorient themselves toward the United States, following in this respect the example of Canada, which more and more is moving away from the influence of England and orienting itself toward the United States. The strengthening of American positions in the Far East could stimulate a similar process in Australia and New Zealand. In the Arabic countries of the Near East, which are striving to emancipate themselves from the British Empire, there are groups within the ruling circles that would not be averse to working out a deal with the United States. It is quite possible that the Near East will become a center of Anglo-American contradictions that will explode the agreements now reached between the United States and England.

The "hard-line" policy with regard to the USSR announced by [Secretary of State James F.] Byrnes after the rapprochement of the reactionary Democrats with the Republicans is at present the main obstacle on the road to cooperation of the Great Powers. It consists mainly of the fact that in the postwar period the United States no longer follows a policy of strengthening cooperation among the Big Three (or Four) but rather has striven to undermine the unity of these countries. The objective has been to impose the will of other countries on the Soviet Union. This is precisely the tenor of the policy of certain countries, which is being carried out with the blessing of the United States, to undermine or completely abolish the principle of the veto in the Security Council of the United Nations. This would give the United States opportunities to form among the Great Powers narrow groupings and blocs directed primarily against the Soviet Union, and thus to split the United Nations. Rejection of the veto by the Great Powers would transform the United Nations into an Anglo-Saxon domain in which the United States would play the leading role.

The present policy of the American government with regard to the USSR is also directed at limiting or dislodging the influence of the Soviet Union from neighboring countries. In implementing this policy in former enemy or Allied countries adjacent to the USSR, the United States attempts, at various international conferences or directly in these countries themselves, to support reactionary forces with the purpose of creating obstacles to the process of democratization of these countries. In so doing, it also attempts to secure positions for the penetration of American capital into their economies. . . .

The American occupation policy [in Germany] does not have the objective of eliminating the remnants of German Fascism and rebuilding German political life on a democratic basis, so that Germany might cease to exist as an aggressive force. The United States is not taking measures to eliminate the monopolistic associations of German industrialists on which German Fascism depended in preparing aggression and waging war. Neither is any agrarian reform being conducted to eliminate large landholders, who were also a reliable support for the Hitlerites. Instead, the United States is considering the possibility of terminating the Allied occupation of German territory before the main tasks of the occupation—the demilitarization and democratization of Germany—have been implemented. This would create the prerequisites for the revival of an imperialist Germany, which the United States plans to use in a future war on its side. One cannot help seeing that such a policy has clearly outlined anti-Soviet edge and constitutes a serious danger to the cause of peace.

The numerous and extremely hostile statements by American government, political, and military figures with regard to the Soviet Union and its foreign policy are very characteristic of the current relationship between the ruling circles of the United States and the USSR. These statements are echoed in an even more unrestrained tone by the overwhelming majority of the American press organs. Talk about a "third war," meaning a war against the Soviet Union, and even a direct call for this war—with the threat of using the atomic bomb—such is the content of the statements on relations with the Soviet Union by reactionaries at public meetings and in the press. . . .

Careful note should be taken of the fact that the preparation by the United States for a future war is being conducted with the prospect of war against the Soviet Union, which in the eyes of American imperialists is the main obstacle in the path of the United States to world domination. This is indicated by facts such as the tactical training of the American army for war with the Soviet Union as the future opponent, the siting of American strategic bases in regions from which it is possible to launch strikes on Soviet territory, intensified training and strengthening of Arctic regions as close approaches to the USSR, and attempts to prepare Germany and Japan to use those countries in a war against the USSR.

6. The Truman Doctrine Calls for Aid to Greece and Turkey to Contain Totalitarianism, 1947

The gravity of the situation which confronts the world today necessitates my appearance before a joint session of the Congress.

The foreign policy and the national security of this country are involved.

One aspect of the present situation, which I present to you at this time for your consideration and decision, concerns Greece and Turkey.

The United States has received from the Greek Government an urgent appeal for financial and economic assistance. Preliminary reports from the American Economic Mission now in Greece and reports from the American Ambassador in Greece corroborate the statement of the Greek Government that assistance is imperative if Greece is to survive as a free nation. . . .

The British Government has informed us that, owing to its own difficulties, it can no longer extend financial or economic aid to Turkey.

As in the case of Greece, if Turkey is to have the assistance it needs, the United States must supply it. We are the only country able to provide that help. . . .

The peoples of a number of countries of the world have recently had totalitarian regimes forced upon them against their will. The Government of the United States has made frequent protests against coercion and intimidation, in violation of the Yalta agreement, in Poland, Rumania, and Bulgaria. I must also state that in a number of other countries there have been similar developments.

At the present moment in world history nearly every nation must choose between alternative ways of life. The choice is too often not a free one.

One way of life is based upon the will of the majority, and is distinguished by free institutions, representative government, free elections, guarantees of individual liberty, freedom of speech and religion, and freedom from political oppression.

The second way of life is based upon the will of a minority forcibly imposed upon the majority. It relies upon terror and oppression, a controlled press and radio, fixed elections, and the suppression of personal freedoms.

I believe that it must be the policy of the United States to support free peoples who are resisting attempted subjugation by armed minorities or by outside pressures.

This document can be found in *Public Papers of the Presidents of the United States, Harry S. Truman, 1947* (Washington, D.C.: U.S. Government Printing Office, 1963), 176–180.

I believe that we must assist free peoples to work out their own destinies in their own way.

I believe that our help should be primarily through economic and financial aid which is essential to economic stability and orderly political processes.

The world is not static, and the *status quo* is not sacred. But we cannot allow changes in the *status quo* in violation of the Charter of the United Nations by such methods as coercion, or by such subterfuges as political infiltration. In helping free and independent nations to maintain their freedom, the United States will be giving effect to the principles of the Charter of the United Nations.

It is necessary only to glance at a map to realize that the survival and integrity of the Greek nation are of grave importance in a much wider situation. If Greece should fall under the control of an armed minority, the effect upon its neighbor, Turkey, would be immediate and serious. Confusion and disorder might well spread throughout the entire Middle East.

Moreover, the disappearance of Greece as an independent state would have a profound effect upon those countries in Europe whose peoples are struggling against great difficulties to maintain their freedoms and their independence while they repair the damages of war. . . .

Should we fail to aid Greece and Turkey in this fateful hour, the effect will be far reaching to the West as well as to the East.

We must take immediate and resolute action.

I therefore ask the Congress to provide authority for assistance to Greece and Turkey in the amount of $400,000,000 for the period ending June 30, 1948. In requesting these funds, I have taken into consideration the maximum amount of relief assistance which would be furnished to Greece out of the $350,000,000 which I recently requested that the Congress authorize for the prevention of starvation and suffering in countries devastated by the war.

In addition to funds, I ask the Congress to authorize the detail of American civilian and military personnel to Greece and Turkey, at the request of those countries, to assist in the tasks of reconstruction, and for the purpose of supervising the use of such financial and material assistance as may be furnished. I recommend that authority also be provided for the instruction and training of selected Greek and Turkish personnel. . . .

This is a serious course upon which we embark.

I would not recommend it except that the alternative is much more serious. The United States contributed $341,000,000,000 toward winning World War II. This is an investment in world freedom and world peace.

The assistance that I am recommending for Greece and Turkey amounts to little more than 1/10 of 1 percent of this investment. It is only common sense that we should safeguard this investment and make sure that it was not in vain.

The seeds of totalitarian regimes are nurtured by misery and want. They spread and grow in the evil soil of poverty and strife. They reach their full growth when the hope of a people for a better life has died.

We must keep that hope alive.

The free peoples of the world look to us for support in maintaining their freedoms.

If we falter in our leadership, we may endanger the peace of the world—and we shall surely endanger the welfare of this Nation.

Great responsibilities have been placed upon us by the swift movement of events.

I am confident that the Congress will face these responsibilities squarely.

7. The Marshall Plan (Economic Cooperation Act) Provides Aid for European Reconstruction, 1948

Recognizing the intimate economic and other relationships between the United States and the nations of Europe, and recognizing that disruption following in the wake of war is not contained by national frontiers, the Congress finds that the existing situation in Europe endangers the establishment of a lasting peace, the general welfare and national interest of the United States, and the attainment of the objectives of the United Nations. The restoration or maintenance in European countries of principles of individual liberty, free institutions, and genuine independence rests largely upon the establishment of sound economic conditions, stable international economic relationships, and the achievement by the countries of Europe of a healthy economy independent of extraordinary outside assistance. The accomplishment of these objectives calls for a plan of European recovery, open to all such nations which cooperate in such plan, based upon a strong production effort, the expansion of foreign trade, the creation and maintenance of internal financial stability, and the development of economic cooperation, including all possible steps to establish and maintain equitable rates of exchange and to bring about the progressive elimination of trade barriers. Mindful of the advantages which the United States has enjoyed through the existence of a large domestic market with no internal trade barriers, and believing that similar advantages can accrue to the countries of Europe, it is declared to be the policy of the people of the United States to encourage these countries through a joint organization to exert sustained common efforts as set forth in the report of the Committee of European Economic Cooperation signed at Paris on September 22, 1947, which will speedily achieve that economic cooperation in Europe which is essential for lasting peace and prosperity. It is further declared to be the policy of the people of the United States to sustain and strengthen principles of individual liberty, free institutions, and genuine independence in Europe through assistance to those countries of Europe which participate in a joint recovery program based upon self-help and mutual cooperation: *Provided,* That no assistance to the participating countries herein contemplated shall seriously impair the economic stability of the United States. It is further declared to be the policy of the United States that continuity of assistance provided by the United States should, at all times, be dependent upon continuity of cooperation among countries participating in the program.

This document can be found in *United States Statutes at Large, 1948* (Washington, D.C.: Government Printing Office, 1949), LXII, 137.

8. The National Security Council Paper No. 68 (NSC-68) Reassesses the Soviet Threat and Recommends a Military Buildup, 1950

Within the past thirty-five years the world has experienced two global wars of tremendous violence. It has witnessed two revolutions—the Russian and the Chinese—of extreme scope and intensity. It has also seen the collapse of five empires—the Ottoman, the Austro-Hungarian, German, Italian, and Japanese—and the drastic decline of two major imperial systems, the British and the French. During the span of one generation, the international distribution of power has been fundamentally altered. For several centuries it had proved impossible for any one nation to gain such preponderant strength that a coalition of other nations could not in time face it with greater strength. The international scene was marked by recurring periods of violence and war, but a system of sovereign and independent states was maintained, over which no state was able to achieve hegemony.

Two complex sets of factors have now basically altered this historical distribution of power. First, the defeat of Germany and Japan and the decline of the British and French Empires have interacted with the development of the United States and the Soviet Union in such a way that power has increasingly gravitated to these two centers. Second, the Soviet Union, unlike previous aspirants to hegemony, is animated by a new fanatic faith, antithetical to our own, and seeks to impose its absolute authority over the rest of the world. Conflict has, therefore, become endemic and is waged, on the part of the Soviet Union, by violent or non-violent methods in accordance with the dictates of expediency. With the development of increasingly terrifying weapons of mass destruction, every individual faces the ever-present possibility of annihilation should the conflict enter the phase of total war. . . .

Our overall policy at the present time may be described as one designed to foster a world environment in which the American system can survive and flourish. It therefore rejects the concept of isolation and affirms the necessity of our positive participation in the world community.

This broad intention embraces two subsidiary policies. One is a policy which we would probably pursue even if there were no Soviet threat. It is a policy of attempting to develop a healthy international community. The other is the policy of "containing" the Soviet system. These two policies are closely interrelated and interact on one another. Nevertheless, the distinction between them is basically valid and contributes to a clearer understanding of what we are trying to do. . . .

As for the policy of "containment," it is one which seeks by all means short of war to (1) block further expansion of Soviet power, (2) expose the falsities of Soviet pretentions, (3) induce a retraction of the Kremlin's control and influence and (4) in general, so foster the seeds of destruction within the Soviet system that the Kremlin is brought at least to the point of modifying its behavior to conform to generally accepted international standards.

This document can be found in U.S. Department of State, *Foreign Relations of the United States, 1950, National Security Affairs; Foreign Economic Policy* (Washington, D.C.: Government Printing Office, 1977), I, 237, 252–253, 262–263, 264, 282, 290.

It was and continues to be cardinal in this policy that we possess superior overall power in ourselves or in dependable combination with other like-minded nations. One of the most important ingredients of power is military strength. In the concept of "containment," the maintenance of a strong military posture is deemed to be essential for two reasons: (1) as an ultimate guarantee of our national security and (2) as an indispensable backdrop to the conduct of the policy of "containment." Without superior aggregate military strength, in being and readily mobilizable, a policy of "containment"—which is in effect a policy of calculated and gradual coercion—is no more than a policy of bluff.

At the same time, it is essential to the successful conduct of a policy of "containment" that we always leave open the possibility of negotiation with the U.S.S.R. A diplomatic freeze—and we are in one now—tends to defeat the very purposes of "containment" because it raises tensions at the same time that it makes Soviet retractions and adjustments in the direction of moderated behavior more difficult. It also tends to inhibit our initiative and deprives us of opportunities for maintaining a moral ascendancy in our struggle with the Soviet system.

In "containment" it is desirable to exert pressure in a fashion which will avoid so far as possible directly challenging Soviet prestige, to keep open the possibility for the U.S.S.R. to retreat before pressure with a minimum loss of face and to secure political advantage from the failure of the Kremlin to yield or take advantage of the openings we leave it.

We have failed to implement adequately these two fundamental aspects of "containment." In the face of obviously mounting Soviet military strength ours has declined relatively. Partly as a byproduct of this, but also for other reasons, we now find ourselves at a diplomatic impasse with the Soviet Union, with the Kremlin growing bolder, with both of us holding on grimly to what we have and with ourselves facing difficult decisions. . . .

It is apparent from the preceding sections that the integrity and vitality of our system is in greater jeopardy than ever before in our history. Even if there were no Soviet Union we would face the great problem of the free society, accentuated many fold in this industrial age, of reconciling order, security, the need for participation, with the requirements of freedom. . . .

It is quite clear from Soviet theory and practice that the Kremlin seeks to bring the free world under its dominion by the methods of the cold war. The preferred technique is to subvert by infiltration and intimidation. Every institution of our society is an instrument which it is sought to stultify and turn against our purposes. Those that touch most closely our material and moral strength are obviously the prime targets, labor unions, civic enterprises, schools, churches, and all media for influencing opinion. . . .

At the same time the Soviet Union is seeking to create overwhelming military force, in order to back up infiltration with intimidation. In the only terms in which it understands strength, it is seeking to demonstrate to the free world that force and the will to use it are on the side of the Kremlin, that those who lack it are decadent and doomed. In local incidents it threatens and encroaches both for the sake of local gains and to increase anxiety and defeatism in all the free world.

The possession of atomic weapons at each of the opposite poles of power, and the inability (for different reasons) of either side to place any trust in the other, puts a premium on a surprise attack against us. It equally puts a premium on a more violent and ruthless prosecution of its design by cold war, especially if the Kremlin is sufficiently objective to realize the improbability of our prosecuting a preventive war. It also puts a premium on piecemeal aggression against others, counting on our unwillingness to engage in atomic war unless we are directly attacked. . . .

A more rapid build-up of political, economic, and military strength and thereby of confidence in the free world than is now contemplated is the only course which is consistent with progress toward achieving our fundamental purpose. The frustration of the Kremlin design requires the free world to develop a successfully functioning political and economic system and a vigorous political offensive against the Soviet Union. These, in turn, require an adequate military shield under which they can develop. It is necessary to have the military power to deter, if possible, Soviet expansion, and to defeat, if necessary, aggressive Soviet or Soviet-directed actions of a limited or total character. The potential strength of the free world is great; its ability to develop these military capabilities and its will to resist Soviet expansion will be determined by the wisdom and will with which it undertakes to meet its political and economic problems. . . .

Our position as the center of power in the free world places a heavy responsibility upon the United States for leadership. We must organize and enlist the energies and resources of the free world in a positive program for peace which will frustrate the Kremlin design for world domination by creating a situation in the free world to which the Kremlin will be compelled to adjust. Without such a cooperative effort, led by the United States, we will have to make gradual withdrawals under pressure until we discover one day that we have sacrificed positions of vital interest.

It is imperative that this trend be reversed by a much more rapid and concerted build-up of the actual strength of both the United States and the other nations of the free world. The analysis shows that this will be costly and will involve significant domestic financial and economic adjustments.

E S S A Y S

In the opening essay, Barton J. Bernstein, a professor of history at Stanford University, analyzes the Roosevelt and Truman administrations' thinking about the atomic bomb's place both as a weapon to defeat Japan and as a lever to pry diplomatic concessions from the Soviet Union. Bernstein agrees with most historians that Truman ordered the use of the atomic bomb against Japanese civilians primarily to end the war quickly and to save American lives. But he also explores the bomb as a diplomatic "bonus" that American leaders believed would enhance U.S. bargaining power in the Cold War, and he explains the detrimental effects of the bomb and atomic diplomacy on Soviet-American relations. In the second essay, Arnold A. Offner of Lafayette College critically assesses President Harry S. Truman's role in the coming of the Cold War. Offner acknowledges that Stalin's ruthless dictatorship and the deep ideological differences between the Soviet Union and the United States contributed to Cold War conflict. But he emphasizes how Truman's own insecurity, parochialism, and nationalism led the president to oversimplify complex issues, exaggerate the Soviet threat, and rely on military preparedness to contain Soviet expansionism. The administration's atomic diplomacy, its insistence on making West Germany the cornerstone for Europe's reconstruction, and deployment of U.S. naval power in the Mediterranean, according to Offner, unnecessarily antagonized Moscow. And while the Marshall Plan helped ensure Western Europe's economic health, it also precluded Soviet participation and further divided the world. Thus Truman's confrontational policies helped provoke the Cold War.

In the last selection, John Lewis Gaddis of Yale University takes issue with those who view the United States and the Soviet Union as equally responsible for the Cold War. Gaddis observes that World War II produced two distinctively different empires. Driven by traditional Russian nationalism and Joseph Stalin's authoritarian communism, the Soviet Union relied on military force and political coercion to fasten its grip on Eastern Europe. U.S. leaders, in contrast, pursued world hegemony reluctantly and extended American influence across Western Europe by peaceful means—mainly through multilateral economic arrangements such as the Marshall Plan. According to Gaddis, the Soviet empire was the more dangerous and destabilizing of the two, and more directly culpable for the onset of the Cold War.

Secrets and Threats: Atomic Diplomacy and Soviet-American Antagonism

BARTON J. BERNSTEIN

When Harry S. Truman became president on April 12, 1945, he was only dimly aware of the existence of the Manhattan Project and unaware that it was an atomic-bomb project. Left uninformed of foreign affairs and generally ignored by Roosevelt in the three months since the inaugural, the new president inherited a set of policies and a group of advisers from his predecessor. While Truman was legally free to reverse Roosevelt's foreign policies and to choose new advisers on foreign policy, in fact he was quite restricted for personal and political reasons. Because Truman was following a very prestigious president whom he, like a great many Americans, loved and admired, the new president was not free psychologically or politically to strike out on a clearly new course. Only a bolder man, with more self-confidence, might have tried critically to assess the legacy and to act independently. But Truman lacked the confidence and the incentive. When, in fact, he did modify policy—for example, on Eastern Europe—he still believed sincerely, as some advisers told him, that he was adhering to his predecessor's agreements and wishes. . . .

In the case of the international-diplomatic policy on the bomb, Truman was even more restricted by Roosevelt's decisions, for the new president inherited a set of reasonably clear wartime policies. Because Roosevelt had already decided to exclude the Soviets from a partnership on the bomb, his successor could not *comfortably* reverse this policy during the war—unless the late president's advisers pleaded for such a reversal or claimed that he had been about to change his policy. They did neither. Consider, then, the massive personal and political deterrents that blocked Truman from even reassessing this legacy. What price might he have paid at home if Americans learned later that he had reversed Roosevelt's policy and had launched a bold new departure of sharing with the Soviets a great weapon that cost

From Barton J. Bernstein, "Roosevelt, Truman, and the Atomic Bomb, 1941–1945: A Reinterpretation," *Political Science Quarterly* 90 (Spring 1975), 23–69. Reprinted by permission.

the United States $2 billion? Truman, in fact, was careful to follow Roosevelt's strategy of concealing from Congress even the dimensions of the secret partnership on atomic energy with Britain. . . .

During his first weeks in office, Truman learned about the project from [Secretary of War Henry] Stimson and from James F. Byrnes, Roosevelt's former director of the Office of War Mobilization and Reconversion who was to become Truman's secretary of state. Byrnes, despite his recent suspicions that the project might be a scientific boondoggle, told Truman, in the president's words, that "the bomb might well put us in a position to dictate our own terms at the end of the war." On April 25, Stimson discussed issues about the bomb more fully with Truman, especially the "political aspects of the S-1 [atomic bomb's] performance." The bomb, the secretary of war explained in a substantial memorandum, would probably be ready in four months and "would be the most terrible weapon ever known in human history [for it] . . . could destroy a whole city." . . .

The entire discussion, judging from Stimson's daily record and [Manhattan Project director General Leslie R.] Groves's memorandum, assumed that the bomb was a legitimate weapon and that it would be used against Japan. The questions they discussed were not *whether* to use the bomb, but its relationship to the Soviet Union and the need to establish postwar atomic policies. Neither Stimson nor Truman sought then to resolve these outstanding issues, and Truman agreed to his secretary's proposal for the establishment of a high-level committee to recommend "action to the executive and legislative branches of our government when secrecy is no longer in full effect." At no time did they conclude that the committee would also consider the issue of whether to use the bomb as a combat weapon. For policy makers, that was not a question; it was an operating assumption.

Nor did Stimson, in his own charge to the Interim Committee, ever *raise* this issue. Throughout the committee's meetings, as various members later noted, all operated on the assumption that the bomb would be used against Japan. They talked, for example, about drafting public statements that would be issued after the bomb's use. They did not discuss *whether* but how to use it. Only one member ultimately endorsed an explicit advance warning to Japan, and none was prepared to suggest that the administration should take any serious risks to avoid using the bomb. At lunch between the two formal meetings on May 31, some members, perhaps only at one table, briefly discussed the possibility of a noncombat demonstration as a warning to Japan but rejected the tactic on the grounds that the bomb might not explode and the failure might stiffen Japanese resistance, or that Japan might move prisoners of war to the target area. . . .

Two weeks later, after the Franck Committee [a scientific advisory group] recommended a noncombat demonstration, Stimson's assistant submitted this proposal to the four-member scientific advisory panel for advice. The panel promptly rejected the Franck Committee proposal: "we can propose no technical demonstration likely to bring an end to the war; we see no acceptable alternative to direct military use." Had the four scientists known that an invasion was not scheduled until November, or had they even offered their judgment after the unexpectedly impressive Alamogordo test on July 16, perhaps they would have given different counsel. But in June, they were not sure that the bomb explosion would be so dramatic, and, like many others in government, they were wary of pushing for a change in tactics if they might be held responsible for the failure of those tactics—especially if that failure could mean the loss of American lives.

A few days after the panel's report, the issue of giving Japan an advance warning about the bomb was raised at a White House meeting with the president, the military chiefs, and the civilian secretaries. On June 18, after they agreed upon a two-stage invasion of Japan, beginning on about November 1, Assistant Secretary of War John J. McCloy became clearly troubled by the omission of the bomb from the discussion and planning. When Truman invited him to speak, the assistant secretary argued that the bomb would make the invasion unnecessary. Why not warn the emperor that the United States had the bomb and would use it unless Japan surrendered? "McCloy's suggestion had appeal," the official history of the AEC [Atomic Energy Commission] later recorded, "but a strong objection developed" to warning Japan in advance, "which no one could refute—there was no assurance the bomb would work." Presumably, like the Interim Committee, they too feared that a warning, followed by a "dud," might stiffen Japan's morale. There was no reason, policy makers concluded, to take this risk.

Though the Interim Committee and high administration officials found no reason not to use the bomb against Japan, many were concerned about the bomb's impact, and its later value, in Soviet-American relations. "[I]t was already apparent," Stimson later wrote, "that the critical questions in American policy toward atomic energy would be directly connected with Soviet Russia." At a few meetings of the Interim Committee, for example, members discussed informing the Soviets of the bomb before its use against Japan. When the issue first arose, [the scientists] Vannevar Bush and [James B.] Conant estimated that the Soviet Union could develop the bomb in about four years and argued for informing the Soviets before combat use as a preliminary to moving toward international control and thereby avoiding a postwar nuclear arms race. Conant and Bush had been promoting this strategy since the preceding September. Even though Roosevelt had cast them to the side in 1943, when he cemented the Anglo-American alliance, the two scientist-administrators had not abandoned hope for their notions. They even circulated to the Interim Committee one of their memoranda on the subject. But at the meetings of May 18 and 31 they again met defeat. General Groves, assuming that America was far more advanced technologically and scientifically and also that the Soviet Union lacked uranium, argued that the Soviets could not build a bomb for about twenty years. He contributed to the appealing "myth" of the atomic secret—that there was a secret and it would long remain America's monopoly. James Byrnes, with special authority as secretary of state–designate and Truman's representative on the committee, accepted Groves's analysis and argued for maintaining the policy of secrecy— which the committee endorsed. Byrnes was apparently very pleased, and Stimson agreed, as he told Truman on June 6, "There should be no revelation to Russia or anyone else of our work on S-1 [the atomic bomb] until the first bomb has been laid successfully on Japan."

At a later meeting on June 21, the Interim Committee, including Byrnes, reversed itself. Yielding to the pleas of Bush and Conant, who were strengthened by the scientific panel's recommendations, the Interim Committee advised Truman to inform the Soviets about the bomb before using it in combat. Like the Franck Committee, the Interim Committee concluded (as the minutes record):

> In the hope of securing effective future control and in view of the fact that general information concerning the project would be made public shortly after the [Potsdam] conference, the Committee *agreed* that there would be considerable advantage, if suitable opportunity arose, in having the President advise the Russians that we were working on this weapon with every prospect of success and that we expected to use it against Japan.
>
> The president might say further that he hoped this matter might be discussed some time in the future in terms of insuring that the weapon would become an aid to peace.

Because of this recommendation, and perhaps also because of the continuing prodding of Bush and Conant, Stimson reversed his own position. He concluded that if the United States dropped the bomb on Japan without first informing the Soviet Union, that act might gravely strain Soviet-American relations. Explaining the committee's position to Truman, Stimson proposed that if the President "thought that Stalin was on good terms with him" at the forthcoming Potsdam conference, he would inform Stalin that the United States had developed the bomb, planned to use it against Japan, knew the Soviets were working on the bomb, and looked forward to discussing international control later. . . .

The issues of the bomb and the Soviet Union had already intruded in other ways upon policy and planning. Awaiting the bomb, Truman had postponed the Potsdam conference, delayed negotiations with Russia, and hoped that atomic energy would pry some concessions from Russia. Truman explained in late May to Joseph Davies, an advocate of Soviet-American friendship, and in early June to Stimson that he was delaying the forthcoming Potsdam conference until the Alamogordo test, when he would know whether the United States had a workable atomic bomb—what Stimson repeatedly called the "mastercard." . . .

At Yalta [in February 1945], Roosevelt had granted the Soviet Union concessions in China in order to secure Soviet entry into the Pacific war, which Stalin promised, within two to three months after V-E Day (May 8). Stalin made it clear that Soviet entry would await a Sino-Soviet pact ratifying these concessions. At the time of Yalta, American military planners were counting on a Soviet attack in Manchuria to pin down the Kwantung army there and hence stop Japan from shifting these forces to her homeland to meet an American invasion.

But by April, war conditions changed and military planners revised their analysis: Japan no longer controlled the seas and therefore could not shift her army, so Soviet entry was not essential. In May, the State Department asked Stimson whether Soviet participation "at the earliest possible moment" was so necessary that the United States should abide by the Far East section of the Yalta agreement. Stimson concluded that the Soviets would enter the war for their own reasons, at their schedule, and with little regard to any American action, that the Yalta concessions would be largely within the grasp of Soviet military power, and that Soviet assistance would be useful, but not essential, if an American invasion was necessary. If there is an invasion, "Russian entry," he wrote, "will have a profound military effect in that almost certainly it will materially shorten the war and thus save American lives." But if the bomb worked, he implied in other discussions, then an invasion would probably not be necessary and Soviet help would be less important. As a result, he urged a delay in settling matters with Russia on the Far East until after the Alamo-gordo test, and the President apparently followed this counsel. . . .

At Potsdam, on July 24, [eight days after the Alamagordo test] Truman told Stalin casually that the United States had developed "a new weapon of unusual destructive force" for use against Japan but did not specify an atomic weapon. Why didn't Truman explicitly inform Stalin about the atomic bomb? Was Truman, as some have suggested, afraid that the news would prompt Stalin to hasten Soviet interven-tion and therefore end the war and make combat use of the bomb impossible? Did Truman simply want to delay Soviet entry and did he, like Byrnes, fear that his news would have the opposite effect? Did Truman think that the destruction wrought by the bomb would not impress the Soviets as forcefully if they were informed in advance? Why did Truman reject the counsel of the Interim Committee, of Stimson, and even of [British prime minister Winston S.] Churchill, who, after the glowing news of the Alamogordo test, "was not worried about giving the Russians informa-tion on the matter but was rather inclined to use it as an argument in our favor in the negotiations"?

Many of these questions cannot be definitively answered on the basis of the presently available evidence, but there is enough evidence to refute one popular in-terpretation: that Truman's tactic was part of an elaborate strategy to prevent or retard Soviet entry *in order* to delay Japan's surrender and *thereby* make combat use of the bomb possible. That interpretation claims too much. Only the first part can be sup-ported by some, albeit indirect, evidence: that he was probably seeking to delay or prevent Soviet entry. Byrnes later said that he feared that Stalin would order an immediate Soviet declaration of war if he realized the importance of this "new weapon"—advice Truman dubiously claimed he never received. Truman was not try-ing to postpone Japan's surrender *in order* to use the bomb. In addition to the reason-able theory that he was seeking to prevent or retard Soviet entry, there are two other plausible, complementary interpretations of Truman's behavior. First, he believed, as had some of his advisers earlier, that a combat demonstration would be more impres-sive to Russia without an advance warning and therefore he concealed the news. Sec-ond, he was also ill-prepared to discuss atomic energy with Stalin, for the president had not made a decision about postwar atomic policy and how to exploit the bomb, and probably did not want to be pressed by Stalin about sharing nuclear secrets. Perhaps all three theories collectively explained Truman's evasive tactics.

Even without explicit disclosure, the bomb strengthened American policy at Potsdam. The Alamogordo test stiffened Truman's resolve, as Churchill told Stim-son after the meeting of the Big Three on July 22: "Truman was evidently much fortified . . . and . . . he stood up to the Russians in a most emphatic and decisive manner, telling them as to certain demands that they absolutely could not have." Probably, also, the bomb explains why Truman pushed more forcefully at Potsdam for the Soviets to open up Eastern Europe. It is less clear whether the bomb changed the substance of American policy at Potsdam. Probably Byrnes endorsed a reparations policy allowing the division of Germany because the bomb replaced Germany as a potential counterweight to possible Soviet expansion. . . .

Scholars and laymen have criticized the combat use of the atomic bomb. They have contended, among other points, that the bombs were not necessary to end the war, that the administration knew or should have known this, that the administration knew that Japan was on the verge of defeat and *therefore* close to surrender, and that the administration was either short-sighted or had other controlling international-political motives (besides ending the war) for using the bomb. These varying contentions usually focus on the alleged failure of the United States to pursue five alternatives, individually or in combination, in order to achieve Japanese surrender before using the bomb: (1) awaiting Soviet entry, a declaration of war, or a public statement of intent (already discussed); (2) providing a warning and/or a noncombat demonstration (already discussed); (3) redefining unconditional surrender to guarantee the Imperial institution; (4) pursuing Japan's "peace feelers"; or (5) relying upon conventional warfare for a longer period. These contentions assume that policy makers were trying, or should have tried, to avoid using atomic bombs—precisely what they were not trying to do. . . .

There were powerful reasons why the fifth alternative—the use of conventional weapons for a longer period *before* using atomic bombs—seemed undesirable to policy makers. The loss of American lives, while perhaps not great, would have been unconscionable and politically risky. How could policy makers have justified to themselves or to other Americans delaying the use of this great weapon and squandering American lives? Consider the potential political cost at home. In contrast, few Americans were then troubled by the mass killing of enemy citizens, especially if they were yellow. The firebombings of Tokyo, of other Japanese cities, and even of Dresden had produced few cries of outrage in the United States. There was no evidence that most citizens would care that the atomic bomb was as lethal as the raids on Dresden or Tokyo. It was unlikely that there would be popular support for relying upon conventional warfare and not using the atomic bomb. For citizens and policy makers, there were few, if any, moral restraints on what weapons were acceptable in war.

Nor were there any powerful advocates within the high councils of the administration who wanted to delay or not use the bomb and rely instead upon conventional warfare—a naval blockade, continued aerial bombings, or both. The advocates of conventional warfare were not powerful, and they did not directly oppose the use of the bomb. Admiral Ernest L. King, chief of Naval Operations, did believe that the invasion and the atomic bomb were not the only alternative tactics likely to achieve unconditional surrender. A naval blockade, he insisted, would be successful. The army, however, he complained, had little faith in sea power and, hence, Truman did not accept his proposal. [Admiral William] Leahy had serious doubts about using the bomb, but as an old explosives expert who had long claimed that the bomb would never work, he carried little weight on this matter. Surprisingly, perhaps, he did not forcefully press his doubts on the president. . . .

For policy makers, the danger was not simply the loss of a few hundred American lives *prior* to the slightly delayed use of the bombs if the United States relied upon conventional warfare for a few more weeks. Rather the risk was that, if the nuclear attacks were even slightly delayed, the scheduled invasion of Kyushu, with perhaps 30,000 casualties in the first month, would be necessary. After the war, it became fashionable to assume that policy makers clearly foresaw and comfortably expected that an atomic bomb or two would shock Japan into a speedy surrender. But the evidence does not support this view. "The abrupt surrender of Japan came more or less as a surprise," Henry H. Arnold, commanding general of the air force, later explained. Policy makers were planning, if necessary, to drop at least three atomic bombs in August, with the last on about August 24, and more in September. . . .

There have been criticisms of the administration for failing to pursue two other alleged opportunities: (1) redefining the unconditional surrender demands before Hiroshima to guarantee the Imperial institution; (2) responding to Japan's "peace feelers," which stressed the need for this guarantee. Byrnes and apparently Truman, however, were fearful at times that concessions might strengthen, not weaken, the Japanese military and thereby prolong, not shorten, the war. Some critics imply that Byrnes and Truman were not sincere in presenting this analysis and that they rejected concessions consciously in order to use the bomb. That is incorrect. Other critics believe that these policy makers were sincere but disagree with their assessment—especially since some intelligence studies implied the need for concessions on peace terms to shorten the war. Probably the administration was wrong, and these latter critics right, but either policy involved risks and some were very unattractive to Truman.

Truman, as a new president, was not comfortable in openly challenging Roosevelt's policy of unconditional surrender and modifying the terms. That was risky. It could fail and politically injure him at home. Demanding unconditional surrender meant fewer risks at home and, according to his most trusted advisers at times, fewer risks in ending the war speedily. . . . After August 10, when Japan made the guarantee the only additional condition, Truman yielded on the issue. He deemed it a tactical problem, not a substantive one. But even then, Byrnes was wary of offering this concession, despite evidence that it would probably end the war promptly— precisely what he wanted in order to forestall Soviet gains in the Far East. . . .

Let us look at the remaining, but connected, alternative—pursuing Japan's "peace feelers." Japan's so-called peace feelers were primarily a series of messages from the foreign minister to his nation's ambassador in Moscow, who was asked to investigate the possibility of having the Soviets serve as intermediaries in negotiating a peace. American intelligence intercepted and decoded all the messages. Most, if not all, were sent on to Potsdam, where Truman and Byrnes had access to them. Both men showed little interest in them, and may not even have read all of them, apparently because the proposed concessions were insufficient to meet American demands and because Truman and Byrnes had already decided that the peace party in Japan could not succeed until American attacks—including atomic bombs—crushed the military's hopes. The intercepted and decoded messages fell short of American expectations. Not only did Japan's foreign minister want to retain the Imperial institution, which was acceptable to some policy makers, but he also wanted a peace that would maintain his nation's "honor and existence," a phrase that remained vague. As late as July 27, the day after the Potsdam Proclamation, when Japan's foreign minister was planning a special peace mission to Russia, he was still unwilling or unable to present a "concrete proposal" for negotiations. . . .

Looking back upon these years, Americans may well lament the unwillingness of their leaders to make some concessions at this time and to rely upon negotiations before using the bombs. That lament, however, is logically separable from the unfounded charges that policy makers consciously avoided the "peace feelers" *because* they wanted to drop the bombs in order to intimidate the Soviets. It is true that

American leaders did not cast policy in order to avoid using the atomic bombs. Given their analysis, they had no reason to avoid using these weapons. As a result, their analysis provokes ethical revulsion among many critics, who believe that policy makers should have been reluctant to use atomic weapons and should have sought, perhaps even at some cost in American lives, to avoid using them. . . .

[One can also suggest that the bomb was used as] retribution against Japan. A few days after Nagasaki, Truman hinted at this theme in a private letter justifying the combat use of the bombs:

> Nobody is more disturbed over the use of Atomic bombs than I am but I was greatly disturbed over the unwarranted attack by the Japanese on Pearl Harbor. The only language they seem to understand is the one that we have been using to bombard them. When you have to deal with a beast you have to treat him as a beast. It is most regrettable but nevertheless true.

In this letter, one can detect strains of the quest for retribution (the reference to Pearl Harbor), and some might even find subtle strains of racism (Japan was "a beast"). The enemy was a beast and deserved to be destroyed. War, as some critics would stress, dehumanized victors and vanquished, and justified inhumanity in the name of nationalism, of justice, and even humanity.

In assessing the administration's failure to challenge the assumption that the bomb was a legitimate weapon to be used against Japan, we may conclude that Truman found no reason to reconsider, that it would have been difficult for him to challenge the assumption, and that there were also various likely benefits deterring a reassessment. For the administration, in short, there was no reason to avoid using the bomb and many reasons making it feasible and even attractive. The bomb was used primarily to end the war *promptly* and thereby to save American lives. There were other ways to end the war, but none of them seemed as effective. They would not produce victory as promptly and seemed to have greater risks. Even if Russia had not existed, the bombs would have been used in the same way. How could Truman, in the absence of overriding contrary reasons, justify not using the bombs, or even delaying their use, and thereby prolonging the war sacrificing American lives? . . .

Did the bomb make a critical difference in shaping the early Cold War? Roosevelt's repeated decisions to bar the Soviets from the nuclear project and Truman's decision to use the bomb in combat without explicitly informing the Soviet Union and inviting her to join in postwar control of atomic energy undoubtedly contributed to the Cold War and helped shape the form that it took. Yet, in view of the great strains in the fragile wartime Soviet-American alliance, historians should not regard America's *wartime* policy on the bomb as *the* cause, but only as one of the causes, of the Cold War. The wartime policy on atomic energy represented one of a number of missed opportunities at achieving limited agreements and at testing the prospects for Soviet-American cooperation on a vital matter.

The atomic bomb, first as prospect and then as reality, did influence American policy. The bomb reduced the incentives for compromise and even stiffened demands by the time of the Potsdam meeting in July 1945 because the weapon gave the United States enhanced power. Without the bomb, policy makers probably would have been more conciliatory after V-J Day in dealing with the Soviet Union, especially about Eastern Europe. The president certainly would have been unable to try to use atomic diplomacy (implied threats) to push the Soviets out of Eastern

Europe. Rather, he might have speedily, though reluctantly, agreed to the dominance of Soviet power and to the closed door in that sector of the world. The bomb, as potential or actual weapon, did *not* alter the administration's conception of an ideal world, but possession of the weapon did strengthen the belief of policy makers in their capacity to move toward establishing their goal: an "open door" world with the Soviets acceding to American demands. This ideal world included free elections, an open economic door, and the reduction of Soviet influence in Eastern Europe. Without the bomb, the Truman administration would not have surrendered these ultimate aims, but policy makers would have had to rely primarily on economic power as a bargaining card to secure concessions from the Soviet Union. And economic power, taken alone, would probably have seemed insufficient—as the record of lend-lease and the Russian loan suggests. . . .

Without the bomb, in summary, American policy after V-J Day would have been more cautious, less demanding, less optimistic. Such restraint would not have prevented the breakdown of the Soviet-American alliance, but probably the cold war would not have taken the form that it did, and an uneasy truce, with less fear and antagonism, might have been possible.

Provincialism and Confrontation: Truman's Responsibility

ARNOLD A. OFFNER

As the twenty-first century [begins], President Harry S. Truman's reputation stands high. This is especially true regarding his stewardship of foreign policy although, ironically, he entered the Oval Office in 1945 untutored in world affairs, and during his last year in the White House Republicans accused his administration of having surrendered fifteen countries and five hundred million people to communism and sending twenty thousand Americans to their "burial ground" in Korea. Near the end of his term, Truman's public "favorable" rating had plummeted to 23 percent.

Within a decade, however, historians rated Truman a "near great" president, crediting his administration with reconstructing Western Europe and Japan, resisting Soviet or Communist aggression from Greece to Korea, and forging collective security through NATO. In the 1970s the "plain speaking" Truman became a popular culture hero. Recently, biographers have depicted him as the allegory of American life, an ordinary man whose extraordinary character led him to triumph over adversity from childhood through the presidency, and even posited a symbiotic relationship between "His Odyssey" from Independence to the White House and America's rise to triumphant superpower status. . . .

Collapse of the Soviet Union and Europe's other Communist states, whose archives have confirmed Truman's belief in 1945 that their regimes governed largely by "clubs, pistols and concentration camps," has further raised the former president's standing. This has encouraged John Lewis Gaddis and others to shift their focus to Stalin's murderous domestic rule as the key determinant of Soviet

Adapted from Arnold A. Offner, "'Another Such Victory': President Truman, American Foreign Policy, and the Cold War," *Diplomatic History,* 23 (Spring 1999), 127–152, 153–155. Reprinted with permission of Blackwell Publishing Ltd.

foreign policy and the Cold War. As Gaddis has contended, Stalin was heir to Ivan the Terrible and Peter the Great, responsible for more state-sanctioned murders than Adolf Hitler, and treated world politics as an extension of domestic politics: a zero sum game in which his gaining security meant depriving all others of it. For Gaddis and others, that is largely the answer to the question of whether Stalin sought or caused the Cold War.

But as Walter LaFeber has said, to dismiss Stalin's policies as the work of a paranoid is greatly to oversimplify the Cold War. Indeed, historians of Stalin's era seem to be of the preponderant view that he pursued a cautious but brutal realpolitik. He aimed to restore Russia's 1941 boundaries, establish a sphere of influence in border states, provide security against a recovered Germany or Japan or hostile capitalist states, and gain compensation, notably reparations, for the ravages of war. Stalin calculated forces, recognized America's superior industrial and military power, put Soviet state interests ahead of Marxist-Leninist ideology, and pursued pragmatic or opportunistic policies in critical areas such as Germany, China, and Korea.

Thus, the time seems ripe, given our increased knowledge of Soviet policies, to reconsider President Truman's role in the Cold War. As Thomas G. Paterson has written, the president stands as the pinnacle of the diplomatic-military establishment, has great capacity to set the foreign policy agenda and to mold public opinion, and his importance, especially in Truman's case, cannot be denied. But contrary to prevailing views, I believe that his policymaking was shaped by his parochial and nationalistic heritage. This was reflected in his uncritical belief in the superiority of American values and political-economic interests and his conviction that the Soviet Union and communism were the root cause of international strife. Truman's parochialism also caused him to disregard contrary views, to engage in simplistic analogizing, and to show little ability to comprehend the basis for other nations' policies. Consequently, his foreign policy leadership intensified Soviet-American conflict, hastened the division of Europe, and brought tragic intervention in Asian civil wars. . . .

Truman's parochialism and nationalism, and significant insecurity, were rooted in his background, despite his claim to have had a bucolic childhood of happy family, farm life, and Baptist religiosity. In fact, young Harry's poor eyesight, extended illness, and "sissy" piano playing alienated him from both his peers and his feisty father and fostered ambivalence in him toward powerful men. On the one hand, Truman deferred to "Boss" Thomas Pendergast, his dishonest political benefactor, and to Secretaries of State George Marshall and Dean Acheson, whose manner and firm viewpoints he found reassuring. On the other hand, he denounced those whose style or ways of thinking were unfamiliar. This included the State Department's "striped pants boys," the military's "brass hats" and "prima donnas," political "fakirs" [sic] such as Teddy and Franklin Roosevelt, and "professional liberals." For Truman, Charles de Gaulle, Josef Stalin, Ernest Bevin, and Douglas MacArthur were each, at one time or another, a "son of a bitch." . . .

Truman's self-tutelage in history derived largely from didactic biographies of "great men" and empires. This enhanced his vision of the globe but provided little sense of complexity or ambiguity and instilled exaggerated belief that current events had exact historical analogues that provided the key to contemporary policy. The new president was "amazed" that the Yalta accords were so "hazy" and fraught with "new meanings" at every reading, which probably contributed to his "lackluster" adherence to them. Shortly, Truman uncritically applied analogues about 1930s appeasement of Nazi Germany to diplomacy with the Soviet Union and crises in Iran, Greece, Turkey, and Korea.

Further, young Harry's Bible reading and church going did not inspire an abiding religiosity or system of morals so much as a conviction that the world was filled with "liars and hypocrites," terms he readily applied to his presidential critics, and a stern belief, as he wrote in 1945, that "punishment always followed transgression," a maxim that he applied to North Korea and the People's Republic of China (PRC).

Truman's early writings disdained non-Americans and minorities ("Chink doctor," "dago," "nigger," "Jew clerk," and "bohunks and Rooshans"), and in 1940 he proposed to deport "disloyal inhabitants." As president in 1945 he questioned the loyalty of "hyphenate" Americans, and in 1947 he signed Executive Order 9835, creating an unprecedented "loyalty" program that jettisoned basic legal procedural safeguards and virtually included a presumption of guilt.

Truman's command of men and bravery under fire in World War I were exemplary but not broadening. He deplored Europe's politics, mores, and food and sought only to return to "God's country." He intended never to revisit Europe: "I've nearly promised old Miss Liberty that she'll have to turn around to see me again," he wrote in 1918, and in 1945 he went reluctantly to Potsdam to his first and only European summit.

Nonetheless, Truman identified with Wilsonian internationalism, especially the League of Nations, and as a senator he supported President Franklin Roosevelt on the World Court, neutrality revision, rearmament, and Lend Lease for Britain and Russia. He rightfully said "I am no appeaser." But his internationalism reflected unquestioned faith in American moral superiority, and his foreign policy proposals largely comprised military preparedness. He was indifferent to the plight of Republican Spain and too quickly blamed international conflict on "outlaws," "savages," and "totalitarians." After Germany invaded the Soviet Union in 1941, he hastily remarked that they should be left to destroy one another—although he opposed Germany's winning—and he likened Russian leaders to "Hitler and Al Capone" and soon inveighed against the "twin blights—atheism and communism." Hence, while Truman supported the fledgling United Nations and the liberalization of world trade, the man who became president in April 1945 was less an incipient internationalist than a parochial nationalist given to excessive fear that appeasement, lack of preparedness, and enemies at home and abroad would thwart America's mission (the "Lord's will") to "win the peace" on its terms.

President Truman inherited an expedient wartime alliance that stood on shaky ground at Yalta in February 1945 and grew more strained over Soviet control in Romania and Poland and U.S. surrender talks with German officials at Bern that aroused Stalin's fears of a separate peace. Truman lamented that "they didn't tell me anything about what was going on." He also had to depend on advisers whose views ranged from Ambassador Averell Harriman's belief that it was time to halt the Russians' "barbarian invasion" of Europe to counsel from FDR emissaries Joseph Davies and Harry Hopkins to try to preserve long-term accord. Truman's desire to appear decisive by making quick decisions and his instinct to be "tough" spurred his belief that he could get "85 percent" from the Russians on important matters and that they could go along or "go to hell."

Initially, the president's abrupt style and conflicting advice produced inconsistent policy. His mid-April call for a "new" government in Poland and his "one-two to the jaw" interview with [Soviet foreign minister Vyacheslav] Molotov brought only a sharp reply from Stalin, after which the United States recognized a predominantly Communist Polish government. In May, Truman approved "getting tough" with the Russians by suddenly curtailing Lend Lease shipments, but Anglo-Soviet protests caused him to countermand the cutoffs. He then refused Prime Minister Winston Churchill's proposal to keep Anglo-American troops advanced beyond their agreed occupation zones to bargain in Germany and soon wrote that he was "anxious to keep all my engagements with the Russians because they are touchy and suspicious of us."

Still, Truman determined to have his way with the Russians, especially in Germany. Tutored in part by Secretary of War Henry L. Stimson, he embraced the emergent War-State Department position that Germany was key to the balance of power in Europe and required some reconstruction because a "poor house" standard of living there meant the same for Europe, and might cause a repeat of the tragic Treaty of Versailles history. Truman replaced Roosevelt's reparations negotiator, Isador Lubin, with conservative oil entrepreneur Edwin Pauley, who brushed off both Soviet claims to Yalta's $20 billion in reparations and State Department estimates that Germany could pay $12–14 billion. Truman also said that when he met with Churchill and Stalin he wanted "all the bargaining power—all the cards in my hands, and the plan on Germany is one of them."

The other card was the atomic bomb, which inspired Truman and [Secretary of State] Byrnes to think that they could win their way in Europe and Asia. Byrnes told the president in April that the bomb might allow them to "dictate our terms" at the war's end and in May indicated his belief that it would make the Russians more "manageable." Stimson counseled Truman that America's industrial strength and unique weapon comprised a "royal straight flush and we mustn't be a fool about how we play it," that it would be "dominant" in any dispute with Russia over Manchuria, and a "weapon" or "master card" in America's hand in its "big stakes" diplomacy with the Russians. . . .

After meeting Stalin [at Potsdam, Germany,] on 17 July Truman wrote that he was unfazed by the Russian's "dynamite" agenda because "I have some dynamite too which I'm not exploding now." The following day he asserted that the "Japs will fold up" before Russia entered the Pacific war, specifically "when Manhattan appears over their homeland." Truman agreed with Byrnes that use of the bomb would permit them to "out maneuver Stalin on China," that is, negate the Yalta concessions in Manchuria and guarantee that Russia would "not get in so much on the kill" of Japan or its occupation. . . .

News of the bomb's power also greatly reinforced Truman's confidence to allow Byrnes to press European negotiations to impasse by refusing the Russians access to the Ruhr, rejecting even their low bid for $4 billion in industrial reparations, and withdrawing the Yalta accords. Convinced that the New Mexico atomic test would allow the United States to "control" events, Byrnes pushed his famous 30 July tripartite ultimatum on German zonal reparations [limiting Soviet reparations mainly to the Soviet occupational zone and reducing the amounts discussed by FDR and Stalin at Yalta], Poland's de facto control over its new western border (including Silesia) with Germany, and Italy's membership in the UN. "Mr. Stalin is stallin'," Truman wrote hours before the American-set deadline on 31 July, but that was useless because

"I have an ace in the hole and another one showing," aces that he knew would soon fall upon Japan.

Truman won his hand, as Stalin acceded to zonal reparations. But Truman's victory was fraught with more long-term consequences than he envisioned. He had not only equated his desire to prevent use of taxpayer dollars to help sustain occupied Germany with the Russians' vital need for reparations but also given them reason to think, as Norman Naimark has written, that the Americans were deaf to their question for a "paltry" $10 billion or less to compensate for Germany's having ravaged their nation. Further, America's insistence on zonal reparations would impede development of common economic policy for all of Germany and increase likelihood of its East-West division. . . .

Truman backed Byrnes's [hard-headed] diplomacy at the London CFM [Council of Foreign Ministers], which deadlocked over Russian control in Eastern Europe and American control in Japan. Truman told Byrnes to "stick to his guns" and tell the Russians "to go to hell." The president then agreed with "ultranationalist" advisers who opposed international atomic accord by drawing misleading analogies about interwar disarmament and "appeasement" and by insisting that America's technological-industrial genius assured permanent atomic supremacy. Truman held that America was the world's atomic "trustee"; that it had to preserve the bomb's "secret"; and that no nation would give up the "locks and bolts" necessary to protect its "house" from "outlaws." The atomic arms race was on, he said in the fall of 1945, and other nations had to "catch up on their own hook."

In the spring of 1946, Truman undercut the Dean Acheson-David Lilienthal plan for international control and development of atomic resources by appointing as chief negotiator Bernard Baruch, whose emphasis on close inspections, sanctions, no veto, and indefinite American atomic monopoly virtually assured Russian refusal. Despite Acheson's protests, Truman analogized that "if Harry Stimson had been back up in Manchuria [in 1931] there would have been no war." And as deadlock neared in July 1946, the president told Baruch to "stand pat."

Ultimately the UN commission weighing the Baruch Plan approved it on 31 December 1946. But the prospect of a Soviet veto in the Security Council precluded its adoption. Admittedly, Stalin's belief that he could not deal with the United States on an equal basis until he had the bomb and Soviet insistence on retention of their veto power and national control of resources and facilities may have precluded atomic accord in 1946. Still, Baruch insisted that the United States could get its way because it had an atomic monopoly, and American military officials sought to preserve a nuclear monopoly as long as possible and to develop a strategy based on air power and atomic weapons. . . .

Meanwhile, Byrnes's diplomacy in Moscow in December 1945 had produced Yalta-style accords on a European peace treaty process, Russian predominance in Bulgaria and Romania and American primacy in China and Japan, and compromise over Korea, with Soviet disputes with Iran and Turkey set aside. But conservative critics cried "appeasement," and in his famous but disputed letter of 5 January 1946, an anxious president charged that Byrnes had kept him "completely in the dark"; denounced Russian "outrage[s]" in the Baltic, Germany, Poland, and Iran and intent to invade Turkey; and said that the Russians understood only an "iron fist" and "divisions" and that he was tired of "babying" them. In fact, Truman knew of most of Byrnes's positions; they had hardly "babied" Russia since Potsdam; and no Russian attack was imminent. The letter reflected Truman's new "get tough" policy, or personal cold war declaration, which, it must be emphasized, came six weeks before George Kennan's Long Telegram and Churchill's Iron Curtain speech.

Strong American protests in 1946 caused the Russians to withdraw their troops from Iran and their claims to joint defense of the Turkish Straits. In the latter case, Truman said he was ready to follow his policy of military response "to the end" to determine if Russia intended "world conquest." Once again he had taken an exaggerated, nationalist stance. No one expected a Russian military advance; America's action rested on its plans to integrate Turkey into its strategic planning and to use it as a base of operations against Russia in event of war. And in September Truman approved announcement of a Mediterranean command that led to the United States becoming the dominant naval power there by year's end.

Meanwhile, Truman ignored Secretary of Commerce Henry Wallace's lengthy memoranda during March–September 1946 that sought to promote economic ties with Russia and questioned America's atomic policies and global military expansiveness. The president then fired Wallace after he publicly challenged Byrnes's speech on 6 September in Stuttgart propounding West German reconstruction and continued American military presence there. The firing was reasonable, but not the rage at Wallace as "a real Commy" and at "parlor pinks and soprano-voiced men" as a "national danger" and "sabotage front" for Stalin.

Equally without reason was Truman's face value acceptance of White House special counsel Clark Clifford's "Russian Report" of September 1946 and accompanying "Last Will of Peter the Great." Clifford's report rested on a hasty compilation of apocalyptic projections of Soviet aim to conquer the world by military force and subversion, and he argued that the United States had to prepare for total war. He wrote in the "black and white" terms that he knew Truman would like and aimed to justify a vast global military upgrade and silence political critics on the left and right. Tsar Peter's will was an old forgery purporting to show that he had a similar design to conquer Eurasia. Truman may have found the report so "hot" that he confined it to his White House safe, but he believed the report and the will and soon was persisting that the governments of the czars, Stalin, and Hitler were all the same. Later he told a mild critic of American policy to read Tsar Peter's will to learn where Russian leaders got their "fixed ideas."

It was a short step, Clifford recalled, from the Russian Report to Truman's epochal request in March 1947 for military aid to Greece and Turkey to help "free peoples" fight totalitarianism. Truman vastly overstated the global-ideological aspects of Soviet-American conflict. Perhaps he sought to fire "the opening gun" to rouse the public and a fiscally conservative Republican Congress to national security expenditures. But he also said that this was "only the beginning" of the "U.S. going into European politics," that the Russians had broken every agreement since Potsdam and would now get only "one language" from him. He added in the fall of 1947 that "if Russia gets Greece and Turkey," it would get Italy and France, the iron curtain would extend to western Ireland, and the United States would have to "come home and prepare for war."

Truman's fears were excessive. Stalin never challenged the Truman Doctrine or Western primacy in Turkey, now under U.S. military tutelage, and Greece. He provided almost no aid to the Greek rebels and told Yugoslavia's leaders in early

1948 to halt their aid because the United States would never allow the Greek Communists to win and break Anglo-American control in the Mediterranean. When Marshal Josip Broz Tito balked, Stalin withdrew his advisers from Yugoslavia and expelled that nation from the Cominform. Tito finally closed his borders to the Greek rebels in July 1949.

Perhaps U.S. officials feared that Britain's retreat from Greece might allow Russia to penetrate the Mediterranean, or that if Greek Communists overthrew the reactionary Greek regime (Turkey was not threatened) they might align Athens with Moscow. Still, the Truman administration's costly policy never addressed the causes of Greece's civil war; instead, it substituted military "annihilation of the enemy for the reform of the social and economic conditions" that had brought civil war. Equally important, Truman's rhetorical division of the world into "free" versus "totalitarian" states . . . created . . . an unfortunate model for later interventions, such as in Korea—"the Greece of the Far East," as Truman would say—and in French Indochina.

The Truman Doctrine led to the Marshall Plan in June 1947, but they were not "two halves of the same walnut," as Truman claimed. State Department officials who drew up the European Recovery Plan (ERP) differentiated it from what they viewed as his doctrine's implications for "economic and ultimately military warfare." The Soviets likened the Truman Doctrine to retail purchase of separate nations and the Marshall Plan to wholesale purchase of Europe.

The Soviet view was narrow, although initially they had interest in participating and perhaps even harbored dreams that the United States would proffer a generous Lend Lease-style arrangement. But as the British quickly saw, Soviet participation was precluded by American-imposed financial and economic controls and, as Michael J. Hogan has written, by the integrated, continental approach to aid rather than a nation-by-nation basis that would have benefited war-devastated Russia. Indeed, in direct talks in Paris, U.S. officials refused concessions, focused on resources to come from Russia and East Europe, and insisted on German contributions to the ERP ahead of reparations payments or a peace treaty—and then expressed widespread relief when the Soviets rejected the ERP for themselves and East Europe.

The Marshall Plan proved to be a very successful geostrategic venture. It helped to spur American-European trade and Western European recovery, bring France into camp with Germany and satisfy French economic and security claims, and revive western Germany industrially without unleashing the 1930s-style "German colossus" that Truman's aides feared. The Marshall Plan was also intended to contain the Soviets economically, forestall German-Soviet bilateral deals, and provide America with access to its allies' domestic and colonial resources. Finally, as the British said, the Truman administration sought an integrated Europe resembling the United States, "God's own country."

The Marshall Plan's excellent return on investment, however, may have cost far more than the $13 billion expended. "The world is definitely split in two," Undersecretary of State Robert Lovett said in August 1947, while Kennan forewarned that for defensive reasons the Soviets would "clamp down completely on Czechoslovakia" to strengthen their hold on Eastern Europe. Indeed, the most recent evidence indicates that Stalin viewed the Marshall Plan as a "watershed" event, signaling an American effort to predominate over all of Europe. This spurred the Soviets into a comprehensive strategy shift. They now rigged the elections in Hungary, proffered [Politburo spokesman] Andrei Zhdanov's "two camps" approach to world policy, created the Cominform, and blessed the Communist coup in Czechoslovakia in February 1948. Truman, in turn, concluded that the Western world confronted the same situation it had a decade earlier with Nazi Germany, and his bristling St. Patrick's Day speeches in March 1948 placed sole onus for the Cold War on the Soviet Union. Subsequently, Anglo-American talks at the Pentagon would culminate in NATO in April 1949.

Meanwhile, the U.S. decision to make western Germany the cornerstone of the ERP virtually precluded negotiations to reunify the country. In fact, when Secretary of State Marshall proposed during a CFM meeting in the spring of 1947 to offer current production reparations to the Russians to induce agreement to unify Germany, the president sternly refused. Marshall complained of lack of "elbow room" to negotiate. But Truman would not yield, and by the time of the next CFM in late 1947 the secretary showed no interest in Russian reparations or Ruhr access. Despite America's public position, Ambassador to Moscow Walter Bedell Smith wrote, "we really do not want nor intend to accept German unification on any terms that the Russians might agree to, even though they seemed to meet most of our requirements."

The Americans were by then onto their London Conference program to create a West German state and, as Stalin said in February 1948, "The West will make Western Germany their own, and we shall turn Eastern Germany into our own state." In June the Soviet dictator initiated the Berlin blockade to try to forestall the West's program, but Truman determined to "stay period." He believed that to withdraw from Berlin would seriously undermine U.S. influence in Europe and the ERP and destroy his presidential standing, and he remained determined to avert military confrontation.

But Truman saw no connection between the London program and the blockade, as Carolyn Eisenberg has written. Further, his belief that "there is nothing to negotiate" and accord with General Lucius Clay's view that to withdraw from Berlin meant "we have lost everything we are fighting for" exaggerated the intent of Stalin's maneuver and diminished even slim chances for compromise on Germany, including Kennan's "Plan A" for a unified, neutralized state with American and Soviet forces withdrawn to its periphery. As Marshall said in August 1948, there would be "no abandonment of our position" on West Germany.

Eventually, Truman and the airlift prevailed over Stalin, who gave in to a face-saving CFM in May 1949 that ended the blockade, with nothing else agreed. The new secretary of state, Acheson, said that the United States intended to create a West German government "come hell or high water" and that Germany could be unified only by consolidating the East into the West on the basis of its incipient Bonn Constitution. Likewise Truman said in June 1949 that he would not sacrifice West Germany's basic freedoms to gain "nominal political unity." . . .

No one leader or nation caused the Cold War. The Second World War generated inevitable Soviet-American conflict as two nations with entirely different political-economic systems confronted each other on two war-torn continents. The Truman administration would seek to fashion a world order friendly to American political and economic interests, to achieve maximum national security by preventing any nation from severing U.S. ties to its traditional allies and vital areas of trade and resources, and to avoid 1930s-style "appeasement." Truman creditably favored creation of the UN, fostered foreign aid and reconstruction, and wished to avert war. . . .

Nonetheless, from the Potsdam Conference through the Korean War, the president contributed significantly to the growing Cold War and militarization of American foreign policy. He assumed that America's economic-military-moral superiority assured that he could order the world on its terms, and he ascribed only dark motives to nations or leaders who resisted America's will. . . .

It is clear that Truman's insecurity with regard to diplomacy and world politics led him to seek to give the appearance of acting decisively and reinforced his penchant to view conflict in black and white terms and to divide nations into free or totalitarian societies. He shied from weighing the complexities of historic national conflicts and local or regional politics. Instead, he attributed nearly every diplomatic crisis or civil war—in Germany, Iran, Turkey, Greece, and Czechoslovakia—to Soviet machination and insisted that the Russians had broken every agreement and were bent on "world conquest." To determine his response he was quick to reach for an analogy, usually the failure of the Western powers to resist Germany and Japan in the 1930s, and to conclude that henceforth he would speak to the Russians in the only language that he thought they understood: "divisions." This style of leadership and diplomacy closed off both advocates and prospects for more patiently negotiated and more nuanced or creative courses of action. . . .

In conclusion, it seems clear that despite Truman's pride in his knowledge of the past, he lacked insight into the history unfolding around him. He often could not see beyond his immediate decision or visualize alternatives, and he seemed oblivious to the implications of his words or actions. More often than not he narrowed rather than broadened the options that he presented to the American citizenry, the environment of American politics, and the channels through which Cold War politics flowed. Throughout his presidency, Truman remained a parochial nationalist who lacked the leadership to move America away from conflict and toward détente. Instead, he promoted an ideology and politics of Cold War confrontation that became the modus operandi of successor administrations and the United States for the next two generations.

Two Cold War Empires:
Imposition vs. Multilateralism

JOHN LEWIS GADDIS

Leaders of both the United States and the Soviet Union would have bristled at having the appellation "imperial" affixed to what they were doing after 1945. But one need not send out ships, seize territories, and hoist flags to construct an empire: "informal" empires are considerably older than, and continued to exist alongside, the more "formal" ones Europeans imposed on so much of the rest of the world from the fifteenth through the nineteenth centuries. During the Cold War years Washington and Moscow took on much of the character, if never quite the charm,

Adapted from John Lewis Gaddis, *We Now Know: Rethinking Cold War History* (New York: Oxford University Press, 1997), 27–39. © by John Lewis Gaddis. Reprinted by permission of Oxford University Press.

of old imperial capitals like London, Paris, and Vienna. And surely American and Soviet influence, throughout most of the second half of the twentieth century, was at least as ubiquitous as that of any earlier empire the world had ever seen.

Ubiquity never ensured unchallenged authority, though, and that fact provides yet another reason for applying an imperial analogy to Cold War history. For contrary to popular impressions, empires have always involved a two-way flow of influence. Imperializers have never simply acted upon the imperialized; the imperialized have also had a surprising amount of influence over the imperializers. The Cold War was no exception to this pattern, and an awareness of it too will help us to see how that rivalry emerged, evolved, and eventually ended in the way that it did.

Let us begin with the structure of the Soviet empire, for the simple reason that it was, much more than the American, deliberately designed. It has long been clear that, in addition to having had an authoritarian vision, Stalin also had an imperial one, which he proceeded to implement in at least as single-minded a way. No comparably influential builder of empire came close to wielding power for so long, or with such striking results, on the Western side.

It was, of course, a matter of some awkwardness that Stalin came out of a revolutionary movement that had vowed to smash, not just tsarist imperialism, but all forms of imperialism throughout the world. The Soviet leader constructed his own logic, though, and throughout his career he devoted a surprising amount of attention to showing how a revolution and an empire might coexist. Bolsheviks could never be imperialists, Stalin acknowledged in one of his earliest public pronouncements on this subject, made in April 1917. But surely in a *revolutionary* Russia nine-tenths of the non-Russian nationalities would not *want* their independence. Few among those minorities found Stalin's reasoning persuasive after the Bolsheviks did seize power later that year, however, and one of the first problems Lenin's new government faced was a disintegration of the old Russian empire not unlike what happened to the Soviet Union after communist authority finally collapsed in 1991.

Whether because of Lenin's own opposition to imperialism or, just as plausibly, because of Soviet Russia's weakness at the time, Finns, Estonians, Latvians, Lithuanians, Poles, and Moldavians were allowed to depart. Others who tried to do so—Ukrainians, Belorussians, Caucasians, Central Asians—were not so fortunate, and in 1922 Stalin proposed incorporating these remaining (and reacquired) nationalities into the Russian republic, only to have Lenin as one of his last acts override this recommendation and establish the multi-ethnic Union of Soviet Socialist Republics. After Lenin died and Stalin took his place it quickly became clear, though, that whatever its founding principles the USSR was to be no federation of equals. Rather, it would function as an updated form of empire even more tightly centralized than that of the Russian tsars.

Lenin and Stalin differed most significantly, not over authoritarianism or even terror, but on the legitimacy of Great Russian nationalism. The founder of Bolshevism had warned with characteristic pungency of "that truly Russian man, the Great-Russian chauvinist," and of the dangers of sinking into a "sea of chauvinistic Great-Russian filth, like flies in milk." Such temptations, he insisted, might ruin the prospects of revolution spreading elsewhere in the world. But Stalin—the implied target of Lenin's invective—was himself a Great Russian nationalist, with all the intensity transplanted nationals can sometimes attain. "The leaders of the revolutionary workers of all countries are avidly studying the most instructive history of the working class of Russia, its past, the past of Russia," he would write in a revealing private letter in 1930, shortly after consolidating his position as Lenin's successor. "All this instills (cannot but instill!) in the hearts of the Russian workers a feeling of revolutionary national pride, capable of moving mountains and working miracles."

The "Stalin constitution" of 1936, which formally specified the right of non-Russian nationalities to secede from the Soviet Union, coincided with the great purges and an officially sanctioned upsurge in Russian nationalism that would persist as a prominent feature of Stalin's regime until his death. It was as if the great authoritarian had set out to validate his own flawed prediction of 1917 by creating a set of circumstances in which non-Russian nationalities would not even *think* of seceding, even though the hypothetical authority to do so remained. The pattern resembled that of the purge trials themselves: one maintained a framework of legality—even, within the non-Russian republics, a toleration of local languages and cultures considerably greater than under the tsars. But Stalin then went to extraordinary lengths to deter anyone from exercising these rights or promoting those cultures in such a way as to challenge his own rule. He appears to have concluded, from his own study of the Russian past, that it was not "reactionary" to seek territorial expansion. His principal ideological innovation may well have been to impose the ambitions of the old princes of Muscovy, especially their determination to "gather in" and dominate all of the lands that surrounded them, upon the anti-imperial spirit of proletarian internationalism that had emanated from, if not actually inspired, the Bolshevik Revolution.

Stalin's fusion of Marxist internationalism with tsarist imperialism could only reinforce his tendency, in place well before World War II, to equate the advance of world revolution with the expanding influence of the Soviet state. He applied that linkage quite impartially: a major benefit of the 1939 pact with Hitler had been that it regained territories lost as a result of the Bolshevik Revolution and the World War I settlement. But Stalin's conflation of imperialism with ideology also explains the importance he attached, following the German attack [on the Soviet Union] in 1941, to having his new Anglo-American allies confirm these arrangements. He had similar goals in East Asia when he insisted on bringing the Soviet Union back to the position Russia had occupied in Manchuria prior to the Russo-Japanese War: this he finally achieved at the 1945 Yalta Conference in return for promising to enter the war against Japan. "My task as minister of foreign affairs was to expand the borders of our Fatherland," Molotov recalled proudly many years later. "And it seems that Stalin and I coped with this task quite well."

From the West's standpoint, the critical question was how far Moscow's influence would extend *beyond* whatever Soviet frontiers turned out to be at the end of the war. Stalin had suggested to [Yugoslav communist] Milovan Djilas that the Soviet Union would impose its own social system as far as its armies could reach, but he was also very cautious. Keenly aware of the military power the United States and its allies had accumulated, Stalin was determined to do nothing that might involve the USSR in another devastating war until it had recovered sufficiently to be certain of winning it. "I do not wish to begin the Third World War over the Trieste question," he explained to disappointed Yugoslavs, whom he ordered to evacuate that territory in June 1945. Five years later, he would justify his decision not to intervene in the Korean War on the grounds that "the Second World War ended not long ago, and we are not ready for the Third World War." Just how far the expansion of Soviet influence would proceed depended, therefore, upon a careful balancing of opportunities against risks. "[W]e were on the offensive," Molotov acknowledged:

> They [presumably the West] certainly hardened their line against us, but we had to consolidate our conquests. We made our own socialist Germany out of our part of Germany, and restored order in Czechoslovakia, Poland, Hungary, and Yugoslavia, where the situations were fluid. To squeeze out capitalist order. This was the cold war.

But, "of course," Molotov added, "you had to know when to stop. I believe in this respect Stalin kept well within the limits."

Who or what was it, though, that set the limits? Did Stalin have a fixed list of countries he thought it necessary to dominate? Was he prepared to stop in the face of resistance within those countries to "squeezing out the capitalist order"? Or would expansion cease only when confronted with opposition from the remaining capitalist states, so that further advances risked war at a time when the Soviet Union was ill-prepared for it?

Stalin had been very precise about where he wanted Soviet boundaries changed; he was much less so on how far Moscow's sphere of influence was to extend. He insisted on having "friendly" countries around the periphery of the USSR, but he failed to specify how many would have to meet this standard. He called during the war for dismembering Germany, but by the end of it was denying that he had ever done so: that country would be temporarily divided, he told leading German communists in June 1945, and they themselves would eventually bring about its reunification. He never gave up on the idea of an eventual world revolution, but he expected this to result—as his comments to the Germans suggested—from an expansion of influence emanating from the Soviet Union itself. "[F]or the Kremlin," a well-placed spymaster recalled, "the mission of communism was primarily to consolidate the might of the Soviet state. Only military strength and domination of the countries on our borders could ensure us a superpower role."

But Stalin provided no indication—surely because he himself did not know—of how rapidly, or under what circumstances, this process would take place. He was certainly prepared to stop in the face of resistance from the West: at no point was he willing to challenge the Americans or even the British where they made their interests clear. Churchill acknowledged his scrupulous adherence to the famous 1944 "percentages" agreement confirming British authority in Greece, and Yugoslav sources have revealed Stalin's warnings that the United States and Great Britain would never allow their lines of communication in the Mediterranean to be broken. He quickly backed down when confronted with Anglo-American objections to his ambitions in Iran in the spring of 1946, as he did later that year after demanding Soviet bases in the Turkish Straits. This pattern of advance followed by retreat had shown up in the purges of the 1930s, which Stalin halted when the external threat from Germany became too great to ignore, and it would reappear with the Berlin Blockade and the Korean War, both situations in which the Soviet Union would show great caution after provoking an unexpectedly strong American response.

What all of this suggests, though, is not that Stalin had limited ambitions, only that he had no timetable for achieving them. Molotov retrospectively confirmed this: "Our ideology stands for offensive operations when possible, and if not, we wait."

Given this combination of appetite with aversion to risk, one cannot help but wonder what would have happened had the West tried containment earlier. To the extent that it bears partial responsibility for the coming of the Cold War, the historian Vojtech Mastny has argued, that responsibility lies in its failure to do just that.

Where Western resistance was unlikely, as in Eastern Europe, Stalin would in time attempt to replicate the regime he had already established inside the Soviet Union. Authority extended out from Moscow by way of government and party structures whose officials had been selected for their obedience, then down within each of these countries through the management of the economy, social and political institutions, intellectuals, even family-relationships. The differentiation of public and private spheres that exists in most societies disappeared as all aspects of life were fused with, and then subordinated to, the interests of the Soviet Union as Stalin himself had determined them. Those who could not or would not go along encountered the same sequence of intimidation, terror, and ultimately even purges, show trials, and executions that his real and imagined domestic opponents had gone through during the 1930s. "Stalin's understanding of friendship with other countries was that the Soviet Union would lead and they would follow," Khrushchev recalled. "[He] waged the struggle against the enemies of the people there in the same way that he did in the Soviet Union. He had one demand: absolute subordination."

Stalin's policy, then, was one of imperial expansion and consolidation differing from that of earlier empires only in the determination with which he pursued it, in the instruments of coercion with which he maintained it, and in the ostensibly anti-imperial justifications he put forward in support of it. It is a testimony to his skill, if not to his morality, that he was able to achieve so many of his imperial ambitions at a time when the tides of history were running against the idea of imperial domination—as colonial offices in London, Paris, Lisbon, and The Hague were finding out—and when his own country was recovering from one of the most brutal invasions in recorded history. The fact that Stalin was able to *expand* his empire when others were contracting and while the Soviet Union was as weak as it was requires explanation. Why did opposition to this process, within and outside Europe, take so long to develop?

One reason was that the colossal sacrifices the Soviet Union had made during the war against the Axis had, in effect, "purified" its reputation: the USSR and its leader had "earned" the right to throw their weight around, or so it seemed. Western governments found it difficult to switch quickly from viewing the Soviet Union as a glorious wartime ally to portraying it as a new and dangerous adversary. President Harry S. Truman and his future Secretary of State Dean Acheson—neither of them sympathetic in the slightest to communism—nonetheless tended to give the Soviet Union the benefit of the doubt well into the early postwar era. A similar pattern developed within the United States occupation zone in Germany, where General Lucius D. Clay worked out a cooperative relationship with his Soviet counterparts and resisted demands to "get tough" with the Russians, even after they had become commonplace in Washington.

Resistance to Stalin's imperialism also developed slowly because Marxism-Leninism at the time had such widespread appeal. It is difficult now to recapture the admiration revolutionaries outside the Soviet Union felt for that country before they came to know it well. "[Communism] was the most rational and most intoxicating, all-embracing ideology for me and for those in my disunited and desperate land who so desired to skip over centuries of slavery and backwardness and to bypass reality itself," Djilas recalled, in a comment that could have been echoed throughout much of what came to be called the "third world." Because the Bolsheviks themselves had overcome one empire and had made a career of condemning others, it would take decades for people who were struggling to overthrow British, French, Dutch, or Portuguese colonialism to see that there could also be such a thing as Soviet imperialism. European communists—notably the Yugoslavs—saw this much earlier, but even to most of them it had not been apparent at the end of the war.

Still another explanation for the initial lack of resistance to Soviet expansionism was the fact that its repressive character did not become immediately apparent to all who were subjected to it. With regimes on the left taking power in Eastern and Central Europe, groups long denied advancement could now expect it. For many who remembered the 1930s, autarchy within a Soviet bloc could seem preferable to exposure once again to international capitalism, with its periodic cycles of boom and bust. Nor did Moscow impose harsh controls everywhere at the same time. Simple administrative incompetence may partially account for this: one Russian historian has pointed out that "[d]isorganization, mismanagement and rivalry among many branches of the gigantic Stalinist state in Eastern Europe were enormous." But it is also possible, at least in some areas, that Stalin did not expect to *need* tight controls; that he anticipated no serious challenge and perhaps even spontaneous support. Why did he promise free elections after the war? Maybe he thought the communists would win them.

One has the impression that Stalin and the Eastern Europeans got to know one another only gradually. The Kremlin leader was slow to recognize that Soviet authority would not be welcomed everywhere beyond Soviet borders; but as he did come to see this he became all the more determined to impose it everywhere. The Eastern Europeans were slow to recognize how confining incorporation within a Soviet sphere was going to be; but as they did come to see this they became all the more determined to resist it, even if only by withholding, in a passive but sullen manner, the consent any regime needs to establish itself by means other than coercion. Stalin's efforts to consolidate his empire therefore made it at once more repressive and less secure. Meanwhile, an alternative vision of postwar Europe was emerging from the other great empire that established itself in the wake of World War II, that of the United States, and this too gave Stalin grounds for concern.

The first point worth noting, when comparing the American empire to its Soviet counterpart, is a striking reversal in the sequence of events. Stalin's determination to create his empire preceded by some years the conditions that made it possible: he had first to consolidate power at home and then defeat Nazi Germany, while at the same time seeing to it that his allies in that enterprise did not thwart his long-term objectives. With the United States, it was the other way around: the conditions for establishing an empire were in place long before there was any clear intention on the part of its leaders to do so. Even then, they required the support of a skeptical electorate, something that could never quite be taken for granted.

The United States had been poised for global hegemony at the end of World War I. Its military forces played a decisive role in bringing that conflict to an end. Its economic predominance was such that it could control both the manner and the rate of European recovery. Its ideology commanded enormous respect, as Woodrow Wilson found when he arrived on the Continent late in 1918 to a series of rapturous public receptions. The Versailles Treaty fell well short of Wilson's principles, to be sure, but the League of Nations followed closely his own design, providing an explicit legal basis for an international order that was to have drawn, as much as anything else, upon the example of the American constitution itself. If there was ever a point at which the world seemed receptive to an expansion of United States influence, this was it.

Americans themselves, however, were not receptive. The Senate's rejection of membership in the League reflected the public's distinct lack of enthusiasm for international peace-keeping responsibilities. Despite the interests certain business, labor, and agricultural groups had in seeking overseas markets and investment opportunities, most Americans saw few benefits to be derived from integrating their economy with that of the rest of the world. Efforts to rehabilitate Europe during the 1920s, therefore, could only take the form of private initiatives, quietly coordinated with the government. Protective tariffs hung on well into the 1930s—having actually increased with the onset of the Great Depression—and exports as a percentage of gross national product remained low in comparison to other nations, averaging only 4.2 per cent between 1921 and 1940. Investments abroad had doubled between 1914 and 1919 while foreign investment in the United States had been cut in half; but this shift was hardly sufficient to overcome old instincts within the majority of the public who held no investments at all that it was better to stand apart from, rather than to attempt to dominate, international politics outside of the Western hemisphere.

This isolationist consensus broke down only as Americans began to realize that a potentially hostile power was once again threatening Europe: even their own hemisphere, it appeared, might not escape the consequences this time around. After September 1939, the Roosevelt administration moved as quickly as public and Congressional opinion would allow to aid Great Britain and France by means short of war; it also chose to challenge the Japanese over their occupation of China and later French Indochina, thereby setting in motion a sequence of events that would lead to the attack on Pearl Harbor. Historians ever since have puzzled over this: why, after two decades of relative inactivity on the world scene, did the United States suddenly become hyperactive? Might the administration have realized that it would never generate public support for the empire American elites had long desired without a clear and present danger to national security, and did it not then proceed to generate one? Can one not understand the origins and evolution of the Cold War in similar terms?

There are several problems with such interpretations, one of which is that they confuse contingency with conspiracy. Even if Roosevelt had hoped to maneuver the Japanese into "firing the first shot," he could not have known that Hitler would seize this opportunity to declare war and thereby make possible American military intervention in Europe. The Pacific, where the United States would have deployed most of its strength in the absence of Hitler's declaration, would hardly have been the platform from which to mount a bid for global hegemony. These explanations also allow little room for the autonomy of others: they assume that Hitler and the Japanese militarists acted *only* in response to what the United States did, and that other possible motives for their behavior—personal, bureaucratic, cultural, ideological, geopolitical—were insignificant. Finally, these arguments fail to meet the test of proximate versus distant causation. The historian Marc Bloch once pointed out that one could, in principle, account for a climber's fall from a precipice by invoking physics and geology: had it not been for the law of gravity and the existence of the mountain, the accidents surely could not have occurred. But would it follow that all who ascend mountains must plummet from them? Just because Roosevelt *wanted* the United States to enter the war and to become a world power afterwards does not mean that his actions made these things happen.

A better explanation for the collapse of isolationism is a simpler one: it had to do with a resurgence of authoritarianism. Americans had begun to suspect, late in the nineteenth century, that the internal behavior of states determined their external behavior; certainly it is easy to see how the actions of Germany, Italy, and Japan during the 1930s could have caused this view to surface once again, much as it had in relations with tsarist Russia and imperial Germany during World War I. Once that happened, the Americans, not given to making subtle distinctions, began to oppose authoritarianism everywhere, and that could account for their sudden willingness to take on several authoritarians at once in 1941. But that interpretation, too, is not entirely adequate. It fails to explain how the United States could have coexisted as comfortably as it did with authoritarianism in the past—especially in Latin America—and as it would continue to do for some time to come. It certainly does not account for the American willingness during the war to embrace, as an ally, the greatest authoritarian of this century, Stalin himself.

The best explanation for the decline of isolationism and the rise of the American empire, I suspect, has to do with a distinction Americans tended to make— perhaps they were more subtle than one might think—between what we might call benign and malignant authoritarianism. Regimes like those of Somoza in Nicaragua or Trujillo in the Dominican Republic might be unsavory, but they fell into the benign category because they posed no serious threat to United States interests and in some cases even promoted them. Regimes like those of Nazi Germany and imperial Japan, because of their military capabilities, were quite another matter. Stalin's authoritarianism had appeared malignant when linked to that of Hitler, as it was between 1939 and 1941; but when directed against Hitler, it could come to appear quite benign. What it would look like once Germany had been defeated remained to be seen.

With all this, the possibility that even malignant authoritarianism might harm the United States remained hypothetical until 7 December 1941, when it suddenly became very real. Americans are only now, after more than half a century, getting over the shock: they became so accustomed to a Pearl Harbor mentality—to the idea that there really are deadly enemies out there—that they find it a strange new world, instead of an old familiar one, now that there are not. Pearl Harbor was, then, the defining event for the American empire, because it was only at this point that the most plausible potential justification for the United States becoming and remaining a global power as far as the American people were concerned—an endangered national security—became an actual one. Isolationism had thrived right up to this moment; but once it became apparent that isolationism could leave the nation open to military attack, it suffered a blow from which it never recovered. The critical date was not 1945, or 1947, but 1941.

It did not automatically follow, though, that the Soviet Union would inherit the title of "first enemy" once Germany and Japan had been defeated. A sense of vulnerability preceded the identification of a source of threat in the thinking of American strategists: innovations in military technology—long-range bombers, the prospect of even longer-range missiles—created visions of future Pearl Harbors before it had become clear from where such an attack might come. Neither in the military nor the political-economic planning that went on in Washington during the war was there consistent concern with the USSR as a potential future adversary. The threat, rather, appeared to arise from war itself, whoever might cause it, and the most likely candidates were thought to be resurgent enemies from World War II.

The preferred solution was to maintain preponderant power for the United States, which meant a substantial peacetime military establishment and a string of bases around the world from which to resist aggression if it should ever occur. But equally important, a revived international community would seek to remove the fundamental causes of war through the United Nations, a less ambitious version of Wilson's League, and through new economic institutions like the International Monetary Fund and the World Bank, whose task it would be to prevent another global depression and thereby ensure prosperity. The Americans and the British assumed that the Soviet Union would want to participate in these multilateral efforts to achieve military and economic security. The Cold War developed when it became clear that Stalin either could not or would not accept this framework.

Did the Americans attempt to impose their vision of the postwar world upon the USSR? No doubt it looked that way from Moscow: both the Roosevelt and Truman administrations stressed political self-determination and economic integration with sufficient persistence to arouse Stalin's suspicions—easily aroused, in any event—as to their ultimate intentions. But what the Soviet leader saw as a challenge to his hegemony the Americans meant as an effort to salvage multilateralism. At no point prior to 1947 did the United States and its Western European allies abandon the hope that the Russians might eventually come around; and indeed negotiations aimed at bringing them around would continue at the foreign ministers' level, without much hope of success, through the end of that year. The American attitude was less that of expecting to impose a system than one of puzzlement as to why its merits were not universally self-evident. It differed significantly, therefore, from Stalin's point of view, which allowed for the possibility that socialists in other countries might come to see the advantages of Marxism-Leninism as practiced in the Soviet Union, but never capitalists. They were there, in the end, to be overthrown, not convinced.

The emergence of an opposing great power bloc posed serious difficulties for the principle of multilateralism, based as it had been on the expectation of cooperation with Moscow. But with a good deal of ingenuity the Americans managed to *merge* their original vision of a single international order built around common security with a second and more hastily improvised concept that sought to counter the expanding power and influence of the Soviet Union. That concept was, of course, containment, and its chief instrument was the Marshall Plan.

The idea of containment proceeded from the proposition that if there was not to be one world, then there must not be another world war either. It would be necessary to keep the peace while preserving the balance of power: the gap that had developed during the 1930s between the perceived requirements of peace and power was not to happen again. If geopolitical stability could be restored in Europe, time would work against the Soviet Union and in favor of the Western democracies. Authoritarianism need not be the "wave of the future"; sooner or later even Kremlin authoritarians would realize this fact and change their policies. "[T]he Soviet leaders are prepared to recognize *situations,* if not arguments," George F. Kennan wrote in 1948. "If, therefore, situations can be created in which it is clearly not to the advantage of their power to emphasize the elements of conflict in their relations with the outside world, then their actions, and even the tenor of their propaganda to their own people, *can* be modified."

This idea of time being on the side of the West came—at least as far as Kennan was concerned—from studying the history of empires. Edward Gibbon had written in *The Decline and Fall of the Roman Empire* that "there is nothing more contrary to nature than the attempt to hold in obedience distant provinces," and few things Kennan ever read made a greater or more lasting impression on him. He had concluded during the early days of World War II that Hitler's empire could not last, and in the months after the war, he applied similar logic to the empire Stalin was setting out to construct in Eastern Europe. The territorial acquisitions and spheres of influence the Soviet Union had obtained would ultimately become a source of *insecurity* for it, both because of the resistance to Moscow's control that was sure to grow within those regions and because of the outrage the nature of that control was certain to provoke in the rest of the world. "Soviet power, like the capitalist world of its own conception, bears within it the seeds of its own decay," Kennan insisted in the most famous of all Cold War texts, his anonymously published 1947 article on the "The Sources of Soviet Conduct." He added, "the sprouting of those seeds is well advanced."

All of this would do the Europeans little good, though, if the new and immediate Soviet presence in their midst should so intimidate them that their own morale collapsed. The danger here came not from the prospect that the Red Army would invade and occupy the rest of the continent, as Hitler had tried to do; rather, its demoralized and exhausted inhabitants might simply vote in communist parties who would then do Moscow's bidding. The initial steps in the strategy of containment—stopgap military and economic aid to Greece and Turkey, the more carefully designed and ambitious Marshall Plan—took place within this context: the idea was to produce instant intangible reassurance as well as eventual tangible reinforcement. Two things had to happen in order for intimidation to occur, Kennan liked to argue: the intimidator had to make the effort, but, equally important, the target of those efforts had to agree to be intimidated. The initiatives of 1947 sought to generate sufficient self-confidence to prevent such acquiescence in intimidation from taking place.

Some historians have asserted that these fears of collapse were exaggerated: that economic recovery on the continent was already underway, and that the Europeans themselves were never as psychologically demoralized as the Americans made them out to be. Others have added that the real crisis at the time was within an American economy that could hardly expect to function hegemonically if Europeans lacked the dollars to purchase its products. Still others have suggested that the Marshall Plan was the means by which American officials sought to project overseas the mutually-beneficial relationship between business, labor, and government they had worked out at home: the point was not to make Wilsonian values a model for the rest of the world, but rather the politics of productivity that had grown out of American corporate capitalism. All of these arguments have merit: at a minimum they have forced historians to place the Marshall Plan in a wider economic, social, and historical context; more broadly they suggest that the American empire had its own distinctive internal roots, and was not solely and simply a response to the Soviet external challenge.

At the same time, though, it is difficult to see how a strategy of containment could have developed—with the Marshall Plan as its centerpiece—had there been nothing to contain. One need only recall the early 1920s, when similar conditions of European demoralization, Anglo-French exhaustion, and American economic predominance had existed; yet no American empire arose as after World War II. The critical difference, of course, was national security: Pearl Harbor created an atmosphere of vulnerability Americans had not known since the earliest days of the republic, and the Soviet Union by 1947 had become the most plausible source of threat. The American empire arose *primarily,* therefore, not from internal causes, as had the Soviet empire, but from a perceived external danger powerful enough to overcome American isolationism.

Washington's wartime vision of a postwar international order had been premised on the concepts of political self-determination and economic integration. It was intended to work by assuming a set of *common* interests that would cause other countries to *want* to be affiliated with it rather than to resist it. The Marshall Plan, to a considerable extent, met those criteria: although it operated on a regional rather than a global scale, it did seek to promote democracy through an economic recovery that would proceed along international and not nationalist lines. Its purpose was to create an American sphere of influence, to be sure, but one that would allow those within it considerable freedom. The principles of democracy and open markets required nothing less, but there were two additional and more practical reasons for encouraging such autonomy. First, the United States itself lacked the capability to administer a large empire: the difficulties of running occupied Germany and Japan were proving daunting enough. Second, the idea of autonomy was implicit in the task of restoring Europeans self-confidence; for who, if not Europeans themselves, was to say when the self-confidence of Europeans had been restored?

Finally, it is worth noting that even though Kennan and the other early architects of containment made use of imperial analogies, they did not see themselves as creating an empire, but rather a restored balance of power. Painfully—perhaps excessively—aware of limited American resources, fearful that the domestic political consensus in favor of internationalism might not hold, they set out to reconstitute *independent* centers of power in Europe and Asia. These would be integrated into the world capitalist system, and as a result they would certainly fall under the influence of its new hegemonic manager, the United States. But there was no intention here of creating satellites in anything like the sense that Stalin understood that term; rather, the idea was that "third forces" would resist Soviet expansionism while preserving as much as possible of the multilateralist agenda American officials had framed during World War II. What the United States really wanted, State Department official John D. Hickerson commented in 1948, was "not merely an extension of US influence but a real European organization strong enough to say 'no' both to the Soviet Union and to the United States, if our actions should seem so to require."

The American empire, therefore, reflected little imperial consciousness or design. An anti-imperial tradition dating back to the American Revolution partially accounted for this: departures from that tradition, as in the Spanish–American War of 1898 and the Philippine insurrection that followed, had only reinforced its relevance—outside the Western hemisphere. So too did a constitutional structure that forced even imperially minded leaders like Wilson and the two Roosevelts to accommodate domestic attitudes that discouraged imperial behavior long after national capabilities had made it possible. And even as those internal constraints diminished dramatically in World War II—they never entirely dropped away—Americans still found it difficult to think of themselves as an imperial power. The idea of remaking the international system in such a way as to transcend empires altogether still lingered, but so too did doubts as to whether the United States was up to the task. In the end it was again external circumstances—the manner in which Stalin managed his own empire and the way in which this pushed Europeans into preferring its American alternative—that brought the self-confidence necessary to administer imperial responsibilities into line with Washington's awareness of their existence.

F U R T H E R   R E A D I N G

Gar Alperovitz, *Atomic Diplomacy* (1965 and 1985)
———, *The Decision to Use the Atomic Bomb* (1995)
Stephen Ambrose and Douglas Brinkley, *Rise to Globalism* (1997)
Christian G. Appy, ed., *Cold War Constructions* (2000)
Volker Berghahn, *America and the Intellectual Cold Wars in Europe* (2001)
Barton J. Bernstein, "The Atomic Bombings Reconsidered," *Foreign Affairs* 74 (1995): 135–142
Kai Bird and Lawrence Lifschultz, *Hiroshima Shadows* (1998)
——— and Martin J. Sherwin, *American Prometheus* (2005) (on J. Robert Oppenheimer)
H. W. Brands, *The Devil We Knew* (1993)
Douglas Brinkley, ed., *Dean Acheson and the Making of U.S. Foreign Policy* (1993)
David Callahan, *Dangerous Capabilities* (1990) (on Paul Nitze)
James Chace, *Acheson* (1998)
Warren I. Cohen, *America in the Age of Soviet Power* (1995)
Committee for the Compilation of Materials on Damage Caused by the Atomic Bombs in Hiroshima and Nagasaki, *Hiroshima and Nagasaki* (1981)
Frank Costigliola, "Unceasing Pressure for Penetration: Gender, Pathology, and Emotion in George Kennan's Formation of the Cold War," *Journal of American History* 83 (1997): 1309–1338
James E. Cronin, *The World the Cold War Made* (1996)
Robert Dean, *Imperial Brotherhood* (2001) (on gender)
John W. Dower, "The Most Terrible Bomb in the History of the World," in James M. McPherson and Alan Brinkely, eds., *Days of Destiny* (2001)
Carol Eisenberg, *Drawing the Line* (1996) (on Germany)
John Fousek, *To Lead the Free World* (2000)
John Lewis Gaddis, *Russia, the Soviet Union, and the United States* (1990)
———, *Strategies of Containment* (2005)
John Gimbel, *Science, Technology, and Reparations* (1990)
Mary E. Glantz, *FDR and the Soviet Union* (2005)
John L. Harper, *American Visions of Europe* (1994)
Tsuyoshi Hasegawa, *Racing the Enemy: Stalin, Truman, and the Surrender of Japan* (2005)
Robert M. Hathaway, *Ambiguous Partnership: Britain and America, 1944–1947* (1981)
Gregg Herken, *The Winning Weapon* (1981)
James Hershberg, *James B. Conant and the Birth of the Nuclear Age* (1994)
Walter Hixson, *George F. Kennan* (1990)

————, *Parting the Curtain: Propaganda, Culture, and the Cold War* (1997)
Michael J. Hogan, *A Cross of Iron: Harry S. Truman and the Origins of the National Security State* (1998)
————, ed., *Hiroshima in History and Memory* (1996)
————, *The Marshall Plan* (1987)
David Holloway, *Stalin and the Bomb* (1994)
Michael Hopkins, *Oliver Franks and the Truman Administration* (2003)
Jeff Hughes, *The Manhattan Project* (2003)
John O. Iatrides and Linda Wrigley, eds., *Greece at the Crossroads* (1995)
Walter Isaacson and Evan Thomas, *The Wise Men* (1986)
Howard Jones, *"A New Kind of War"* (1989)
Arthur David Kahn, *Experiment in Occupation* (2004) (on Germany)
Lawrence S. Kaplan, *The United States and NATO* (1984)
Frank Kofsky, *Harry S. Truman and the War Scare of 1948* (1993)
Richard Kuisel, *Seducing the French* (1993) (on cultural relations)
Peter J. Kuznik and James Gilbert, eds., *Rethinking Cold War Culture* (2001)
Walter LaFeber, *America, Russia, and the Cold War* (2002)
Deborah Larson, *Anatomy of Distrust* (1997)
Melvyn Leffler, *A Preponderance of Power* (1992)
Ralph Levering et al., *Debating the Origins of the Cold War* (2002)
————, *The Cold War* (1994)
Scott Lucas, *Freedom's War* (1999)
Gier Lundestad, *Empire by Integration* (1998)
Shane J. Maddock, ed., *The Nuclear Age* (2001)
Robert J. McMahon, *The Cold War* (2003)
Robert J. Maddox, *Weapons for Victory* (1995) (on atomic bombings)
Vojtech Mastny, *The Cold War and Soviet Insecurity* (1996)
David Mayers, *The Ambassadors and America's Soviet Policy* (1995)
Richard L. Merritt, *Democracy Imposed* (1995) (on Germany)
Robert S. Norris, *Racing for the Bomb* (2002) (on General Leslie Groves)
Arnold A. Offner, *Another Such Victory* (2002)
David S. Painter, *The Cold War* (1999)
Thomas G. Paterson, *Soviet-American Confrontation* (1973)
————, *Meeting the Communist Threat* (1988)
————, *On Every Front: The Making and Unmaking of the Cold War* (1992)
Richard Pells, *Not Like Us* (1997) (on U.S.-European cultural relations)
Edvard Radzinsky, *Stalin* (1996)
David Reynolds, ed., *The Origins of the Cold War in Europe* (1994)
Thomas A. Schwartz, *America's Germany* (1991)
Michael S. Sherry, *In the Shadow of War: The United States Since the 1930s* (1995)
Martin J. Sherwin, *A World Destroyed* (1975)
Joseph Smith, ed., *The Origins of NATO* (1990)
John Spanier, *American Foreign Policy Since World War II* (1997)
Ronald Steel, *Walter Lippmann and the American Century* (1980)
"Symposium: Soviet Archives: Recent Revelations and Cold War Historiography," *Diplomatic History* 21 (1997): 215–305
Ronald Takaki, *Hiroshima* (1995)
Adam Ulam, *The Rivals* (1971)
Dimitri Volkogonov, *Stalin* (1991)
J. Samuel Walker, *Prompt and Utter Destruction* (1997) (on atomic bombings)
Irwin M. Wall, *The United States and the Making of Postwar France* (1991)
Graham White and John Maze, *Henry A. Wallace* (1995)
Allan M. Winkler, *Life Under a Cloud* (1993)
Lawrence S. Wittner, *American Intervention in Greece, 1943–1949* (1982)
Thomas W. Zeiler, *Unconditional Defeat* (2003)
Vladislav Zubok and Constantine Pleshakov, *Inside the Kremlin's Cold War* (1996)

C H A P T E R
11

Cold War Culture and
the "Third World"

As several of the selections and documents in previous chapters demonstrate, historians of American foreign relations in recent years have become increasingly interested in the cultural aspects of international relations. The word culture is difficult to
define. Anthropologists and cultural theorists have advanced a working definition
that describes culture as a constellation of values, beliefs, symbols, and language
around which a society develops and maintains a sense of identity and a means of
interpreting the outside world. Since the eighteenth century, cultural identity has
usually intersected with national identity, or, in the words of the international studies
scholar Benedict Anderson, the imagined community in which modern men and
women feel a sense of commonality and communion. The history of international
relations lends itself to analysis of identities. We live in an age of globalization, where
economic, technological, environmental, political, cultural, and other developments
have connected people, nations, and regions in distant parts of the world. Although
globalization has roots reaching back to the age of European exploration, twentieth-
century developments in transportation and communications, and most recently the
computer revolution, have brought together the world's peoples as never before—
sometimes producing culture clash, and at other times spawning cooperation. This
chapter explores the cultural dynamics of U.S. relations with the "Third World," or
non-Western world, during the early post–World War II years.

The era of intensified globalization was also the era of the Cold War and decolonization in Asia, the Middle East, and Africa. The decline of colonialism transformed international politics—creating thirty-seven new nations between 1945
and 1960. U.S. officials and the American public at times sympathized with the
anticolonial movements, which reminded them of their own break from the British
Empire in 1776. But national security officials refrained from embracing the new
states when doing so undermined the position of colony-holding allies, unleashed
unrest that threatened U.S. economic and strategic interests, or created opportunities for Soviet expansion. They assigned the label "Third World" to the emerging
nations—and to Latin America, a Cold War term that signified their geopolitical
location outside of U.S. and Soviet spheres in Europe, their "less-developed"
economies, and their political instability. But the terminology lent a misleading

324

coherence to the mosaic of regions, peoples, and cultures that comprised the non-Western world. To influence the new states Washington during the early Cold War relied on a number of mechanisms: trade agreements and cultural exchanges; military and economic assistance; diplomatic nonrecognition (China 1949 and Cuba 1961); covert operations and coup attempts—Iran (1953), Guatemala (1954), British Guiana (1959), Cuba (1961), and Chile (1973); and military interventions—Korea (1950–1953), Lebanon (1958), the Dominican Republic (1965), and South Vietnam (1954–1975).

Historians of American foreign relations examine several manifestations of cultural interaction. First, they explore the many ways in which cultural perceptions of self and of "others" can influence foreign policy decisionmaking. Although national security experts pride themselves on their ability to rationally assess power, interests, and threats, cultural analysis suggests that policymakers can be swayed by nonrational or irrational factors. Societies engage in what theorists call cultural discourses or, more simply put, ongoing conversations about shared beliefs and assumptions, such as notions of class, race, gender, and sexuality; attitudes toward sexuality; or perhaps the meaning of nationhood and civilization itself. The discourse is dominated by society's most powerful, and in twentieth-century America that has usually meant upper-class white males. When U.S. policymakers during the early Cold War confronted difficult-to-fathom non-Western leaders, they often considered Third World friends and foes alike to be backward and inferior, unmanly, or annoyingly obstinate. Fiery nationalists, such as Prime Minister Mohammed Mossadeq of Iran, or President Kwame Nkrumah of Ghana, might be written off as childlike, or effeminate. Distinguishing between nationalists and communists often challenged U.S. officials, in part due to the fact that the Soviets did cultivate Third World friends and allies, but more often due to the misreading of unfamiliar cultural and linguistic terrain. Cultural perceptions did not necessarily trump political, strategic, or economic considerations in policymaking. But they provided context that significantly shaped U.S. attitudes and actions.

A second arena of cultural interaction that is the object of study is the internationalization of culture itself. Whether it be the widespread popularity of rock 'n roll, English's status as an international language, or the worldwide love affair with the cell phone, peoples of the world increasingly show evidence of building a common culture. The immigration and emigration of peoples encourages the sharing of customs and traditions. International travel and tourism, student exchange programs, and multinational business transactions blur boundaries and national identities. Peace movements, the women's rights lobby, and human rights organizations operate globally. Following World War II, the Afro-Asian struggle for decolonization dovetailed with the African-American struggle for civil rights in the United States. In the early 1960s, just before the United States geared up for a domestic War on Poverty, President John F. Kennedy launched the Peace Corps, a program that sent thousands of young, idealistic volunteers to Africa, Asia, Latin America, and the Middle East to promote education and economic development. European, Soviet, and Canadian youth participated in similar humanitarian efforts. Thus, societies are capable of intercultural cooperation as well as culture clash. Indeed, some analysts speculate that for better or worse the world's cultures are becoming less distinct and more homogeneous. Others disagree and point to enduring ethnic and religious conflicts, the continuing power of nationalism, and contrasting codes of etiquette, gender relations, and family structure as evidence that cultural differences survive and thrive. Skeptics are quick to observe, moreover, that even the most noble American overseas undertakings, *including the Peace Corps, have usually contributed to Washington's self-interested global agenda.*

How do cultural perceptions, and misperceptions, influence the conduct of American foreign policy and relations? How important is culture to the making of U.S. diplomacy? To what extent is culture becoming globalized? These questions are essential to an understanding of modern international relations.

D O C U M E N T S

Although the subject of U.S. relations with the Third World is expansive, three examples illustrate key themes in Cold War cultural interactions. First, Iran's nationalist prime minister Mohammed Mossadeq struck a blow against British imperialism in June 1951 when he nationalized the Anglo-Iranian Oil Company. Concerned that the flow of Middle East oil to postwar Europe and Japan might be disrupted, the Truman administration worked to arbitrate the dispute between Tehran and London. Document 1 is a letter from Prime Minister Mohammed Mossadeq to President Truman, dated June 11, 1951, in which the Iranian leader denounces the exploitative practices of the British-owned oil firm and offers to consider any proposal that is not contrary to the principle of nationalization. As the crisis dragged on, American sympathy for Iran dwindled. On July 28, 1952, U.S. ambassador Loy Henderson vented his frustration in a telegram to the State Department in Washington, D.C., reprinted here as Document 2. The cable lamented Mossadeq's anti-Americanism and questioned the prime minister's mental stability. Scholars have noted the Western tendency to dismiss non-Western adversaries by stereotyping them as "emotional" and "unstable." When the administration of Dwight D. Eisenhower took command in early 1953, Washington became alarmed by Mossadeq's contacts with Iran's Communist Tudeh party, and CIA operatives worked covertly with Iranian supporters of the Shah Reza Pahlavi to depose the prime minister. The new regime reversed the nationalization of the oil industry, and U.S. oil companies received lucrative concessions. The United States remained a stalwart ally of the Shah's pro-Western regime—until its overthrow by Islamic followers of the Ayatollah Khomeni in 1979.

A second example of cultural relations, President John F. Kennedy's Peace Corps, generated a very different kind of interaction. First proposed on the presidential campaign trail in the fall of 1960, Kennedy launched the Peace Corps by executive order on March 1, 1961, and named his brother-in-law Sargent Shriver as director. The president's statement upon signing the order appears here as Document 3. As a U.S. senator and presidential candidate, Kennedy had voiced support for Third World nationalism and economic development, both of which he viewed as antidotes to communism. After becoming president, he took a special personal interest in the Peace Corps. Document 4 is a photograph of Kennedy meeting with some of the program's earliest recruits. Soon thousands of youthful volunteers fanned out across the globe—assisting economic development and educational projects, representing America abroad, and learning firsthand about non-Western cultures and peoples. Of course, volunteers' experiences varied widely, but although many governments distanced themselves from U.S. Cold War policies, relations between Peace Corps volunteers and local populations tended to be warm. In a letter written to Peace Corps headquarters, Document 5, a young male volunteer, one of the first to be stationed in the African nation of Ghana, offered advice to future volunteers. Knowledge of the local language, an acceptance of hard work, and a sense of humor seemed to win Ghanaian approval.

A third example of cultural interaction, the rising tide of North American tourism in the only partially autonomous U.S.-sponsored Commonwealth of Puerto Rico during the 1950s and 1960s, illustrates that cultural relations also occur on a people-to-people basis. The Commonwealth of Puerto Rico used its newly acquired authority to invest public funds, subsidies, and tax breaks to jump-start its tourism industry. Document 6 is a memo from Estebán A. Bird, a Puerto Rican tourism official, to Governor Luis Muñoz Marín, dated January 17, 1949, that lays out the Commonwealth's carefully planned strategy to woo North American visitors. Over the next decade the island's tourism boomed—especially after Fidel Castro's revolution in the late 1950s discouraged travel to Cuba, and advertisers portrayed Puerto Rico as a Cold War paradise. Document 7 is a photograph of the Caribe Hilton Hotel shortly after its opening in December 1949. The luxurious ocean-front resort captured the essence of modernity that appealed to U.S. travelers, yet it was owned and built by the Commonwealth government. Although many Puerto Ricans welcomed the tourists as a source of income and prestige, others viewed the influx of vacationers as a second Yankee invasion. Document 8 is a political cartoon that appeared in San Juan's Spanish-language *independentista* newspaper *Claridad.* It pokes fun at American tourists who blame the omnipresence of American street names in Puerto Rico on the island's unimaginative natives. The rickshaw image symbolizes the exploitative nature of the tourist trade.

1. Iranian Prime Minister Mohammed Mossadeq Defends the Nationalization of Oil, 1951

Concerning the nationalization of the oil industry in Iran I have to assure you, Mr. President, that the Government and Parliament of Iran, like yourself desire that the interests of the countries, which hitherto have used the Iranian oil should not suffer in the slightest degree. As, however, you have expressed the apprehension of the United States and it would seem that the matter is not fully clear to you, I ask permission to avail myself of the opportunity to put before you a cursory history of the case of the measures which have now been adopted.

For many years the Iranian Government have been dissatisfied with the activities of the former Anglo-Iranian Oil Company, but I feel it would be beyond the scope of this letter and would cause you undue trouble if I attempted to set forth in detail the exactions of that company and to prove with unshakable documentary evidence that the accounts of the company have not corresponded with the true facts and that even in their disclosed accounts, the share they have earmarked for the Iranian people, the sole owners of the oil, has been so meagre as to rouse the indignation of all fair-minded persons.

The Iranian people have suffered these events for a good many years, with the result that they are now in the clutches of terrible poverty and acute distress, and it has become impossible to continue this tolerance, especially with the situation brought into existence in this country by the second world war.

This document can be found in Text of Message from Prime Minister Mosadeq to President Truman, June 11, 1951, Papers of Harry S. Truman, President's Secretary Files, Harry S. Truman Library, Independence, Mo. It can also be found in Dennis Merrill, ed., *Documentary History of the Truman Presidency* (Bethesda, Md.: University Publications of America, 2000), XXIX, 55–59.

No doubt you will recall, Mr. President, that during the war Iran collaborated fully and most sincerely with the Allies for the ultimate triumph of right, justice and world freedom, and that she suffered untold hardships and made many sacrifices. During the war all our productive resources were directed day and night to carrying out large-scale plans for the transfer of ammunitions, the supply of foodstuffs and other requirements of the Allied armies. These heavy burdens, borne for several years, disorganized and weakened our finance and economy and brought us up against a series of very grave economic problems, with the result that the labouring classes of this country who had toiled for the Allies throughout the war, were faced with an unbearable rise in prices and wide-spread unemployment.

Had we been left alone, after the termination of war, we could have dealt with the situation brought about by the war, restored normal conditions and managed to move back to the depopulated villages the peasants who had been drawn to war work on roads and in factories, thus improving agriculture.

Had we been given outside help like other countries which suffered from war, we could soon have revived our economy, and even without that help, could have succeeded in our efforts had we not been hampered by the greed of the company and by the activities of its agents.

The company, however, always strove by restricting our income to put us under heavy financial pressure, and by disrupting our organizations to force us to ask its help and, as a consequence, to submit to whatever it desired to force upon us.

Secret agents on the one hand paralysed our reform movements by economic pressure, and on the other hand, on the contention that the country had enormous sources of wealth and oil, prevented us from enjoying the help which was given to other countries suffering from the effects of war.

I ask you in fairness, Mr. President, whether the tolerant Iranian people, who, whilst suffering from all these hardships and desperate privations, have so far withstood all kinds of strong and revolutionary propaganda, without causing any anxiety to the world, are not worthy of praise and appreciation, and whether they had any other alternative but recourse to the nationalization of the oil industry, which will enable them to utilize the natural wealth of their country and will put an end to the unfair activities of the company.

Having thus given a short summary of the motives which have led to nationalization of the oil industry in Iran, I wish to refer you, Mr. President, to the text of the law, and I hope you will agree that the two Houses of the Iranian Parliament have not deviated from the path of right and justice, and that the law, as repeatedly announced from the tribunes of both Houses and in various interviews, does not authorize the confiscation and seizure of property, but on the contrary envisages and gives security for the repayment of damages and losses, and that furthermore, it gives special consideration to the continuation of oil supplies to those countries hitherto using Iranian oil, and explicitly safeguards the viewpoints of former customers.

It is now a month since the law and the method of execution of the principle of the nationalization of the oil industry in Iran were ratified by both Houses of Parliament and received the Royal signature, and, although the law has decreed an immediate dispossession, and the government is under extraordinary pressure from public opinion impatiently demanding the dispossession of the former oil company, the government and the mixed committee appointed by the two Houses of Parliament have given careful study to the means of putting the law into force in the best possible way so that no disruption may occur in the exploitation of oil from the various centers and in the continuity of the flow of export.

The first evidence of the truth of this contention and the good-will of the Imperial Iranian Government is to be found in the provisions which have been communicated to the representatives of the former oil company, the most important of which are mentioned below:

1. So long as the status of the National Iranian Oil Company is not approved by the two Houses of the Iranian Parliament, the basis of operations of the temporary board of directors shall be the regulation devised by the former oil company (except insofar as such regulation [*sic*] are contrary to the law of nationalization of the oil industry).
2. The foreign and Iranian experts, employees and labourers of the former oil company shall remain in service as before, and shall henceforth be recognized as employees of the National Iranian Oil Company.
3. The temporary board of directors will take the utmost care to execute existing programmes and to increase the production of oil so that the level of production and exploitation shall be raised above the present level. . . .

Lastly the former oil company has been given the opportunity to submit immediate proposals, provided they are not contrary to the principle of the nationalization of the oil industry, and the government has promised to consider these proposals.

The aim of the Iranian Government and the mixed committee in adopting the above measures has been the continuation of the flow of oil to the consumer countries—an aim which has been your immediate concern.

You may rest assured, Mr. President, that the Iranian people are desirous of maintaining their friendship with all nations and especially with those, like the British nation, which have had age-long relations with them. . . .

I avail myself of this opportunity to offer to you, Mr. President, the expressions of my highest and most sincere regards and to wish the continuous progress and prosperity of the great American nation.

2. U.S. Ambassador Loy Henderson Questions Mossadeq's Mental Stability, 1952

During last two days I have recd various hints, including one from son, that Mosadeq was ready for me to call. Accordingly, I visited him yesterday evening. Our conversation, which lasted nearly two and half hours, was both exhausting and depressing. As I listened to him I cld not but be discouraged at thought that person

This document can be found in The Ambassador in Iran (Henderson) to the Department of State, 28 July 1952, *Foreign Relations of the United States 1952–1954* (Washington, D.C.: Government Printing Office, 1989), X, 416–421.

so lacking in stability and clearly dominated by emotions and prejudices shld represent only bulwark left between Iran and communism. As during several previous conversations, I had feeling at times that I was talking with someone not quite sane and that therefore he shld be humored rather than reasoned with. On occasions he resorted to such silly exaggerations and extravagances it seemed almost useless to talk further. At one point I almost decided to abandon our conv when he rptd again and again in monotone that "Iran wld never, never want UK and US to have any differences over it. Iran wld prefer go Communist than cause any trouble between US and UK." There were periods during our talk when he seemed lucid and sensible. Gen impression which he left was however one of deterioration. I have noticed in past that in evenings he is likely to be more tired and to have less control over his emotions. I can only hope his behavior last evening was due to strain of recent events and fatigue and does not indicate serious degeneration.

I shall not attempt to outline conversation but will merely touch on those portions which seem to me to be more important and which may enable Dept have better understanding his present frame of mind. . . .

Mosadeq launched into bitter attack upon US foreign policy. He said US had no diplomacy. US in Mid-East was merely agent Brit. Manifestations of anti-Americans as witnessed during recent days had shown how great had been failure so-called US diplomacy in Iran. US had given billion dollars aid to Turkey and yet when Iran was bankrupt and on verge communism, it had refused finan assistance first because it feared that if Iran shld be able operate its own oil industry US oil interests in Saudi Arabia and elsewhere might suffer and, secondly, because it was afraid of Brit displeasure. I told Mosadeq that American interests in internatl oil were really of secondary nature and did not govern our policies re Iran.

Mosadeq said even certain Brit were charging that US, because of fear of effect of US oil concessions in other countries, did not wish Brit to compromise in oil dispute with Iran. I again emphasized that effects of possible settlement on US oil concessions in various parts world did not play major role in our policies re Iran. I added that in any event it did not seem likely that countries in which there were Amer oil concessions wld be tempted follow Iran's example. I had already on various occasions tried to make clear to him it wld not be in interest free world for us to give Iran finan aid in circumstances which might cause Brit and Amer public opinion to believe that US was subsidizing Iran's position re oil dispute. At this point Mosadeq began to chant that Iran wld prefer to go Communist that for US and UN [*UK*] to have differences of opinion with regard to it. Eventually, I was able to tell him that US choice was not merely between US–UK friction and Iran going Communist. I stressed that if serious misunderstandings shld develop in present world situation between US and UK, Iran wld go Communist anyway. . . .

Mosadeq placed great stress on Communist danger facing Iran. He said Iranian army was no longer stabilizing factor. It was now hated by all Iranians. Iranian army, under orders [of former prime minister Ahmad] Qavam, who was Brit agent, had fired on and killed hundreds Iranians. Iranian people, therefore, considered army as tool Brit. I asked Mosadeq if he as MinWar, wld not be able by certain measures restore prestige army. He insisted too late. Nothing cld save army now. In fact, army was now danger to country since many officers and men, humiliated at their present unpopularity, might at any moment try to get back into public favor by taking leadership in revolt of Communist character. This revolt might not be fomented gradually. It might break out at any moment.

I asked Mosadeq if there was anything he cld tell me re future mil aid and mil missions. Various kinds rumors were afloat re his attitude on these subjects. He replied he not prepared to talk to me at present. He wld take matter up later. Any recommendations which might be circulated had no basis. He had not discussed his intention re mil missions and aid with anyone. . . .

Reverting to oil problem Mosadeq described briefly suggestion which he had made to [British Counsellor George] Middleton. He made no request of me and I stated that I was glad that direct conversation on subject had been opened with Brit.

As I was preparing depart, Mosadeq said he hoped I wld not take amiss frankness his comments to me. It had been his practice to talk on personal basis rather than that of PriMin addressing Amb. He believed his country and govt were in great danger and he cld not understand why US, which was supposed to be so friendly to Iran shld not show friendship by action. I told Mosadeq that US was in many ways trying to help Iran. He laughed and said if we were really trying assist by other than words, we were certainly succeeding in hiding our helpful activities.

3. President John F. Kennedy Launches the Peace Corps, 1961

I have today signed an Executive Order providing for the establishment of a Peace Corps on a temporary pilot basis. I am also sending to Congress a message proposing authorization of a permanent Peace Corps. This Corps will be a pool of trained American men and women sent overseas by the U.S. Government or through private institutions and organizations to help foreign countries meet their urgent needs for skilled manpower.

It is our hope to have 500 or more people in the field by the end of the year.

The initial reactions to the Peace Corps proposal are convincing proof that we have, in this country, an immense reservoir of such men and women—anxious to sacrifice their energies and time and toil to the cause of world peace and human progress.

In establishing our Peace Corps we intend to make full use of the resources and talents of private institutions and groups. Universities, voluntary agencies, labor unions and industry will be asked to share in this effort—contributing diverse sources of energy and imagination—making it clear that the responsibility for peace is the responsibility of our entire society.

We will only send abroad Americans who are wanted by the host country— who have a real job to do—and who are qualified to do that job. Programs will be developed with care, and after full negotiation, in order to make sure that the Peace Corps is wanted and will contribute to the welfare of other people. Our Peace Corps

This document can be found in Statement by the President upon Signing Order Establishing Peace Corps, 1 March 1961, *Public Papers of the President: John F. Kennedy, 1961* (Washington, D.C.: Government Printing Office, 1962), 134–135.

is not designed as an instrument of diplomacy or propaganda or ideological conflict. It is designed to permit our people to exercise more fully their responsibilities in the great common cause of world development.

Life in the Peace Corps will not be easy. There will be no salary and allowances will be at a level sufficient only to maintain health and meet basic needs. Men and women will be expected to work and live alongside the nationals of the country in which they are stationed—doing the same work, eating the same food, talking the same language.

But if the life will not be easy, it will be rich and satisfying. For every young American who participates in the Peace Corps—who works in a foreign land—will know that he or she is sharing in the great common task of bringing to man that decent way of life which is the foundation of freedom and a condition of peace.

4. JFK Enlists Youth and Idealism in the Peace Corps, 1961

Photo from Abbie Rowe, National Park Service/John Fitzgerald Kennedy Library, Boston.

5. A Peace Corps Volunteer Describes
Life in Ghana, 1964

What is the reaction of different groups to the Peace Corps volunteers? The students tend to be very much in favor of the volunteers. I have heard of no instances of trouble with anti-American students. On the contrary, they try to emulate you in every way possible. This may manifest itself in a broad American accent, or in an attempt to copy the teacher's mannerisms. They are also interested in any and all things American. American music is extremely popular, especially rock and roll and the twist.

The great majority of Ghanaians also show a great liking for the Americans. I leave the newspapers out of this, because the two party newspapers, the *Evening News* (C.P.P. paper) and the *Ghana Times* (official government paper), tend to take a neutral to pro-Eastern stand on most matters. However, you will find, I think, a great well of good feeling for us here. I must say that the Peace Corps has not hurt this feeling. It certainly has not hurt for us to know some of the Twi language.

The knowledge of their language has a profound effect on the villagers. You don't have to know too much, but if you have the proper answer to a greeting, it raises your prestige a great deal. They will laugh at you but they are proud that you are making the attempt to speak their language. Oh yes, the proper answer to '*Broni*' when it is yelled at you, is '*Bibini.*' This seems to make a big hit, in my area anyway.

As for the British and American communities in Ghana, for the most part you will find them to be very friendly and helpful people. Of course, there is bound to be the individual who makes your hackles rise. There is one Englishman who makes me angry every time I see him, but he has the same effect on the British, so I am not too worried. You will find that this type of person is in a distinct minority. The British tend to be a little distrustful of most Americans, because they tend to raise the cost of living by paying exorbitant prices to workers and traders. This cannot be said of the volunteers, though, as we don't get the salaries other Americans do and have to watch our money fairly carefully.

The Americans have been willing to give us any help we may desire. They are generally a pleasant bunch of people, again with the occasional exception to the rule, and will bend over backwards to make you comfortable. The only people who are hard to get to know are the Russians. There are a great many here, and more are coming. At present, most of them are up north, or in Accra. They travel in groups and talk little, if at all, with anyone outside the group. They are the closest thing I have seen to the so-called Ugly American image.

They are even somber when they go to the Lido. The Lido is a local nightspot which has a bad reputation as a place for pickups. Naturally, this is where all the Peace Corps volunteers go for an evening of high life. Actually, they have a

This document can be found in Iris Luce, ed., *Letters from the Peace Corps* (Washington, D.C.: Robert B. Luce, Inc., 1964), 108–110, 112–113.

fine band, and the drinks are not too expensive. A few other places that are nice to go for drinks and good food are the Star Hotel and the Ambassador. The Glamour gives you fine Indian curry, while the Casanova gives you belly-dancers with your meal.

The biggest dance here is the 'high-life.' Everyone who comes here must learn it. It is akin to West Indian Calypso and entails a mass of bodies shuffling around a cement dance floor. It ruins shoes, but it is fun. If you like, you may learn classical high-life but if you are like me, you learn bush high-life. This is a no-holds-barred type of dance, where you may use any step you like, as long as you remain relatively in step and don't knock anyone down. Oh yes, we also have the twist here. The Ghanaians do it very well, as do most volunteers. Typically, I managed to hurt myself doing the twist, but that will come under the medical section, so I shan't say anymore along that line here. . . .

For those of you who think you are escaping the nine-to-five grind; you are! You work from seven to two. Life does not change as much as you think it will. You are doing a job that requires that you do the same type of work, day after day, through the months that you are here. Life will not be very exotic after the first excitement wears off. There will be the occasional exciting events, but it runs about the same as home.

Looking back over the last eight months, I find that my taste has dulled considerably. Movies that I wouldn't be caught dead seeing in the States help to kill an evening once a week. You also lose contact with all the new trends in books, plays, etc. Then there are the women. In eight months I have seen some remarkable changes in the expatriate and African women nearby. They seem to change for the better every month.

Before I start crying over the typewriter, though, I will move on to the running of your home. If you live alone, in a Ghana Trust house, life is not bad. My house has two bedrooms, a living room, dining room, den, kitchen, bathroom, and toilet.

As far as running the house is concerned, mine seems to run itself. My pay covers the electric bill, water bill, conservancy fees, rent, and a few nonessential luxuries such as food and tobacco. Clothing is no great problem and doesn't cost a great deal. Medical fees are virtually nonexistent.

This leads into the matter of health in Ghana. With all the shots you will be getting, you will probably think that you are entering the nearest thing to the Black Hole of Calcutta. This just does not prove true. I have heard of very few volunteers who have been very sick. Of course, you have your cases of malaria, dengue fever, dysentery, and sand fly fever, but strict adherence to the major rules will make life relatively illness-free.

If you do get sick, Bill C——, the Peace Corps doctor, usually has the remedy. If he doesn't, he at least smiles as he tells you. Seriously, there have been only a few things that have warranted any real notice. One fellow came down with hepatitis— he drank bad water—and was hospitalized for a while, and I have the distinction of having the Ghana Peace Corps' first and second operations. The first one removed a cyst, and the second patched me up after I tore myself open again doing the twist in the Lido.

6. The Commonwealth of Puerto Rico
Plans for Tourism, 1949

Puerto Rico has all the basic requirements for a large scale tourist industry.

Climate   Close to ideal. Sunshine all but four or five days a year. Winter temperatures 68° to 78°, summer 70° to 88° and always cooled by the trade winds. . . .

Beauty   The island has great natural beauty varying from the coastal belt to the mountainous areas, including the two national forests with heights to nearly 5,000 feet. The scenic variety delights visitors and encourages their stay in Puerto Rico. Tropical flowers and fruits abound throughout the year.

Interest   The island is large, 100 miles by 35 miles. The old city of San Juan is outstanding with its 400 year old walls and fortifications. There are numerous old towns and cities around the island with their typical Spanish plazas; the town of San German with Porta Coeli—one of the oldest churches in the Western Hemisphere— is exceptionally interesting; Phosphorescent Bay near La Parguera has been called "unrivalled"; the many activities of the people are of great interest—sugar plantations; coffee fincas, tobacco farms, the salt evaporation marshes, handicrafts. . . .

Activities and Attractions   Attractions and activities suitable to the semi-tropics all exist or can be started. Puerto Rico is ringed by beaches, many of them superlative. There are literally hundreds of miles of beaches. There is good golf; there is tennis; there is magnificent swimming; Puerto Rico is superb for horseback riding; boating is good; and fishing is potentially excellent. There is first class baseball; horse racing on three tracks, cockfighting. Gambling has been legalized for tourist development; there are night clubs, bars and restaurants. Shopping—magnificent embroidered articles and handicrafts.

Transportation   In San Juan—taxis all metered; ample bus service at 5¢ fare. The island has an excellent system of roads, the best in the Caribbean. . . .

Geographical Location   The air hub of the Eastern Caribbean—8–9 hours from New York by DC4; 6–7 hours by Constellation; 5 hours by DC4 from Miami; 4–4½ by Constellation; the easiest point to get to in the Caribbean from main population centers of United States with possible exception of Havana; the nearest place from the New York area where warm winter climate can be assured. . . .

People   The people of Puerto Rico are naturally kind and anxious to assist the visitor. Mayor O'Dwyer, of New York, said: "Puerto Rico is alive with historic interest, beautiful climates from seacoast to mountain tops, pleasant vistas and a hospitable

---

This document can be found in "Puerto Rico's Tourist & Business," Estebán A. Bird (Tourist Advisory Board) to Governor," 17 January 1949, Oficina del Gobernador, Archivo General de Puerto Rico, San Juan, P.R.

people. The tourist looking for a combination of the romantic past and the serious business of modern living will find them both in Puerto Rico." . . .

The Government's Commitment

The Government of Puerto Rico is committed to a policy of developing a major tourist industry. This is part of its program of economic betterment of the island. It is also intended to improve understanding with, and to promote closer cultured ties with the Mainland of the United States.

It has taken positive steps to implement this policy. Among these are:

1. It has created the Tourist Advisory Board which is a part of the Puerto Rico Industrial Development Company. The Board operates through the Office of Tourism. . . .
2. The Government has appropriated $200,000 for the development and promotion expenses of the Board and Office of Tourism during the fiscal year 1948–1949.
3. The present legislature has legalized gambling to promote tourism.
4. Resort hotels are listed among the businesses entitled to 15 year tax exemption in the tax exemption law passed to encourage the industrialization of Puerto Rico. Commercial hotels receive 50% tax exemption on the same basis. . . .

The [Tourism Advisory] Board Has a Long Range and a Short Range Program

There follows here a partial listing of these programs particularly those that are already under way.

1. STAFF—It employed April 1, 1948, J. Stanton Robbins, who has an international reputation in the transportation and travel field extending over the last 25 years. Mr. Robbins has a staff of assistants in the Office of Tourism to implement the Board's program.
2. ACCOMMODATIONS—Places to stay in San Juan and in Puerto Rico are inadequate both in quantity and quality for a large tourist industry. This has been and is one of the Board's chief preoccupations. Here is what has been done.
   a) In cooperation with the Puerto Rico Industrial Development Company the Caribe-Hilton Hotel is being built—300 rooms—all air conditioned—in an ideal location with its own beach and sea-side swimming pool—twelve acres of grounds—in the middle of San Juan. It will open in late 1949 under Hilton management at [the government's] cost of over $5,000,000. It will be the finest hotel in the Caribbean.
   b) The Board has approved a short range program which includes the improvement and enlargement of existing hotels in Puerto Rico. . . .

   The Board's longer range programs envisions 3,500 hotel rooms in Puerto Rico by 1960 (2,500 in San Juan) accommodating over 6,000 visitors at one time. For projects approved by the Board financial assistance in the form of loans or participation by local capital are [*sic*] often possible. . . .

i) The Board has cooperated with Eastern Air Lines and Tramp Trips in developing a special all expense trip covering Puerto Rico, the Dominican Republic and the Virgin Islands.

j) The Transportation Authority and the Board are working together to make the new passenger terminal at the Isla Grande airport an attractive "front door" to Puerto Rico.

7. Modernity Goes on Display: San Juan's Caribe Hilton Hotel, 1949

Photo from Conrad N. Hilton Collection, Hospitality Industry Archives, University of Houston, Houston, Texas.

8. A Puerto Rican Cartoon Satirizes U.S. Tourists, 1960

Courtesy of Claridad/Latin American Collection, Doe Library, University of California, Berkeley, CA.

ESSAYS

In the first essay, Mary Ann Heiss of Kent State University examines how cultural perceptions, especially gender-based views of Iran's prime minister Mohammed Mossadeq, influenced the U.S. response to the Anglo-Iranian oil controversy, 1951–1953. According to Heiss, the Iranian's manner of attire (especially his practice of wearing pajamas in daytime), his political passion, and his public display of tears marked the prime minister as effeminate and unstable by Western standards. U.S. and British officials also used gender-coded language that described Mossadeq with words commonly associated with females in masculine Western culture: *moody, impractical,* and *unrealistic.* Heiss concludes that gendered perceptions of Mossadeq buttressed claims of Western superiority over Iranian and other Middle East peoples, undergirded Washington's pro-British stand in the oil dispute, and justified the Anglo-American overthrow of Mossadeq in 1953.

Whereas Heiss's study highlights the perils of culture clash, the second essay by Elizabeth Cobbs Hoffman of San Diego State University, concludes that President Kennedy's Peace Corps promoted cross-cultural cooperation. Her examination of the Peace Corps in Ghana, an excerpt from her book *All You Need Is Love: The Peace Corps and the Spirit of the 1960s,* concludes that the innovative program overcame the political reservations of Ghana's left-leaning nationalist president, Kwame Nkrumah, and fostered a positive image of the United States. The Peace Corps proved successful in Ghana because Nkrumah's government prioritized education, as did Peace Corps leaders and volunteers. Ghanaian culture, moreover, prized community-wide cooperation and did not shun outside aid. Peace Corps volunteers derived satisfaction from the effort because they were assigned well-structured responsibilities as teachers and demon-strated a willingness to know and respect another culture.

In the final selection, Dennis Merrill of the University of Missouri-Kansas City, ex-plores how international tourists and their hosts negotiate cultural differences. Focusing on Puerto Rico, Merrill depicts the travel boom of the early Cold War as a manifestation of modernity, which he defines as the main cultural direction for global development. While visitors and hosts clashed over their cultural differences—class, language, race, and sexuality—each group negotiated benefits from tourism. The commonwealth government planned and regulated the trade to serve Puerto Rico's economic and cul-tural interests. U.S. officials and tourists perceived Puerto Rico not only as a tourist mecca but as a model for noncommunist development and modernization in the tumultuous Caribbean region.

Culture Clash: Gender, Oil, and Iranian Nationalism

MARY ANN HEISS

Between 1951 and 1953, Iran struggled to gain control of its oil industry—and the considerable wealth it generated—from the British-owned Anglo-Iranian Oil Com-pany (AIOC). The AIOC and its predecessor, the Anglo-Persian Oil Company (APOC), had run Iran's oil industry since the first decade of the twentieth century. During the First World War, the British government had purchased a large amount of APOC stock, and by the time of the oil crisis it held slightly more than half—or a controlling interest—in that company's successor. The relationship between the Iranian government and the oil company was never particularly harmonious. Finan-cial arrangements, especially the relatively low level of royalties the company paid to Iran, the almost total lack of Iranians in high-ranking positions within the com-pany, and the overall aura of secrecy that pervaded the company's operations, led to Iranian discontent. Added to these practical complaints was the growing sense of Iranian nationalism after the Second World War. Nationalism, rather than simply a desire for greater oil revenues, motivated Iranian policy and sustained that policy when its fruits proved bitter. It helps to explain why Iran wanted Britain to abandon its exclusive control of the Iranian oil industry and why the Iranians persisted in spite of tremendous economic hardship. . . .

The Anglo-Iranian oil dispute seemed irresolvable from the start. Each side saw the conflict through the prism of its own history and perspective, and neither showed much willingness to compromise. The AIOC and the British Foreign Office empha-sized legal issues, denied that Iran had the right to nationalize its oil industry, and sought to protect the considerable British financial stake in Iranian oil. Between 1945

"Culture Clash: Gender, Oil, and Iranian Nationalism," excerpted from Mary Ann Heiss, "Real Men Don't Wear Pajamas: Anglo-American Cultural Perceptions of Mohammed Mossadeq and the Iranian Oil Nationalization Debate," in Peter Hahn and Mary Ann Heiss, eds., *Empire and Revolution: The United States and the Third World Since 1945* (Columbus: Ohio State University Press, 2001), pp. 178–191. Copyright © 2001 by Ohio State University Press. Reprinted with permission.

and 1950, the AIOC earned £250 million from its Iranian operations. Iran's oil fields provided Britain with twenty-two million tons of oil products and seven million tons of crude oil annually, including 85 percent of the fuel needed by the British Admiralty. In other words, the British position stressed the company's value as an economic asset of great importance and the contribution that the AIOC made to Britain's overall Middle Eastern and world position. For British officials, this last consideration was paramount, as the crux of the matter for them was the danger that Iranian nationalization posed to their nation's status as a great power. As Britain's largest overseas investment, the refinery at Abadan and the AIOC's Iranian operations symbolized Britain's power in the Middle East. Losing control of these assets would be a deadly blow to British prestige the world over, especially considering Britain's recent withdrawals from India and Palestine. It might also imperil other British holdings around the world, foremost among them the Suez Canal. At a time when British policy makers were keenly aware of their diminishing status as a global power, it is not surprising that they were sensitive to anything that might undermine their position in Iran, particularly surrendering control of the nation's oil industry to the Iranians. . . .

By way of contrast, the Iranian stance during the oil dispute stressed politics and national independence. Although Iranian nationalists complained bitterly about the relatively small profits they received from the AIOC's Iranian operations—their royalties between 1945 and 1950 totaled only £90 million, slightly more than one-third of what the AIOC earned from its Iranian operations—what most galled them was the imperious way the company used its oil concession to dominate and control their nation almost as a colony. Convinced that the AIOC and the British government had interfered in Iran's internal affairs for decades by bribing legislators, influencing elections, and essentially holding the country hostage financially, nationalists like Prime Minister Mohammed Mossadeq asserted that such interference would stop only after Iran had gained control of its rich oil holdings. Mossadeq was ultimately willing to make concessions on price, production levels, and other technical details, but he would not budge on the central point that operational control of the oil industry had to rest in Iranian hands. Unless British officials were willing to concede that point, the prime minister was prepared to see his nation's oil industry shut down. "Tant pis pour nous. Too bad for us," was his usual response when Anglo-American officials warned him that his refusal to reach a resolution of the oil dispute might shut down the industry. . . .

It was the inability of the British and the Iranians to resolve the oil dispute on their own that ultimately brought the United States into the conflict. U.S. officials saw the oil crisis as [a] potentially destabilizing force in Iran—and perhaps throughout the entire Middle East—that could lead to communist advances and provide the Soviets with an inroad to the oil-rich Persian Gulf. As the only direct land barrier between the Soviet Union and the Persian Gulf, Iran served as a vital link in the Western security chain; Soviet control of its territory would make the defense of Greece, Turkey, and the eastern Mediterranean all but impossible. Compounding Iran's importance were its rich oil reserves, which U.S. officials considered crucial to the reconstruction and rearmament of Western Europe. Loss of these resources would have dire consequences. In the short term, it would create serious shortages of aviation gasoline and other fuels needed for the military effort in Korea and would raise the specter of civilian rationing in the United States and throughout the West. In the long term it might compromise the West's ability to fight a protracted war with the Soviets, force augmentation of its military establishments, and result in an expansion of Soviet military bases in the Middle East.

Initially, the Truman administration acted as an honest broker in the search for a settlement that paid lip service to the idea of nationalization but also recognized the contractual rights of the AIOC. On the one hand, U.S. policy makers called for a firm, commercially acceptable agreement that did not set a dangerous precedent or encourage nationalization elsewhere. On the other, they advocated a flexible approach to the nationalization dispute that would make a settlement possible before Iran collapsed internally or succumbed to Soviet penetration. To this end, President Harry S. Truman and his secretary of state, Dean Acheson, lobbied for concessions from both sides, warning that "too much 'take'" on the part of the Iranians was as dangerous as "too little 'give'" on the part of the British.

As the dispute dragged on, however, and as the chance of destabilization in Iran became increasingly likely, officials in the Truman administration abandoned their middle-of-the-road stance and decided to prop up the British position in Iran, just as they were doing in Egypt and would soon do for the French in Indochina. By the summer of 1952, Truman went so far as to join British Prime Minister Winston S. Churchill in a joint Anglo-American proposal to Mossadeq that wedded the U.S. government to the British position in Iran. President Dwight D. Eisenhower and Secretary of State John Foster Dulles continued this pro-British position when they assumed office in January 1953, ultimately joining the British in a covert operation against Mossadeq late that summer. Administration officials justified this coup as necessary to save Iran from communism. The prolonged oil crisis was beginning to take its toll on the Iranian economy, and economic dislocation was spawning mass demonstrations that U.S. officials feared would grow into full-scale revolution. Making matters worse, Mossadeq was forging closer ties with the Communist Tudeh Party and moving his country closer to the Soviet Union through new trade agreements. He was even threatening to sell Iranian oil to the Soviet Union and its satellites. In truth, Mossadeq was a staunch anticommunist who hoped such moves would win U.S. assistance for his financially strapped government. Given the anticommunist hysteria of the early 1950s, however, officials in Washington could not easily dismiss the prime minister's apparent flirtation with communism. . . .

In addition to collaborating to remove Mossadeq from office, over the course of the oil dispute, Anglo-American officials came to a common way of looking at Mossadeq that used many of his personal characteristics, habits, and negotiating tactics, as well as some of his policy positions themselves, to justify a view of him as unmanly and unfit for office. Because Anglo-American officials did not view Mossadeq as their equal, they found it easy to dismiss him as an unworthy adversary whose position did not matter. Although these Anglo-American conceptions and descriptions of Mossadeq were not the sole, or even the most important, factor influencing policy, they deserve scholarly consideration because they helped to shape the context within which officials formulated policy. They buttressed claims of Western superiority over Iranian and other Middle Eastern peoples by perpetuating the idea that those peoples were weak and incapable. And their cumulative effect was to paint Mossadeq and others like him in unfavorable ways that rationalized and justified Western control. . . .

The analysis presented in this essay . . . postulates that Anglo-American officials joined to formulate a gender-based view of Mossadeq that denigrated him for departing from what they considered to be acceptable Western norms and that worked against their stated goal of seeking a resolution to the vexing oil imbroglio. It should not be construed as a complete picture of the Iranian oil crisis, and it certainly does not purport to be the only way of looking at what happened in Iran during the early 1950s. On the contrary, it utilizes the concepts of gender and culture as tools for examining the oil crisis in new ways.

When *Time* magazine designated Mossadeq as its 1951 Man of the Year, it proclaimed the Iranian prime minister to be "by Western standards an appalling caricature of a statesman." "His tears, his tantrums," and "his grotesque antics" led the magazine to dub Mossadeq a "dizzy old wizard" who "put Scheherazade in the petroleum business" by nationalizing the Anglo-Iranian Oil Company in the spring of 1951. *Time*'s editors accurately reflected the prevailing sentiment in the West and unknowingly echoed what British and U.S. government officials had been telling each other for quite some time. Influenced by long-standing stereotypes that justified Western superiority and sought to maintain Western control, Anglo-American policy makers consistently employed what Edward Said has termed "Orientalism" when dealing with Mossadeq, whom they considered inferior, childlike, and feminine. They often referred to him with gendered language that revealed their conviction that he was neither manly enough for international politics nor fit to hold the office of prime minister. They condemned as unacceptable examples of Mossadeq's unmanliness what were accepted forms of behavior in Iran, failed to see Mossadeq as their equal, and dismissed him as an unworthy adversary whose position did not matter. . . . The end result of the Orientalization of Mossadeq was an increasingly rigid Anglo-American position on the oil crisis that eschewed compromise or concessions and ultimately saw removing him from office as the only acceptable course of action.

Anglo-American officials found Mossadeq different from themselves in many ways, and these differences affected the way they dealt with him during his premiership. One startling difference concerned the way the prime minister dressed and his preferred place of conducting business. Because of his age and poor health, Mossadeq usually worked from his bed while dressed in pajamas, thereby presenting Anglo-American officials with a situation so strange that they took to including the color of his pajamas in their reports home. Some days, in fact, they noted that the prime minister wore two sets of pajamas on top of each other—khaki and green one day, blue and khaki another. Officials also thought it significant to note, sometimes with veiled sarcasm, those occasions when Mossadeq was up and about. U.S. ambassador Loy Henderson, for example, described one meeting in which Mossadeq "received me fully dressed (not pajama clad) as though for [a] ceremonial occasion." Officials from the International Bank for Reconstruction and Development, who went to Iran seeking to arrange an oil settlement in 1952, made the same point by expressing shock one day to find the prime minister "alert" and "on his feet." On another occasion they were astonished that Mossadeq actually "got out of bed, put on his slippers, and escorted us to the hall," as if the prime minister and his iron-framed bed had somehow become conjoined. The cultural assumptions behind such remarks are clear: Real leaders are expected to wear suits or other professional attire when conducting business, not pajamas, and they are expected to conduct their business from an upright position, not while reclining in their beds. Never mind that Winston Churchill often wore pajamas and worked from his bed. That Mossadeq did so marked him as an "eccentric" at best, a "lunatic" at worst, and contributed to a mounting Anglo-American conviction that what Mossadeq had to say from his bed was unimportant.

Another thing that U.S. and British officials had difficulty dealing with was what they termed Mossadeq's "fragile" and "emotional" temperament. On many occasions throughout his premiership, Mossadeq became teary eyed when speaking of the plight of the Iranian people, sometimes during private discussions, sometimes during public appearances. In part, these outbursts were genuine reflections of his outrage at the sufferings wrought upon the Iranians by the "evil" Anglo-Iranian Oil Company. In part, though, these episodes were carefully choreographed plays to the balcony designed to garner important popular support for the prime minister during the long and economically devastating oil crisis. Anglo-American officials did not give enough credence to the possibility that Mossadeq's tears might have stemmed from something other than uncontrolled emotionalism. To them, they were signs of weakness and effeminacy that diminished Mossadeq's standing as a statesman and absolved them of the responsibility of dealing with him as an equal.

Mossadeq's tears were not the only thing that made him feminine in Western eyes. The prime minister also displayed a host of other traits that earned him the opprobrium of officials in the Foreign Office and State Department and that yielded descriptions thick with gender-coded language. He was "moody," "impractical," and "unrealistic," they said. He lacked the capacity "to carry on complicated negotiations for any length of time in a single direction." He had a tendency "to change his mind, to forget, to become confused." He approached "international politics from [an] emotional point of view" rather than from a "rational" one. All of these descriptions painted Mossadeq in feminine terms and seemed to brand him unworthy of playing the role of an international statesman. Sometimes Anglo-American officials even went beyond simply gender-coded language to explicit and obvious characterization, as when they railed against the prime minister's "negative and feminine [negotiating] tactics." This description came during the failed mission of British Lord Privy Seal Sir Richard Stokes to arrange an oil settlement during the summer of 1952 and apparently meant that like most women, Mossadeq had trouble making up his mind, sought to avoid final decisions, and always wanted something better. The cumulative result of such characterizations was the conclusion that Mossadeq was an irrational and fickle adversary who was prone to emotional outbursts, often changed his mind, and could not be trusted. It seemed to follow that any permanent, realistic settlement required his removal from office and the appointment of a more reasonable and reliable prime minister.

Many of Mossadeq's policies contributed to Western descriptions of him as weak and incapable. By eschewing the economic gains that would come from a compromise settlement and insisting on total Iranian control of the oil industry, even if that meant operating at a reduced output, Mossadeq saw himself as safeguarding his nation's independence against the rapacious imperialism of the West. Anglo-American officials, however, saw things differently. For them, such a stance was further proof of Mossadeq's simple mind and unfitness for office. . . .

Mossadeq's effort to steer a middle course in the Cold War, which at the time took the name of "negative equilibrium," also made him look weak in Western eyes. Such a course turned the traditional Iranian policy of playing the Great Powers against each other on its head by proclaiming instead that no foreign power should have influence in Iran. As the prime minister saw it, what would later come to be called "nonalignment" was the only way to protect Iran from the kind of interference that the AIOC had practiced throughout Iran and thereby to ensure the attainment of the nation's true independence. For U.S. officials, though, refusing to stand with the West against the communist menace was unmanly, even perfidious. In the "if you're not with us you're against us" climate that characterized the early 1950s, especially once the Republicans returned to power in 1953, Mossadeq's neutralism only further confirmed suspicions that his regime was leading Iran toward disaster.

Also telling were the frequent Anglo-American references to Mosasdeq's child-ishness and immaturity and the attendant assumption that the West needed to save Iran from his unrealistic and naive policies. The prime minister was called "insolent" and "intransigent" when he refused to accept British and U.S. plans for resolving the oil crisis, and during negotiations he allegedly had to be "humored" like "a frac-tious child." In contrast to the British, who had been "'saints'" throughout the oil crisis, Mossadeq had "'been the naughty boy'" who needed to be disciplined. Such descriptions were dripping with the arrogance and superiority of Western colonial-ism and are perfect examples of the Orientalist thinking that pervaded Western policy-making circles. . . .

Anglo-American officials used yet another category of descriptors to denigrate and dismiss Mossadeq: the language of psychology and mental illness. The docu-mentary record on the oil crisis is replete with references to Mossadeq as "crazy," "sick," "mad," "hysterical," "neurotic," "demented," "periodically unstable," and "not quite sane." Because he was "suspicious" and "entirely impervious to reason," the ordinary rules [of] logic" were useless when dealing him. In the discourse of the 1950s, terms like *hysterical* and *neurotic* were usually reserved for females, and their use in this context reflects an Anglo-American proclivity to see Mossadeq as femi-nine as well as demented—and indeed to link the two, to consider Mossadeq's sup-posed effeminacy and his apparent mental illness as part and parcel of the same problem and to see both as reasons for dismissing him and what he had to say. Anglo-American references to Mossadeq's mental state also reflected a tendency by British and U.S. officials to practice pop psychology on the prime minister, to ascribe to him medical conditions they were certainly not qualified to diagnose, and to use those diagnoses to justify their refusal to take what he said seriously. "If Mr. Mossadiq is as mad as he seems," they concluded, talking and reasoning with him were futile. These characterizations of Mossadeq as mentally ill continued through the planning for the coup that ultimately overthrew him: Secretary of State John Foster Dulles reportedly exclaimed, "So this is how we get rid of that madman Mossadegh" when the opera-tion was laid out for him in June 1953. Mossadeq's "madness," it seemed, truly was grounds for the Anglo-American operation against him.

Finally, Anglo-American officials revealed their cultural biases when describ-ing Iranian society and the Iranian people in general. Mossadeq's supporters were termed little more than "mad and suicidal . . . lemmings" who needed to be saved from their folly by Western benevolence. It was difficult to negotiate an agreement with Tehran because of "characteristic defects in the Persian mode of conducting business." And any thought that the Iranians could operate the Abadan refinery in the absence of British technicians was roundly dismissed by Averell Harriman, sent by President Truman to arrange an oil settlement in the summer of 1951, as "lunacy."

Anglo-American officials also wrote often about the "Iranian mentality" and the "Oriental mind," vague, undefined terms that became all-too-easy rationalizations for the failure to reach an acceptable oil agreement and prevented Western officials from searching for the real root of the impasse in oil talks. Blaming the inability to reach a settlement on inherent differences between the Iranians and themselves offered Anglo-American officials what they considered an honorable way to escape responsibility for the continued stalemate. It wasn't their fault there was no oil agreement; the fault lay with the Iranians, whose way of thinking was so different from the Anglo-American one that no settlement was possible. . . .

In characterizing Mossadeq as feminine and incapable, Anglo-American officials made two serious mistakes. One was their failure to recognize that Iranian standards of acceptable and normal behavior differed greatly from those that prevailed in the West. Whereas Mossadeq's tears symbolized weakness and emotionalism to them, for the Iranian people they were proof of Mossadeq's deep concern for the welfare of the country, concern that was so strong that he was driven to tears when he thought about the plight of his fellow countrymen. Whereas his proclivity to conduct business from his bed while dressed in pajamas proved his quirkiness to Westerners, for the Iranians these things were, as Andrew F. Westwood has noted, "deeply symbolic . . . of their personal plight and that of their nation, symbolic of the frailty of righteousness beset by powerful forces of evil." And whereas his fainting spells were for the Anglo-Americans something to mock and laugh about, they were the kinds of public displays of emotion and feeling that Iranians expected from a leader. In other words, the Iranian people found nothing wrong with Mossadeq's behavior. On the contrary, they respected and admired him for being so concerned about the plight of his nation that he was driven to faint and cry about it.

Anglo-American officials also erred by not giving enough weight to the possibility that Mossadeq's emotionalism might have been intentional, something he employed to serve his own ends: Maybe he fainted and cried on purpose. In fact, there is evidence to suggest that this is precisely what the prime minister did. The best example of the depth of Mossadeq's theatrical talent came from a Majlis deputy who related the following personal experience. One day during an emotional speech on the floor of the Majlis, Mossadeq collapsed in a heap. Fearing that the elderly premier had suffered a heart attack, the deputy, who also happened to be a medical doctor, rushed to check Mossadeq's pulse, when he expected to find weak and fluttering. He was quite surprised when it was strong and regular, and even more surprised when the prime minister opened one eye and winked at him, as if to say, "My trick has worked. You were taken in, and so were the others. I have won you over." . . .

Like all of us, policy makers in London and Washington judged others, including Mossadeq, in relation to how they saw themselves. They developed in their own minds standards of acceptable behavior, action, and appearance and used these standards as a yardstick to measure others. Those who met the minimum were respected as equals; those who did not were denigrated and dismissed. As scholars such as Carol Cohn and Emily Rosenberg have noted, these standards consisted largely of opposing pairs of traits and behaviors with the positive element of each pair denoting acceptable (or Western) norms and the negative element signifying unacceptable (or Other) norms. For Westerners, the positive traits were coded as male, the negative traits as female. Thus, in the pairs "strong and weak," rational and irrational," and "realistic and emotional," "strong," "rational," and "realistic" were seen as male, and therefore desirable, traits, while "weak," "irrational," and "emotional" were seen as female, and therefore undesirable, traits.

In the case of Mossadeq, everything he did fed Western perceptions of him as weak and unmanly, which in turn made it much easier for Anglo-American officials to discount his position—and that of his country. Because Mossadeq neither looked nor acted like a Western leader and refused to kow-tow to Western pressures for continued control of Iran's oil industry, he was described as an irrational lunatic unfit to hold the office of prime minister. . . .

Assessing the immediate influence of Western characterizations of Mossadeq on the formulation of Anglo-American policy is tricky because it is not possible to determine a direct causal relationship between Anglo-American perceptions and prejudices and specific events. We cannot say, for example, that Western stereotypes led linearly to the coup that removed Mossadeq from office in the summer of 1953. But this does not mean that these stereotypes were unimportant. On the contrary, by shaping the mind-set of Anglo-American officials, they were part of the context within which those officials formulated policy. They buttressed claims of Western superiority over Iranian and other Middle Eastern peoples by perpetuating the idea that those peoples were weak and incapable. And their cumulative effect was to paint Mossadeq and others like him in unfavorable ways that rationalized and justified Western control.

The British and U.S. officials charged with negotiating an oil settlement with Mossadeq were probably not aware of the role cultural perceptions played in circumscribing their ability to reach such a settlement. But as this essay has demonstrated, those perceptions did constitute important obstacles to a negotiated resolution of the oil crisis on terms that Western officials would have considered acceptable. To be sure, there were many other contexts surrounding the oil crisis besides gender and culture—the East-West Cold War, Anglo-American relations, and decolonization and the rise of Third World nationalism, to name only three—and each of these contexts provided its own obstacles to an acceptable oil agreement. But in seeking a complete understanding of the Anglo-Iranian oil crisis, and especially the reasons why resolution proved so difficult, scholars should not discount the role of cultural perceptions. . . .

Without question, Mossadeq committed his own errors of perception. He misread the willingness of U.S. officials to come to Iran's assistance in its struggle against Britain, the difficulties of selling nationalized oil on the open market, and the degree of British opposition to surrendering control of Iranian oil. He also miscalculated the usefulness of communism as a way to win U.S. support. But of much greater consequence were the misperceptions of British and U.S. officials about Mossadeq—that he was senile, mentally unbalanced, and unfit for office. Because key U.S. Foreign Service officers had little understanding of Iranian history, culture, or tradition, they did not appreciate the role that emotion or public tears played in the political culture of Iran or why Mossadeq might have worn pajamas and worked from his bed. Instead of taking Mossadeq on his own terms, Western leaders chose to judge him according to their own standards and to dismiss him when he failed to measure up to expectations. This tendency was not unique to Iran, of course, but applied throughout the world's developing countries. It reflected an Anglo-American sense of cultural superiority over developing world leaders who sought to maintain their nations' independence and helps to explain why the Anglo-Iranian oil crisis, which was at its heart a North-South conflict, ultimately proved so difficult to resolve.

Cultural Cooperation: The Peace Corps in Ghana

ELIZABETH COBBS HOFFMAN

Beginning in 1958, Ghanaians requested help with a national commitment of their own: to make better use of their own human resources and to diminish through a national system of education the kinds of tribal rivalries that in the past had fed the slave trade and that thirty years later would make Rwanda a symbol of genocide. In the four decades since independence this commitment has been imperfectly realized, but the extent to which it has been is due to important part to the convergence of the free world and African goals that brought [President] Kwame Nkrumah together with the Peace Corps. . . .

Since winning its independence peacefully in 1957, the government of the former Gold Coast had promoted the slogan it used against the British, "Self Government Now," throughout colonial Africa. More than a dozen new nations emerged in the following three years, and they looked admiringly to Ghana as a model. Recognized by the United States as "the then leading spokesman for African nationalism," President Kwame Nkrumah also headed the continental movement for African unity, confering regularly with other independence leaders such as Sekou Touré of Guinea, Julius Nyerere of Tanganyika, and Patrice Lumumba of the Congo. . . .

The ten years he had spent as a student in the United States, from 1935 to 1945, gave Nkrumah a unique perspective. His first-hand experience of American segregation encouraged a race-consciousness (including exposure to the ideas of Marcus Ga[r]vey and W. E. B. Du Bois) he might otherwise not have attained. But while certain experiences rankled (such as being shown to the garden hose when he asked for a drink in a restaurant), others inspired him. Nkrumah, like many other Ghanaians, admired what the United States had made of itself since independence from Britain. "Forget about slavery," one early education officer later said; "we knew that Americans had struggled to achieve." Ghanaians also recognized America's historic resistance to Britain. . . .

Nkrumah also admired the American schooling system, in which he had studied for his bachelor's and doctoral degrees in education. Nkrumah was unusual in this respect, since at the time most Ghanaians considered the British school system far superior to the American. His close companion Kojo Botsio later attested that Nkrumah believed that when it came to practical training, "You couldn't beat America." Nkrumah himself wrote in an article for the Penn State University journal of education in 1943 that "the colonial school program of Africa . . . should give way to a new process of training and educating in life and current social, political, technical, and economic ideals now in vogue in progressive schools in America, China, and Russia."

This reference to the trio of "America, China, and Russia," then allies in World War II, foreshadowed the most important source of conflict between Ghana and the United States following independence. From the start, when Nkrumah with British approval invited China to attend Ghana's independence day celebrations instead of

---

Taiwan, the United States objected to the sympathies of his government, which formally adopted socialism in 1962. Nkrumah, however, wanted to be free to pick and choose what he thought best in each system: for example, American education and technology and Russian economic planning. In the context of the cold war, however, that meant playing the Americans against the Russians and vice versa to obtain aid from both. . . .

When the first Peace Corps volunteers stepped off the Pan Am prop jet on August 30, 1961, wearing summer suits and light cotton dresses, the steamy, wood-smoke-tinged air of Accra signaled their arrival in a place far, far from home. The . . . minister of education . . . waited on the sizzling black tarmac with other dignitaries to greet them. Quietly forming themselves into a group, the volunteers sang as best they could the Ghanaian national anthem "Yen Ara Asaasa Ni" (This Is Our Homeland) in Twi, the local language they had studied. A gesture that appeared corny and inept to a later, more bruised generation of Americans struck Ghanaians as original and heartfelt—which is undoubtedly how it was meant at the time. Radio Ghana taped the performance and aired it repeatedly. Years later a Ghanaian associate of the Peace Corps program called it "a singular gesture of friendship, goodwill and understanding which . . . more than any official statement could convey, signaled to Ghanaians and to the world the deep respect and concern that the very first group of volunteers had for the people of the first country it was to serve." . . .

By American standards, and by the British standards that Ghana's Ministry of Education struggled to maintain, the majority of Peace Corps teachers were not qualified for the job. Most were neither education majors nor majors in the fields they were assigned to teach. But by the standards of Ghana's secondary schools, the volunteers were far better qualified than the local peer instructor alternative. The teachers were needed, and their willingness to try scaling the cultural barrier—to sing in Twi, as it were—was deeply appreciated. But perhaps the strongest proof of the value that members of the government placed on Peace Corps volunteers was the fact that Kwame Nkrumah never asked them to leave.

The government of Ghana had accepted word for word the Peace Corps contract presented by the American ambassador, with one amendment: "The Peace Corps program in Ghana may be terminated by either government ninety days after the date of written notification of such intent." Nkrumah made it clear that the Peace Corps would not be tolerated if volunteers sought to have a political effect or tried to "propagandize or spy or . . . subvert the Ghanaian system." The minister of Nigeria commented, when pressed by U.S. officials to commit to the program, that it was "naive to assume that for a government to invite the Peace Corps into its country was not a political act." For Kwame Nkrumah, under whom 93 percent of the National Assembly voted for socialism and one-party rule in 1962, this "political act" contradicted his economic policy at the same time that it moved forward his educational policy. It contradicted as well the trend of his foreign policy, which became increasingly cool toward the United States.

Answerable only to himself once "insults" of the "Osagyefo" were outlawed in 1961, Nkrumah never had to resolve these contradictions to anyone's satisfaction but his own. The result was that he kept the Peace Corps, even praised it, while taking steps to minimize its potential to stir dissent. At first, Nkrumah welcomed the volunteers enthusiastically. He gave them a party on arrival at which, one volunteer later recalled, "he danced with us and taught us the 'high life,'" then a popular dance step. On the following New Year's Day, without mentioning the Peace Corps by name, the president broadcast to the nation his expectation that Ghanaians would embrace volunteers who had "left homes and friends to come work among us." Ghana, he noted, had "invited [them] here to assist us to develop our country. . . . Those who have such a spirit deserve our co-operation and support in all they do for the good of the nation, and we should do nothing to discourage them." . . .

Nkrumah's satisfaction with the Peace Corps could also be seen through the press, controlled by the government. Yaw Agyeman-Badu has noted in his research comparing attitudes toward the United States in Ghana and Nigeria from 1960 to 1977 that Nkrumah's pan-African, socialist policies constantly "put him at variance" with American policies toward Africa. The only aspect of U.S. policy toward either Africa or third world development given even "neutral" press coverage in the Nkrumah years was the Peace Corps.

Agyeman-Badu's assessment of the press coverage as generally "neutral," rather than actually "favorable" up until the president's overthrow in 1966, reflects Nkrumah's growing suspicion after 1962 that the Peace Corps was a front for the Central Intelligence Agency. "Nkrumah was made to believe," according to K. B. Asante, "that many of them were CIA agents. Therefore he became very cool." Rumors of a link between the CIA and Peace Corps persisted for decades in many countries, and could at times approach the absurd—as when soldiers in Zaire confiscated one volunteer's maps of Africa and then examined a tampon from another one's suitcase. ("They dropped it like a hot potato when they found out what it was for," a compatriot wryly noted.) Such misgivings were natural considering the infamy of the agency's covert techniques. In the pursuit of victory in the cold war, the United States would stop at nothing to beat the Soviet Union, third world countries well understood. Even though the Ghanaian government never uncovered any evidence of CIA infiltration of the Peace Corps, and members of the regime later concluded that it had likely never occurred, in 1963 a suspicious Nkrumah took steps to counter the volunteers' influence.

One step was to bar the Peace Corps from teaching English and history. Nkrumah pointedly did not extend the restriction to Canadian volunteers. According to George Ayi-Bonte, an associate director of the Ghana Peace Corps program for twenty years, some of the Americans had been using George Orwell's *Animal Farm* in their classes and members of the government got wind of it. Peace Corps country director George Carter never knew, however, what precisely made Nkrumah believe that the volunteers had overstepped the bounds of math, science, and "neutral" English language instruction. . . .

Why did Kwame Nkrumah never expel the Peace Corps, which he thought might be CIA-infiltrated, as neighboring Guinea did when it was annoyed with U.S. policies? Perhaps because, as one of the volunteers suspended from teaching English said, "If it were really thought we were 'agents' of the C.I.A. type, I don't think we would be in Ghana at all." But the most important reason was probably just that the Peace Corps was too helpful. . . .

A Peace Corps proverb in the sixties, often repeated by veterans, was that volunteers who went to Asia came back meditating, volunteers who went to Latin America came back as revolutionaries, and volunteers who went to Africa came back laughing.

Volunteers in Africa left "laughing" for various reasons, and one of them is the attitude expressed by the proverbs of the Africans themselves. As the scholar Kwame Gyekye has observed, the philosophy of the Akan (a collection of tribes encompassing the Ashanti, among others) has been handed down to each generation through proverbs that are both spoken and printed. The proverbs are guides to personal and collective behavior, reinforcing the values esteemed by the Akan. Chief among them is care of the family and the community. This value led many African villages to embrace young volunteers as one of their own turning odd-looking "obroni" (whites) into members of the community addressed as "brother" and "sister." . . .

The cultural traditions of Ghana, in particular, made for a hospitable environment. "Within the framework of Akan social and humanistic ethics," according to Gyekye, "what is morally good is generally that which promotes social welfare, solidarity, and harmony in human relationships." This emphasis on collectivity and reciprocity, rather than individuality and autonomy, was expressed in proverbs such as "the left arm washes the right arm and the right arm washes the left arm," and "man is not a palm tree that he should be . . . self-sufficient." For volunteers, this meant entering into a society that welcomed, accepted, and cared for them as members of a community quite unlike the industrialized societies from which they had come. One volunteer later summed up an experience common to many: "I was well looked after by concerned Ghanaian friends. One of the most remarkable and wonderful characteristics of the Ghanaian people is the way they look after their guests."

The other aspect of Ghanaian communalism that enhanced the volunteer experience was the cultural openness to "help." Ironically, the volunteers themselves came from a cultural context where the need to be helped was frequently interpreted as a sign of weakness or insufficiency. Symbols like the frontiersman bespoke a cultural admiration for "going it alone," for helping others, perhaps, but not needing help oneself—for being, in the words of Ralph Waldo Emerson, "self-reliant." Fortunately for the Peace Corps, the cultural ethos in Ghana was nearly the opposite.

Akan philosophy, while recognizing that not everyone contributed equally to society, still asserted the necessity, dignity, and rights of each member. "The fingers of the hand are not equal in length," one proverb said, complemented by the related saying, "One finger cannot lift up a thing." In Ghanaian society, gift giving and mutual aid were customary. And when a gift was given, it was considered rude to reciprocate too quickly, lest one appear to be trying to "pay off" the obligation of friendship. Thus aid that might have been resented in other cultures seemed natural to many African villagers who, having welcomed volunteers into their midst, accepted and appreciated the Americans' contributions to the life of the group. . . .

Volunteers raised on stories of hardy pioneers and frontier heroes also admired, as they frequently reported, the extraordinary work ethic of West Africans. Teachers noted that students worked in the fields before and after class. Community development workers were often amazed at the Herculean efforts of those students' parents to wrest sustenance from the sea or soil. Mike Tidwell, who advised the local chief on building his own fish pond, later said: "I knew that no man would ever command more respect from me than one who, to better feed his children, moves 4,000 cubic feet of dirt with a shovel."

One result was a significantly lower early termination rate in Ghana than in many other countries. Worldwide, the rate of early termination for Peace Corps volunteers, including those who did not make it through training, averaged 30 percent by the mid-1990s, whereas in Ghana the rate hovered around 20 percent. The reason for this, in addition to Ghanaian hospitality, was the placement itself, usually in teaching. According to Charles Peters, the happiest, least frustrated volunteers on average were teachers—"most were in Africa"—who had "structured jobs with a clear set of tasks to perform." In Africa, work usually consisted of six periods of high school English, algebra, or chemistry—enough to satisfy the passion of almost any idealistic college graduate.

Reasonable living conditions also helped ease the path of the Peace Corps in Ghana. For most Americans, far away and with almost no history of trade or missionary work there, Africa was truly *terra incognita* in 1961. Tarzan movies, museum exhibits, and *National Geographic* photos displays of bare-breasted villagers were as close as most Americans had ever come to the mysterious "dark continent." Volunteers and their terrified parents knew somewhat more, much in the form of medical horror stories told by trainers determined to lose as few young Americans as possible. In addition to prescriptions on how to minimize the risk of cholera, malaria, yellow fever, typhoid, rabies, dysentery, meningitis, and giardia, which one could catch in any third world country, Peace Corps staff warned volunteers going to Africa of the even stranger maladies and dangers to be found there: the guinea worm, which could grow up to a meter long in the body before emerging from a skin blister (through which it could then be extracted by wrapping the worm around a matchstick and carefully pulling on it for a month, wrapping a little more of its length each time); or "schisto" worms, which burrowed into the skin in five minutes but stayed thirty years, rapidly aging the unlucky host; or "oncho," also called river blindness, whereby one could lose one's sight forever by taking an ill-considered dip in a lake or river. Going to Africa in the early 1960s "took a bunch of guts," in the words of George Carter, whose number one concern was "that I come back with [the same] 52 kids." And not all volunteers to Africa did return. The worst that usually happened was a case of malaria or severe dysentery. But over the years a number died in motorcycle or car crashes, and one twenty-five-year-old volunteer in Ethiopia even suffered the gruesome fate of being eaten by a crocodile.

Thus when daily conditions for teachers in Africa turned out to be relatively "civilized"—bungalows built for British teachers and other expatriates—volunteers gained confidence in their ability to endure the experience. "What they found when they got there was such a relief!" Carter recalled. Although some had to dig their own latrines, most volunteers were issued small gas-powered refrigators, kerosene lamps, and rooms complete with screens against mosquitoes. Food was simple and strange, but plentiful and often wonderfully tasty—pineapples so sweet that they smelled like coconut, chicken stewed with red peppers and peanuts, platains fried until the natural sugar in them crystallized, bland cassava pounded into gelatinous "fufu" and served with steaming palm fruit soup. . . .

For many volunteers, the physical pleasures they experienced were sometimes tinged with guilt or at least uneasiness. Throughout the 1960s volunteers battled within themselves and with Washington over the expectation that being in the Peace Corps meant living in mud huts, being best friends with the natives, and generally changing the world single-handedly. Physical comfort did not fit in the Peace Corps self-image. . . . Sargent Shriver made his first trip to inspect the volunteers' assignment in 1962, and he challenged the volunteers to reject the amenities offered by the Ghanaian community. . . .

[O]ver the next several years Peace Corps administrators gradually fine-tuned policy by . . . reducing volunteer living stipends and taking away jeep privileges from the few volunteers who had them.

Beyond the occasional defensiveness over "Sarge's" disappointment that they were not really roughing it, many volunteers were disturbed by the sense that the Peace Corps administration did not value teachers nearly as much as the heroes of community development. Both the American media and the Peace Corps newsletter, *The Volunteer,* tended to highlight those volunteers who either were in unusual or daring placements, or who—quite aside from their demanding jobs as teachers—had also managed to start so-called secondary projects such as libraries, craft cooperatives, adult literacy programs, or community gardens. From the attention these projects received, many volunteers drew the conclusion that the Peace Corps considered these projects not secondary but, rather, as the primary justification for placing young Americans in what otherwise seemed rather staid jobs. The volunteers felt that the newsletter "was implicitly criti[ci]zing them," George Carter wrote to Washington headquarters in 1962, "because they were not involved in a project which involved hacking one's way though the bush with a bolo knife." . . .

The Peace Corps stayed in education because African governments requested it and because Sargent Shriver himself strongly supported the Peace Corps role in education. A former chairman of Chicago's Board of Education, Shriver had a natural compatibility with the emphasis of the Kennedy family and the Kennedy administration on achievement through education. Joseph and Rose Kennedy had sent their sons to the best schools money could buy and, having attained the presidency, John Kennedy built his Cabinet with professors from the Ivy League. In the United States as a whole, this was the post-Sputnik era of the "new math" and the "new physics," the era of the president's Commission on Physical Fitness and of growing federal aid to colleges, universities, and medical schools. Indeed, free compulsory education was the oldest of Yankee traditions. . . .

One result was a program in which, by the end of the 1960s, 90 percent of volunteers reported that they were "moderately" or "very" satisfied with their Peace Corps experience. Clearly structured jobs in response to a clear need, plus the support of the local culture, made the experience a good one in spite of occasional guilt about not doing enough, or loving enough, or sacrificing enough. One volunteer who taught high school English and ran an enormously popular Shakespeare festival in the nearby Nigerian bush said decades later: "My Peace Corps assignment was so perfect I hesitate to talk about it even now, fearing that someone will yet take it away." One woman wrote home from Ghana in 1962, "I'm more pleased with the world and humans and myself than previously." From Africa, volunteers came back laughing. . . .

Canada and Britain also . . . [sent] volunteers to Ghana, and their experiences in many ways paralleled those of the Americans. Indeed, what was perhaps most remarkable about the overlap among the Peace Corps, [the British] Voluntary Service Overseas, and Canadian University Service Overseas was how similar they were, quite unintentionally, in their placements, organizational cultures, and political outlook. At the same time, the programs had differences. Those differences place in perspective the sometimes hypercritical treatment of the Peace Corps by scholars who wish to demythologize Kennedy's Camelot or to show the essential flaws of all U.S. foreign policy during the Vietnam era. Comparing the Peace Corps with its Anglo counterparts alters the significance of some of these complaints.

The historian Gary May, for example, says that Peace Corps language instruction "was almost legendary for its poor quality" and that "Peace Corps incompetence and ignorance" in the field of volunteer health created a "nightmare." In comparison with other programs, however, the Peace Corps not only gave volunteers extensive training on safety and hygiene (too much, some volunteers protested), but also innovated the practice of preventive gamma globulin shots (later adopted by the Canadians) and sent medical personnel to each country to attend to the volunteers. CUSO and VSO volunteers received relatively little of this kind of staff support, with the result that they suffered from a much higher incidence of potentially deadly hepatitis, dysentery, and malaria in the early 1960s than did Peace Corps volunteers. VSO volunteers thirty years later still complained about the lack of medical support compared with that given to American volunteers. . . .

Still, in fundamental ways, the experience of American, Canadian, and British volunteers in Ghana paralleled one another remarkably, and they generally got what they came for: a chance to know the existentialist "Other" and to deny his or her essential differentness: a chance to express the individual initiative central to their own Anglo-derived cultures yet seemingly threatened by mass society; a chance to try on preindustrial life and the values of communalism often associated with it; and, last but not least, a chance for old-fashioned adventure and heroism. . . .

For their part, Ghanaians welcomed the assistance of VSO in 1958 and the Peace Corps and CUSO in 1961. They continued to welcome volunteers decades later. The contributions in education stood out especially to Africans. "The importance of the Peace Corps programme to Ghana cannot be over-emphasized," the national director of secondary education told volunteers in 1995, echoing the assessment of other officials. Sheer numbers told part of the story: approximately 675,000 Ghanaians had American teachers between 1961 and 1991. Out of a population of 14 million, this equaled roughly 5 percent of all Ghanaians. Indeed, in Ghana it was difficult to find a person who had achieved white-collar status who had not had a Peace Corps teacher at some point.

Peace Corps also helped introduce educational innovations, such as the "new math" and learning by reasoning rather than by rote. These innovations did not all spread, however. Lacking books that could serve as an aid to memory, Ghanaian students continued to rely on copying down and memorizing the facts necessary to pass state exams. Julius Amin, a former Peace Corps student in nearby Cameroon, later wrote: "Memorization provided the . . . [village] student with a feeling of being knowledgeable" in an environment that was otherwise unfamiliar and intimidating. Still, he noted in in-depth research on Cameroon, the volunteers designed both textbooks and curricula more attuned to the needs of the rural students than those of the British system they helped transform, and laid the foundation for a national testing center that replaced the London-based exam board in 1977. Throughout West Africa, volunteers also started libraries, equipped rudimentary science labs and technical workshops, built school latrines, initiated athletic programs, conducted science fairs, and organized academic clubs. Even though many Peace Corps teachers taught subjects for which they had not prepared in college, "they made a difficult job look easy," according to Julius Amin. "Whatever the weaknesses of the volunteers, it remains true that their services were essential." . . .

Perhaps the most compelling contribution of the Peace Corps, however, was indeed its simple existence. As one Cameroonian later expressed it, "these Americans had their weaknesses but just the fact that these Kennedy boys came to struggle with us, I think, is the most important thing." Ghanaians often characterized the Peace Corps meaning to Ghana as one of morale. From the first singing of the national anthem in Twi to the volunteers in the 1990s who still reported to village chiefs before starting their assignments, the Peace Corps continuously impressed West Africans with its willingness to enter into the life of the villages "under all sort of conditions."

To K. B. Asante and Kojo Botsio, the individual, intangible effect had enriched particular lives as well as the life of the nation. Ghana, in its totality, may not have become measurably different, but many Ghanaians had. "The individual's effort seeps into society," according to Asante. Asante himself served a stint as Ghana's education minister in the 1970s and was "so impressed" with the American Peace Corps volunteers—working in remote places "where Ghanaians wouldn't go"—who came to his office to ask for supplies for their schools. To Kojo Botsio, who had weathered every political and economic crisis between 1951 and 1991 (from imprisonment by the British to a death sentence by a post-Nkrumah regime), the final judgment on the Peace Corps' thirty years in his country was simple: "We wanted to bring up the standard of education of the people and it contributed quite a lot . . . no doubt about it." . . .

In Ghana, the Peace Corps had not changed the world, but it had met its own stated goals: to serve the needs of another country, to promote local understanding of America, and to foster Americans' understanding of other people. Indeed, it had triumphed.

Cultural Negotiation: U.S. Tourism in Puerto Rico

DENNIS MERRILL

The postwar era witnessed an unprecedented boom in international tourism. Pushed along by American affluence, liberalized employee vacation benefits, easy credit, affordable air travel, and growing communications links, tourism—once the privilege of an elite few—became a crucial element in the global economy and a component of international relations. During the early 1960s Americans alone spent $3 billion per year traveling overseas. By the mid-1990s, international tourism generated as much as $3.4 trillion annually, vying with oil as the world's largest industry.

Although U.S. visitors traveled to Puerto Rico in pursuit of fun and relaxation, they unavoidably became participants in a Cold War cultural experience. Commonwealth Puerto Rico, the advertising read, was a postcolonial territory tutored in democratic capitalism by the United States and generously granted autonomy. It had forsworn the turbulence that swept much of the Third World, denounced Castroism, and peacefully pursued private investment and economic development. The image

Adapted from Dennis Merrill, "Negotiating Cold War Paradise: U.S. Tourism, Economic Planning, and Cultural Modernity in the Twentieth Century Puerto Rico," *Diplomatic History,* 25 (Spring 2001), 179–214. Reprinted with permission of Blackwell Publishing Ltd.

juxtaposed the island's tropical allure and its material progress, its yearning for change and its stability. In short, Pueto Rico shone as a Cold War paradise, an outpost for liberal capitalism in a world seemingly tempted by the promises of communism.

Depicting tourism as a one-way street, where visitors bestowed progress upon hosts, the advertising hype oversimplified the give-and-take inherent to tourism. Local communities, in fact, are not static and often seize upon tourism as a means to display their existence and establish their power. Travel narratives and popular discourses of tourism illuminate how governments, media, businesses, workers, and consumers ultimately engage in the globalization of cultural modernity—a consciousness, or value system, that elevates urbanism, science, consumerism, and mastery over nature. To be modern, the theorist Marshall Berman has posited, is to find ourselves in an environment that promises economic and technological advance, yet to feel threatened by the loss of revered customs and life ways. Modernity is not simply imposed from the outside, but rather represents "the main cultural direction for global development." It is transmitted through many channels: trade, communications, diplomacy, and the migration of people. Tourism serves as a battleground on which hosts and visitors contest and negotiate their modern identities.

Acquired and awarded colonial status following the U.S. victory over Spain in 1898, Puerto Rico ranked with Cuba, Haiti, Jamaica, and the Dominican Republic as a featured tropical attraction for an affluent and adventurous leisure class. In the days before mass tourism, most who traveled to Puerto Rico went by steamship from New York, a four-day voyage by the 1920s that cost about $75. The early guidebooks, what the scholar Edward Said has termed a literature of exploration and discovery, highlighted Puerto Rico's natural beauty and colonial charm.

Early travel writers also paid homage to the United States's civilizing and modernizing powers. Philip Marsden's *Sailing South* explained to readers that the United States had acquired Puerto Rico as an afterthought following the crusade to free Cuba, but had brought to it modern health care, highways, civil administration, and English-language education. Tourism would enhance these benefits by promising an influx of capital, technology, and travel conveniences. By the early 1930s the beachfront capital city of San Juan boasted two foreign-owned tourist hotels, a handful of restaurants, and several nightclubs and casinos. . . .

Meanwhile, colonialism and tourism made the island a meeting ground for distinctive cultures. A few American visitors during these years developed an appreciation for Puerto Rico. Most of the travel literature, however, advanced a derogatory set of perceptions. Guidebooks disparaged the island's poverty, illiteracy, and health problems, and depicted a helpless, dependent people, a foreign "other," who lived outside the boundaries of the civilized world. U.S. travel writers, reflecting the mores of the Jim Crow era, typically portrayed Puerto Ricans as a "mongrel race," among whom the Iberian tradition of mañana obstructed reform and progress.

The 1930s witnessed the first effort by U.S. officials to package Puerto Rico for mass tourism. It was a colonial enterprise, imposed on the island. The U.S. governor Blanton Winship viewed the industry as the centerpiece of a new economy—to replace the island's declining sugar plantations. In addition to launching a road beautification program, and expanding accommodations, Winship hired a public relations firm to churn out travel brochures highlighting Puerto Rico's beaches, golf courses, and deep sea fishing. The campaign portrayed Puerto Rico in condescending terms: a poverty stricken land whose simple people awaited the opportunity to serve their benefactors. It accented popular constructions of gender, with posters featuring attractive female models posed in swimsuits: "beautiful señoritas at the Canto de Piedras," one caption read. Colonial tourism literature commonly depicted Puerto Rico as a generous hostess, accepting of male domination, and eager to pamper her paying guests.

Winship's campaign failed to take hold, in part because of the depression-plagued 1930s economy, but also due to the rising nationalism that shaped Puerto Rican politics during the decade. The nationalist movement was associated with the name Pedro Albizu Campos, a graduate of Harvard Law School, a former U.S. Army officer, and leader of the Nationalist party. In the harsh depression atmosphere, compounded by punishing hurricanes in 1928 and 1932, Albizu's denunciation of U.S. colonial rule and call to arms found a receptive audience. At the same time, the "1930s generation" of Puerto Rican intellectuals decried the forced instruction of English in public schools and celebrated the island's Spanish-American, "hispanidad" culture. Winship's tourism activities, particularly his imposition of a subservient identity on the island, won the wrath of both political and cultural nationalists.

In this context, Puerto Rico first experienced the innovative leadership of Luis Muñoz Marín. The son of Luis Muñoz Rivera, Puerto Rico's resident commissioner in Washington, the younger Muñoz had been educated in the United States. After a stint as an independentista, Muñoz's pragmatism led him to champion commonwealth status, an ill-defined middle ground between independence and colonialism. In 1938 he organized the Popular Democratic party (Partido Populare Democratica, or PPD), which melded his moderate commonwealth cause with a leftist economic program, promising land redistribution and new, job-producing, state-owned industries. A talented politician, Muñoz echoed others during the 1940 legislative elections in denouncing Winship's tourism initiatives. When charges of casino corruption arose, he even demanded that San Juan's slot machines be tossed into the sea.

The PPD's smashing victory at the polls in 1940 foreshadowed Muñoz's domination of Puerto Rican politics for nearly three decades, and set the stage for a locally based, planned tourist industry. Prerequisite to the effort was a redefinition of Puerto Rico's political status. After becoming the island's first elected governor in 1948, Muñoz negotiated with Washington Public Law 600, which conferred on Puerto Rico limited self-government. Washington kept control of the island's judiciary and military, but San Juan gained the power to tax and regulate Puerto Rico's economy. Puerto Ricans maintained U.S. citizenship (first granted by the Jones Act of 1917), but did not receive the right to vote in U.S. elections. The legislation won popular approval in a 1951 plebiscite that offered a choice only between commonwealth or colonial status, much to the dismay of statehood and independence advocates. Nationalism remained a central impulse on the island, and profoundly shaped future tourism, but the independence party (Partido Independentista Puertorriqueño, or PIP) steadily lost ground in elections over the next decade—overtaken by Muñoz's populism and victimized by repression enforced by Commonwealth and U.S. authorities alike.

As he reshaped Puerto Rico's political identity, Muñoz also refined his economic agenda. Again, he sought greater self-reliance for the island without severing ties to the United States. With his American-educated economic adviser, Teodoro Moscoso, Muñoz established Puerto Rico's Economic Planning Board, or "Fomento." The two abandoned their preference for state-owned enterprises, and used their newly acquired taxing authority to offer exemptions to private investors undertaking new ventures.

The goal was to transform Puerto Rico from a sugar-producing, colonial entity to a job-producing industrial workshop. Muñoz's modernist vision included public-private collaboration, state subsidies for key industries, and access to U.S. federal welfare programs for the poor. The strategy became known as "Operation Bootstrap."

Muñoz delegated to Fomento's Teodoro Moscoso the restructuring of the tourist industry. The effort would not be left solely to private, foreign investors, but instead draw on government subsidies and local capital. Planners estimated in 1949 that a modest, public investment of $1.7 million annually for staff, advertising, and subsidies would generate roughly $15,600,000 in revenue and create four thousand new jobs. In contrast to the colonial authority's earlier efforts to make tourism the island's economic mainstay, Fomento officials envisioned the industry's share of gross product topping off at 5 to 10 percent. That figure contrasted with other Atlantic-Caribbean retreats, such as the Bahamas and the U.S. Virgin Islands, which relied on travel for up to 80 percent of their national incomes. Manufacturing constituted the core of Operation Bootstrap.

The effort first required a tourism infrastructure. It was the availability of affordable air travel that made modern, mass tourism possible. Pan American Airlines inaugurated daily nonstop flights between New York and San Juan in 1946. Three years later, construction commenced on San Juan's $15 million Isla Verde airport, capable of handling more than five hundred flights per day. Then, a breakthrough came in 1951 when the U.S. Bureau of Civil Aviation granted authorization to Eastern Airlines to land in San Juan, breaking PanAm's monopoly and spurring lower airfares. By 1952 the Puerto Rico advertised six- to eight-hour flights from New York for $128 roundtrip; and ten-hour flights from Chicago for $275. Daily jet service, commencing in late 1959, reduced travel time from New York to three and one-half hours.

Another turning point came in 1949 when Moscoso hired J. Stanton Robbins, an American who had worked on Virginia's colonial Williamsburg, to head Fomento's Office of Tourism. Soon, the office was publishing *Qué Pasa in Puerto Rico,* a glossy magazine, still in print today, that featured photographs and articles on leading attractions. Equally important, the bureau established schools for hotel and restaurant employees and developed a survey system for departing tourists that helped fine-tune its promotional efforts. Tourism officials also prepared the island for legalized gambling, citing the nineteen-year-old Nevada experiment to argue that regulation countered infiltration by organized crime. Puerto Rico legalized casino gambling in late 1948, created a gambling division within the Tourism Office, and hired a corps of inspectors. Despite protests from smaller hotels, the government licensed only establishments larger than two hundred rooms. Consistent with Muñoz's antigambling posture in the 1940 elections, the government refused to sanction slot machines.

Infrastructure alone could not spark mass tourism. Critical to the undertaking, and a pivotal component of cultural modernity, was the refashioning of Puerto Rico's image. For more than a half century the island's people had been portrayed in narratives as dependent and subservient "others." Stereotypes had been reinforced by the migration of roughly fifty thousand Puerto Ricans annually, mainly to New York and the urban northeast, during the late 1940s and 1950s. A 1947 pictorial essay in *Life* magazine described the migration and dramatized the health, housing, and employment problems of the immigrants. In popular culture, the 1958 Broadway musical *West Side Story* reinforced these images by choreographing its characters as hot-tempered, knife-wielding juvenile delinquents. The musical drew an even less flattering image of Puerto Rico itself, a place, according to song, devoid of modern symbols such as washing machines, highways, and Buicks.

In 1948 the commonwealth contracted the New York public relations firm Hamilton Wright to engineer a media blitz. An army of journalists descended upon the island, where they were chauffeured about, given access to the governor, and fed a steady diet of government press releases. Publications such as *Travel, Saturday Review,* and the travel page of the *New York Times* filled with articles that accented Puerto Rico's climate, architecture, and natural beauty. Tropical images had been central to earlier advertising, but commonwealth officials also conveyed an image of an island in the throes of modernity. An array of publications told the story of "Operation Bootstrap," the name itself a powerful metaphor in Yankee culture for self-reliance. Under Muñoz annual earnings had risen from $125 per capita in 1940 to $514 by 1960, second only to Venezuela in Latin America. In the years 1958–59 alone 237 firms had signed contracts with Fomento.

The reinvention of Puerto Rico required above all the construction and advertisement of a glamorous tourist zone. At the end of World War II, Moscoso and Fomento surveyed the city for hotel sites, and targeted the Condado area, along the city's northern beach-lined coast, as the island's primary tourist district. The Condado's first new hotel, the stunning $7.2 million Caribe Hilton, was entirely government financed, built, and owned. The entrepreneur Conrad Hilton accepted a joint venture with the commonwealth government that placed management in company hands, reserved ownership for the government, and arranged a sharing of profits. When completed in late 1949, the ten-story, three-hundred-room, Caribe Hilton stood out on Old San Juan peninsula. Its dazzling white facade contrasted with the sparkling blue sea, and its modernity juxtaposed the centuries old San Gerónimo fort nearby. A testimony to technology, it had a swimming pool carved out of coral stone that held salt water replaced by attendants every four hours. The beachfront was also human-engineered, of powdery, coral sand so as not to stick uncomfortably to sunbathers. The hotel's open-air entrance took visitors through a manicured garden, signifying the taming of the tropics, and the interior's controlled environment, air-conditioned throughout, consisted of a collage of stone, glass, and stainless steel.

The Caribe Hilton inaugurated San Juan's tourism make-over. Soon after its opening, the World War I era Condado Beach hotel, only a few blocks from the Caribe, received a government-assisted $1.3 million facelift. Then other hotel projects followed and the landscape of Ashford Avenue, the Condado's main thoroughfare, filled with shops, restaurants, and clubs. For the commonwealth government, the Condado represented a source of revenue and an important symbol of Puerto Rican modernity. For affluent, Cold War Americans, the Caribe and other high-rises seemed to demonstrate that the American Dream had universal application. "San Juan is a new Miami with a Spanish accent," gloated the *Saturday Review* in 1952.

Puerto Rico's lunge toward modernity did not go uncontested. The editors of the influential Spanish-language daily *El Mundo* decried the Caribe Hilton as a sell-out to foreigners. Even some members of Muñoz's PPD denounced casino gambling and questioned the allocation of public funds to the leisure industry. Muñoz and Moscoso defended both the Hilton deal and tourism as a whole. "How do you expect to pay for public education and social welfare," Moscoso chided his critics, "if the commonwealth is barred from earning revenue?" The journal *Architectural*

Forum emphasized the role of New York consultants Warner Leeds and Associates in overseeing the project, commenting that the hotel had "the color, texture, and finish demanded by Americans off to the semi-tropics." But Moscoso and others emphasized that the Caribe had been designed by a local San Juan firm, headed by architects Osvaldo Toto and Miguel Ferrer, and reflected a unique Puerto Rican style—functional, clean, and modern.

Antitourism sentiment would intensify as the industry grew, but during the early 1950s it remained only an undercurrent in Puerto Rican cultural discourse. After all, the PPD easily captured majorities in the island's first several elections, and its main competitor, the Republican Statehood party (PER), favored close ties to the United States and applauded tourism. Commonwealth officials, moreover, eased the transition to modernity by promoting the island's rustic and traditional attractions—for both foreign and local tourists. Drawing on the European bed and breakfast model, Fomento extended tax breaks to smaller, more affordable inns outside of San Juan, and travel publications began to emphasize that three thousand miles of road allowed visitors to escape the city and discover the less heav[il]y touristed, more authentic "outer island."

To tap the tourist's thirst for authenticity, the government also initiated the restoration of Old San Juan, consisting of eight blocks of Spanish colonial residences, churches, and fortresses. In the spring of 1949 Tourist Bureau Director Stanton Robbins invited a group of former colleagues from colonial Williamsburg to San Juan to advise the project. The legislature designated Old San Juan an "ancient and historical zone," and in 1955 the government created the Institute of Puerto Rican Culture, which advised property owners on structural design and decor. Fomento granted tax incentives and loans to building owners who undertook restorations. By 1962 twenty-five major structures, dating to the sixteenth, seventeenth, and eighteenth centuries, had been rehabilitated and the ancient city bustled with restaurants, gift shops, and tourists. The traveler's taste for the elemental and the exotic did not conflict with the worship of modernity. As the sociologist Dean MacCannell has put it: "the best indication of the final victory of modernity over other sociocultural arrangements is not the disappearance of the nonmodern world, but its artificial preservation and reconstruction in modern society." The maintenance of a reconstructed past, or "staged authenticity," reaffirmed rather than denied the march of progress.

History and modernity converged with Cold War politics as neighboring Cuba descended into revolution. While Havana had nurtured a tourist boom for over three decades, it had accumulated massive problems during the 1950s. The authoritarian government of Fulgencio Batista had adopted a free-wheeling, laissez faire policy toward the industry, content to leave matters to private interests, as long as it received its share of casino revenue. Cuba's capital had become synonymous with the darker side of tourism: mob-controlled gambling, drunkenness, and prostitution. The incongruities of tourism intensified domestic discontent, fed anti-Yankee sentiment, and contributed to Fidel Castro's communist revolution. In June 1960 Castro's government seized the landmark Havana Hilton, and relations with the tourist industry disintegrated.

As Castro's shadow stretched across the Caribbean, U.S. officials and the press heaped more praise than ever on Puerto Rico's "peaceful revolution." The *Saturday*

Review editorialized in 1962 that the commonwealth had no revolutionary past—the island was managed pragmatically and democratically. "Under way here is an American-style revolution that really works," observed *U.S. News and World Report*, that stood "in sharp contrast to the violent revolution in nearby Cuba." At the center of it all was Muñoz Marín, whose picture graced the cover of *Time* in June 1958. Guidebooks and articles praised Puerto Rico's "success story," and Muñoz's Tourist Bureau made the island's economic progress, and the contrast to Cuba, a selling point.

Puerto Rico also won support from U.S. politicians. Richard Nixon found refuge there in 1958. The following year presidential hopeful Senator Hubert Humphrey (D-MN) visited the island and lauded it as a model for liberal development in the Third World. President Dwight D. Eisenhower made Puerto Rico the first stop on his Latin American tour in February 1960, and captured headlines when he took to the fairways of the recently opened, Rockefeller-owned Dorado Beach Club, east of San Juan. John F. Kennedy forged the strongest bond. In December 1958 he visited the island and made his first major speech on Latin America as a presidential candidate. Following his election he picked two of Muñoz's closest associates, Teodoro Moscoso and Arturo Morales Carrión, to serve on a task force on Latin American affairs and later appointed each to high-ranking administration positions. When the young president made his first trip to Latin America in December 1961, Puerto Rico topped the itinerary.

Cuba's turmoil also catapulted Puerto Rico into a leadership position among Caribbean vacation retreats. The Condado underwent another spurt of hotel construction, and the island's beach hotels booked for months ahead. Wrote *Time* magazine in December 1958, Puerto Rico is aimed to please the crowd "bored with Miami and scared of going to Havana because of the Cuban revolution." By 1964 the number of American tourists reached five hundred thousand; and five years later it surpassed the one million mark, second only to Mexico in Latin America.

The tourist binge received mixed reviews on the island. Part of the misgivings arose from economic inequalities. In a less developed country, where the technicalities of commonwealth status did not veil continued colonial power, the prospect of using tourism to attain economic progress encountered skepticism. Operation Bootstrap's accomplishments notwithstanding, much of Puerto Rico remained desperately poor. U.S.-based companies that took advantage of tax-free inducements often pulled up stakes when moratorium periods ended, and unemployment hovered at 10 to 12 percent, figures that did not consider the added problem of partial employment.

No issue better illustrated the intersection between tourism and class structure than the continuous effort to remove the inhabitants and demolish the slum dwellings of "La Perla." Perched along the rockbound shore, adjacent to Old San Juan, the neighborhood was immortalized by the sociologist Oscar Lewis's study of Puerto Rican poverty *La Vida*. In 1949 government tourist planners recommended clearance of the area, but community organizers mobilized and political pressure prevented action. The prostitute Soledad in *La Vida* related how her work and travels took her back and forth from ghetto to the stylish Condado and spoke of "the pain one feels after being in a nice hotel and walking past the Caribe Hilton" only to return home to the nearby slum. "They live in separate worlds, the poor and the rich," she observed.

Economic disparities constituted only one irritant. As the flood of tourists mounted, charges of "cultural imperialism" echoed across the island. Particularly abrasive was the tourist's disregard for the Spanish language. "The trouble with you Americans," one reader addressed the English-language *Puerto Rico World Journal,* "is that when you come to Puerto Rico you want to be understood in your own language, but don't give a damn to learn our language." Governor Muñoz wrote Hilton executives about a trip to the Castellano Hilton in Spain where menus were printed in Spanish and English. Could a similar practice be implemented in San Juan? Such a menu, he suggested, would be handy in a bilingual society, and provide tourists a point of interest. Hilton menus, however, remained English-only. Responding to the *World Journal,* an indignant American observed that the island's use of U.S. currency accorded him special rights. Until the commonwealth minted its own coins, he lectured, you "better damn well learn the language of the country that feeds you."

Of all the affronts that accompanied tourism, few touched as sensitive a chord as racism. Although Puerto Rican society had never been free of racial prejudice, the island had no history of rigid, racial separation until U.S. military units instituted the practice. In late 1949 rumors swirled that the Caribe Hilton would implement the color bar. The Caribe in fact shunned segregation, but reports surfaced throughout the 1950s that San Juan's hotel beaches prohibited black sunbathers and swimmers. Racism, moreover, manifested itself in other ways. Shortly after the Caribe's opening, Carl Hilton penned a letter to his brother Conrad decrying the work habits of the labor force. The hired "peons," he wrote, were "child-like or even dog-like; it is not what you say when directing their efforts it is your tone of voice that counts."

Gender and sexual relations also stirred tension. Although travel literature historically depicted Puerto Rico as an alluring woman, female tourists frequently encountered the island's patriarchy. Most common were complaints of sexual harassment, assaults, and rapes. The Condado beachfront, one letter to an island newspaper complained, had become a gathering place for "degenerates" who "are exposing themselves, masturbating, and saying ugly, filthy things to women." Of course, male sexism was a frequently cited problem at beachside in the United States as well. Still, a Puerto Rican woman wrote back to the paper and expressed contempt for the American women who walk the beaches in "tight bathing suits," and then complain of being harassed: "Do the Puerto Rican gentlemen let their women walk on the beaches alone?" she asked. Then a lecture: "Remember, you are a guest and a foreigner in this country and therefore abide with the customs and culture."

Other commentators turned their sights on the sexual prerogatives exercised by male vacationers. Puerto Rico never achieved the fame accorded Cuba as a zone for sexual license. Government surveys indicated that most tourists were married and came to the island as couples. North American men—businessmen, tourists, and sailors—were nonetheless often observed in the company of prostitutes. The Condado became a well-known meeting ground, and Puerto Ricans and tourists alike complained of overt solicitation outside bars and casinos. Other writers noted with alarm the presence of homosexuals. Old San Juan developed one of the few gay scenes in the Caribbean in the fifties, and as tourism flourished, a small homosexual subculture of hotels, restaurants, and clubs arose. Although most Puerto Ricans seemed willing to tolerate the subculture, it upset traditionalists. One concerned citizen lamented the turning of the capital into a "slum, a haven for all kinds of undesirable characters," including "the tight pant wiggle-walking homosexuals."

While tourism at times seemed a predatory force, the reality was more complex. The industry unleashed unease across the island, but antitourism sentiment never boiled over into organized protest. Hosts and tourists struggled to adapt to modernity, all the while sensing the discomfort of traditions lost. But the difference between cultural loss and cultural imposition is critical because it speaks to the difference between the globalization of culture and coercive colonialism. Puerto Ricans resented their subjugated past, and expressed uncertainty about the globalized future, but found in cultural modernity a reality that might be regulated, manipulated, and negotiated. As agents of change they both accepted and resisted tourism.

For its part, the Muñoz administration never abandoned state planning, and cited the Caribe Hilton as an example of its benefits. The joint venture handed over day-to-day operation of the hotel to Hilton, but secured ownership for the commonwealth government. The contract, moreover, specified that Hilton purchase the resort's furnishings and equipment, cover losses incurred in the first year's operation, and be barred from opening a competing hotel on the island. Finally, the arrangements guaranteed the government 66⅔ percent of the operating profit. Hilton Corporation certainly felt that Fomento had driven a hard bargain. Predicting success for the hotel, Caribe manager Frank Wangeman wrote to Conrad Hilton six months after the opening: "I think we have a gold mine here. Let's buy this hotel before they [the commonwealth] realize how prosperous it is going to be." Muñoz and Moscoso would have nothing of it. By 1953 the enterprise netted $1 million annually for the government.

Tourism workers also wrung concessions from the industry. A strike at two San Juan hotels, including the Caribe Hilton, erupted in January 1955 when negotiations with an American Federation of Labor affiliate collapsed due to disputes over wages, medical and vacation benefits, and overtime compensation. Five hundred workers, including maids, waiters and waitresses, bartenders, and kitchen workers, walked off the job. Tensions mounted as hotel managers accused the strikers, a majority of whom were female in this traditionally sex-segregated industry, of sabotaging company cars suspected of transporting strikebreakers. The strike organizers, in turn, accused police of siding with the hoteliers and trying to intimidate them away from the picket lines. The Muñoz administration first interceded with the police and then arbitrated the impasse, persuading Hilton to provide a 2 percent pay raise, a 4 percent increase in medical and insurance benefits, and liberalized overtime pay. After the settlement, strikers wrote to express their gratitude, informing Muñoz they were willing "morir por nuestro Gobernador" [to die for our Governor].

As tourism flourished, Puerto Ricans found countless ways to assert themselves. Although exit surveys showed a high level of tourist satisfaction, complaints about slow service in restaurants and hotels became commonplace. And while the petty crime that swept the island may have had no particular cultural significance, it rattled the nerves of some tourists. The English-language *Island Times* filled with letters decrying the island's "crime wave" from Yankee travelers and expatriots. Humor also registered as a form of resistance. The independentista organ *Claridad* regularly featured satirical cartoons with Yankees in tourist attire (bermuda shorts, flowered dresses, straw hats, and cameras) demanding royal treatment. One Spanish-language cartoon depicted a tour group, ignorant of imperial history, making disparaging remarks about Puerto Rico's Americanized street names while being pulled by a human-drawn rickshaw.

While the commonwealth tried to steer tourism to its economic advantage, it also grappled with the industry's cultural consequences. The most significant initiatives were undertaken by the Institute of Puerto Rican Culture, the agency that coordinated the reconstruction of Old San Juan. The institute's initial projects showcased the island's European heritage, especially its Spanish-built fortresses, residences, and churches. But by the later 1950s, it shifted focus and promoted indigenous Taíno-Indian art forms and Afro-Caribbean traditions. In the township of Loíza Aldea, the institute's scholars traced the origins of the popular drum-driven dance rhythms known as the "bomba" to the area's runaway African slave population. Archeological digs elsewhere recovered artifacts of the long-since decimated native Taíno people. The recovery of the island's distant past facilitated the representation of Puerto Rican culture as a harmonious blending of European, African, and Indian influences. Thus the PPD not only preserved, but manufactured a national identity—no small feat for a commonwealth denied full national sovereignty. . . .

Ambivalence toward tourism remained a fixture of Puerto Rican life. Still, by 1969 Fomento estimated that tourism contributed $200 million annually to the gross national product, and that hotels alone created nearly ten thousand jobs. Nor had the industry became a controlling factor in the Puerto Rican economy, ranking below both manufacturing and agriculture as a producer of wealth. Puerto Ricans and Yankees continued to grate on one another, but few could take issue with Teodoro Moscoso, who told a conference in April 1961: "In the jargon of the advertising trade, an image has been created; we have emerged from anonymity. That, for a tiny island halfway across the Atlantic, is no mean accomplishment."

In many ways mass tourism is theater, a dramatic and comedic play in which hosts and guests choreograph their responses to cultural modernity. Americans who traveled to Puerto Rico during the early Cold War years found in the island's hotels and restaurants confirmation that global uplift could best be achieved through U.S. consumerism rather than Soviet communism. By the late 1960s Puerto Rico had become synonymous with beachfront luxury, bootstrap capitalism, anticommunism, and old world charm: a mix of old and new, material and spiritual, the mythic and the trivial. Puerto Ricans also placed on stage an idealized self, at once rooted in a glorified past, and looking toward a capitalist future. In fact, tourism both reinforced and undermined U.S. and Puerto Rican identities. It globalized culture, blurred the line between inside and outside, and demonstrated the fragility of national identity in a mobile world.

FURTHER READING

Benedict Anderson, *Imagined Communities: Reflections of the Origins and Spread of Nationalism* (1991)
Carol Anderson, *Eyes Off the Prize* (2003) (on civil rights and foreign relations)
Ali Ansari, *A History of Modern Iran* (2003)
James A. Bill, *The Eagle and the Lion* (1988) (on Iran)
Scott L. Bills, *Empire and Cold War* (1990)
Thomas Borstelmann, *The Cold War and the Color Line* (2002)
H. W. Brands, *The Specter of Neutralism* (1988)
D. Clayton Brown, *Globalization and America Since 1945* (2003)
Liping Bu, *Making the World like Us* (2003) (on international education programs)

Arturo Morales Carrión, *Puerto Rico* (1983)

Nick Cullather, *Secret History* (1999) (on Guatemala)

———, "Development? It's History," *Diplomatic History* 24 (Fall 2000): 641–654

Andrew DeRoche, *Black, White, and Chrome* (2001) (on Zimbabwe)

Mary L. Dudziak, *Cold War and Civil Rights* (2000)

Christopher Endy, *Cold War Holidays: American Tourism in France* (2004)

David Engerman, "Research Agenda for the History of Tourism," *American Studies International* 32 (1994): 3–31

——— et al., *Staging Growth* (2003)

Arturo Escobar, *Encountering Development* (1995)

Max Paul Friedman, "Retiring Puppets, Bringing Latin America Back In: Recent Scholarship on United States-Latin American Relations," *Diplomatic History* 5 (November 2003): 621–636

Mark Gasiorowski, *U.S. Foreign Policy and the Shah* (1991)

Jessica C.E. Gienow-Hecht and Frank Schumacher, *Culture and International History* (2003)

James Goode, *The United States and Iran* (1997)

Mary Ann Heiss, *Empire and Nationhood* (1997) (on Iran)

Gerald C. Horne, *From the Barrel of a Gun* (2001) (on Zimbabwe)

Stephen Kinzer, *All the Shah's Men* (2003)

Christina Klein, *Cold War Orientalism* (2003) (on Asia)

Gabriel Kolko, *Confronting the Third World* (1988)

Michael Krenn, *Black Diplomacy* (1999)

Rob Kroes, *If You've Seen One, You've Seen the Mall: Europeans and American Mass Culture* (1996)

Michael Latham, *Modernization and Ideology* (2000)

Mark Hamilton Lytle, *The Origins of the Iranian-American Alliance* (1987)

Dean MacCannell, *The Tourist* (1999)

Alan McPherson, *Yankee No! Anti-Americanism in U.S.–Latin American Relations* (2003)

Gary May, "Passing the Torch and Lighting Fires: The Peace Corps," in *Kennedy's Quest for Victory,* ed. Thomas G. Paterson (1989), 284–316

Louis A. Pérez Jr., *On Becoming Cuban* (1999)

Frederick B. Pike, *The United States and Latin America* (1992)

Brenda Gayle Plummer, *Rising Wind: Black Diplomats and U.S. Foreign Policy, 1935–1960* (1996)

Stephen G. Rabe, *Eisenhower and Latin America* (1989)

———, *The Most Dangerous Area of the World* (1999) (on JFK and Latin America)

———, *U.S. Intervention in British Guiana* (2005)

T. Zane Reeves, *The Politics of the Peace Corps and Vista* (1988)

Yale Richmond, *Cultural Exchange and the Cold War* (2003)

Darlene Rivas, *Missionary Capitalist* (2002) (on Nelson Rockefeller)

Andrew Rotter, "Saidism Without Said: *Orientalism* in U.S. Diplomatic History," *American Historical Review* 105 (October 2000): 1205–1217

Edward Said, *Orientalism* (1978)

———, *Culture and Imperialism* (1993)

Frances Saunders, *The Cultural Cold War* (2000)

David E. Schmitz, *Thank God They're on Our Side* (1999) (on the U.S. and dictators)

Rosalie Schwartz, *Pleasure Island* (1997) (on Cuban tourism)

James F. Seikmeir, *Aid, Nationalism, and InterAmerican Relations* (2001)

Amy L.S. Staples, "Seeing Diplomacy Through Bankers' Eyes: The World Bank, the Anglo-Iranian Oil Crisis, and the Aswan High Dam," *Diplomatic History* 26 (2002): 397–418

John A. Tomlinson, *Globalization and Culture* (1999)

Penny M. Von Eschen, *Race Against Empire* (1997)

———, *Satchmo Blows Up the World: Jazz Ambassadors Play the Cold War* (2005)

Reinhold Wagnleitner and Elaine Tyler May, eds., *"Here, There, and Everywhere"* (2000)

Thomas Zeiller and Alfred Eckes Jr., *Globalization and the American Century* (2003)

CHAPTER
1 2

Cuba and the Missile Crisis

In October 1962, American U-2 reconnaissance planes photographed missile sites installed by the Soviets on the Caribbean island of Cuba. The missiles could carry nuclear weapons capable of striking the United States. After meeting with his advisers and deciding to announce U.S. policy in a televised address, President John F. Kennedy demanded withdrawal of the missiles and imposed a blockade around Cuba. Exchanges of diplomatic letters, rallying of allies, exhausting meetings, and military preparations soon followed. While a dangerous, superpower nuclear arms race was already an established feature of the Cold War, and each side's deadly arsenal continued to grow after the crisis passed, the face-off over Cuba was the closest the United States and the Soviet Union even came to nuclear war.

In the end, Premier Nikita Khrushchev and President Kennedy settled the confrontation, without consulting Cuban premier Fidel Castro. The United States promised not to invade Cuba (as it had done using Cuban exiles in April 1961, at the Bay of Pigs) and assented to the removal of its Jupiter missiles from Turkey. In return, Moscow agreed to remove its missiles from Cuba. The U.S. no-invasion pledge never took effect because Castro refused to permit United Nations inspections. But the Soviets dismantled their missiles and the Jupiters in Turkey came down.

Beneath the missile crisis lay years of Cuban-American antagonism. On taking power in 1959, Fidel Castro launched a revolution that challenged major U.S. interests on the island, including mob-run casinos, U.S. military missions, and investments worth over a billion dollars. Castro decried the history of U.S. hegemony over Cuba, especially the hated Platt Amendment, and he vowed a restructuring of society to reduce Cuba's dependence on the United States. Washington became alarmed, too, because Castro's call for revolution across Latin America carried popular appeal throughout the region. When the United States instituted trade sanctions against Cuba in 1960, the Cubans looked to the Soviet Union as an economic and political partner. In January 1961 the United States broke diplomatic relations with Havana. In 1961–1962 came the Bay of Pigs expedition, covert operations designed to cripple the Cuban economy through sabotage, Central Intelligence Agency (CIA) assassination plots against Castro, and threatening U.S. military maneuvers. Because it occurred during a particularly tense time in the Cold War, the U.S.-Cuba contest held international consequences.

In recent years a greater proportion of the documentary record on the missile crisis in the archives of the United States, Russia, and Cuba has opened for research,

*and crisis participants have gathered in meetings to reexamine the 1962 confronta-
tion. Explaining the origins of the Soviet-American face-off, some analysts emphasize
the importance of Moscow's global strategic goals: obtaining nuclear parity, or the
appearance of parity, with the United States; or perhaps creating an atmosphere
conducive to a favorable settlement of the Berlin crisis. Others accent the importance
of the Cuban setting, especially the bad blood that ran between Washington and
Havana. The interpretive differences are distinct. From one perspective the missile
crisis stemmed from Soviet Cold War expansionism. The other side contends that the
incident arose primarily from a long history of U.S. hegemony in the Caribbean
and Latin America. Which imperialism triggered the dangerous drama—Soviet
or American? Or both?*

*Scholars also disagree in assessing how the crisis was handled. Some writers
have lavished praise on the Kennedy team for its "crisis management" skills. The
young president surrounded himself with a small group of talented advisers, the
Executive Committee of the National Security Council, or ExComm, that according
to analysts carefully weighed options and deployed a mix of diplomacy and military
force to coerce peacefully an outcome favorable to the United States. Critics, however,
charge that Kennedy, a Cold War hawk eager to prove his mettle, shunned quiet,
behind-the-scenes diplomacy in favor of public bravado and a naval blockade that
heightened tensions. Instead of cool-headed, calibrated deliberation, the president
and ExComm operated under heavy stress and on several occasions nearly lost control of policy to subordinates. The critics contend that the crisis eased not when the
Kremlin decided to submit to Washington's demands, but when Kennedy belatedly
agreed to a secret removal of U.S. Jupiter missiles from Turkey—following a string
of near-misses involving both Soviet and American military mishaps.*

*What exactly brought about this very-near human catastrophe? Did American
and Soviet leaders grasp the magnitude of the crisis and rise to the occasion with
forceful but effective diplomacy? Or did they overreact, misjudge, and in the end
simply luck out? What lessons about international behavior can be drawn from
the Cuban missile crisis?*

🌐 D O C U M E N T S

Document 1 is drawn from a November 1975 report by the U.S. Senate Select Committee
to Study Governmental Operations with Respect to Intelligence Activities. Chaired by
Senator Frank Church of Idaho, this committee detailed CIA assassination plots against
Fidel Castro. Document 2, dated March 14, 1962, constitutes the initial guidelines for
Operation Mongoose, the CIA's conspiracy to overthrow the Castro government through
"indigenous sources" and possibly U.S. military intervention. President Kennedy
apparently approved this secret document, and his brother, Attorney General Robert F.
Kennedy, became the primary overseer of the spoiling operation.

Document 3 includes significant parts of the transcribed record of Kennedy's first
two meetings with his high-level advisers on October 16, 1962, the day intelligence
officials presented him with photographs showing Soviet missile sites under construction in Cuba. Document 4 is Kennedy's October 22 television address to the nation and
the world. The president insisted on removal of the missiles and announced the U.S.
"quarantine" of Cuba. On October 26 Premier Khrushchev replied to a Kennedy letter
of the preceding day that had reiterated the U.S. case against the missile bases. The
Khrushchev letter, reprinted here as Document 5, denounces the blockade and claims
that the Soviet weapons had been sent to defend Cuba against a U.S. invasion. The

Soviet leader also offered a deal: He would remove the "armaments" from Cuba if the United States pledged not to invade Cuba.

On October 27 Khrushchev sent another letter to Kennedy, included here as Document 6. Adding to his earlier request for a no-invasion promise, Khrushchev asked for the removal of American Jupiter missiles from Turkey. President Kennedy again convened his advisers—now called the Executive Committee (ExComm)—to discuss this new request. A record of part of their meeting of October 27 is found in Document 7. Kennedy decided to pull the Jupiters out of Turkey; Robert Kennedy soon privately conveyed this concession to the Soviets, and the crisis dissipated. Document 8, from Russian archives, reports conversations between the high-ranking Soviet official Anastas I. Mikoyan and Fidel Castro in Havana on November 4 and 5. Standing out in these intense exchanges are Soviet claims of victory and Cuban protests against both superpowers for their ending the crisis without consulting the Cuban government.

1. CIA Assassination Plots Against Cuban Leader Fidel Castro (1960–1965), 1975

Efforts against Castro did not begin with assassination attempts.

From March through August 1960, during the last year of the Eisenhower Administration, the CIA considered plans to undermine Castro's charismatic appeal by sabotaging his speeches. According to the 1967 Report of the CIA's Inspector General, an official in the Technical Services Division (TSD) recalled discussing a scheme to spray Castro's broadcasting studio with a chemical which produced effects similar to LSD, but the scheme was rejected because the chemical was unreliable. During this period, TSD impregnated a box of cigars with a chemical which produced temporary disorientation, hoping to induce Castro to smoke one of the cigars before delivering a speech. The Inspector General also reported a plan to destroy Castro's image as "The Beard" by dusting his shoes with thallium salts, a strong depilatory that would cause his beard to fall out. The depilatory was to be administered during a trip outside Cuba, when it was anticipated Castro would leave his shoes outside the door of his hotel room to be shined. TSD procured the chemical and tested it on animals, but apparently abandoned the scheme because Castro cancelled his trip. . . .

A notation in the records of the Operations Division, CIA's Office of Medical Services, indicates that on August 16, 1960, an official was given a box of Castro's favorite cigars with instructions to treat them with lethal poison. The cigars were contaminated with a botulinum toxin so potent that a person would die after putting one in his mouth. The official reported that the cigars were ready on October 7, 1960; TSD notes indicate that they were delivered to an unidentified person on February 13, 1961. The record does not disclose whether an attempt was made to pass the cigars to Castro.

In August 1960, the CIA took steps to enlist members of the criminal underworld with gambling syndicate contacts to aid in assassinating Castro. . . .

——————

This document can be found in U.S. Senate, Select Committee to Study Governmental Operations with Respect to Intelligence Activities, *Alleged Assassination Plots Involving Foreign Leaders: An Interim Report* (Washington, D.C.: Government Printing Office, November 1975), 71–77, 79–80, 83–85, 148.

The earliest concrete evidence of the operation is a conversation between DDP [Deputy Director for Plans Richard] Bissell and Colonel Sheffield Edwards, Director of the Office of Security. Edwards recalled that Bissell asked him to locate someone who could assassinate Castro. Bissell confirmed that he requested Edwards to find someone to assassinate Castro and believed that Edwards raised the idea of contacting members of a gambling syndicate operating in Cuba. . . .

Edwards and the Support Chief [of the Office of Security] decided to rely on Robert A. Maheu to recruit someone "tough enough" to handle the job. Maheu was an ex-FBI agent who had entered into a career as a private investigator in 1954. A former FBI associate of Maheu's was employed in the CIA's Office of Security and had arranged for the CIA to use Maheu in several sensitive covert operations in which "he didn't want to have an Agency person or a government person get caught.". . .

Sometime in late August or early September 1960, the Support Chief approached Maheu about the proposed operation. As Maheu recalls the conversation, the Support Chief asked him to contact John Rosselli, an underworld figure with possible gambling contacts in Las Vegas, to determine if he would participate in a plan to "dispose" of Castro. The Support Chief testified, on the other hand, that it was Maheu who raised the idea of using Rosselli. . . .

According to Rosselli, he and Maheu met at the Brown Derby Restaurant in Beverly Hills in early September 1960. Rosselli testified that Maheu told him that "high government officials" needed his cooperation in getting rid of Castro, and that he asked him to help recruit Cubans to do the job. Maheu's recollection of that meeting was that "I informed him that I had been asked by my Government to solicit his cooperation in this particular venture." . . .

A meeting was arranged for Maheu and Rosselli with the Support Chief at the Plaza Hotel in New York. The Inspector General's Report placed the meeting on September 14, 1960. Rosselli testified that he could not recall the precise date of the meeting, but that it had occurred during Castro's visit to the United Nations, which the New York Times Index places from September 18 through September 28, 1960. . . .

It was arranged that Rosselli would go to Florida and recruit Cubans for the operation. Edwards informed Bissell that contact had been made with the gambling syndicate. . . .

Maheu handled the details of setting up the operation and keeping the Support Chief informed of developments. After Rosselli and Maheu had been in Miami for a short time, and certainly prior to October 18, Rosselli introduced Maheu to two individuals on whom Rosselli intended to rely: "Sam Gold," who would serve as a "back-up man," or "key" man and "Joe," whom "Gold" said would serve as a courier to Cuba and make arrangements there. The Support Chief, who was using the name "Jim Olds," said he had met "Sam" and "Joe" once, and then only briefly.

The Support Chief testified that he learned the true identities of his associates one morning when Maheu called and asked him to examine the "Parade" supplement to the *Miami Times*. An article on the Attorney General's ten-most-wanted criminals list revealed that "Sam Gold" was Momo Salvatore Giancana, a Chicago-based gangster, and "Joe" was Santos Trafficante, the Cosa Nostra chieftain in Cuba. The Support Chief reported his discovery to Edwards, but did not know whether Edwards reported this fact to his superiors. The Support Chief testified that this incident occurred after "we were up to our ears in it," a month or so after Giancana had been brought into the operation, but prior to giving the poison pills to Rosselli. . . .

The Inspector General's Report described conversations among Bissell, Edwards, and the Chief of the Technical Services Division (TSD), concerning the most effective method of poisoning Castro. There is some evidence that Giancana or Rosselli originated the idea of depositing a poison pill in Castro's drink to give the "asset" a chance to escape. The Support Chief recalled Rosselli's request for something "nice and clean, without getting into any kind of out and out ambushing," preferably a poison that would disappear without a trace. . . .

Edwards rejected the first batch of pills prepared by TSD because they would not dissolve in water. A second batch, containing botulinum toxin, "did the job expected of them" when tested on monkeys. The Support Chief received the pills from TSD, probably in February 1961, with assurances that they were lethal, and then gave them to Rosselli.

The record clearly establishes that the pills were given to a Cuban for delivery to the island some time prior to the Bay of Pigs invasion in mid-April 1961. There are discrepancies in the record, however, concerning whether one or two attempts were made during that period, and the precise date on which the passage[s] occurred. The Inspector General's Report states that in late February or March 1961, Rosselli reported to the Support Chief that the pills had been delivered to an official close to Castro who may have received kickbacks from the gambling interests. The Report states that the official returned the pills after a few weeks, perhaps because he had lost his position in the Cuban Government, and thus access to Castro, before he received the pills. The Report concludes that yet another attempt was made in April 1961, with the aid of a leading figure in the Cuban exile movement. . . .

In early April 1962, [Operation Mongoose task force chief William K.] Harvey, who testified that he was acting on "explicit orders" from [Director of Operations Richard] Helms, requested Edwards to put him in touch with Rosselli. The Support Chief first introduced Harvey to Rosselli in Miami, where Harvey told Rosselli to maintain his Cuban contacts, but not to deal with Maheu or Giancana, whom he had decided were "untrustworthy" and "surplus." The Support Chief recalled that initially Rosselli did not trust Harvey although they subsequently developed a close friendship.

Harvey, the Support Chief and Rosselli met for a second time in New York on April 8–9, 1962. A notation made during this time in the files of the Technical Services Division indicates that four poison pills were given to the Support Chief on April 18, 1962. The pills were passed to Harvey, who arrived in Miami on April 21, and found Rosselli already in touch with the same Cuban who had been involved in the pre–Bay of Pigs pill passage. He gave the pills to Rosselli, explaining that "these would work anywhere and at any time with anything." Rosselli testified that he told Harvey that the Cubans intended to use the pills to assassinate Che Guevara as well as Fidel and Raul Castro. According to Rosselli's testimony, Harvey approved of the targets, stating "everything is all right, what they want to do."

The Cuban requested arms and equipment as a *quid pro quo* for carrying out the assassination operation. With the help of the CIA's Miami station which ran covert operations against Cuba (JM/WAVE), Harvey procured explosives, detonators, rifles, handguns, radios, and boat radar costing about $5,000. . . .

Harvey met Rosselli in Miami on September 7 and 11, 1962. The Cuban was reported to be preparing to send in another three-man team to penetrate Castro's bodyguard. Harvey was told that the pills, referred to as "the medicine," were still "safe" in Cuba.

Harvey testified that by this time he had grave doubts about whether the operation would ever take place, and told Rosselli that "there's not much likelihood that this is going anyplace, or that it should be continued." The second team never left for Cuba, claiming that "conditions" in Cuba were not right. During early January 1963, Harvey paid Rosselli $2,700 to defray the Cuban's expenses. Harvey terminated the operation in mid-February 1963. . . .

As [for the question of authorization], both Helms and the high Kennedy Administration officials who testified agreed that no direct order was ever given for Castro's assassination and that no senior Administration officials, including [CIA head John A.] McCone, were informed about the assassination activity. Helms testified, however, that he believed the assassination activity was permissible and that it was within the scope of authority given to the Agency. McCone and other Kennedy Administration officials disagreed, testifying that assassination was impermissible without a direct order and that Castro's assassination was not within the bounds of the MONGOOSE operation [the covert U.S. operation designed to undermine the Castro government].

As DDP, Helms was in charge of covert operations when the poison pills were given to Rosselli in Miami in April 1962. Helms had succeeded to this post following Bissell's retirement in February 1962. He testified that after the Bay of Pigs:

> Those of us who were still [in the agency] were enormously anxious to try and be successful at what we were being asked to do by what was then a relatively new Administration. We wanted to earn our spurs with the President and with other officers of the Kennedy Administration.

2. Guidelines for Operation Mongoose, 1962

1. Operation Mongoose will be developed on the following assumptions:
   a. In undertaking to cause the overthrow of the target government, the U.S. will make maximum use of indigenous resources, internal and external, but recognizes that final success will require decisive U.S. military intervention.
   b. Such indigenous resources as are developed will be used to prepare for and justify this intervention, and thereafter to facilitate and support it.
2. The immediate priority objective of U.S. efforts during the coming months will be the acquisition of hard intelligence on the target area. Concurrently, all other political, economic and covert actions will be undertaken short of those reasonably calculated to inspire a revolt within the target area, or other development

---

This document can be found in Document 6, Guidelines for *Operation Mongoose,* 14 March 1962; Alleged Assassination Plots Involving Foreign Leaders, 20 November 1975, 145–147, 159, "The Cuban Missile Crisis: The Making of U.S. Policy," National Security Archive Microfiche Collection, National Security Archive, Washington, D.C. It can also be found in Lawrence Chang and Peter Kornbluh, eds., *The Cuban Missile Crisis: A National Security Archive Documents Reader* (New York: New Press, 1992), 38–39.

which would require armed U.S. intervention. These actions, insofar as possible, will be consistent with overt policies of isolating the [two words illegible on the document but probably are "Cuban leader"] and of neutralizing his influence in the Western Hemisphere.

3. Missiles Photographed in Cuba:
President John F. Kennedy Meets with His Advisers,
October 16, 1962

Meeting of 11:50 A.M.–12:57 P.M.

Lundahl*: This is a result of the photography taken Sunday, sir.

JFK: Yeah.

Lundahl: There's a medium-range ballistic missile launch site and two new military encampments on the southern edge of Sierra del Rosario in west central Cuba.

JFK: Where would that be?

Lundahl: Uh, west central, sir. That. . . .

JFK: Yeah. . . .

Lundahl: Well, one site on one of the encampments contains a total of at least fourteen canvas-covered missile trailers measuring 67 feet in length, 9 feet in width. The overall length of the trailers plus the tow-bars is approximately 80 feet. The other encampment contains vehicles and tents but with no missile trailers. . . .

JFK: How far advanced is this? . . . How do you know this is a medium-range ballistic missile?

Lundahl: The length, sir. . . .

JFK: Is this ready to be fired?

Graybeal**: No, sir.

JFK: How long have we got. . . . We can't tell, I take it . . .

Graybeal: No, sir.

JFK: . . . how long before it can be fired?

Graybeal: That depends on how ready the . . .

JFK: But, what does it have to be fired from?

Graybeal: It would have to be fired from a stable hard surface. This could be packed dirt; it could be concrete or, or asphalt. The surface has to be hard, then you put a flame deflect-, a deflector plate on there to direct the missile.

McNamara***: Would you care to comment on the position of nuclear warheads—this is in relation to the question from the president—explain when these can be fired?

This document can be found in Presidential Records, Transcripts, President's Office Files, John F. Kennedy Presidential Papers, John F. Kennedy Library, Boston, Mass. It can also be found in U.S. Department of State, *Foreign Relations of the United States, 1961–1963, Cuban Missile Crisis and Aftermath* (Washington, D.C.: Government Printing Office, 1996), XI, 31–45, 49–93.

*Art Lundahl, National Photograhic Interpretation Center.
**Sidney Graybeal.
***Robert McNamara, secretary of defense.

Graybeal: Sir, we've looked very hard. We can find nothing that would spell nuclear warhead in terms of any isolated area or unique security in this particular area. The mating of the nuclear warhead to the missile from some of the other short range missiles there would take about, uh, a couple of hours to do this.

McNamara: This is not defensed, I believe, at the moment?

Lundahl: Not yet, sir. . . .

Rusk*: Don't you have to assume these are nuclear? . . .

McNamara: There's no question about that. The question is one of readiness of the, to fire and—and this is highly critical in forming our plans—that the time between today and the time when the readiness to fire capability develops is a very important thing. To estimate that we need to know where these warheads are, and we have not yet found any probable storage of warheads and hence it seems extremely unlikely that they are now ready to fire or may be ready to fire within a matter of hours or even a day or two. . . .

JFK: Secretary Rusk?

Rusk: Yes. [Well?], Mr. President, this is a, of course, a [widely?] serious development. It's one that we, all of us, had not really believed the Soviets could, uh, carry this far. . . . Now, uhm, I do think we have to set in motion a chain of events that will eliminate this base. I don't think we [can?] sit still. . . . The thing that I'm, of course, very conscious of is that there is no such thing, I think, as unilateral action by the United States. It's so [eminently or heavily?] involved with 2 allies and confrontation in many places, that any action that we take, uh, will greatly increase the risks of direct action involving, uh, our other alliances and our other forces in other parts of the world. Uhm, so I think we, we have to think very hard about two major, uh, courses of action as alternatives. One is the quick strike. The point where we [make or think?], that is the, uh, overwhelming, overriding necessity to take all the risks that are involved doing that. I don't think this in itself would require an invasion of Cuba. I think that with or without such an invasion, in other words if we make it clear that, uh, what we're doing is eliminating this particular base or any other such base that is established. We ourselves are not moved to general war, we're simply doing what we said we would do if they took certain action. Uh, or we're going to decide that this is the time to eliminate the Cuban problem by actually eliminating the island.

The other would be, if we have a few days—from the military point of view, if we have the whole time—uh, then I would think that, uh, there would be another course of action, a combination of things that, uh, we might wish to consider. Uhm, first, uh, that we, uh, stimulate the OAS [Organization of American States] procedure immediately for prompt action to make it quite clear that the entire hemisphere considers that the Rio Pact [the hemispheric Cold War military alliance] has been violated [and actually?] what acts should [we take or be taken?] in, under the terms of the Rio Pact. . . .

I think also that we ought to consider getting some word to Castro, perhaps through the Canadian ambassador in Havana or through, uh, his representative at the U.N. Uh, I think perhaps the Canadian ambassador would be best, the better

---

*Dean Rusk, secretary of state.

channel to get to Castro [apart?] privately and tell him that, uh, this is no longer support for Cuba, that Cuba is being victimized here, and that, uh, the Soviets are preparing Cuba for destruction or betrayal. . . .

And I think there are certain military, uhm, uh, actions that we could, we might well want to take straight away. First, to, uh, to call up, uh, highly selective units [no more than?] 150,000. Unless we feel that it's better, more desirable to go to a general national emergency so that we have complete freedom of action. If we announce, at the time that we announce this development—and I think we do have to announce this development some time this week—uh, we announce that, uh, we are conducting a surveillance of Cuba, over Cuba, and we will enforce our right to do so. We reject the mission of secrecy in this hemisphere in any matters of this sort. We, we reinforce our forces in Guantánamo. We reinforce our forces in the southeastern part of the United States—whatever is necessary from the military point of view to be able to give, to deliver an overwhelming strike at any of these installations, including the SAM [surface-to-air missile] sites. And, uh, also, to take care of any, uh, MiGs or bombers that might make a pass at Miami or at the United States. Build up heavy forces, uh, if those are not already in position. . . .

I think also that we need a few days, uhm, to alert our other allies, for consultation with NATO [North Atlantic Treaty Organization]. I'll assume that we can move on this line at the same time to interrupt all air traffic from free world countries going into Cuba, insist to the Mexicans, the Dutch, that they stop their planes from coming in. Tell the British, who, and anyone else who's involved at this point, that, uh, if they're interested in peace, that they've got to stop their ships from Cuban trade at this point. Uh, in other words, isolate Cuba completely without at this particular moment a, uh, a forceful blockade. . . .

But I think that, by and large, there are, there are these two broad alternatives: one, the quick strike; the other, to alert our allies and Mr. Khrushchev that there is utterly serious crisis in the making here, and that, uh. . . . Mr. Khrushchev may not himself really understand that or believe that at this point. I think we'll be facing a situation that could well lead to general war. . . .

McNamara: Mr. President, there are a number of unknowns in this situation I want to comment upon, and, in relation to them, I would like to outline very briefly some possible military alternatives and ask General Taylor to expand upon them.

But before commenting on either the unknowns or outlining some military alternatives, there are two propositions I would suggest that we ought to accept as, uh, foundations for our further thinking. My first is that if we are to conduct an air strike against these installations, or against any part of Cuba, we must agree now that we will schedule that prior to the time these missile sites become operational. I'm not prepared to say when that will be, but I think it is extremely important that our talk and our discussion be founded on this premise: that any air strike will be planned to take place prior to the time they become operational. Because, if they become operational before the air strike, I do not believe we can state we can knock them out before they can be launched; and if they're launched there is almost certain to be, uh, chaos in part of the east coast or the area, uh, in a radius of six hundred to a thousand miles from Cuba.

Uh, secondly, I, I would submit the proposition that any air strike must be directed not solely against the missile sites, but against the missile sites plus the airfields plus the aircraft which may not be on the airfields but hidden by that time plus all potential nuclear storage sites. . . .

Taylor*: Uh, we're impressed, Mr. President, with the great importance of getting a, a strike with all the benefits of surprise, uh, which would mean *ideally* that we would have all the missiles that are in Cuba above ground where we can take them out. Uh, that, that desire runs counter to the strong point the secretary made if the other optimum would be to get every missile before it could, becomes operational. Uh, practically, I think the, our knowledge of the timing of the readiness is going to be so, so, uh, difficult that we'll never have the, the exact permanent, uh, the perfect timing. . . .

I would also mention among the, the military actions we should take that once we have destroyed as many of these offensive weapons as possible, we should, should prevent any more coming in, which means a naval blockade. . . .

JFK: What is the, uh, advant-. . . . Must be some major reason for the Russians to, uh, set this up as a. . . . Must be that they're not satisfied with their ICBMs [Intercontinental Ballistic Missiles]. What'd be the reason that they would, uh. . . .

Taylor: What it'd give 'em is primary, it makes the launching base, uh, for short range missiles against the United States to supplement their rather [deceptive?] ICBM system, for example. . . .

Rusk: Still, about why the Soviets are doing this, uhm, Mr. McCone** suggested some weeks ago that one thing Mr. Khrushchev may have in mind is that, uh, uh, he knows that we have a substantial nuclear superiority, but he also knows that we don't really live under fear of his nuclear weapons to the extent that, uh, he has to live under fear of ours. Also we have nuclear weapons nearby, in Turkey and places like that.

JFK: How many weapons do we have in Turkey?

Taylor?: We have Jupiter missiles. . . .

McNamara?: About fifteen, I believe it is. . . .

Rusk: . . . I think also that, uh, Berlin is, uh, very much involved in this. Uhm, for the first time, I'm beginning really to wonder whether maybe Mr. Khrushchev is entirely rational about Berlin. We've [hardly?] talked about his obsession with it. And I think we have to, uh, keep our eye on that element. But, uh, they may be thinking that they can either bargain Berlin and Cuba against each other, or that they could provoke us into a kind of action in Cuba which would give an umbrella for them to take action with respect to Berlin. . . .

JFK: Uh, eh, well, this, which . . . What you're really talking about are two or three different, uh, [tense?] operations. One is the strike just on this, these three bases. One, the second is the broader one that Secretary McNamara was talking about, which is on the airfields and on the SAM sites and on anything else connected with, uh, missiles. Third is doing both of those things and also at the same time launching a blockade, which requires really the, uh, the, uh, third and which is a larger step. And then, as I take it, the fourth question is the, uh, degree of consultation.

RFK***: Mr. President.

JFK: Yes.

---

*General Maxwell Taylor, chairman of the Joint Chiefs of Staff.
**John A. McCone, director of the Central Intelligence Agency.
***Robert F. Kennedy.

RFK: We have the fifth one, really, which is the invasion. I would say that, uh, you're dropping bombs all over Cuba if you do the second, uh, air, the airports, knocking out their planes, dropping it on all their missiles. You're covering most of Cuba. You're going to kill an awful lot of people, and, uh, we're going to take an awful lot of heat on it . . .

JFK: I don't believe it takes us, at least, uh. . . . How long did it take to get in a position where we can invade Cuba? Almost a month? Two months?

McNamara: No, sir. . . .

JFK: I think we ought to, what we ought to do is, is, uh, after this meeting this afternoon, we ought to meet tonight again at six, consider these various, uh, proposals. In the meanwhile, we'll go ahead with this maximum, whatever is needed from the flights, and, in addition, we will. . . . I don't think we got much time on these missiles. They may be. . . . So it may be that we just have to, we can't wait two weeks while we're getting ready to, to roll. Maybe just have to just take *them out,* and continue our other preparations if we decide to do that. That may be where we end up. I think we ought to, beginning right now, be preparing to. . . . Because that's what we're going to do *anyway.* We're certainly going to do number one; we're going to take out these, uh, missiles. Uh, the questions will be whether, which, what I would describe as number two, which would be a general air strike. That we're not ready to say, but we should be in preparation for it. The third is the, is the, uh, the general invasion. At least we're going to do number one, so it seems to me that we don't have to wait very long. We, we ought to be making *those* preparations.

Bundy*: You want to be clear, Mr. President, whether we have *definitely* decided *against* a political [i.e., diplomatic] track. I, myself, think we ought . . .

Taylor?: Well, we'll have . . .

Bundy: . . . to work out a contingency on that.

Taylor?: We, we'll develop both tracks.

Meeting of 6:30–7:55 P.M.

McNamara: Mr. President, could I outline three courses of action we have considered and speak very briefly on each one? The first is what I would call the political course of action, in which we, uh, follow some of the possibilities that Secretary Rusk mentioned this morning by approaching Castro, by approaching Khrushchev, by discussing with our allies. An overt and open approach politically to the problem [attempting, or in order?] to solve it. This seemed to me likely to lead to no satisfactory result, and it almost stops subsequent military action. . . .

A second course of action we haven't discussed but lies in between the military course we began discussing a moment ago and the political course of action is a course of action that would involve declaration of open surveillance; a statement that we would immediately impose an, uh, a blockade against *offensive* weapons entering Cuba in the future; and an indication that with our open-surveillance reconnaissance which we would plan to maintain indefinitely for the future. . . .

---

*McGeorge Bundy, assistant for national security affairs.

But the third course of action is any one of these variants of military action directed against Cuba, starting with an air attack against the missiles. The Chiefs are strongly opposed to so limited an air attack. But even so limited an air attack is a very extensive air attack. It's not twenty sorties or fifty sorties or a hundred sorties, but probably several hundred sorties. Uh, we haven't worked out the details. It's very difficult to do so when we lack certain intelligence that we hope to have tomorrow or the next day. But it's a substantial air attack. . . . I don't believe we have considered the consequences of any of these actions satisfactorily, and because we haven't considered the consequences, I'm not sure we're taking all the action we ought to take now to minimize those. I, I don't know quite what kind of a world we live in after we've struck Cuba, and we, we've started it. . . .

Taylor: And you'll miss some [missiles].

McNamara: And you'll miss some. That's right. Now after we've launched sorties, what kind of a world do we live in? How, how do we stop at that point? I don't know the answer to this. I think tonight State and we ought to work on the consequences of any one of these courses of actions, consequences which I don't believe are entirely clear. . . .

JFK: If the, uh, it doesn't increase very much their strategic, uh, strength, why is it, uh, can any Russian expert tell us why they. . . . After all Khrushchev demonstrated a sense of caution [thousands?] . . .

Speaker?: Well, there are several, several possible . . .

JFK: . . . Berlin, he's been cautious, I mean, he hasn't been, uh . . .

Ball*: Several possibilities, Mr. President. One of them is that he has given us word now that he's coming over in November to, to the UN. If, he may be proceeding on the assumption, and this lack of a sense of *apparent* urgency would seem to, to support this, that this *isn't* going to be discovered at the moment and that, uh, when he comes over this is something he can do, a ploy. That here is Cuba armed against the United States, or possibly use it to try to trade something in Berlin, saying he'll disarm Cuba, if, uh, if we'll yield some of our interests in Berlin and some arrangement for it. I mean, that this is a, it's a trading ploy.

Bundy: I would think one thing that I would still cling to is that he's not likely to give Fidel Castro nuclear warheads. I don't believe that has happened or is likely to happen.

JFK: Why does he put these in there though?

Bundy: Soviet-controlled nuclear warheads [of the kind?] . . .

JFK: That's right, but what is the advantage of that? It's just as if we suddenly began to put a major number of MRBMs [Medium-Range Ballistic Missiles] in Turkey. Now that'd be goddam dangerous, I would think.

Bundy: Well, we *did,* Mr. President. . . .

JFK: Yeah, but that was five years ago. . . .

Ball: Yes, I think, I think you, you look at this possibility that this is an attempt to, to add to his strategic capabilities. A second consideration is that it is simply a trading ploy, that he, he wants this in so that he could, he could [words unintelligible]. . . .

---

*George W. Ball, undersecretary of state.

JFK: Well, it's a goddam mystery to me. I don't know enough about the Soviet Union, but if anybody can tell me any other time since the Berlin blockade where the Russians have given us so clear provocation, I don't know when it's been, because they've been awfully cautious really. The Russians, I never. . . . Now, maybe our mistake was in not saying some time *before* this summer that if they do this we're [word unintelligible] to act.

4. Kennedy Addresses the Nation, October 22, 1962

This urgent transformation of Cuba into an important strategic base—by the presence of these large, long-range, and clearly offensive weapons of sudden mass destruction—constitutes an explicit threat to the peace and security of all the Americas, in flagrant and deliberate defiance of the Rio Pact of 1947, the traditions of this nation and hemisphere, the Joint Resolution of the 87th Congress, the Charter of the United Nations, and my own public warnings to the Soviets on September 4 and 13.

This action also contradicts the repeated assurances of Soviet spokesmen, both publicly and privately delivered, that the arms buildup in Cuba would retain its original defensive character and that the Soviet Union had no need or desire to station strategic missiles on the territory of any other nation.

The size of this undertaking makes clear that it has been planned for some months. Yet only last month, after I had made clear the distinction between any introduction of ground-to-ground missiles and the existence of defensive antiaircraft missiles, the Soviet Government publicly stated on September 11 that, and I quote, "The armaments and military equipment sent to Cuba are designed exclusively for defensive purposes," and, and I quote the Soviet Government, "There is no need for the Soviet Government to shift its weapons for a retaliatory blow to any other country, for instance Cuba," and that, and I quote the Government, "The Soviet Union has so powerful rockets to carry these nuclear warheads that there is no need to search for sites for them beyond the boundaries of the Soviet Union." That statement was false.

Only last Thursday, as evidence of this rapid offensive buildup was already in my hand, Soviet Foreign Minister Gromyko told me in my office that he was instructed to make it clear once again, as he said his Government had already done, that Soviet assistance to Cuba, and I quote, "pursued solely the purpose of contributing to the defense capabilities of Cuba," that, and I quote him, "training by Soviet specialists of Cuban nationals in handling defensive armaments was by no means offensive," and that "if it were otherwise," Mr. Gromyko went on, "the Soviet Government would never become involved in rendering such assistance." That statement also was false.

Neither the United States of America nor the world community of nations can tolerate deliberate deception and offensive threats on the part of any nation, large or small. We no longer live in a world where only the actual firing of weapons represents a sufficient challenge to a nation's security to constitute maximum peril.

This document can be found in *Department of State Bulletin* 47 (November 12, 1962): 715–720.

Nuclear weapons are so destructive and ballistic missiles are so swift that any sub-stantially increased possibility of their use or any sudden change in their deploy-ment may well be regarded as a definite threat to peace. . . .

[T]his secret, swift, and extraordinary buildup of Communist missiles—in an area well known to have a special and historical relationship to the United States and the nations of the Western Hemisphere, in violation of Soviet assurances, and in defiance of American and hemispheric policy—this sudden, clandestine decision to station strategic weapons for the first time outside of Soviet soil—is a deliber-ately provocative and unjustified change in the *status quo* which cannot be accepted by this country if our courage and our commitments are ever to be trusted again by either friend or foe.

The 1930's taught us a clear lesson: Aggressive conduct, if allowed to grow unchecked and unchallenged, ultimately leads to war. This nation is opposed to war. We are also true to our word. Our unswerving objective, therefore, must be to pre-vent the use of these missiles against this or any other country and to secure their withdrawal or elimination from the Western Hemisphere. . . .

I have directed that the following *initial* steps be taken immediately:

First: To halt this offensive buildup, a strict quarantine on all offensive mili-tary equipment under shipment to Cuba is being initiated. All ships of any kind bound for Cuba from whatever nation or port will, if found to contain cargoes of offensive weapons, be turned back. This quarantine will be extended, if needed, to other types of cargo and carriers. We are not at this time, however, denying the ne-cessities of life as the Soviets attempted to do in their Berlin blockade of 1948.

Second: I have directed the continued and increased close surveillance of Cuba and its military buildup. The Foreign Ministers of the OAS in their commu-niqué of October 3 rejected secrecy on such matters in this hemisphere. Should these offensive military preparations continue, thus increasing the threat to the hemisphere, further action will be justified. I have directed the Armed Forces to prepare for any eventualities; and I trust that, in the interest of both the Cuban people and the Soviet technicians at the sites, the hazards to all concerned of continuing this threat will be recognized.

Third: It shall be the policy of this nation to regard any nuclear missile launched from Cuba against any nation in the Western Hemisphere as an attack by the Soviet Union on the United States, requiring a full retaliatory response upon the Soviet Union.

Fourth: As a necessary military precaution I have reinforced our base at Guantánamo, evacuated today the dependents of our personnel there, and ordered additional military units to be on a standby alert basis.

Fifth: We are calling tonight for an immediate meeting of the Organ of Con-sultation, under the Organization of American States, to consider this threat to hemispheric security and to invoke articles 6 and 8 of the Rio Treaty in support of all necessary action. The United Nations Charter allows for regional security arrangements—and the nations of this hemisphere decided long ago against the military presence of outside powers. Our other allies around the world have also been alerted.

Sixth: Under the Charter of the United Nations, we are asking tonight that an emergency meeting of the Security Council be convoked without delay to take action against this latest Soviet threat to world peace. Our resolution will call for the prompt dismantling and withdrawal of all offensive weapons in Cuba, under the supervision of U.N. observers, before the quarantine can be lifted.

Seventh and finally: I call upon Chairman Khrushchev to halt and eliminate this clandestine, reckless, and provocative threat to world peace and to stable relations between our two nations. I call upon him further to abandon this course of world domination and to join in an historic effort to end the perilous arms race and transform the history of man. He has an opportunity now to move the world back from the abyss of destruction—by returning to his Government's own words that it had no need to station missiles outside its own territory, and withdrawing these weapons from Cuba—by refraining from any action which will widen or deepen the present crisis—and then by participating in a search for peaceful and permanent solutions.

This nation is prepared to present its case against the Soviet threat to peace, and our own proposals for a peaceful world, at any time and in any forum—in the OAS, in the United Nations, or in any other meeting that could be useful—without limiting our freedom of action. . . .

But it is difficult to settle or even discuss these problems in an atmosphere of intimidation. That is why this latest Soviet threat—or any other threat which is made either independently or in response to our actions this week—must and will be met with determination. Any hostile move anywhere in the world against the safety and freedom of peoples to whom we are committed—including in particular the brave people of West Berlin—will be met by whatever action is needed.

Finally, I want to say a few words to the captive people of Cuba, to whom this speech is being directly carried by special radio facilities. I speak to you as a friend, as one who knows of your deep attachment to your fatherland, as one who shares your aspirations for liberty and justice for all. And I have watched and the American people have watched with deep sorrow how your nationalist revolution was betrayed and how your fatherland fell under foreign domination. Now your leaders are no longer Cuban leaders inspired by Cuban ideals. They are puppets and agents of an international conspiracy which has turned Cuba against your friends and neighbors in the Americas. . . .

Many times in the past the Cuban people have risen to throw out tyrants who destroyed their liberty. And I have no doubt that most Cubans today look forward to the time when they will be truly free—free from foreign domination, free to choose their own leaders, free to select their own system, free to own their own land, free to speak and write and worship without fear or degradation. And then shall Cuba be welcomed back to the society of free nations and to the associations of this hemisphere.

My fellow citizens, let no one doubt that this is a difficult and dangerous effort on which we have set out. No one can foresee precisely what course it will take or what costs or casualties will be incurred. Many months of sacrifice and self-discipline lie ahead—months in which both our patience and our will will be tested, months in which many threats and denunciations will keep us aware of our dangers. But the greatest danger of all would be to do nothing.

5. Soviet Premier Nikita Khrushchev Asks for a U.S. No-Invasion Pledge, October 26, 1962

I see, Mr. President, that you too are not devoid of a sense of anxiety for the fate of the world, [not without an] understanding . . . of what war entails. What would a war give you? You are threatening us with war. But you well know that the very least which you would receive in reply would be that you would experience the same consequences as those which you sent us. And that must be clear to us, people invested with authority, trust, and responsibility. We must not succumb to intoxication and petty passions, regardless of whether elections are impending in this or that country, or not impending. These are all transient things, but if indeed war should break out, then it would not be in our power to stop it, for such is the logic of war. I have participated in two wars and know that war ends when it has rolled through cities and villages, everywhere sowing death and destruction.

In the name of the Soviet Government and the Soviet people, I assure you that your conclusions regarding offensive weapons on Cuba are groundless. It is apparent from what you have written me that our conceptions are different on this score, or rather, we have different estimates of these or those military means. Indeed, in reality, the same forms of weapons can have different interpretations.

You are a military man and, I hope, will understand me. Let us take for example a simple cannon. What sort of means is this: offensive or defensive? A cannon is a defensive means if it is set up to defend boundaries or a fortified area. But if one concentrates artillery, and adds to it the necessary number of troops, then the same cannons do become an offensive means, because they prepare and clear the way for infantry to attack. The same happens with missile-nuclear weapons as well, with any type of this weapon. . . .

You have now proclaimed piratical measures, which were employed in the Middle Ages, when ships proceeding in international waters were attacked, and you have called this "a quarantine" around Cuba. Our vessels, apparently, will soon enter the zone which your Navy is patrolling. I assure you that these vessels, now bound for Cuba, are carrying the most innocent peaceful cargoes. Do you really think that we only occupy ourselves with the carriage of so-called offensive weapons, atomic and hydrogen bombs? Although perhaps your military people imagine that these [cargoes] are some sort of special type of weapon, I assure you that they are the most ordinary peaceful products.

Consequently, Mr. President, let us show good sense. I assure you that on those ships, which are bound for Cuba, there are no weapons at all. The weapons

---

This document can be found in *Problems of Communism,* Special Issue: "Back from the Brink," 41 (Spring 1992): 37–45. It can also be found in U.S. Department of State, *Foreign Relations of the United States, 1961–1963, Cuban Missile Crisis and Aftermath* (Washington, D.C.: Government Printing Office, 1996), XL, 235–240.

which were necessary for the defense of Cuba are already there. I do not want to say that there were not any shipments of weapons at all. No, there were such shipments. But now Cuba has already received the necessary means of defense. . . .

Let us normalize relations. We have received an appeal from the Acting Secretary General of the UN, U Thant, with his proposals. I have already answered him. His proposals come to this, that our side should not transport armaments of any kind to Cuba during a certain period of time, while negotiations are being conducted—and we are ready to enter such negotiations—and the other side should not undertake any sort of piratical actions against vessels engaged in navigation on the high seas. I consider these proposals reasonable. This would be a way out of the situation which has been created, which would give the peoples the possibility of breathing calmly.

You have asked what happened, what evoked the delivery of weapons to Cuba? You have spoken about this to our Minister of Foreign Affairs. I will tell you frankly, Mr. President, what evoked it.

We were very grieved by the fact—I spoke about it in Vienna [at the 1961 summit meeting]—that a landing took place [Bay of Pigs], that an attack on Cuba was committed, as a result of which many Cubans perished. You yourself told me then that this had been a mistake. . . .

Why have we proceeded to assist Cuba with military and economic aid? The answer is: we have proceeded to do so only for reasons of humanitarianism. At one time, our people itself had a revolution when Russia was still a backward country. We were attacked then. We were the target of attack by many countries. The USA participated in that adventure. . . .

You once said that the United States was not preparing an invasion. But you also declared that you sympathized with the Cuban counterrevolutionary emigrants, that you support them and would help them to realize their plans against the present government of Cuba. It is also not a secret to anyone that the threat of armed attack, aggression, has constantly hung, and continues to hang over Cuba. It was only this which impelled us to respond to the request of the Cuban government to furnish it aid for the strengthening of the defensive capacity of this country.

If assurance were given by the President and the government of the United States that the USA itself would not participate in an attack on Cuba and would restrain others from actions of this sort, if you would recall your fleet, this would immediately change everything. I am not speaking for Fidel Castro, but I think that he and the government of Cuba, evidently, would declare demobilization and would appeal to the people to get down to peaceful labor. Then, too, the question of armaments would disappear, since, if there is no threat, then armaments are a burden for every people. Then, too, the question of the destruction, not only of the armaments which you call offensive, but of all other armaments as well, would look different. . . .

Let us therefore show statesmanlike wisdom. I propose: we, for our part, will declare that our ships, bound for Cuba, will not carry any kind of armaments. You would declare that the United States will not invade Cuba with its forces and will not support any sort of forces which might intend to carry out an invasion of Cuba. Then the necessity for the presence of our military specialists in Cuba would disappear.

Mr. President, I appeal to you to weigh well what the aggressive, piratical actions, which you have declared the USA intends to carry out in international waters, would lead to. You yourself know that any sensible man simply cannot agree with this, cannot recognize your right to such actions.

If you did this as the first step towards the unleashing of war, well then, it is evident that nothing else is left to us but to accept this challenge of yours. If, however, you have not lost your self-control and sensibly conceive what this might lead to, then, Mr. President, we and you ought not now to pull on the ends of the rope in which you have tied the knot of war, because the more the two of us pull, the tighter that knot will be tied. And a moment may come when that knot will be tied so tight that even he who tied it will not have the strength to untie it, and then it will be necessary to cut that knot. And what that would mean is not for me to explain to you, because you yourself understand perfectly of what terrible forces our countries dispose.

Consequently, if there is no intention to tighten that knot and thereby to doom the world to the catastrophe of thermonuclear war, then let us not only relax the forces pulling on the ends of the rope, let us take measures to untie that knot. We are ready for this.

6. Khrushchev Requests U.S. Removal of Jupiter Missiles from Turkey, October 27, 1962

You are worried over Cuba. You say that it worries you because it lies at a distance of 90 miles across the sea from the shores of the United States. However, Turkey lies next to us. Our sentinels are pacing up and down and watching each other. Do you believe that you have the right to demand security for your country and the removal of such weapons that you qualify as offensive, while not recognizing this right for us?

You have stationed devastating rocket weapons, which you call offensive, in Turkey literally right next to us. How then does recognition of our equal military possibilities tally with such unequal relations between our great states? This does not tally at all. . . .

This is why I make this proposal: We agree to remove those weapons from Cuba which you regard as offensive weapons. We agree to do this and to state this commitment in the United Nations. Your representatives will make a statement to the effect that the United States, on its part, bearing in mind the anxiety and concern of the Soviet state, will evacuate its analogous weapons from Turkey. . . .

The U.S. Government will . . . declare that the United States will respect the integrity of the frontiers of Cuba, its sovereignty, undertakes not to intervene in its domestic affairs, not to invade and not to make its territory available as place d'armes for the invasion of Cuba, and also will restrain those who would think of launching an aggression against Cuba either from U.S. territory or from the territory of other states bordering on Cuba.

This document can be found in *Problems of Communism,* Special Issue: "Back from the Brink," 41 (Spring 1992): 45–50. It can also be found in U.S. Department of State, *Foreign Relations of the United States, 1961–1963, Cuban Missile Crisis and Aftermath* (Washington, D.C.: Government Printing Office, 1996), XI, 257–260.

7. Kennedy and ExComm Consider Trading the Jupiter Missiles in Turkey, October 27, 1962

JFK (reading): "Premier Khrushchev told President Kennedy yesterday he would withdraw offensive missiles from Cuba if the United States withdrew its rockets from Turkey."

Speaker?: He didn't really say that, did he? . . .

JFK: That wasn't in the letter [of October 26] we received, was it?

Speaker?: No. . . .

JFK: We're going to be in an insupportable position on this matter if this becomes his proposal. In the first place, we last year tried to get the [Jupiter] missiles out of there [Turkey] because they're not militarily useful, number one. Number two, it's going to—to any man at the United Nations or any other rational man it will look like a very fair trade. . . .

I think you're going to find it very difficult to explain why we are going to take hostile military action in Cuba, against these [missile] sites—what we've been thinking about—the thing that he's saying is, if you'll get yours out of Turkey, we'll get ours out of Cuba. I think we've got a very tough one here. . . .

He's put this out in a way that's caused maximum tension and embarrassment. It's not as if it was a private proposal, which would give us an opportunity to negotiate with the Turks. He's put it out in a way that the Turks are bound to say they don't agree to this. . . .

They've got a very good card. This one is going to be very tough, I think, for us. It's going to be tough in England, I'm sure—as well as other places on the continent—we're going to be forced to take action, that might seem, in my opinion, not a blank check but a pretty good check to take action in Berlin on the grounds that we were wholly unreasonable. Most think—people think that if you're allowed an even trade you ought to take *advantage* of it. Therefore it makes it much more difficult for us to move with world support. These are all the things that—uh—why this is a pretty good play of his. . . .

I'm just thinking about what—what we're going to have to do in a day or so, which is [deleted] sorties and [deleted] days, and possibly an invasion, all because we wouldn't take missiles out of Turkey, and we all know how quickly everybody's courage goes when the blood starts to flow, and that's what's going to happen in NATO, when they—we start these things, and they grab Berlin, and everybody's going to say, "Well that was a pretty good proposition." Let's not kid ourselves that we've got—that's the difficulty. Today it sounds great to reject it, but it's not going to, after we do something. . . .

Thompson*: The important thing for Khrushchev, it seems to me, is to be able to say, I saved Cuba, I stopped an invasion—and he can get away with this, if he wants to, and he's had a go at this Turkey thing, and that we'll discuss later. . . .

This document can be found in Presidential Recordings, Transcripts, President's Office Files, John F. Kennedy Presidential Papers, John F. Kennedy Library, Boston, Mass. It can also be found in David A. Welch and James G. Blight, "October 27, 1962: Transcript of the Meetings of the ExComm," *International Security* XII (Winter 1987–1988): 30–92.

*Llewellyn E. Thompson, U.S. ambassador to the Soviet Union, July 16, 1957–July 27, 1962; U.S. ambassador-at-large, October 3, 1962–1966.

LBJ*: Bob [McNamara], if you're willing to give up your missiles in Turkey, you think you ought to [words unclear] why don't you say that to him and say we're cutting a trade—make the trade there? [mixed voices] save all the invasion, lives and—

Speaker?: The State Department, they invite them—we talked about this, and they said they'd be *delighted* to trade those missiles in Turkey for the things in Cuba.

McNamara: I said I thought it was the realistic solution to the problem.

LBJ: Sure. What we were afraid of was he'd never offer this, but what he'd want to do was trade [mixed voices] *Berlin.* . . .

JFK: We can't very well invade Cuba with all its toil, and long as it's going to be, when we could have gotten them out by making a deal on the same missiles in Turkey. If that's part of the record I don't see how we'll have a very good war. . . .

Well, let's see—uh—let's give him [Khrushchev] an explanation of what we're trying to do. We're trying to get it back on the original proposition of last night, and—because we don't want to get into this trade. If we're unsuccessful, then we—it's *possible* that we may have to get back on the Jupiter thing.

8. Soviet Official Anastas I. Mikoyan and Fidel Castro Debate and Review the Crisis, November 4–5, 1962

Mikoyan-Castro Meeting in Havana, November 4, 1962

[Mikoyan:] I remember that after visiting Bulgaria [in May 1962], Nikita Khrushchev told you that all through his stay in that country he had been thinking of Cuba, fearing that the Americans might mount armed intervention with the aid of reactionary Latin American governments or commit outright aggression. They refuse to allow Cuba to grow stronger, Nikita Khrushchev told us, and if Cuba were defeated, the whole world revolutionary movement would suffer a heavy blow. We must thwart the American imperialists' plans, he said. . . .

The only purpose of shipping Soviet troops and strategic arms to Cuba was to strengthen your defences. Ours was a containment plan, a plan intended to discourage the imperialists from playing with fire in regard to Cuba. Had we developed strategic arms in secrecy, with America knowing nothing about those arms' presence in Cuba, they would have served as a strong deterrent. That was the assumption we started from. Our military told us that Cuba's palm forests made it possible to dependably camouflage strategic missiles against detection from the air. . . .

[Despite the U.S. detection of the missiles] Kennedy agreed to Soviet troops being left in Cuba and as the Cubans kept powerful weapons and anti-aircraft missiles, we may consider that he made a concession for his part.

Kennedy's statement about nonaggression against Cuba by the United States and Latin American countries is another concession. If we take these reciprocal concessions and all other factors into account, we will see that we've won a big victory. Never before have the Americans made such statements. This is why we

---

This document can be found in "Documents: Dialogue in Havana. The Caribbean Crisis," *International Affairs* (Moscow) 10 (1992): 109–111, 114, 115, 116, 117, 122, 123.

*Lyndon B. Johnson, vice president.

came to the conclusion that we were achieving the main goal, which is to preserve Cuba. There will be no attack on Cuba. Nor will there be any war. We are winning more favourable positions.

Of course, we should have sent our draft decision to Cuba, should have consulted you and secured your consent before publishing it. We would actually have done so in a normal situation. Fidel Castro wrote us in his letter [of October 26] that aggression within the next 24 hours was imminent. When we received the letter and discussed the situation, the start of aggression was only 10 to 12 hours away.

Let us compare the situation today with what it was before the crisis. At that time the Americans were planning armed intervention against Cuba. But now they have committed themselves not to attack Cuba. This is a great achievement. . . .

Frankly speaking, we had not at all been thinking about the bases in Turkey. But when discussing the dangerous situation that had developed, we received information from the United States saying that, from what [the journalist Walter] Lippmann wrote in his column, the Russians might raise the question of abolishing the US bases in Turkey. The possibility of our putting forward such a demand was discussed among Americans. The idea was debated in the United States. That was how that demand came to be advanced. Subsequently, however, we stopped insisting on it because the US bases in that country are no problem for us. The Turkish bases are of little significance as we see it. They will be destroyed in case of war. Of course, they have some political significance but we don't pay them any particular attention although we plan to press for their elimination.

Mikoyan-Castro Meeting in Havana, November 5, 1962

[Castro:] We have no doubt that had the siting of the strategic weapon been completed in secret, we would have obtained in that way a powerful deterrent against American plans for attack on our country. That would have meant achieving goals pursued by both the Soviet government and the government of the Republic of Cuba. We consider, however, that the deployment of Soviet missiles in Cuba was important in that it served the interests of the whole socialist camp. Even assuming that their deployment provided no military advantage, it was important politically and psychologically for the effort to contain imperialism and prevent it from implementing its plans for aggression. It follows that the strategic weapon was deployed in Cuba in the interest of defending not only Cuba but the socialist camp as a whole. It was a move made with our full consent.

We were well aware of the significance of that move and consider that it was the right thing to do.

We fully agree that war is inadmissible. We are not against the fact that the measures adopted had a twofold purpose, namely, preventing an attack on Cuba and staving off a world war. We fully subscribe to these aims pursued by the Soviet Union.

What gave rise to misunderstanding was the form in which the matter was discussed. We realise, however, that there were circumstances demanding prompt action and that the situation was not normal. . . .

The United States could have been told that the Soviet Union was ready to dismantle the facility but wanted to discuss the matter with the Cuban government. We believe you should have decided the question that way rather than issuing instructions at once on the removal of the strategic weapon. Such an approach would have eased international tension and made it possible to discuss the problem with the Americans in a more favourable context. It would have enabled us not only to bring about a lessening of international tension and discuss the matter in more favourable conditions but to secure the signing of a declaration.

E S S A Y S

In the first essay, Robert Dallek of Boston University, a recent biographer of John F. Kennedy, acknowledges that the Kennedy administration's attempts to overthrow Fidel Castro soured Cuban-American relations, but he assigns primary responsibility for the Cuban missile crisis to Soviet leader Nikita Khrushchev. According to Dallek, Khrushchev recklessly used Cuban-American hostilities as an opportunity to place medium-range nuclear missiles in Cuba, redress the global balance of power with the United States, and increase Moscow's bargaining leverage on Cold War issues such as Berlin. Examining the administration's decisionmaking, Dallek exalts President Kennedy as a model for wise statesmanship by highlighting the president's role in the Executive Committee of the National Security Council, where he sidetracked calls for immediate military action and forged a consensus in favor of patient diplomacy and measured pressure. The president's determination and America's nuclear superiority, Dallek concludes, convinced Khrushchev to remove the missiles.

Thomas G. Paterson, professor emeritus at the University of Connecticut, disagrees. In the second essay, Paterson emphasizes the centrality of Cuban-American relations to the Cold War missile crisis. Conspicuous, repeated, and threatening U.S. actions incited Cuban fears of an invasion. Cuba's quest for defense joined with Soviet objectives to prompt the mid-1962 Cuban-Soviet agreement to deploy missiles on the island. Paterson next explores the management of the crisis. Noting the near misses and accidents, the severe stress experienced by administration officials, and the Executive Committee's inflated record, Paterson questions the thesis that Kennedy's leadership represents a superb example of crisis management. Rather, fear of events spinning out of control—of a nuclear doomsday—mattered as much as anything else in bringing the crisis to a close. Paterson concludes that the near miss did little to chasten Kennedy, whose fixation with Cuba quickly reasserted itself after the Soviet-American crisis had passed.

Patient Diplomacy and Measured Pressure: JFK's Finest Hour

ROBERT DALLEK

[Soviet leader Nikita] Khrushchev saw multiple benefits from the deployment of Soviet missiles abroad. It would deter a U.S. attack on Cuba, keep the island in Moscow's orbit, and give him greater leverage in bargaining with Washington over Berlin. Yet such a substantial change in the balance of power seemed likely to provoke a crisis and possibly a war with the United States. Khrushchev convinced himself, however, that the "intelligent" Kennedy "would not set off a thermonuclear war

From Robert Dallek, *An Unfinished Life: John F. Kennedy, 1917–1963* (Boston: Little, Brown and Company, 2003), pp. 535–539, 542–574. Copyright © 2003 by Robert Dallek. By permission of Little, Brown and Company, Inc.

if there were our warheads there, just as they put their warheads on missiles in Turkey." These seventeen intermediate-range Jupiter missiles under U.S. command, which became operational in 1962, had indeed frightened Moscow, but Khrushchev did not anticipate using his missiles. "Every idiot can start a war," Khrushchev told Kremlin associates, "but it is impossible to win this war. . . . Therefore the missiles have one purpose—to scare them, to restrain them . . . to give them back some of their own medicine." The deployment would equalize "what the West likes to call 'the balance of power.' The Americans had surrounded our country with military bases and threatened us with nuclear weapons, and now they would learn just what it feels like to have enemy missiles pointing at [them]." . . .

Khrushchev's aim was to hide the buildup in Cuba until after the American elections, when he planned to attend the U.N. General Assembly and see Kennedy. He would then reveal the existence of the Cuban missile base and extract concessions from the president over Berlin and Cuba. As historians Aleksandr Fursenko and Timothy Naftali concluded, borrowing from JFK, it was "one hell of a gamble." . . .

In August 1962, U.S. intelligence reported increased Soviet military equipment going to Cuba, where it was transported to the interior of the island under Soviet guards. U.S. national security officials concluded that the Soviets were installing SA-2 missiles, a modern anti-aircraft weapon with a thirty-mile range. The report noted that the SA-2s could be fit with nuclear warheads, "but there is no evidence that the Soviet government had ever provided nuclear warheads to any other state, on any terms. It seems unlikely that such a move is currently planned—but," the analysts warned, "there is also little reason to suppose that the Soviets would refuse to introduce such weapons if the move could be controlled in the Soviet interest."

Soviet private and public statements also gave Kennedy assurances that the military buildup represented a change in degree but not in kind. In April 1961, after the Bay of Pigs invasion, Khrushchev had told Kennedy, "We have no bases in Cuba, and do not intend to establish any." On July 30, 1962, in order to reduce the likelihood of exposure, Khrushchev asked Kennedy, "for the sake of better relations," to stop reconnaissance flights over Soviet ships in the Caribbean. Eager to avoid any international crisis during the election campaign, Kennedy ostensibly agreed. . . .

However much Kennedy wished to believe the Soviet professions of restraint, he could not take their assurances at face value; their deviousness in secretly preparing renewed nuclear tests had made him suspicious of anything they said. Besides, [CIA director John] McCone and Bobby [the president's brother and attorney general] were asserting that the "defensive" buildup might presage offensive missile deployments, and even if not, they saw the expanding Soviet presence in Cuba as reason to topple Castro's regime as quickly as possible. Complaints from Republicans about timid responses to the Cuban danger joined with the McCone-Bobby warnings to heighten Kennedy's concerns. . . .

On September 4, Kennedy and his advisers spent several hours preparing a statement about Soviet missiles in Cuba. To be as clear as possible, Kennedy expanded an admonition about "offensive weapons" to include a warning against "ground-to-ground missiles." He also eliminated any mention of the Monroe Doctrine and kept references to Cuba to a minimum. He wanted the statement to focus on Soviet aggression and not on U.S. power in the Western Hemisphere or on the administration's eagerness to topple [Fidel] Castro's regime. . . .

On October 1, [however, Secretary of Defense Robert S.] McNamara and the Joint Chiefs received disturbing information about offensive weapons in Cuba. On September 21, the Defense Intelligence Agency had learned of "a first-hand sighting on September 12 of a truck convoy of 20 objects 65 to 70 feet long which resembled large missiles." The convoy had "turned into an airport on the southwest edge of Havana." Because early reports of a similar nature had proved false, the DIA described the information as only "potentially significant." However, photographs received in the last week of September and reports of surface-to-air missile (SAM) sites produced "a hypothesis that MRBM [medium-range ballistic missile] sites were under preparation in Pinar del Rio province." . . .

October 9, Kennedy approved a U-2 [spy plane] mission to take place as soon as weather permitted. Clear visibility up to seventy-four thousand feet, the U-2's altitude, did not occur until October 14. In the meantime, on October 10, [Senator Kenneth] Keating [R-NY] publicly announced that he had evidence of six IRBM (intermediate-range ballistic missile) sites in Cuba. The IRBMs, which could reach targets twenty-one hundred miles away, had twice the range of MRBMs. . . .

To Kennedy's distress, the October 14 U-2 flight over the island, which lasted six minutes and produced 928 photographs, revealed conclusive evidence of offensive weapons: three medium-range ballistic missile sites under construction; one additional MRBM site discovered at San Cristobal; and two IRBM sites at Guanajay. The photos also revealed twenty-one crated IL-28 medium-range bombers capable of delivering nuclear bombs. The CIA's report on the discoveries reached [National Security Adviser McGeorge] Bundy on the evening of October 15, but he decided to wait until morning to present this "very big news" to the president, when enlargements of the photographs would be available. . . .

At 8:45 on the morning of the sixteenth, Bundy brought the bad news to Kennedy in his bedroom. The president ordered Bundy to set up a White House meeting in the Cabinet Room before noon and ticked off the names of the national security officials he wanted there. He then called Bobby, who had been first on his list. "We have some big trouble. I want you over here," the president told him. Determined not to create a public crisis and demands for press comments before he had had a chance to consider his options, Kennedy kept his early-morning appointments. . . .

At 11:45 A.M., thirteen men joined the president in the Cabinet Room for an hour-and-ten-minute discussion. The group came to be called Ex Comm, the Executive Committee of the National Security Council. Kennedy sat in the center of an oblong table, with [Secretary of State Dean] Rusk, [Undersecretary of State George] Ball, and Deputy Undersecretary of State U. Alexis Johnson to his immediate right and McNamara, [Deputy Defense Secretary Roswell] Gilpatric, Joint Chiefs chairman Maxwell Taylor, and acting CIA director Marshall Carter (McCone was at a family funeral) to his immediate left. Bundy, [Treasury Secretary Douglas] Dillon, Bobby, and [Vice-president Lyndon] Johnson sat across from the president. Two experts on aerial photography, Arthur Lundahl and Sidney Graybeal, briefed the group on the U-2 photos, which were propped on easels. . . .

The principal focus on the meeting was on how to eliminate the missiles from Cuba. Rusk thought that they could do it by a "sudden, unannounced strike of some sort," or by a political track in which they built up the crisis "to the point where the other side has to consider very seriously about giving in." Perhaps they could talk sense to Castro through an intermediary, Rusk suggested. "It ought to be said to

Castro that this kind of a base is intolerable. . . . The time has now come when he must, in the interests of the Cuban people . . . break cleanly with the Soviet Union and prevent this missile base from becoming operational." The alternative to the quick strike, Rusk said, was "to alert our allies and Mr. Khrushchev that there is an utterly serious crisis in the making here. . . . We'll be facing a situation that could well lead to a general war. . . . We have an obligation to do what has to be done, but to do it in a way that gives everybody a chance to pull away from it before it gets too hard."

For the moment, Kennedy was not thinking about any political or diplomatic solution; his focus was on military options and how to mute the crisis until they had some clear idea of what to do. He saw four possible military actions: an air strike against the missile installations; a more general air attack against a wide array of targets; a blockade; and an invasion. He wanted preparations for the second, third, and fourth possibilities, decisions on which could come later. But "we're certainly going to do number one," he said. "We're going to take out these missiles." Just when, he did not say, but he wanted knowledge of the missiles limited to as few offiials as possible. He believed that the news would leak anyway in two or three days. But even when it became known, he wanted policy decisions to remain secret. "Otherwise," he said, "we bitch it up."

He scheduled another Ex Comm meeting for 6:30 that evening. . . .

The evening meeting included the morning's participants as well as [speech writer Theodore] Sorensen and Edwin Martin, a State Department expert on Latin America. Kennedy . . . [expressed] his puzzlement over Khrushchev's actions. Khrushchev had, all things considered, been cautious over Berlin, so how did the Russian experts explain his willingness to risk a war by putting nuclear missiles in Cuba, especially if, as some believed, it did not reduce America's military advantage over the USSR? "Well, it's a goddamn mystery to me," Kennedy admitted. "I don't know enough about the Soviet Union, but if anybody can tell me any other time since the Berlin blockade where the Russians have given so clear a provocation, I don't know when it's been, because they've been awfully cautious, really."

Ball, Bundy, and Alex Johnson saw the Soviets as trying to expand their strategic capabilities. But McNamara was not so sure. The Joint Chiefs thought the Soviet missile deployments "substantially" changed the strategic balance, but McNamara believed it made no difference. Taylor acknowledged that the missiles in Cuba meant "just a few more missiles targeted on the United States," but he considered them "a very, a rather important, adjunct and reinforcement" to Moscow's "strike capability." . . .

The question that remained, then, was how to remove the missiles without a full-scale war. Despite his earlier certainty, Kennedy had begun to have doubts about a surprise air strike and may already have ruled this out as a sensible option. When he asked at the morning meeting, "How effective can the take-out be?" Taylor had answered, "It'll never be 100 percent, Mr. President, we know. We hope to take out the vast majority in the first strike, but this is not just one thing—one strike, one day—but continuous air attack for whenever necessary, whenever we discover a target." Kennedy picked up on the uncertain results of such an operation: "Well, let's say we just take out the missile bases," he said. "Then they have some more there. Obviously they can get them in by submarine and so on. I don't know whether you just keep high strikes on." . . .

The only new idea put forth at the evening meeting came from McNamara. He suggested a middle ground between the military and political courses they had been discussing. He proposed a "declaration of open surveillance: a statement that we would immediately impose a blockade against offensive weapons entering Cuba in the future, and an indication that, with our open surveillance reconnaissance, which we would plan to maintain indefinitely for the future, we would be prepared to immediately attack the Soviet Union in the event that Cuba made any offensive move against this country."

After a long day of discussions, Kennedy was no closer to a firm decision on how to proceed. On Wednesday, the seventeenth, while he continued to hide the crisis from public view by meeting with West Germany's foreign minister, eating lunch with Libya's crown prince, and flying to Connecticut to campaign for Democratic candidates, his advisers held nonstop meetings. But first he saw McCone, who had returned to Washington, at 9:30 in the morning. The CIA director gained the impression that Kennedy was "inclined to act promptly if at all, without warning, targeting on MRBMs and possible airfields." McCone may have been hearing what he wanted to hear, or, more likely, Kennedy created this impression by inviting McCone to make the case for prompt air strikes.

As part of his balancing act, Kennedy invited [U.S. ambassador to the U.N.] Adlai Stevenson into the discussion. After learning about the crisis from the president, who showed him the missile photos on the afternoon of the sixteenth, Stevenson predictably urged Kennedy not to rush into military action. When Kennedy said, "I suppose the alternatives are to go in by air and wipe them out, or to take other steps to render the weapons inoperable," Stevenson replied, "Let's not go into an air strike until we have explored the possibilities of a peaceful solution." . . .

When Ex Comm met again on Thursday morning, October 18, additional reconnaissance photos revealed construction of IRBM launching pads. They had now discovered five different missile sites. McCone reported that the Soviets could have between sixteen and thirty-two missiles ready to fire "within a week or slightly more." Concerned about convincing the world of the accuracy of their information, Kennedy wanted to know if an untrained observer would see what the experts saw in the photos. Lundahl doubted it. "I think the uninitiated would like to see the missile, in the tube," he said.

Sensing the president's hesitancy about quick action without clear evidence to convince the world of its necessity, Rusk asked whether the group thought it "necessary to take action." He believed it essential. The Soviets were turning Cuba into "a powerful military problem" for the United States, he said, and a failure to respond would "undermine our alliances all over the world." Inaction would also encourage Moscow to feel free to intervene wherever they liked and would create an unmanageable problem in sustaining domestic support for the country's foreign policy commitments. Rusk then read a letter from [former U.S. ambassador to the Soviet Union Charles] Bohlen urging diplomatic action as a prelude to military steps. An attack on Cuba without a prior effort at diplomatic pressure to remove the missiles, Bohlen said, would alienate all America's allies, give Moscow credibility for a response against Berlin, and "greatly increase the probability of general war."

Bohlen's argument echoed Kennedy's thinking. People saw the United States as "slightly demented" about Cuba, the president said. "No matter how good our films are . . . a lot of people would regard this [military action] as a mad act by the United States." They would see it as "a loss of nerve because they will argue that taken at its worst, the presence of those missiles really doesn't change the [military] balance."

But the evidence of additional missile sites had convinced the Joint Chiefs to urge a full-scale invasion of Cuba. Kennedy stubbornly resisted. "Nobody knows what kind of success we're going to have with this invasion," he said. "Invasions are tough, hazardous. We've got a lot of equipment, a lot of—thousands of—Americans get killed in Cuba, and I think you're in much more of a mess than you are if you take out these . . . bases." And if Bobby's opinion remained a reflection of his brother's thinking, Kennedy also opposed unannounced air strikes. Ball made what Bobby called "a hell of a good point." "If we act without warning," Ball said, "without giving Khrushchev some way out . . . that's like Pearl Harbor. It's the kind of conduct that one might expect of the Soviet Union. It is not conduct that one expects of the United States." The way we act, Bobby asserted, speaks to "the whole question of . . . what kind of a country we are." Ball saw surprise air strikes as comparable to "carrying the mark of Cain on your brow for the rest of your life." Bobby echoed the point: "We've fought for 15 years with Russia to prevent a first strike against us. Now . . . we do that to a small country. I think it is a hell of a burden to carry."

Kennedy had not ruled out military action, but his remarks at the meetings on October 18 revealed a preference for a blockade and negotiations. He wanted to know what would be the best way to open talks with Khrushchev—through a cable, a personal envoy? He also asked, if we established a blockade of Cuba, what would we do about the missiles already there, and would we need to declare war on Havana? [U.S. ambassador to the Soviet Union] Llewellyn Thompson, who had joined the Thursday morning discussion, addressed Kennedy's first concern by suggesting Kennedy press Khrushchev to dismantle the existing missile sites and warn him that if they were armed, our constant surveillance would alert us, and we would eliminate them. As for a declaration of war, Kennedy thought it would be unwise: "It seems to me that with a declaration of war our objective would be an invasion."

To keep up the facade of normality, Kennedy followed his regular schedule for the rest of the day, including a two-hour meeting with Soviet foreign minister Andrei Gromyko. Nothing was said about the offensive missiles by Gromyko or Kennedy. But they gave each other indirect messages. Gromyko ploddingly read a prepared statement. He emphasized that they were giving Cuba "armaments which were only defensive—and he wished to stress the word defensive—in character." After the meeting, Kennedy told [former Secretary of Defense] Bob Lovett about Gromyko, "who, in this very room not over ten minutes ago, told more barefaced lies than I have ever heard in so short a time. All during his denial that the Russians had any missiles or weapons, or anything else, in Cuba, I had the . . . pictures in the center drawer of my desk, and it was an enormous temptation to show them to him." Instead, Kennedy told Gromyko that the Soviet arms shipments had created "the most dangerous situation since the end of the war." . . .

Kennedy reconvened his advisers at a secret late-night meeting on the second floor of the executive mansion. He wanted to hear the results of the day's deliberations. Bundy now argued the case for doing nothing. He believed that any kind of action would bring a reprisal against Berlin, which would divide the NATO alliance.

But Kennedy thought it was impossible to sit still. As he had said earlier in the day, "Somehow we've got to take some action. . . . Now, the question really is . . . what action we take which lessens the chances of a nuclear exchange which obviously is the final failure." They agreed that a blockade against Soviet shipments of additional offensive weapons would be the best starting point. Instead of air strikes or an invasion, which was tantamount to a state of war, they would try to resolve the crisis with "a limited blockade for a limited purpose."

On Friday, October 19, Kennedy kept his campaign schedule, which took him to Cleveland and Springfield, Illinois, and Chicago. . . .

In the morning, however, he held a secret forty-five-minute meeting with the Joint Chiefs. The discussion was as much an exercise in political hand-holding as in advancing a solution to the crisis. Kennedy knew that the Chiefs favored a massive air strike and were divided on whether to follow it with an invasion. He saw their counsel as predictable and not especially helpful. His memories of the navy brass in World War II, the apparent readiness of the Chiefs to risk nuclear war in Europe and their unhelpful advice before the Bay of Pigs . . . deepened his distrust of their promised results.

Nevertheless, Kennedy candidly discussed his concerns with the Chiefs. An attack on Cuba would provoke the Soviets into blocking or taking Berlin, he said. And our allies would complain that "we let Berlin go because we didn't have the guts to endure a situation in Cuba." Moreover, we might eliminate the danger in Cuba, but the Berlin crisis would likely touch off a nuclear war.

Taylor respectfully acknowledged the president's dilemma but asserted the need for military action. Without it, we would lose our credibility, he said, and "our strength anyplace in the world is the credibility of our response. . . . And if we don't respond here in Cuba, we think the credibility is sacrificed."

[Air Force general] Curtis LeMay was even more emphatic. He did not share the president's view "that if we knock off Cuba, they're going to knock off Berlin." Kennedy asked, "What do you think their reply would be?" LeMay did not think there would be one. He saw military intervention as the only solution. "This blockade and political action," he predicted, "I see leading into war. I don't see any other solution. It will lead right into war. This is almost as bad as the appeasement at Munich." . . .

At a late-morning gathering of the Ex Comm, [former Secretary of State Dean] Acheson, Bundy, Dillon, and McCone lined up with the Chiefs in favor of an air strike. McNamara, undoubtedly alerted to the president's preference, favored a blockade over air action. Bobby, grinning, said that he had spoken with the president that morning and thought "it would be very, very difficult indeed for the President if the decision were to be for an air strike, with all the memory of Pearl Harbor. . . . A sneak attack was not in our traditions. . . .

For two hours and forty minutes, beginning at 2:30 P.M., on Saturday, October 20, Kennedy and the National Security Council reviewed their options. None impressed him as just right, but under the president's prodding the group agreed to a blockade or, rather, a "quarantine," which could more readily be described as less than an act of war and seemed less likely to draw comparisons to the Soviets' 1948 Berlin blockade. The announcement of the quarantine was to coincide with a demand for removal of the offensive missiles from Cuba and preparations for an air strike should Moscow not comply. Kennedy was willing to discuss the removal of U.S.

missiles from Turkey or Italy in exchange, but only if the Soviets raised the issue. Should the United States make this concession, he intended to assure the Turks and Italians that Polaris submarines would become their defense shield. . . .

Kennedy spent Monday working to create a national and international consensus for the blockade. . . . [H]e told Taylor, "I know you and your colleagues are unhappy with this decision, but I trust that you will support me." Kennedy telephoned former presidents Hoover, Truman, and Eisenhower and consulted advisers about messages to foreign heads of state and his planned evening address. . . .

A meeting with congressional leaders for an hour before he spoke to the nation heightened his doubts about being able to generate the strong support he felt essential in the crisis. Their opposition to a blockade was as intense as that voiced by the Chiefs and seemed more likely to become public; unlike the military, congressional barons were not under presidential command. Senator Richard Russell saw a blockade as a weak response to the Soviet action. "It seems to me that we are at a crossroads," he said. "We're either a first-class power or we're not." Since Russell believed that a war with Russia was "coming someday," he thought that the time to fight was now. William Fulbright also favored an invasion. . . .

Kennedy saw his speech to the country and the world explaining the crisis and his choice of a blockade as crucial not only in bringing Americans together but also in pressuring Khrushchev to accede to his demands. He also sent Khrushchev a letter, which [Soviet ambassador Anatoly] Dobrynin received at the State Department an hour before Kennedy spoke. He had an ongoing concern, Kennedy wrote, that "your Government would not correctly understand the will and determination of the United States in any given situation." He feared a Soviet miscalculation, "since I have not assumed that you or any other sane man would, in this nuclear age, plunge the world into war which it is crystal clear no country could win and which could only result in catastrophic consequences to the whole world, including the aggressor." . . .

Kennedy's seventeen-minute speech Monday night reached one hundred million Americans, who had been alerted to the crisis by the media; it was the largest audience ever up to that point for a presidential address. The president's words matched his grim demeanor. Looking drawn and tired, he spoke more deliberately than usual, making clear the gravity of what the United States and USSR, and, indeed, the whole world faced. Moscow had created a "nuclear strike capability" in Cuba. The missiles could hit Washington, D.C., or any other city in the southeastern United States. IRBMs, when installed, could strike most of the major cities in the Western Hemisphere. Kennedy bluntly condemned the Soviets for lying: The deployment represented a total breach of faith with repeated Soviet promises to supply Cuba with only defensive weapons. The United States, Kennedy announced, could not tolerate this threat to its security and would henceforth quarantine Cuba to block all offensive weapons from reaching the island. A Soviet failure to stop its buildup would justify additional U.S. action. Any use of the missiles already in Cuba would bring retaliatory attacks against the Soviet Union. Kennedy demanded prompt dismantling and withdrawal of all offensive weapons in Cuba under U.N. supervision. . . .

A reply from Khrushchev, which reached the president by noon [Tuesday], gave little hope of a peaceful settlement. Khrushchev complained that Kennedy's speech and letter to him represented a "serious threat to peace." A U.S. quarantine would be a "gross violation of . . . international norms." Khrushchev reaffirmed that the weapons going to Cuba were defensive and urged Kennedy to "renounce actions pursued by you, which could lead to catastrophic consequences." . . .

In his eagerness to find a way out of the crisis, Bobby had asked journalists Frank Holeman and Charles Barlett to tell [Soviet military attaché Georgi] Bolshakov that the White House might be receptive to dismantling Jupiter missiles in Turkey if the Soviets removed the missiles in Cuba. But the American move could come only after the Soviets had acted—"in a time of quiet and not when there is the threat of war." When Bobby reported to Kennedy, the president suggested that his brother directly approach Dobrynin, which he did that evening. Telling the ambassador that he was there on his own, without instructions from the president, Bobby angrily accused him and Khrushchev of "hypocritical, misleading and false" actions. Bobby asked "if the ships were going to go through to Cuba." Dobrynin believed they would. As he left, Bobby declared, "I don't know how all this will end, but we intend to stop your ships."

At the morning Ex Comm meeting on the twenty-fourth, the group feared that they were on the brink of an unavoidable disaster. The Soviets were making "rapid progress" in the completion of their missile sites and bringing their military forces "into a complete state of readiness." In fact, by the morning of the twenty-fourth, all of the Soviet MRBMs and their warheads were in Cuba and close to operational. In addition, Soviet ships were continuing on course, and two of them, which seemed to be carrying "offensive weapons," would approach the quarantine line by about noon, or in two hours. The presence of Soviet submarines screening the ships made it "a very dangerous situation." U.S. forces had increased their state of readiness from Defense Condition 3 to DEFCON2, only one level below readiness for a general war. . . .

Only a State Department intelligence report gave a glimmer of hope. Khrushchev's "public line," the analysts advised—which continued to be that Moscow had no offensive weapons in Cuba—"seems designed to leave him with some option to back off, if he chooses." A written report handed to McCone during the meeting suggested that Khrushchev might be doing just that. "Mr. President," McCone interrupted McNamara, who was explaining how the navy would deal with the Soviet subs, "I have a note just handed to me. . . . It says we've just received information through ONI [Office of Naval Intelligence] that all six Soviet ships currently identified in Cuban waters—and I don't know what that means—have either stopped or reversed course." McCone left the room to ask for clarification on what "Cuban waters" meant: Were these ships approaching or leaving Cuba? The good news that it was indeed ships heading toward Cuba momentarily broke the mood of dire concern. "We're eyeball to eyeball," Rusk whispered to Bundy, "and I think the other fellow just blinked." But no one saw this as an end to the crisis. . . .

In the afternoon, McNamara went to the navy's command center in the Pentagon, a secure room under constant marine guard. McNamara learned that it had taken hours for some of the information on Soviet ship movements to reach the White House. He began chiding the duty officers for the delay, when Admiral George Anderson, the navy's representative on the Joint Chiefs, entered. Mindful of the president's concern about unauthorized navy action, McNamara began interrogating Anderson about procedures for dealing with the Soviet ships. Anderson saw the president's instructions as an unwarranted interference in the navy's freedom to do its job. Anderson told McNamara that his local commanders would decide on the details of how to deal with Soviet ships crossing the quarantine line, and said,

"We've been doing this ever since the days of John Paul Jones." He waved the navy regulations manual at McNamara, saying, "It's all in there." McNamara heatedly replied, "I don't give a damn what John Paul Jones would have done. I want to know what you are going to do, now." The objective was to deter Khrushchev and avert a nuclear war, McNamara explained. Anderson answered that they would shoot across the bow, and if the ship did not stop, they would disable its rudder. Anderson defiantly added, "Now, Mr. Secretary, if you and your deputy will go back to your offices, the navy will run the blockade." McNamara ordered him not to fire at anything without his permission and left. . . .

Khrushchev put a fresh damper on hopes that Moscow would not challenge the quarantine, with a letter arriving on the night of the twenty-fourth. His language was harsh and uncompromising. He objected to the U.S. "ultimatum" and threat of "force," described U.S. actions toward Cuba as "the folly of degenerate imperialism," and refused to submit to the blockade. We intend "to protect our rights," he wrote, and ominously declared, "We have everything necessary to do so." . . .

An unyielding reply from Kennedy to Khrushchev's letter, which reached Moscow on the morning of the twenty-fifth, plus indications that the Americans might invade Cuba, convinced Khrushchev it was time to negotiate an end to the crisis. More than anything else, it was Khrushchev's concern with Soviet military inferiority that compelled him to back down. "He could not go to war in the Caribbean with any hope of prevailing," Fursenko and Naftali write. . . .

Kennedy spent the twenty-fifth temporizing. Since a dozen Soviet ships had turned away from the quarantine line, the White House had some time to consider which remained Cuba-bound ships to stop and inspect. Kennedy told the morning Ex Comm meeting that he did not want "a sense of euphoria to get around. That [October 24] message of Khrushchev is much tougher than that." At the same time, however, a proposal from U.N. secretary general U Thant for a cooling-off period, during which Moscow and Washington would avoid tests of the quarantine, persuaded Kennedy to temporarily suspend a decision to board a Soviet ship. . . .

Yet Kennedy was doubtful that U Thant's initiative would come to much. On the afternoon of the twenty-fifth, he watched a televised confrontation at the U.N. between Stevenson and Soviet ambassador Valerian Zorin. When Stevenson pressed Zorin to say whether the Soviets had put offensive missiles in Cuba, he replied, "I am not in an American courtroom, and therefore I do not wish to answer a question that is put to me in the fashion in which a prosecutor puts questions." Stevenson would not let him evade the question. "You are in the courtroom of world opinion right now, and you can answer yes or no," Stevenson shot back. "You will have your answer in due course," Zorin answered. "I am prepared to wait for my answer until hell freezes over," Stevenson said. He then embarrassed the Russians by putting U-2 photos of the missiles before the Security Council. "I never knew Adlai had it in him," Kennedy said of his performance. . . .

At the Ex Comm meeting at 10:00 A.M. on the twenty-sixth, it was clear that the quarantine was no longer the central issue. There were no ships close to the quarantine line; nor did they expect any "quarantine activity with respect to Soviet ships . . . in the next few days." The concern now was the continuing missile buildup in Cuba. . . . He told [British prime minister Harold] Macmillan that evening, "If at the end of 48 hours we are getting no place, and the missile sites continue to be constructed, then we are going to be faced with some hard decisions."

But Kennedy did not have to wait two days. Within two hours after talking to Macmillan, he received a long, rambling letter from Khrushchev, which Llewellyn Thompson, who was with the president when he read it, believed Khrushchev had written in a state of near panic without consultation. It was an unmistakable plea for a settlement. He justified Soviet help to Cuba as preserving its right of self-determination against U.S. aggression, and he continued to dispute Kennedy's characterization of the missiles as offensive weapons, but declared, "Let us not quarrel now. It is apparent that I will not be able to convince you of this." He had no interest in mutual destruction. It was time for "good sense." To that end, he proposed an exchange: If the United States promised not to invade or support an invasion of Cuba and would recall its fleet, the Soviet Union would no longer see a need for armaments on the island—"the presence of our military specialists in Cuba would disappear." He urged Kennedy to avoid the catastrophe of a nuclear war, but warned, should there be one, "We are ready for this." . . .

But fresh evidence of Soviet progress on the missile sites, coupled with reports that six Soviet and three satellite ships remained on course toward the quarantine line, put a damper on Khrushchev's negotiating proposal. "We cannot permit ourselves to be impaled on a long negotiating hook while the work goes on on these bases," Kennedy told the Ex Comm at the October 27 morning meeting. They feared that Khrushchev's letter might be a ploy for engaging them in drawn-out talks that would allow Soviet completion of the missile sites.

A new initiative from Moscow, which reached Kennedy during the morning Ex Comm discussions, deepened their suspicions. The Kremlin had released a more polished version of Khrushchev's October 26 letter to the press. It now included a proposal that the United States remove its Jupiter missiles from Turkey in return for the dismantling of what "you regard as offensive weapons" in Cuba. The revised letter also maintained the demand for a pledge against invading Cuba and reliance on the U.N. as an intermediary. . . .

For almost four hours beginning at 4:00 P.M. on Saturday the twenty-seventh, the Ex Comm agonized over Khrushchev's Cuba-for-Turkey missile swap. With the Cuban missile sites nearing completion and reports that a SAM had shot down a U-2 flying over Cuba and killed its pilot, the Joint Chiefs were pressing for a massive air strike no later than Monday morning, the twenty-ninth, to be followed by an invasion in seven days. Kennedy and his advisers saw Khrushchev's proposal as possibly the last chance to reach a settlement and avoid military action that could lead to a nuclear exchange. . . .

Nevertheless, Kennedy's advisers convinced him to omit any mention of Turkey in his written reply to Khrushchev—in other words, to answer the first letter and largely ignore the second. He told Khrushchev that he first had to stop work on offensive missile bases in Cuba, make all offensive weapons systems there "inoperable," and halt the further introduction of such weapons. All of it was to be done under U.N. supervision. In return, the United States would end the quarantine and give assurances against an invasion of Cuba. Such a settlement "would enable us to work toward a more general arrangement regarding 'other armaments,' as proposed in your second letter which you made public. . . .

At the same time Kennedy cabled his letter to Moscow, he had Bobby hand deliver it to Dobrynin. By using his brother as the messenger, Kennedy was indicating that this was no committee or bureaucratic response but a statement of his personal eagerness to end the crisis on the terms described in the letter. Bobby's mission was also meant to signal the urgency of a positive response from Khrushchev to relieve Pentagon pressure on the president for military action. As is clear from a memo Bobby subsequently made of his conversation with Dobrynin, he left no question that a failure to agree to the proposed exchange would have disastrous consequences. Bobby told him that the attack on the U-2 and death of the pilot compelled the administration "to make certain decisions within the next 12 or possibly 24 hours. There was very little time left. If the Cubans were shooting at our planes, then we were going to shoot back." . . .

When Dobrynin asked about Khrushchev's proposal on Turkey, Bobby was ready with an answer. At a meeting with the president and several of his advisers just before he met with the ambassador, Bobby was instructed by Kennedy and Rusk to say that "while there could be no deal over the Turkish missiles, the President was determined to get them out and would do so once the Cuban crisis was resolved." The group agreed that knowledge of this commitment would be a closely guarded secret, since "this unilateral private assurance might appear to betray an ally." Bobby was also told to make plain to Dobrynin that if Moscow revealed this pledge, it would become null and void. On October 27, Kennedy secretly instructed Rusk to telephone Andrew Cordier, a Columbia University dean, who had served under U Thant at the U.N., and ask him to be prepared to give the secretary general a statement proposing the simultaneous removal of the missiles in Turkey and Cuba. Although this contingency plan was never activated and Rusk did not reveal its existence until 1987, it leaves no doubt that the president would have publicly given up the Jupiters for an end to the crisis. . . .

At a meeting of the entire Soviet presidium in a Moscow suburb, Khrushchev declared the need for a "retreat" in order to save Soviet power and the world from a nuclear catastrophe. As a prelude to a discussion on how to respond to Kennedy's offer, the presidium authorized Soviet forces to repel a U.S. attack on Cuba if there were no settlement. During the presidium discussion, the arrival of Dobrynin's report on his meeting with Bobby created a sense of urgency about ending the crisis. Khrushchev immediately dictated a letter accepting Kennedy's terms and instructed that it be broadcast on the radio to ensure its prompt receipt in Washington before some incident triggered military action. At the same time, Khrushchev sent the president a secret communication expressing satisfaction at Kennedy's promise to remove the Jupiters from Turkey in four or five months and promised to hold this agreement in confidence.

The Soviet broadcast, which was heard in Washington at 9:00 A.M. Sunday morning, lifted a pall of apprehension from Kennedy and his Ex Comm advisers. Only the Joint Chiefs refused to take Khrushchev's "surrender" at face value. Led by LeMay, they sent the president a letter recommending execution of the planned air strikes on Monday followed by the invasion unless there were "irrefutable evidence" of immediate Soviet action to remove the missile sites. . . .

Kennedy told his advisers that the quarantine would continue until they could be sure that the terms of the agreement were met. He would remain uncomfortable with the continued presence of Soviet IL-28 bombers in Cuba, which had been omitted from the required elimination of offensive weapons. He also anticipated no end to communist subversion in the hemisphere and expected the two sides would be "toe to toe on Berlin" by the end of November. But for the moment, the danger of a Soviet-American war had receded. . . .

In refusing to declare the crisis at an end, Kennedy wished to avoid an embarrassing possible reversal, which would be a political disaster and an irresistible prod to military action. He planned to officially end the quarantine after the Soviets dismantled the launching sites and shipped the missiles back to Russia. He also wanted the IL-28 bombers removed. . . .

Kennedy received justifiable plaudits for resolving the crisis. Yet he had no illusion that his response was the principal reason for success. Rather, America's local military superiority, Moscow's limited national security stake in keeping missiles in Cuba, and the Soviets' difficulty justifying to world opinion a possible nuclear conflict over Cuba were of greater importance in persuading Khrushchev to back down. Still, Kennedy's resistance to pressure from military chiefs for air attacks and an invasion, and his understanding that patient diplomacy and measured pressure could persuade the Soviets to remove the missiles were essential contributions to the peaceful outcome of the crisis. . . .

Forty years after the crisis, historians almost uniformly agree that this was the most dangerous moment in the forty-five-year Cold War. Moreover, despite his part in provoking the crisis, they generally have high praise for Kennedy's performance. His restraint in resisting a military solution that would almost certainly have triggered a nuclear exchange makes him a model of wise statesmanship in a dire situation. One need only compare his performance with that of Europe's heads of government before World War I—a disaster that cost millions of lives and wasted unprecedented sums of wealth—to understand how important effective leadership can be in times of international strife. October 1962 was not only Kennedy's finest hour in the White House; it was also an imperishable example of how one man prevented a catastrophe that may yet afflict the world.

Spinning Out of Control: Kennedy's War Against Cuba and the Missile Crisis

THOMAS G. PATERSON

"My God," muttered Richard Helms of the Central Intelligence Agency, "these Kennedys keep the pressure on about [Fidel] Castro." Another CIA officer heard it straight from John F. and Robert F. Kennedy: "Get off your ass about Cuba." Defense Secretary Robert McNamara remembered that "we were hysterical about Castro at the time of the Bay of Pigs and thereafter." When White House assistant Arthur Schlesinger, Jr., returned from an early 1962 overseas trip, he told the president that

This essay is based on Thomas G. Paterson, "Fixation with Cuba: The Bay of Pigs, Missile Crisis, and Covert War Against Castro," in *Kennedy's Quest for Victory: American Foreign Policy, 1961–1963,* ed. Thomas G. Paterson (New York: Oxford University Press, 1989), 123–155, 343–352; Thomas G. Paterson, "The Defense-of-Cuba Theme and the Missile Crisis," *Diplomatic History* 14 (Spring 1990): 249–256; Thomas G. Paterson, *Contesting Castro: The United States and the Triumph of the Cuban Revolution* (New York: Oxford Univeristy Press, 1994); and documents declassified and studies published since the publication of these works.

people abroad thought that the administration was "obsessed with Cuba." President Kennedy himself acknowledged during the missile crisis that "most allies regard [Cuba] as a fixation of the United States."

This essay seeks, first, to explain the U.S. "fixation" with Cuba in the early 1960s, identifying the sources and negative consequences of the Kennedy administration's multitrack war against Cuba. Second, to demonstrate the considerable American responsibility for the onset of the dangerous missile crisis of fall 1962. Third, to explore Kennedy's handling of the crisis, questioning the thesis of deft, cautious management. And, last, to illustrate the persistence of the "fixation" by studying the aftermath of the missile crisis, when the revitalization of the U.S. war against Castro's government set Cuban-American relations on a collision course for decades.

A knowledgeable and engaged President Kennedy spent as much or more time on Cuba as on any other foreign-policy problem. Cuba stood at the center of his administration's greatest failure, the Bay of Pigs, and its alleged greatest success, the missile crisis. Why did President Kennedy and his chief advisers indulge such an obsession with Cuba and direct so many U.S. resources to an unrelenting campaign to monitor, harass, isolate, and ultimately destroy Havana's radical regime? One answer springs from a candid remark by the president's brother, Robert F. Kennedy, who later wondered "if we did not pay a very great price for being more energetic than wise about a lot of things, especially Cuba." The Kennedys' famed eagerness for action became exaggerated in the case of Cuba. They always wanted to get moving on Cuba, and Castro dared them to try. The popular, intelligent, but erratic Cuban leader, who in January 1959 overthrew the U.S. ally Fulgencio Batista, hurled harsh words at Washington and defiantly challenged the Kennedy model of evolutionary, capitalist development so evident in the Alliance for Progress. As charismatic figures charting new frontiers, Kennedy and Castro often personalized the Cuban-American contest. To Kennedy's great annoyance, Castro could not be wheedled or beaten.

Kennedy's ardent war against *fidelismo* may also have stemmed from his feeling that Castro had double-crossed him. As a senator, Kennedy had initially joined many Americans in welcoming the Cuban Revolution as an advancement over the "oppressive" Batista dictatorship. Kennedy had urged a "patient attitude" toward the new government, which he did not see as Communist. Denying repeatedly that he was a Communist, Castro had in fact proclaimed his allegiance to democracy and private property. But in the process of legitimizing his revolution and resisting U.S. pressure, Castro turned more and more radical. Americans grew impatient with the regime's highly-charged anti-Yankeeism, postponement of elections, jailing of critics, and nationalization of property.

Richard N. Goodwin, the young White House and State Department official, provided another explanation for the Kennedy "fixation" with Cuba. He remarked that "the entire history of the Cold War, its positions and assumptions, converged upon the 'problem of Cuba.'" The Cold War dominated international politics, and as Cuban-American relations steadily deteriorated, Cuban-Soviet relations gradually improved. Not only did Americans come to believe that a once-loyal ally had jilted them for the tawdry embrace of the Soviets; they also grew alarmed that Castro sneered at the Monroe Doctrine by inviting the Soviet military to the island. When Castro, in late 1961, declared himself a Marxist-Leninist, Americans who had long denounced him as a Communist then felt vindicated.

American politics also influenced the administration's Cuba policy. In the 1960 presidential campaign, Kennedy had seized the Cuban issue to counter Richard Nixon's charge that the inexperienced Democratic candidate would abandon Zinmen (Quemoy) and Mazu (Matsu) in the Taiwan Strait to Communism and prove no match for the hard-nosed Khrushchev. "In 1952 the Republicans ran on a program of rolling back the Iron Curtain in Eastern Europe," Kennedy jabbed. "Today the Iron Curtain is 90 miles off the coast of the United States." He asked in private, "How would *we* have saved Cuba if we had [had] the power," but he nonetheless valued the political payback from his attack. "What the hell," he informed his aides, "they never told us how they would have saved China." Apparently unaware that President Dwight D. Eisenhower had initiated a clandestine CIA program to train Cuban exiles for an invasion of the island, candidate Kennedy bluntly called for just such a project. After exploiting the Cuban issue, Kennedy, upon becoming president, could not easily have retreated.

Overarching all explanations for Kennedy's obsession with Cuba is a major phenomenon of the second half of the twentieth century: the steady erosion of the authority of imperial powers, which had built systems of dependent, client, and colonial governments. The strong currents of decolonization, anti-imperialism, revolutionary nationalism, and social revolution, sometimes in combination, undermined the instruments the imperial nations had used to maintain control and order. The Cuban Revolution exemplified this process of breaking up and breaking away. American leaders reacted so hostilely to this revolution not simply because Castro and his 26th of July Movement taunted them or because domestic politics and the Cold War swayed them, but also because Cuba, as symbol and reality, challenged U.S. hegemony in Latin America. The specter of "another Cuba" haunted President Kennedy, not just because it would hurt him politically, but because "the game would be up through a good deal of Latin America," as Under Secretary of State George Ball put it. The Monroe Doctrine and the U.S. claim to political, economic, and military leadership in the hemisphere seemed at stake. As Castro once remarked, "the United States *had* to fight his revolution."

The Eisenhower Administration bequeathed to its successor an unproductive tit-for-tat process of confrontation with Cuba and a legacy of failure. In November 1959, President Eisenhower decided to encourage anti-Castro groups within Cuba to "replace" the revolutionary regime and thus end an anti-Americanism that was "having serious adverse effects on the United States position in Latin America and corresponding advantages for international Communism." In March 1960 Eisenhower ordered the CIA to train Cuban exiles for an invasion of their homeland— this shortly after Cuba signed a trade treaty with the Soviet Union. The CIA, as well, hatched assassination plots against Castro and staged hit-and-run attacks along the Cuban coast. As Cuba undertook land reform that struck at American interests and nationalized American-owned industries, the United States suspended Cuba's sugar quota and forbade American exports to the island, drastically cutting a once-flourishing commerce. On January 3, 1961, fearing an invasion and certain that the U.S. embassy was a "nest of spies" aligned with counterrevolutionaries who were burning cane fields and sabotaging buildings, Castro demanded that the embassy staff be greatly reduced. Washington promptly broke diplomatic relations with Havana.

The plan to invade Cuba at the Bay of Pigs began to unravel from the start. As the brigade's old, slow freighters plowed their way to the island, B-26 airplanes took to the skies from Nicaragua. On April 15, D-Day-minus-2, the brigade pilots destroyed several parked planes of Castro's meager air force. That same day, as part of a pre-invasion ploy, a lone, artificially damaged B-26 flew directly to Miami, where its pilot claimed that he had defected from the Cuban military and had just bombed his country's airfields. But the cover story soon cracked. Snooping journalists noticed that the nose cone of the B-26 was metal; Cuban planes had plastic noses. They observed too that the aircraft's guns had not been fired. The American hand was being exposed. The president, still insistent upon hiding U.S. complicity, decided to cancel a second D-Day strike against the remnants of the Cuban air force.

Shortly after midnight on April 17, more than 1,400 commandoes motored in small boats to the beaches at Bahía de Cochinos. The invaders immediately tangled with Castro's militia. Some commandoes never made it, because their boats broke apart on razor-sharp coral reefs. In the air, Castro's marauding airplanes shot down two brigade B-26s and sank ships carrying essential communications equipment and ammunition. Fighting ferociously, the brigade nonetheless failed to establish a beachhead. Would Washington try to salvage the mission? Kennedy turned down desperate CIA appeals to dispatch planes from the nearby U.S.S. *Essex,* but he did permit some jets to provide air cover for a new B-26 attack from Nicaragua. Manned this time by American CIA pilots, the B-26s arrived an hour after the jets had come and gone. Cuban aircraft downed the B-26s, killing four Americans. With Castro's boasting that the *mercenarios* had been foiled, the final toll proved grim: 114 of the exile brigade dead and 1,189 captured. One hundred-and-fifty Cuban defenders died.

The most controversial operational question remains the cancelled second D-day air strike. Post-crisis critics have complained that the president lost his nerve and made a decision that condemned the expedition to disaster. Cuban air supremacy did prove important to Cuba's triumph. But was it decisive? A preemptive strike on D-Day against the Cuban air force would not have delivered victory to the invaders. After the first air attack, Castro had dispersed his planes; the brigade's B-26s would have encountered considerable difficulty in locating and destroying them. And, even if a D-Day assault had disabled all of Castro's planes, then what? The brigade's 1,400 warriors would have had to face Castro's army of 25,000 and the nation's 200,000 militia. The commandoes most likely would not have survived the overwhelming power of the Cuban military.

Critical to understanding the frightening missile crisis of fall 1962 is the relationship between post–Bay of Pigs U.S. activities and the Soviet/Cuban decisions to place on the island nuclear-tipped missiles that could strike the United States, endangering the lives of 92 million people. In late April, after hearing from Cuban leaders that they expected a direct U.S. invasion and sought Soviet help to resist an attack, and after protesting the deployment of U.S. intermediate-range Jupiter missiles in Turkey, Nikita Khrushchev began to think about a missile deployment in Cuba; in late May, after dismissing the skepticism of some key advisers who judged his plan provocative to the United States and therefore highly explosive, he made the offer of missiles to Fidel Castro, who quickly accepted them. . . . The plan called for the Soviets' installation on the island of forty-eight medium-range ballistic missiles (SS-4s with a range of 1,020 miles), thirty-two intermediate-range ballistic missiles (SS-5s with a range of 2,200 miles), 144 surface-to-air missiles (SAMs), theater-nuclear weapons (Lunas), forty-eight IL-28 light bombers (with a range of 600 miles), and 42,000 Soviet combat troops.

After the Bay of Pigs, the Kennedy administration launched a multitrack program of covert, economic, diplomatic, and propagandistic elements calculated to overthrow the Castro government. This multidimensional project prompted the Cuban/Soviet decisions of mid-1962. Secretary of Defense Robert McNamara said later: "If I had been in Moscow or Havana at that time [1961–1962], I would have believed the Americans were preparing for an invasion." Indeed, Havana had to fear a successful Bay of Pigs operation conducted by U.S. forces.

Encouraged by the White House, the CIA created a huge station in Miami called JMWAVE to recruit and organize Cuban exiles. In Washington, Robert Kennedy became a ramrod for action. At a November 4, 1961, White House meeting, the Attorney General insisted: "stir things up on the island with espionage, sabotage, general disorder. . . ." The president himself asked Colonel Edward Lansdale to direct Operation Mongoose—"to use our available assets . . . to help Cuba overthrow the Communist regime." Operation Mongoose and JMWAVE, although failing to unseat Castro, punished Cubans. CIA-handled saboteurs burned cane fields and blew up factories and oil storage tanks. In a December 1961 raid, for example, a seven-man team blasted a railroad bridge, derailed an approaching train, and torched a sugar warehouse. One group, Agrupacíon Montecristi, attacked a Cuban patrol boat off the northern coast of the island in May 1962. Directorio Revolutionario Estudiantil, another exile organization, used two boats to attack Cuba in August, hoping to hit a hotel where Castro was dining.

The CIA, meanwhile, devised new plots to kill Castro with poisonous cigars, pills, and needles. To no avail. Did the Kennedys know about these death schemes? In May 1961, Federal Bureau of Investigation Director J. Edgar Hoover informed Robert Kennedy that the CIA had hired mafia boss Sam Giancana to do some "dirty business" in Cuba. Kennedy noted on the margin of the Hoover memorandum that this information should be "followed up vigorously." A year later, the CIA briefed the attorney general about its use of mafia gangsters to assassinate Castro. If his brother Robert knew about these CIA assassination plots, the president surely did, for Robert was John's closest confidant. They kept little if anything from one another. President Kennedy apparently never directly ordered the assassination of Castro—at least no trail of documents leads to the White House. But, of course, nobody uttered the word "assassination" in the presence of the president or committed the word to paper, thereby honoring the principle of plausible deniability. Advisers instead simply mentioned the need to remove Castro. "And if killing him was one of the things that was to be done in this connection," assassination was attempted because "we felt we were acting within the guidelines," said the CIA's Richard Helms.

Intensified economic coercion joined these covert activities. The Kennedy administration, in February 1962, banned most imports of Cuban products. Washington also pressed its North Atlantic Treaty Organization allies to support the "economic isolation" of Cuba. The embargo hurt. Cuba had to pay higher freight costs, enlarge its foreign debt, and suffer innumerable factory shut-downs due to the lack of spare parts once bought in the United States. Cuba's economic woes also stemmed from the flight of technicians and managers, a decline in tourism, high workers' absenteeism rates, the drying up of foreign capital investment, hastily conceived policies to diversify the economy, and suffocating government controls.

A contemporary document, this one from the chairman of the Joint Chiefs of Staff, General Maxwell Taylor, noted in spring 1962 that the Mongoose plan to overthrow the Cuban government would be undertaken largely by "indigenous resources," but "recognizes that final success will require decisive U.S. military intervention." Because the plan also required close cooperation with Cuban exiles, it is very likely that Castro's spies picked up from the Cuban community in Miami leaks that the U.S. military contemplated military action against Cuba. As CIA agents liked to joke, there were three ways to transmit information rapidly: telegraph, telephone, and tell-a-Cuban. Cuban officials have claimed, in fact, that their intelligence agency had infiltrated anti-Castro exile groups and had learned about some of the activities associated with Lansdale's scheme. Although they surely did not know the details of President Kennedy's National Security Action Memorandum No. 181 (NSAM-181), dated August 23, a directive to engineer an internal revolt that would be followed by U.S. military intervention, the Cubans no doubt began to observe accelerated U.S. actions to achieve that goal.

By the late spring and early summer of 1962, then, when Havana and Moscow discussed defensive measures that included missiles with nuclear warheads, Cuba felt besieged from several quarters. The Soviet Union had become its trading partner, and the Soviets, after the Bay of Pigs, had begun military shipments of small arms, howitzers, machine guns, armored personnel carriers, patrol boats, tanks, and MiG jet fighters. Yet all of this weaponry had not deterred the United States. And, given the failure of Kennedy's multitrack program to unseat Castro, "were we right or wrong to fear direct invasion" next, asked Fidel Castro. As he said in mid-1962, shortly after striking the missile-deployment agreement with the Soviets: "We must prepare ourselves for that direct invasion."

Had there been no exile expedition at the Bay of Pigs, no destructive covert activities, no assassination plots, no military maneuvers and plans, and no economic and diplomatic steps to harass, isolate, and destroy the Castro government in Havana, there would not have been a Cuban missile crisis. The origins of the October 1962 crisis derived largely from the concerted U.S. campaign to quash the Cuban Revolution. To stress only the global dimension (Soviet-American competition in the nuclear arms race) is to slight the local origins of the conflict. To slight these sources by suggesting from very incomplete declassified Soviet records that the "thought of deterring a U.S. invasion figured only incidentally" in Moscow's calculations, as argued by Ernest R. May and Philip D. Zelikow, editors of the tape recordings that Kennedy made during the crisis, is to overlook the substantial evidence of Soviet (and Cuban) preoccupation with the defense of Cuba and is to miss the central point that Premier Nikita Khrushchev would never have had the opportunity to install dangerous missiles in the Caribbean if the United States had not been attempting to overthrow the Cuban government. This interpretation does not dismiss the view that the emplacement of nuclear missiles in Cuba also served the Soviet strategic goal of catching up in the nuclear arms race. Rather, the interpretation in this essay emphasizes that both Cuba and the Soviet Union calculated that their interests would be served by putting nuclear-capable rockets on the island.

Why did the Cubans and Soviets decide on nuclear-tipped ballistic missiles instead of a military pact, conventional (non-nuclear) forces, or just the battlefield Lunas—in short, weapons that Washington could not label "offensive" because they could not reach the United States? The Cubans sought effective deterrence, or what the historian Mark White has called "the *ultimate* deterrent." One thinks here of similar American thinking, near the end of the Second World War, that the Japanese were so fanatical that only the threat of annihilation from atomic bombs would persuade them to surrender. The Cubans, in fact, looking for an immediate deterrent effect, had wanted to make the 1962 missile agreement public, but the Soviets, guessing that the deployment could be camouflaged until the missiles became operational, preferred secrecy.

On October 14, an American U-2 plane photographed missile sites in Cuba, thus providing the first "hard" evidence, as distinct from the "soft" reports of exiles, that the island was becoming a nuclear base. "He can't do that to me!" snapped Kennedy when he saw the pictures on the 16th. He had warned the Soviets that the United States would not suffer "offensive" weapons in Cuba, although the warnings had come after the Cuban-Soviet agreement of early summer. Shortly before noon on October 16, the president convened his top advisers (a group eventually called the Executive Committee, or ExComm). His first questions focused on the firing readiness of the missiles and the probability that they carried nuclear warheads. The advisers gave tentative answers. All agreed that the missiles could become operational in a brief time. Discussion of military options (invasion? air strike?) dominated this first meeting. Kennedy's immediate preference became clear: "We're certainly going . . . to take out these . . . missiles." Kennedy showed little interest in negotiations. Perhaps his initial tilt toward military action derived from his knowledge of the significant U.S. military plans, maneuvers, and movement of forces and equipment undertaken after he signed NSAM-181, thus making it possible for the United States to respond with military effectiveness.

At a second meeting on the 16th, Secretary of State Dean Rusk argued against the surprise air strike that General Taylor had bluntly advocated. Rusk recommended instead "a direct message to Castro." At the close of Rusk's remarks, Kennedy immediately asked: "Can we get a little idea about what the military thing *is*?" Bundy then asked: "How gravely does this change the strategic balance?" McNamara, for one, thought "not at all," but Taylor disputed him. Kennedy himself seemed uncertain, but he did complain that the missile emplacement in Cuba "makes them look like they're co-equal with us." And, added Treasury Secretary C. Douglas Dillon, who obviously knew the president's competitive personality, the presence of the missiles made it appear that "we're scared of the Cubans."

Then the rambling discussion turned to Khrushchev's motivation. The Soviet leader had been cautious on Berlin, Kennedy said. "It's just as if we suddenly began to put a major number of MRBMs in Turkey," the President went on. "Now that'd be goddam dangerous. . . ." Bundy jumped in: "Well, we *did,* Mr. President." Not liking the sound of a double standard, Kennedy lamely answered, "Yeah, but that was five years ago." Actually, the American Jupiter missiles in Turkey were IRBMs (intermediate-range ballistic missiles) which, under a 1959 agreement with Ankara, had gone into launch position in mid-1961—during the Kennedy administration—and were turned over to Turkish forces on October 22, 1962, the very day Kennedy informed Moscow that it must withdraw its missiles from Cuba.

For the next several days, ExComm met frequently in tight secrecy and discussed four policy options: "talk them out," "squeeze them out," "shoot them out," or "buy them out." In exhausting sessions marked by frank disagreement and changing minds, the president's advisers weighed the advantages and disadvantages of invasion, bombing, quarantine, and diplomacy. The president gradually moved with a majority of ExComm toward a quarantine or blockade of Cuba: incoming ships would be stopped and inspected for military cargo. When queried if an air strike would knock out all of the known missiles General Taylor said that "the best we can offer you is to destroy 90%. . . ." In other words, some missiles in Cuba would remain in place for firing against the United States. Robert Kennedy also worried that the Soviets might react unpredictably with military force, "which could be so serious as to lead to general nuclear war." In any case, the attorney general insisted, there would be no "Pearl Harbor type of attack" on his brother's record.

By October 22 the president had made two decisions. First, to quarantine Cuba to prevent further military shipments and to impress the Soviets with U.S. resolve to force the missiles out. If the Soviets balked, other, more drastic, measures would be undertaken. Second, Kennedy decided to inform the Soviets of U.S. policy through a television address rather than through diplomatic channels. Several advisers dubiously argued that a surprise public speech was necessary to rally world opinion behind U.S. policy and to prevent Khrushchev from issuing an ultimatum, but some ExComm participants recommended that negotiations be tried first. Former ambassador to the Soviet Union Charles Bohlen advised that Moscow would have to retaliate against the United States if its technicians died from American bombs. A stern letter to Khrushchev should be "tested" as a method to gain withdrawal of the missiles. "I don't see the urgency of military action," Bohlen told the president. And ambassador to the United Nations Adlai Stevenson appealed to an unreceptive Kennedy: "the existence of nuclear missile bases anywhere is negotiable before we start anything." Stevenson favored a trade: withdrawing the U.S. Jupiter missiles from Turkey and evacuating the Guantánamo naval base, turning it over to Cuba, in exchange for withdrawal of the Soviet missiles from Cuba. The president, according to the minutes of an October 20 ExComm meeting, "sharply rejected" Stevenson's proposal, especially on the issue of Guantánamo.

In his evening television speech of October 22, Kennedy demanded that the Soviets dismantle the missiles in Cuba, and he announced the Caribbean quarantine as an "initial" step. Later that evening, in a telephone conversation, he told British prime minister Harold Macmillan that U.S. credibility was on the line; if he had not acted, America's resolve to defend Berlin might be questioned and Soviet success in deploying the missiles "would have unhinged us in all of Latin America." The missile crisis soon became an international war of nerves. More than sixty American ships began patrols to enforce the blockade. The Strategic Air Command went on nuclear alert, moving upward to Defense Condition (DEFCON) 2 for the first time ever (the next level is deployment for combat). B-52 bombers, loaded with nuclear weapons, stood ready, while men and equipment moved to the southeastern United States to prepare for an invasion. The Soviets did not mobilize or redeploy their huge military, nor did they take measures to make their strategic forces less vulnerable. The Soviets also refrained from testing the quarantine: Their ships turned around and went home. But what next? On the 26th, Kennedy and some ExComm members, thinking that the Soviets were stalling, soured on the quarantine. Sentiment for military action strengthened.

On the afternoon of the 26th, an intelligence officer attached to the Soviet embassy, Aleksandr Feklisov (alias Fomin), met with ABC television correspondent John Scali and suggested a solution to the crisis: The Soviet Union would withdraw the missiles if the United States would promise not to invade Cuba. Scali scurried to Secretary of State Dean Rusk, who sent him back to Feklisov with the reply that American leaders were interested in discussing the proposal. As it turns out, and unbeknownst to American leaders, Feklisov was acting on his own and a report of his conversations with Scali did not reach the Soviet foreign secretary in Moscow until the late afternoon of October 27. Feklisov's independent intervention, in other words, did not influence the writing of the two critical letters that Khrushchev sent to Washington on the 26th and 27th, but ExComm thought the Feklisov initiative and Khrushchev's letters were linked, thus clearly signaling an earnest Soviet desire to settle.

Khrushchev's first letter, a rambling emotional private message that ruminated on the horrors of war, offered to withdraw the missiles if the United States pledged not to invade Cuba. The Soviet premier defended the initial installation of the missiles with the argument that the United States had been threatening the island. In the morning of October 27, another Khrushchev letter reached the president. Khrushchev now upped the stakes: He would trade the missiles in Cuba for the American missiles in Turkey. Kennedy felt boxed, because "we are now in the position of risking war in Cuba and in Berlin over missiles in Turkey which are of little military value." At first, Kennedy hesitated to accept a swap—because he did not want to appear to be giving up anything in the face of Soviet provocation; because he knew that the proud Turks would recoil from the appearance of being "traded off in order to appease an enemy"; and because acceptance of a missile trade would lend credence to charges that the United States all along had been applying a doubling standard. Kennedy told ExComm that Khrushchev's offer caused "embarrassment," for most people would think it "a very fair trade." Indeed, Moscow had played "a very good card."

In the afternoon of the 27th, more bad news rocked the White House. An American U-2 plane overflew the eastern part of the Soviet Union, probably because its equipment malfunctioned. "There is always some son of a bitch who doesn't get the word," the president remarked. Soviet fighters scrambled to intercept the U-2, and American fighter jets from Alaska, carrying Falcon missiles with nuclear warheads, took flight to protect the errant aircraft. Although the spy plane flew home without having sparked a dog fight, the incident carried the potential of sending the crisis to a more dangerous level.

Also on the 27th, a U-2 was shot down over Cuba and its pilot killed by a surface-to-air missile (SAM). The shoot-down constituted a serious escalation. A distressed McNamara, not knowing that the order to shoot was made independently by the Soviet air defense commander in Cuba without orders from Moscow, now thought "invasion had become almost inevitable." He urged that U.S. aircraft "go in and take out that SAM site." But Kennedy hesitated to retaliate, surely scared about taking a step in toward a nuclear nightmare. The president decided to ignore Khrushchev's second letter and answer the first. The evening of the 27th, he also dispatched his brother Robert to deliver an ultimatum to Soviet Ambassador Anatoly Dobrynin: Start pulling out the missiles within forty-eight hours or "we would remove them." After Dobrynin asked about the Jupiters in Turkey, Robert Kennedy presented an important American concession: They would be dismantled if the problem in Cuba were resolved. As the president had said in an ExComm meeting, "we can't very well invade Cuba with all its toil . . . when we could have gotten them out by making a deal on the same missiles in Turkey." But, should the Soviets leak word of a "deal," Robert Kennedy told the Soviet ambassador, the United States would disavow the offer. Dobrynin, who judged President Kennedy a "hot-tempered gambler," cabled an account of the meeting to Moscow, pointing out that the "very upset" president's brother insisted that "time is of the essence" and that if another U.S. plane were shot at, the United States would return fire and set off "a chain reaction" toward "a real war."

On October 28, faced with an ultimatum and a concession, and fearful that the Cubans might precipitate a greater Soviet-American conflagration, Khrushchev retreated and accepted the American offer: the Soviet Union would dismantle its missiles under United Nations supervision and the United States would pledge not to invade Cuba. The crisis had ended—just when the nuclear giants seemed about to stumble over the brink.

Many analysts give John F. Kennedy high marks for his handling of the Cuban missile crisis, applauding a stunning success, noble statesmanship, and model of crisis management. Secretary Rusk lauded Kennedy for having "ice water in his veins." The journalist Hugh Sidey has gushed over "the serene leader who guides the nation away from nuclear conflict." Arthur Schlesinger, Jr., has effusively written that Kennedy's crisis leadership constituted a "combination of toughness and restraint, of will, nerve, and wisdom, so brilliantly controlled, so matchlessly calibrated." May and Zelikow celebrate Kennedy's "finest hours," sketching a "lucid" and "calm" president, who, in the end, steps back from the brink.

Kennedy's stewardship of policymaking during the crisis actually stands less as a supreme display of careful crisis management and more as a case of near misses, close calls, narrow squeaks, physical exhaustion, accidents, and guesses that together scared officials on both sides into a settlement, because, in the words of McGeorge Bundy, the crisis was "so near to spinning out of control." When McNamara recalled those weeks, he questioned the entire notion of crisis management because of "misinformation, miscalculation, misjudgment, and human fallibility." "We were in luck," Ambassador John Kenneth Galbraith ruminated, "but success in a lottery is no argument for lotteries."

Danger lurked too in the way the commander of the Strategic Air Command issued DEFCON 2 alert instructions. He did so in the clear, instead of in code, because he wanted to impress the Soviets. Alerts serve to prepare American forces for war, but they may also provoke an adversary to think that the United States might launch a first strike. Under such circumstances, the adversary might be tempted to strike first. The Navy's antisubmarine warfare activities also carried the potential of escalating the crisis. Soviet submarines prowled near the quarantine line, and, following standing orders, Navy ships forced several of them to surface. In one case, a Navy commander exercised the high-risk option of dropping a depth charge on a Soviet submarine. As in so many of these examples, decisionmakers in Washington actually lost some control of the crisis to personnel at the operational level.

ExComm members represented considerable intellectual talent and experience, but a mythology of grandeur, illusion of control, and embellishment of performance have obscured the history of the committee. ExComm debated alternatives under "intense strain," often in a "state of anxiety and emotional exhaustion," recalled Under Secretary Ball. McGeorge Bundy told Ball on October 24 that he (Bundy) was getting "groggy." Two advisers may have suffered such stress that they became less able to perform their responsibilities. An assistant to Adlai Stevenson recalled that he had had to become an ExComm "back-up" for the ambassador because, "while he could speak clearly, his memory wasn't very clear. . . ." Asked if failing health produced this condition, Vice Admiral Charles Wellborn answered that the "emotional state and nervous tension that was involved in it [missile crisis] had this effect." Stevenson was feeling "pretty frightened." So apparently was Dean Rusk. The president scratched on a notepad during an October 22 meeting: "Rusk rather quiet & somewhat fatigued." Robert Kennedy remembered that the secretary of state "had a virtually complete breakdown mentally and physically." Once, when Rusk's eyes swelled with tears, Dean Acheson barked at him: "Pull yourself together, . . . you're the only secretary of state we have." We cannot determine how stress affected the advice ExComm gave Kennedy, but at least we know that its members struggled against time, sleep, exhaustion, and themselves, and they did not always think clearheadedly at a time when the stakes were very high.

What about the president himself, gravely ill from Addison's disease and often in severe pain because of his ailing back? Dr. Max Jacobson, known as "Dr. Feelgood" by the Hollywood crowd that paid for his services, and a frequent visitor to the White House, administered amphetamines and steroids to President Kennedy during the first days of the missile crisis. Medical doctors have reported that the effect of these unorthodox injections might have been supreme confidence and belligerence. One might speculate that JFK's inclination toward a bold military response at the start of the crisis was influenced by the doses of potent drugs he was taking. . . .

As for the Soviets, they too worried about their decisionmaking process and the crisis spinning out of control. Khrushchev, of course, had miscalculated from the outset. He somehow thought that the Americans would not discover the missiles until after all of them had become operational. He had no fallback plan once they were photographed. Because he had never informed his own embassy in Washington that missiles were being placed in Cuba, he had cut himself off from critical advice—counsel that would have alerted him to the certain vigorous U.S. response to the emplacement.

Add to these worries the Soviet premier's troubles with Fidel Castro, who demanded a bold Soviet response to U.S. actions and who might provoke an incident with the United States that could escalate the crisis. Castro pressed the Soviets to use nuclear weapons to save Cuba should the United States attack. Soviet leaders urged Castro not to "initiate provocations" and to practice "self-restraint." Such "adventurists," remarked a Soviet decisionmaker about the Cubans. Khrushchev sternly told his advisers: "You see how far things can go. We've got to get those missiles out of there before a real fire starts."

President Kennedy helped precipitate the missile crisis by harassing Cuba through his multitrack program. Then he reacted to the crisis by suspending diplomacy in favor of public confrontation. In the end, with the management of the crisis disintegrating, he frightened himself. In order to postpone doomsday, or at least to prevent a high-casualty invasion of Cuba, he moderated the American response and compromised. Khrushchev withdrew his mistake, while gaining what ExComm member Ambassador Llewellyn Thompson thought was the "important thing" all along for the Soviet leader: being able to say, "I saved Cuba. I stopped an invasion."

After the missile imbroglio, the pre-crisis "fixation" reasserted itself. For example, the State Department's Policy Planning Council on November 7 urged a "maximal U.S. strategy" to eliminate the Castro regime. The messy ending to the crisis—no formal accord was reached, no formal document signed—also left the Kennedy administration room to hedge on the no-invasion promise. Using the argument that the United States had agreed not to invade the island only if the missiles were withdrawn under United Nations inspection and that Castro had blocked such inspection, Kennedy refused to give an unqualified no-invasion pledge. . . .

Kennedy's retreat to an ambiguous no-invasion promise reflected his administration's unrelenting determination to oust Castro. In early January 1963, the CIA director noted that "Cuba and the Communist China nuclear threat" were the two most prominent issues on Kennedy's foreign-policy agenda. Later that month, the president himself told the National Security Council that Cuba must become a U.S. hostage. "We must always be in a position to threaten Cuba as a possible riposte to Russian pressure against us in Berlin. We must always be ready to move immediately against Cuba" should the Soviets move against Berlin. "We can use Cuba to limit Soviet actions," he concluded. The administration set about once again to threaten Cuba, to "tighten the noose" around Cuba, although Kennedy grew impatient with exile attacks, because they did not deliver "any real blow at Castro."

In June 1963, the National Security Council approved a new sabotage program. The CIA quickly cranked up destructive plots and revitalized its assassination option by making contact with a traitorous Cuban official, Rolando Cubela. Codenamed AM/LASH, he plotted with CIA operatives to kill Fidel Castro.

After President Kennedy's death, the new Johnson administration decided to put some "marginal" and "tenuous" Cuban-American contacts that Kennedy had explored "on ice." President Johnson also instructed his advisers to avoid "high risk actions" toward Cuba. Throughout the 1960s, as the United States became hostage to the war in Vietnam, Cuba receded as a top priority. Fidel Castro may have been correct when he remarked a decade after the missile crisis that Cuba "was saved by Vietnam. Who can say whether the immense American drive that went into Vietnam . . . would not have been turned against Cuba?" Except for a thaw in the mid to late-1970s, U.S.-Cuba relations remained frozen in hostility. Kennedy's "fixation" with Cuba fixed itself on U.S. Cuba policy for decades.

🌐 *F U R T H E R   R E A D I N G*

Graham Allison, *Essence of Decision* (1971)
—— and Philip Zelikow, *Essence of Decision* (1999; 2d ed.)
Jules Benjamin, *The United States and the Origins of the Cuban Revolution* (1990)
Barton J. Bernstein, "The Cuban Missile Crisis: Trading the Jupiters in Turkey?" *Political Science Quarterly* 95 (1980): 97–125
Michael Beschloss, *The Crisis Years* (1991)
James G. Blight and Philip Brenner, *Sad and Luminous Days* (2002)
——, et al., *Cuba on the Brink* (2003)
Don Bohning, *The Castro Obsession* (2005)
Dino Brugioni, *Eyeball to Eyeball* (1991)
McGeorge Bundy, *Danger and Survival* (1988)
Laurence Chang and Peter Kornbluh, eds., *The Cuban Missile Crisis, 1962* (1992)
Jorge I. Domínguez, *To Make a World Safe for Revolution* (1989)
Max Frankel, *High Noon in the Cold War* (2004)
Lawrence Freedman, *Kennedy's Wars* (2002)
Aleksandr Fursenko and Timothy Naftali, *"One Hell of a Gamble": Khrushchev, Castro, and Kennedy, 1958–1964* (1997)
Raymond L. Garthoff, *Reflections on the Cuban Missile Crisis* (1989)
——, "Berlin 1961: The Record Corrected," *Foreign Policy* 84 (1991): 142–156
Alexander George, *Avoiding War: Problems of Crisis Management* (1991)
Alice L. George, *Awaiting Armageddon* (2003)
James N. Giglio, *The Presidency of John F. Kennedy* (1991)
—— and Stephen G. Rabe, *Debating the Kennedy Presidency* (2003)
Piero Gleijeses, "Ships in the Night: The C.I.A., The White House, and the Bay of Pigs," *Journal of Latin American Studies* 27 (1995): 1–42
——, *Conflicting Missions: Havana, Washington, and Africa, 1959–1976* (2001)
Maurice Halperin, *The Taming of Fidel Castro* (1981)
Mary N. Hampton, *The Wilsonian Impulse* (1996) (on U.S.-Germany)
Hope Harrison, "Ulbricht and the Concrete 'Rose': New Archival Evidence on the Dynamics of Soviet-East German Relations and the Berlin Crisis, 1958–1961," Working Paper #5 (May 1993), *Cold War International History Project Bulletin,* Woodrow Wilson International Center for Scholars
Seymour Hersh, *The Dark Side of Camelot* (1997)
James G. Hershberg, "Before 'The Missiles of October': Did Kennedy Plan a Military Strike Against Cuba?" *Diplomatic History* 14 (1990): 163–198
Trumbull Higgins, *The Perfect Failure* (1987) (on the Bay of Pigs invasion)
Irving L. Janis, *Groupthink* (1982)
Donna Rich Kaplowitz, *Anatomy of a Failed Embargo: U.S. Sanctions Against Cuba* (1998)
Montague Kern, Patricia W. Levering, and Ralph B. Levering, *The Kennedy Crises: The Press, the Presidency, and Foreign Policy* (1983)
Richard Ned Lebow and Janice Gross Stein, *We All Lost the Cold War* (1993)
Ernest R. May and Philip D. Zelikow, *The Kennedy Tapes* (1997)
Frank A. Mayer, *Adenauer and Kennedy: A Study in German-American Relations, 1961–1963* (1996)
Morris Morley, *Imperial State and Revolution: The United States and Cuba, 1952–1987* (1987)
Philip Nash, *The Other Missiles of October* (1997) (on Jupiters)
James A. Nathan, *Anatomy of the Cuban Missile Crisis* (2001)
Kendrick Oliver, *Kennedy, Macmillan, and the Nuclear Test Ban Treaty* (1998)
Herbert S. Parmet, *JFK* (1983)
Thomas G. Paterson, *Contesting Castro* (1994)
——, ed., *Kennedy's Quest for Victory* (1989)

———— and William T. Brophy, "October Missiles and November Elections: The Cuban Missile Crisis and American Politics, 1962," *Journal of American History* 73 (1986): 87–119

Louis A. Pérez, Jr., *Cuba and the United States* (1997)

Richard M. Pious, "The Cuban Missile Crisis and the Limits of Crisis Management," *Political Science Quarterly* 116 (2001): 81–105

Scott D. Sagan, *The Limits of Safety* (1993)

Arthur M. Schlesinger Jr., *A Thousand Days* (1965)

————, *Robert Kennedy and His Times* (1978)

Thomas J. Schoenbaum, *Waging Peace and War* (1988) (on Rusk)

Len Scott and Steve Smith, "Lessons of October: Historians, Political Scientists, Policy-makers, and the Cuban Missile Crisis," *International Affairs* 70 (1994): 659–684

Glenn T. Seaborg and Benjamin J. Loeb, *Kennedy, Khrushchev, and the Test Ban* (1981)

Sheldon Stern, *Averting the Final Failure* (2003)

Tad Szulc, *Fidel* (1986)

Marc Trachtenberg, *History and Strategy* (1991)

Lucien S. Vandenbroucke, *Perilous Options* (1993)

Robert Weisbrot, *Maximum Danger* (2002)

Richard E. Welch, Jr., *Response to Revolution* (1985)

Mark J. White, *The Kennedys and Cuba* (1999)

————, *Missiles in Cuba* (1997)

Peter Wyden, *Bay of Pigs* (1979)

CHAPTER
13

The Vietnam War

After World War II, the United States' engagement in the Indochinese country of Vietnam deepened over a thirty-year period. In 1945 the Truman administration tolerated the reimposition of French colonialism, and in early 1950, following the triumph of Mao Zedong's (Mao Tse-tung) communist forces in the Chinese civil war, Washington began giving aid to the French to quell the patriot Ho Chi Minh's nationalistic, communist-led insurgency. U.S. military intervention in the Korean War (1950–1953) heightened Washington's role in Asia, and aid to French Indochina steadily increased. After the French defeat in 1954, the United States supported the division of Vietnam at the seventeenth parallel, and the Eisenhower administration helped to organize, and to prop up, a noncommunist regime in the South. In 1961 President John F. Kennedy deployed U.S. military personnel to combat missions in South Vietnam; then in 1964, Kennedy's successor, Lyndon B. Johnson, launched an air war against North Vietnam. Over the next three years the Johnson administration also dramatically increased the level of ground forces in Vietnam. Following the North Vietnamese–Vietcong Tet offensive in 1968, peace talks began, and in 1973 Washington and Hanoi reached a settlement that permitted the United States to continue to support the South Vietnamese regime. But in 1975 communist forces drove Americans pell-mell from Vietnam and seized Saigon, the southern capital, which they renamed Ho Chi Minh City.

By the end, more than 58,000 American servicemen and women had died in Vietnam, and the United States had spent more than $175 billion in Southeast Asia. Millions of Asians perished, hundreds of thousands of others became refugees, and the countries of Indochina—Vietnam, Cambodia, and Laos—lay in ruins. The war also polarized Americans at home. Peace demonstrations swept the United States during the 1960s and early 1970s. U.S. leaders ultimately responded by withdrawing American forces, but the passionate Vietnam debate nonetheless unhinged a twenty-five-year-old Cold War consensus on foreign policy.

Considering the war's length and historical significance, it is not surprising that scholars debate all aspects of the conflict. Perhaps the most fundamental question is: Why did the United States intervene in Vietnam and become so deeply involved? Some scholars stress that a blinding Cold War anticommunism led U.S. officials to downplay Ho Chi Minh's anticolonial nationalism and exaggerate Hanoi's ties to Moscow and Beijing. Cold War calculations similarly made Washington conclude that America's prestige and credibility across the world required the survival of a noncommunist South Vietnam. Other analysts argue that a flawed decisionmaking

CHINA

Mengzi

Nanning
Guixian

Lao Cai
Cao Bang

Thai
Nguyen
Pingxiang
Loc
Binh

Dien
Bien Phu
Hanoi ✪
Haiphong
Zhanjiang

BURMA

Nam Dinh
(Harbor Mined, 1972)

NORTH
Thanh
Hoa
*Gulf of
Tonkin*

Luang
Prabang
Plain
of
Jars
*(Maddox
attacked, 1964)*

HAINAN

Chiang
Mai
Nan
*(Pathet Lao
Victory, 1975)*
VIETNAM
Vinh

Vientiane
U.S. SEVENTH FLEET

L

A

MU GIA
PASS

*Demarcation Line,
July 1954*

Udon Thani
Nakhon
Phanom

17°

Phitsanulok

Sépone
Khe Sanh
DEMILITARIZED
ZONE

Khon Kaen
Hué
Da Nang

THAILAND

O

My Lai
Chu Lai
Quang Ngai

Ta Khli

Ubon
Ratchathani

Dak To
Kontum

Rachasima

Ban San
Keo
Pleiku
An Khe
Qui Nhon

Don Muang

Vietnamese Invasion, 1978
Duc Co
Central

Bangkok ✪

SOUTH

Sattahip

*Tonle
Sap*
Pursat
CAMBODIA
Highlands
VIETNAM

Khe
Sanh
Quang Tri
Hué

U.S. Invasion, 1970
Nha Trang
Dalat

THAILAND

Lang Vei
A Chau
Da Nang

Kompong Cham
Bu Dop
Cam Ranh
Bay

LOS

Hoian
Kham Duc

*Gulf
of
Siam*
Phnom
Penh ✪
*(Khmer Rouge
Victory, 1975)*
Bien Hoa
Long Binh

SOUTH
CHINA
SEA

Dak
To
Quang
Ngai
Kontum

Cholon

Tan Son Nhut
Saigon

Pleiku

Wai
Is.
*(Mayaguez
Incident
1975)*
My Tho
Vinh Long
Vung Tau

SOUTH
Qui
Nhon

CAMBODIA
Ban Me
Thuot
Tuy
Hoa

Can Tho
Ben Tre

*U.S. Withdrawal,
1975*

Tonle Sap
VIETNAM
Nha
Trang

Ca Mau
Peninsula
Mekong Delta

Dalat

Cholon
Bien Hoa

*"Boat People"
Refugees After
1975*

Chau Duc
My
Tho
Saigon

Southeast Asia and the
Vietnam War

Vinh Long
Ben Tre

Can Tho
Ca Mau

■ Major U.S. bases during the Vietnam War

The Tet Offensive
January-February
1968

0   100   200   300

☆ Major battles

miles

MALAYSIA

*process, a bureaucracy that prized consensus, an "imperial" presidency, and a com-
pliant Congress drew the United States into the quagmire. Historians of a radical
bent challenge the notion that the war stemmed from mistaken judgment or bureaucratic morass, and assert that the Americanization of the Vietnam War arose from
an aggressive drive for global hegemony—a post–World War II ambition to make
the world safe for markets, capital investment, and military bases. Another school of
thought posits that cultural arrogance, whether expressed in terms of race, machismo,
or national mission, served as a principal motivating force for intervention.*

*Americans have also long debated the military conduct of the war. The most
nagging question remains: Was the Vietnam War winnable? Some experts maintain
that the United States was on the right track with its deployment of air power, "search
and destroy" campaigns, and war of attrition, but that domestic political pressures, the
antiwar movement, and the media forced U.S. leaders to retreat. Others argue that
U.S. forces could have been victorious, but only with a change in strategy. A more
rapid escalation, unrestricted bombing, an invasion of North Vietnam, the sealing of
the Vietnamese-Laotian border, and a more vigorous counterinsurgency effort have
all been cited as possible alternative strategies. Still, some analysts conclude that the
American effort in Vietnam was doomed from the start. A corrupt and unpopular
South Vietnamese government and military, a highly skilled guerrilla opponent, a
debilitating climate and harsh terrain, and an inflexible U.S. command structure
made the war unwinnable for the United States. Expanded military operations above
the seventeenth parallel ran the additional risk of inviting war with neighboring
China. Not only was the war unwinnable, but the widespread use of air power, and
intensive village warfare, led to atrocities and a staggering level of civilian casualties.*

*Why did Americans fight? Why did they lose? What lessons were learned?
These questions have haunted an entire generation of Americans, and continue to
challenge historians.*

D O C U M E N T S

Resistance to foreigners is an enduring theme in Vietnamese history. For example, during
World War II, the Vietnamese battled the Japanese. On September 2, 1945, Ho Chi Minh
and other nationalists wrote a Declaration of Independence for the Democratic Republic
of Vietnam. Reprinted here as Document 1, it resembled the 1776 American declaration.
The French attempt to reimplement colonial rule during the early postwar period, however, led to the first Indochinese War between Ho Chi Minh's nationalist-communist
insurgency and the French military. Fearing that a communist victory in Indochina would
lead to a communist-dominated Asia—the so-called domino theory—the United States
provided the French with assistance. The beleaguered French ultimately decided to withdraw from Vietnam, and at the Geneva Conference of May 8–July 21, 1954, the warring
parties and their allies, including the United States, prepared peace terms for Indochina.
The Geneva Accords that were set down in the final declaration are reprinted here as
Document 2. Thereafter, Ho's communists governed North Vietnam, and the United
States, which refused to accept the Geneva Accords, backed a regime in the south.

Despite U.S. aid, the government of South Vietnam was plagued by rampant corruption, inefficiency, and inadequate popular support. By 1960 a communist-led insurgency, the National Liberation Front (NLF), had gained widespread support in the
south and gained North Vietnamese assistance. In Document 3, dated from 1961, North
Vietnamese general Vo Nguyen Giap explains the strategy of "people's war," whereby
a smaller, weaker force could achieve military victory over a stronger, imperialist power.
The Tonkin Gulf Resolution, Document 4, which the U.S. Senate passed on August 10,

1964, with only two dissenting votes, authorized the president to use the force he deemed necessary in Vietnam. American war managers interpreted this important document as equivalent to a declaration of war. Just prior to President Lyndon Johnson's landslide victory at the polls in November 1964, a National Security Council Working Group weighed U.S. options for addressing the deteriorating political conditions in South Vietnam. Document 5, a memorandum to Undersecretary of State George Ball from his assistant Thomas Ehrlich, laments the Working Group's focus on military action and its neglect of proposals for a negotiated withdrawal: "these things seem quickly to develop a bureaucratic life of their own," he concludes. The Working Group ultimately sent its findings to an NSC Executive Committee consisting of Secretary of State Dean Rusk, Secretary of Defense Robert McNamara, National Security Adviser McGeorge Bundy, and CIA chief John McCone; the committee made its final recommendations to President Johnson on December 2, 1964. The "Position Paper on Southeast Asia," Document 6, provided a blueprint for the first phase of U.S. military activity along North Vietnamese supply lines in Laos and north of the seventeenth parallel. It also laid plans for a more extensive second phase of "graduated military pressures" against the Democratic Republic of Vietnam, including U.S. air strikes in reprisal for Vietcong provocations. Johnson approved the policy paper the following day. After a Vietcong attack against the U.S. helicopter base in Pleiku, South Vietnam, on February 7, 1965, the United States initiated Operation Rolling Thunder, a sustained bombing campaign against North Vietnam. President Johnson soon ordered an increase in U.S. combat troops, an escalation that was paralleled by increases in both Soviet and Chinese assistance to Hanoi.

Document 7, drawn from Chinese archives, is a translation of Chairman Mao Zedong's presentation to a visiting delegation of North Vietnamese officials, dated October 20, 1965. Mao praises the Vietnamese for fighting an "excellent war" against the United States, discourages negotiations, and confirms that Chinese assistance will continue. J. William Fulbright, chair of the Senate Foreign Relations Committee, became a vocal critic of the Vietnam War. In Document 8, a speech of May 5, 1966, he protests an American "arrogance of power." In Document 9, an excerpt from Robert S. McNamara's controversial 1995 memoir, *In Retrospect,* the former secretary concludes that he and the Johnson administration erred badly in July 1965 when they escalated U.S. military intervention in Vietnam.

1. The Vietnamese Declaration of Independence, 1945

All men are created equal. They are endowed by their Creator with certain inalienable rights, among these are Life, Liberty and the pursuit of Happiness.

This immortal statement was made in the Declaration of Independence of the United States of America in 1776. In a broader sense, this means: All the peoples on the earth are equal from birth, all the peoples have a right to live, to be happy and free.

The Declaration of the French Revolution made in 1791 on the Rights of Man and the Citizen also states: "All men are born free and with equal rights, and must always remain free and have equal rights."

Those are undeniable truths.

Nevertheless, for more than eighty years, the French imperialists, abusing the standard of Liberty, Equality and Fraternity, have violated our Fatherland and oppressed our fellow-citizens. They have acted contrary to the ideals of humanity and justice.

This document can be found in Information Service, Viet-Nam Delegation in France, *The Democratic Republic of Viet-Nam* (Paris: Imprimerie Centrale Commerciale, 1948), 3–5.

In the field of politics, they have deprived our people of every democratic liberty.

They have enforced inhuman laws; they have set up three distinct political regimes in the North, the Centre and the South of Viet Nam in order to wreck our national unity and prevent our people from being united.

They have built more prisons than schools. They have mercilessly slain our patriots; they have drowned our uprisings in rivers of blood.

They have fettered public opinion; they have practised obscurantism against our people.

To weaken our race they have forced us to use opium and alcohol.

In the field of economics, they have fleeced us to the backbone, impoverished our people and devastated our land.

They have robbed us of our ricefields, our mines, our forests and our raw materials. They have monopolized the issuing of banknotes and the export trade.

They have invented numerous unjustifiable taxes and reduced our people, especially our peasantry, to a state of extreme poverty.

They have hampered the prospering of our national bourgeoisie; they have mercilessly exploited our workers. . . .

For these reasons, we, members of the Provisional Government, representing the whole Vietnamese people, declare that from now on we break off all relations of a colonial character with France; we repeal all the international obligation[s] that France has so far subscribed to on behalf of Viet Nam and we abolish all the special rights the French have unlawfully acquired in our Fatherland.

The whole Vietnamese people, animated by a common purpose, are determined to fight to the bitter end against any attempt by the French colonialists to reconquer their country.

We are convinced that the Allied nations which at Teheran and San Francisco have acknowledged the principles of self-determination and equality of nations, will not refuse to acknowledge the independence of Viet Nam.

A people who have courageously opposed French domination for more than eighty years, a people who have fought side by side with the Allies against the fascists during these last years, such a people must be free and independent.

For these reasons, we, members of the Provisional Government of the Democratic Republic of Vietnam, solemnly declare to the world that Viet Nam has the right to be a free and independent country—and in fact it is so already. The entire Vietnamese people are determined to mobilize all their physical and mental strength, to sacrifice their lives and property in order to safeguard their independence and liberty.

2. Final Declaration of the Geneva Conference on Indochina, 1954

1. The Conference takes note of the agreements ending hostilities in Cambodia, Laos and Viet Nam and organising international control and the supervision of the execution of the provisions of these agreements. . . .

This document can be found in *Department of State Bulletin* 31 (August 2, 1954): 164.

4. The Conference takes note of the clauses in the agreement on the cessation of hostilities in Viet Nam prohibiting the introduction into Viet Nam of foreign troops and military personnel as well as of all kinds of arms and munitions. . . .

5. The Conference takes note of the clauses in the agreement on the cessation of hostilities in Viet Nam to the effect that no military base under the control of a foreign State may be established in the regrouping zones of the two parties [above and below the seventeenth parallel], the latter having the obligation to see that the zones allotted to them shall not constitute part of any military alliance and shall not be utilised for the resumption of hostilities or in the service of an aggressive policy. . . .

6. The Conference recognises that the essential purpose of the agreement relating to Viet Nam is to settle military questions with a view to ending hostilities and that the military demarcation line [at the seventeenth parallel] is provisional and should not in any way be interpreted as constituting a political or territorial boundary. The Conference expresses its conviction that the execution of the provisions set out in the present declaration and in the agreement on the cessation of hostilities creates the necessary basis for the achievement in the near future of a political settlement in Viet Nam.

7. The Conference declares that, so far as Viet Nam is concerned, the settlement of political problems, effected on the basis of respect for the principles of independence, unity and territorial integrity, shall permit the Vietnamese people to enjoy the fundamental freedoms, guaranteed by democratic institutions established as a result of free general elections by secret ballot. In order to ensure that sufficient progress in the restoration of peace has been made, and that all of the necessary conditions obtain for free expression of the national will, general elections shall be held in July 1956, under the supervision of an international commission composed of representatives of the Member States of the International Supervisory Commission, referred to in the agreement on the cessation of hostilities. Consultations will be held on this subject between the competent representative authorities of the two zones from July 20, 1955, onwards. . . .

12. In their relations with Cambodia, Laos and Viet Nam, each member of the Geneva Conference undertakes to respect the sovereignty, the independence, the unity and the territorial integrity of the above-mentioned States, and to refrain from any interference in their internal affairs.

3. North Vietnamese General Vo Nguyen Giap Outlines His People's War Strategy, 1961

The Vietnamese people's war of liberation [against France] was a just war, aiming to win back the independence and unity of the country, to bring land to our peasants and guarantee them the right to it, and to defend the achievements of the August [1945] Revolution. That is why it was first and foremost a people's war. To educate, mobilise, organise and arm the whole people in order that they might take part in the Resistance was a crucial question.

This document can be found in Vo Nguyen Giap, *People's War, People's Army* (Hanoi: Foreign Languages Publishing House, 1961), 27–30.

The enemy of the Vietnamese nation was aggressive imperialism, which had to be overthrown. . . .

A backward colonial country which had only just risen up to proclaim its independence and install people's power, Viet Nam only recently possessed armed forces, equipped with still very mediocre arms and having no combat experience. Her enemy, on the other hand, was an imperialist power which has retained a fairly considerable economic and military potentiality despite the recent German occupation [during World War II] and benefited, furthermore, from the active support of the United States. The balance of forces decidedly showed up our weaknesses against the enemy's power. The Vietnamese people's war of liberation had, therefore, to be a hard and long-lasting war in order to succeed in creating conditions for victory. All the conceptions born of impatience and aimed at obtaining speedy victory could only be gross errors. It was necessary to firmly grasp the strategy of a long-term resistance, and to exalt the will to be self-supporting in order to maintain and gradually augment our forces, while nibbling at and progressively destroying those of the enemy; it was necessary to accumulate thousands of small victories to turn them into a great success, thus gradually altering the balance of forces in transforming our weakness into power and carrying off final victory. . . .

From the point of view of directing operations, our *strategy and tactics had to be those of a people's war and of a long-term resistance.*

Our strategy was, as we have stressed, to wage a long-lasting battle. A war of this nature in general entails several phases; in principle, starting from a stage of contention, it goes through a period of equilibrium before arriving at a general counter-offensive. In effect, the way in which it is carried on can be more subtle and more complex, depending on the particular conditions obtaining on both sides during the course of operations. Only a long-term war could enable us to utilise to the maximum our political trump cards, to overcome our material handicap and to transform our weakness into strength. To maintain and increase our forces, was the principle to which we adhered, contenting ourselves with attacking when success was certain, refusing to give battle likely to incur losses to us or to engage in hazardous actions. We had to apply the slogan: to build up our strength during the actual course of fighting.

The forms of fighting had to be completely adapted that is, to raise the fighting spirit to the maximum and rely on heroism of our troops to overcome the enemy's material superiority. In the main, especially at the outset of the war, we had recourse to guerilla fighting. In the Vietnamese theatre of operations, this method carried off great victories: it could be used in the mountains as well as in the delta, it could be waged with good or mediocre material and even without arms, and was to enable us eventually to equip ourselves at the cost of the enemy. Wherever the Expeditionary Corps came, the entire population took part in the fighting; every commune had its fortified village, every district had its regional troops fighting under the command of the local branches of the Party and the people's administration, in liaison with the regular forces in order to wear down and annihilate the enemy forces.

Thereafter, with the development of our forces, guerilla warfare changed into a mobile warfare—a form of mobile warfare still strongly marked by guerilla warfare—which would afterwards become the essential form of operations on the main front, the northern front. In this process of development of guerilla warfare and of accentuation of the mobile warfare, our people's army constantly grew and passed from the stage of combats involving a section or company, to fairly large-scale campaigns bringing into action several divisions. Gradually, its equipment improved, mainly by the seizure of arms from the enemy—the materiel of the French and American imperialists.

From the military point of view, *the Vietnamese people's war of liberation proved that an insufficiently equipped people's army, but an army fighting for a just cause, can, with appropriate strategy and tactics, combine the conditions needed to conquer a modern army of aggressive imperialism.*

4. The Tonkin Gulf Resolution Authorizes the President to Use Force, 1964

To promote the maintenance of international peace and security in southeast Asia.

Whereas naval units of the Communist regime in Vietnam, in violation of the principles of the Charter of the United Nations and of international law, have deliberately and repeatedly attacked United States naval vessels lawfully present in international waters, and have thereby created a serious threat to international peace; and

Whereas these attacks are part of a deliberate and systematic campaign of aggression that the Communist regime in North Vietnam has been waging against its neighbors and the nations joined with them in the collective defense of their freedom; and

Whereas the United States is assisting the peoples of southeast Asia to protect their freedom and has no territorial, military or political ambitions in that area, but desires only that these peoples should be left in peace to work out their own destinies in their own way: Now, therefore, be it *Resolved by the Senate and House of Representatives of the United States of America in Congress assembled,* That the Congress approves and supports the determination of the President, as Commander in Chief, to take all necessary measures to repel any armed attack against the forces of the United States and to prevent further aggression.

Sec. 2. The United States regards as vital to its national interest and to world peace the maintenance of international peace and security in southeast Asia. Consonant with the Constitution of the United States and the Charter of the United Nations and in accordance with its obligations under the Southeast Asia Collective Defense Treaty, the United States is, therefore, prepared, as the President determines, to take all necessary steps, including the use of armed force, to assist any member or protocol state of the Southeast Asia Collective Defense Treaty requesting assistance in defense of its freedom.

Sec. 3. This resolution shall expire when the President shall determine that the peace and security of the area is reasonably assured by international conditions created by action of the United Nations or otherwise, except that it may be terminated earlier by concurrent resolution of the Congress.

This document can be found in *Department of State Bulletin* 51 (August 24, 1964): 268.

5. A Bureaucratic Insider Laments the Momentum Against Negotiation, November 1964

Mr. Bundy has circulated the attached papers concerning "courses of action in Southeast Asia" to Secretary [of State Dean] Rusk, Secretary [of Defense Robert] McNamara, [CIA Director] Mr. [John] McCone, and General [Earl] Wheeler. A meeting with Secretary Rusk, Secretary McNamara, you, and McGeorge and William Bundy to review these papers is scheduled for next Tuesday. After further meetings next Thursday and Friday, a meeting with the President is scheduled for December 1.

I think that the approach taken in these papers will cause you serious concern. Three "broad options" are considered. *First,* to "continue present policies of maximum assistance with SVN [South Vietnam] and limited external actions in Laos and by the GVN [Government of Vietnam] coherently against North Viet-Nam;" and, possibly, specific individual reprisal actions. "Basic to this option is the continued rejection of negotiation in the hope that the situation will improve." *Second,* "present policies plus a systematic program of military pressures against the north, meshing at some point with negotiation, but with pressure actions to be continued until we achieve our central present objectives." *Third,* "present policies plus additional forceful measures and military moves, followed by negotiations in which we would seek to maintain a believable threat of still further military pressures but would not actually carry out such pressures to any marked degree during the negotiations."

These papers conclude with a proposed recommendation to the President that we follow "a program of immediate actions within the next few weeks" and that, "if the Communist side does not respond favorably" to these actions, we adopt the third alternative early next year. The "basic ingredients" of the "immediate actions during the next few weeks" would be: (1) "talking tough;" (2) "vigorous actions within our current policy" including: (a) a strong 34–A MAROPS [covert U.S.–South Vietnamese sabotage against North Vietnam] schedule; (b) continued strong air activity in the Panhandle area of Laos, including at least a few United States armed reconnaissance strikes; (c) continued strong air activity in central Laos; (d) perhaps a DeSoto patrol [a covert electronic spying program against North Vietnam] early in December; and (e) "consider explicit use of US air in South Viet-Nam if a lucrative target appears;" (3) reprisals in the event of future serious incidents; (4) "consultations with the GVN to improve its performance;" and (5) "miscellaneous actions clearly foreshadowing stronger actions."

Nowhere in these papers is there a consideration of your proposal for negotiations within the near future and without increased military action (although with the threat of such action). In fact, the first option (to continue present policies) specifically excludes negotiations. Furthermore, although the outline of the papers calls for a separate section concerning "alternative forms of negotiation" no draft of this

---

This document can be found in Memorandum from the Under Secretary of State's Special Assistant (Ehrlich) to the Under Secretary of State (Ball), 18 November 1964, *Foreign Relations of the United States, 1964–1968, I: Vietnam 1964* (Washington, D.C.: Government Printing Office, 1992), 912–913.

section was prepared. Rather, "various working papers on negotiations . . . have been woven into" the other sections.

I think there are a number of significant gaps in reasoning and questions unanswered throughout these papers. As we have discussed, the third option is full of dangers—I do not believe that they have received sufficient consideration in these papers. Most serious, however, is the lack of any real analysis of a negotiating track. In my judgment, at the very least, a paper on this track should be prepared as a fourth option.

I am particularly concerned because policy proposals like these seem quickly to develop a bureaucratic life of their own unless immediate action is taken.

6. President Lyndon B. Johnson's Advisers Chart the Path to Military Escalation, December 1964

A. US objectives in South Vietnam (SVN) are unchanged. They are to:

1. Get Hanoi and North Vietnam (DRV) support and direction removed from South Vietnam, and, to the extent possible, obtain DRV cooperation in ending Viet Cong (VC) operations in SVN.

2. Re-establish an independent and secure South Vietnam with appropriate international safeguards, including the freedom to accept US and other external assistance as required.

3. Maintain the security of other non-Communist nations in Southeast Asia including specifically the maintenance and observance of the Geneva Accords of 1962 in Laos.

B. We will continue to press the South Vietnamese Government (GVN) in every possible way to make the government itself more effective and to push forward with the pacification program. We will also press upon leaders and members of all groups in that country the overriding need for national unity.

C. We will join at once with the South Vietnamese and Lao Governments in a determined action program aimed at DRV activities in both countries and designed to help GVN morale and to increase the costs and strain on Hanoi, foreshadowing still greater pressures to come. Under this program the *first phase* actions within the next thirty days will be intensified forms of action already under way, plus possibly U.S. air protection of Lao aircraft making strikes in the Corridor, US armed air reconnaissance and air strikes against infiltration routes in Laos, and GVN and possibly US air strikes against the DRV as reprisal against any major or spectacular Viet Cong action in the south, whether against US personal and installations or not. We would be prepared to stop the flow of dependents to Vietnam at the same time as US strikes in Laos were conducted.

This document can be found in paper prepared by the Executive Committee, "Position Paper on Southeast Asia," 2 December 1964, *Foreign Relations of the United States, 1964–1968, I: Vietnam 1964* (Washington, D.C.: Government Printing Office, 1992), 969–970, 973.

D. Beyond the thirty-day period, first phase actions may be continued without change. Alternatively, additional military measures may be taken, including deployment of a large number of US aircraft to the area, low-level reconnaissance of infiltration targets in the DRV near the borders, and the possible initiation of strikes a short distance across the border against the infiltration routes from the DRV. . . .

E. Thereafter, if the GVN improves its effectiveness to an acceptable degree and Hanoi does not yield on acceptable terms, the US is prepared—at a time to be determined—to enter into a *second phase* program, in support of the GVN and RLG [Royal Laotian Government], of graduated military pressures directed systematically against the DRV. Such a program would consist principally of progressively more serious air strikes, of a weight and tempo adjusted to the situation as it develops (possibly running from two to six months) and of appropriate US deployments to handle any contingency. Targets in the DRV would start with infiltration targets south of the 19th parallel and work up to targets north of that point. This could eventually lead to such measures as air strikes on all major military-related targets, aerial mining of DRV ports, and a US naval blockade of the DRV. The whole sequence of military actions would be designed to give the impression of a steady, deliberate approach, and to give the US the option at any time (subject to enemy reaction) to proceed or not, to escalate or not, and to quicken the pace or not. Concurrently, the US would be alert to any sign of yielding by Hanoi, and would be prepared to explore negotiated solutions that attain US objectives in an acceptable manner. . . .

I. *Reprisal Actions*

For any VC provocation similar to the following, a reprisal will be undertaken, preferably within 24 hours, against one or more selected targets in the DRV. GVN forces will be used to the maximum extent, supplemented as necessary by US forces. The exact reprisal will be decided at the time, in accordance with a quick-reaction procedure which will be worked out.

The following may be appropriate occasions for reprisals, but we should be alert for any appropriate occasion:

1. Attacks on airfields.
2. Attack on Saigon.
3. Attacks on provincial or district capitals.
4. Major attacks on US citizens.
5. Attacks on major POL [Petroleum, oil, lubricants] facilities.
6. Attacks on bridges and railroad lines after the presently damaged facilities have been restored and warning given.
7. Other "spectaculars" such as earlier attack on a US transport carrier at a pier in Saigon.

In these or similar cases, the reprisal action would be linked as directly as possible to DRV infiltration, so that we have a common thread of justification. VC attacks on transportation facilities, in addition to being related to DRV infiltration, would provide the occasion for attacks on DRV communications on a parallel basis.

A flexible list of reprisal targets has been prepared running from infiltration targets in the southern part of the DRV up to airfields, ports, and naval bases also located south of the 19th parallel.

7. Chinese Leader Mao Zedong Urges the North Vietnamese to Fight On, 1965

You are fighting an excellent war. Both the South and the North are fighting well. The people of the whole world, including those who have already awakened and those who have not awakened, are supporting you. The current world is not a peaceful one. It is not you Vietnamese who are invading the United States, neither are the Chinese who are waging an aggressive war against the United States.

Not long ago the Japanese *Asahi Shimbum* and *Yomiuri Shimbun* published several reports filed by Japanese correspondents from South Vietnam. U.S. newspapers described these reports as unfair, thus provoking a debate. I am not referring to the Japanese Communist newspaper, *Akahata*. I am talking about Japanese bourgeois newspapers. This shows that the direction of the media is not favorable to the United States. Recently the demonstration by the American people against the American government's Vietnam policy has developed. At the moment it is primarily American intellectuals who are making trouble.

But all this are external conditions. In fact what will solve the problem is the war you are fighting. Of course you can conduct negotiations. In the past you held negotiations in Geneva. But the American did not honor their promise after the negotiations. We have had negotiations with both [Chinese Nationalist] Chiang Kaishek and the United States. . . . But we stick to one point: the United States must withdraw from Taiwan, and after that all other problems can be easily resolved. The United States does not accept this point. China and the United States have been negotiating for ten years and we are still repeating the same old words. . . .

You withdrew your armed forces from the South in accordance with the Geneva Accords. As a result, the enemy began to kill people in the South, and you revived armed struggle. At first you adopted political struggle as a priority supplemented by armed struggle. We supported you. In the second stage when you were carrying out political and armed struggles simultaneously, we again supported you. In the third stage when you are pursuing armed struggle as a priority supplemented by political struggle, we still support you. In my view, the enemy is gradually escalating the war: so are you. In the next two and three years you may encounter difficulties. But it is hard to say, and it may not be so. We need to take this possibility into consideration. So long as you have made all kinds of preparations, even if the most difficult situation emerges, you will not find it too far from your initial considerations. Isn't this a good argument? Therefore there are two essential points: the first is to strive for the most favorable situation, and the second to prepare for the worst. . . .

I have not noticed what issues you have negotiated with the United States. I only pay attention to how you fight the Americans and how you drive the Americans out. You can have negotiations at certain time[s], but you should not lower your tones. You should raise your tones a little higher. Be prepared that the enemy may deceive you.

From "Mao's Conversation with the Party and Government Delegation of the Democratic Republic of Vietnam," 20 October, 1965, translated by Qiang Zhai, in *Cold War International History Project Bulletin* (Winter 1995–1996), pp. 245–246. Copyright © 1996. Reprinted with permission.

We will support you until your final victory. The confidence in victory comes from the fighting you have done and from the struggle you have made. For instance, one experience we have is that the Americans can be fought. We obtained this experience only after fighting the Americans [in the Korean War]. The Americans can be fought and can be defeated. We should demolish the myth that the Americans cannot be fought and cannot be defeated. Both of our two parties have many experiences. Both of us have fought the Japanese. You have also fought the French. At the moment you are fighting the Americans. . . .

The Chinese people and the people of the whole world support you. The more friends you have, the better you are.

8. Senator J. William Fulbright Decries the "Arrogance of Power," 1966

The attitude above all others which I feel sure is no longer valid is the arrogance of power, the tendency of great nations to equate power with virtue and major responsibilities with a universal mission. The dilemmas involved are preeminently American dilemmas, not because America has weaknesses that others do not have but because America is powerful as no nation has ever been before and the discrepancy between its power and the power of others appears to be increasing. . . .

We are now engaged in a war to "defend freedom" in South Vietnam. Unlike the Republic of Korea, South Vietnam has an army which [is] without notable success and a weak, dictatorial government which does not command the loyalty of the South Vietnamese people. The official war aims of the United States Government, as I understand them, are to defeat what is regarded as North Vietnamese aggression, to demonstrate the futility of what the communists call "wars of national liberation," and to create conditions under which the South Vietnamese people will be able freely to determine their own future. I have not the slightest doubt of the sincerity of the President and the Vice President and the Secretaries of State and Defense in propounding these aims. What I do doubt—and doubt very much—is the ability of the United States to achieve these aims by the means being used. I do not question the power of our weapons and the efficiency of our logistics; I cannot say these things delight me as they seem to delight some of our officials, but they are certainly impressive. What I do question is the ability of the United States, or France or any other Western nation, to go into a small, alien, undeveloped Asian nation and create stability where there is chaos, the will to fight where there is defeatism, democracy where there is no tradition of it and honest government where corruption is almost a way of life. Our handicap is well expressed in the pungent Chinese proverb: "In shallow waters dragons become the sport of shrimps."

Early last month demonstrators in Saigon burned American jeeps, tried to assault American soldiers, and marched through the streets shouting "Down with the

This document can be found in *Congressional Record,* CXII (May 17, 1966), 10805–10810.

American imperialists," while one of the Buddhist leaders made a speech equating the United States with the communists as a threat to South Vietnamese independence. Most Americans are understandably shocked and angered to encounter such hostility from people who by now would be under the rule of the Viet Cong but for the sacrifice of American lives and money. Why, we may ask, are they so shockingly ungrateful? Surely they must know that their very right to parade and protest and demonstrate depends on the Americans who are defending them.

The answer, I think, is that "fatal impact" of the rich and strong on the poor and weak. Dependent on it though the Vietnamese are, our very strength is a reproach to their weakness, our wealth a mockery of their poverty, our success a reminder of their failures. What they resent is the disruptive effect of our strong culture upon their fragile one, an effect which we can no more avoid than a man can help being bigger than a child. What they fear, I think rightly, is that traditional Vietnamese society cannot survive the American economic and cultural impact. . . .

The cause of our difficulties in southeast Asia is not a deficiency of power but an excess of the wrong kind of power which results in a feeling of impotence when it fails to achieve its desired ends. We are still acting like boy scouts dragging reluctant old ladies across the streets they do not want to cross. We are trying to remake Vietnamese society, a task which certainly cannot be accomplished by force and which probably cannot be accomplished by any means available to outsiders. The objective may be desirable, but it is not feasible. . . .

If America has a service to perform in the world—and I believe it has—it is in large part the service of its own example. In our excessive involvement in the affairs of other countries, we are not only living off our assets and denying our own people the proper enjoyment of their resources; we are also denying the world the example of a free society enjoying its freedom to the fullest. This is regrettable indeed for a nation that aspires to teach democracy to other nations, because, as [Edmund] Burke said, "Example is the school of mankind, and they will learn at no other.". . .

There are many respects in which America, if it can bring itself to act with the magnanimity and the empathy appropriate to its size and power, can be an intelligent example to the world. We have the opportunity to set an example of generous understanding in our relations with China, of practical cooperation for peace in our relations with Russia, of reliable and respectful partnership in our relations with Western Europe, of material helpfulness without moral presumption in our relations with the developing nations, of abstention from the temptations of hegemony in our relations with Latin America, and of the all-around advantages of minding one's own business in our relations with everybody. Most of all, we have the opportunity to serve as an example of democracy to the world by the way in which we run our own society; America, in the words of John Quincy Adams, should be "the well-wisher to the freedom and independence of all" but "the champion and vindicator only of her own.". . .

If we can bring ourselves so to act, we will have overcome the dangers of the arrogance of power. It will involve, no doubt, the loss of certain glories, but that seems a price worth paying for the probable rewards, which are the happiness of America and the peace of the world.

9. Former Secretary of Defense Robert S. McNamara Concludes That He Erred, 1995

We of the Kennedy and Johnson administrations who participated in the decisions on Vietnam acted according to what we thought were the principles and traditions of this nation. We made our decisions in light of those values.

Yet we were wrong, terribly wrong. . . .

Looking back, I clearly erred by not forcing—then or later, in either Saigon or Washington—a knock-down, drag-out debate over the loose assumptions, unasked questions, and thin analyses underlying our military strategy in Vietnam. I had spent twenty years as a manager identifying problems and forcing organizations—often against their will—to think deeply and realistically about alternative courses of action and their consequences. I doubt I will ever fully understand why I did not do so here.

On July 21 [1965], I returned to Washington and presented the report I had prepared along the way to the president. It began with a frank but disturbing assessment:

> The situation in South Vietnam is worse than a year ago (when it was worse than a year before that). After a few months of stalemate, the tempo of the war has quickened. A hard VC push is now on to dismember the nation and to maul the army. . . . Without further outside help, the ARVN* is faced with successive tactical reverses, loss of key communication and population centers particularly in the highlands, piecemeal destruction of ARVN units . . . and loss of civilian confidence.

I continued:

> There are no signs that we have throttled the inflow of supplies for the VC or can throttle the flow while their material needs are as low as they are. . . . Nor have our air attacks in North Vietnam produced tangible evidence of the willingness on the part of Hanoi to come to the conference table in a reasonable mood. The DRV/VC [Democratic Republic of North Vietnam/Vietcong] seem to believe that South Vietnam is on the run and near collapse; they show no signs of settling for less than a complete take-over.

I then reviewed the three alternatives we had examined so many times before: (1) withdraw under the best conditions obtainable—almost certainly meaning something close to unconditional surrender; (2) continue at the present level—almost certainly forcing us into Option 1 later; or (3) expand our forces to meet Westy's request** while launching a vigorous effort to open negotiations—almost certainly staving off near-term defeat but also increasing the difficulty and cost of withdrawal later.

I was driven to Option 3, which I considered "prerequisite to the achievement of any acceptable settlement." I ended by expressing my judgment that "the course of action recommended in this memorandum—if the military and political moves are properly integrated and executed with continuing vigor and visible determination—stands a good chance of achieving an acceptable outcome within a reasonable time." Subsequent events proved my judgment wrong.

---

*The Army of the Republic of South Vietnam
**General William Westmoreland requested 175,000 troops by year's end and another 100,000 in 1966.

ESSAYS

In the first essay, Robert Buzzanco of the University of Houston places the Vietnam War in a global context—the post–World War II competition between international capitalism and communism—and argues that the United States's pursuit of an integrated world capitalist market dictated U.S. opposition to Vietnam's nationalism and communism and ultimately direct military intervention. According to Buzzanco, U.S. policymakers, from Truman through Johnson, deemed Vietnam essential to U.S. efforts to promote its post–World War II interests in Europe and Japan. Although never a puppet to external communist powers, Vietnam became a Cold War battleground when the Soviet Union and the People's Republic of China began to aid Ho Chi Minh's anticolonial movement. Ironically, the war became so expensive that it generated a severe global monetary crisis and undermined American hegemony. It also unmasked deep divisions within the socialist camp.

In the second essay, Fredrik Logevall of Cornell University disputes that Vietnam policy was driven primarily by either U.S. economic needs or Cold War containment. He instead deconstructs the decisionmaking process of late 1964 and concludes that President Johnson and his highest-ranking advisers equated U.S. national interests with their own personal reputations and therefore chose military escalation to forestall an embarrassing retreat. Johnson's ego and machismo led him to demand victory in Vietnam even though intelligence reports minimized the chances for military success and even though numerous foreign leaders, journalists, and Democrats urged disengagement. The administration's midlevel working group on Southeast Asia and its most senior advisers fell in line with the president's wishes, partly out of conviction, but also to maintain their status within the bureaucracy. Thus presidential power and bureaucratic politics set the stage for a military debacle in Vietnam.

In the final piece, Robert K. Brigham of Vassar College uses recently declassified Chinese and Vietnamese sources to reassess the U.S. military defeat in Vietnam. Brigham identifies three strategies commonly cited as alternatives to gradual escalation and attrition: a U.S. invasion of North Vietnam; American incursion into neighboring Laos; and the concentration of U.S. forces in defensive enclaves in South Vietnam. He concludes that none would have brought victory because each failed to take into account the indigenous nature of the South Vietnamese insurgency and the multiple deficiencies of the Saigon government. An attack on the north carried the added disadvantage of virtually guaranteeing a costly U.S. war with Hanoi's neighbor and ally, the People's Republic of China. Given the nature of a people's war, Brigham concludes that no American strategy could have reversed the war's outcome.

International Capitalism and Communism Collide with Vietnamese Nationalism

ROBERT BUZZANCO

Vietnam became an important *international* issue only after World War II. During those years in the late 1940s, U.S. officials were trying to reestablish a stable world system but at the same time restructure it according to U.S. needs. The United States believed it imperative to rebuild former enemies like Germany and Japan along

Excerpts from Robert Buzzanco, "The United States and Vietnam: Capitalism, Communism, and Containment," in Peter Hahn and Mary Ann Heiss, eds., *Empire and Revolution: The United States and the Third World Since 1945* (Columbus: Ohio State University Press, 2001), pp. 95–105, 107–115. Copyright © 2001 by Ohio State University Press. Reprinted with permission.

capitalist and democratic lines. In this effort to create a new world (liberal) order, smaller countries, like Vietnam, became objects of interest. Future economic prosperity, if not hegemony, would depend on creating an integrated world market. Where colonial areas earlier in the twentieth century might have been attractive principally as sources of raw materials or cheap labor, in the postwar economic environment they would serve as important areas for investment and regional development. Vietnam's development along anticommunist lines, for instance, would be essential for the re-creation of capitalism in Japan and to keep the French appeased in Europe. Thus, this [essay] will, more than most studies, pay attention to the economic factors involved in the Vietnam War: the need to use all of Southeast Asia, not just Vietnam, as a means of rebuilding Japan, and ultimately the drain on U.S. resources that the war would become. It will also stress the global nature of the war. In the past few years, documents from archives in ex-communist nations and from China have begun to increase our understanding of the Cold War and, in the case of places like Vietnam, the hot wars that attended it. . . .

[P]erhaps the United States's greatest blunder was its inability to recognize both the nationalist *and* socialist nature of the Vietnamese resistance, later organized as the Viet Minh. Never doctrinaire, Ho merged a class analysis and a program for land redistribution (the key issue in Vietnamese society) with popular front politics and an appeal to *all* anti-French elements to join the cause. Ho himself had no inherent animus against the United States either; in fact, encouraged by Woodrow Wilson's call for self-determination during the Great War, the expatriate in Paris had tried to get an audience with the U.S. president during the postwar conference at Versailles. In 1945, when Ho declared Vietnamese independence after the defeat of the Japanese, he had positive relations with U.S. military and intelligence officials, quoted at length from the U.S. Declaration of Independence during his own address marking Vietnamese sovereignty on 2 September 1945, and even sent telegrams to President Harry S. Truman seeking U.S. amity and recognition. . . .

Though U.S. leaders had mounted anticolonial rhetoric in World War II, the White House and State Department had supported the return of France to power in Indochina in 1945–46. Fearing the emergence of communist parties and trade union movements in Western Europe, and especially in France where the Communist Party and labor were strong, the United States would placate the French by acquiescing in their renewed control over Vietnam. For U.S. foreign policy makers, this was a no-brainer, since a French role in containing the European Left was exponentially more important than Vietnamese autonomy. Ironically, however, U.S. military officials, who agreed on the primacy of French interests, argued *against* supporting their return to Indochina, claiming that it would divert resources and attention away from their principal mission, containment at home. The civilians won out, however, and the United States began to back the French, sending about $25 million in 1950, which rose to nearly $1 billion by 1954.

The Vietnamese, however, continued to resist the French, politically and militarily from 1946 to 1954, so the U.S. aid did not rescue France's position in Indochina. By 1954, then, the Viet Minh were on the verge of victory; hence the expedient agreement at Geneva to divide the country, *temporarily,* until nationwide elections could be held in 1956. That plebiscite never happened, though. Aware of Ho's popularity and support on both sides of the seventeenth parallel, U.S. officials and their

Vietnamese allies canceled the vote, ensuring the continued partition of Vietnam, with a disgruntled nationalist-communist state—the Democratic Republic of Vietnam (DRV)—in the north and an artificial "country"—the Republic of Vietnam (RVN)—cobbled together by the United States in the south. Complicating U.S. efforts at containment in Vietnam, the southern regime was led by an autocratic mandarin, Ngo Dinh Diem, whose repression and corruption would be a great recruiting tool for the enemy Viet Minh. By the mid-1950s, then, the United States was on a collision course with the forces of liberation and revolution in Vietnam. . . .

The most pressing [global] problem facing the United States after World War II was the so-called dollar gap. The United States was the only power to emerge from the hostilities stronger than it entered and was producing more goods than domestic markets could absorb (as in the 1890s). But European nations lacked adequate dollars to purchase the U.S. surplus. The United States needed to somehow get dollars into foreign hands so that other nations could in turn buy U.S. goods, but Congress, especially after appropriating $17 billion in Marshall Plan money in 1948, was reluctant to expend another huge sum of money on foreign aid. Still, without some type of support, U.S. officials feared, the Europeans would probably erect trade barriers against U.S. goods as they did during the 1930s, thereby exacerbating the Great Depression.

Complicating, and connecting, such matters, the United States had also been subsidizing Japanese recovery since 1945 but by 1950 was hoping to wean Japan off U.S. funding and to connect it, as before the war, with other Far Eastern economies such as those in Southeast Asia, including Vietnam. On this issue—the need for Southeast Asian markets—European and Japanese interests merged. Not only could the Japanese profit from trade with other Asians, especially since plans to link the Japanese and Chinese economies fell by the wayside with Mao's victory, but British recovery was linked to Southeast Asia as well. In the aftermath of the Second World War, British debt was growing rapidly, to a large extent because the flow of dollars from its colony in Malaya had been cut off, first because of the Japanese occupation during the war and then because of reconstruction difficulties afterward. To remedy Malaya's economic ills, the British began to pour money—£86 million between 1945 and 1949—into the country and to pressure the United States to offer economic aid and to increase imports of Malayan tin and rubber. U.S. purchases would then provide the dollars that the British could use to purchase goods from the United States. As Seymour Harris, an economist on the government dole at the time, explained, "A gradual transfer of aid from Western Europe to the underdeveloped areas [such as Southeast Asia] will contribute towards a solution of the dollar problems of both Europe and the underdeveloped areas." "A vigorous foreign aid program," Harris concluded, was necessary "for a prosperous America." Southeast Asia, then, could serve a dual purpose: providing markets and materials to Japan and helping fix the dollar gap for Europeans.

Vietnam was crucial to this process for two reasons. First, it too could provide raw materials and become a source of dollars for the French and could become a market for and offer materials to Japan. Second, the issue of communism in Asia touched directly on Vietnam. Within Southeast Asia after World War II, there were two communist insurgencies directed against European colonial powers—in Malaya against the British and in Vietnam against the French. While British leaders were not enthusiastic about France's return to Indochina, they even more feared that Ho's revolution would succeed and that Laos, Cambodia, Burma, and Thailand would then, like falling dominoes, fall to the Reds as well, thereby putting intense and direct pressure on Malaya. Once more, Ho's movement for national liberation became a target of U.S. opposition not because of events in Vietnam so much as because of the United States's need to develop a world system in which capitalist markets would be protected and nationalist-communist movements would be contained.

While the Vietnam War was being fought in the 1960s and 1970s, U.S. leaders contended that it was imperative to fight there to defeat communism. But there were then, and there remain today, important questions about Ho's own version of communism, his commitment to expand Vietnamese control elsewhere, and his relationship with other communist states. . . .

In the late 1950s, both the Soviet Union and the PRC were urging Ho to be cautious with regard to any forced attempt to unify Vietnam—advice that dovetailed nicely with Ho's own conservative tendencies on that matter. After a Vietnamese request to analyze their plans for the south, Chinese communist leaders responded that the "most fundamental, the most crucial, and the most urgent" task was to rebuild and develop socialism above the seventeenth parallel. In the south, PRC officials advised Ho, the anti-Diem activists should conduct "long-term" preparations and "wait for opportunities." Although dispensing advice freely, the communist powers, as General Tran Van Don, an aide to Diem in the south, conceded, were giving only limited material support to Ho, still dramatically less than the United States was supplying to the RVN. In the south, however, remnants of the Viet Minh, suffering under the Diemist repression, were pleading with the communist leadership in Hanoi to sponsor and fund an armed insurgency in the south. Ho, as [the historian] William Duiker's work over the years has shown, wanted to move more slowly than the southern insurgents, and the RVN itself did not fear northern aggression below the partition line or a significant increase in DRV aid to the anti-Diem movement. Apparently, the new documents show, the Chinese and Ho were on the same page.

By 1960, however, both Ho and the Chinese began to see the efficacy of armed struggle against Diem, with Hanoi acquiescing at the end of the year to the establishment of the southern-based National Liberation Front (NLF). It is not clear whether one side convinced the other or the PRC and DRV came to the same conclusion about armed insurgency on their own (which is probably more likely), but in a May 1960 meeting, [PRC Foreign Minister] Zhou Enlai, [Mao's eventual successor] Deng Xiaoping, and the Vietnamese now saw the need for combining intensified political organization with armed struggle. By 1961, with a new U.S. president ready to significant[ly] expand the U.S. role in Vietnam, communists in Vietnam, and China, were prepared to meet John Kennedy's challenge. During a 1961 visit by the DRV's premier, Pham Van Dong, to China, Mao Zedong expressed general support for armed struggle in southern Vietnam. The war in Vietnam was about to expand.

As U.S. support and aid to the RVN increased and its military involvement grew correspondingly, Ho continued to make contacts with the PRC and Soviet Union and looked to them for more assistance as well. The Chinese especially had been helping the Viet Minh and NLF in the 1950s and early 1960s, providing the DRV and NLF with 270,000 guns, over 10,000 artillery pieces and millions of artillery shells, thousands of wire transmitters, over 1,000 trucks, aircraft, warships, and uniforms; in fact, one of the U.S. justifications for its own increased role in Vietnam was such PRC involvement. . . . Remembering Korea, Mao feared a U.S. military role in Vietnam, so close to the PRC's own borders, and was ideologically committed to supporting the Vietnamese liberation movement. . . .

In October 1964, Pham Van Dong, Ho's closest adviser, met with Mao in Beijing and explained that his strategy was to restrict the war in the south "to the sphere of special war" (i.e., insurgency war), avoid provoking a larger U.S. intervention, and prevent the war from expanding above the seventeenth parallel. Mao was unimpressed by the U.S. potential to thwart the insurgency in the south and predicted that, if it engaged the DRV, the United States would "fight for one hundred years, and its legs will be trapped." Mao accordingly approved of the Vietnamese plans and suggested to Pham Van Dong that "you must not engage your main force in a head-to-head confrontation with [U.S. forces], and must well maintain our main force. My opinion is that so long as the green mountain is there, how can you ever lack firewood?" . . . General [Vo Nguyen] Giap already understood this approach and was adept throughout the war at drawing U.S. forces into battles in which the PAVN [Peoples Army of Vietnam] held the initiative and was able to inflict heavy casualties. Ironically, one U.S. war leader, Defense Secretary McNamara, saw the war in similar ways to Mao and Pham Van Dong. In November 1965, after the so-called victory of U.S. forces at Ia Drang, he recognized that the PAVN was avoiding main-force engagements and was attacking only at opportune moments. Even with a larger concentration of U.S. forces in Vietnam, as military commanders were requesting, Giap's strategic successes made it more likely "that we will be faced with a 'no-decision' at an even higher level."

McNamara's fear, an expanded war in Southeast Asia, was, conversely, China's threat and advantage. Promising to "go to Vietnam if Vietnam is in need, as we did in Korea," Zhou [Enlai] warned that "the war will have no limits if the US expands it into Chinese territory. The US can fight an air war. Yet, China can also fight a ground war." Lyndon Johnson understood that as well, and prudently . . . did avoid provoking the PRC to the point of intervention. Indeed, during discussions with his military chiefs regarding reinforcements in 1967, the president asked, "At what point does the enemy ask for [Chinese] volunteers?" General Earle Wheeler, the chair of the Joint Chiefs of Staff, could not reassure Johnson, agreeing that China could easily send troops into Vietnam in support of the DRV-NLF effort. . . .

While the PRC maintained a high level of interest in the war in Vietnam from the outset of the war of liberation in the 1950s, the other communist power, the Soviet Union (USSR), was initially more distant from the conflict. While offering recognition and some support to the DRV, the Soviets did not match the level of Chinese interest. In the aftermath of the 1962 Cuban missile crisis, U.S.-Soviet relations had improved noticeably, and the Soviets had minimized their role in Vietnam, which—along with Soviet suspicions that Ho was too close to Mao—caused a chill in the Kremlin's contacts with the DRV through 1964. That year, however, the ouster of Nikita Khrushchev and Leonid Brezhnev's assumption of power prompted the USSR to reevaluate its Vietnam policies and become more deeply involved in support of the DRV. In part, the Soviets did not want to lose influence in Southeast Asia or relinquish their role as primary communist power to the PRC. Toward that end, the Soviets began to publicly denounce the "American aggression" in Vietnam and to increase their military and economic assistance to the DRV and NLF. Between 1963 and 1967, the Soviets sent over one billion rubles worth of military supplies to the Vietnamese, shipped German-, and then Soviet-, made arms to their "Vietnamese friends," and sent surface-to-air missiles, jets, rockets, field artillery, and air defense technology to Ho. Economic aid flowed as freely, with the Soviets providing 50 percent of all aid to the DRV by 1968, with a total package to that point of over 1.8 billion rubles. The Vietnamese, while appreciative of Russian help, tried to exploit the friendship of both the Chinese and the Soviets. Vietnamese leaders Le Duan, Pham Van Dong, and Vo Nguyen Giap, among others, formed a working group in 1964–65 to determine ways to gain support from both communist powers while avoiding Chinese imperialism and an overreliance on the USSR. . . .

Ho, the master strategist who had played off France, China, Japan, and the United States for several decades already, had once again done so, acquiring significant aid from both the Soviet Union and China but never relinquishing Vietnamese sovereignty in the process. Meanwhile, the war against the United States raged on, with the stakes for all sides increasing on a steady basis.

By the late 1960s, U.S. leaders had been monitoring the economic effects of military intervention in Vietnam for some time already. The war was exacerbating a deep deficit in the U.S. balance of payments (BOP)—the amount of U.S. money moving abroad, in the form of tourist dollars, investment capital, or military spending, for instance—thereby weakening the dollar and prompting foreign governments to cash in their U.S. currency for gold, which in turn undermined the international monetary structure. The eminent business historian Louis Galambos has argued that Vietnam "was the most debilitating episode in the nation's entire history, more expensive in its own special way than World Wars I and II combined." An examination of the economic legacy of Vietnam in the 1960s offers ample evidence to support such claims.

After World War II, the United States had established global hegemony based on the confluence of its military power, economic growth, and political liberalism, and for a generation afterward it maintained a dominant position in the world political economy. By the mid-1960s, however, the United States's role was changing, principally as participation in the Vietnam War grew and caused greater BOP deficits and shortages in U.S. gold reserves. By 1968, the postwar system was entering a crisis phase as the Tet Offensive and the so-called gold crisis converged to transform the international system and create new political relationships at home. The events of 1967–68, it is not an exaggeration to suggest, marked the evolution of the United States's postwar role from that of unrivaled and prosperous imperial power to "first among equals" in a system of "shared hegemony." At home, the spiraling economic growth brought on by two decades of military Keynesianism could not be sustained in wartime, and U.S. capital began to flow overseas, to the detriment of domestic workers. By itself, Vietnam was calling into question the United States's military power and world leadership. At the same time, the Bretton Woods system experienced the greatest crisis since its founding. Created near the end of World War II, the Bretton Woods system established the dollar as the world's currency, fully convertible to gold at $35 per ounce and exchangeable with other currencies at stable rates based on the gold standard. Throughout the Vietnam War, however, the world monetary system was in disequilibrium or disarray, both as a result of the chronic and escalating BOP problem and, more critically, because of continuing runs on U.S. gold. . . .

Throughout 1966 and 1967 . . . the BOP deficits grew, [and] gold continued to leave the United States. . . . Inflation was rising as well, causing a major increase in the cost of the war, increasing import demand, and decreasing exports. The U.S. share of world trade, which had approached 50 percent after World War II, was down to 25 percent in 1964 and fell to just 10 percent by 1968. Treasury officials also estimated that the BOP deficit would continue to soar due "entirely to our intensified effort in Southeast Asia" while "a further $200 million increase in [military] expenditures may occur next year [FY 67] and worsen the projected deficit by that amount." . . .

Indeed, U.S. leaders could no longer avoid meeting the "overall problem" of Vietnam and economic calamity, and in early 1968 they had to confront the most serious U.S. crisis, military or economic, of the postwar era. In Vietnam, the enemy launched the Tet Offensive, a countrywide series of attacks that undermined [General William] Westmoreland's claim of "light at the end of the tunnel." Enemy forces, breaking a Tet holiday cease-fire, struck virtually every center of political or military significance in the RVN. Though suffering heavy losses—which U.S. officials would cite to claim victory during the offensive—the NLF and PAVN had in fact gained a major politico-strategic victory, exposing both the shaky nature of ARVN forces, who deserted in large numbers, and the bankruptcy of U.S. strategy, for U.S. forces could not even protect their own installations, even the embassy, in southern Vietnam. The shock of Tet, especially after respected newsman Walter Cronkite appeared on national television in late February 1968 urging an end to the war, forced U.S. leaders to finally reevaluate their approach to Vietnam. . . .

But, just as importantly, the world economic crisis peaked in early 1968 as well, and money and war were on a collision course. The military's request for massive reinforcement—206,000 more troops and the activation of 280,000 reserves—McNamara warned, would require additional appropriations of $25 billion in fiscal year 1969–70 alone, without the likelihood, let alone the promise, of turning the corner in Vietnam. At the same time, the Europeans, fearing the economic effects of another escalation in Vietnam, began cashing in their dollars for gold. During the last week of February, the gold pool sold $119 million in hard currency; on 3 and 4 March, losses totaled $141 million; and by early March the new chair of the Council of Economic Advisers, Arthur Okun, describing "a bad case of the shakes" in world financial markets, reported that the BOP deficit for the first week of March had risen to $321 million while gold losses soared to $395 million, including $179 million on 8 March alone. Should such withdrawals continue to mount, as [the historian] Thomas McCormick has explained, the depletion of gold reserves could have caused a devaluation of the dollar, which could have ignited a series of currency devaluations not unlike the 1930s. Then, with the absence of stable exchange rates, businesses would suffer globally.

With the crisis intensifying, the administration scrambled for a response. An Advisory Committee established by [Treasury Secretary] Henry Fowler, headed by Douglas Dillon and including various leaders of the Washington and Wall Street establishments, insisted that Johnson press hard for a 10 percent surcharge on corporate and individual income taxes, a move Johnson had been hoping to avoid since late 1965; retain the $35 price of gold despite European calls for an increase; and, if the problems deepened, consider closing the gold pool. "My own feeling," [National Security Adviser Walt] Rostow admitted, "is that the moment of truth is close upon us." He was right. On 14 March the gold pool lost $372 million—bringing the March losses to date to $1.26 billion—and U.S. officials anticipated that the next day's withdrawals could top $1 billion. The administration, as Rostow lamented, "can't go on as is, hoping that something will turn up." The Europeans were also pressuring the United States to act, so Johnson, on the 15th, closed the London gold market for the day, a Friday—typically the heaviest trading day of the week—and called an emergency meeting of central bankers. That weekend, governors of the central banks of the United States, the United Kingdom, Germany, Italy, Belgium, the Netherlands, and Switzerland—but not France [which had sharply criticized U.S. policy]—met in Washington to deliberate world monetary conditions. The governors, not for the first time, called on the United States and the United Kingdom to improve their BOP positions, urged the president to retain the official price of gold, and called for a "two-tiered" system for gold in which private markets could float their rates. Perhaps the major reform emerging from the crisis was the establishment of Special Drawing Rights (SDR). Created by the International Monetary Fund, these international reserve units—"paper" gold—provided the world monetary system with internationally managed liquid assets to avoid future massive hard currency withdrawals.

While the governors had stemmed the crisis with such action, LBJ was feeling more political heat than ever. . . . Rostow and Economic Adviser Ernest Goldstein told the president to anticipate additional costs for Vietnam in the $6 to $8 billion range for fiscal year 1969. And, in a biting analysis, Presidential Aide Harry McPherson berated Johnson for asking the U.S. people to keep supporting a war that was already excessively costly and had no end in sight. Lyndon Johnson, however, did not have to be told how bad the situation had turned. . . .

The alliance and military survived much better than Johnson. In a 31 March speech to the nation, he announced limited reinforcements for Vietnam, curtailed bombing above the twentieth parallel, discussed the world monetary crisis, and stressed the need for a tax surcharge. At the end of his address he stunned the nation by withdrawing from the 1968 campaign. Although the war in Vietnam would continue for five more years, Johnson was admitting failure in early 1968. . . .

The communist nations were not without their own crises in 1968, however, for the PRC, Soviet Union, and Vietnam all fell into conflict with each other just as the DRV-NLF war was attaining its greatest success. The Soviet Union was [now] trying to persuade Ho to negotiate with the United States and had denounced Hanoi for rejecting Lyndon Johnson's late 1967 "San Antonio Formula," which had promised a bombing pause if the Vietnamese would talk. The Soviet embassy even advised Moscow to inform the DRV that the USSR could not afford political brinksmanship with the United States by deepening its involvement in Vietnam and that an end to hostilities in 1968 would be in both Vietnamese and Soviet interests. But the PRC, wanting to maintain a high level of antagonism between the Soviet Union and the United States, feared that negotiations could end the war, which would raise the prospects of Chinese-Vietnamese tension again and would remove the U.S. counterbalance in Asia against the Soviets. . . .

For their part, the Vietnamese did not appreciate PRC pressure and began to distance themselves from the Chinese, especially during the Czech crisis of mid-1968. The USSR, believing it had to take a leadership role in global affairs regarding socialist countries, sent troops into Czechoslovakia to stem a liberalization movement there. The Chinese had repeatedly accused the Soviet Union of deviating from the Marxist, revolutionary line and of collusion with the West, so, as Ilya Gaiduk explained, "the Kremlin had to defend its policy not only by strong words, but also by deeds." The DRV, amid an intense anti-Soviet campaign out of Beijing, supported the Czech invasion, angering the Chinese but bringing praise from Moscow. Hanoi's support of the Soviets, open and explicit, was a signal to the USSR that the DRV was moving closer to it and remaining independent of the PRC. Thus the Soviet Union urged—and the Vietnamese agreed—that negotiations, then under way in Paris, should be taken seriously to try to end the war. . . .

What had begun in the aftermath of World War II as a war of national liberation waged by the Viet Minh against the French Union had become a global affair, with the world's major powers involved.

Because of the escalation of the conflict in Vietnam—by the United States, by Vietnam, by the Soviet Union, and by China too—the world was transformed. U.S. military and economic power, the events of the mid- to late 1960s showed, was limited. Washington no longer had fiat over the world as it seemed to have had in the 1940s and 1950s. Apparently unable or unwilling to distinguish between nationalism and communism, the United States, for reasons of credibility and capitalist expansion, tried to crush a liberation-cum-revolution in Vietnam with dire consequences. Not only was the United States's world position undermined, but, much worse, tens of thousands of U.S. citizens died fighting in Indochina, while, worse still, a small nation in Indochina was destroyed beyond feasible reconstruction. The Vietnamese, for their part, finally reached their goal. After 1968 it was clear that the United States did not possess the means or the will to "win" in Vietnam, and though troops remained until 1973 and the United States supported the RVN until 1975, Tet had effectively become the U.S. obituary in Vietnam. As for the communist world, the Vietnam War exposed divisions between the PRC and the USSR that were evident prior to the 1960s but not as obvious. By 1968, talk of "monolithic communism" was simply absurd; the major powers were more concerned with the political war they were fighting among themselves than with the shooting war between Vietnam and the United States.

Lyndon Johnson and His Advisers Pursue Personal Credibility and War

FREDRIK LOGEVALL

There can be no doubt that millions who cast their ballots for Johnson [in the 1964 presidential election] did so precisely because he was not Barry Goldwater. The Republican candidate scared them with his ideologically tinged speeches and his seeming proclivity for a direct confrontation with communist forces in Vietnam. In contrast, Johnson ran as the candidate of peace, as the man who would continue to support South Vietnam but also keep the United States out of a major war in Southeast Asia. Notwithstanding the attempt by White House speechwriters to leave slightly ajar the door to a larger American involvement in the conflict, the dominant impression left by LBJ in the final weeks of the campaign was that of a president telling

Lyndon Johnson and His Bureaucracy Choose War from Fredrik Logevall, *Choosing War: The Lost Chance for Peace and the Escalation of War in Vietnam* (Berkeley: University of California Press, 1999), pp. 253–260, 266–271, 383, 387–395. Reprinted by permission of the University of California Press.

voters that if they wanted to avoid a larger war in Vietnam, he was their man. "If any American president had ever promised anything to the American people," Thomas Powers has written, "then Lyndon Johnson had promised to keep the United States out of the war in Vietnam." . . .

And disengagement was a policy option that won many new adherents in the United States in the wake of the election, less because of American than because of South Vietnamese political developments. November and December 1964 witnessed the almost total unraveling of the South Vietnamese socio-political fabric. Internal factional struggles among Saigon officials reached new levels of intensity, and intelligence agencies reported widespread support for some form of neutralist settlement leading to a coalition government. War-weariness became still more pervasive among the peasantry and many urban dwellers, and there occurred a pronounced increase in anti-American rhetoric, some of it uttered by top GVN [Government of Vietnam] officials. To longtime proponents of early negotiations these developments only confirmed what they had always said: that any American attempt to secure a GVN military victory over the Vietcong would inevitably fail, and that it was foolish to pretend otherwise.

Significantly, these critics now found vastly increased support for their views. In December 1964, dozens of newspapers across the United States, some of which had hitherto been unquestioning supporters of the American commitment (and would be again after the Americanization of the war in 1965), began to express deep doubts about the enterprise. Many of them endorsed a negotiated disengagement from the war. Others would not go that far but still explicitly ruled out any deeper American involvement. A troubling question began to echo in editorials across the land: Just what was America doing supporting a government and a people so demonstrably unwilling to contribute to their own defense? On Capitol Hill, meanwhile, support increased for a full-fledged reexamination of the country's commitment to South Vietnam. . . .

On some level, Lyndon Johnson understood that he had options regarding Vietnam and that the immediate postelection period would present an opportunity to examine those options closely. The day before the election, he ordered the creation of an NSC "Working Group" to study "immediately and intensively" the American alternatives in Southeast Asia. The group, to be chaired by Assistant Secretary of State William P. Bundy, would be composed of eight middle-level officials from the State Department, the Pentagon, and the CIA—in addition to Bundy, they were Marshall Green, Robert H. Johnson, and Michael Forrestal, all from the State Department, John McNaughton and Vice Admiral Lloyd Mustin from the Pentagon, and Harold Ford and George Carver from the CIA. These men would report their conclusions to a group of NSC "principals" (Secretary of Defense Robert McNamara, Secretary of State Dean Rusk, National Security Adviser McGeorge Bundy, CIA Director John McCone, Undersecretary of State George Ball, and Joint Chiefs of Staff Chairman General Earle Wheeler), who would in turn make recommendations to the president. It resembled a bureaucratic layer cake, which suited the president fine—it allowed him to create something close to unanimity among his advisers.

Herein lay the crux of the matter. Lyndon Johnson not only wanted consensus on which way to proceed in Vietnam; he also wanted victory in the war, or at least something other than defeat. In the wake of his campaign triumph, he was no less adamant than before that he would not be the president who lost Vietnam. As William Bundy put it in a memorandum on 5 November, LBJ emerged from the election "clearly thinking in terms of maximum use of a Gulf of Tonkin rationale" to show American determination. Presidential advisers, whether in the top or middle level, understood this Johnsonian idée fixe perfectly well, and it must have hung like a heavy blanket over the planning that November. In addition, almost all of these advisers had developed a deep stake in the success of the war effort. For several years in many cases, they had trumpeted the need to stand firm and proclaimed the certainty of ultimate victory; to suggest a new course now would mean going against all their previous recommendations and analyses. Vested interest, in other words, produced bias.

These pressures explain what in hindsight is the most defining characteristic of the postelection deliberations: their highly circumscribed nature. Whatever freedom of action other observers may have thought Johnson possessed after the crushing victory over Goldwater, it quickly became clear that there remained little latitude for reopening the basic questions about American involvement in Vietnam—about whether the struggle needed to be won or whether it could be won. NSAM [National Security Action Memo] 288, issued in March 1964, which committed the United States to defending and preserving an independent, noncommunist South Vietnam, remained the bedrock upon which all proposals were to be built. . . .

Before the NSC Working Group held its first meeting, in fact even before the election, this future direction of American policy could be seen. On 1 November, a State Department cable approved by Secretary of Defense Robert McNamara and by the White House asked Ambassador Maxwell Taylor in Saigon to recommend actions that would give the "right signal level to the North and keep up morale in the South." The cable requested Taylor's opinion about the use of air strikes against Vietcong units in South Vietnam and about the deployment of American ground forces, suggesting that such forces could give "the desirable appearance of securing decks for action." The following day, on the eve of the election, a second cable, authored by the Working Group's chairman, William Bundy, and approved by the White House, informed Taylor that the administration intended to seek the "earliest possible preparation for a later decision" to begin expanded action, and to authorize "interim actions" that would demonstrate America's unbending determination in the war. The cable added that the administration would try to have the various alternatives for wider action ready as soon as possible. . . .

The Working Group thus began its work with the general assessment that an increased American participation in the war would be useful and necessary. The three basic options were outlined immediately and, with some modifications, were the ones presented to the principals in the final week of November. Option A would be to continue present policies, including, in John McNaughton's words, "maximum assistance within South Vietnam and limited external actions in Laos and by the GVN covertly against North Vietnam." Any American reprisal actions would be for the purpose of punishing large Vietcong actions in the South enough to deter future activity but not so much as to bring about strong international negotiating pressures. Basic to this option would be the "continued rejection of negotiating in the hope the situation will improve." Option B would be early, heavy military pressure against the North, called "fast/full squeeze" by McNaughton. The actions would continue at a rapid pace and without interruption until the United States achieved its present objectives (that is, an end to the insurgency). At some point, Option B activity would be meshed with negotiation, Bundy and McNaughton wrote, "but we would approach any discussions or negotiations with absolutely inflexible insistence on our present objectives."

Option C took the middle road between A and B. It called for a continuation of existing policies but with added military pressure. There would be communication with Hanoi, Beijing, or both, and graduated military moves against infiltration routes in Laos and North Vietnam and then against additional targets in the North. "The scenario should give the impression of a steady deliberate approach," McNaughton suggested. "It would be designed to give the U.S. the option at any point to proceed or not, to escalate or not, and to quicken the pace or not." Under Option C, the question of negotiations would be "played by ear," though the administration should probably indicate a willingness to talk under the right conditions. McNaughton and Bundy, the two dominant members of the Working Group, both preferred this option. Smart bureaucrats that they were, they plainly sought to control the outcome of the deliberations by utilizing what has been called the "Goldilocks principle," in which one choice is portrayed as too soft, one too hard, and one just right. The two men could reasonably expect the principals to join them in favoring the "just right" choice, Option C.

Though these three options framed the debate throughout the Working Group's deliberations, there are intriguing hints that early in the process at least fleeting consideration was given to a "fall-back" position, to what we might call an "Option D," under which the United States would seek to disengage from the war. The unspoken rationale behind this line of thinking was that defeat in Vietnam was certain, or almost certain, regardless of what the administration did. An early position paper, drafted by William Bundy . . . acknowledged that most of the world had written off South Vietnam and Laos in 1954; that South Vietnam was uniquely poor ground on which to make a stand, for reasons of geography, demography, and history; and that the present situation looked dismal. American policy had always been based on the notion that the South Vietnamese would care about defending themselves, the paper said, yet in the view of much of the world this will was precisely the lacking element in South Vietnam. . . .

It is not clear if any members of the Working Group actually thought this fall-back positions merited serious consideration, but the group's intelligence panel held views that, if nothing else, seemed to confirm its pessimistic conclusions. The panel members noted that "the basic elements of Communist strength in South Vietnam remain indigenous" and that "even if severely damaged," North Vietnam could continue to support the insurgency at a reduced level. Equally important, Hanoi would endure great pain in any "test of wills with the United States over the course of events in South Vietnam." . . .

Nevertheless, Bundy and McNaughton remained committed to pressing ahead, regardless of the odds. In this conviction they were joined by the Joint Chiefs of Staff's representative to the group, Vice Admiral Lloyd Mustin, who called for an end to the "dallying and delaying" in favor of expanded military action. Mustin's forceful advocacy no doubt helped remove any chance that serious consideration be given the "fall-back" position, but it meant less to the deliberations than the position articulated in the cables of his former boss, Saigon ambassador Maxwell Taylor. Still a voice of major influence in American policy making on Vietnam, Taylor by the last two months of 1964 had become fully convinced that an air campaign against the

North represented the magical missing ingredient in the war effort. . . . On 9 November, for example, the ambassador called such action the only way to revive a "despondent country grown tired of the strains of the counterinsurgency struggle." He theorized that bombing could inflict significant damage on "the sources of VC strength" in North Vietnam and along the infiltration routes in Laos and that this damage would boost southern morale. . . .

In reality, unstoppable momentum had developed in favor of bombing the North, and early negotiations leading to withdrawal had been ruled out. The fact that senior officials continued to refer to [Undersecretary of State George] Ball's activity as a "devil's advocate" exercise suggests how little intellectual weight they attached to it. . . . Likewise, Ball's mid-November suggestion that the administration develop a diplomatic strategy in the event of an imminent collapse by the Saigon regime got nowhere—the centerpiece of this strategy, an early great-power conference on the war convened by the British, at which the United States would play the best it could with lousy cards, was anathema to officials who still refused to contemplate seriously a retreat from core aims laid down in NSAM 288.

Nor was Ball alone in hoping to restrain the move to a larger war. Several mid-level officials shared his basis [*sic*] position, among them James C. Thomson Jr. of the NSC; Thomas L. Hughes, who headed the Bureau of Intelligence and Research at the State Department; Allen Whiting, deputy director of the East Asian desk at the State Department; Carl Salans of the Legal Adviser's Office at the State Department; and the Working Group's Robert Johnson. No less than Ball, these men were distressed by the continuing administration pursuit of a military solution and by the complete unwillingness to negotiate on any terms except those that amounted to Hanoi's unconditional surrender. The United States was in no position to bargain from strength, they believed, and yet the administration had adopted a totally unyielding position on the question of negotiations. . . .

Paul Kattenburg, whose suggestion of withdrawal back in the late summer of 1963 had been so swiftly quashed, later outlined the numerous disadvantages that such individuals worked from in terms of what he called the "bureaucratic-political warfare within the U.S. government." To begin with, Kattenburg argued, with the exception of Ball they were all middle- or lower-ranking officials, which meant that they lacked pulling power against the president's senior advisers. (Even Ball, Kattenburg might have noted, stood outside the inner circle occupied by only Rusk, McNamara, McGeorge Bundy, and perhaps Taylor.) In addition, these men did not make up a coherent group within the bureaucracy but rather worked individually and apart, and they did not actively try to alter this situation by seeking allies in other agencies like the Defense Department or the CIA. Finally, in Kattenburg's view, they were all "just sufficiently career oriented not to dare pit their personal futures" on the single aim of stopping the momentum toward bombing.

Kattenburg suggested that George Ball was the only one of the group not constrained by career considerations, but in fact the undersecretary was as anxious as anyone to preserve his position in the administration. Maintaining the posture to which he had adhered all year, Ball in November and December always took care not to rock the boat too much and to voice his strongest doubts outside Johnson's presence. This may explain why Ball, who attended the 19 November meeting at the White House, said nothing when McGeorge Bundy spoke of the growing consensus around Option C, and why he raised no objection to Bundy's use of the phrase "devil's advocate exercise" to describe what he was doing. . . .

By Thanksgiving, when Ambassador Taylor returned to Washington to take part in the shaping of the final report to be presented to Johnson on 1 December, a solid consensus had developed among the principals in favor of expanded action and against early negotiations. . . . The ambassador's visit was thus extraordinarily important . . . he more than anyone could have challenged the consensus for escalation. He did not. He was, to be sure, a troubled man as he boarded the plane for Washington, and he carried with him a gloomy report he had written detailing the desperate military situation, the weakness of the GVN ("It is impossible to foresee a stable and effective government under any name in anything like the near future"), and the pronounced and mounting war-weariness and hopelessness that pervaded South Vietnam. At the same time, the report maintained that the United States should persist in its efforts in Vietnam and indeed should expand them, by working to "establish" a stronger Saigon government and by bombing the North. . . .

Johnson's top advisers were in agreement that, if necessary, the new measures should be undertaken regardless of the strength of the regime, but they conceded that a more viable political foundation in South Vietnam had to be in place before too long. They accordingly recommended a two-phase policy, consistent with the general approach outlined in Option C. The first phase involved "armed reconnaissance strikes" against infiltration routes in Laos as well as retaliatory strikes against the North in the event of a Vietcong "spectacular" such as the one at Bienhoa [site of a Vietcong rocket attack against a U.S. air base on November 1, 1964], and the second phase would see "graduated military pressure" against North Vietnam. Phase one would begin as soon as possible. Phase two would come later, after thirty days, provided the Saigon government had bettered its effectiveness "to an acceptable degree." However, unwilling to contemplate the implications if the regime should fail to meet this standard, the advisory team then proceeded to waive this requirement: "If the GVN can only be kept going by stronger action," the final recommendations read, then "the U.S. is prepared . . . to enter into a second phase program." Escalation, in other words, should be undertaken regardless of the political picture in Saigon, either to reward the GVN or to keep it from disintegrating.

Enter Lyndon Johnson. On 19 November, the president had indicated his general agreement with the Working Group's early thinking; now, almost two weeks later, he had the final recommendations in front of him. His decision was never in serious doubt, though he plainly did not relish making it. At a long White House meeting on 1 December, he worried about the absence of governmental stability in Saigon ("Basic to anything is stability," he said) and complained that he did not want to send "Johnson City boys" out to die for a bunch of politicians who could not get their act together. "Why not say, 'This is it?'" and withdraw, he wondered aloud. These comments could be taken as proof that LBJ in this period remained deeply uncertain about which way to proceed in the war, but his subsequent comments in the same meeting suggest that he still shared the same mixture of gloom and determination that he and his top aides had possessed throughout 1964. It would be "easy to get in or out," he lectured the men in the room, "but hard to be patient." The United States had to stick it out." The plans you've got now," he said, referring to the Working Group's recommendations, "[are] all right." Johnson insisted that Taylor "do [his] damnedest in South Vietnam" before the administration moved into the second phase, but he signaled his intention to go ahead regardless. If the Saigon situation failed to improve, he declared, looking at JCS chairman Wheeler, "then I'll be talking to you, General." . . .

It would be hard to overestimate the importance of this presidential decision. Johnson opted to fundamentally alter the American involvement in Vietnam. Like his ambassador in Saigon, he was unhappy about the prospect of moving against the North without a stronger South Vietnamese government, but like him, he was prepared to do so if necessary. The decision contained deep contradictions. Washington policymakers had for a long time conceded among themselves that the keys to victory in the war lay in the South, but now they were seeking a solution through striking the North, despite general skepticism in the intelligence community that such a policy would yield results. They had consistently preached the need for stable, effective government in Saigon prior to any action north of the seventeenth parallel, but now they were opting to try to bring about that stability by bombing the North. They had always declared that Americans should not be sent to fight in the war, and yet such a deployment looked more and more likely—the position paper that emerged out of the 1 December meeting included the cryptic but suggestive line that the escalatory program would include "appropriate U.S. deployments to handle any contingency."

And as always, there was the stark contradiction between the administration's publicly stated willingness to pursue a peaceful solution to the war and its profound private fear of such an outcome. American officials had always proclaimed their commitment to the notion of South Vietnamese self-determination, but the deliberations in November revealed just how empty that claim had become—"The U.S. would oppose any independent South Vietnamese moves to negotiate," said the report that Johnson approved. The establishment of a National Assembly in South Vietnam should be delayed as long as possible, because it might be dominated by pro-peace elements. It is clear that neither LBJ nor his top aides were prepared to accept the idea that to win the people, you had to let them express themselves, which meant risking a government that might negotiate an end to the war. Plainly put, the self-determination Washington claimed to be defending was what it feared most. . . .

Seen in this light, the Americanization of the war becomes difficult to understand. The isolation of the United States on the war among its international allies at the end of 1964; the thin nature of domestic American popular support for the Vietnam commitment; the downright opposition to a larger war among many elite American voices; the spreading war-weariness and anti-Americanism in urban and rural areas of South Vietnam; and the political chaos in Saigon—add all these elements together, along with the fact that senior officials in Washington knew of them and worried about them, and you have a policy decision that is far less easily explained than many would suggest (and this author used to believe). This does not mean it is impossible to explain. . . .

For the key consideration behind the decision for war we must look to [a] . . . rationale articulated by policymakers: *credibility* and the need to preserve it by avoiding defeat in Vietnam. This was the explanation typically advanced by officials when they addressed knowledgeable audiences in off-the-record meetings—one finds scant references to "moral obligations" or "defending world freedom" in the records of their interaction with congressional committees, with foreign government leaders, with journalists in private sessions. In these settings, the emphasis was almost always on abstract (and closely related) notions of prestige, reputation, and credibility and how these were on the line in Vietnam. Even here, however, the picture that emerges is incomplete, inasmuch as the "credibility" referred to was always a purely national concept, having to do with the position of the United States on the world stage. That is, it was *American* credibility that was at stake in Southeast Asia, *American* prestige that needed to be upheld there. Though it can be right and proper to define the credibility imperative in exclusively national terms; it will not suffice as an explanation for policy making in Vietnam. For Vietnam a broader definition is essential, one that also includes domestic political credibility and even personal credibility. For it was not merely the United States that had a stake in the outcome in Vietnam; so did the Democratic Party (or at least so Kennedy and Johnson believed), and so did the individuals who had helped shape the earlier commitment and who were now charged with deciding the next move.

We may go further and argue that, within this three-part conception of the credibility imperative, the national part was the least important. Geostrategic considerations were not the driving force in American Vietnam policy in . . . 1964, either before the election or after; partisan political considerations were; individual careerist considerations were. True, some officials did see Vietnam as a vital theater in the larger Cold War struggle against world communism, did see American credibility as very much on the line—Dean Rusk was one, Walt Rostow another. Most, however, were more dubious. William Bundy and John McNaughton, two of the key players in the policy deliberations in late 1964, not only shared much of George Ball's pessimism about the long-term prospects in the war but on several occasions endorsed his relatively benign view of the likely consequences of defeat in South Vietnam. . . . So why did they favor Americanization? Less out of concern for America's credibility, I believe, than out of fears for their own personal credibility. For more than three years, McNamara and Bundy had counseled the need to stand firm in the war (a relatively easy thing to do in, say, 1962, when the commitment was small and the Cold War situation considerably more tense), and to go against that now would be to expose themselves to potential humiliation and to threaten their careers. . . .

Johnson was always first among equals, as the internal record makes clear. If his top Vietnam aides intimidated him with their accomplishments and academic pedigrees, he also intimidated them with his forceful presence and his frequent resort to bullying tactics, and he established firm control of his administration from the start. Furthermore, no president is a prisoner to his advisers—Eisenhower and Kennedy had rejected policy recommendations on Vietnam, and Johnson might have done the same had he so desired. (He showed a capacity to do so on non-Vietnam issues.) He did not. What, then, drove Johnson's approach to the Vietnam issue? Chiefly its potential to do harm to his domestic political objectives and to his personal historical reputation. Both concerns were there from the start—he determined already in late 1963 that Vietnam would be kept on the back burner in 1964, so as to avoid giving Republicans an issue with which to beat up on Democrats in an election year, and he vowed only hours after the Dallas assassination that he would not be the president who lost Vietnam.

Understanding this duality in Johnson's thinking about the war, in which partisan calculations competed for supremacy with concerns for his personal reputation, is essential to understanding the outcome of the policy process in Washington in the fifteen months that followed his taking office as president. The former explains his determination to keep Vietnam from being lost in an election year, a year in which he also sought to pass major pieces of the Democratic Party's legislative agenda. But it cannot by itself explain his willingness to proceed with a major military intervention—whose importance and viability he himself doubted—after the glorious election results, which brought not only a smashing victory over Barry Goldwater but also huge Democratic majorities in both houses of Congress. . . .

For this reason it would be wrong to overemphasize the importance of the Great Society in the decision to escalate the conflict—that is, to give too much weight to the idea that LBJ took the nation to war because of fears that if he did not, Republicans and conservative Democrats would oppose and possibly scuttle his beloved domestic agenda. Concerns along these lines certainly existed within Johnson, and they directly influenced the *way* in which he expanded the war—in particular, they dictated that the escalation be as quiet as possible so as to avoid the need for choosing between the war and the programs, between guns and butter. But strategizing of this sort cannot be considered the primary *cause* of the decision for escalation. . . .

Lyndon Johnson was a hawk on Vietnam, and he was so for reasons that went beyond immediate domestic political or geostrategic advantage. For it was not merely his country's and his party's reputation that Johnson took to be on the line, but also his own. His tendency to personalize all issues relating to the war, so evident in the later years, in 1966 and 1967 and 1968, was there from the start, from the time he vowed to not be the first American president to lose a war. From the beginning, he viewed attacks on the policy as attacks on himself, saw American credibility and his own credibility as essentially synonymous. In so doing he diminished his capacity to render objective judgment, to retain the necessary level of detachment. . . .

Had Johnson been concerned only with, or even primarily with, preserving *American* credibility and/or *Democratic* credibility, he surely would have ordered extensive contingency planning for some kind of fig leaf for withdrawal in the months leading up to escalation, when the outlook looked grimmer than ever. He would have actively sought, rather than actively avoided, the advice of allied leaders like [British prime minister] Harold Wilson and [Canadian prime minister] Lester Pearson and given much deeper reflection to the urgings of anti-Americanization voices on Capitol Hill and in the press community. His dislike of the war was hardly less intense than theirs, after all, his evaluation of the Saigon government's potential was not significantly more rosy. But the end result of the scenario these critics espoused—American withdrawal without victory—was one Johnson could not contemplate, largely because of the damage such an outcome could do to his own personal reputation.

The concern here went deeper than merely saving his political skin. In private LBJ would sometimes say that he could not withdraw from Vietnam because it would lead to his impeachment, but he was too smart a politician to really believe such a thing. What he really feared was the personal humiliation that he believed would come with failure in Vietnam. He saw the war as a test of his own manliness. Many have commented on the powerful element of *machismo* in Johnson's world view, rooted in his upbringing and fueled by his haunting fear that he would be judged insufficiently manly for the job, that he would lack courage when the chips were down. In his world there were weak and strong men; the weak men were the skeptics, who sat around contemplating, talking, criticizing; the strong men were the doers, the activists, the ones who were always tough and always refused to back down. Thus [Senator Mike] Mansfield could be dismissed as spineless, as "milque-toast"; thus [Senator J. William] Fulbright could be castigated as a "crybaby." Though Johnson on occasion showed himself quite capable of asking probing questions in policy meetings, he had little patience with those who tried to supply probing answers. His macho ethos extended to relations among states. "If you let a bully come into your front yard one day," he liked to say, in reference to the lesson of Munich, "the next day he will be up on your porch and the day after that he will rape your wife in your own bed." In such a situation, retreat was impossible, retreat was cowardly. Johnson's approach did not make him reckless on Vietnam—he was, in fact, exceedingly cautious—but it made him quite unable to contemplate extrication as anything but the equivalent of, as he might put it, "tucking tail and running."

This personal insecurity in Johnson, so much a feature of the recollections of those who knew him and worked with him, might have been less important in Vietnam policy if not for the way it reinforced his equally well documented intolerance of dissent. Even in the early months of his presidency he was incredulous to learn that some Americans might be opposed to his policy of fully supporting South Vietnam; it was un-American, he believed, to make an issue during the Cold War of national security matters. Throughout his career Johnson had made his way in politics by intimidation, by dominating those around him, and he did not change this modus operandi once he got the White House. "I'm the only president you have," he told those who opposed his policies. His demand for consensus and loyalty extended to his inner circle of advisers, a reality that, when combined with his powerful personality, must have had a chilling effect on anyone inclined to try to build support for a contrary view. . . .

In this way, while responsibility for the outcome of the policy process rested with all of those who participated in it, it rested chiefly with the president. Johnson, no one else, ensured that the critical decisions on Vietnam were made by a small and insular group of individuals who by the latter part of 1964 had been involved in policy making for several years in most cases, who had overseen the steady expansion in the U.S. commitment to the war, and who had a large personal stake in seeing that commitment succeed. . . . Johnson was poorly served by his advisory system, but it was a system he in large measure created.

An Unwinnable War

ROBERT K. BRIGHAM

Three alternative military strategies have been put forward since the end of the Vietnam War as missed opportunities for a U.S. military victory. They are: (1) invasion of North Vietnam; (2) incursion into Laos; and (3) concentration of U.S. forces on defense of "enclaves."

When each is reexamined carefully, in light of recently released information from new Chinese and Vietnamese sources, we find that none of them would likely have produced a better outcome for the United States.

An Unwinnable War excerpted from Robert K. Brigham, "Three Alternative U.S. Strategies in Vietnam: A Reexamination Based on New Chinese and Vietnamese Sources," in Robert S. McNamara, *Argument Without End: In Search of Answers to the Vietnam Tragedy* (New York: Public Affairs, 1999), pp. 409–419. Copyright © 1999 by McNamara, Blight, Bingham, Biersteker and Schandler. Reprinted by permission of PublicAffairs, a member of Perseus Books, L.L.C.

An invasion of North Vietnam was enthusiastically advanced by some in the U.S. Army. They believed that the United States should have attacked the North directly, north of the demilitarized zone (DMZ) at the 17th parallel. Military leaders who supported this strategy, however, overlooked the threat of China and, on occasion, even appeared eager for a direct confrontation. Secretary of Defense Robert S. McNamara was convinced, in contrast, that an invasion of the North carried an unacceptable risk of bringing the Chinese into the war. He reasoned that Beijing would act in its own self-interest and would never surrender its buffer area to the West. Gen. Bruce Palmer Jr., Gen. William Westmoreland's deputy in Vietnam, agrees. He argues in his book *The Twenty-Five Year War* that "one cannot quarrel with the decision not to invade North Vietnam because it was too close to China." In addition, as Palmer recognized, a war with China would have had little to do with American objectives in Vietnam and could even have led to millions of unnecessary deaths.

New documentary evidence from Hanoi and Beijing supports the worst U.S. predictions. We now know that North Vietnam asked for and received security commitments from Beijing from 1960 onward. In 1962 a Vietnamese delegation headed by Ho Chi Minh and Gen. Nguyen Chi Thanh visited China, requesting aid for the southern struggles. The Chinese communists pledged an additional 230 battalions to the Vietnamese if needed. The following year, Beijing's military chief of staff, Luo Ruiqing, visited Hanoi. He told Ho that if the Americans were to attack the North, China would come to its defense. In June 1964 the North Vietnamese Army's chief of staff, Van Tien Dung, received Beijing's pledge of "unconditional military support." During the Tonkin Gulf crisis of August 1964, Chinese communists placed their naval units stationed in the area on combat readiness and ordered them to "pay close attention to the movement of American forces" and be prepared to "cope with any possible sudden attack." The Chinese air command went on alert, and the Seventh Army's air force was moved to the Vietnamese border, where it remained for several years. Four other air divisions were also moved closer to the border, and Beijing built two new airstrips in anticipation of an American invasion. American intelligence reports also detected the Chinese movement of nearly forty MiG fighters to the North Vietnamese airfield at Phuc Yen.

In 1965, when the sustained bombing of the North began under Operation "ROLLING THUNDER," the Chinese agreed to step up their commitment to Vietnam as a rear area and deterrent. Beijing pledged repeatedly that it would avoid a direct military conflict with the United States as long as possible, but it would not back away from a confrontation. On March 25, 1965, an editorial in the Party's official newspaper announced that China had offered Hanoi "any necessary material support, including the supply of weapons and all kinds of military materials." It stated further that, if necessary, China was prepared to "send its personnel to fight together with the Vietnamese people to annihilate the American aggressors." Shortly after these statements, China sent the first wave of its combat engineers to Vietnam to aid in the construction of antiaircraft batteries, railroads, airports, bridges, and roads. By 1968, the number of Chinese serving within North Vietnam's borders reached 200,000. . . .

Some analysts have suggested that China may have backed away from its military commitments to Vietnam during the Cultural Revolution. New material from communist archives suggests, however, that China never would have allowed an American invasion of North Vietnam to go unanswered. In fact, as Beijing looked inward during the mid-1960s, its line concerning the United States in Vietnam actually

hardened. Until the end of 1964, China's official policy concerning U.S. planes flying into its airspace was to avoid a direct confrontation. By mid-1965, however, this
policy had been reversed. Accordingly, there were nearly two hundred confrontations
between China and the United States, resulting in the destruction of twelve American
fighters. Even after relations between Vietnam and China had soured, the evidence
indicates that Beijing's own self-interest would have led it to defend its "buffer zone"
in Indochina. . . .

China was motivated to aid Vietnam by its own foreign policy needs. Beijing
hoped to use its support of the war in Vietnam to stimulate mass mobilization within
China for the Cultural Revolution. Chinese leaders claimed that Beijing was the center for continuous revolutions and that the United States threatened that central role.
China repeatedly claimed that it would support Vietnam by any means necessary,
"even at the expense of heavy national sacrifice." Accordingly, when a Vietnamese
delegation visited Beijing in April 1965, China pledged to aid Hanoi economically
and militarily. Aid came in the form of armored vehicles, small arms and ammunition, uniforms, shoes, rice, and even recreation equipment for North Vietnamese
soldiers. Chinese communist sources claim that more than $200 million in material
aid was sent to Hanoi annually beginning in 1965.

At the time, other considerations were also thought to preclude taking the war
to the North. During the early years of the war, the Sullivan Group, a presidential
advisory group, had concluded that attacking the North would do little to reduce its
support for the war in the South. For example, the group predicted:

> It is not likely that North Vietnam would (if it could) call off the war in the South even
> though U.S. actions would in time have serious economic and political impact. Overt ac-
> tion against North Vietnam would be unlikely to produce reduction in Viet Cong activity
> sufficiently to make victory on the ground possible in South Vietnam unless accompanied
> by new U.S. bolstering actions in South Vietnam and considerable improvement in the
> government there.

Indeed, the war had always been fundamentally about the political future of
Vietnam south of the 17th parallel, and a direct attack by U.S. ground forces against
North Vietnam would have had little or no positive effect on meeting this objective.
The United States came to understand too late that the insurgency in the South was
primarily indigenous. During the early days of the insurgency, we now know, it was
the southern cadres who pressed Hanoi to allow them to move toward the armed
struggle. Attacking the North to stop the insurgency was strategically meaningless,
given the U.S. objective of preserving the *South* Vietnamese government in Saigon.
By 1968 it was understood in Washington that the NLF would have continued to
carry the fight to the South Vietnamese Army, and it would have remained in control
in the countryside no matter what happened in North Vietnam.

Many southern cadres felt betrayed because of the 1954 partition of Vietnam,
which left them vulnerable to the brutal efforts of the anticommunist Ngo Dinh Diem
to exterminate them. Thereafter, the southerners tended to stress the need for a decisive battlefield victory prior to engaging in peace talks. Communist documents show
overwhelmingly that southerners were more offensive-minded than many of their
colleagues in Hanoi—in fact that they were prepared to carry on the struggle against
the United States and its Saigon ally no matter what decisions were made by Hanoi.

Writing after the war in a special issue of a military history journal, Le Duc Tho, a longtime member of the Party's political bureau, noted that southerners often engaged in offensive struggles "in spite of orders to the contrary by northern cadres." This is especially true after Gen. Nguyen Chi Thanh became director of the Central Office South Vietnam—the mobile command post in the South—in 1965. Nguyen Chi Thanh was a southerner who had long advocated a more military pursuit of the war effort. During the early 1960s, he argued that victory over the South Vietnamese and their American backers would come only on the battlefield. "If we feared the United States," Nguyen Chi Thanh declared, "we would have called on the people of southern Vietnam to wait and coexist peacefully with the U.S.-Diem clique. We are not afraid of the United States. . . ."

An attack against the North, therefore, was a losing strategy on several counts. It virtually guaranteed a war with China. If China intervened, one could only surmise what the Soviets would do, in an attempt to retain their leadership of the world communist movement. Neither did such a strategy take account of the irrelevance of an invasion of the North regarding saving the South Vietnamese government from collapse. And finally, neither did such a strategy acknowledge the probable consequences—north and south—for U.S. forces. The probable casualties would have dwarfed the actual U.S. casualties from the war, leading in all likelihood to severely hostile reactions in the U.S. Congress and American body politic.

Former U.S. Army Col. Harry Summers has long been one of the most outspoken advocates of the invasion of Laos. Summers argues that a combined military action into Laos could have blocked the Laotian panhandle from being used as a base by North Vietnamese forces. After blocking the flow of men and supplies south, Summers contends, the South Vietnamese forces could have isolated the battlefield from communist incursions originating in Laos and destroyed the NLF.

The U.S. Army actually considered this proposal during the war but ultimately rejected it as unacceptable. When Army Chief of Staff Harold K. Johnson explored the option, he concluded that it would require support services beyond U.S. capabilities. For example, he found that such an operation demanded the astounding total of 18,000 engineer troops to make the operation feasible. Alas, the United States did not have available 18,000 engineer troops for assignment to Vietnam and Laos. Furthermore, U.S. intelligence reports reliably reported that, until mid-1969, the majority of communist forces in the South were actually southerners, who had not need of a sanctuary in Laos in which they might prepare to "invade" South Vietnam. They were already there.

The Trong Son, or Ho Chi Minh Trail, ran through the Laotian panhandle. Advocates of the Laotian invasion strategy believe that by invading Laos the United States could have effectively cut off the trail, stopped supplies heading from North Vietnam to South Vietnam, and thus won the war. But it is clear now, years later, that the southern insurgency could have survived without the Ho Chi Minh Trail. All the conditions that created the insurgency would still have been present.The NLF was never dependent on the North for its sustenance, in any case.

Finally, the force that Summers proposed would probably have met with the same fate as those U.S. forces who operated along the DMZ, nearest to North Vietnam's territory. These troops experienced unusually high casualty rates—mainly from mortars and heavy artillery. The same sort of phenomenon had already occurred in Laos, where U.S. combat losses were higher in a relative sense than those within the territory of Vietnam. Thus, the "barrier across Laos" strategy ignores the reality of jungle war and the extraordinary disadvantages the U.S. would have had in such a war with the NLF and North Vietnamese. . . .

Leading military strategists in Hanoi agree that cutting off the Ho Chi Minh Trail via an invasion of Laos would have accomplished nothing for the United States. Gen. Doan Chuong, director of Hanoi's Institute for Strategic Studies, recently addressed the issue as follows:

> If the supply route had been truly cut off during the war, this would have been a very serious development. That is why the strategic Truong Son Road [Ho Chi Minh Trail] was constructed and involved such elaborate precautions, as you know. We not only had trials on land, we also had a "sea trail." In addition to the East Truong Son Road, there was a West Truong Son Road, with numerous criss-cross pathways, like a labyrinth. So it would have been hard to cut it off completely. As you know the U.S. applied various measures to block it: bombing, defoliating, sending in commandos, setting up a fence called "McNamara's Line," concentrating air strikes on the panhandle area, and so on. Still, the route remained open. . . . We could not, and in fact did not, allow the Trail to be cut off. . . .

William C. Westmoreland, the U.S. field commander from 1964–1968, opposed the Laotian invasion strategy. In his memoirs, General Westmoreland recalls with amazement that many of his critics—within the military and without—"considered it practicable to seal land frontiers against North Vietnamese infiltration. . . . Yet small though South Vietnam is," he pointed out, "its land frontier extended for more than 900 miles." To have defended that entire frontier, according to General Westmoreland, would have required "many millions of troops."

A cardinal error of advocates of the Laos incursion, it would appear, is their use of the U.S. experience in Korea as a model for what they believe should have been done in Vietnam. But the Korean Peninsula presented problems for the infiltration of men and supplies far different from what was faced in Vietnam. Surrounded by water on three sides, the actual Korean *frontier* was quite limited. Not only is the Vietnamese frontier, in this sense, almost 1,000 miles long, or roughly the distance from Boston to Chicago; in addition, the Truong Son Mountains of Indochina, along which supplies moved north to south, are home to the largest triple-canopy jungle in the world outside of the Amazon Basin. Detection and interdiction of the movement of supplies is nearly impossible in such conditions, which can create almost total darkness at noon on a sunny day.

A third alternative U.S. strategy in Vietnam—gathering U.S. forces into enclaves located in or near strategic assets—is in some ways more sophisticated than the invasion strategies directed at North Vietnam and Laos. Those advocating this strategy showed that they understood the nature of the war on the ground in South Vietnam: a fundamentally indigenous insurgency that could be successfully combated, if at all, by the application of counterinsurgency techniques in the South.

At the heart of this notion is the idea that U.S. troops would occupy a supporting role by controlling the densely populated coastal areas. The South Vietnamese forces would thereby be free to move inland from coastal bases, where they would confront the NLF. Proponents of the enclave strategy argued that U.S. troops could join the fight as long as the coastal bases remained protected and secure.

This strategy was based on some realistic assumptions about the war: (1) Basically, the war in the countryside had to be won by the South Vietnamese; and (2) the communists would never be strong enough to drive the U.S. Army into the sea. At worst, its adherents claimed (as some still claim), the enclave strategy would have bought time for South Vietnam to become stabilized, at minimum cost in American lives and material. An added feature, it is claimed, is that the insurgency itself would actually weaken once U.S. troops secured the heavily populated coast.

The enclave strategy, however, like the other alternatives, has not been without its strident critics. They assert that herding U.S. forces into enclaves would have disallowed the Americans from taking maximum advantage of their most potent weapon—superior firepower. Considerable doubt has also been expressed as to the ability of the South Vietnamese Army to carry the battle inland to the NLF. Time and again, the South Vietnamese proved they were no match for the NLF's committed guerrillas.

General Westmoreland was absolutely opposed to the enclave strategy. He believed bringing American combat troops into the major coastal cities of the South, including Saigon, would constitute a huge mistake. He saw the potential for them to get embroiled in the daily street demonstrations and other political conflicts that plagued the South. When Gen. Earle Wheeler, the chairman of the Joint Chiefs of Staff, recommended the enclave strategy to Westmoreland as one that would free the South Vietnamese for offensive operations in the countryside, the field commander pointed out that approximately 40 percent of the South Vietnamese forces were always available for, or committed to, combat operations in any case. . . .

In fact, a variant of the enclave strategy had been tried before, by the French, and it had failed miserably. Col. Quach Hai Luong, deputy director of Hanoi's Institute for Strategic Studies, recently argued that the Americans would have met a similar fate if they had withdrawn to enclaves: "That would conjure up a situation that was similar to what happened during the French war. The French had also concentrated their forces in the big cities. If you do that, then you would be able to control various outlets [i.e., ports] and economic and political headquarters. If you want to occupy a country for a long time, as the French did, then that's what you would do." As Quach Hai Luong went on to point out, however, the Americans had no wish to occupy Vietnam in the traditional sense, as the French did. To him, this meant that the strategy of enclaves would make even less sense for the Americans than it did for the French. At least the French goal—long-term occupation of Vietnam—was consistent with the strategy, even though it failed. But for the Americans, he could see no benefits to it whatsoever.

Many who have compared the American and French military experiences in Vietnam agree. Bernard Fall, a French journalist and scholar with vast experience in Indochina, wrote in 1961 that the enclave strategy invited disaster because it concentrated conventional forces in an area where it could not dispense its weapons, for fear of alienating the local population. Revolutionaries, according to Fall, could isolate enemy forces for attack and simply use the village or rural area as a sanctuary. This was certainly the French experience along the central Vietnamese coast on Highway 1—*La Rue Sans Joie,* or "The Street Without Joy."

After the war, Harry Summers recalled an encounter with a North Vietnamese general in which Summers said that the Americans won every battle in Vietnam.

The general replied, "That may be so, but it is also irrelevant." *Why* it was irrelevant is something that has been insufficiently grasped by advocates of one or more
of the alternative strategies just reexamined. In short, the U.S. forces arrived in
Vietnam prepared to turn back an invasion of South Vietnam by North Vietnam. If
that had been the nature of the problem, the United States might have been successful. But what they encountered, and what some analysts still find it impossible
to accept, is a war in the South that was fundamentally a war among southerners.
Each side had a more powerful patron—the NLF was allied to Hanoi and the South
Vietnamese government to the United States. And in this kind of war, the United
States, along with its uninspired and hapless South Vietnamese allies, did not
"know the territory."

Any strategy, including those just reexamined, would have required for its success a viable South Vietnamese government with credibility in the eyes of the South
Vietnamese people. No government in Saigon after November 1963, when Diem was
assassinated, was credible in this sense. From 1965, therefore, when U.S. combat
troops first arrived, the situation in Saigon was politically untenable. In the end, no
American strategy could have reversed the outcome in Vietnam, because the NLF
and its North Vietnamese allies had committed to total war. Each was prepared to
sustain casualties, far beyond American estimates, without giving up the fight. Any
war would have been a war of attrition on the ground. And it is obvious, looking
back, which side was willing, as John Kennedy said during his inaugural address, to
"pay any price, bear any burden."

FURTHER READING

David L. Anderson, ed., *The Human Tradition in the Vietnam Era* (2000)
———, *Shadow on the White House* (1993)
———, *Trapped by Success: The Eisenhower Administration and Vietnam, 1953–1961*
    (1991)
Christian G. Appy, *Patriots: The Vietnam War Remembered from All Sides* (2003)
David M. Barrett, *Uncertain Warriors* (1993)
Eric M. Bergerud, *Red Thunder, Tropic Lightning* (1993)
Larry Berman, *Lyndon Johnson's War* (1989)
Irving Bernstein, *Guns or Butter: The Presidency of Lyndon Johnson* (1996)
Michael R. Beschloss, *Taking Charge* (1997) (on the LBJ White House)
Melanie Billings-Yun, *Decision Against War: Eisenhower and Dien Bien Phu, 1954* (1988)
Anne Blair, *Lodge in Vietnam* (1995)
Mark Philip Bradley, *Imagining Vietnam* (2000)
Peter Braestrup, *Big Story* (1977)
Robert Brigham, *The NLF's Foreign Relations and the Vietnam War* (1999)
Peter Busch, *All the Way with JFK?* (2003)
Robert Buzzanco, *Masters of War* (1996)
Timothy Castle, *At War in the Shadow of Vietnam* (1993) (on Laos)
James W. Clinton, *The Loyal Opposition* (1995)
Robert Dallek, *Flawed Giant* (1998) (on LBJ)
Charles DeBenedetti with Charles Chatfield, *An American Ordeal: The Antiwar Movement
    of the Vietnam Era* (1990)
William J. Duiker, *Sacred War* (1995)
———, *Ho Chi Minh* (2000)

Ronald B. Frankum, Jr., *Like Rolling Thunder* (2005) (on air war)
Marc Frey et al., *The Transformation of Southeast Asia* (2003) (on decolonization)
Ilya V. Gaiduk, *The Soviet Union and the Vietnam War* (1996)
Lloyd C. Gardner, *Approaching Vietnam* (1988)
———, *Pay Any Price* (1995) (on LBJ)
Leslie H. Gelb and Richard K. Betts, *The Irony of Vietnam* (1979)
Marc Jason Gilbert, ed., *Why the North Won the Vietnam War* (2002)
David Halberstam, *The Best and the Brightest* (1972)
Daniel C. Hallin, *The "Uncensored War"* (1986)
Ellen J. Hammer, *A Death in November: America in Vietnam, 1963* (1988)
Kenneth Heineman, *Campus Wars* (1993)
George C. Herring, *America's Longest War* (1996)
Michael H. Hunt, *Lyndon Johnson's War* (1996)
Richard H. Immerman, "The United States and the Geneva Conference of 1954: A New Look," *Diplomatic History* 14 (1990): 43–66
"International Dimensions of the Vietnam War," *Diplomatic History* 27 (2003): 35–149
Susan Jeffords, *The Remasculinization of America: Gender and the Vietnam War* (1989)
Howard Jones, *Death of a Generation* (2002) (on the JFK and Diem assassinations)
Matthew Jones, *Conflict and Confrontation in Southeast Asia* (2001)
George McT. Kahin, *Intervention* (1986)
David Kaiser, *American Tragedy* (2000)
Lawrence S. Kaplan, Denise Artaud, and Mark R. Rubin, eds., *Dienbienphu and the Crisis in Franco-American Relations, 1954–1955* (1990)
Stanley Karnow, *Vietnam* (1983)
Jeffrey Kimball, *The Vietnam War Files* (2004) (on the Nixon administration)
Douglas Kinnard, *The Certain Trumpet: Maxwell Taylor and the American Experience in Vietnam* (1991)
Katherine Kinney, *Friendly Fire* (2000)
Gabriel Kolko, *Anatomy of a War* (1985)
Walter LaFeber, *The Deadly Bet* (2005) (on the 1968 election)
Mark Lawrence, *Constructing Vietnam* (2004) (on decolonization)
Guenter Lewy, *America in Vietnam* (1978)
Michael Lind, *Vietnam: The Necessary War* (2000)
Robert Mann, *A Grand Delusion* (2001)
David Maraniss, *They Marched into Sunlight* (2003)
Robert J. McMahon, "Contested Memory: The Vietnam War and American Society, 1975–2001," *Diplomatic History* 26 (2002): 159–184
H. R. McMaster, *Dereliction of Duty* (1997)
Edwin F. Moise, *Tonkin Gulf and the Escalation of the Vietnam War* (1996)
Richard R. Moser, *The New Winter Soldiers* (1996)
Charles E. Neu, ed., *After Vietnam* (2000)
Don Oberdofer, *Tet* (2001)
Gregory A. Olson, *Mansfield and Vietnam* (1995)
James S. Olson and Randy Roberts, *Where the Domino Fell* (1996)
Bruce Palmer, Jr., *The 25-Year War* (1984)
Douglas Pike, *PAVN: People's Army of Vietnam* (1986)
———, *Vietnam and the Soviet Union* (1987)
Norman Podhoretz, *Why We Were in Vietnam* (1982)
John Prados, *The Blood Road: The Ho Chi Minh Trail and the Vietnam War* (1998)
———, *Operation Vulture* (2002) (on Eisenhower)
William Prochnau, *Once Upon a Distant Star* (1995)
Andrew J. Rotter, *The Path to Vietnam* (1987)
Howard B. Schaffer, *Ellsworth Bunker* (2003)
Robert D. Schulzinger, *A Time for War* (1997)
William Shawcross, *Sideshow: Kissinger, Nixon, and the Destruction of Cambodia* (1979)
Neil Sheehan, *A Bright Shining Lie* (1988)

Melvin Small, *Antiwarriors: The Vietnam War and the Battle for America's Hearts and Minds* (2002)
Ronald H. Spector, *The United States Army in Vietnam* (1983)
———, *After Tet* (1992)
Harry G. Summers, *On Strategy* (1981)
Sandra Taylor, *Vietnamese Women at War* (1999)
Robert R. Tomes, *Apocalypse Then: American Intellectuals and the Vietnam War* (1998)
Kathleen J. Turner, *Lyndon Johnson's Dual War* (1985) (on the press)
James Westheider, *Fighting on Two Fronts: African Americans and the Vietnam War* (1997)
James H. Willbanks, *Abandoning Vietnam* (2004)
Francis X. Winters, *The Year of the Hare* (1997)
Randall Woods, *Fulbright* (1995)
———, ed., *Vietnam and the American Political Tradition* (2003)
Marilyn B. Young, *The Vietnam Wars* (1991)
Qiang Zhai, *China and the Vietnam Wars* (2000)

CHAPTER
14

The Cold War Ends and the Post–Cold War Era Begins

Even before the Vietnam War ended, the Soviet-American Cold War had eased. The reconstruction of post–World War II Western Europe and Japan, along with decolonization in the Third World, contributed to a diffusion of global political and economic power. At the same time, the rising cost of the Cold War arms race spurred both superpowers during the latter 1960s and 1970s to pursue a policy of détente. Enunciated by President Richard M. Nixon (1969–1973) and his foreign policy adviser Henry Kissinger, détente did not signal an end to the Cold War, but it did entail new, less aggressive tactics for pursuing national interests, including Soviet-American arms control treaties, the diplomatic recognition of the People's Republic of China, and increased trade and cultural exchanges with Moscow and Beijing. Skeptics derided the Nixon administration—and its successor, the Gerald Ford administration (1974–1977)—for their blind spot on international human rights and the continued arms buildup allowed by agreements arising from the Strategic Arms Limitation Talks (SALT). President Jimmy Carter worked to advance SALT, but by the close of his administration (1977–1981) arms negotiations had stalled, the Soviets had invaded Afghanistan, and Carter had set into motion plans to modernize and expand the nation's nuclear arsenal. Iran's Islamic revolution, rising oil prices and economic recession, and the taking of U.S. embassy personnel hostage in Tehran added to Carter's woes. Some scholars wrote of America's decline in the world system.

Republican candidate Ronald Reagan charged during the 1980 presidential election that Carter had let American power slip. Following his electoral victory, Reagan spurned arms control talks, increased military budgets, and supported anti-communist movements around the world. Reagan sent U.S. troops to Lebanon and Granada, ordered bombing raids against terrorist-supporting Libya, financed the contra war against the communist-led government in Nicaragua, armed the rebel Muslim mujahadeen in Afghanistan, and announced the Strategic Defensive Initiative (SDI, a space-based anti-missile defense system). Critics at home and abroad decried what they viewed as wasteful spending and dangerous militarism. Under pressure, Reagan proposed a new approach: arms reduction instead of arms control. Doubters viewed the president's stance as a delaying tactic.

453

Then, a new, younger, reform-minded generation of Soviet officials came to power in Moscow in 1985, led by General Secretary of the Communist Party Mikhail Gorbachev. Gorbachev worked to restructure the moribund Soviet economy (perestroika), liberalize politics (glasnost), reduce military forces, and loosen controls over the Eastern European satellite states. Soon Gorbachev and Reagan were arranging summit meetings, discussing substantial cuts in nuclear weapons, and in 1987 signing the Intermediate-Range Nuclear Forces Treaty to disband all American and Soviet intermediate-range missiles. Although the treaty covered only 4 percent of superpower arsenals, it ranked as the world's first nuclear arms reduction accord.

Long-simmering protest in communist-ruled Eastern Europe and East Germany exploded in this new atmosphere of reform, and Gorbachev refrained from suppressing dissent. Thus, communist regimes collapsed one after another in 1989—Poland, Hungary, East Germany, Czechoslovakia, and Romania. In November, one of the infamous pillars of the Cold War, the Berlin Wall, came down. And by the end of the year, Gorbachev had pulled Soviet troops out of Afghanistan. In his State of the Union address in 1990, the new American president, George Bush, proclaimed communism to be a remnant of the past. By summer 1991, the Soviet Communist party disbanded, and the Union of Soviet Socialist Republics dissolved.

In the decade that followed U.S. power was unmatched. When the forces of Iraqi dictator Saddam Hussein invaded neighboring, oil-rich Kuwait in August 1990, Bush assembled a multinational military coalition that in early 1991 ousted Hussein's troops. Bush boasted that the United States stood poised to lead a "new world order" based on self-determination and collective security. But over the next decade, a proliferation of challenges tested U.S. power. Ethnic and religious wars in the former Yugoslavia, tribal genocide in African Rwanda, and drug trafficking in Latin America defied easy solutions. Acid rain, global warming, and deforestation endangered the world's environment. Terrorism and the spread of weapons of mass destruction loomed as international menaces. Throughout the presidencies of Republican George Bush (1989–1993), Democrat Bill Clinton (1993–2001), and Republican George W. Bush (2001–), U.S. officials struggled to define America's role in the post–Cold War era. Sometimes the United States deployed its military power unilaterally to bring American values and order to the rest of the world; at other times it worked with other states and multilateral institutions to promote global security. Either way, U.S. military interventions—Panama (1991), Somalia (1992–1993), Haiti (1993), and the former Yugoslavia (1995 and 1999)—multiplied.

The end of the Cold War also sparked a renewed American dedication to the expansion of capitalism. President Clinton emphasized trade arrangements such as the North American Free Trade Agreement or NAFTA (1993) and the World Trade Organization or WTO (1994). The U.S. economy grew throughout the 1990s, but recessions in Japan and East Asia, Russia's postcommunist financial morass, new competition from the recently formed European Union, and instability in the oil-producing Middle East generated fears that the United States might falter in the global marketplace. George W. Bush succeeded Clinton in 2001 touting free enterprise and quickly won Congressional approval for large tax cuts to stimulate investment. U.S. corporations, however, continued to "outsource" jobs, the federal budget deficit soared, and the nation's economic health remained uncertain.

Although few predicted the startling reversals that produced the post–Cold War era, scholars have offered competing explanations for the end of the Cold War. One school of thought claims that President Reagan's tough anticommunism, especially his military expansion and strategy of negotiating through strength, broke the *bank and the spirit of the Soviet system. According to the "Reagan victory" thesis, America emerged from fifty years of anticommunist containment as the undisputable winner of the Cold War. Others look inside the Soviet system for an explanation, and stress communism's economic and political failures as the key factor in ending the Cold War. According to this perspective, it was Mikhail Gorbachev who took the initiative in dramatically changing Soviet-American relations as he sought internal reforms with reduced arms expenditures in order to revive a decaying command economy. Still others have emphasized the importance of external, or international, developments: the relative decline of both the Soviet Union and the United States in the international system; the weakening of superpower alliances; and global economic competition. Rather than a sudden, cataclysmic event, the ending of the Cold War evolved out of a long-term, systemic process that produced no clear winners.*

Nor is there agreement on the state of the world following the Cold War's demise. Many commentators have proclaimed a new unipolar era in which a triumphant United States wields overwhelming military, economic, and cultural strength. Thus, Washington has an opportunity to impose unilaterally its preference for free market economies and to dictate political solutions to troubled states and regions. Others see a more murky global reality where America's power remains limited and challenged on many fronts. According to this view, the dispersal of international economic power and global cultural differences have forced Washington to seek allies and multilateral arrangements to safeguard its interests and promote international peace and prosperity.

Why and how did the Cold War end? Why was the post–Cold War world so unstable? The debate over these questions will undoubtedly shape American foreign relations in the twenty-first century.

D O C U M E N T S

President Richard M. Nixon and his chief foreign policy adviser Henry A. Kissinger, both self-proclaimed realists, assumed power in 1969 determined to reconfigure America's foreign policy by reducing tensions with the Soviet Union and China and redeploying U.S. power to protect the nation's vital interests. In Document 1, taken from testimony before the Senate Foreign Relations Committee, September 19, 1974, Secretary of State Kissinger, defined détente and reviewed its accomplishments. Détente endured through the 1970s, but ongoing U.S.-Soviet competition in the Third World, bitter exchanges over Moscow's human rights record, and growing opposition from hardline anticommunists in the United States undermined détente during the presidencies of Gerald Ford and Jimmy Carter. When Soviet troops invaded Afghanistan to bolster a Marxist client government in December 1979, President Carter, already beleaguered by a declining economy and Iran's anti-American, Islamic revolution, vowed strong action to safeguard U.S. interests in Southwest Asia. In an address to the nation on January 4, 1980 (Document 2) he condemned Soviet aggression and announced that United States would shelve the second Strategic Arms Limitations Treaty (SALT II) and embargo U.S. grain shipments to the Soviet Union. He also threatened a boycott of the summer Olympic games in Moscow—a threat he later carried out. Détente seemed a relic of the past.

The election of Republican Ronald Reagan to the presidency in November 1980 marked a historic shift to the right in American politics and a further intensification of Soviet-American rivalry. In Document 3, comprising press conference comments from January 19, 1981, the newly inaugurated, president denounces the Soviet Union, setting the Cold War confrontational style of his early administration. Following the rise of Mikhail Gorbachev to power in Moscow in 1985, however, the two superpowers took the first tentative steps toward ending the Cold War. Reagan and Gorbachev met at Geneva in 1985, and again at Reykjavík, Iceland, in October 1986. At Rekjavík, they came close to a major agreement on terminating nuclear weapons, but Gorbachev refused to accept Reagan's plans to develop a new antinuclear defensive system called the Strategic Defense Initiative, or SDI. Their opposing positions are presented in Documents 4 and 5, both televised addresses—Reagan's on October 13 and Gorbachev's on October 22. The momentum for diplomacy intensified throughout the second half of the 1980s. Document 6, a concluding part of Yale University historian Paul Kennedy's best-selling *The Rise and Fall of the Great Powers* (1987), discusses the relationship between military spending and the relative economic decline of the United States, and suggests that "imperial overstretch" had eroded national security. Some observers noted that both superpowers had been driven to the negotiating table by economic necessity. Document 7, from interviews conducted over 1987–1989 with Georgi Arbatov, the Soviet Union's preeminent scholar of America and a reformer who emerged with Gorbachev, provides a glimpse into the "new thinking" in Moscow.

President George Bush officially ushered in the post–Cold War era in September 1990, roughly one year after the collapse of the Berlin Wall. In Document 8, the president's State of the Union address, Bush applauded the rebirth of freedom in formerly Soviet-dominated Eastern Europe, rallied Americans to support the ideal of liberty worldwide, and credited Harry Truman's policy of anticommunist containment for patiently outlasting Soviet communism. The administration of President William J. Clinton also trumpeted America's post–Cold War mission to advance American values abroad. Document 9 consists of remarks given by Clinton at a breakfast meeting on October 6, 1995, a day after signing a cease-fire agreement for war-torn and ethnically divided Bosnia. In his comments, the president highlighted America's role as peacemaker and world leader, and he warned against the danger of isolationism. Document 10 is a letter from President George W. Bush to Senate Republican leaders, dated March 13, 2001, in which the new president explains his opposition to the international Kyoto Protocol on carbon dioxide emissions. It demonstrates the importance of environmental issues in world affairs, the new administration's emphasis on global free enterprise, and President Bush's skepticism about multilateral initiatives, especially when they impinge on U.S. interests.

1. Secretary of State Henry A. Kissinger Defines Détente, 1974

[W]e must be clear at the outset on what the term "détente" entails. It is the search for a more constructive relationship with the Soviet Union. It is a continuing process, not a final condition. And it has been pursued by successive American leaders though the means have varied as have world conditions.

Some fundamental principles guide this policy:

The United States does not base its policy solely on Moscow's good intentions. We seek, regardless of Soviet intentions, to serve peace through a systematic resistance to pressure and conciliatory responses to moderate behavior.

This document can be found in U.S. Senate, Committee on Foreign Relations, *Détente* (Washington, D.C.: U.S. Government Printing Office, 1975), 247–248, 251–254, 256.

We must oppose aggressive actions, but we must not seek confrontations lightly.

We must maintain a strong national defense while recognizing that in the nuclear age the relationship between military strength and politically usable power is the most complex in all history.

Where the age-old antagonism between freedom and tyranny is concerned, we are not neutral. But other imperatives impose limits on our ability to produce internal changes in foreign countries. Consciousness of our limits is a recognition of the necessity of peace—not moral callousness. The preservation of human life and human society are moral values, too.

We must be mature enough to recognize that to be stable a relationship must provide advantages to both sides and that the most constructive international relationships are those in which both parties perceive an element of gain. . . .

To set forth principles of behavior in formal documents is hardly to guarantee their observance. But they are reference points against which to judge actions and set goals.

The first of the series of documents is the Statement of Principles signed in Moscow in 1972. It affirms: (1) the necessity of avoiding confrontation; (2) the imperative of mutual restraint; (3) the rejection of attempts to exploit tensions to gain unilateral advantages; (4) the renunciation of claims of special influence in the world; and (5) the willingness, on this new basis, to coexist peacefully and build a firm long-term relationship.

An Agreement on the Prevention of Nuclear War based on these Principles was signed in 1973. But it emphasizes that this objective presupposes the renunciation of any war or threat of war not only by the two nuclear superpowers against each other, but also against allies or third countries. In other words, the principle of restraint is not confined to relations between the United States and the U.S.S.R. It is explicitly extended to include all countries. . . .

One of the features of the current phase of United States–Soviet relations is the unprecedented consultation between leaders either face to face or through diplomatic channels. . . .

It was difficult in the past to speak of a United States–Soviet bilateral relationship in any normal sense of the phrase. Trade was negligible. Contacts between various institutions and between the peoples of the two countries were at best sporadic. Today, by joining our efforts even in such seemingly apolitical fields as medical research or environmental protection, we and the Soviets can benefit not only our two peoples, but all mankind. . . .

We have approached the question of economic relations with deliberation and circumspection and as an act of policy not primarily of commercial opportunity. As political relations have improved on a broad basis, economic issues have been dealt with on a comparably broad front. A series of interlocking economic agreements with the U.S.S.R. has been negotiated, side by side with the political progress already noted. The 25-year-old lend-lease debt was settled; the reciprocal extension of the most-favored-nation treatment was negotiated, together with safeguards against the possible disruption of our markets and a series of practical arrangements to facilitate the conduct of business; our Government credit facilities were made available for trade with the U.S.S.R.; and a maritime agreement regulating the carriage of goods has been signed. . . .

Over time, trade and investment may leaven the autarkic tendencies of the Soviet system, invite gradual association of the Soviet economy with the world economy, and foster a degree of interdependence that adds an element of stability to the political relationship.

We cannot expect to relax international tensions or achieve a more stable international system should the two strongest nuclear powers conduct an unrestrained strategic arms race. Thus, perhaps the single most important component of our policy toward the Soviet Union is the effort to limit strategic weapons competition.

The competition in which we now find ourselves is historically unique:

Each side has the capacity to destroy civilization as we know it.

Failure to maintain equivalence could jeopardize not only our freedom but our very survival. . . .

The prospect of a decisive military advantage, even if theoretically possible, is politically intolerable; neither side will passively permit a massive shift in the nuclear balance. Therefore, the probable outcome of each succeeding round of competition is the restoration of a strategic equilibrium, but at increasingly higher and more complex levels of forces.

The arms race is driven by political as well as military factors. While a decisive advantage is hard to calculate, the appearance of inferiority—whatever its actual significance—can have serious political consequences. Thus, each side has a high incentive to achieve not only the reality but the appearance of equality. In a very real sense each side shapes the military establishment of the other. . . .

Détente is admittedly far from a modern equivalent to the kind of stable peace that characterized most of the 19th century. But it is a long step away from the bitter and aggressive spirit that has characterized so much of the post-war period. When linked to such broad and unprecedented projects as SALT, détente takes on added meaning and opens prospects of a more stable peace. SALT agreements should be seen as steps in a process leading to progressively greater stability. It is in that light that SALT and related projects will be judged by history.

2. President Jimmy Carter Condemns the Soviet Invasion of Afghanistan, 1980

I come to you this evening to discuss the extremely important and rapidly changing circumstances in Southwest Asia.

I continue to share with all of you the sense of outrage and impatience because of the kidnapping of innocent American hostages and the holding of them by militant terrorists with the support and the approval of Iranian officials. Our purposes continue to be the protection of the long-range interests of our Nation and the safety of the American hostages. . . .

Recently, there has been another very serious development which threatens the maintenance of the peace in Southwest Asia. Massive Soviet military forces have invaded the small, nonaligned, sovereign nation of Afghanistan, which had hitherto not been an occupied satellite of the Soviet Union.

This document can be found in *Public Papers of the Presidents, Jimmy Carter, 1980* (Washington, D.C.: U.S. Government Printing Office, 1981), 21–24.

Fifty thousand heavily armed Soviet troops have crossed the border and are now dispersed throughout Afghanistan, attempting to conquer the fiercely independent Muslim people of that country.

The Soviets claim, falsely, that they were invited into Afghanistan to help protect that country from some unnamed outside threat. But the President, who had been the leader of Afghanistan before the Soviet invasion, was assassinated—along with several members of his family—after the Soviets gained control of the capital city of Kabul. Only several days later was the new puppet leader even brought into Afghanistan by the Soviets.

This invasion is an extremely serious threat to peace because of the threat of further Soviet expansion into neighboring countries in Southwest Asia and also because such an aggressive military policy is unsettling to other peoples throughout the world.

This is a callous violation of international law and the United Nations Charter. It is a deliberate effort of a powerful atheistic government to subjugate an independent Islamic people.

We must recognize the strategic importance of Afghanistan to stability and peace. A Soviet-occupied Afghanistan threatens both Iran and Pakistan and is a steppingstone to possible control over much of the world's oil supplies. . . .

The successful negotiation of the SALT II treaty has been a major goal and a major achievement of this administration, and we Americans, the people of the Soviet Union, and indeed the entire world will benefit from the successful control of strategic nuclear weapons through the implementation of this carefully negotiated treaty.

However, because of the Soviet aggression, I have asked the United States Senate to defer further consideration of the SALT II treaty so that the Congress and I can assess Soviet actions and intentions and devote our primary attention to the legislative and other measures required to respond to this crisis. As circumstances change in the future, we will, of course, keep the ratification of SALT II under active review in consultation with the leaders of the Senate.

The Soviets must understand our deep concern. We will delay opening of any new American or Soviet consular facilities, and most of the cultural and economic exchanges currently under consideration will be deferred. Trade with the Soviet Union will be severely restricted. . . .

The 17 million tons of grain ordered by the Soviet Union in excess of that amount which we are committed to sell will not be delivered. This grain was not intended for human consumption but was to be used for building up Soviet livestock herds. . . .

Although the United States would prefer not to withdraw from the Olympic games scheduled in Moscow this summer, the Soviet Union must realize that its continued aggressive actions will endanger both the participation of athletes and the travel to Moscow by spectators who would normally wish to attend the Olympic games. . . .

History teaches, perhaps, very few clear lessons. But surely one such lesson learned by the world at great cost is that aggression, unopposed, becomes a contagious disease.

The response of the international community to the Soviet attempt to crush Afghanistan must match the gravity of the Soviet action.

With the support of the American people and working with other nations, we will deter aggression, we will protect our Nation's security, and we will preserve the peace. The United States will meet its responsibilities.

3. President Ronald Reagan Denounces the Soviet Union, 1981

So far détente's been a one-way street that the Soviet Union has used to pursue its own aims. I don't have to think of an answer as to what I think their intentions are; they have repeated it. I know of no leader of the Soviet Union since the revolution, and including the present leadership, that has not more than once repeated in the various Communist congresses they hold their determination that their goal must be the promotion of world revolution and a one-world Socialist or Communist state, whichever word you want to use.

Now, as long as they do that and as long as they, at the same time, have openly and publicly declared that the only morality they recognize is what will further their cause, meaning they reserve unto themselves the right to commit any crime, to lie, to cheat, in order to attain that, and that is moral, not immoral, and we operate on a different set of standards, I think when you do business with them, even at a détente, you keep that in mind.

4. Reagan Defends SDI After the Reykjavík Summit Meeting, 1986

We proposed the most sweeping and generous arms control proposal in history. We offered the complete elimination of all ballistic missiles—Soviet and American—from the face of the Earth by 1996. While we parted company with this American offer still on the table, we are closer than ever before to agreements that could lead to a safer world without nuclear weapons. . . .

Some years ago, the United States and the Soviet Union agreed to limit any defense against nuclear missile attacks to the emplacement in one location in each country of a small number of missiles capable of intercepting and shooting down incoming nuclear missiles [the Anti-ballistic Missile Treaty (ABM)] . . . a policy called mutual assured destruction, meaning if one side launched a nuclear attack, the other side could retaliate. And this mutual threat of destruction was believed to be a deterrent against either side striking first. So here we sit, with thousands of nuclear warheads targeted on each other and capable of wiping out both our countries. The Soviets deployed the few antiballistic missiles around Moscow as the treaty permitted. Our country didn't bother deploying because the threat of nationwide annihilation made such a limited defense seem useless.

For some years now we've been aware that the Soviets may be developing a nationwide defense. They have installed a large, modern radar at Krasnoyarsk, which

Document 3 can be found in *Public Papers of the Presidents, Ronald Reagan, 1981* (Washington, D.C.: U.S. Government Printing Office, 1982), 57.

Document 4 can be found in *Public Papers of the Presidents, Ronald Reagan, 1986* (Washington, D.C.: U.S. Government Printing Office, 1989), Book II, 1367–1370.

we believe is a critical part of a radar system designed to provide radar guidance for antiballistic missiles protecting the entire nation. Now, this is a violation of the ABM treaty. Believing that a policy of mutual destruction and slaughter of their citizens and ours was uncivilized, I asked our military, a few years ago, to study and see if there was a practical way to destroy nuclear missiles after their launch but before they can reach their targets, rather than just destroy people. Well, this is the goal for what we call SDI, and our scientists researching such a system are convinced it is practical and that several years down the road we can have such a system ready to deploy. Now incidentally, we are not violating the ABM treaty, which permits such research. If and when we deploy, the treaty also allows withdrawal from the treaty upon 6 months' notice. SDI, let me make it clear, is a nonnuclear defense. . . .

I offered a proposal that we continue our present [SDI] research. And if and when we reached the stage of testing, we would sign, now, a treaty that would permit Soviet observation of such tests. And if the program was practical, we would both eliminate our offensive missiles, and then we would share the benefits of advanced defenses. I explained that even though we would have done away with our offensive ballistic missiles, having the defense would protect against cheating or the possibility of a madman, sometime, deciding to create nuclear missiles. After all, the world now knows how to make them. I likened it to our keeping our gas masks, even though the nations of the world had outlawed poison gas after World War I. We seemed to be making progress on reducing weaponry, although the General Secretary [Gorbachev] was registering opposition to SDI and proposing a pledge to observe ABM for a number of years. . . .

The Soviets had asked for a 10-year delay in the deployment of SDI programs. In an effort to see how we could satisfy their concerns—while protecting our principles and security—we proposed a 10-year period in which we began with the reduction of all strategic nuclear arms, bombers, air-launched cruise missiles, intercontinental ballistic missiles, submarine-launched ballistic missiles and the weapons they carry. They would be reduced 50 percent in the first 5 years. During the next 5 years, we would continue by eliminating all remaining offensive ballistic missiles, of all ranges. And during that time, we would proceed with research, development, and testing of SDI—all done in conformity with ABM provisions. At the 10-year point, with all ballistic missiles eliminated, we could proceed to deploy advanced defenses, at the same time permitting the Soviets to do likewise.

And here the debate began. The General Secretary wanted wording that, in effect, would have kept us from developing the SDI for the entire 10 years. In effect, he was killing SDI. And unless I agreed, all that work toward eliminating nuclear weapons would go down the drain—canceled. I told him I had pledged to the American people that I would not trade away SDI, there was no way I could tell our people their government would not protect them against nuclear destruction. . . .

I realize some Americans may be asking tonight: Why not accept Mr. Gorbachev's demand? Why not give up SDI for this agreement? Well, the answer, my friends, is simple. SDI is America's insurance policy that the Soviet Union would keep the commitments made at Reykjavík. SDI is America's security guarantee if the Soviets should—as they have done too often in the past—fail to comply with their solemn commitments. SDI is what brought the Soviets back to arms control talks at Geneva and Iceland. SDI is the key to a world without nuclear weapons. The Soviets understand this. They have devoted far more resources, for a lot longer time than we, to their own SDI. The world's only operational missile defense today surrounds Moscow, the capital of the Soviet Union.

What Mr. Gorbachev was demanding at Reykjavík was that the United States agree to a new version of a 14-year-old ABM treaty that the Soviet Union has already violated. I told him we don't make those kinds of deals in the United States. And the American people should reflect on these critical questions: How does a defense of the United States threaten the Soviet Union or anyone else? Why are the Soviets so adamant that America remain forever vulnerable to Soviet rocket attack? As of today, all free nations are utterly defenseless against Soviet missiles—fired either by accident or design. Why does the Soviet Union insist that we remain so—forever?

5. Soviet General Secretary Mikhail Gorbachev Criticizes SDI After the Reykjavík Summit Meeting, 1986

Reykjavík generated not hopes alone. Reykjavík also highlighted the hardships on the road to a nuclear-free world. . . .

Quarters linked with militarism and arms race profits are clearly scared. They are doing their utmost to cope with the new situation and, coordinating their actions, are trying in every way to mislead the people, to control the sentiment of broad sections of the world public, to suppress their quest for peace, to hinder governments from taking a clear-cut position at this decisive moment in history. . . .

Far-reaching and interconnected, they [the Soviet proposals presented at the Reykjavík meeting] constitute an integrated package and are based on the program we announced on 15 January for the elimination of nuclear weapons by the year 2000.

The first proposal is to cut by half all strategic arms, without exception.

The second proposal is to fully eliminate Soviet and US medium-range missiles in Europe and immediately set about talks on missiles of this type in Asia, as well as on missiles with a range of less than a thousand kilometres. We suggested freezing the number of such missiles immediately.

The third proposal is to consolidate the ABM Treaty and to start full-scale talks on a total ban on nuclear tests. . . .

The US Administration is now trying in every possible way to convince people that a possible major success with concrete agreements was not achieved owing to Soviet unyieldingness over the program of the so-called Strategic Defence Initiative (SDI).

It is even being asserted that we allegedly lured the President into a trap by putting forward "breathtaking" proposals on cutting down strategic offensive arms and medium-range missiles, and that later on we ostensibly demanded in an ultimatum form that SDI be renounced.

But the essence of our stand and of our proposals is as follows: we are for reduction and then complete elimination of nuclear weapons and are firmly against a new stage in the arms race and against its transfer to outer space.

This document can be found in M. S. Gorbachev, *Speeches and Writings* (Oxford: Pergamon Press, 1986), II, 64–70.

Hence we are against SDI and are for consolidation of the ABM Treaty.

It is clear to every sober-minded person that if we embark upon the road of deep cuts and then complete elimination of nuclear weapons, it is essential to rule out any opportunity for either the Soviet or US side to gain unilateral military superiority.

We perceive the main danger of SDI precisely in a transfer of the arms race to a new sphere, and in endeavours to go out into space with offensive arms and thereby achieve military superiority.

SDI has become an obstacle to ending the arms race, to getting rid of nuclear weapons, and is the main obstacle to a nuclear-free world. . . .

In upholding the position that thwarted the reaching of agreement in Reykjavík, the President asks rhetorical questions: Why do the Russians so stubbornly demand that America forever remain vulnerable to a Soviet missile strike? Why does the Soviet Union insist that we remain defenceless forever?

I am surprised at such questions, I must say. They have the air of indicating that the American President has an opportunity to make his country invulnerable, to give it secure protection against a nuclear strike.

As long as nuclear weapons exist and the arms race continues, he does not have such an opportunity. The same, naturally, applies to ourselves.

If the President counts on SDI in this respect, he does so in vain. The system would be effective only if all missiles were eliminated. But then, one might ask, why the anti-missile defence altogether? Why build it? I need not mention the money wasted, the cost of the system—according to some estimates, it will run into several trillion dollars.

So far, we have been trying to persuade America to give up that dangerous undertaking. We are urging the American Administration to look for invulnerability and for protection in another way—the way of total elimination of nuclear weapons and the establishment of a comprehensive system of international security that would preclude all war—nuclear and conventional. . . .

It is hard to reconcile oneself to the loss of a unique chance—that of saving mankind from the nuclear threat. Bearing precisely this in mind, I told the press conference in Reykjavík that we did not regard the dialogue as closed and hoped that President Reagan, on returning home, would consult Congress and the American people and adopt decisions logically necessitated by what had been achieved in Reykjavík.

Quite a different thing has happened. Besides distorting the entire picture of the Reykjavík negotiations—I will speak about that later—they have in recent days taken actions that look simply wild in the normal human view after such an important meeting between the two countries' top leaders.

I mean the expulsion of another fifty-five Soviet embassy and consular staff from the United States. We will take measures in response, of course—very tough measures on an equal footing. We are not going to put up with such outrageous practices. But for now let me say the following.

What kind of government is this? What can one expect from it in other affairs in the international arena? To what limits does the unpredictability of its actions go?

It turns out that it has no constructive proposals on key disarmament issues and that it does not even have a desire to maintain the atmosphere essential for a normal continuation of the dialogue. It appears that Washington is not prepared for any of these. . . .

An unattractive portrait of the Administration of that great country, of an Administration quick to take disruptive actions, is coming into view. Either the President is unable to cope with an entourage which literally breathes hatred for the Soviet Union and for everything that may lead international affairs into a calm channel or he himself wants that. At all events, there is no keeping the "hawks" in the White House in check. And this is very dangerous. . . .

Let me say once again: when SDI is preferred to nuclear disarmament, only one conclusion is possible: it is that through that military program efforts are being made to disprove the axiom of international relations of our epoch expressed in the simple and clear-cut words under which the US President and I put our signatures last year [at the Geneva summit conference]. Here are those words: nuclear war must not be fought and it cannot be won.

Let me say in conclusion: the Soviet Union has put the maximum of goodwill into its proposals. We are not removing these proposals, they still stand! Everything that has been said by the way of their substantiation and development remains in force.

6. Paul Kennedy on "Imperial Overstretch" and the Relative Decline of the United States, 1987

Although the United States is at present still in a class of its own economically and perhaps even militarily, it cannot avoid confronting the two great tests which challenge the *longevity* of every major power that occupies the "number one" position in world affairs: whether, in the military/strategic realm, it can preserve a reasonable balance between the nation's perceived defense requirements and the means it possesses to maintain those commitments; and whether, as an intimately related point, it can preserve the technological and economic bases of its power from relative erosion in the face of the ever-shifting patterns of global production. This test of American abilities will be the greater because it, like Imperial Spain around 1600 or the British Empire around 1900, is the inheritor of a vast array of strategical commitments which had been made decades earlier, when the nation's political, economic, and military capacity to influence world affairs seemed so much more assured. In consequence, the United States now runs the risk, so familiar to historians of the rise and fall of previous Great Powers, of what might roughly be called "imperial overstretch"; that is to say, decision-makers in Washington must face the awkward and enduring fact that the sum total of the United States' global interests and obligations is nowadays far larger than the country's power to defend them all simultaneously. . . .

This brings us, inevitably, to the delicate relationship between slow economic growth and high defense spending. The debate upon "the economics of defense spending" is a highly controversial one, and—bearing in mind the size and variety of the American economy, the stimulus which can come from large government contracts, and the technical spin-offs from weapons research—the evidence does not point simply in one direction. But what is significant for our purposes is the comparative dimension. Even if (as is often pointed out) defense expenditures formed

10 percent of GNP under Eisenhower and 9 percent under Kennedy, the United States' relative share of global production and wealth was at that time around *twice* what it is today; and, more particularly, the American economy was not then facing the challenges to either its traditional or its high-technology manufactures. Moreover, if the United States at present continues to devote 7 percent or more of its GNP to defense spending while its major economic rivals, especially Japan, allocate a far smaller proportion, then *ipso facto* the latter have potentially more funds "free" for civilian investment; if the United States continues to invest a massive amount of its R&D activities into military-related production while the Japanese and West Germans concentrate upon commercial R&D; and if the Pentagon's spending drains off the majority of the country's scientists and engineers from the design and production of goods for the world market while similar personnel in other countries are primarily engaged in bringing out better products for the civilian consumer, then it seems inevitable that the American share of world manufacturing will steadily decline, and also likely that its economic growth rates will be slower than in those countries dedicated to the marketplace and less eager to channel resources into defense.

It is almost superfluous to say that these tendencies place the United States on the horns of a most acute dilemma over the longer term. Simply because it is *the* global superpower, with far more extensive military commitments than a regional Power like Japan or West Germany, it requires much larger defense forces—in just the same way as imperial Spain felt it needed a far larger army than its contemporaries and Victorian Britain insisted upon a much bigger navy than any other country. Furthermore, since the USSR is seen to be the major military threat to American interests across the globe and is clearly devoting a far greater proportion of *its* GNP to defense, American decision-makers are inevitably worried about "losing" the arms race with Russia. Yet the more sensible among these decision-makers can also perceive that the burden of armaments is debilitating the Soviet economy; and that if the two superpowers continue to allocate ever-larger shares of their national wealth into the unproductive field of armaments, the critical question might soon be: "Whose economy will decline *fastest*, relative to such expanding states as Japan, China, etc.?" A low investment in armaments may, for a globally overstretched Power like the United States, leave it feeling vulnerable everywhere; but a very heavy investment in armament, while bringing greater security in the short term, may so erode the commercial competitiveness of the American economy that the nation will be *less* secure in the long term.

7. Soviet Reformer Georgi Arbatov Explains the "New Thinking" in the Soviet Union, 1989

Personally I share the radical view that *perestroika* means building a new model of Soviet socialism. We have to go all the way in democratization, *glasnost,* and economic reforms, not halfway. This bothers some people, but the reasons aren't hard to understand. The Soviet Union is a young country—just over seventy years old.

Georgi Arbatov Explains the "New Thinking" in the Soviet Union, 1989, from *Voices of Glasnost: Interviews with Gorbachev's Reformers* by Stephen F. Cohen and Katrina vanden Heuvel. Copyright © 1989 by Stephen F. Cohen and Katrina vanden Heuvel. Reprinted by permission of W. W. Norton & Company, Inc.

During those years we have lived through so many extraordinary circumstances—the Revolution, the Civil War, Stalinism, the world war, the Cold War—that our structures, psychology, and behavior acquired extraordinary characteristics. It was like growing up under martial law. Even Stalinism was shaped by extraordinary circumstances—the threats of German fascism and Japanese militarism in the 1930s, the burden of the Cold War. So it's not surprising that we haven't yet built the socialist model we intended and believe in.

Now we have to rid ourselves of all those things that arose in those extraordinary times—things in which we used to believe, things we thought were intrinsic to socialism. This isn't easy, partly because many people will believe in all those things but also because the old economic model worked rather well in its time and for certain purposes. If the old economic model had completely failed, if the country had not developed from being a very backward country, it would be easier to change today. It would be easier to give up the obsolete thinking and policies that led the country into a dead end and that had such a negative impact on international relations. I can't think of any other country or government that now is so self-critical and demanding in looking at its own past and learning from the sufferings of the past.

That's why I argue against some of our officials who are guarded or worried about *glasnost*. The anti-*glasnost* tradition was imposed on the country during Stalinism, and it has had very negative effects in our domestic policies—but also in foreign policy. In fact, improvements brought by the Twentieth Party Congress back in the 1950s barely touched foreign policy. I don't mean that everything in our foreign policy stagnated in the years that followed. There were achievements—the beginnings of détente, arms control steps, and other things. But the tradition of secrecy, silence, and the absence of *glasnost* fossilized much of our defense and foreign policy thinking and decision making. When I argue for greater openness, some of our people say that exposing our problems will hurt us abroad. I tell them that the world knew about our problems before *glasnost;* we can't hide them. Moreover, *glasnost* has helped us abroad because more people there understand we are serious about our reforms. If there is an attempt to curtail *glasnost*, it will be harmful and counterproductive. . . .

The main priority of our foreign policy is to create the best international circumstances for the reforms going on inside our country. For us, economic and social progress is the most important thing. Of course, there still are some people here who cling to old ideas about the priority of promoting revolutions abroad—people who still think we can work miracles when foreign Marxists ask us for help. But it doesn't work. The best way to influence other countries is by reforming our own system. *Perestroika* involves a new way of thinking about foreign policy which begins with seeing realities as they are, not as we want them to be. We must face the truth, no matter how bitter it is. Our basic conception of the world has changed. We no longer view it in terms of "we" and "they" but as one humanity that has to live or die together. The nuclear world is too fragile for the use of military force, any kind of serious misbehavior, any geopolitical adventures, or an unlimited arms race. That is a basic principle of our new thinking. . . .

[W]e now believe that what unites different countries, their common interests, is more important than the conflicts and differences between them. We also realized that we relied too much on military power for security. Both the Soviet Union and the United States have far more military power than they can use for any reasonable purpose. Militarism on the part of all countries is the real danger. We all must rely for security more on political means—on negotiations, for example. Our mutual task is to reverse the militarization of life. We have no need for all these weapons and huge armies. We also now understand that we cannot obtain national security at the expense of the other side—at your [U.S.] expense—and the same is true for you. This is our concept of mutual security. Our security depends on you feeling secure, and yours depends on us feeling secure. Now we also understand better that the lagging economic development of the Third World is a global problem, and despite our limited resources we have to make our contribution to solving this problem. . . .

I know that some Americans dislike them [Soviet domestic reforms] and I understand why. Since 1945 many American institutions have needed a foreign enemy—an evil empire. Indeed, the general framework of American foreign policy has been constructed on the premise of this enemy. The Cold War was built on a kind of black-and-white, religious fundamentalism. There was the American paradise and the Soviet hell. When hell disappears, when the enemy image erodes, the whole structure becomes shaky. Some Americans fear this. But they will just have to find ways to live without the image of the Soviet enemy. America also needs *perestroika* and new thinking of her own. . . .

The Cold War is a living corpse. It died sometime in the 1960s and has been kept alive by political injections of myths and fantasies about the Soviet threat— like a body kept alive on an artificial heart-and-lung machine. It is time to lay it to rest. Neither of us can any longer afford to squander money on fake problems, false stereotypes, and pointless suspicions. Both of us have plenty of real problems at home.

8. President George Bush Proclaims Cold War Victory, 1990

There are singular moments in history, dates that divide all that goes before from all that comes after. And many of us in this Chamber have lived much of our lives in a world whose fundamental features were defined in 1945; and the events of that year decreed the shape of nations, the pace of progress, freedom or oppression for millions of people around the world.

Nineteen forty-five provided the common frame of reference, the compass points of the postwar era we've relied upon to understand ourselves. And that was our world, until now. The events of the year just ended, the Revolution of '89, have been a chain reaction, changes so striking that it marks the beginning of a new era in the world's affairs.

Think back—think back just 12 short months ago to the world we knew as 1989 began.

This document can be found in "Address Before a Joint Session of the Congress on the State of the Union," 31 January 1990, *Public Papers of the Presidents, George Bush 1990* (Washington, D.C.: Government Printing Office, 1991), Book I, 129–134.

One year—one year ago, the people of Panama lived in fear, under the thumb of a dictator. Today democracy is restored; Panama is free. Operation Just Cause has achieved its objective. The number of military personnel in Panama is now very close to what it was before the operation began. And tonight I an announcing that well before the end of February, the additional numbers of American troops, the brave men and women of our Armed Forces who made this mission a success, will be back home.

A year ago in Poland, Lech Walesa declared that he was ready to open a dialog with the Communist rulers of that country; and today, with the future of a free Poland in their own hands, members of Solidarity lead the Polish Government.

A year ago, freedom's playwright, Václav Havel, languished as a prisoner in Prague. And today it's Václav Havel, President of Czechoslovakia.

And 1 year ago, Erich Honecker of East Germany claimed history as his guide, and he predicted the Berlin Wall would last another hundred years. And today, less than 1 year later, it's the Wall that's history.

Remarkable events—events that fulfill the long-held hopes of the American people; events that validate the longstanding goals of American policy, a policy based on a single, shining principle: the cause of freedom.

America, not just the nation but an idea, alive in the minds of people every-where. As this new world takes shape, America stands at the center of a widening circle of freedom—today, tomorrow, and into the next century. Our nation is the enduring dream of every immigrant who ever set foot on these shores, and the mil-lions still struggling to be free. This nation, this idea called America, was and always will be a new world—our new world. . . .

There is a new world of challenges and opportunities before us, and there's a need for leadership that only America can provide. Nearly 40 years ago, in his last address to the Congress, President Harry Truman predicted such a time would come. He said: "As our world grows stronger, more united, more attractive to men on both sides of the Iron Curtain, then inevitably there will come a time of change within the Communist world." Today, that change is taking place.

For more than 40 years, America and its allies held communism in check and ensured that democracy would continue to exist. And today, with communism crum-bling, our aim must be to ensure democracy's advance, to take the lead in forging peace and freedom's best hope: a great and growing commonwealth of free nations. And to the Congress and to all Americans, I say it is time to acclaim a new consensus at home and abroad, a common vision of the peaceful world we want to see. . . .

We are in a period of great transition, great hope, and yet great uncertainty. We recognize that the Soviet military threat in Europe is diminishing, but we see little change in Soviet strategic modernization. Therefore, we must sustain our own strate-gic offense modernization and the Strategic Defense Initiative.

But the time is right to move forward on a conventional arms control agreement to move us to more appropriate levels of military forces in Europe, a coherent defense program that ensures the U.S. will continue to be a catalyst for peaceful change in Europe. And I've consulted with leaders of NATO. In fact, I spoke by phone with President Gorbachev just today.

I agree with our European allies that an American military presence in Europe is essential and that it should not be tied solely to the Soviet military presence in Eastern

Europe. But our troop levels can still be lower. And so, tonight I am announcing a major new step for a further reduction in U.S. and Soviet manpower in Central and Eastern Europe to 195,000 on each side. This level reflects the advice of our senior military advisers. It's designed to protect American and European interests and sustain NATO's defense strategy. A swift conclusion to our arms control talks—conventional, chemical, and strategic—must now be our goal. And that time has come.

Still, we must recognize an unfortunate fact: In many regions of the world tonight, the reality is conflict, not peace. Enduring animosities and opposing interests remain. And thus, the cause of peace must be served by an America strong enough and sure enough to defend our interests and our ideals. It's this American idea that for the past four decades helped inspire this Revolution of '89.

9. President William J. Clinton Applauds America's Globalism and Warns Against a New Isolationism, 1995

You know, in 1991 I sought the presidency because I believed it was essential to restore the American dream for all Americans and to reassert America's leadership in the post-cold-war world. As we move from the industrial to the information age, from the cold war world to the global village, we have an extraordinary opportunity to advance our values at home and around the world. But we face some stiff challenges in doing so as well. . . .

We see the benefits of American leadership in the progress now being made in Bosnia. In recent weeks, our military muscle through NATO, our determined diplomacy throughout the region, have brought the parties closer to a settlement than at any time since this terrible war began 4 years ago. Yesterday, we helped to produce an agreement on a Bosnia-wide cease-fire. Now, the parties will come to the United States to pursue their peace talks mediated by our negotiating team and our European and Russian counterparts.

We have a long way to go, and there's no guarantee of success. But we will use every ounce of our influence to help the parties make a peace that preserves Bosnia as a single democratic state and protects the rights of all citizens, regardless of their ethnic group. . . .

We also saw the benefits of America's leadership last week at the White House where leaders from all over the Middle East gathered to support the agreement between Israel and the Palestinian Authority. For nearly a half-century now, Democratic and Republican administrations have worked to facilitate the cause of peace in the Middle East. The credit here belongs to the peacemakers. But we should all be proud that at critical moments along the way, our efforts helped to make the difference between failure and success.

It was almost exactly a year ago that the United States led the international effort to remove Haiti's military regime and give the people of Haiti a real chance at democracy. We've succeeded because we've backed diplomacy with sanctions

This document can be found in "Remarks at Freedom House," 6 October 1995, *Public Papers of the Presidents of the United States, William J. Clinton, 1995* (Washington, D.C.: U.S. Government Printing Office, 1996), Book II, 1544–1551.

and ultimately with force. We've succeeded because we understood that standing up for democracy in our own hemisphere was right for the Haitian people and right for America.

American efforts in Bosnia, the Middle East, and Haiti and elsewhere have required investments of time and energy and resources. They've required persistent diplomacy and the measured use of the world's strongest military. They have required both determination and flexibility in our efforts to work as leaders and to work with other nations. And sometimes they've called on us to make decisions that were, of necessity, unpopular in the short run, knowing that the payoff would not come in days or weeks but in months or years. Sometimes they have been difficult for many Americans to understand because they have to be made, as many decisions did right after World War II, without the benefit of some overarching framework, the kind of framework the bipolar cold war world provided for so many years.

To use the popular analogy of the present day, there seems to be no mainframe explanation for the PC world in which we're living. We have to drop the abstractions and dogma and pursue, based on trial and error and persistent experimentation, a policy that advances our values of freedom and democracy, peace, and security. . . .

Throughout what we now call the American century, Republicans and Democrats disagreed on specific policies, often heatedly from time to time, but we have always agreed on the need for American leadership in the cause of democracy, freedom, security, and prosperity. Now that consensus is truly in danger, and interestingly enough, it is in danger in both parties. Voices from the left and the right are calling on us to step back from, instead of stepping up to, the challenges of the present day. They threaten to reverse the bipartisan support for our leadership that has been essential to our strength for 50 years. Some really believe that after the cold war the United States can play a secondary role in the world, just as some thought we could after World War II, and some made sure we did after World War I.

But if you look at the results from Bosnia to Haiti, from the Middle East to Northern Ireland, it proves once again that American leadership is indispensable and that without it our values, our interests, and peace itself would be at risk.

It has now become a truism to blame the current isolationism on the end of the cold war because there is no longer a mainframe threat in this PC world. . . .

The isolationists are simply wrong. The environment we face may be new and different, but to meet it with the challenges and opportunities it presents and to advance our enduring values, we have to be more engaged in the world, not less engaged in the world. That's why we have done everything we could in our administration to lead the fight to reduce the nuclear threat, to spread democracy in human rights, to support peace, to open markets, to enlarge and defend the community of nations around the world, to share our aspirations and our values. . . .

The American people are good people. They have common sense. They care when people are being murdered around the world. They understand that a war somewhere else could one day involve our sons and daughters. They know that we cannot simply pretend that the rest of the world is not there. But many of them have their own difficulties. We must work and work and work on the basic values and interests and arguments until we beat back the forces of isolation, with both intense passion and reason.

10. President George W. Bush Jettisons the Multilateral Kyoto Protocol on the Environment, 2001

Thank you for your letter of March 6, 2001, asking for the Administration's view on global climate change, in particular the Kyoto Protocol and efforts to regulate carbon dioxide under the Clean Air Act. My Administration takes the issue of global climate change very seriously.

As you know, I oppose the Kyoto Protocol because it exempts 80 percent of the world, including major population centers such as China and India, from compliance, and would cause serious harm to the U.S. economy. The Senate's vote, 95–0, shows that there is a clear consensus that the Kyoto Protocol is an unfair and ineffective means of addressing global climate change concerns.

As you also know, I support a comprehensive and balanced national energy policy that takes into account the importance of improving air quality. Consistent with this balanced approach, I intend to work with the Congress on a multipollutant strategy to require power plants to reduce emissions of sulfur dioxide, nitrogen oxides, and mercury. And such strategy would include phasing in reductions over a reasonable period of time, providing regulatory certainty, and offering market-based incentives to help industry meet the targets. I do not believe, however, that the government should impose on power plants mandatory emissions reductions for carbon dioxide, which is not a "pollutant" under the Clean Air Act.

A recently released Department of Energy Report, "Analysis of Strategies for Reducing Multiple Emissions from Power Plants," concluded that including caps on carbon dioxide emissions as part of a multiple emissions strategy would lead to an even more dramatic shift from coal to natural gas for electric power generation and significantly higher electricity prices compared to scenarios in which only sulfur dioxide and nitrogen oxides were reduced.

This is important new information that warrants a reevaluation, especially at a time of rising energy prices and a serious energy shortage. Coal generates more than half of America's electricity supply. At a time when California has already experienced energy shortages, and other Western states are worried about price and availability of energy this summer, we must be very careful not to take actions that could harm consumers. This is especially true given the incomplete state of scientific knowledge of the causes of, and solutions to, global climate change and the lack of commercially available technologies for removing and storing carbon dioxide.

Consistent with these concerns, we will continue to fully examine global climate change issues—including the science, technologies, market-based systems, and innovative options for addressing concentrations of greenhouse gases in the atmosphere. I am very optimistic that, with the proper focus and working with our friends and allies, we will be able to develop technologies, market incentives, and other creative ways to address global climate change.

This document can be found in George W. Bush to Senators Hagel, Helms, Craig, and Roberts, 13 March 2001, *Public Papers of the Presidents of the United States, George W. Bush, 2001* (Washington, D.C.: U.S. Government Printing Office, 2002), Book I, 235.

I look forward to working with you and others to address global climate change issues in the context of a national energy policy that protects our environment, consumers, and economy.

🌐 E S S A Y S

In the first essay, a statement representative of the Reagan victory school, the historian John Lewis Gaddis credits Reagan's leadership skills, especially his ability to balance ideological vision with operational pragmatism, for reducing Cold War tensions. Reagan capitalized on Soviet decline and shrewdly used America's military buildup and his SDI initiative to bring the Soviets to the bargaining table. In the new Soviet leader Mikhail Gorbachev, Reagan gained a Russian partner who shared his goal of reducing, not just controlling, nuclear weapons. Gaddis concludes that Reagan's critics, on both the left and the right, vastly underestimated the president's determination to negotiate from strength and build a domestic political base in favor of détente.

In the second essay, Raymond L. Garthoff, a former diplomat and senior fellow at the Brookings Institution in Washington D.C., disagrees with the Reagan victory thesis. Garthoff maintains that the Cold War ended because Soviet leader Mikhail Gorbachev abandoned the Marxist-Leninist dogma of inevitable conflict, sought to restructure Soviet politics and economics, and took the lead in proposing steep cuts in superpower nuclear and conventional weapons. According to Garthoff, Reagan's strident Cold War rhetoric and arms buildup had little impact on the Kremlin. It was only when Reagan administration pragmatists won out over ideological "essentialists," that Washington finally engaged the new generation of Soviet leadership—enabling the two superpowers to advance beyond the limited détente of the 1960s and end of the Cold War.

President Ronald Reagan's Successful Strategy of Negotiating from Strength

JOHN LEWIS GADDIS

To say that the Reagan administration's policy toward the Soviet Union is going to pose special challenges to historians is to understate the matter: rarely has there been a greater gap between the expectations held for an administration at the beginning of its term and the results it actually produced. The last thing one would have anticipated at the time Ronald Reagan took office in 1981 was that he would use his eight years in the White House to bring about the most significant improvement in Soviet-American relations since the end of World War II. I am not at all sure that President Reagan himself foresaw this result. And yet, that is precisely what happened, with—admittedly—a good deal of help from Mikhail Gorbachev. . . .

President Reagan in March, 1983, made his most memorable pronouncement on the Soviet Union: condemning the tendency of his critics to hold both sides responsible for the nuclear arms race, he denounced the U.S.S.R. as an "evil empire"

President Ronald Reagan's Strategy of Negotiating from Strength from John Lewis Gaddis, *The United States and the End of the Cold War: Implications, Reconsiderations, Provocations* (Oxford University Press, 1992), pp. 119, 122–132. Copyright © 1992 by John Lewis Gaddis. Used by permission of Oxford University Press, Inc.

and as "the focus of evil in the modern world." Two weeks later, the President surprised even his closet associates by calling for a long-term research and development
program to create defense against attacks by strategic missiles, with a view, ultimately, to "rendering these nuclear weapons impotent and obsolete." The Strategic
Defense Initiative was the most fundamental challenge to existing orthodoxies on
arms control since negotiations on that subject had begun with the Russians almost
three decades earlier. Once again it called into question the President's seriousness in
seeking an end to—or even a significant moderation of—the strategic arms race.

Anyone who listened to the "evil empire" speech or who considered the implications of "Star Wars" might well have concluded that Reagan saw the Soviet-
American relationship as an elemental confrontation between virtue and wickedness
that would allow neither negotiation nor conciliation in any form; his tone seemed
more appropriate to a medieval crusade than to a revival of containment. Certainly
there were those within his administration who held such views, and their influence,
for a time, was considerable. But to see the President's policies solely in terms of
his rhetoric, it is now clear, would have been quite wrong.

For President Reagan appears to have understood—or to have quickly learned—
the dangers of basing foreign policy solely on ideology: he combined militancy with
a surprising degree of operational pragmatism and a shrewd sense of timing. To the
astonishment of his own hard-line supporters, what appeared to be an enthusiastic return to the Cold War in fact turned out to be a more solidly based approach to détente
than anything the Nixon, Ford, or Carter administrations had been able to accomplish.

There had always been a certain ambivalence in the Reagan administration's
image of the Soviet Union. On the other hand, dire warnings about Moscow's growing military strength suggested an almost Spenglerian gloom about the future: time,
it appeared, was on the Russians' side. But mixed with this pessimism was a strong
sense of self-confidence, growing out of the ascendancy of conservatism within the
United States and an increasing enthusiasm for capitalism overseas, that assumed
the unworkability of Marxism as a form of political, social, and economic organization: "The West won't contain communism, it will transcend communism," the
President predicted in May, 1981. "It won't bother to . . . denounce it, it will dismiss
it as some bizarre chapter in human history whose last pages are even now being
written." By this logic, the Soviet Union had already reached the apex of its strength
as a world power, and time in fact was on the side of the West.

Events proved the optimism to have been more justified than the pessimism,
for over the next four years the Soviet Union would undergo one of the most rapid
erosions both of internal self-confidence and external influence in modern history;
that this happened just as Moscow's long and costly military buildup should have
begun to pay political dividends made the situation all the more frustrating for the
Russians. It may have been luck for President Reagan to have come into office at a
peak in the fortunes of the Soviet Union and at a trough in those of the United States:
things would almost certainly have improved regardless of who entered the White
House in 1981. But it took more than luck to recognize what was happening, and to
capitalize on it to the extent that the Reagan administration did.

Indications of Soviet decline took several forms. The occupation of Afghanistan
had produced only a bloody Vietnam-like stalemate, with Soviet troops unable to
suppress the rebellion, or to protect themselves and their clients, or to withdraw. In

Poland a long history of economic mismanagement had produced, in the form of the Solidarity trade union, a rare phenomenon within the Soviet bloc: a true workers' movement. Soviet ineffectiveness became apparent in the Middle East in 1982 when the Russians were unable to provide any significant help to the Palestinian Liberation Organization during the Israeli invasion of Lebanon; even more embarrassing, Israeli pilots using American-built fighters shot down over eighty Soviet-supplied Syrian jets without a single loss of their own. Meanwhile, the Soviet domestic economy which [former Soviet premier Nikita] Khrushchev had once predicted would overtake that of the United States, had in fact stagnated during the early 1980s, Japan by some indices actually overtook the U.S.S.R. as the world's second largest producer of goods and services, and even China, a nation with four times the population of the Soviet Union, now became an agricultural exporter at a time when Moscow still required food imports from the West to feed its own people.

What all of this meant was that the Soviet Union's appeal as a model for Third World political and economic development—once formidable—had virtually disappeared, indeed as Moscow's military presence in those regions grew during the late 1970s, the Russians increasingly came to be seen, not as liberators, but as latter-day imperialists themselves. The Reagan administration moved swiftly to take advantage of this situation by funneling military assistance—sometimes openly sometimes covertly—to rebel groups (or "freedom fighters," as the President insisted on calling them) seeking to overthrow Soviet-backed regimes in Afghanistan, Angola, Ethiopia, Cambodia, and Nicaragua; in October, 1983, to huge domestic acclaim but with dubious legality Reagan even ordered the direct use of American military forces to overthrow an unpopular Marxist government on the tiny Caribbean island of Grenada. The Reagan Doctrine, as this strategy became known, sought to exploit vulnerabilities the Russians had created for themselves in the Third World: this latter-day effort to "roll back" Soviet influence would, in time, produce impressive results at minimum cost and risk to the United States.

Compounding the Soviet Union's external difficulties was a long vacuum in internal leadership occasioned by [President Leonid] Brezhnev's slow enfeeblement and eventual death in November, 1982; by the installation as his successor of an already-ill Yuri Andropov, who himself died in February 1984; and by the installation of his equally geriatric successor, Konstantin Chernenko. At a time when a group of strong Western leaders had emerged—including not just President Reagan but also Prime Minister Margaret Thatcher in Great Britain, President François Mitterrand in France, and Chancellor Helmut Kohl in West Germany—this apparent inability to entrust leadership to anyone other than party stalwarts on their deathbeds was a severe commentary on what the sclerotic Soviet system had become. "We could go no further without hitting the end," one Russian later recalled of Chernenko's brief reign. "Here was the General Secretary of the party who is also the Chairman of the Presidium of the Supreme Soviet, the embodiment of our country, the personification of the party and he could barely stand up."

There was no disagreement within the Reagan administration about the desirability under these circumstances, of pressing the Russians hard. Unlike several of their predecessors, the President and his advisers did not see containment as requiring the application of sticks and carrots in equal proportion; wielders of sticks definitely predominated among them. But there were important differences over what the purpose of wielding the sticks was to be.

Some advisers, like [Secretary of Defense Caspar] Weinberger, [Assistant Secretary of Defense for International Security Policy Richard] Perle, and [chief Soviet specialist on the National Security Council Richard] Pipes, saw the situation as a historic opportunity to exhaust the Soviet system. Noting that the Soviet economy was already stretched to the limit, they advocated taking advantage of American technological superiority to engage the Russians in an arms race of indefinite duration and indeterminate cost. Others, including [the arms negotiator Paul] Nitze, the Joint Chiefs of Staff, career Foreign Service officer Jack Matlock, who succeeded Pipes as chief Soviet expert at the NSC, and—most important—[Secretary of State Alexander M.] Haig's replacement after June, 1982, the unflamboyant but steady George Shultz, endorsed the principle of "negotiation from strength": the purpose of accumulating military hardware was not to debilitate the other side, but to convince it to negotiate.

The key question, of course, was what President Reagan's position would be. Despite his rhetoric, he had been careful not to rule out talks with the Russians once the proper conditions had been met: even while complaining, in his first press conference, about the Soviet propensity to lie, cheat, and steal, he had also noted that "when we can, . . . we should start negotiations on the basis of trying to effect an actual reduction in the numbers of nuclear weapons. That would be real arms reduction." But most observers—and probably many of his own advisers—assumed that when the President endorsed negotiations leading toward the "reduction," as opposed to the "limitation," of strategic arms, or the "zero option" in the INF [intermediate-range nuclear forces] talks, or the Strategic Defense Initiative, he was really seeking to avoid negotiations by setting minimal demands above the maximum concessions the Russians could afford to make. He was looking for a way they believed, to gain credit for cooperativeness with both domestic and allied constituencies without actually having to give up anything.

That would turn out to be a gross misjudgment of President Reagan, who may have had cynical advisers but was not cynical himself. It would become apparent with the passage of time that when the Chief Executive talked about "reducing" strategic missiles he meant precisely that; the appeal of the "zero option" was that it really would get rid of intermediate-range nuclear forces; the Strategic Defense Initiative might in fact, just as the President had said, make nuclear weapons "impotent and obsolete." A simple and straightforward man, Reagan took the principle of "negotiation from strength" literally: once one had built strength, one negotiated.

The first indications that the President might be interested in something other than an indefinite arms race began to appear in the spring and summer of 1983. Widespread criticism of his "evil empire" speech apparently shook him: although his view of the Soviet system itself did not change, Reagan was careful, after that point, to use more restrained language in characterizing it. Clear evidence of the President's new moderation came with the Korean airliner incident [downed when it strayed into Soviet airspace] of September, 1983. Despite his outrage, Reagan did not respond—as one might have expected him to—by reviving his "evil empire" rhetoric; instead he insisted that arms control negotiations would continue, and in a remarkably conciliatory television address early in 1984 he announced that the United States was "in its strongest position in years to establish a constructive and realistic working relationship with the Soviet Union." The President concluded this address by speculating on how a typical Soviet couple—Ivan and Anya—might find that they had much in common with a typical American couple—Jim and Sally: "They might even have decided that they were all going to get together for dinner some evening soon."

It was possible to construct self-serving motives for this startling shift in tone. With a presidential campaign under way the White House was sensitive to Democratic charges that Reagan was the only postwar president not to have met with a Soviet leader while in office. Certainly it was to the advantage of the United States in its relations with Western Europe to look as reasonable as possible in the face of Soviet intransigence. But events would show that the President's interest in an improved relationship was based on more than just electoral politics or the needs of the alliance: it was only the unfortunate tendency of Soviet leaders to die upon taking office that was depriving the American Chief Executive—himself a spry septuagenarian—of a partner with whom to negotiate.

By the end of September, 1984—and to the dismay of Democratic partisans who saw Republicans snatching the "peace" issue from them—a contrite Soviet Foreign Minister Andrei Gromyko had made the pilgrimage to Washington to re-establish contacts with the Reagan administration. Shortly after Reagan's landslide re-election over Walter Mondale in November, the United States and the Soviet Union announced that a new set of arms control negotiations would begin early the following year, linking together discussions on START [Strategic Arms Reduction Talks], INF, and weapons in space. And in December, a hitherto obscure member of the Soviet Politburo, Mikhail Gorbachev, announced while visiting Great Britain that the U.S.S.R. was prepared to seek "radical solutions" looking toward a ban on nuclear missiles altogether. Three months later, Konstantin Chernenko, the last in a series of feeble and unimaginative Soviet leaders, expired, and Gorbachev—a man who was in no way feeble and unimaginative—became the General Secretary of the Communist Party of the Soviet Union. Nothing would ever be quite the same again. . . .

Whatever the circumstances that led to it, the accession of Gorbachev reversed almost overnight the pattern of the preceding four years: after March, 1985, it was the Soviet Union that seized the initiative in relations with the West. It did so in a way that was both reassuring and unnerving at the same time: by becoming so determinedly cooperative as to convince some supporters of containment in the United States and Western Europe—uneasy in the absence of the intransigence to which they had become accustomed—that the Russians were now seeking to defeat that strategy by depriving it, with sinister cleverness, of an object to be contained.

President Reagan, in contrast, welcomed the fresh breezes emanating from Moscow and moved quickly to establish a personal relationship with the new Soviet leader. Within four days of Gorbachev's taking power, the President was characterizing the Russians as "in a different frame of mind than they've been in the past. . . . [T]hey, I believe, are really going to try and, with us, negotiate a reduction in armaments." And within four months, the White House was announcing that Reagan would meet Gorbachev at Geneva in November for the first Soviet-American summit since 1979.

The Geneva summit, like so many before it, was long on symbolism and short on substance. The two leaders appeared to get along well with one another: they behaved, as one Reagan adviser later put it, "like a couple of fellows who had run into each other at the club and discovered that they had a lot in common." The President agreed to discuss deep cuts in strategic weapons and improved verification, but he made it clear that he was not prepared to forgo development of the Strategic Defense Initiative in order to get them. His reason—which Gorbachev may not have taken seriously until this point—had to do with his determination to retain SDI as a means ultimately of rendering nuclear weapons obsolete. The President's stubbornness on this point precluded progress, at least for the moment, on what was coming to be called the "grand compromise": Paul Nitze's idea of accepting limits on SDI in return for sweeping reductions in strategic missiles. But it did leave the way open for an alert Gorbachev, detecting the President's personal enthusiasm for nuclear abolition, to surprise the world in January, 1986, with his own plan for accomplishing that objective: a Soviet-American agreement to rid the world of nuclear weapons altogether by the year 2000.

It was easy to question Gorbachev's motives in making so radical a proposal in so public a manner with no advance warning. Certainly any discussion of even reducing—much less abolishing—nuclear arsenals would raise difficult questions for American allies, where an abhorrence of nuclear weapons continued to coexist uneasily alongside the conviction that only their presence could deter superior Soviet conventional forces. Nor was the Gorbachev proposal clear on how Russians and Americans could ever impose abolition, even if they themselves agreed to it, on other nuclear and non-nuclear powers. Still, the line between rhetoric and conviction is a thin one: the first Reagan-Gorbachev summit may not only have created a personal bond between the two leaders; it may also have sharpened a vague but growing sense in the minds of both men that, despite all the difficulties in constructing an alternative, an indefinite continuation of life under nuclear threat was not a tolerable condition for either of their countries, and that their own energies might very well be directed toward overcoming that situation.

That both Reagan and Gorbachev were thinking along these lines became clear at their second meeting, the most extraordinary Soviet-American summit of the postwar era, held on very short notice at Reykjavik, Iceland, in October, 1986. The months that preceded Reykjavik had seen little tangible progress toward arms control; there had also developed, in August, an unpleasant skirmish between intelligence agencies on both sides as the KGB, in apparent retaliation for the FBI's highly publicized arrest of a Soviet United Nations official in New York on espionage charges, set up, seized, and held *USNEWS* correspondent Nicholas Daniloff on trumped-up accusations for just under a month. It was a sobering reminder that the Soviet-American relationship existed at several different levels, and that cordiality in one did not rule out the possibility of confrontation in others. The Daniloff affair also brought opportunity though, for in the course of negotiations to settle it Gorbachev proposed a quick "preliminary" summit, to be held within two weeks, to try to break the stalemate in negotiations over intermediate-range nuclear forces in Europe, the aspect of arms control where progress at a more formal summit seemed likely. Reagan immediately agreed.

But when the President and his advisers arrived at Reykjavik, they found that Gorbachev had much more grandiose proposals in mind. These included not only an endorsement of 50 percent cuts in Soviet and American strategic weapons across the broad, but also agreement not to demand the inclusion of British and French nuclear weapons in these calculations—a concession that removed a major stumbling block to START—and acceptance in principle of Reagan's 1981 "zero option" for intermediate-range nuclear forces, all in return for an American commitment not to undermine SALT I's ban on strategic defenses for the next ten years. Impressed by the scope of these concessions, the American side quickly put together a compromise that would have cut ballistic missiles to zero within a decade in return for the right, after that time, to deploy strategic defenses against the bomber and cruise missile forces that would be left. Gorbachev immediately countered by proposing the abolition of *all* nuclear weapons within ten years, thus moving his original deadline from the year 2000 to 1996. President Reagan is said to have replied: "*All* nuclear weapons? Well, Mikhail, that's exactly what I've been talking about all along. . . . That's always been my goal."

A series of events set in motion by a Soviet diplomat's arrest on a New York subway platform and by the reciprocal framing of an American journalist in Moscow had wound up with the two most powerful men in the world agreeing—for the moment, and to the astonishment of their aides—on the abolition of all nuclear weapons within ten years. But the moment did not last. Gorbachev went on to insist, as a condition for nuclear abolition, upon a ban on the laboratory testing of SDI, which Reagan immediately interpreted as an effort to kill strategic defense altogether. Because the ABM treaty does allow for some laboratory testing, the differences between the two positions were not all that great. But in the hothouse atmosphere of this cold-climate summit no one explored such details, and the meeting broke up in disarray, acrimony, and mutual disappointment. . . .

Negotiations on arms control continued in the year that followed Reykjavik, however, with both sides edging toward the long-awaited "grand compromise" that would defer SDI in return for progress toward a START agreement. Reagan and Gorbachev did sign an intermediate-range nuclear forces treaty in Washington in December, 1987, which for the first time provided that Russians and Americans would actually dismantle and destroy—literally before each other's eyes—an entire category of nuclear missiles. There followed a triumphal Reagan visit to Moscow in May, 1988, featuring the unusual sight of a Soviet general secretary and an American president strolling amiably through Red Square, greeting tourists and bouncing babies in front of Lenin's tomb, while their respective military aides—each carrying the codes needed to launch nuclear missiles at each other's territory—stood discreetly in the background. Gorbachev made an equally triumphal visit to New York in December, 1988, to address the United Nations General Assembly: there he announced a *unilateral* Soviet cut of some 500,000 ground troops, a major step toward moving arms control into the realm of conventional forces. . . .

[A]s the Reagan administration prepared to leave office the following month, in an elegaic mood very different from the grim militancy with which it had assumed its responsibilities eight years earlier, the actual prospect of a nuclear holocaust seemed more remote than at any point since the Soviet-American nuclear rivalry had begun. Accidents, to be sure, could always happen. Irrationality though blessedly rare since 1945, could never be ruled out. There was reason for optimism, though, in the fact that as George Bush entered the White House early in 1989, the point at issue no longer seemed to be "how to fight the Cold War" at all, but rather "is the Cold War over?"

The record of the Reagan years suggests the need to avoid the common error of trying to predict outcomes from attributes. There is no question that the President and his advisers came into office with an ideological view of the world that appeared to allow for no compromise with the Russians; but ideology has a way of evolving to accommodate reality especially in the hands of skillful political leadership. Indeed a good working definition of leadership might be just this—the ability to accommodate ideology to practical reality—and by that standard, Reagan's achievements in relations with the Soviet Union will certainly compare favorably with, and perhaps even surpass, those of Richard Nixon and Henry Kissinger.

Did President Reagan intend for things to come out this way? That question is, of course, more difficult to determine, given our lack of access to the archives. But a careful reading of the public record would, I think, show that the President was expressing hopes for an improvement in Soviet-American relations from the moment he entered the White House, and that he began shifting American policy in that direction as early as the first months of 1983, almost two years before Mikhail Gorbachev came to power. Gorbachev's extraordinary receptiveness to such initiatives—as distinct from the literally moribund responses of his predecessors—greatly accelerated the improvement in relations, but it would be a mistake to credit him solely with the responsibility for what happened: Ronald Reagan deserves a great deal of the credit as well.

Critics have raised the question, though, of whether President Reagan was responsible for, or even aware of, the direction administration policy was taking. This argument is, I think, both incorrect and unfair. Reagan's opponents have been quick enough to hold him personally responsible for the failures of his administration; they should be equally prepared to acknowledge his successes. And there are points, even with the limited sources now available, where we can see that the President himself had a decisive impact upon the course of events. They include, among others: the Strategic Defense Initiative, which may have had its problems as a missile shield but which certainly worked in unsettling the Russians; endorsement of the "zero option" in the INF talks and real reductions in START, the rapidity with which the President entered into, and thereby legitimized, serious negotiations with Gorbachev once he came into office; and, most remarkably of all, his eagerness to contemplate alternatives to the nuclear arms race in a way no previous president had been willing to do.

Now, it may be objected that these were simple, unsophisticated, and, as people are given to saying these days, imperfectly "nuanced" ideas. I would not argue with that proposition. But it is important to remember that while complexity, sophistication, and nuance may be prerequisites for intellectual leadership, they are not necessarily so for political leadership, and can at times actually get in the way. President Reagan generally meant precisely what he said: when he came out in favor of negotiations from strength, or for strategic arms reductions as opposed to limitations, or even for making nuclear weapons ultimately irrelevant and obsolete, he did not do so in the "killer amendment" spirit favored by geopolitical sophisticates on the right; the President may have been conservative but he was never devious. The lesson here ought to be to beware of excessive convolution and subtlety in strategy, for sometimes simplemindedness wins out, especially if it occurs in high places.

Finally President Reagan also understood something that many geopolitical sophisticates on the left have not understood: that although toughness may or may not be a prerequisite for successful negotiations with the Russians—there are arguments for both propositions—it is absolutely essential if the American people are to lend their support, over time, to what has been negotiated. Others may have seen

in the doctrine of "negotiation from strength" a way of avoiding negotiations altogether, but it now seems clear that the President saw in that approach the means of
constructing a domestic political base without which agreements with the Russians
would almost certainly have foundered, as indeed many of them did in the 1970s.
For unless one can sustain domestic support—and one does not do that by appearing weak—then it is hardly likely that whatever one has arranged with any adversary
will actually come to anything.

There is one last irony to all of this: it is that it fell to Ronald Reagan to preside
over the belated but decisive success of the strategy of containment George F. Kennan had first proposed more than four decades earlier. For what were Gorbachev's
reforms if not the long-delayed "mellowing" of Soviet society that Kennan had
said would take place with the passage of time? The Stalinist system that had required outside adversaries to justify its own existence now seemed at last to have
passed from the scene; Gorbachev appeared to have concluded that the Soviet Union
could continue to be a great power in world affairs only through the introduction of
something approximating a market economy, democratic political institutions, official
accountability, and respect for the rule of law at home. And that, in turn, suggested an
even more remarkable conclusion: that the very survival of the ideology Lenin had
imposed on Russia in 1917 now required infiltration—perhaps even subversion—by
precisely the ideology the great revolutionary had sworn to overthrow.

I have some reason to suspect that Professor Kennan is not entirely comfortable with the suggestion that Ronald Reagan successfully completed the execution
of the strategy he originated. But as Kennan the historian would be the first to acknowledge, history is full of ironies, and this one, surely, will not rank among the
least of them.

Mikhail Gorbachev's Bold Initiative and Reagan's Modest Response

RAYMOND L. GARTHOFF

The West did not, as is widely believed, win the Cold War through geopolitical
containment and military deterrence. Still less was the Cold War won by the Reagan
military buildup and the Reagan Doctrine, as some have suggested. Instead, "victory"
came when a new generation of Soviet leaders realized how badly their system at
home and their policies abroad had failed. What containment did do was to successfully preclude any temptations by Moscow to advance Soviet hegemony by military
means. It is doubtful that any postwar Soviet leadership would have deliberately resorted to war. That was not, however, so clear to many at the time. Deterrence may
have been redundant, but at least it was highly successful in providing reassurance
to the peoples of Western Europe. For over four decades it performed the historic
function of holding Soviet power in check, or being prepared to do so, until the internal seeds of destruction in the Soviet Union and its empire could mature. At that

Gorbachev's Bold Initiative and Reagan's Modest Response from Raymond L. Garthoff, *The Great Transition: American-Soviet Relations and the End of the Cold War* (Washington, D.C.: The Brookings Institution, 1994), pp. 753–755, 758–762, 764–771. Reprinted by permission of The Brookings Institution.

point, however, Mikhail Gorbachev and the transformation of Soviet policy brought the Cold War to an end.

Despite the important differences among them, all Soviet leaders from Lenin until Gorbachev had shared a belief in an ineluctable conflict between socialism and capitalism. Although Gorbachev remained a socialist, and in his own terms even a communist, he renounced the Marxist-Leninist-Stalinist idea of inevitable world conflict. His avowed acceptance of the interdependence of the world, of the priority of all-human values over class values, and of the indivisibility of common security marked a revolutionary ideological change. That change, which Gorbachev publicly declared as early as February 1986 (though it was then insufficiently noted), manifested itself in many ways during the next five years, in deeds as well as words, including policies reflecting a drastically reduced Soviet perception of the Western threat and actions to reduce the Western perception of a Soviet threat.

In 1986, for example, Gorbachev made clear his readiness to ban all nuclear weapons. In 1987 he signed the INF [Intermediate Nuclear Forces] Treaty, eliminating not only the Soviet and American missiles deployed since the late 1970s but also the whole of the Soviet strategic theater missile forces that had faced Europe and Asia for three decades. What is more, the treaty instituted an intrusive and extensive system of verification. In 1988 Gorbachev proposed conventional arms reductions in Europe under a plan that would abandon the Soviet Union's numerical superiority, and he also launched a substantial unilateral force reduction. In 1988–89 he withdrew all Soviet forces from Afghanistan. At about the same time, he encouraged the ouster of the old communist leadership in Eastern Europe and accepted the transition of the former Soviet-allied states into noncommunist neutral states. By 1990 Gorbachev had signed the CFE [Conventional Forces in Europe] Treaty accepting Soviet conventional arms levels in Europe to the Urals that were much lower than the levels for NATO. By that time he had not only accepted Germany's reunification but also the membership of a unified Germany in NATO. Within another year he had jettisoned the Warsaw Pact and the socialist bloc and agreed in START [Strategic Arms Reduction Treaty] I to verified deep cuts in strategic nuclear forces.

Although Gorbachev had not expected the complete collapse of communism (and Soviet influence) in Eastern Europe that occurred in 1989 and 1990, he had made clear to the Twenty-seventh Congress of the Soviet Communist Party as early as February 1986 that a new conception of security had to replace the previous one, and that the confrontation of the Cold War had to end. . . . The goal, he asserted, should be the "creation of a comprehensive system of international security" that embraced economic, ecological, and humanitarian, as well as political and military, elements. Hence, the Soviet decision to give new support to the United Nations, including collective peacekeeping, and to join the world economic system. Hence, the cooperative Soviet efforts to resolve regional conflicts in Central America, Southern Africa, the Horn of Africa, Cambodia, Afghanistan, and the Middle East, not to mention the Soviet Union's support for the collective UN-endorsed action against Iraq in 1991. . . .

Gorbachev, to be sure, seriously underestimated the task of changing the Soviet Union, and this led to policy errors that contributed to the failure of his program for the transformation of Soviet society and polity. His vision of a resurrected socialism built on the foundation of successful *perestroika* and *demokratizatsiya* was never a realistic possibility. He knew deep economic reform was necessary, and he tried; he did not find the solution. A revitalized Soviet political union was perhaps beyond realization as well. The reasons for Gorbachev's failure were primarily objective, not subjective; that is, they were real obstacles he was unable to overcome—internal opposition, powerful inertia, intractable problems of economic transformation, and the politically charged problem of redefining a democratic relationship between a traditional imperial center and the rest of the country, *not* unwillingness or inability to give up or modify his ideological presuppositions and predispositions. . . .

As the preceding discussion suggests, the American role in ending the Cold War was necessary but not primary. There are several reasons for this conclusion, but the basic one is that the American worldview was derivative of the communist worldview. Containment was hollow without an expansionist power to contain. In this sense, it was the Soviet threat, partly real and partly imagined, that generated the American dedication to waging the Cold War. . . .

Although the Reagan administration did launch U.S. policy, and especially policy toward the Soviet Union, on a new path, it also borrowed much from other approaches. Even its slogans (which were, unexpectedly, often the best guide to policy) were largely borrowed. "Peace through strength" was the term [President Gerald] Ford had turned to after shelving the word détente (in his primary contest with Reagan in 1976). "Reciprocity" was borrowed from [President Jimmy] Carter and [National Security adviser Zbigniew] Brzezinski; "negotiations" and "dialogue" from [President Richard] Nixon and [foreign policy adviser Henry] Kissinger. The confrontation rhetoric was the most original, though much (a "crusade," negotiation from "positions of strength") was vintage 1950s. It was also the least useful for any purpose except to satisfy internal political-psychological drives and to mollify a hard-line constituency. It created a new barrier that could only be partly dispelled by its partial abandonment after 1984.

Most of the foreign policy successes of the administration involved the later neutralization of problems the administration itself had generated. China policy, for example, got back on track by 1983–84 after travails largely caused by the Reagan administration's agitation of the Taiwan issue in 1980–81. Relations with the West Europeans were restored in 1983–84 after being aggravated by U.S. assaults on European détente and economic interests in 1981–82. The United States disentangled itself and withdrew its surviving Marines from Lebanon in early 1984 after ensnaring itself there in 1982 in the first place. The deepening involvements in Central American from 1981 through 1985 slowly moved on to a path toward resolution in the latter half of the 1980s only because Congress kept the administration from excessive commitments to covert warfare. . . .

To understand the policy of the Reagan administration toward the Soviet Union, one must first understand the nature of the administration, especially Reagan's role. Reagan was unusually detached and distant from the daily implementation (and formulation) of policy, even though he ultimately determined its direction. [Secretary of State Alexander] Haig, failing to understand this arrangement so different from the Nixon administration, rather than becoming Reagan's "vicar" for foreign policy soon fell by the wayside. [Haig's successor George] Schultz understood and persisted quietly in pursuing a low-key policy of engagement. Reagan was in many ways like a ceremonial monarch, entirely dependent on his viziers and courtiers for his limited knowledge of what was going on in the outside world—and even in his own domain and court. For example, he was disbelieving when a reporter at a news conference informed him that the United States under his administration had become the world's greatest debtor nation. Similarly, ignorance and absence of interest in knowing the facts, rather than deliberate design, on the part of Reagan and many of his entourage led to unprecedented irresponsibility with respect to many charges against the Soviet Union. The message and "the script," based on his presumptions, were more important to him than the facts. Yet this indifference to reality not only impeded understanding but also undercut understanding between him and the Soviet leaders. For example, Reagan could not understand why Gorbachev would not believe him when Reagan offered to share the fruits of his strategic defense initiative (SDI)—unaware that not one of his own cabinet officers, members of Congress, or allied governments believed that either. . . .

As the Soviets appraised American policy during the first half of the 1980s they concluded that the turning point, in what they saw as a continuing process of change in the United States since 1976, was not the beginning of the Reagan administration in January 1981 but the sharp shift by President Carter in January 1980. From the standpoint of the Soviet leaders, first Carter and then Reagan had kicked over the card table, when all they had been doing (in their view) was playing the game—and not necessarily even winning, much less cheating. They were angered and perplexed. They naturally tended to see a dark design by the American leaders—a turn to militarism.

When the Soviet leaders described the change as a turn to "militarism" that term was not simply an epithet, but represented the common element in what they saw as mutually reinforcing changes in four crucial aspects of American policy toward the Soviet Union, and a fifth with respect to Soviet interests in the Third World.

First, the U.S. political line was seen as having shifted decisively, after several years of growing inclination, to an abandonment of détente. President Carter's across-the-board reaction to the Soviet intervention in Afghanistan was not recognized as having been caused by that event, but at most precipitated by it (most Soviet analysts described Afghanistan as but a pretext). Carter abandoned détente in practice in January 1980; Reagan disavowed détente explicitly. But Reagan then went on to replace the quest for political cooperation mixed with containment with a crusade against the communist system. In the Soviet view, a principal reason that détente was dropped by the United States was to stir up a more militant anti-Soviet atmosphere to gain public and congressional support for a major military buildup and assertion of global American hegemony.

Second, then, was the U.S. military program launched by President Carter in 1980, and again intensified by Reagan. In fact, the U.S. and NATO military buildup was traced to 1978, but only with the intermediate missile deployment decision in December 1979 and major U.S. military budget increases in 1980 was it really underway. In expenditures, if less in capabilities, it grew greatly until the mid-1980s. And this put pressure on the strained Soviet economy in its attempt to ensure continued parity.

Third was an ominous change in U.S. military doctrine, abandoning mutual deterrence based on parity and substituting a drive for superiority in war-waging capabilities in order to provide escalation dominance at all levels of nuclear and nonnuclear engagement. President Directive (PD)-59 under Carter in 1980 was the touchstone. . . . Again, the NATO missile deployment decision was seen as related to the war-waging capabilities sought to implement PD-59. Moreover, the American turn to seek war-waging superiority came after an explicit Soviet modification of military doctrine and renunciation of superiority and winnability of war in the nuclear age. The Reagan administration added the strategic defense initiative (SDI), seen as an attempt to neutralize the Soviet deterrent and give the United States a commanding superiority.

Fourth, rounding out the other three, was U.S. abandonment of arms control with the shelving of the SALT II Treaty by Carter in January 1980, confirmed by its explicit rejection by Reagan in 1981. The fact that the Carter administration faced serious difficulties in ratification even before Afghanistan was seen as largely owing to its own actions (in particular, stirring up a storm over a small Soviet military contingent in Cuba after years of ignoring its presence). Moreover, the Carter administration was prepared (even suspiciously ready) to pay for ratification with a major increase in military outlays. . . .

The Reagan administration abandoned all arms control efforts, only going through the motions of INF and START negotiations in 1982–83 to satisfy Western public opinion sufficiently to keep support for the INF deployment in Europe and for massive military programs at home. In 1983 came the challenge of a technological end run through the SDI. By 1985 the United States demonstratively abandoned the de facto acceptance of the SALT II force levels and sought to undermine the ABM [Anti-Ballistic Missile] Treaty by spurious reinterpretation. Again, after the Soviet Union had developed a serious interest in negotiating strategic arms limitations in the SALT process, the United States dropped out.

The fifth change was in U.S. resort to military force in the Third World to block or roll back what the Soviets regarded as progressive revolutionary change. The Carter Doctrine was seen as only the first step in an intensification of American reliance on military means to secure what were called "vital interests" but seemed to extend to any area, even where U.S. interests earlier had been minimal. It was a repudiation of the Nixon Doctrine [which had depended on allies to promote stability] and reflected an end to the "Vietnam syndrome" and restraint. And the Carter Doctrine was a robust challenge that sought to roll back the modestly favorable shift in the correlation of forces that the Soviet leaders had seen in this arena.

The Reagan administration took this legacy of a shift in American policy and drove it home. Reagan himself, and by and large the American people, saw the Reagan administration from 1981 through 1985 as pursuing a policy of peace through strength, containment of Soviet expansion, "restoration" of military power that had languished, a peaceful assertion of democratic values in an ideological challenge, and readiness to negotiate (from a strong position). But from Moscow it appeared that the Reagan administration sought to acquire military superiority in order to roll back a changing correlation of forces in the world, to negotiate if at all by exerting pressure, for a political-economic-ideological offensive against socialism and the USSR under the shadow of growing military power, and thus to attempt to reassert American dominance in the world against the Soviet Union. Finally, the Soviet Union was charged with being a focus of evil and an Evil Empire—in other words, the legitimacy of the very existence of Soviet rule and of the socialist system was challenged.

Even as the Reagan administration became less strident in its rhetoric, and more ready to negotiate, it also articulated the Reagan Doctrine on the reversibility of socialist revolutions and acted to encourage (and even instigate) insurgencies aimed at overthrowing Third World regimes aligned with the Soviet Union, and to call for democratic (noncommunist) government in the socialist commonwealth (Soviet bloc) itself. Thus in 1982–88 American assistance to groups seeking to overthrow the regimes in Nicaragua and Afghanistan increased in openness and in scale, and the United States began a more direct role in supporting similar efforts in Angola and Kampuchea.

The Carter administration after vacillation and then the Reagan administration with undisguised enthusiasm were seen to have chosen confrontation over détente and a striving for military superiority over mutual arms limitation.

As the Soviet leaders assessed the possibilities for improving or even stabilizing relations with the United States, still a Soviet aim, they thus remained skeptical. The one element they regarded as potentially the most significant but still quite uncertain was that political realities in the United States and the world might lead "realists" in U.S. ruling circles to shift back to a policy akin to what Nixon came to call "hardheaded détente," represented most closely by the positions held first by Haig and later Schultz, and at least rhetorically by Reagan after 1984. . . .

Despite the huge Reagan military buildup in the first half of the 1980s and the threat of the American SDI, Soviet defense spending continued from 1985 through 1988 to remain roughly constant as a share of Soviet gross national product (GNP). From 1989 through 1991, when Gorbachev was politically able to do it, Soviet military spending and procurement were cut sharply. The American impetus to the arms race, and still more the domestic influence of the Soviet military-industrial complex, kept Soviet expenditures from being cut earlier but did not lead to a matching increase. As the Soviet leaders in the mid-1980s contemplated the possible requirements to meet future American deployment of a strategic antimissile defense, they decided on an asymmetrical rather than a matching response. Even that would only have to occur to meet the contingency of an actual American deployment of ABM defense. The nature of the countermeasures would depend on the precise nature of the American deployment program. But as the 1980s progressed the SDI seemed less and less likely to yield a deployable defense system. Thus while the Soviet leaders in the mid-1980s were genuinely worried about a situation arising in which they would have to increase spending to offset an American strategic antiballistic missile defense, that prospect and that concern diminished. Moreover, the contingent future nature of any response, as well as its asymmetrical nature, neutralized and prevented the heavy burden on the Soviet defense budget and economy that the United States had expected and sought.

In retrospect, clearly the United States overrelied on deterrence and on intimidation in arms control. There was no consideration whatsoever by the Soviet leadership of any actions that the American military buildup deterred. Nor were the Soviet leaders in the first half of the 1980s intimidated into any political, military, or arms control concessions because of the American policy of negotiation from positions of strength. That this was the intention of the American leadership was not secret. For example, in the speech in which he introduced the SDI President Reagan had bragged of negotiating for strategic arms reductions from a "position of strength" based on enhanced strategic forces. Similarly, Secretary of State George Shultz spoke of how he and President Reagan were "determined to make American strength serve the cause of serious negotiations on behalf of American interests."

To be sure, in the late 1980s the Soviet leadership under Gorbachev did make concessions to many tough American positions in arms reduction negotiations: it settled for no more than its own unilateral reaffirmation of the ABM Treaty in its restrictive interpretation, it conceded many points in the strategic arms reductions talks (START) in order to get agreement, and it accepted the one-sided zero option for the Intermediate-range Nuclear Forces (INF) Treaty. These have often been cited as examples of Soviet capitulation to American firmness in negotiation and negotiation from a position of strength based on a military buildup the Soviet Union could not match. Yet if the Soviet leaders had not wanted such an outcome, they were not forced to accept it; they could simply have done without those arms control agreements. Moreover, they did not simply cave in to meet tough American positions. Gorbachev repeatedly took the initiative to go beyond American positions, to make greater sacrifices of Soviet military advantages than those called for by the United States, both in unilateral actions and in pushing the United States to go further in negotiations. He used the early Reagan propaganda stance on zero INF missiles rather than giving in to it (and he added the second zero for shorter-range INF missiles even though there too the Soviet Union had to destroy a far larger number of weapons). Gorbachev was ready to accept, and even to seek, a reduced Soviet weight in the balance of military power because he understood the broader political and even historical gains from overcoming the action-reaction arms race, irrespective of whether the arms competition was in pursuit of strategic advantage or merely to ensure a strategic deterrent balance. He sought not mutual deterrence, but mutual assurance. His goal was to end the arms race and the Cold War that spawned it, not merely to stabilize a perpetual deterrent balance (and still less to seek a phantom strategic superiority). . . .

In my earlier volume *Détente and Confrontation,* analyzing the rise and fall of the détente in American-Soviet relations in the 1970s, I adopted from other political scientists a categorization of three schools of thought in American approaches to dealing with the Soviet Union (with analogues in Soviet policy advocacy).

Those in the first school of policy, dominant in American policymaking in the early 1980s for the first time since the formative years of Cold War containment strategy in the 1950s, were called the essentialists. Ronald Reagan was the first president to come to office as a classical essentialist, that is, he saw the Soviet Union, in his words, as "an Evil Empire," led by leaders committed to an ideology sanctioning any means to attain its immutable aims, including absolute power and a communist world. The Soviet system was seen as totalitarian and exceedingly powerful and dangerous. Such an approach could not envisage anything but a protracted conflict, with no possibility for real accommodation and little if any positive value in negotiation. The appropriate America[n] policy was therefore confrontation with the Soviet Union, building American military power, and rallying the Western alliance and the whole Free World under American leadership to face the global communist menace.

The second school focused on Soviet behavior, rather than the essence of the Soviet system and its ideology. Though regarding the Soviet Union as an adversary, the advocates of this approach perceived the Soviet threat as primarily geopolitical. Although they saw a Soviet aim to expand Soviet influence in the world, they also regarded the Soviet Union as prudent and opportunistic, and responsive to incentives and to risks and costs. Hence, while skeptical of accommodation, the practitioners of this approach, who may be called mechanists or pragmatists, saw opportunities for U.S. policy to be used to manipulate American power and negotiation to influence and even to "manage" Soviet foreign policy behavior.

Advocates of the third, or interactionist, approach saw the sources of Soviet-American conflict not only as rooted in conflicting aims and ambitions, and in geopolitical more than ideological terms, as did the mechanists, but also as stemming from the dynamics of the competition itself. The conflict was driven by mutual perceptions and misperceptions as well as conflicts of interest. As with the mechanists conflict was seen more in geopolitical than ideological terms. Adherents of this approach varied in assessments of Soviet intentions and capabilities, but they tended to find an important reactive element in Soviet policy and interactive element in Soviet-American relations. Also pragmatists, interactionists agreed with mechanists that Soviet behavior was subject to external influence, but saw much wider possibilities for change and for American influence. They tended to find greater diversity in internal Soviet politics and therefore greater potential for evolution of the Soviet system. They also believed there was a greater learning process and feedback in foreign relations and greater interaction between the actions and policies of the two sides. While the mechanists relied on linkage and leverage with sticks and carrots (incentives and penalties) orchestrated by the United States to manage Soviet behavior, the interactionists saw less efficacy in attempts by the United States to manipulate Soviet policy and more need to deal with the Soviets directly on the basis of a balance of respective interests. Soviet policy was viewed not only as pursuing Soviet aims and objectives, but also as realistic and reactive and influenced by experience. Interactionists saw possibilities, and a need, for negotiation of common constraints, arms control, and rules of the game or a code of conduct to contain geopolitical competition. They also saw less opportunity and greater risks in unilateral American actions to impose constraints on the Soviet Union from a position of strength.

Although in practice many variations existed within these approaches, clearly the détente policy of Nixon and Kissinger, the diluted détente policy of Brzezinski, and the post-détente policy advocated by Haig, then Shultz, and later [Secretary of State James] Baker and [President George] Bush were within the mechanistic school. In the Carter administration, policy controversy stemmed from tension between the mechanistic geopolitical approach of Brzezinski and the interactionist approach of Vance. In the Reagan administration, Reagan set a confrontational tone with his essentialist declarations about the Soviet system as the focus of evil, although he proved less consistent in practice, and the tension of his administration shifted to a tug of war between mechanists and essentialists. Haig and Shultz were the main exponents of the mechanist approach, and [anti-Communist hardliners] William P. Clark, Richard Pipes, William Casey, Donald Regan, Caspar Weinberger, Richard Perle, and Jeane Kirkpatrick were among the most prominent essentialists. But what counted was Reagan himself, and he moved from being an essentialist in 1981–83 to becoming a mechanist after 1985 and ultimately even an interactionist. George Bush, too, and James Baker, from an initial mechanist position when they entered office in 1989, after nearly a year began, belatedly, to act more as interactionists, though still with mechanist tendencies, in 1990 and 1991. . . .

Although Ronald Reagan personified and dominated the years of confrontation, 1981 through 1983, Mikhail Gorbachev dominated the interactionist years of Soviet-American relations from 1986 through 1991. Moreover, the Soviet Union under Gorbachev moved from what had been a weak reactive posture in 1981–84 to assume the initiative from 1987 through 1989. By 1990–91, while U.S. policy remained largely reactive, so too did Gorbachev's leadership—but now both powers were reacting to events in Eastern Europe and the Soviet Union over which Gorbachev was losing control undercutting his ability to maintain the initiative with the United States.

In the post–Cold War years, under President Boris Yeltsin in Russia and both President Bush in 1992 and subsequently President Bill Clinton, American-Russian relations . . . continued to be based on an interactionist pattern.

In retrospect, it is clear that the single most significant factor not only in turning American-Soviet relations back from confrontation to détente and even beyond during the decade of the 1980s was the impact of Mikhail Gorbachev. Given the policies pursued by Reagan and later Bush, without Gorbachev American-Soviet relations throughout the 1980s and into the 1990s would almost certainly have continued on the same basic course as they did in 1984–85, with minor variations in a pattern of continuing competition. What made the difference was Gorbachev's determination to change the whole Soviet relationship with the world, to enter into the interdependent real world rather than continue a conflict between "two worlds," socialism and capitalism. Gorbachev was not merely an advocate of renewed détente. Détente, after all, was an easing of Cold War tensions between adversaries. Gorbachev did not merely want to reduce tensions; he set out to end the Cold War, to create a "common European home," to turn down decisively the arms race and demilitarize the East-West relationship, and to disengage from Soviet involvement in a geopolitical-ideological struggle in the Third World. To do this he was prepared to sacrifice Soviet political hegemony and military preponderance in Eastern Europe, to make disproportionate concessions in arms control (INF, START, and CFE), to withdraw Soviet troops from Afghanistan and Soviet support for Cuban troops in Angola and Ethiopia and Vietnamese troops in Cambodia, to work for resolution of regional conflicts and greater international cooperation in and through the United Nations and in many other ways, and to make "socialist" regimes everywhere stand or fall on the basis of accomplishment and popular mandate. He also was determined to press for radical transformation of the whole Soviet social-political-economic system. He advocated steps relevant to his changed international course: reducing military forces and outlays, reducing secrecy and control, meeting international standards of human rights, and reforming the Soviet economy so that it could enter the international economic system. . . .

Initially, . . . from 1985 to 1988 and to some extent to the end (1991), Gorbachev thought it possible to reform and revitalize the ideology of socialism, the Soviet social-economic-political system, the Communist Party, and the Union of Soviet Socialist Republics. But as he found various of his initial premises invalid, he changed them and was prepared to change his stand. He did not swim with the tide, although at times (especially from October 1990 to April 1991) he made tactical concessions on the pace of reform. He remained throughout an advocate of "socialism" and of democracy, which he regarded as mutually reinforcing. But he came eventually to see that the Communist Party of the Soviet Union was not able to reform itself. At first he had counted on a reformed party to lead *perestroika;* later he successfully neutralized the party as a potential obstacle, engineered its loss of a monopoly of power, and shunted it to the sidelines in 1990. He was not, as has sometimes been alleged, a prisoner of devotion to the Communist Party or to socialism in its Marxist-Leninist form. Gorbachev was ultimately stymied not by limits on his vision or his readiness to revise his understanding and his programs, but by opposition and ultimately by his inability to control the forces unleashed by his destruction of the old order. Hence, eventually the Soviet socialist system, the Soviet Union itself, and Gorbachev fell.

F U R T H E R   R E A D I N G

Timothy Garton Ash, *Free World* (2004)

Andrew J. Bacevich, *American Empire* (2002)

Robert H. Baker, *Hollow Victory* (2001)

Richard J. Barnet and John Cavanaugh, *Global Dreams: Imperial Corporations and the New World Order* (1994)

Donald C. Baucom, *The Origins of SDI, 1944–1983* (1992)

Larry Berman, ed., *Looking Back at the Reagan Presidency* (1990)

Paul Berman, *A Tale of Two Utopias* (1996)

William G. Berman, *America's Right Turn* (1994)

———, *From the Center to the Edge* (2001) (on the Clinton presidency)

Michael A. Bernstein et al., *Understanding America's Economic Decline* (1994)

Michael R. Beschloss and Strobe Talbott, *At the Highest Levels* (1993)

Jane Boulden, *Peace Enforcement: The United Nations Experience in Congo, Somalia, and Bosnia* (2002)

Paul Boyer, ed., *Reagan as President* (1990)

Seyom Brown, *The Illusion of Control* (2003)

Lester H. Brune, *The United States and Post Cold War Interventions* (1998)

David Callahan, *Between Two Worlds* (1994) (on post–Cold War affairs)

Fraser Cameron, *U.S. Foreign Policy After the Cold War* (2002)

Lou Cannon, *President Reagan* (1991)

James Chace, *The Consequences of Peace* (1992)

Noam Chomsky, *Hegemony or Survival* (2004)

Stephen Cohen, *Failed Crusade,* (2000)

Michael Cox, *U.S. Foreign Policy After the Cold War* (1999)

Ivo H. Daalder and James M. Lindsay, *America Unbound* (2003) (on George W. Bush)

Matthew Evangelista, *Unarmed Forces: The Transnational Movement to End the Cold War* (1999)

John Feffer, ed., *Power Trip* (2003)

Niall Ferguson, *Colossus: The Rise and Fall of the American Empire* (2005)

Beth A. Fisher, *The Reagan Reversal* (1997)

Frances Fitzgerald, *Way Out There* (2000) (on *Star Wars*)

Frederick H. Fleitz Jr., *Peacekeeping Fiascos of the 1990s* (2002)

Francis Fukuyama, *State-Building: Governance and World Order in the 21st Century* (2004)

Raymond L. Garthoff, *Détente and Confrontation* (1994)

Robert Gates, *From the Shadows* (1996)

Misha Glenny, *The Fall of Yugoslavia* (1992)

John Robert Greene, *The Presidency of George Bush* (2000)

David Halberstam, *War in a Time of Peace* (2001)

Stefan Halper and Jonathan Clarke, *America Alone: The Neo-Conservatives and the Global Order* (2004)

Jussi Hanhimaki, *The Flawed Architect* (2004) (on Kissinger)

Jim Hanson, *The Decline of the American Empire* (1993)

Erwin C. Hargrove, *Jimmy Carter as President* (1988)

Joan Hoff, *Nixon Reconsidered* (1994)

Stanley Hoffman, *World Disorders* (1999)

Michael J. Hogan, ed., *The End of the Cold War* (1992)

Samuel P. Huntington, *The Clash of Civilizations and the Remaking of World Order* (1996)

William G. Hyland, *Clinton's World* (1999)

John G. Ikenberry, ed., *America Unrivaled* (2002)

Walter Isaacson, *Kissinger* (1992)

William M. D. Jackson, "Soviet Assessments of Ronald Reagan," *Political Science Quarterly* 113 (1998–1999): 617–644

Robert Jervis and Seweryn Bialer, eds., *Soviet-American Relations After the Cold War* (1991)

Chalmers Johnson, *The Sorrow of Empire* (2004)

Haynes Johnson, *Sleepwalking Through History* (1991) (on Reagan)

———, *The Best of Times: America in the Clinton Years* (2002)

Charles O. Jones, *The Trusteeship Presidency* (1988) (on Carter)

Robert Kagan, *Of Paradise and Power* (2003) (on the U.S. and Europe)

Robert G. Kaiser, *How Gorbachev Happened* (1991)

George F. Kennan, "On American Principles," *Foreign Affairs* 75 (1995): 116–126

Paul Kennedy, *Preparing for the Next Century* (1993)

Ronald Kessler, *A Matter of Character* (2004) (on George W. Bush)

Henry A. Kissinger, *Does America Need a Foreign Policy?* (2000)

Stephen Kotkin, *Armageddon Averted* (2001)

Charles A. Kupchan, *The End of the American Era* (2002)

Richard Ned Lebow, *We All Lost the Cold War* (1994)

Robert J. Leiber, *Eagle Adrift* (1997)

Thomas Lippman, *Madeleine Albright and the New American Diplomacy* (2000)

Matthew McAllester, *Beyond the Mountains of the Damned: The War Inside Kosovo* (2002)

Michael McCgwire, *Perestroika and Soviet National Security* (1991)

Robert J. McMahon, "Making Sense of American Foreign Policy During the Reagan Years," *Diplomatic History* 19 (1995): 367–384

John J. Mearshimer, *The Tragedy of Great Power Politics* (2001)

Morris Morley, *Crisis and Confrontation* (1988)

Henry R. Nau, *The Myth of America's Decline* (1990)

Joseph S. Nye Jr., *The Paradox of American Power* (2002)

Don Oberdorfer, *From the Cold War to a New Era* (1998)

William E. Odom and Robert Dujarric, *America's Inadvertent Empire* (2004)

S. Victor Papacosma et al., *NATO After Fifty Years* (2001)

Herbert S. Parmet, *George Bush* (1998)

Joseph E. Persico, *Casey* (1990)

Kevin Phillips, *American Dynasty* (2004) (on the Bush family)

Richard Pipes, *U.S.-Soviet Relations in the Era of Détente* (1981)

Ronald E. Powaski, *Return to Armageddon* (2003)

John Prados, *President's Secret Wars* (1996)

Clyde Prestowicz, *Rogue Nation* (2004) (on U.S. unilateralism)

Miron Rezan, *Europe's Nightmare: The Struggle for Kosovo* (2001)

Richard Rosencrance, *America's Economic Resurgence* (1990)

Michael Schaller, *Reckoning with Reagan* (1992)

Peter Schweitzer, *Reagan's War* (2002)
Melvin Small, *The Presidency of Richard Nixon* (1999)
Gaddis Smith, *Morality, Reason, and Power* (1986) (on Carter)
Leonard S. Spector, *Nuclear Ambitions* (1990)
James Gustave Speth, *Red Sky at Morning* (2004) (on the global environment)
Ronald Steel, *Temptations of a Superpower* (1996)
Robert Strong, *Working in the World* (2002) (on Carter)
Ralph Summy and Michael E. Salla, *Why the Cold War Ended* (1995)
Jeremi Suri, *Power and Protest: Global Revolution and the Rise of Détente* (2004)
William K. Tabb, *Economic Governance in the Age of Globalization* (2004)
Emmanuel Todd, *After the Empire* (2004)
Robert W. Tucker and David C. Hendrickson, *The Imperial Temptation* (1992)
Peter Wallison, *Ronald Reagan* (2002)
Garry Wills, "Habits of Hegemony," *Foreign Affairs* 78 (1999): 50–59
Vladislav M. Zubok, "New Evidence on the 'Soviet Factor' in the Peaceful Revolutions of 1989," *Cold War International History Project Bulletin* 12–13 (2001): 5–14

CHAPTER
15

September 11, 2001, and Anti-Americanism in the Muslim World

On September 20, 2001, nine days after the horrific attacks on the World Trade
Center in New York City and the Pentagon in Washington, D.C., President George W.
Bush addressed a joint session of Congress. Over the previous week the press reported
that the deadliest terrorist attack in U.S. history, with nearly 3,000 casualties, had
been executed by an Islamic group known as al Qaeda, a shadowy, global network
led by Osama bin Laden, a wealthy Saudi Arabian. "Why do they hate us?" the
president asked. Resentment of American freedom? Hatred for U.S. backed governments in the Middle East? Intolerance for Christians and Jews? The president's
question spoke to an ongoing scholarly debate. Was Islamic culture inherently
violent? Or had al Qaeda hijacked the religion? Was Muslim anger a response to
U.S. policies in the Middle East? Or did it spring from political and cultural conflicts that had long wracked the region?

    The United States is only the most recent external power to exercise influence
in the Middle East. From the sixteenth century until World War I, the Ottoman
Turks ruled most of the region. Following the Turks' defeat in World War I, the
victorious British and French forged a new political order in the Middle East by
creating new states, redrawing boundaries, and striking alliances with local
rulers. American missionaries established a presence in the Arab world during
the nineteenth century, but it was World War II that eroded European imperialism and ushered U.S. power into the region. During the war, President Franklin
Roosevelt anointed King Ibn Saud's Saudi Arabia—which had earlier granted
a concession to the Standard Oil Company of California—as America's favored
Middle East oil supplier. Then, in 1946, after blunting Soviet influence in oil-rich
Iran, Washington initiated a partnership with Shah Mohammed Reza Pahlavi.
While oil fueled America's military and drove global capitalism, petroleum politics strengthened corrupt autocracies, widened the gap between rich and poor,
and embittered many Muslims.

U.S. support for Israel also stirred discord. After World War II, the United
Nations backed a partition of the British mandate in Palestine and the creation
of two political entities—one Jewish and one Palestinian. Israelis, however,
in May 1948, unilaterally declared the creation of a Jewish state, and won diplomatic recognition from both Washington and Moscow. Hundreds of thousands
of Palestinian refugees spilled across borders; and Egypt, Jordan, and Syria
sent armies into Palestine to engage Israeli forces in the first Arab-Israeli War
(1948–1949).

During the 1950s and 1960s Washington's anticommunist containment
policies increasingly impinged on the region. Arab nationalists applauded Egypt's
Gamal Abdel Nasser's denunciations of U.S.-sponsored military alliances, his nationalization of the British- and French-run Suez Canal, and his showdown with
a British-French-Israeli invasion during the Suez Crisis. The Eisenhower administration applied pressure on U.S. allies to abandon their military operation, but
viewed Nasser's rising stature with alarm. In 1957 the Congress approved the
Eisenhower Doctrine, authorizing the dispatch of U.S. troops to any Mideast nation
that requested help in resisting international communism. The following year
U.S. Marines landed on Lebanon's shores to bolster a pro-Western regime. Arab
frustrations mounted following Nasser's devastating setback in the Six Day War
of June 1967, when victorious Israeli troops seized Jordan's West Bank, including the Holy City of Jerusalem, Syria's Golan Heights, and Egypt's Sinai Peninsula and Gaza Strip. Washington's willingness to supply Israel with advanced
weaponry, and Tel Aviv's cool response to UN peace initiatives, fed a growing
anti-Americanism in the region.

The Arab-Israeli conflict escalated following the Six Day War. Palestinians
living under Israeli occupation in the West Bank and Gaza looked to Yasir Arafat
and the militant Palestinian Liberation Organization (PLO) for leadership. But
not a third Arab-Israeli clash, the Yom Kippur War of October 1973, or an oil embargo orchestrated by the Organization of Petroleum Exporting Countries (OPEC)
dislodged the Israelis or blocked new Jewish settlements in the former Arab lands.
The Camp David Accords between Egypt's Anwar Sadat and Israel's Menachem
Begin in 1978, brokered by President Jimmy Carter (1977–1981), provided for
Israel's withdrawal from the Sinai, and Egypt's recognition of the Jewish state,
but left unresolved the status of other occupied territories.

In early 1979, Iran's Islamic revolution unseated Shah Reza Pahlavi and
unleashed a torrent of anti-American fury. The Soviet invasion and occupation of
Afghanistan (1979–1989) prompted resistance from an extremist Taliban theocracy
that eventually took power in Kabul. Israel's invasion of Lebanon (1982), terrorist
retribution by the PLO, Hamas, and Hezbollah—including the bombing of a U.S.
Marine barracks in Beirut—and the Iran-Iraq War (1980–1985) further unhinged
the region. Iraq's invasion of oil-rich Kuwait in August 1990 momentarily aligned
Israel, Egypt, Saudi Arabia, and Syria in a U.S.-led coalition that turned back
Saddam Hussein's war machine, but neither the administration of George Bush
(1989–1993) nor that of Bill Clinton (1993–2001) succeeded in sealing an Arab-
Israeli peace. In the 1993 Oslo Accords, Tel Aviv agreed to hand over Gaza and the
West Bank city of Jericho to a transitional Palestinian Authority. But negotiations
for additional land transfers and Palestinian statehood stalled over the question of
permanent borders, the status of Jerusalem, and the return of Palestinian refugees.
A Palestinian Intifada or uprising, in the occupied territories in September 2000,
and Israel's military crackdown, further dimmed the prospects for peace.

Nor did the U.S. triumph over Iraq in 1991 pacify the Gulf region. Hussein survived the war, and the Saudi kingdom, a home for U.S. military bases, became a recruiting ground for Osama bin Laden's al Qaeda. When the attacks of September 11, 2001, came, the George W. Bush administration (2001–) vowed an unrelenting war against global terrorism. By December, the U.S. military demolished the Taliban regime in Afghanistan, which had provided haven to al Qaeda, but bin Laden eluded capture. Bush next proclaimed Iraq, Iran, and North Korea an "axis of evil," citing their nuclear weapons programs and their links to terrorism, and in November 2002, Congress approved the use of force against Iraq. The UN Security Council found Baghdad in breach of post–Gulf War resolutions prohibiting development of weapons of mass destruction, but the Iraqi dictator denied the charges and readmitted UN weapons inspectors, whom he had ousted in 1998. When the Security Council refused to back a war resolution, Bush assembled a coalition of willing allies and launched a war on Iraq on March 20, 2003. The coalition quickly toppled and arrested Saddam Hussein, but a deadly guerrilla resistance to the U.S.-led occupation ensued. U.S. troops failed to turn up Iraqi nuclear weapons, and the bipartisan September 11 Commission, appointed by the president, disputed the alleged ties between Iraq and al Qaeda. President Bush nonetheless won a victory in the 2004 presidential election, in which he defended the war on Iraq as an integral part of America's war on terror and the spread of democracy worldwide.

The chronology of events supports conflicting explanations for Middle Eastern anti-Americanism. Some scholars argue that deep cultural differences separate the West and the Muslim world. The "clash of civilizations" thesis posits that Islamic leaders have dodged the need for democratic reform and deflected criticism by denouncing all vestiges of Westernization. Others trace Muslim rage primarily to U.S. policies in the Middle East: the pursuit of oil, single-minded anticommunism, support for corrupt Arab autocracies, and Washington's staunch backing for Israel. Some analysts fault European and U.S. officials for feeding into cultural stereotypes by interpreting the Muslim world through the prism of "orientalism," a set of perceptions that highlight the Middle East's exoticism and "otherness." Finally, some observers see in Arab terrorism an anguished response to the dislocation inflicted by economic, political, and cultural globalization—the revenge of the territorially dispossessed and economically disadvantaged.

Why do they hate us? The answers are many. America's ability and willingness to formulate a historically based understanding of Muslim anger may determine the long-term security of the United States.

🌐 D O C U M E N T S

In February 1945, President Roosevelt met with King Abdul Aziz Ibn Saud, head of the state of Saudi Arabia, aboard the USS *Quincy* in the Suez Canal. The two established the fundamentals of an enduring relationship: The United States pledged to provide for Saudi security needs in exchange for access to Saudi oil. The monarch also raised concerns about the growing presence of Jewish settlers in Palestine. Document 1 is a reprint of a letter from Roosevelt to Ibn Saud, dated April 5, 1945, in which FDR assured the king that no decision would be taken on Palestine's future without consultation with both Jews and Arabs. World War II and Nazi genocide, however, increased pressure for a Jewish homeland in the British mandate of Palestine. When the British announced their intention to withdraw from the Holy Land, the United State backed a UN resolution on November 29, 1947, to partition Palestine into separate Jewish and Arab states. But mounting violence between Jews and Arabs in the territory raised American concerns. Document 2 is a draft National Security Council memorandum, penned in February 1948, which weighs the pros and cons of partition and its alternatives. The NSC recommended that partition be delayed, but on May 14, 1948, the state of Israel was proclaimed, and the White House extended diplomatic recognition within hours. Critics at the time suspected that Truman was seeking Jewish votes in the upcoming election—a charge the president denied.

During the mid-1950s and early 1960s Egyptian president Gamal Abdel Nasser emerged as a leading voice for Arab nationalism. In 1955, when the Cold War neutralist accepted arms from the Soviet camp, the administration of Dwight D. Eisenhower canceled loans intended to help build the Aswan Dam. Nasser, in turn, nationalized the Suez Canal. Document 3, is drawn from a July 28, 1956, speech in which Nasser blasts European imperialism and justifies Egypt's takeover of the canal. Israel's decisive victory over Egypt and its allies in the Six Day War of June 1967 tarnished Nasser's image. After supporting Israel in the conflict, the Lyndon B. Johnson administration tried to soothe Arab anti-Americanism by backing UN Resolution 242, which called upon Israel to relinquish recently occupied territories in exchange for recognition and peace. Meanwhile, the Palestinian Liberation Organization (PLO) took up the cause of displaced Arabs and issued its National Covenant, Document 4, in July 1968—a strident condemnation of "Zionist invasion" and Western imperialism.

During the 1970s Islamic extremism shook the Middle East. In 1979 the U.S.-backed Shah of Iran was swept aside by the Ayatollah Khomeini's Islamic revolution. In November, Iranian students stormed the American embassy in Tehran and took U.S. citizens hostage, initiating an excruciating fourteen month–long hostage crisis. In December 1979, Soviet troops marched into neighboring Afghanistan to bolster a client Marxist government. President Jimmy Carter extended covert support for the anti-communist Afghan *mujahadeen,* a program that was expanded by the Reagan administration. Document 5 is an excerpt from Carter's State of the Union address, delivered on January 23, 1980, in which the president enunciated the "Carter Doctrine"—the United States would use military force to counter aggression by outside forces in the Persian Gulf. In Document 6, an address to Congress on September 11, 1990, President George Bush emphasized both principle and U.S. interest in Persian Gulf oil to rally the nation against Iraq's conquest of Kuwait and build a "new world order" based on the rule of law.

Saddam Hussein's defeat in the Persian Gulf War was followed by momentary progress in the Arab-Israeli peace process. In September 1993 President Bill Clinton welcomed Israeli Prime Minister Yitzhak Rabin and PLO chairman Yasir Arafat to Washington to sign the Oslo Accords that arranged a transfer of occupied land to the Palestinian Authority. Document 7 is Rabin's plea for peace made at the White House signing ceremony on September 13, 1993. Rabin was later assassinated by an Israeli extremist, and his Labor party was voted out of office and replaced by a conservative Likud government.

As hopes for an Arab-Israeli peace faded, a new wave of global terrorism targeted the United States. Based in post-Soviet Afghanistan, al Qaeda launched its first attack on New York's World Trade Center in 1993 when a truck bomb killed seven and injured more than a thousand others. Five years later bin Laden's forces engineered the simultaneous bombing of U.S. embassies in Dar es Salaam, Tanzania, and Nairobi, Kenya, killing 258 people. In 2000 a suicide attack on the USS *Cole* off the coast of Yemen killed

17 U.S. servicemen. Then came the attacks on the World Trade Center and Pentagon on September 11, 2001. On September 20, President George W. Bush addressed the Congress and the nation, demanding that Afghanistan's Islamic, Taliban government deliver al Qaeda's leaders to U.S. authorities and declaring a "war on terror." Bush also posed the question: Why do they hate us? The speech is reprinted here as Document 8. On October 7, 2001, after the United States had begun military operations in Afghanistan, the Arab television news network al Jezeera broadcast a defiant speech from Osama bin Laden (Document 9). The Bush administration next charged that Iraq's nuclear weapons program and ties to international terrorism posed an imminent threat to the United States. U.S. and coalition forces in March 2003 launched a preemptive war that ousted Saddam Hussein from power and engaged a ferocious guerrilla insurgency. When U.S. authorities acknowledged the nonexistence of Iraq's alleged nuclear weapons, a chorus of critics questioned the war's legitimacy. Undeterred, the Bush White House refused to set a timetable for withdrawal of U.S. troops and prodded Iraq's provisional government to hold elections for a transitional national assembly. In Document 10, an excerpt from Bush's State of the Union address on February 2, 2005, the president worked to bolster his defense of the war by pledging that the U.S. military effort would democratize Iraq and spread liberty across the Middle East.

1. President Franklin D. Roosevelt
Befriends King Ibn Saud, 1945

I have received the communication which Your Majesty sent me under date of March 10, 1945, in which you refer to the question of Palestine and to the continuing interest of the Arabs in current developments affecting that country.

I am gratified that Your Majesty took this occasion to bring your views on this question to my attention and I have given the most careful attention to the statements which you make in your letter. I am also mindful of the memorable conversation which we had not so long ago and in the course of which I had an opportunity to obtain so vivid an impression of Your Majesty's sentiments on this question.

Your Majesty will recall that on previous occasions I communicated to you the attitude of the American Government toward Palestine and made clear our desire that no decision be taken with respect to the basic situation in that country without full consultation with both Arabs and Jews. Your Majesty will also doubtless recall that during our recent conversation I assured you that I would take no action, in my capacity as Chief of the Executive Branch of this Government, which might prove hostile to the Arab people.

It gives me pleasure to renew to Your Majesty the assurances which you have previously received regarding the attitude of my Government and my own, as Chief Executive, with regard to the question of Palestine and to inform you that the policy of this Government in this respect is unchanged.

I desire also at this time to send you my best wishes for Your Majesty's continued good health and for the welfare of your people.

This document can be found in *Department of State Bulletin* (21 October 1945): 623.

2. The National Security Council Weighs
U.S. Options in the Middle East, 1948

The United States Government, on the basis of high motives and in consideration of conditions existing at the time, voted in favor of the General Assembly Resolution of 29 November 1947, recommending the Plan for Partition of Palestine. In so doing our government assumed a moral obligation, along with the other members of the UN who voted for the resolution, to lend its support honestly and courageously to the implementation of that resolution. Our government cannot without cause fail to fulfill this moral obligation. The most impelling cause for any change in our position on the Palestine problem would be a demonstration of the incompatibility of our present position with the security of our own nation.

The greatest threat to the security of the United States and to international peace is the USSR and its aggressive program of Communist expansion.

In meeting this threat, the United States cannot take steps which disregard the following considerations:

a. Unrestricted access to the oil resources of the Middle east is essential to the complete economy of the United States and to the economic recovery of Europe under the ERP [European Recovery Program].
b. In the event of war, the oil and certain strategic areas of the Middle East will figure prominently in the successful prosecution of such a war by the United States.
c. A friendly or at least a neutral attitude by the Arab peoples toward the US and its interests is requisite to the procurement of adequate quantities of oil for the purposes as stated and to the utilization of strategic areas without prohibitive cost in the event of war.

The United States cannot afford to allow the USSR to gain a lodgment in the Eastern Mediterranean. The Joint Chiefs of Staff have emphasized their view that, of all the possible eventualities in the Palestine situation, the most unfavorable in the security interests of the United States would be the intrusion of Soviet forces and, second only to that the introduction of US troops in opposition to possible Arab resistance. . . .

The affirmative vote of the United States upon the UN Plan for Partition of Palestine, and the pressure applied to other governments by various US groups and individuals, have antagonized the Arab peoples to an unprecedented degree. Competent observers of Arab psychology predict that increasing animosity will attend each further manifestation of US leadership in or support of implementation of the Plan for Partition. Consideration must be given to the fact that the Arab people sincerely believe in the righteousness of their opposition to Palestine partition, which imposes upon them the major initial cost of attempting a solution to the international problem of Zionism. . . .

This document can be found in Draft: "The Position of the United States with Respect to Palestine," 17 February 1948, Papers of Clark M. Clifford, Harry S. Truman Library, Independence, Missouri. It can also be found in Dennis Merrill, ed., *Documentary History of the Truman Presidency,* (Bethesda, Md.: University Publications of America, 1998) XXVI, 49–64.

Fundamental to the Plan for Partition of Palestine is economic union between the proposed Jewish and Arab States. The Arabs have announced their implacable opposition to the establishment of the contemplated Arab State in Palestine, and there is no indication that the Jews and Arabs of Palestine have made any conciliatory moves to effect a compromise solution. Severe fighting has broken out between the Jews and Arabs of Palestine. These and other developments, since the General Assembly adoption of the Palestine resolution, raise grave doubts that the proposed solution to the Palestine problem is the one most conducive to the security of the US, the increased prestige of the UN, and to the peace of the world. . . .

The security of the United States, the peace of the world, and the preservation of the UN, dictate that all possible courses of action by this government be reexamined to determine the one with most promise of success to each of these objectives.

Alternative US courses of action with respect to the Palestine question are:

a. Fully support the partition plan with all the means at our disposal, including the use of armed forces under the United Nations.

Under this course of action, the United States would have to take steps to grant substantial economic assistance to the Jewish authorities and to afford them support through the supply of arms, ammunition and implements of war. In order to enable the Jewish state to survive in the face of wide-scale resistance from the Arabs in Palestine, from the neighboring Arab States, and possibly from other Moslem countries, the United States would be prepared ultimately to utilize its naval units and military forces for this purpose. . . .

(1) Advantages.

(a) Maintains UN and US policy constant in the eyes of the world.

(b) Contributes to the settlement of the displaced Jews of Europe.

(2) Disadvantages.

(a) Alienates the Moslem world with the resultant threat of:

1. Suspension or cancellation of US air base rights and commercial concessions including oil, and drastic curtailment of US trade in the area.

2. Loss of access to British air, military and naval facilities in the area, affecting our strategic position in the Middle East and Mediterranean.

3. Closing of our educational, religious and philanthropic institutions in the area.

4. Possible deaths, injuries and damages arising from acts of violence against individual US citizens and interests throughout the Middle East.

5. A serious impediment to the success of the European Recovery Program, which is dependent on increased production of Middle East oil.

(b) Provides a vehicle for Soviet expansion into an area vital to our security interests.

(c) Deploys US troops in a situation where there is high probability of loss of American lives and which might result in war. . . .

b. Continuation of support for the Partition Plan in the United Nations by all measures short of the use of outside armed force to impose the Plan upon the people of Palestine.

In this course of action United States representatives in the UN Security Council, the Trusteeship Council and the Economic and Social Council would continue to support the implementation of the General Assembly recommendations on Palestine. Such support should take into account, however, that the Charter does not authorize the imposition of a recommended settlement upon the people directly concerned by armed action of the United Nations or its Members. . . .

(1) Advantages.
  (a) Maintains the announced policy of the United States with respect to Palestine so long as such policy appears to have any reasonable opportunity for implementation.
  (b) Retains the responsibility for consideration of the Palestine question within the framework of the United Nations, distributes the responsibility throughout the UN membership, and prevents it from becoming still further a matter of United States responsibility.
  (c) Assures a certain amount of political support from elements in the major political parties within the United States.
  (d) Contributes to the settlement of the displaced Jews of Europe.
(2) Disadvantages.
  (a) Leads to continued deterioration of Arab relations with the United States. . . .
  (b) Permits further exploitation of the interests of world Zionism by the USSR.
  (c) Entails further loss of life while waiting for a conclusive demonstration that outside force will be required to preserve law and order within Palestine.
  (d) Encourages the Arabs within Palestine to increase their resistance by all available means.
  (e) In the event of implementation of partition, provides a vehicle for Soviet expansion into an area vital to our interests.
  (f) Threatens the success of the European Recovery Program, which is dependent on increased production of Middle East oil.

c. Adopt a passive or neutral role, taking no further steps to aid or implement partition.

This course of action would involve maintenance and enforcement of the present United States embargo on arms to Palestine and the neighboring countries. The United States would give no unilateral assistance to either the proposed Jewish or Arab States financially, militarily or otherwise, and insofar as possible, the United States would require an attitude of neutrality to be observed by all persons or organizations under US jurisdiction. The United States would oppose sending armed forces into Palestine by the United Nations or any member thereof for the purpose of implementing partition, and would oppose the recruitment of volunteers for this purpose.

Such a course of action would rest on the assumption that implementation of the General Assembly resolution was a collective responsibility of the United Nations and that no leadership in the matter devolved upon the United States. . . .

(1) Advantages.

    (a) Maintains United Nations and United States policy constant in the eyes of the world.

    (b) Avoids employment of US troops in Palestine.

(2) Disadvantages.

    (a) Surrenders US initiative in the solution of the Palestine problem.

    (b) Permits communist encouragement of chaos.

    (c) Possibly results in Russian intervention on a unilateral basis.

    (d) Exposes the United States to possible curtailment of air base rights and commercial concessions including oil, and to a lesser degree to drastic curtailment of US trade in the area.

d. Alter our previous policy of support for partition and seek another solution to the problem.

This course of action would call for a special session of the General Assembly to reconsider the situation. Abandoning US support of partition as impracticable and unworkable in view of the demonstrated inability of the people of Palestine to assume the responsibilities of self-government, and in view of the report of the [UN] Palestine Commission that outside military forces would be required, the United States would, under this course of action, attempt to seek a constructive solution of the problem. . . .

Specifically the United States would endeavor to bring about conciliation of the problem. The United States would propose that while working for such conciliation or arbitration, a special session of the General Assembly be called to consider a new solution in the form of

(1) An international trusteeship or

(2) A federal state,

with provision for Jewish immigration in either case, and preferably excluding the use of either US or USSR troops.

A trusteeship could take one of several forms; a three-power trusteeship of the US, UK and France, and joint US-UK trusteeship either with or without some of the smaller states, or a general UN trusteeship with the Trusteeship Council as administering authority. Alternatively, a federal state with cantonization, a plan which the British originally favored as having the greatest chance of success, could be discussed.

(1) Advantages.

    (a) Assists in preventing Communist expansion into the Middle East and the Mediterranean.

    (b) Improves our strategic position in the Middle East, thereby enhancing our overall national security.

    (c) Opens the way for restorations of US friendship and influence in the Arab world.

    (d) Opens the way for a solution to the Palestine problem more acceptable to the people of Palestine.

(e) Lessens probability of use of US military forces in combat in Palestine.

(f) Protects our philanthropic and educational interests, investments and oil interests.

(2) Disadvantages.

(a) Produces violent Zionist opposition.

(b) Gives Russia and its Communist satellites a sounding board for further vitriolic vituperations.

(c) Requires the General Assembly to find another solution for the Palestine question without any present assurance of success.

3. Egypt's Gamal Abdel Nasser Justifies Nationalizing the Suez Canal, 1956

The uproar which we anticipated has been taking place in London and Paris. This tremendous uproar is not supported by reason or logic. It is backed only by imperialist methods, by the habits of blood-sucking and of usurping rights, and by interference in the affairs of other countries. An unjustified uproar arose in London, and yesterday Britain submitted a protest to Egypt. I wonder what was the basis of this protest by Britain to Egypt? The Suez Canal Company is an Egyptian company, subject to Egyptian sovereignty. When we nationalized the Suez Canal Company, we only nationalized an Egyptian limited company, and by doing so we exercised a right which stems from the very core of Egyptian sovereignty. What right has Britain to interfere in our internal affairs? What right has Britain to interfere in our affairs and our questions? When we nationalized the Suez Canal Company, we only performed an act stemming from the very heart of our sovereignty. The Suez Canal Company is a limited company, awarded a concession by the Egyptian Government in 1865 to carry out its tasks. Today we withdraw the concession in order to do the job ourselves.

Although we have withdrawn this concession, we shall compensate shareholders of the company, despite the fact that they usurped our rights. Britain usurped 44 per cent of the shares free of charge. Today we shall pay her for her 44 per cent of the shares. We do not treat her as she treated us. We are not usurping the 44 per cent as she did. We do not tell Britain that we shall usurp her right as she usurped ours, but we tell her that we shall compensate her and forget the past.

The Suez Canal would have been restored to us in 12 years. What would have happened in 12 years' time? Would an uproar have been raised? What has happened now has disclosed hidden intentions and has unmasked Britain. If the canal was to fall to us in 12 years, why should it not be restored to us now? Why should it cause an uproar? We understand by this that they had no intention of fulfilling this pledge 12 years from now. What difference is it if the canal is restored to us now or in 12 years' time? Why should Britain say this will affect shipping in the canal? Would it have affected shipping 12 years hence?

This document can be found in the *Summary of World Broadcasts,* Part IV, Daily Series, 6, 30 July 1956, British Broadcasting Corporation, London, UK. It can also be found in T. G. Fraser, *The Middle East, 1914–1979* (New York: St. Martin's Press, 1980), 88–89.

Shipping in the Suez Canal has been normal for the past 48 hours from the time of nationalization until now. Shipping continued and is normal. We nationalized the company. We have not interfered with shipping, and we are facilitating shipping matters. However, I emphatically warn the imperialist countries that their tricks, provocations and interference will be the reason for any hindrance to shipping. I place full responsibility on Britain and France for any curtailment of shipping in the Suez Canal when I state that Egypt will maintain freedom of shipping in the Suez Canal, and that since Egypt nationalized the Suez Canal Company shipping has been normal. Even before that we maintained freedom of shipping in the canal. Who has protected the canal? The canal has been under Egyptian protection because it is part of Egypt and we are the ones who should ensure freedom of shipping. We protect it today, we protected it a month ago, and we protected it for years because it is our territory and a part of our territory. Today we shall continue to protect the canal. But, because of the tricks they are playing, I hold Britain and France responsible for any consequences which may affect shipping.

Compatriots, we shall maintain our independence and sovereignty. The Suez Canal Company has become our property, and the Egyptian flag flies over it. We shall hold it with our blood and strength, and we shall meet aggression with aggression and evil with evil. We shall proceed towards achieving dignity and prestige for Egypt and building a sound national economy and true freedom. Peace be with you.

4. The Palestinian National Covenant Calls for the Liberation of Palestine, 1968

Palestine is the homeland of the Palestinian Arab people and an integral part of the great Arab homeland, and the people of Palestine is a part of the Arab nation.

Palestine with its boundaries that existed at the time of the British mandate is an integral regional unit.

The Palestinian Arab people possesses the legal right to its homeland, and when the liberation of its homeland is completed it will exercise self-determination solely according to its own will and choice.

The Palestinian personality is an innate, persistent characteristic that does not disappear, and it is transferred from fathers to sons. The Zionist occupation, and the dispersal of the Palestinian Arab people as a result of the disasters which came over it, do not deprive it of its Palestinian personality and affiliation and do not nullify them.

The Palestinians are the Arab citizens who were living permanently in Palestine until 1947, whether they were expelled from there or remained. Whoever is born to a Palestinian Arab father after this date, within Palestine or outside it, is a Palestinian.

Jews who were living permanently in Palestine until the beginning of the Zionist invasion will be considered Palestinians.

The Palestinian affiliation and the material, spiritual and historical tie with Palestine are permanent realities. The upbringing of the Palestinian individual in an Arab and revolutionary fashion, the undertaking of all means of forging consciousness and

This document can be found in Walter Laqueur and Barry Rubin, eds., *The Israel-Arab Reader: A Documentary History of the Middle East Conflict* (New York: Penguin Books, 1995), 218–222.

training the Palestinian, in order to acquaint him profoundly with his homeland, spiritually and materially, and preparing him for the conflict and the armed struggle, as well as for the sacrifice of his property and his life to restore his homeland, until the liberation of all this is a national duty.

The phase in which the people of Palestine is living is that of national struggle for the liberation of Palestine. Therefore, the contradictions among the Palestinian national forces are of secondary order which must be suspended in the interest of the fundamental contradiction between Zionism and colonialism on the one side and the Palestinian Arab people on the other. On this basis, the Palestinian masses, whether in the homeland or in places of exile, organizations and individuals, comprise one national front which acts to restore Palestine and liberate it through armed struggle.

Armed struggle is the only way to liberate Palestine and is therefore a strategy and not tactics. The Palestinian Arab people affirms its absolute resolution and abiding determination to pursue the armed struggle and to march forward towards the armed popular revolution, to liberate its homeland and return to it [to maintain] its right to a natural life in it, and to exercise its right of self-determination in it and sovereignty over it. . . .

The Palestinian Arab people believes in Arab unity. In order to fulfill its role in realizing this, it must preserve, in this phase of its national struggle, its Palestinian personality and the constituents thereof, increase consciousness of its existence and resist any plan that tends to disintegrate or weaken it. . . .

The destiny of the Arab nation, indeed the very Arab existence, depends upon the destiny of the Palestine issue. The endeavour and effort of the Arab nation to liberate Palestine follows from this connection. The people of Palestine assumes its vanguard role in realizing this sacred national aim.

The liberation of Palestine, from an Arab viewpoint, is a national duty to repulse the Zionist, Imperialist invasion from the great Arab homeland and to purge the Zionist presence from Palestine. Its full responsibility falls upon the Arab nation, peoples and governments, with the Palestinian Arab people at their head. For this purpose, the Arab nation must mobilize all its military, human, material and spiritual capacities to participate actively with the people of Palestine in the liberation of Palestine. They must especially in the present stage of armed Palestinian revolution, grant and offer the people of Palestine all possible help and every material and human support, and afford it every sure means and opportunity enabling it to continue to assume its vanguard role in pursuing its armed revolution until the liberation of its homeland.

The liberation of Palestine, from a spiritual viewpoint, will prepare an atmosphere of tranquillity and peace for the Holy Land in the shade of which all the Holy Places will be safeguarded, and freedom of worship and visitation to all will be guaranteed, without distinction or discrimination of race, colour, language or religion. For this reason, the people of Palestine looks to the support of all the spiritual forces in the world.

The liberation of Palestine, from a human viewpoint, will restore to the Palestinian man his dignity, glory and freedom. For this, the Palestinian Arab people looks to the support of those in the world who believe in the dignity and freedom of man.

The liberation of Palestine, from an international viewpoint is a defensive act necessitated by the requirements of self-defence. For this reason the Arab people of Palestine, desiring to befriend all peoples, looks to the support of the states which love freedom, justice and peace in restoring the legal situation to Palestine, establishing security and peace in its territory, and enabling its people to exercise national sovereignty and national freedom. . . .

To realize the aims of this covenant and its principles the Palestine Liberation Organization will undertake its full role in liberating Palestine.

The Palestine Liberation Organization, which represents the forces of the Palestinian revolution, is responsible for the movement of the Palestinian Arab people in its struggle to restore its homeland, liberate it, return to it and exercise the right of self-determination in it. This responsibility extends to all military, political and financial matters, and all else that the Palestine issue requires in the Arab and international spheres.

The Palestine Liberation Organization will cooperate with all Arab States, each according to its capacities, and will maintain neutrality in their mutual relations in the light of and on the basis of, the requirements of the battle of liberation and will not interfere in the internal affairs of any Arab State.

5. The Carter Doctrine Announces U.S. Intention to Repel Aggression in the Persian Gulf, 1980

This last few months has not been an easy time for any of us. As we meet tonight, it has never been more clear that the state of our Union depends on the state of the world. And tonight, as throughout our own generation, freedom and peace in the world depend on the state of our Union. . . .

At this time in Iran, 50 Americans are still held captive, innocent victims of terrorism and anarchy. Also at this moment, massive Soviet troops are attempting to subjugate the fiercely independent and deeply religious people of Afghanistan. These two acts—one of international terrorism and one of military aggression—present a serious challenge to the United States of America and indeed to all the nations of the world. Together, we will meet these threats to peace. . . .

Three basic developments have helped to shape our challenges: the steady growth and increased projection of Soviet military power beyond its own borders; the overwhelming dependence of the Western democracies on oil supplies from the Middle East; and the press of social and religious and economic and political change in the many nations of the developing world, exemplified by the revolution in Iran. . . .

If the American hostages are harmed, a severe price will be paid. We will never rest until every one of the American hostages are released.

But now we face a broader and more fundamental challenge in this region because of the recent military action of the Soviet Union. . . .

The Soviet Union has taken a radical and an aggressive new step. It's using its great military power against a relatively defenseless nation. The implications of the Soviet invasion of Afghanistan could pose the most serious threat to the peace since the Second World War. . . .

This document can be found in "President Jimmy Carter's State of the Union Address Before Congress, 23 January 1980," *Public Papers of the Presidents, 1980–1981* (Washington, D.C.: Government Printing Office, 1981), 194–199.

While this invasion continues, we and the other nations of the world cannot conduct business as usual with the Soviet Union. That's why the United States has imposed stiff economic penalties on the Soviet Union. . . .

The region which is now threatened by Soviet troops in Afghanistan is of great strategic importance: It contains more than two-thirds of the world's exportable oil. The Soviet effort to dominate Afghanistan has brought Soviet military forces to within 300 miles of the Indian Ocean and close to the Straits of Hormuz, a waterway [connecting the Persian Gulf to the Indian Ocean] through which most of the world's oil must flow. The Soviet Union is now attempting to consolidate a strategic position, therefore, that poses a grave threat to the free movement of Middle East oil.

This situation demands careful thought, steady nerves, and resolute action, not only for this year but for many years to come. It demands collective efforts to meet this new threat to security in the Persian Gulf and in Southwest Asia. It demands the participation of all those who rely on oil from the Middle East and who are concerned with global peace and stability. And it demands consultation and close cooperation with countries in the area which might be threatened.

Meeting this challenge will take national will, diplomatic and political wisdom, economic sacrifice, and, of course, military capability. We must call on the best that is in us to preserve the security of this crucial region.

Let our position be absolutely clear: An attempt by any outside force to gain control of the Persian Gulf region will be regarded as an assault on the vital interests of the United States of America, and such an assault will be repelled by any means necessary, including military force. . . .

The crises in Iran and Afghanistan have dramatized a very important lesson: Our excessive dependence on foreign oil is a clear and present danger to our Nation's security. The need has never been more urgent. At long last, we must have a clear, comprehensive energy policy for the United States. . . .

The single biggest factor in the inflation rate last year, the increase in the inflation rate last year, was from one cause: the skyrocketing prices of OPEC [Organization of Petroleum Exporting Countries] oil. We must take whatever actions are necessary to reduce our dependence on foreign oil.

6. President George Bush Declares a New World Order During the Persian Gulf Crisis, 1990

We stand today at a unique and extraordinary moment. The crisis in the Persian Gulf, as grave as it is, also offers a rare opportunity to move toward an historic period of cooperation. Out of these troubled times, . . . a new world order can emerge: a new era—freer from the threat of terror, stronger in the pursuit of justice, and more secure in the quest for peace. An era in which the nations of the world, East and West, North and South, can prosper and live in harmony. A hundred generations have searched for this elusive path to peace, while a thousand wars raged across the span of human endeavor. Today that new world is struggling to be born, a world

This document can be found in "Address to Congress on Persian Gulf Crisis," 11 September 1990, *Public Papers of the Presidents of the United States, George Bush, 1990* (Washington, D.C.: U.S. Government Printing Office, 1991), Book II, 1218–1222.

quite different from the one we've known. A world where the rule of law supplants the rule of the jungle. A world in which nations recognize the shared responsibility for freedom and justice. A world where the strong respect the rights of the weak. This is the vision that I shared with [Soviet] President Gorbachev in Helsinki. He and other leaders from Europe, the Gulf, and around the world understand that how we manage this crisis today could shape the future for generations to come.

The test we face is great, and so are the stakes. This is the first assault on the new world that we seek, the first test of our mettle. Had we not responded to this first provocation with clarity of purpose, if we do not continue to demonstrate our determination, it would be a signal to actual and potential despots around the world. America and the world must defend common vital interests—and we will. America and the world must support the rule of law—and we will. America and the world must stand up to aggression—and we will. And one thing more: In the pursuit of these goals America will not be intimidated.

Vital issues of principle are at stake. Saddam Hussein is literally trying to wipe a country [Kuwait] off the face of the Earth. We do not exaggerate. Nor do we exaggerate when we say Saddam Hussein will fail. Vital economic interests are at risk as well. Iraq itself controls some 10 percent of the world's proven oil reserves. Iraq plus Kuwait controls twice that. An Iraq permitted to swallow Kuwait would have the economic and military power, as well as the arrogance, to intimidate and coerce its neighbors— neighbors who control the lion's share of the world's remaining oil reserves. We cannot permit a resource so vital to be dominated by one so ruthless. And we won't.

Recent events have surely proven that there is no substitute for American leadership. In the face of tyranny, let no one doubt American credibility and reliability.

7. Israeli Prime Minister Yitzhak Rabin Pleads for Peace, 1993

We, the soldiers who have returned from battles stained with blood; we who have seen our relatives and friends killed before our eyes; we who have attended their funerals and cannot look in the eyes of their parents; we who have come from a land where parents bury their children; we who have fought against you, the Palestinians—we say to you today, in a loud and a clear voice: enough of blood and tears. Enough.

8. President George W. Bush Asks, "Why Do They Hate Us?" 2001

On September the 11th, enemies of freedom committed an act of war against our country. Americans have known wars, but for the past 136 years they have been wars on foreign soil, except for one Sunday in 1941. Americans have known the casualties of war, but not at the center of a great city on a peaceful morning. . . .

Document 7 can be found at Israeli Prime Minister Speech at the White House, 13 September 1993, *http://www.bartleby.com/66/28/45828.html.*

Document 8 can be found in President Bush Address to Congress, 20 September 2001, *Journal of the House of Representatives,* 107th Congress, 1st Session, Vol. 1 (Washington, D.C.: Government Printing Office, 2002), 1081–1083.

Americans have many questions tonight. Americans are asking, "Who attacked our country?"

The evidence we have gathered all points to a collection of loosely affiliated terrorist organizations known as al Qaeda. They are some of the murderers indicated for bombing American embassies in Tanzania and Kenya and responsible for bombing the USS Cole.

Al Qaeda is to terror what the Mafia is to crime. But its goal is not making money, its goal is remaking the world and imposing its radical beliefs on people everywhere.

The terrorists practice a fringe form of Islamic extremism that has been rejected by Muslim scholars and the vast majority of Muslim clerics; a fringe movement that prevents the peaceful teachings of Islam.

The terrorists' directive commands them to kill Christians and Jews, to kill all Americans and make no distinction among military and civilians, including women and children. This group and its leader, a person named Osama bin Laden, are linked to many other organizations in different countries, including the Egyptian Islamic Jihad, the Islamic Movement of Uzbekistan. . . .

The leadership of al Qaeda has great influence in Afghanistan and supports the Taliban regime in controlling most of that country. In Afghanistan we see al Qaeda's vision for the world. Afghanistan's people have been brutalized, many are starving and many have fled.

Women are not allowed to attend school. You can be jailed for owning a television. Religion can be practiced only as their leaders dictate. A man can be jailed in Afghanistan if his beard is not long enough. The United States respects the people of Afghanistan—after all, we are currently its largest source of humanitarian aid—but we condemn the Taliban regime.

It is not only repressing its own people, it is threatening people everywhere by sponsoring and sheltering and supplying terrorists.

By aiding and abetting murder, the Taliban regime is committing murder. And tonight the United States of America makes the following demands on the Taliban:
• Deliver to United States authorities all of the leaders of Al Qaeda who hide in your land.
• Release all foreign nationals, including American citizens you have unjustly imprisoned.
• Protect foreign journalists, diplomats and aid workers in your country.
• Close immediately and permanently every terrorist training camp in Afghanistan. And hand over every terrorist and every person and their support structure to appropriate authorities.
• Give the United States full access to terrorist training camps, so we can make sure they are no longer operating.

These demands are not open to negotiation or discussion.

The Taliban must act and act immediately.

They will hand over the terrorists or they will share in their fate. I also want to speak tonight directly to Muslims throughout the world. We respect your faith. It's practiced freely by many millions of Americans and by millions more in countries that America counts as friends. Its teachings are good and peaceful, and those who commit evil in the name of Allah blaspheme the name of Allah.

The terrorists are traitors to their own faith, trying, in effect, to hijack Islam itself. . . .

Our war on terror begins with al Qaeda, but it does not end there.

It will not end until every terrorist group of global reach has been found, stopped and defeated.

Americans are asking "Why do they hate us?"

They hate what they see right here in this chamber: a democratically elected government. Their leaders are self-appointed. They hate our freedoms: our freedom of religion, our freedom of speech, our freedom to vote and assemble and disagree with each other.

They want to overthrow existing governments in many Muslim countries such as Egypt, Saudi Arabia and Jordan. They want to drive Israel out of the Middle East. They want to drive Christians and Jews out of vast regions of Asia and Africa.

These terrorists kill not merely to end lives, but to disrupt and end a way of life. With every atrocity, they hope that America grows fearful, retreating from the world and forsaking our friends. They stand against us because we stand in their way.

We're not deceived by their pretenses to piety.

We have seen their kind before. They're the heirs of all the murderous ideologies of the 20th century. By sacrificing human life to serve their radical visions, by abandoning every value except the will to power, they follow the path of fascism, Nazism and totalitarianism. And they will follow that path all the way to where it ends in history's unmarked grave of discarded lies. Americans are asking, "How will we fight and win this war?"

We will direct every resource at our command—every means of diplomacy, every tool of intelligence, every instrument of law enforcement, every financial influence, and every necessary weapon of war—to the destruction and to the defeat of the global terror network.

Now, this war will not be like the war against Iraq a decade ago, with a decisive liberation of territory and a swift conclusion. It will not look like the air war above Kosovo two years ago, where no ground troops were used and not a single American was lost in combat.

Our response involves far more than instant retaliation and isolated strikes. Americans should not expect one battle, but a lengthy campaign unlike any other we have ever seen. It may include dramatic strikes visible on TV and covert operations secret even in success.

We will starve terrorists of funding, turn them one against another, drive them from place to place until there is no refuge or no rest.

And we will pursue nations that provide aid or safe haven to terrorism. Every nation in every region now has a decision to make: Either you are with us or you are with the terrorists. . . .

This is not, however, just America's fight. And what is at stake is not just America's freedom. This is the world's fight. This is civilization's fight. This is the fight of all who believe in progress and pluralism, tolerance and freedom.

We ask every nation to join us. . . .

I will not forget the wound to our country and those who inflicted it. I will not yield, I will not rest, I will not relent in waging this struggle for freedom and security for the American people. The course of this conflict is not known, yet its outcome is certain. Freedom and fear, justice and cruelty, have always been at war, and we know that God is not neutral between them.

9. Osama bin Laden Proclaims, "God Has Given Them Back What They Deserve," 2001

Thanks to God, he who God guides will never lose. And I believe that there's only one God. And I declare I believe there's no prophet but Mohammed.

This is America, God has sent one of the attacks by God and has attacked one of its best buildings. And this is America filled with fear from the north to south and east to west, thank God.

And what America is facing today is something very little of what we have tasted for decades. Our nation, since nearly 80 years is tasting this humility. Sons are killed, and nobody answers the call.

And when God has guided a bunch of Muslims to be at the forefront and destroyed America, a big destruction, I wish God would lift their position.

And when those people have defended and retaliated to what their brothers and sisters have suffered in Palestine and Lebanon, the whole world has been shouting.

And there are civilians, innocent children being killed every day in Iraq without any guilt, and we never hear anybody. We never hear any fatwah from the clergymen of the government.

And every day we see the Israeli tanks going to Jenin, Ramallah, Beit Jalla and other lands of Islam. And, no, we never hear anybody objecting to that.

So when the swords came after eight years to America, then the whole world has been crying for those criminals who attacked. This is the least which could be said about them. They are people. They supported the murder against the victim, so God has given them back what they deserve.

I say the matter is very clear, so every Muslim after this, and after the officials in America, starting with the head of the infidels, Bush. And they came out with their men and equipment and they even encouraged even countries claiming to be Muslims against us.

So, we run with our religion. They came out to fight Islam with the name of fighting terrorism.

People—event of the world—in Japan, hundreds of thousands of people got killed. This is not a war crime. Or in Iraq, what our—who are being killed in Iraq. This is not a crime. And those, when they were attacked in my Nairobi, and Dar es Salaam, Afghanistan, and Sudan were attacked.

I say these events have split the whole world into two camps: the camp of belief and the disbelief. So every Muslim shall take—shall support his religion.

And now with the winds of change has blown up now, has come to the Arabian Peninsula.

And to America, I say to it and to its people this: I swear by God the Great, America will never dream nor those who in America will never taste security and safety unless we feel security and safety in our land and in Palestine.

This document can be found at "Bin Laden: America 'Filled with Fear,'" 7 October 2001, *http://cnn.com.* © 2004 Cable News Network LP, LLLP.

10. President Bush Vows to Democratize Iraq, 2005

Our generational commitment to the advance of freedom, especially in the Middle East, is now being tested and honored in Iraq. That country is a vital front in the war on terror, which is why the terrorists have chosen to make a stand there. Our men and women in uniform are fighting terrorists in Iraq, so we do not have to face them here at home. And the victory of freedom in Iraq will strengthen a new ally in the war on terror, inspire democratic reformers from Damascus to Tehran, bring more hope and progress to a troubled region, and thereby lift a terrible threat from the lives of our children and grandchildren.

We will succeed because the Iraqi people value their own liberty—as they showed the world last Sunday. Across Iraq, often at great risk, millions of citizens went to the polls and elected 275 men and women to represent them in a new Transitional National Assembly. A young woman in Baghdad told of waking to the sound of mortar fire on election day, and wondering if it might be too dangerous to vote. She said, "Hearing those explosions, it occurred to me—the insurgents are weak, they are afraid of democracy, they are losing. So I got my husband, and I got my parents, and we all came out and voted together."

Americans recognize that spirit of liberty, because we share it. In any nation, casting your vote is an act of civic responsibility; for millions of Iraqis, it was also an act of personal courage, and they have earned the respect of us all. . . .

The terrorists and insurgents are violently opposed to democracy, and will continue to attack it. Yet, the terrorists' most powerful myth is being destroyed. The whole world is seeing that the car bombers and assassins are not only fighting coalition forces, they are trying to destroy the hopes of Iraqis, expressed in free elections. And the whole world now knows that a small group of extremists will not overturn the will of the Iraqi people.

We will succeed in Iraq because Iraqis are determined to fight for their own freedom, and to write their own history. As Prime Minister [Ayad] Allawi said in his speech to Congress last September, "Ordinary Iraqis are anxious to shoulder all the security burdens of our country as quickly as possible." That is the natural desire of an independent nation, and it is also the stated mission of our coalition in Iraq. The new political situation in Iraq opens a new phase of our work in that country.

At the recommendation of our commanders on the ground, and in consultation with the Iraqi government, we will increasingly focus our efforts on helping prepare more capable Iraqi security forces—forces with skilled officers and an effective command structure. As those forces become more self-reliant and take on greater security responsibilities, America and its coalition partners will increasingly be in a supporting role. In the end, Iraqis must be able to defend their own country—and we will help that proud, new nation secure its liberty.

Recently an Iraqi interpreter said to a reporter, "Tell America not to abandon us." He and all Iraqis can be certain: While our military strategy is adapting to circumstances, our commitment remains firm and unchanging. We are standing for the

From President George W. Bush State of the Union Address, 2 February 2005, *http://www.whitehouse. gov/news/releases/2005/02/print/20050202-11.html.*

freedom of our Iraqi friends, and freedom in Iraq will make America safer for generations to come. We will not set an artificial timetable for leaving Iraq, because that
would embolden the terrorists and make them believe they can wait us out. We are
in Iraq to achieve a result: A country that is democratic, representative of all its
people, at peace with its neighbors, and able to defend itself. And when that result
is achieved, our men and women serving in Iraq will return home with the honor
they have earned.

E S S A Y S

The first essay, by Bernard Lewis, a professor emeritus at Princeton University, is
representative of the "clash of civilizations" thesis that attributes much of Muslim anti-
Americanism to the vast cultural differences that separate the West and the Middle
East. According to Lewis, the religiously based Muslim civilization is tradition bound
and resistant to modernity, secularism, and democracy. Unable to form stable, popularly
based nation-states in the postcolonial era, most of the region's rulers have blamed outsiders for their shortcomings, especially Britain, France, Israel, and the United States.
Although some Muslims admire America for its promise of human rights and free institutions, a historical consciousness based on anti-Westernism and antimodernity has
become central to Muslim identity, and in recent years has fueled the rise of Islamic
extremism and terrorism.

Ussama Makdisi of Rice University strongly disagrees with the clash of civilizations thesis. In the second essay, Makdisi argues that hatred of the United States and the
West is not embedded in Muslim culture, but finds expression among a growing seg-
ment of Arabs who oppose America's foreign policies. The United States was widely
admired by Arabs in the nineteenth and early twentieth centuries as a consequence of its
educational philanthropy and Woodrow Wilson's support for self-determination after
World War I. But as its power grew with the passing decades, the United States increasingly allied itself with corrupt oil kingdoms, opposed popular nationalist movements,
and abandoned all pretense of neutrality in the Arab-Israeli conflict by its strong
backing of Tel Aviv. Makdisi concludes that September 11 was ultimately a perverted,
or hijacked, expression of widespread Arab anger at the United States.

The Revolt of Islam

BERNARD LEWIS

I. Making History

President Bush and other Western politicians have taken great pains to make it
clear that the war in which we are engaged is a war against terrorism—not a war
against Arabs, or, more generally, against Muslims, who are urged to join us in this
struggle against our common enemy. Osama bin Laden's message is the opposite.
For bin Laden and those who follow him, this is a religious war, a war for Islam

---

"The Revolt of Islam" first appeared in *The New Yorker*, November 19, 2001 and then a more extended
version was published in Professor Lewis's book entitled *The Crisis of Islam: Holy War and Unholy
Terror*, New York 2003. Reprinted with permission of the author.

and against infidels, and therefore, inevitably, against the United States, the greatest power in the world of the infidels.

In his pronouncements, bin Laden makes frequent references to history. One of the most dramatic was his mention, in the October 7th videotape, of the "humiliation and disgrace" that Islam has suffered for "more than eighty years." Most American—and, no doubt, European—observers of the Middle Eastern scene began an anxious search for something that had happened "more than eighty years" ago, and came up with various answers. We can be fairly sure that bin Laden's Muslim listeners—the people he was addressing—picked up the allusion immediately and appreciated its significance. In 1918, the Ottoman sultanate, the last of the great Muslim empires, was finally defeated—its capital, Constantinople, occupied, its sovereign held captive, and much of its territory partitioned between the victorious British and French Empires. The Turks eventually succeeded in liberating their homeland, but they did so not in the name of Islam but through a secular nationalist movement. One of their first acts, in November, 1922, was to abolish the sultanate. The Ottoman sovereign was not only a sultan, the ruler of a specific state; he was also widely recognized as the caliph, the head of all Sunni Islam, and the last in a line of such rulers that dated back to the death of the Prophet Muhammad, in 632 A.D. After a brief experiment with a separate caliph, the Turks, in March, 1924, abolished the caliphate, too. During its nearly thirteen centuries, the caliphate had gone through many vicissitudes, but it remained a potent symbol of Muslim unity, even identity, and its abolition, under the double assault of foreign imperialists and domestic modernists, was felt throughout the Muslim world.

Historical allusions such as bin Laden's, which may seem abstruse to many Americans, are common among Muslims, and can be properly understood only within the context of Middle [E]astern perceptions of identity and against the background of Middle Eastern history. Even the concepts of history and identity require redefinition for the Westerner trying to understand the contemporary Middle East. In current American usage, the phrase "that's history" is commonly used to dismiss something as unimportant, of no relevance to current concerns, and, despite an immense investment in the teaching and writing of history, the general level of historical knowledge in our society is abysmally low. The Muslim peoples, like everyone else in the world, are shaped by their history, but, unlike some others, they are keenly aware of it. In the nineteen-eighties, during the Iran-Iraq war, for instance, both sides waged massive propaganda campaigns that frequently evoked events and personalities dating back as far as the seventh century. These were not detailed narratives but rapid, incomplete allusions, and yet both sides employed them in the secure knowledge that they would be understood by their target audiences—even by the large proportion of that audience that was illiterate. Middle Easterners' perception of history is nourished from the pulpit, by schools, and by the media, and, although it may be—indeed, often is—slanted and inaccurate, it is nevertheless vivid and powerfully resonant.

But history of what? In the Western world, the basic unit of human organization is the nation, which is then subdivided in various ways, one of which is by religion. Muslims, however, tend to see not a nation subdivided into religious groups but a religion subdivided into nations. This is no doubt partly because most of the nation-states that make up the modern Middle East are relatively new creations, left over from the era of Anglo-French imperial domination that followed the defeat of the

Ottoman Empire, and they preserve the state-building and frontier demarcations of their former imperial masters. Even their names reflect this artificiality: Iraq was a medieval province, with borders very different from those of the modern republic; Syria, Palestine, and Libya are names from classical antiquity that hadn't been used in the region for a thousand years or more before they were revived and imposed by European imperialists in the twentieth century; Algeria and Tunisia do not even exist as words in Arabic—the same name serves for the city and the country. Most remarkable of all, there is no word in the Arabic language for Arabia, and modern Saudi Arabia is spoken of instead as "the Saudi Arab kingdom" or "the peninsula of the Arabs," depending on the context. This is not because Arabic is a poor language—quite the reverse is true—but because the Arabs simply did not think in terms of combined ethnic and territorial identity. Indeed, the caliph Omar, the second in succession after the Prophet Muhammad, is quoted as saying to the Arabs, "Learn your genealogies, and do not be like the local peasants who, when they are asked who they are, reply: 'I am from such-and-such a place.'"

In the early centuries of the Muslim era, the Islamic community was one state under one ruler. Even after that community split up into many states, the ideal of a single Islamic polity persisted. The states were almost all dynastic, with shifting frontiers, and it is surely significant that, in the immensely rich historiography of the Islamic world in Arabic, Persian, and Turkish, there are histories of dynasties, of cities, and, primarily, of the Islamic state and community, but no histories of Arabia, Persia, or Turkey. Both Arabs and Turks produced a vast literature describing their struggles against Christian Europe, from the first Arab incursions in the eighth century to the final Turkish retreat in the twentieth. But until the modern period, when European concepts and categories became dominant, Islamic commentators almost always referred to their opponents not in territorial or ethnic terms but simply as infidels (*kafir*). They never referred to their own side as Arab or Turkish; they identified themselves as Muslims. This perspective helps to explain, among other things, Pakistan's concern for the Taliban in Afghanistan. The name Pakistan, a twentieth-century invention, designates a country defined entirely by its Islamic religion. In every other respect, the country and people of Pakistan are—as they have been for millennia—part of India. An Afghanistan defined by its Islamic identity would be a natural ally, even a satellite, of Pakistan. An Afghanistan defined by ethnic nationality, on the other hand, could be a dangerous neighbor, advancing irredentist claims on the Pashto-speaking areas of northwestern Pakistan and perhaps even allying itself with India.

II. The House of War

In the course of human history, many civilizations have risen and fallen—China, India, Greece, Rome, and, before them, the ancient civilizations of the Middle East. During the centuries that in European history are called medieval, the most advanced civilization in the world was undoubtedly that of Islam. Islam may have been equalled—or even, in some ways, surpassed—by India and China, but both of those civilizations remained essentially limited to one region and to one ethnic group, and their impact on the rest of the world was correspondingly restricted. The civilization of Islam, on the other hand, was ecumenical in its outlook, and explicitly so in its aspirations. One of the basic tasks bequeathed to Muslims by the

Prophet was jihad. This word, which literally means "striving," was usually cited in the Koranic phrase "striving in the path of God" and was interpreted to mean armed struggle for the defense or advancement of Muslim power. In principle, the world was divided into two houses: the House of Islam, in which a Muslim government ruled and Muslim law prevailed, and the House of War, the rest of the world, still inhabited and, more important, ruled by infidels. Between the two, there was to be a perpetual state of war until the entire world either embraced Islam or submitted to the rule of the Muslim state.

From an early date, Muslims knew that there were certain differences among the peoples of the House of War. Most of them were simply polytheists and idolaters, who represented no serious threat to Islam and were likely prospects for conversion. The major exception was the Christians, whom Muslims recognized as having a religion of the same kind as their own, and therefore as their primary rival in the struggle for world domination—or, as they would have put it, world enlightenment. It is surely significant that the Koranic and other inscriptions on the Dome of the Rock, one of the earliest Muslim religious structures outside Arabia, built in Jerusalem between 691 and 692 A.D., include a number of directly anti-Christian polemics: "Praise be to God, who begets no son, and has no partner," and "He is God, one, eternal. He does not beget, nor is he begotten, and he has no peer." For the early Muslims, the leader of Christendom, the Christian equivalent of the Muslim caliph, was the Byzantine emperor in Constantinople. Later, his place was taken by the Holy Roman Emperor in Vienna, and his in turn by the new rulers of the West. Each of these, in his time, was the principal adversary of the jihad.

In practice, of course, the application of jihad wasn't always rigorous or violent. The canonically obligatory state of war could be interrupted by what were legally defined as "truces," but these differed little from the so-called peace treaties the warring European powers signed with one another. Such truces were made by the Prophet with his pagan enemies, and they became the basis of what one might call Islamic international law. In the lands under Muslim rule, Islamic law required that Jews and Christians be allowed to practice their religions and run their own affairs, subject to certain disabilities, the most important being a poll tax that they were required to pay. In modern parlance, Jews and Christians in the classical Islamic state were what we would call second-class citizens, but second-class citizenship, established by law and the Koran and recognized by public opinion, was far better than the total lack of citizenship that was the fate of non-Christians and even of some deviant Christians in the West. The jihad also did not prevent Muslim governments from occasionally seeking Christian allies against Muslim rivals—even during the Crusades, when Christians set up four principalities in the Syro-Palestinian area. The great twelfth-century Muslim leader Saladin, for instance, entered into an agreement with the Crusader king of Jerusalem, to keep the peace for their mutual convenience.

Under the medieval caliphate, and again under the Persian and Turkish dynasties, the empire of Islam was the richest, most powerful, most creative, most enlightened region in the world, and for most of the Middle Ages Christendom was on the defensive. In the fifteenth century, the Christian counterattack expanded. The Tatars were expelled from Russia, and the Moors from Spain. But in southeastern Europe, where the Ottoman sultan confronted first the Byzantine and then the Holy Roman Emperor, Muslim power prevailed, and these setbacks were seen as minor and peripheral. As late as the seventeenth century, Turkish pashas still ruled in Budapest and Belgrade, Turkish armies were besieging Vienna, and Barbary corsairs were raiding lands as distant as the British Isles and, on one occasion, in 1627, even Iceland.

Then came the great change. The second Turkish siege of Vienna, in 1683, ended in total failure followed by headlong retreat—an entirely new experience for the Ottoman armies. A contemporary Turkish historian, Silihdar Mehmet Aga, described the disaster with commendable frankness: "This was a calamitous defeat, so great that there has been none like it since the first appearance of the Ottoman state." This defeat, suffered by what was then the major military power of the Muslim world, gave rise to a new debate, which in a sense has been going on ever since. The argument began among the Ottoman military and political élite as a discussion of two questions: Why had the once victorious Ottoman armies been vanquished by the despised Christian enemy? And how could they restore the previous situation?

There was good reason for concern. Defeat followed defeat, and Christian European forces, having liberated their own lands, pursued their former invaders whence they had come, the Russians moving into North and Central Asia, the Portuguese into Africa and around Africa to South and Southeast Asia. Even small European powers such as Holland and Portugal were able to build vast empires in the East and to establish a dominant role in trade.

For most historians, Middle Eastern and Western alike, the conventional beginning of modern history in the Middle East dates from 1798, when the French Revolution, in the person of Napoleon Bonaparte, landed in Egypt. Within a remarkably short time, General Bonaparte and his small expeditionary force were able to conquer, occupy, and rule the country. There had been, before this, attacks, retreats, and losses of territory on the remote frontiers, where the Turks and the Persians faced Austria and Russia. But for a small Western force to invade one of the heartlands of Islam was a profound shock. The departure of the French was, in a sense, an even greater shock. They were forced to leave Egypt not by the Egyptians, nor by their suzerains the Turks, but by a small squadron of the British Royal Navy, commanded by a young admiral named Horatio Nelson. This was the second bitter lesson the Muslims had to learn: not only could a Western power arrive, invade, and rule at will but only another Western power could get it out.

By the early twentieth century—although a precarious independence was retained by Turkey and Iran and by some remoter countries like Afghanistan, which at that time did not seem worth the trouble of invading—almost the entire Muslim world had been incorporated into the four European empires of Britain, France, Russia, and the Netherlands. Middle Eastern governments and factions were forced to learn how to play these mighty rivals off against one another. For a time, they played the game with some success. Since the Western allies—Britain and France and then the United States—effectively dominated the region, Middle Eastern resisters naturally looked to those allies' enemies for support. In the Second World War, they turned to Germany; in the Cold War, to the Soviet Union.

And then came the collapse of the Soviet Union, which left the United States as the sole world superpower. The era of Middle Eastern history that had been inaugurated by Napoleon and Nelson was ended by [Soviet President Mikhail] Gorbachev and the elder George Bush. At first, it seemed that the era of imperial rivalry had ended with the withdrawal of both competitors: the Soviet Union couldn't play the imperial role, and the United States wouldn't. But most Middle Easterners didn't see it that way. For them, this was simply a new phase in an old imperial game, with America as the latest in a succession of Western imperial overlords, except that this overlord had no rival—no Hitler or Stalin—whom they could use either to damage or influence the West. In the absence of such a patron, Middle Easterners found themselves obligated to mobilize their own force of resistance. Al Qaeda—its leaders, its sponsors, its financiers—is one such force.

III. "The Great Satan"

America's new role—and the Middle East's perception of it—was vividly illustrated by an incident in Pakistan in 1979. On November 20th, a band of a thousand Muslim religious radicals seized the Great Mosque in Mecca and held it for a time against the Saudi security forces. Their declared aim was to "purify Islam" and liberate the holy land of Arabia from the royal "clique of infidels" and the corrupt religious leaders who supported them. Their leader, in speeches played from loudspeakers, denounced Westerners as the destroyers of fundamental Islamic values and the Saudi government as their accomplices. He called for a return to the old Islamic traditions of "justice and equality." After some hard fighting, the rebels were suppressed. Their leader was executed on January 9, 1980, along with sixty-two of his followers, among them Egyptians, Kuwaitis, Yemenis, and citizens of other Arab countries.

Meanwhile, a demonstration in support of the rebels took place in the Pakistani capital, Islamabad. A rumor had circulated—endorsed by Ayatollah Khomeini, who was then in the process of establishing himself as the revolutionary leader in Iran—that American troops had been involved in the clashes in Mecca. The American Embassy was attacked by a crowd of Muslim demonstrators, and two Americans and two Pakistani employees were killed. Why had Khomeini stood by a report that was not only false but wildly improbable?

These events took place within the context of the Iranian revolution of 1979. On November 4th, the United States Embassy in Teheran [was] seized, and fifty-two Americans were taken hostage; those hostages were then held for four hundred and forty-four days, until their release on January 20, 1981. The motives for this, baffling to many at the time, have become clearer since, thanks to subsequent statements and revelations from the hostage-takers and others. It is now apparent that the hostage crisis occurred not because relations between Iran and the United States were deteriorating but because they were improving. In the fall of 1979, the relatively moderate Iranian Prime Minister, Mehdi Bazargan, had arranged to meet with the American national-security adviser, Zbigniew Brzezinski, under the aegis of the Algerian government. The two men met on November 1st, and were reported to have been photographed shaking hands. There seemed to be a real possibility—in the eyes of the radicals, a real danger—that there might be some accommodation between the two countries. Protesters seized the Embassy and took the American diplomats hostage in order to destroy any hope of further dialogue.

For Khomeini, the United States was "the Great Satan," the principal adversary against whom he had to wage his holy war for Islam. America was by then perceived—rightly—as the leader of what we like to call "the free world." Then, as in the past, this world of unbelievers was seen as the only serious force rivalling and preventing the divinely ordained spread and triumph of Islam. But American observers, reluctant to recognize the historical quality of the hostility, sought other reasons for the anti-American sentiment that had been intensifying in the Islamic world for some time. One explanation which was widely accepted, particularly in American foreign-policy circles, was that America's image had been tarnished by its wartime and continuing alliance with the former colonial powers of Europe.

In their country's defense, some American commentators pointed out that, unlike the Western European imperialists, America had itself been a victim of colonialism; the United States was the first country to win freedom from British rule. But the hope that the Middle Eastern subjects of the former British and French Empires would accept the American Revolution as a model for their own anti-imperialist struggle rested on a basic fallacy that Arab writers were quick to point out. The American Revolution was fought not by Native American nationalists but by British settlers, and, far from being a victory against colonialism it represented colonialism's ultimate triumph—the English in North America succeeded in colonizing the land so thoroughly that they no longer needed the support of the mother country.

It is hardly surprising that former colonial subjects in the Middle East would see America as being tainted by the same kind of imperialism as Western Europe. But Middle Eastern resentment of imperial powers has not always been consistent. The Soviet Union, which extended the imperial conquests of the tsars of Russia, ruled with no light hand over tens of millions of Muslim subjects in Central Asian states and in the Caucasus; had it not been for American opposition and the Cold War, the Arab world might well have shared the fate of Poland and Hungary, or, more probably, that of Uzbekistan. And yet the Soviet Union suffered no similar backlash of anger and hatred from the Arab community. Even the Russian invasion of Afghanistan in 1979—a clear case of imperialist aggression, conquest, and domination—triggered only a muted response in the Islamic world. The P.L.O. observer at the United Nations defended the invasion, and the Organization of the Islamic Conference did little to protest it. South Yemen and Syria boycotted a meeting held to discuss the issue, Libya delivered an attack on the United States, and the P.L.O. representative abstained from voting and submitted his reservations in writing. Ironically, it was the United States, in the end, that was left to orchestrate an Islamic response to Soviet imperialism in Afghanistan.

As the Western European empires faded, Middle Eastern anti-Americanism was attributed more and more to another cause: American support for Israel, first in its conflict with the Palestinian Arabs, then in its conflict with the neighboring Arab states and the larger Islamic world. There is certainly support for this hypothesis in Arab statements on the subject. But there are incongruities, too. In the nineteenthirties, Nazi Germany's policies were the main cause of Jewish migration to Palestine, then a British mandate, and the consequent reinforcement of the Jewish community there. The Nazis not only permitted this migration; they facilitated it until the outbreak of the war, while the British, in the somewhat forlorn hope of winning Arab good will, imposed and enforced restrictions. Nevertheless, the Palestinian leadership of the time, and many other Arab leaders, supported the Germans, who sent the Jews to Palestine, rather than the British, who tried to keep them out.

The same kind of discrepancy can be seen in the events leading to and following the establishment of the State of Israel, in 1948. The Soviet Union played a significant role in procuring the majority by which the General Assembly of the United Nations voted to establish a Jewish state in Palestine, and then gave Israel immediate de-jure recognition. The United States, however, gave only de-facto recognition. More important, the American government maintained a partial arms embargo on Israel, while Czechoslovakia, at Moscow's direction, immediately sent a supply of weaponry, which enabled the new state to survive the attempts to strangle it at birth. As late as the war of 1967, Israel still relied for its arms on European, mainly French, suppliers, not on the United States.

The Soviet Union had been one of Israel's biggest supporters. Yet, when Egypt announced an arms deal with Russia, in September of 1955, there was an overwhelmingly enthusiastic response in the Arab press. The Chambers of Deputies in Syria, Lebanon, and Jordan met immediately and voted resolutions of congratulation to President [Gamal Abdel] Nasser; even Nuri Said, the pro-Western ruler of Iraq, felt obliged to congratulate his Egyptian colleague—this despite the fact that the Arabs had no special love of Russia, nor did Muslims in the Arab world or elsewhere wish to invite either Communist ideology or Soviet power to their lands. What delighted them was that they saw the arms deal—no doubt correctly—as a slap in the face for the West. The slap, and the agitated Western response, reinforced the mood of hatred and spite toward the West and encouraged its exponents. It also encouraged the United States to look more favorably on Israel, now seen as a reliable and potentially useful ally in a largely hostile region. Today, it is often forgotten that the strategic relationship between the United States and Israel was a consequence, not a cause, of Soviet penetration.

The Israeli-Palestinian conflict is only one of many struggles between the Islamic and non-Islamic worlds—on a list that includes Nigeria, Sudan, Bosnia, Kosovo, Macedonia, Chechnya, Sinkiang, Kashmir, and Mindanao—but it has attracted far more attention than any of the others. There are several reasons for this. First, since Israel is a democracy and an open society, it is much easier to report—and misreport—what is going on. Second, Jews are involved, and this can usually secure the attention of those who, for one reason or another, are for or against them. Third, and most important, resentment of Israel is the only grievance that can be freely and safely expressed in those Muslim countries where the media are either wholly owned or strictly overseen by the government. Indeed, Israel serves as a useful stand-in for complaints about the economic privation and political repression under which most Muslim people live, and as a way of deflecting the resulting anger.

IV. Double Standards

This raises another issue. Increasingly in recent decades, Middle Easterners have articulated a new grievance against American policy: not American complicity with imperialism or with Zionism but something nearer home and more immediate—American complicity with the corrupt tyrants who rule over them. For obvious reasons, this particular complaint does not often appear in public discourse. Middle Eastern governments, such as those of Iraq, Syria, and the Palestine Authority, have developed great skill in controlling their own media and manipulating those of Western countries. Nor, for equally obvious reasons, is it raised in diplomatic negotiation. But it is discussed, with increasing anguish and urgency, in private conversations with listeners who can be trusted, and recently even in public. (Interestingly, the Iranian revolution of 1979 was one time when this resentment was expressed openly. The Shah was accused of supporting America, but America was also attacked for imposing an impious and tyrannical leader as its puppet.)

Almost the entire Muslim world is affected by poverty and tyranny. Both of these problems are attributed, especially by those with an interest in diverting attention from themselves, to America—the first to American economic dominance and exploitation, now thinly disguised as "globalization"; the second to America's support for the many so-called Muslim tyrants who serve its purposes. Globalization has become a major theme in the Arab media, and it is almost always raised in connection with American economic penetration. The increasingly wretched economic situation in most of the Muslim world, relative not only to the West but also to the tiger economies of East Asia, fuels these frustrations. American paramountcy, as Middle Easterners see it, indicates where to direct the blame and the resulting hostility.

There is some justice in one charge that is frequently leveled against the United States: Middle Easterners increasingly complain that the United States judges them by different and lower standards than it does Europeans and Americans, both in what is expected of them and in what they may expect—in terms of their financial well-being and their political freedom. They assert that Western spokesmen repeatedly overlook or even defend actions and support rulers that they would not tolerate in their own countries. As many Middle Easterners see it, the Western and American governments' basic position is: "We don't care what you do to your own people at home, so long as you are coöperative in meeting our needs and protecting our interests."

The most dramatic example of this form of racial and cultural arrogance was what Iraqis and others see as the betrayal of 1991, when the United States called on the Iraqi people to revolt against Saddam Hussein. The rebels of northern and southern Iraq did so, and the United States forces watched while Saddam, using the helicopters that the ceasefire agreement had allowed him to retain, bloodily suppressed them, group by group. The reasoning behind this action—or, rather, inaction—is not difficult to see. Certainly, the victorious Gulf War coalition wanted a change of government in Iraq, but they had hoped for a coup d'état, not a revolution. They saw a genuine popular uprising as dangerous—it could lead to uncertainty or even anarchy in the region. A coup would be more predictable and could achieve the desired result—the replacement of Saddam Hussein by another, more amenable tyrant, who could take his place among America's so-called allies in the coalition. The United States' abandonment of Afghanistan after the departure of the Soviets was understood in much the same way as its abandonment of the Iraqi rebels.

Another example of this double standard occurred in the Syrian city of Hama and in refugee camps in Sabra and Shatila. The troubles in Hama began with an uprising headed by the radical group in Muslim Brothers in 1982. The government responded swiftly. Troops were sent, supported by armor, artillery, and aircraft, and within a very short time they had reduced a large part of the city to rubble. The number killed was estimated, by Amnesty International, at somewhere between ten thousand and twenty-five thousand. The action, which was ordered and supervised by the Syrian President, Hafiz al-Assad, attracted little attention at the time and did not prevent the United States from subsequently courting Assad, who received a long succession of visits from American Secretaries of State James Baker, Warren

Christopher, and Madeleine Albright, and even from President [Bill] Clinton. It is hardly likely that Americans would have been so eager to propitiate a ruler who had perpetrated such crimes on Western soil, with Western victims.

The massacre of seven hundred to eight hundred Palestinian refugees in Sabra and Shatila that same year was carried out by Lebanese militiamen, led by a Lebanese commander who subsequently became a minister in the Syrian-sponsored Lebanese government, and it was seen as a reprisal for the assassination of the Lebanese President Bashir Gemayyel. Ariel Sharon, who at the time commanded the Israeli forces in Lebanon, was reprimanded by an Israeli commission of inquiry for not having foreseen and prevented the massacre, and was forced to resign from his position as Minister of Defense. It is understandable that the Palestinians and other Arabs should lay sole blame for the massacre on Sharon. What is puzzling is that Europeans and Americans should do the same. Some even wanted to try Sharon for crimes against humanity before a tribunal in Europe. No such suggestion was made regarding either Saddam Hussein or Hafiz al-Assad, who slaughtered ten of thousands of their compatriots. It is easy to understand the bitterness of those who see the implication here. It was as if the militia who had carried out the deed were animals, not accountable by the same human standards as the Israelis.

Thanks to modern communications, the people of the Middle East are increasingly aware of the deep and widening gulf between the opportunities of the free world outside their borders and the appalling privation and repression within them. The resulting anger is naturally directed first against their rulers, and then against those whom they see as keeping those rulers in power for selfish reasons. It is surely significant that most of the terrorists who have been identified in the September 11th attacks on New York and Washington come from Saudi Arabia and Egypt—that is, from countries whose rulers are deemed friendly to the United States.

V. A Failure of Modernity

If America's double standards—and its selfish support for corrupt regimes in the Arab world—have long caused anger among Muslims, why has that anger only recently found its expression in acts of terrorism? In the nineteenth and twentieth centuries, Muslims responded in two ways to the widening imbalance of power and wealth between their societies and those of the West. The reformers or modernizers tried to identify the sources of Western wealth and power and adapt them to their own use, in order to meet the West on equal terms. Muslim governments—first in Turkey, then in Egypt and Iran—made great efforts to modernize, that is, to Westernize, the weaponry and equipment of their armed forces; they even dressed them in Western-style uniforms and marched them to the tune of brass bands. When defeats on the battlefield were matched by others in the marketplace, the reformers tried to discover the secrets of Western economic success and to emulate them by establishing industries of their own. Young Muslim students who were sent to the West to study the arts of war also came back with dangerous and explosive notions about elected assemblies and constitutional governments.

All attempts at reform ended badly. If anything, the modernization of the armed forces accelerated the process of defeat and withdrawal, culminating in the humiliating failure of five Arab states and armies to prevent a half million Jews from building a new state in the debris of the British Mandate in Palestine in 1948. With rare exceptions, the economic reforms, capitalist and socialist alike, fared no better. The Middle Eastern combination of low productivity and high birth rate makes for an unstable mix, and by all indications the Arab countries, in such matters as job creation, education, technology, and productivity, lag ever farther behind the West. Even worse, the Arab nations also lag behind the more recent recruits to Western-style modernity, such as Korea, Taiwan, and Singapore. Out of a hundred and fifty-five countries ranked for economic freedom in 2001, the highest-ranking Muslim states are Bahrain (No. 9), the United Arab Emirates (No. 14), and Kuwait (No. 42). According to the World Bank, in 2000 the average annual income in the Muslim countries from Morocco to Bangladesh was only half the world average, and in the nineties the combined gross national products of Jordan, Syria, and Lebanon—that is, three of Israel's Arab neighbors—were considerably smaller than that of Israel alone. The per-capita figures are worse. According to United Nations statistics, Israel's per-capita G.D.P. was three and a half times that of Lebanon and Syria, twelve times that of Jordan, and thirteen and a half times that of Egypt. The contrast with the West, and now also with the Far East, is even more disconcerting.

Modernization in politics has fared no better—perhaps even worse—than in warfare and economics. Many Islamic countries have experimented with democratic institutions of one kind or another. In some, as in Turkey, Iran, and Tunisia, they were introduced by innovative native reformers; in others, they were installed and then bequeathed by departing imperialists. The record, with the possible exception of Turkey, is one of almost unrelieved failure. Western-style parties and parliaments almost invariably ended in corrupt tyrannies, maintained by repression and indoctrination. The only European model that worked, in the sense of accomplishing its purpose, was the one-party dictatorship. The Baath Party, different branches of which have rules [*sic*] Iraq and Syria for decades, incorporated the worst features of its Nazi and Soviet models. Since the death of Nasser, in 1970, no Arab leader has been able to gain extensive support outside his own country. Indeed, no Arab leader has been willing to submit his claim to power to a free vote. The leaders who have come closest to winning pan-Arab approval are Qaddafi in the seventies and, more recently, Saddam Hussein. That these two, of all Arab rulers, should enjoy such wide popularity is in itself both appalling and revealing.

In view of this, it is hardly surprising that many Muslims speak of the failure of modernization. The rejection of modernity in favor of a return to the sacred past has a varied and ramified history in the region and has given rise to a number of movements. The most important of these, Wahhabism, has lasted more than two and a half centuries and exerts a significant influence on Muslim movements in the Middle East today. Its founder, Muhammad ibn Abd al-Wahhab (1703–87), was a theologian from the Najd area of Arabia. In 1744, he launched a campaign of purification and renewal. His purpose was to return the Muslim world to the pure and authentic Islam of the Prophet, removing and, where necessary, destroying all later accretions. The Wahhabi cause was embraced by the Saudi rulers of Najd, who promoted it, for a while successfully, by force. In a series of campaigns, they carried their rule and their faith to much of central and eastern Arabia, before being rebuffed, at the end of the eighteenth century, by the Ottoman sultan, whom the Saudi ruler had denounced as a backslider from the true faith and a usurper in the Muslim state. The second alliance of Wahhabi doctrine and Saudi force began in the last years of the Ottoman Empire and continued after the collapse. The Saudi conquest of the Hejaz, including the holy cities of Mecca and Medina, increased the prestige of the House of Saud and gave new scope to the Wahhabi doctrine, which spread, in a variety of forms, throughout the Islamic world.

From the nineteen-thirties on, the discovery of oil in the eastern provinces or Arabia and its exploitation, chiefly by American companies, brought vast new wealth and bitter new social tensions. In the old society, inequalities of wealth had been limited, and their effects were restrained, on the one hand, by the traditional social bonds and obligations that linked rich and poor and, on the other hand, by the privacy of Muslim home life. Modernization has all too often widened the gap, destroyed those social bonds, and, through the universality of the modern media, made the resulting inequalities painfully visible. All this has created new and receptive audiences for Wahhabi teachings and those of other like-minded groups, among them the Muslim Brothers in Egypt and Syria and the Taliban in Afghanistan.

It has now become normal to designate these movements as "fundamentalist." The term is unfortunate for a number of reasons. It was originally an American Protestant term, used to designate Protestant churches that differed in some respects from the mainstream churches. These differences bear no resemblance to those that divide Muslim fundamentalists from the Islamic mainstream, and the use of the term can therefore be misleading. Broadly speaking, Muslim fundamentalists are those who feel that the troubles of the Muslim world at the present time are the result not of insufficient modernization but of excessive modernization. From their point of view, the primary struggle is not against the Western enemy as such but against the Westernizing enemies at home, who have imported and imposed infidel ways on Muslim peoples. The task of the Muslims is to depose and remove these infidel rulers, sometimes by defeating or expelling their foreign patrons and protectors, and to abrogate and destroy the laws, institutions, and social customs that they have introduced, so as to return to a purely Islamic way of life, in accordance with the principles of Islam and the rules of the Holy Law.

VI. The Rise of Terrorism

Osama bin Laden and his Al Qaeda followers may not represent Islam, and their statements and their actions directly contradict basic Islamic principles and teachings, but they do arise from within Muslim civilization, just as Hitler and the Nazis arose from within Christian civilization, so they must be seen in their own cultural, religious, and historical context.

If one looks at the historical record, the Muslim approach to war does not differ greatly from that of Christians, or that of Jews in the very ancient and very modern periods when the option was open to them. While Muslims, perhaps more frequently than Christians, made war against the followers of other faiths to bring them within the scope of Islam, Christians—with the notable exception of the Crusades, which were themselves an imitation of Muslim practice—were more prone to fight internal religious wars against those whom they saw as schismatics or heretics. Islam, no doubt owing to the political and military involvement of its founder, takes what one might call a more pragmatic view than the Gospels of the realities of societal relationships. Because war for the faith has been a religious obligation within Islam from the beginning, it is elaborately regulated. Islamic religious law, or the Sharia, deals in some detail with such matters as the opening, conclusion, and resumption of hostilities, the avoidance of injury to noncombatants, the treatment of prisoners, the division of booty, and even the types of weapons that may be used. Some of these rules have been explained away by modern radical commentators who support the fundamentalists; others are simply disregarded.

What about terrorism? Followers of many faiths have at one time or another invoked religion in the practice of murder, both retail and wholesale. Two words deriving from such movements in Eastern religions have even entered the English language: "thug," from India, and "assassin," from the Middle East, both commemorating fanatical religious sects whose form of worship was to murder those whom they regarded as enemies of the faith. The question of the lawfulness of assassination in Islam first arose in 656 A.D., with the murder of the third caliph, Uthman, by pious Muslim rebels who believed they were carrying out the will of God. The first of a succession of civil wars was fought over the question of whether the rebels were fulfilling or defying God's commandment. Islamic law and tradition are very clear on the duty of obedience to the Islamic ruler. But they also quote two sayings attributed to the Prophet: "There is no obedience in sin" and "Do not obey a creature against his creator." If a ruler orders something that is contrary to the law of God, then the duty of obedience is replaced by a duty of disobedience. The notion of tyrannicide—the justified removal of a tyrant—was not an Islamic innovation; it was familiar in antiquity, among Jews, Greeks, and Romans alike, and those who performed it were often acclaimed as heroes.

Members of the eleventh-to-thirteenth-century Muslim sect known as the Assassins, which was based in Iran and Syria, seem to have been the first to transform the act that was named after them into a system and an ideology. Their efforts, contrary to popular belief, were primarily directed not against the crusaders but against their own leaders, whom they saw as impious usurpers. In this sense, the Assassins are the true predecessors of many of the so-called Islamic terrorists of today, some of whom explicitly make this point. The name Assassins, with its connotation of "hashish-taker," was given to them by their Muslim enemies. They called themselves *fidayeen*—those who are ready to sacrifice their lives for their cause. The term has been revived and adopted by their modern imitators. In two respects, however—in their choice of weapons and of victims—the Assassins were markedly different from their modern successors. The victim was always an individual—a highly placed political, military, or religious leader who was seen as the source of evil. He, and he alone, was killed. This action was not terrorism in the current sense of that term but, rather, what we would call "targeted assassination." The method was always the same: the dagger. The Assassins disdained the use of poison, crossbows, and other weapons that could be used from a distance, and the Assassin did not expect—or, it would seem, even desire—to survive his act, which he believed would insure him eternal bliss. But in no circumstance did he commit suicide. He died at the hands of his captors.

The twentieth century brought a renewal of such actions in the Middle East, though of different types and for different purposes, and terrorism has gone through several phases. During the last years of the British Empire, imperial Britain faced terrorist movements in its Middle Eastern dependencies that represented three different cultures: Greeks in Cyprus, Jews in Palestine, and Arabs in Aden. All three acted from nationalist, rather than religious, motives. Though very different in their backgrounds and political circumstances, the three were substantially alike in their tactics. Their purpose was to persuade the imperial power that staying in the region was not worth the cost in blood. Their method was to attack the military and, to a lesser extent, administrative personnel and installations. All three operated only within their own territory and generally avoided collateral damage. All three succeeded in their endeavors.

Thanks to the rapid development of the media, and especially of television, the more recent forms of terrorism are targeted not at specific and limited enemy objectives but at world opinion. Their primary purpose is not to defeat or even to weaken the enemy militarily but to gain publicity—a psychological victory. The most successful group by far in this exercise has been the Palestine Liberation Organization. The P.L.O. was founded in 1964 but became important in 1967, after the defeat of the combined Arab armies in the Six-Day War. Regular warfare had failed; it was time to try other methods. The targets in this form of armed struggle were not military or other government establishments, which are usually too well guarded, but public places and gatherings of any kind, which are overwhelmingly civilian, and in which the victims do not necessarily have a connection to the declared enemy. Examples of this include, in 1970, the hijacking of three aircraft—one Swiss, one British, and one American—which were all taken to Amman; the 1972 murder of Israeli athletes at the Munich Olympics; the seizure in 1973 of the Saudi Embassy in Khartoum, and the murder there of two Americans and a Belgian diplomat; and the takeover of the Italian cruise ship Achille Lauro, in 1985. Other attacks were directed against schools, shopping malls, discothèques, pizzerias, and even passengers waiting in line at European airports. These and other attacks by the P.L.O. were immediately and remarkably successful in attaining their objectives—the capture of newspaper headlines and television screens. They also drew a great deal of support in sometimes unexpected places, and raised their perpetrators to starring roles in the drama of international relations. Small wonder that others were encouraged to follow their example—in Ireland, in Spain, and elsewhere.

The Arab terrorists of the seventies and eighties made it clear that they were waging a war for an Arab or Palestinian cause, not for Islam. Indeed, a significant proportion of the P.L.O. leaders and activists were Christian. Unlike socialism, which was discredited by its failure, nationalism was discredited by its success. In every Arab land but Palestine, the nationalists achieved their purposes—the defeat and departure of imperialist rulers, and the establishment of national sovereignty under national leaders. For a while, freedom and independence were used as more or less synonymous and interchangeable terms. The early experience of independence, however, revealed that this was a sad error. Independence and freedom are very different, and all too often the attainment of one meant the end of the other.

Both in defeat and in victory, the Arab nationalists of the twentieth century pioneered the methods that were later adopted by religious terrorists, in particular the lack of concern at the slaughter of innocent bystanders. This unconcern reached new proportions in the terror campaign launched by Osama bin Laden in the early nineties. The first major example was the bombing of two American embassies in East Africa in 1998. In order to kill twelve American diplomats, the terrorists were willing to slaughter more than two hundred Africans, many of them Muslims, who happened to be in the vicinity. The same disregard for human life, on a vastly greater scale, underlay the action in New York on September 11th.

There is no doubt that the foundation of Al Qaeda and the consecutive declarations of war by Osama bin Laden marked the beginning of a new and ominous phase in the history of both Islam and terrorism. The triggers for bin Laden's actions, as he himself has explained very clearly, were America's presence in Arabia during the Gulf War—a desecration of the Muslim Holy land—and America's use of Saudi Arabia as a base for an attack on Iraq. If Arabia is the most symbolic location in the world of Islam, Baghdad, seat of the caliphate for half a millennium and the scene of some of the most glorious chapters in Islamic history, is the second.

There was another, perhaps more important, factor driving bin Laden. In the past, Muslims fighting against the West could always turn to the enemies of the West for comfort, encouragement, and material and military help. With the collapse of the Soviet Union for the first time in centuries there was no such useful enemy. There were some nations that had the will, but they lacked the means to play the role of the Third Reich or the Soviet Union. Bin Laden and his cohorts soon realized that, in the new configuration of world power, if they wished to fight America they had to do it themselves. Some eleven years ago, they created Al Qaeda, which included many veterans of the war in Afghanistan. Their task might have seemed daunting to anyone else, but they did not see it that way. In their view, they had already driven the Russians out of Afghanistan, in a defeat so overwhelming that it led directly to the collapse of the Soviet Union itself. Having overcome the superpower that they had always regarded as more formidable, they felt ready to take on the other; in this they were encouraged by the opinion, often expressed by Osama bin Laden, among others, that America was a paper tiger.

Muslim terrorists had been driven by such beliefs before. One of the most surprising revelations in the memoirs of those who held the American Embassy in Teheran from 1979 to 1981 was that their original intention had been to hold the building and the hostages for only a few days. They changed their minds when statements from Washington made it clear that there was no danger of serious action against them. They finally released the hostages, they explained, only because they feared that the new President, Ronald Reagan, might approach the problem "like a cowboy."

Bin Laden and his followers clearly have no such concern, and their hatred is neither constrained by fear nor diluted by respect. As precedents, they repeatedly cite the American retreats from Vietnam, from Lebanon, and—the most important of all, in their eyes—from Somalia. Bin Laden's remarks in an interview with John Miller, of ABC News, on May 28, 1998, are especially revealing:

> We have seen in the last decade the decline of the American government and the weakness of the American soldier, who is ready to wage cold wars and unprepared to fight long wars. This was proven in Beirut when the Marines fled after two explosions. It also proves they can run in less than twenty-four hours, and this was also repeated in Somalia. . . . The youth were surprised at the low morale of the American soldiers. . . . After a few blows, they ran in defeat. . . . They forgot about being the world leader and the leader of the new world order. [They] left, dragging their corpses and their shameful defeat, and stopped using such titles.

Similar inferences are drawn when American spokesmen refuse to implicate—and sometimes even hasten to exculpate—parties that most Middle Easterners believe to be deeply involved in the attacks on America. A good example is the repeated official denial of any Iraqi involvement in the events of September 11th. It may indeed be true that there is no evidence of Iraqi involvement, and that the Administration is unwilling to make false accusations. But it is difficult for Middle Easterners to resist the idea that this refusal to implicate Saddam Hussein is due less to a concern for legality than to a fear of confronting him. He would indeed be a formidable adversary. If he faces the prospect of imminent destruction, as would be inevitable in a real confrontation, there is no knowing what he might do with his already considerable arsenal of unconventional weapons. Certainly, he would not be restrained by any scruples, or by the consideration that the greatest victims of any such attack would be his own people and their immediate neighbors.

For Osama bin Laden, 2001 marks the resumption of the war for the religious dominance of the world that began in the seventh century. For him and his followers, this is a moment of opportunity. Today, America exemplifies the civilization and embodies the leadership of the House of War, and, like Rome and Byzantium, it has become degenerate and demoralized, ready to be overthrown. Khomeini's designation of the United States as "the Great Satan" was telling. In the Koran, Satan is described as "the insidious tempter who whispers in the hearts of men." This is the essential point about Satan: he is neither a conqueror nor an exploiter—he is, first and last, a tempter. And for the members of Al Qaeda it is the seduction of America that represents the greatest threat to the kind of Islam they wish to impose on their fellow-Muslims.

But there are others for whom America offers a different kind of temptation—the promise of human rights, of free institutions, and of a responsible and elected government. There are a growing number of individuals and even some movements that have undertaken the complex task of introducing such institutions in their own countries. It is not easy. Similar attempts, as noted, led to many of today's corrupt regimes. Of the fifty-seven member states of the Organization of the Islamic Conference, only one, the Turkish Republic, has operated democratic institutions over a long period of time and, despite difficult and ongoing problems, has made progress in establishing a liberal economy and a free society and political order.

In two countries, Iraq and Iran, where the regimes are strongly anti-American, there are democratic oppositions capable of taking over and forming governments. We could do much to help them, and have done little. In most other countries in the region, there are people who share our values, sympathize with us, and would like to share our way of life. They understand freedom, and want to enjoy it at home. It is more difficult for us to help those people, but at least we should not hinder them. If they succeed, we shall have friends and allies in the true, not just the diplomatic, sense of these words.

Meanwhile, there is a more urgent problem. If bin Laden can persuade the world of Islam to accept his views and his leadership, then a long and bitter struggle lies ahead, and not only for America. Sooner or later, Al Qaeda and related groups will clash with the other neighbors of Islam—Russia, China, India—who may prove less squeamish than the Americans in using their power against Muslims and their sanctities. If bin Laden is correct in his calculations and succeeds in his war, then a dark future awaits the world, especially the part of it that embraces Islam.

A Clash with U.S. Foreign Policy

USSAMA MAKDISI

[T]his essay turns to history to answer the oft-asked question "Why do they hate us?" It offers a brief, synthetic, interpretive account of Arab and American interactions over the past two centuries. I recognize from the outset the limits of generalizing about 280 million Arabs, living in a host of Arab countries, each with its own tradition and history. Nonetheless, I seek to place the rise of anti-American sentiment in the Arab world within a historical and political context often neglected, misunderstood, or ignored by proponents of a "clash of civilizations" thesis.

Anti-Americanism is a recent phenomenon fueled by American foreign policy, not an epochal confrontation of civilizations. While there are certainly those in both the United States and the Arab world who believe in a clash of civilizations and who invest politically in such beliefs, history belies them. Indeed, at the time of World War I the image of the United States in the Arab provinces of the Ottoman Empire was generally positive; those Arabs who knew of the country saw it as a great power that was not imperialist as Britain, France, and Russia were. Those Americans who lived in the region—missionaries and their descendants and collaborators—were pioneers in the realm of higher education. Liberal America was not simply a slogan; it was a reality encountered and experienced by Arabs, Turks, Armenians, and Persians in the hallways of the Syrian Protestant College (later renamed the American University of Beirut), Robert College in Istanbul, the American College in Persia, and the American University in Cairo. But over the course of the twentieth century, American policies in the region profoundly complicated the meaning of America for Arabs.

Among the vast majority of Arabs today, the expression of anti-American feelings stems less from a blind hatred of the United States or American values than from a profound ambivalence about America: at once an object of admiration for its affluence, its films, its technology (and for some its secularism, its law, its order) and a source of deep disappointment given the ongoing role of the United States in shaping a repressive Middle Eastern status quo. Anti-Americanism is not an ideologically consistent discourse—its intensity, indeed, its coherence and evidence, vary across the Arab world. Yet to the extent that specifically anti-American sentiments are present, never more obviously so to Americans than in the aftermath of the attacks of September 11, 2001, it is imperative to understand their nature and origins.

American involvement with the Arab world began inauspiciously in 1784 when an American ship, the *Betsey,* was seized in the Mediterranean Sea by Moroccan privateers. A year later Algerians captured more American vessels and imprisoned their crews. Thus were inaugurated the negotiations, skirmishes, and legends known collectively as the Barbary wars, which culminated in the capture of the U.S. frigate *Philadelphia* in 1803, Stephen Decatur's famous but quite ineffectual raid on Tripoli in 1804, and the ransom and release of the American captives in 1805. The episodes sparked debates between Thomas Jefferson and John Adams about whether it was necessary to go to war, rather than pay ransom to the Barbary states, in order to

A Clash with U.S. Foreign Policy, excerpted from Ussama Makdisi, "Anti-Americanism in the Arab World: An Interpretation of a Brief History," *Journal of American History,* 89 (September 2002), 538–557.

uphold the values of the newly independent republic. As Robert J. Allison has noted in his work on the image of Islam in the early-nineteenth-century United States, the Barbary wars, and especially the myriad captivity narratives that emerged from them, crystallized existing negative Western images of the Muslim and Ottoman world. The discourse of the despotic "Turk" functioned as one foil to early republican identity just as the more entrenched discourse of "Mohammedanism" as imposture signified the antithesis of true religion, that is to say, Christianity, at a time when complex political and sectarian battle lines were being etched into a rapidly changing American landscape.

Such perspectives were amplified in the nineteenth century by the advent of U.S. travelers' discourses of the Orient and, specifically, of Palestine. Hilton Obenzinger has described a "Holy Land mania" that gripped American travelers, artists, and writers who toured and laid claim to Palestine. The Arab inhabitants of Palestine (and the surrounding areas) were acknowledged to be paradoxically there—animating accounts of the Holy Land as Levantine dragomans, dirty natives, impious Mohammedans, or "nominal" Christians—yet not there in any meaningful historical or spiritual sense. During his post–Civil War tour of the Ottoman Empire, for example, Mark Twain irreverently satirized American travelers' religious obsession with Palestine and their enchantment with the East more generally.

In the United States itself books by Twain and by missionaries, landscapes by such artists as Frederic Church, as well as novels such as Robert Smythe Hichens's 1904 *The Garden of Allah* (which went into forty-four editions over the next forty years), contributed to the rise of a specifically American genre of orientalism. It exoticized the East as premodern, conceived of it as dreamy yet often experienced it as squalid, separated the sacred landscape of the Holy Land from its native Arab inhabitants, and commodified the Orient through promotions, advertisements, trinkets, novels, photographic exhibits, postcards, and ultimately films.

There was, however, an American encounter with the Arabs that was far more direct and had a far greater impact on early Arab attitudes toward the United States. This was the missionary encounter led mostly by New England men and women. They shared many of the prejudices that characterized nineteenth-century American travelers; indeed, the roots of their missionary effort lay in part in their disavowal of a growing liberalism in New England religious thought. They were impelled by a sense of patrimony in the Holy Land and feelings of superiority to the natives as they sought to reclaim the lands of the Bible from Muslim and Eastern Christian control. Yet, motivated by "disinterested benevolence," they were also the first Americans to engage with the local populations in a serious and sustained manner— they wanted to change the Ottoman world, not just to describe or experience it. Their spiritual preoccupation with the Holy Land was premised, not on overlooking the natives, but on recognizing their presence on the land and on proclaiming the urgent need to save the "perishing souls" of the East. The first American missionaries to the Arab world were associated with the American Board of Commissioners for Foreign Missions. They departed Boston in 1819 and arrived in the Levant in 1820. Failing to establish themselves in Jerusalem, they settled on Beirut as the center of a missionary enterprise to Syria in 1823. . . .

Had the missionaries devoted themselves only to direct proselytizing, their impact on the region would have been scarcely noticeable and their later achievements impossible. But the missionaries also functioned as a bridge between cultures. Not only did they seek to introduce the Ottoman Arab world to Protestant notions of piety and individual salvation, they also brought with them American manners and customs, clothes, education, and medicine. Simultaneously, they sought to introduce Americans to a world unknown to them—to actual inhabitants, societies, histories, and geographies normally excluded by the alternatively sacred and exotic discourse of American orientalism. . . .

The missionaries . . . served as ethnographers of Arabs to Americans. . . . The missionaries themselves changed in the crucible of encounter, especially after it became clear that the proselytizing dimension of their enterprise had failed. Thus an evangelical effort that rejected a current liberalism growing in early-nineteenth-century New England was transformed—by the labors of missionaries and natives alike—into a major project of essentially secular liberal higher education embodied in institutions such as the 1866 Syrian Protestant College in Beirut and in 1863 Robert College in Istanbul. Nowhere was the fruit of this transformation by actual experience in the Orient more evident than in the words of the famous American missionary-turned-college president Daniel Bliss. When he laid the cornerstone of College Hall at the Syrian Protestant College in 1871, Bliss spoke words as revolutionary in America as they were in the Ottoman Empire:

> This College is for all conditions and classes of men without regard to colour, nationality, race or religion. A man white, black or yellow; Christian, Jew, Mohammedan or heathen, may enter and enjoy all the advantages of this institution for three, four, or eight years; and go out believing in one God, or in many Gods, or in no God. But it will be impossible for any one to continue with us long without knowing what we believe to be the truth and our reasons for that belief.

This conversion from direct proselytization that was openly intolerant of other faiths to more liberal persuasion was fraught with tension. The secularization of the missionary enterprise coincided with and reflected a dramatic increase in Western ascendancy in the non-Western world in the late nineteenth century. That ascendancy led to a codification of national and racial prejudices—from designations of professors, to differential pay scales, to the insistence that only the English language could be a medium of modern instruction—that discriminated against Arabs even as it offered them educational opportunities that they readily grasped. Students of the Syrian Protestant College—known locally as the "American college" long before it changed its name to the American University of Beirut in 1920—played a crucial role in building a thriving late Ottoman Arab print culture, and its medical graduates greatly contributed to the development of modern health care in Lebanon and the Arab world. Innovative modern education and the absence of American government imperialism in the late Ottoman Empire contributed to the benevolent image of the United States in such places as Beirut, Istanbul, and Tehran. For example, the famous nineteenth-century Egyptian advocate of women's liberation, Qasim Amin, extolled American virtues and praised the freedom of women in America. . . .

The influence of an idea of a benevolent America reached its apex among Arabs during and immediately after World War I. Not only were Americans identified with educational efforts in the region, they were also central to relief efforts amid a terrible wartime famine in Beirut and the surrounding region of Mount Lebanon.

Moreover, President Woodrow Wilson's proclamations on self-determination reinforced a notion among nationalist elites in the Arab world that the United States was different from the European powers, which had agreed to partition the postwar Middle East much as they had partitioned Africa in the late nineteenth century, with the notable difference that Africa was partitioned openly while the Arab world was carved up secretly. Most egregious from an Arab perspective was the Balfour Declaration of 1917, which promised British support for the establishment of a Jewish "national home" in Palestine despite the fact that the overwhelming majority of the native inhabitants—90 percent—were Arabs who opposed what they saw as European colonialism bent on dispossessing them of their land. . . . In 1919 Howard Bliss, son of Daniel Bliss and then president of the Syrian Protestant College, urged Wilson to form a mission to find out what the Arab peoples wanted, an idea that squarely contradicted the spirit of the Balfour Declaration and the colonial wisdom on which it was based.

The American section of the resultant Inter-Allied Commission on Mandates in Turkey was popularly known as the King-Crane commission, headed as it was by two Americans: Charles Crane, a Chicago industrialist and contributor to Wilson's presidential campaign, and Henry King, president of Oberlin College. The British and the French opposed it from the outset, reluctant to participate in what they regarded as American meddling in their imperial spheres of influence. Zionist leaders regarded it with "deepest disquietude," for travel to Palestine and interviews with natives threatened to expose a fundamental (and still often unacknowledged) problem of the Zionist project in Palestine: Namely, by what right could one create a Jewish state in a land where the vast majority of the indigenous population was not Jewish? The King-Crane commission represented the tension between two strands of nineteenth-century American experience of the Arab world. On the one hand, the commissioners by their own admission began with a "predisposition" to the Zionist perspective: they were well informed about the passionate claims to Palestine made by Jews. At the outset of their mission, therefore, they reflected a dominant nineteenth-century American view of Palestine that overlooked the Arab reality on the ground or dismissed it as marginal to the allegedly true Judeo-Christian heritage of the land or to its modern civilized future. . . .

[However] after conducting interviews with local mayors and municipal councils and professional and trade organizations and making an extensive tour of Palestine and Syria, the King-Crane commission issued a final report that outraged British and French imperial sentiments as well as Zionist aspirations. It recommended an independent unified Arab state in Syria, Palestine, and Lebanon that, if necessary, should be placed under American mandatory control. In recommending an American mandate, the commissioners drew on a discourse of American exceptionalism and a history of American missionary contributions to higher education in the region that, they claimed, had led Arabs to know and trust the United States. The Arab people, noted the final report, "declared that their choice was due to knowledge of America's record: the unselfish aims with which she had come into the war; the faith in her felt by multitudes of Syrians who had been in America; the spirit revealed in American educational institutions in Syria, especially the College in Beirut, . . . their belief that America had no territorial or colonial ambitions;" and finally "her genuinely democratic spirit; and her ample resources." . . .

The King-Crane report fell on deaf ears in Washington, London, and Paris. Wilson, who had already committed himself to the Balfour Declaration and to British imperial interests, did not publish the report officially. The British and the French proceeded with their predetermined partition of the Arab world. In 1920 Palestine became a British mandate formally committed to the terms of the Balfour Declarations, and the French dismantled the fledgling Arab state in Syria, exiling its leader, who became instead king of the newly constituted British-dominated state of Iraq. . . .

The discovery of oil in Saudi Arabia in 1938 pushed the United States into a more direct role in the Middle East. It was in oil, not in mandatory Palestine or Syria, that the United States had a strategic stake. And unlike the largely passive U.S. Middle Eastern policy of the immediate post–World War I decades, post–World War II policy was far more extensive and direct. The result was a symbiotic relationship between American oil companies, the U.S. government, and the emerging Saudi state. The brilliant novel *Cities of Salt* (1984) by Abdelrahman Munif depicts the extraordinary political transformations entailed by the almost overnight conversion of an Arab tribal society into an oil kingdom, the corruption it induced, and the alienation created as rulers became increasingly independent of their subjects and dependent on oil companies and foreign protection. The novel explores the historical tensions between the American racialist paternalism toward Arabs, epitomized in the white American compounds from which natives were barred, and the collaboration between Americans and Arabs to explore for, market, and profit from oil.

The Saudi state became an oil frontier not only for American companies, as the political scientist Robert Vitalis has argued, but also for thousands of Arabs from the Levant and tens of thousands of migrant workers from South Asia. It was from this oil frontier that the Saudi regime emerged in its present form, on the one hand deeply dependent on expatriates and on the government of the United States, and on the other hand constantly emphasizing its Islamic (and hence non-American) heritage and mandate in an effort to maintain its legitimacy with its own people. The autocratic Saudi state has sought to co-opt and outflank domestic opposition both by appearing to uphold a "pure" version of Islam and by using oil profits to build a modern infrastructure of highways, hospitals, airports, schools, and electricity grids for its citizens. The American-Saudi relationship inaugurated a U.S. involvement with the Arab world far more secular in form, strategic in conception, and nationalist in interest than the nineteenth-century spiritual and educational missionary enterprise. Henceforth, while the United States remained a land of opportunity for many Arabs and American oil companies were instrumental in realizing the undreamed-of profits for many Gulf Arab states (as well as for themselves), the U.S. government saw itself far less as a force for liberal or democratic change than as a guarantor of the status quo.

The Cold War exacerbated the suspicion felt by U.S. policy makers toward any potentially destabilizing force in the Middle East, particularly populist secular Iranian and Arab nationalisms. In Iran, for example, after the parliament nationalized the British-dominated Anglo-Iranian Oil Company in 1951, the Central Intelligence Agency (CIA) organized the overthrow in 1953 of the nationalist prime minister Mohammed Mossadeq. Thereafter, the United States supported the absolutist dictatorship of Mohammed Reza Shah Pahlavi, rationalizing or ignoring the tremendous popular disaffection with Pahlavi rule. As late as New Year's Eve 1978,

Jimmy Carter lavishly praised "the great leadership of the Shah," which, he insisted, had turned Iran into "an island of stability in one of the more troubled areas of the world." The United States helped the shah establish (with Israeli advisers) the infamous SAVAK internal security agency that rounded up and tortured political prisoners. The historian Nikki R. Keddie concluded her study of the Iranian revolution of 1979 by noting that it was American policies in Iran that led to a marked increase in anti-American feeling.

A similar process unfolded in the Arab world. American hostility to Mossadeq paralleled American animosity toward the secular Pan-Arab nationalism of Gamal Abdel Nasser in Egypt. Despite some initial sympathy, American policy makers were ultimately unwilling to interpret his nationalist Pan-Arab rhetoric within the context of the recent history of British and French colonial exploitation of the Arab world. Nasser saw Israel as the greatest threat to the Arabs, whereas the Americans focused on the dangers of alleged Soviet intrusion into the Middle East. Thus they perceived Nasser within a Cold War logic that dismissed his attempt at nonalignment. Although much of the Arab world, indeed, the Third World, saw in Nasser a genuinely charismatic leader and an authentic voice for Arab aspirations, for the Palestinian people, and for Egypt, Americans portrayed him as dangerously ambitious. They regarded his 1955 decision to seek arms from the eastern block (after being rebuffed by the West) and his 1956 nationalization of the Suez Canal (after the United States suddenly pulled out of financing the Aswan Dam project) as destabilizing to pro-Western regimes in the region, including Saudi Arabia and Iraq (whose monarchy was indeed overthrown). When the Iraqi monarchy fell in July 1958, 14,000 American troops were immediately dispatched to a Lebanon embroiled in civil conflict. They were sent to shore up the pro-Western regime of Camille Chamoun and also to signal U.S. determination to stave off perceived radical Arab nationalism and Soviet expansionism. This politicization of the United States on the side of conservative autocratic regimes fostered a first round of anti-American sentiment in the Arab world that was similar to the anti-Americanism then evident in Latin America and Asia, where the United States more often than not sided with dictatorships in the name of fighting Communism and radical nationalism.

This anti-Americanism was not characterized by hatred of America or things American as much as by a relatively new identification of American power as a force for repression rather than liberation in the Arab world. . . .

The secular anti-imperialist rhetoric of student movements, leftist intellectuals, and "progressive" governments such as Nasser's now regarded the U.S. government as a representative of the historic force of colonialism and imperialism (and capitalism) and as a power holding the Arab world back from its rightful place at the eagerly anticipated postcolonial "rendezvous of victory." Enormous differences within the secularist camp notwithstanding (Nasser's regime, for example, persecuted Communists), this secular criticism of perceived American imperialism was based ultimately, not on a theory about a clash of civilizations, but on a discourse about a historic clash between the reactionary forces of imperialism and the progressive forces of revolution. It interpreted politics as a struggle between two stages of a single teleological reading of history in which the United States supported allegedly retrograde regimes, be it in the shah's Iran or in Chamoun's Lebanon and Nuri Said's Iraq in 1958 against supposedly more progressive ones. Anti-imperialist mobilization involved anti-American rhetoric, but its characterizations were broad, its criticism tempered by the fact that the United States as a nation remained a promised land for many, a source of admiration for still more, and on occasion—as during the Suez crisis in 1956 when President Dwight D. Eisenhower reversed a British, French, and Israeli invasion of Egypt following Nasser's nationalization of the Suez Canal—a symbol of hope for a new kind of relationship between the Third World and the great powers.

For the most part secular anti-imperialist rhetoric prevailed from Cairo to Baghdad, especially in the 1960s as the secular Arab nationalism represented by Nasser remained ascendant. But there also existed an undercurrent of Islamist dissidence from the autocratic governments of the Arab world and Iran. Unlike secularists, Islamists (who were also split into many ideological factions) framed their politics as a response to the violation of an alleged tradition and envisioned a revival of an ostensibly pure Islamic state and society. Unlike many of the great nineteenth-century Islamist reformers such as Jamal al-Din al-Afghani and Muhammad 'Abdu, who had tried to reconcile Islam and the West, many Islamists now regarded the West as a representative of an antagonistic secular and un-Islamic history, culture, and civilization. They witnessed the Arab inability to prevent the loss of Palestine and the dispersion of the Palestinian people—the first of which was justified, and the second largely ignored, by the West. They also seethed at the corruption of post-colonial Arab regimes. [Egypt's Sayyid] Qutb, who had once awkwardly admired certain facets of the United States, turned away from it in the 1950s because of its materialism and its support for Israel. He was further radicalized following his arrest in 1954 after a failed assassination attempt on Nasser by a member of the Muslim Brotherhood to which Qutb belonged. Qutb suffered, as did many other Egyptians, at the hands of Nasser's secret police. . . . It was not freedom or temptation per se that Qutb opposed; it was what he saw as the degradation, corruption, injustice, authoritarianism, and materialism imposed on Muslims by their enemies. Qutb was hanged by Nasser's regime in 1966.

A year later Nasser's regime and secular Arab nationalism were shaken by Israel's success in the June 1967 war. The Israeli defeat of Nasser and secular Arab nationalism, which by then had amassed a dismal human rights and economic record, and the Iranian revolution of 1979 sapped secularist rhetoric and galvanized the Islamist alternative. What Qutb, an adherent of the dominant Sunni branch of Islam, advocated in Egypt, Ayatollah Ruhollah Khomeini succeeded in accomplishing in predominantly Shiite Iran. Not surprisingly, when the shah of Iran finally fell in 1979, an intense power struggle between Islamists and secularists and among Islamists themselves began not only in Iran but also in the Arab world. Many self-styled spokesmen for Islam denounced American and Western culture, and some have also criticized and on occasion persecuted those women, minorities, and Muslim men who did not conform to "proper" Islamic codes of conduct. In the Arab world, however, Islamist movements have remained oppositional forces to authoritarian governments. In Iran the Islamists led by Khomeini triumphed and ushered in the "Islamic Revolution" and with it the most sustained challenge to U.S. regional hegemony. Khomeini did not hide his antipathy to the West and the United States in particular for propping up the shah's repressive regime. "With the support of America," Khomeini wrote in 1978, "and with all the infernal means at his disposal, the Shah has fallen on our oppressed people, turning Iran into one vast graveyard."

But unlike Nasser, and unlike Islamists such as Ali Shariati who promoted an Islamic liberation theology, Khomeini mobilized and channeled revolutionary aspirations into a Manichaean theocracy that viewed Islam and America as totally antithetical civilizations. The taking of American hostages in 1980 dramatically illustrated the gulf that separated the revolutionary Iranian sense of an "imperialist" America and the U.S. image of itself as a benevolent nation. Khomeini's fiery denunciation of America in 1980 drew on a history of American overseas politics of which most Americans were ignorant but that Iranians and Arabs encountered on a daily basis. "The most important and painful problem confronting the subjugated nations of the world, both Muslim and non-Muslim," Khomeini said, "is the problem of America." . . .

The Islamist anti-American sentiment that came to the fore during the Iranian revolution was ironically and unintentionally exacerbated by covert U.S. and Saudi mobilization, training, and financing of Muslim fighters to repel the Soviet invasion of Afghanistan. Their victory over one "imperialist" superpower turned their attention to another. Indeed, the United States loomed in the 1980s and 1990s ever more clearly as the unequivocal regional hegemon, the largest arms seller to the Middle East (particularly the gulf Arab states), an increasingly staunch supporter of Israel, and the guarantor of the authoritarian status quo in the gulf states (the wealthiest Arabs) and, since [the peace accords at] Camp David, in Egypt (the most populous Arab nation). And the United States military firmly planted itself in Saudi Arabia following the Gulf War . . . to oversee a stringent sanctions regime against Iraq. It is in this context of Iranian revolutionary upheaval, the defeat of the Soviets in Afghanistan, and the rise of U.S. dominance in the Persian Gulf that some Saudi Islamists, for example, have incorporated a militant anti-Americanism into their opposition to an increasingly obvious dependency of Saudi Arabia and to the "unjust" regional order that the United States has overseen. Their specific political anti-Americanism is inextricably bound up with their religious defensiveness and their more general repudiation of secular culture. Their anti-Americanism is not, however, simply a reaction against the basing of U.S. "infidels" near Mecca and Medina; nor is it simply fury at long-lost Muslim ascendancy. Such Islamists see the United States as a leader of a new crusade, a term that in the Arab world is replete not only with religious connotations of spiritual violation but equally with political ideas of occupation and oppression, in short, of worldly *injustice*. . . .

On no issue is Arab anger at the United States more widely and acutely felt than that of Palestine. And on *no* issue, arguably, has there been more misunderstanding and less candor in mainstream commentaries purporting to explain Arab anger to American audiences following September 11. For it is over Palestine that otherwise antithetical Arab secularist and Islamist interpretations of history converge in their common perception of an immense gulf separating official American avowals of support for freedom from actual American policies. No account of anti-Americanism in the Arab world that does not squarely address the Arab understanding of Israel can even begin to convey the nature, the depth, and the sheer intensity of Arab anger at the United States.

Viewed from an exclusively Western perspective, the creation of the state of Israel represented Jewish national redemption, both because of a history of European anti-Semitism (especially the Holocaust) and because of the centrality of the

Jewish presence (and the marginality of Islam) in Christian, particularly evangelical, thought about Palestine. But from an Arab perspective, Israel never has been and never could have been so understood. Zionism in Palestine, a land whose overwhelming majority was Arab at the turn of the twentieth century and for over a thousand years before that, caused the destruction of Palestinian society and the dispossession of its Arab inhabitants. . . .

Compounding the original uprooting of the Palestinians in 1948 from their homes and lands—what Palestinians refer to as the *nakba* (catastrophe)—has been Israel's 1967 military occupation of the West Bank, Gaza, East Jerusalem, and the Golan Heights, an occupation that remains in full force today. Successive Israeli governments, Labor and Likud alike, have steadily confiscated more and more Palestinian land, demolished Palestinian homes, and exiled Palestinians, thus dismantling an Arab reality in Palestine and transforming it into a Jewish one. In the immediate aftermath of the 1948 war, for example, the new state of Israel razed approximately four hundred Palestinian villages; today Jewish settlements continue to be built on expropriated Palestinian land in East Jerusalem and the West Bank. Because of this, Israel represents, for Arabs, a gross injustice. The contradictions and nuances within Israeli society are lost in the fact that Israel's creation and its persistence in its present form came and *continues* to come at the expense of the indigenous inhabitants of the land. From an Arab perspective, the creation of Israel marked the triumph of Western colonialism over native Arabs at a time when India and much of Africa and Asia were freeing themselves from European colonial rule. The specific question of Palestine has always been a broader Arab one as well, both because of the hundreds of thousands of Palestinian refugees in several Arab countries and because of a common history, language, culture, and politics that leads Arabs—Muslim and Christian—to identify with Palestinians.

American support for Israel has several foundations, ranging from the evangelical to the secular, from putative Judeo-Christian affinity to Cold War strategy, from passionate belief in the necessity of a Jewish state to opportunistic appeal to American Jewish voters, and from memory of the Holocaust to a perception of Israel as a small democratic nation surrounded by hostile Arab nations. For those reasons American financial support for Israel currently stands at nearly $3 billion a year, making it by far the single largest recipient of U.S. foreign aid. But as Kathleen Christison, a former CIA analyst, has recently put it, "the singular U.S. focus on Israel's perspective in the conflict renders the United States unable to perform the role it has always set for itself as ultimate mediator and peacemaker." In the United States (unlike most other parts of the world, including Europe) and among most Americans, the cumulative costs borne by Palestinians particularly and Arabs more generally for the violent creation of a Jewish state in the Arab world against the explicit wishes of the indigenous population are rarely acknowledged in public debate. To the extent that Arab hostility to Israel is known, it is often assumed to be based on age-old or irrational hatreds, anti-Semitism, or an intrinsic antidemocratic Arab sensibility. Just as support for Israel has become fundamental to an American imagination of the Middle East, particularly following the 1967 war, it is largely through Israel that most Arabs have come to judge the United States politically (although within often contradictory secular and Islamist narratives and hence with different implications). Satellite television stations such as Al-Jazeera daily beam pictures of

Palestinian *suffering* under Israeli *occupation* directly into Arab households at a time when American television represents the Palestinian-Israeli conflict largely as Arab *violence* against Israel and Israeli *retaliation* against this violence.

It is not lost on Arabs that current American government officials describe the United States as an "honest broker." But those officials (and those in administrations before them) have explicitly condemned Palestinian terror against Israeli civilians while remaining largely silent when Palestinian civilians in far greater numbers are killed by Israeli terror. This American silence is seen in the Arab world as complicity in Israeli occupation—particularly when it is American planes, helicopters, and bombs that enforce the thirty-five-year-old occupation. The dominant view in the Arab world is that American foreign policy regarding the Arab-Israeli conflict is shaped by the pro-Israel lobby, notably the American Israel Public Affairs Committee (AIPAC). Even regimes considered "pro-American" such as those of Saudi Arabia, Jordan, and post–Camp David Egypt are embarrassed by their apparent inability to make any significant impact on this state of affairs. . . .

[C]ondemnations of an evident U.S. bias toward Israel rarely acknowledge the Arabs own role in solidifying that affinity, given the lack of democratic governance in the Arab world and the consequent inability of Arab leaders (and recently of Yasir Arafat) to articulate the moral and political nature of the Palestinian struggle for self-determination in terms that will resonate with the American public. Nor is it to deny that many Arab regimes and opposition parties have ruthlessly exploited the Palestinian question or that those regimes treat Palestinians and their own citizens callously. Nor is it to suggest that Arab convergence on the question of Palestine indicates unanimity on how to resolve the Arab-Israeli conflict. On that question, as on so many others, Arabs are deeply divided. Nor is it to deny that the Palestinians' own leadership under Yasir Arafat has successively alienated Arab people after people, beginning in Jordan, going on to Lebanon, and most recently in Kuwait, both tarnishing the image and immensely complicating the meaning of the Palestinian struggle within the Arab world. Nor is it, finally, to deny that criticism of Israel covers up a multitude of Arab sins, from the suppression of democratic opposition, the torture and banishment of dissidents, and the rampant corruption of state institutions to the cultivation of one-party and, indeed, one-family rule in Arab regimes (pro-American or not) from Saudi Arabia to Syria. Yet it *is* testament to the unresolved simplicity of the basic underlying issue that fuels this struggle—Arab natives evicted from their homes by Zionists, languishing stateless in refugee camps, and still suffering under Israeli occupation—that Arabs, from Morocco to Yemen and from all walks of life, still strongly sympathize with the Palestinians as a people for their half century of tribulations and exile from their land.

Whatever good Americans and the United States as a nation do in the region—from food aid to technological assistance to educational outreach to efforts at bilateral Arab-Israeli peacemaking—has been constantly overshadowed and tainted in Arab eyes by the continuation of the Arab-Israeli conflict, in which Arabs do not see the United States as evenhanded. Anti-American sentiment stemming from American support for Israel has been compounded in the past decade by the punitive American-dominated United Nations (UN) sanctions regime against Iraq put in place following the second Gulf War [in 1991]. The sanctions have contributed—according to UN statistics—to the deaths of several hundred thousand Iraqi civilians.

In 1996 CBS correspondent Lesley Stahl noted a report that "half a million children" had died in Iraq as a result of sanctions and asked then secretary of state Madeleine Albright, "Is the price worth it?" Albright replied, "I think this is a very hard choice, but the price, we think the price is worth it." Americans see the image of Saddam Hussein and hear about frightening "weapons of mass destruction." Arabs see a flagrant double standard—Iraq punished and humiliated for invading Kuwait; Israel effusively supported despite its far longer occupation of Lebanon (which began in 1978 and ended in April 2000 because of a successful resistance campaign waged by Hezbollah), both occupations in clear defiance of UN resolutions. In the Arab world, therefore, the hope in America evident at the beginning of the twentieth century was transformed by the mid-twentieth century into disillusionment and by the end of the twentieth century into outright anger and hostility.

Most Arabs do not and will not act on this anger at U.S. policy in the region, like other people, most Arabs try to get on with their daily lives and, when they do turn to politics, can and do separate what they think of American culture, of Americans, and of American foreign policy. Yet September 11 is ultimately a mutilated and hijacked expression of immense Arab anger at the United States. Osama bin Laden is no more representative of Arabs than David Koresh or Timothy McVeigh were representative of Americans. But bin Laden *is* a manifestation of a deeply troubled Arab world beset by Arab government authoritarianism, a rise of Islamic fundamentalism, Israeli occupation and settlement of Arab lands, continuing Palestinian exile, and, finally, by American policies toward the region during and after the Cold War that have done little to encourage justice or democracy. . . .

The merest familiarity with modern history, then, would indicate that widespread Arab opposition to America is a sign of the times. It is based, not on *longstanding hatred* of "American" values, but on more *recent anger* at American policies in the region, especially toward Israel. Anti-Americanism is therefore not civilizationally rooted, even if it is at times expressed in civilizational terms.

F U R T H E R   R E A D I N G

Fouad Ajami, *The Dream Palace of the Arab's Dream* (1999)

Graham Allison, *Nuclear Terrorism* (2004)

Robert J. Allison, *The Crescent Obscured: The United States and the Muslim World, 1776–1815* (1995)

Isaac Alteras, *Eisenhower and Israel* (1993)

Mustafa Aydin and Cagri Erhan, eds., *Turkish-American Relations* (2004)

Robert Baer, *Sleeping with the Devil* (2003) (on Saudi Arabia)

George Ball and Douglas Ball, *The Passionate Attachment* (1992) (on Israel)

James Bamford, *A Pretext for War* (2004) (on the Iraq War)

Warren Bass, *Support Any Friend: Kennedy's Middle East and the Making of the U.S.-Israeli Alliance* (2004)

Daniel Benjamin and Steven Simon, *The Age of Sacred Terror* (2003)

Michael Benson, *The United States and the Founding of Israel* (1997)

Abraham Ben-Zvi, *Decade of Transition: Eisenhower, Kennedy, and the Origins of the American-Israeli Alliance* (1998)

Paul Berman, *Terror and Liberalism* (2003)

Hans Blix, *Disarming Iraq* (2004)

H. W. Brands, *Into the Labyrinth* (1994)

Teresa Brennan, *Globalism and Its Terrors* (2002)

Zbigniew K. Brzezinski, *The Choice: Global Domination or Global Leadership* (2004)

Richard J. Chasdi, *Tapestry of Terror* (2002)

Noam Chomsky, *Middle East Illusions* (2004)

Kathleen Christison, *Perceptions of Palestine* (1999)

Nathan Citino, *From Arab Nationalism to OPEC* (2002) (on Saudi Arabia)

Richard A. Clarke, *Against All Enemies* (2004)

Michael Cohen, *Truman and Israel* (1990)

Steve Coll, *Ghost Wars* (2004) (on the C.I.A. and Afghanistan)

Anthony H. Cordesman, *Terrorism, Asymmetric Warfare, and Weapons of Mass Destruction* (2001)

———, *The Iraq War* (2003)

Richard Crockett, *America Embattled* (2003)

"Diplomatic History Roundtable: The Bush Administration's Foreign Policy in Historical Perspective," *Diplomatic History* 29 (2005): 393–444

Herbert Druks, *The Uncertain Alliance* (2001) (on Israel)

Khaled Abou El Fadl, *The Place of Tolerance in Islam* (2002)

Charles Enderlin, *Shattered Dreams* (2003) (on the Oslo peace process)

David L. Esposito, *Unholy War: Terror in the Name of Islam* (2002)

David Farber, *Taken Hostage* (2004) (on the Iran hostage crisis)

"Fifty Years of U.S.-Israeli Relations: A Roundtable," *Diplomatic History* 22 (1998): 231–283

Glen Frankel, *Beyond the Promised Land* (1996)

Lawrence Freedman and Ephraim Karsh, *The Gulf Conflict, 1990–1991* (1993)

Thomas L. Friedman, *The Lexus and the Olive Tree* (2000)

———, *Longitudes and Attitudes* (2003)

David Fromkin, *A Peace to End All Peace* (2001) (on the Ottoman Empire)

John Lewis Gaddis, *Surprise, Security, and the American Experience* (2004)

Irene L. Gendzier, *Notes from the Minefield* (1997)

Fawaz A. Gerges, *America and Political Islam* (1999)

Philip Gordon and Jeremy Shapiro, *Allies at War* (2004)

Peter L. Hahn, *Caught in the Middle East* (2004)

———, *Crisis and Crossfire* (2005)

David Harris, *The President, the Prophet, and the Shah* (2004)

Parker T. Hart, *Saudi Arabia and the United States* (1999)

Seymour M. Hersh, *Chain of Command: The Road from 9/11 to Abu Ghraib* (2004)

Dilip Hiro, *War Without End* (2002) (on terrorism)

Christopher Hitchens, *A Long Short War* (2003) (on the Iraq War)

Bruce Jentleson, *With Friends Like These: Reagan, Bush, and Saddam* (1994)

Chalmers Johnson, *Blowback* (2000)

Robert Kaplan, *The Arabists* (1996)

Nikki R. Keddie, *Modern Iran* (2003)

John Keegan, *The Iraq War* (2004)

Gilles Kepel, *Jihad* (2002)

———, *The War for Muslim Minds* (2004)

Jane E. Krasno and James D. Sutterlin, *The United Nations and Iraq* (2002)

Audrey Kurth, "Behind the Curve: Globalization and International Terrorism," *International Security* 3 (Winter 2002–2003): 30–58

Walter LaQueur, *The New Terrorism* (1999)

Bernard Lewis, *What Went Wrong?* (2001)

———, *The Crisis of Islam* (2003)

Douglas Little, *American Orientalism* (2004)

Robert S. Litwak, *Rogue States and US Foreign Policy* (2000)

William Maley, *The Afghanistan Wars* (2002)

Mahmood Mamdani, *Good Muslim, Bad Muslim* (2004)

James Mann, *Rise of the Vulcans* (2004) (on the Bush administration)

Michelle Mart, "Tough Guys and American Cold War Policy: Images of Israel, 1948–1960," *Diplomatic History* 20 (Summer 1996): 357–380

Melani McAlister, *Epic Encounters* (2001) (on the U.S. media and the Middle East)

Joanne Meyerowitz, ed., *History and September 11th* (2003)

John P. Migetta, *American Alliance Policy in the Middle East* (2002)

Benny Morris, *Israel's Border Wars, 1949–1956* (1993)

Williamson Murray and Robert H. Schlesinger Jr., *The Iraq War* (2003)

Donald Neff, *Fallen Pillars: US Policy Toward Palestine and Israel Since 1945* (1995)

David S. New, *Holy War* (2002)

Michael B. Oren, *Six Days of War* (2002)

David Painter, *Oil and the American Century* (1986)

Monte Palmer and Princess Palmer, *At the Heart of Terror* (2005)

Ibn Pappe, *The Israel/Palestine Question* (1999)

Daniel Pipes, *Militant Islam Reaches America* (2002)

Kenneth M. Pollack, *The Threatening Storm* (2002) (on Iraq)

———, *The Persian Puzzle* (2004) (on Iran)

Gerald L. Posner, *Why America Slept* (2004) (on 9/11)

John Prados, ed., *America Confronts Terrorism* (2002)

William B. Quandt, *Peace Process* (1993)

Ahmed Rashid, *Taliban* (2001)

———, *Jihad* (2002) (on Central Asia)

"The Road to and from September 11th: A Roundtable," *Diplomatic History* 26 (Fall 2002): 541–644

Jeffrey J. Roberts, *The Origins of Conflict in Afghanistan* (2002)

Barry Rubin, *The Fragmentation of Afghanistan* (2002)

Edward W. Said, *The Question of Palestine* (1979)

Yezid Sayigh, *Armed Struggle and the Search for State* (1998) (on the Palestinians)

Michael Scheuer, *Imperial Hubris* (2004)

———, *Through Our Enemies' Eyes* (2005)

Stephen Schwartz, *The Two Faces of Islam* (2003)

David K. Shipler, *Arab and Jew* (2002)

Geoff Simons, *Libya and the West* (2003)

Strobe Talbot and Nayan Chanda, eds., *The Age of Terror* (2002)

Shibley Telhami, *The Stakes: America and the Middle East* (2003)

Bernard E. Trainor, *The General's War* (1995) (on the 1990 Gulf War)

Robert Vitalis, "Black Gold, White Crude: An Essay on American Exceptionalism, Hierarchy, and Hegemony in the Gulf," *Diplomatic History* 26 (Spring 2002): 185–213

David C. Wills, *The First War on Terrorism* (2003) (on the Reagan era)

Bob Woodward, *Bush at War* (2003)

———, *Plan of Attack* (2004)

Robin Wright, *The Last Great Revolution* (2001) (on Iran)

Salim Yaqub, *Containing Arab Nationalism* (2004)

Daniel Yergin, *The Prize* (1991) (on oil)